Florence Kelley

and the Nation's

Work

Florence Kelley

and the Nation's Work

The Rise of Women's
Political Culture, 1830–1900

Kathryn Kish Sklar

Yale University Press New Haven & London

Published with the support of a grant from the National Endowment for the Humanities,
an independent federal agency.
Published with assistance from the foundation established in memory of Philip Hamilton
McMillan of the Class of 1894, Yale College.

Designed by Deborah Dutton.
Set in Monotype Fournier by Tseng Information Systems, Inc.
Printed in the United States of America by Thomson-Shore, Dexter, Michigan.

Library of Congress Cataloging-in-Publication Data
Sklar, Kathryn Kish.
Florence Kelley and the nations work : the rise of women's political
culture, 1830–1900 / Kathryn Kish Sklar.
v.   cm.
Includes bibliographical references and index.
Contents: v. 1. Doing the nation's work, 1830–1900 —
ISBN 0-300-05912-4 (cloth)
0-300-07285-6 (pbk.)
1. Kelley, Florence, 1859–1932   2. Women social reformers — United
States — Biography   3. Feminists — United States — Biography.
I. Title.
HQ1413.K45S58   1995
305.42'092 — dc20   94-22725
[B]   CIP

A catalogue record for this book is available from the British Library.

⊗ The paper in this book meets the guidelines for permanence and durability of the Committee on
Production Guidelines for Book Longevity of the Council on Library Resources.

10 9 8 7 6 5 4 3 2

To Tom
Partner and friend

Contents

Part Three
Agency

Illustrations

Preface

This is the story of a remarkable woman whose vision and energy did much to recast governmental responsibility for human welfare in the United States between 1890 and 1930. This volume, the first of two, considers her life against the background of the civil traditions dominant from 1830 to 1900. During that large share of the nineteenth century, women's public culture matured into a vital force in American life. Florence Kelley's participation in that process illuminates women's entry into public activism after 1870, as well as the gendered contours of American civil society that both invited and inhibited women's participation.

Many of the social, economic, and cultural issues during the first four decades of Florence Kelley's life were shaped by the publication of Charles Darwin's *Origin of Species* in 1859, the year of her birth. Arguing that humankind evolved from material substance and random mutations rather than from the plan of an omnipotent deity, Darwin fastened uncertainty at the core of human destiny and made progress immanent within material life. His conclusions fit well with the increasing materialism of day-to-day life during the industrial revolution and the culture's deepening engagement with the contingencies of the economic marketplace.

The generation born in the urban north of the United States around 1859 met this new uncertainty in various ways. Some formed groups—corporations among the wealthy and trade unions among wage earners—to diminish the effects of risks in their lives. Middle-class people turned to each other in a search for answers that carried both women and men into civil society and new civic institutions. They, even more than the founding generation of the Republic one hundred years earlier, confronted changes that threatened the existence of their social institutions and values. Could the nation's democratic institutions survive the social strains created by unregulated industrial capitalism? Did the negation of religious explanations of human origins also annul the moral and ethical obligations of Judeo-Christian traditions? Were individual liberties compatible with community welfare? Only a generation removed from the transformative power of Evangelical religion, Florence Kelley's contemporaries answered many of these questions with what we might call moral materialism—values that accepted the materialism of the post-Darwin world but imbued it with meanings carried forward from an earlier era.

Florence Kelley's life offers a revealing lens through which to view her generation's construction of moral materialism. Her example takes us deep into the process by which middle-class Americans sought to recast their society by reshaping the civil space that stretched between the state and the economy.[1] During this watershed of American history marking the transition from preindustrial to industrial society, civil society and its myriad voluntary associations offered potential openings for the middle-class reconquest of government and the economic marketplace. For two hundred years, the power of the "middling sort" in American society had been rooted in this civil terrain. Now it became the arena where they grappled with alarming new forces of unprecedented power.

In this project, the public culture of middle-class women held two distinct advantages over that of middle-class men: women were not as deeply implicated in the war between capital and labor that seemed to immobilize civil society; nor were they as compromised by urban political machines. The exclusion of most middle-class women from wage earning and of all women from electoral activity situated them differently from men in civil society. In this book, I explore that difference and the opportunities it opened.

I rely on Thomas Bender's definition of "public culture" as "a forum where power in its various forms, including meaning and aesthetics, is elaborated and made authoritative." My perspective draws on Gramscian-inspired cultural studies that emphasize the continuous dialectic between knowledge and power, between values and actions, between beliefs and institutions.[2] I am particularly interested in the process through which gendered (perceived as "natural") cultural categories gave rise to conscious mobilization. That process brought new energy and creativity into civic life at a crucial moment in American history, greatly expanding the power of civil society, especially its capacity to shape the state and the economy.

My views have been informed by the work of Jürgen Habermas, which has helped me understand when and under what conditions the arguments of groups not endowed with state power can gain public authority. Especially important in this regard is the notion that the state and the economy are both rivals for dominance with the democratic public sphere and work by power not by discourse. How discourse can gain ascendancy under these conditions is a problem I aspire to address.[3]

By women's public culture or women's political culture, I mean women's participation in public culture and the separate institutions women built to facilitate their participation. While the concept of public culture implies a distinction between public and private, the border between these realms was always porous. As a category of historical analysis, women's public culture rests on the assumption that women's experience was by no means exclusively private. The equation of women with private and men with public life was an ideological construct that lost much of its power during the 1870s, when Florence Kelley's generation came of age. This occurred at the same time that public dialogue over slavery was replaced by dialogue over the relationship between capital and labor. Focusing on women's public culture between 1830 and 1900, I analyze the sources of that construct's decline among its chief subjects—white middle-class women—and its replacement between 1880 and 1900 with a vision of women as the embodiment of virtue within civil society.

Women's public culture—even that dominated by white middle-class women—was never a homogeneous entity. Rather, it was constantly changing, depending on time, place, the processes of class formation, race, other forms of social identity, and the opportunities for coalition across those divisions. At its moments of greatest power, women's public culture fostered coalitions among diverse social identities, especially diverse class identities. Only cross-race cooperation was virtually unknown in the urban north, where the African-American population remained small before 1900 and the race segregation of the Jim Crow era affected women as well as men. White women had access to the state and its resources; black women did not. Yet, except for race, women's public culture had the capacity to bridge social differences just as much if not more than did men's electoral culture.

All women had access to some form of public culture shaped by their gender. Poor women congregated on stoops or in the street to pool resources and share information. Wage-earning women and women in propertied families gathered in clubs to do the same. The crucial difference between their era and our own was the existence of gender distinctions defining the public spaces of women and men. Although examples to the contrary abounded—including churches, trade unions and schools—sex-segregated socializing or gatherings in which members of one gender greatly outnumbered the other were far more common in the lives of nineteenth-century women than were groups that included men and women in similar proportions. Sex-segregated work reinforced this reality.

At its weakest, women's public culture was merely an extension of social identities shared with men—women's auxiliaries of male organizations being an example—but even in this guise women's groups had the potential to amplify their power by affiliating with other women's groups. Thus, although limited to the social identities of the women drawn together at any particular time and place, women's public culture was as pervasive as nineteenth-century gender distinctions themselves and was not restricted to any one group.[4]

The goals of women's public culture took many forms. The woman suffrage movement battled women's second-class citizenship. For some in that movement, the state remained an enemy that denied women's rightful place alongside men in public life. However, many women activists sought expanded citizenship for women not as an abstract test of women's equality but as a vehicle for concrete ways of changing their society. For example, women trade unionists organized against class oppression. For them, the state could be positive as easily as negative. The movement for race progress among African-American women also occasionally turned to the white-dominated state to represent the interests of their race and gender. I trace the strand of women's public culture that ran closest to the state: coalitions of white middle-class and working-class women who sought social justice for working people at the same time that they claimed a larger voice for women within public life.

Women's public culture matters to historians because it was a means by which social resources were distributed. Among poor women, child care might be such a resource; among trade-union women, mutual aid during illness; among propertied women, new forms of knowledge. Through collective action, women could transcend the limitations they encountered as individuals. Thus by viewing them collectively we gain new insights into women's historical agency.

Women's public culture strongly interests historians of women because it was frequently the medium within which women's consciousness changed, especially their consciousness of gender identity and the structures that maintained it. Thus study of this phenomenon offers opportunities for analyzing the intersection between women's struggles with their personal identities and their engagement with the forces constructing those identities.

Although Florence Kelley began and ended her public activism in affiliation with other women, she searched for alternatives to this form of expression within European socialism. Her search helps us situate women's public culture in a larger framework of late-nineteenth-century state formation. White middle-class women were too central to the state-building process to be ignored, even by Kelley at her most alienated. The whys and wherefores of her and other women's nation-building power is another subject of this book.

Quite apart from her gender identity, Kelley's experience helps us see an important fact about contemporary public life—it was experienced in group terms. Citizenship, for all its rhetorical emphasis on the individual, was actually a process by which individuals combined to pursue a shared vision. Where there was no group and no shared vision of the personal good, there was also no sense of collective right or justice or of effective citizenship. The construction of Kelley's political identity, important as it was to her personal sense of self, was part of a collective dynamic.[5]

Florence Kelley's female identity complicated her participation in American public life. Her experience shows that the mobilization of middle-class and working-class women had enormous consequences for the redefinition of what was considered good and right in public life both before and after her generation emerged around 1880. The novelty of women's activism after 1880 lay in its scale and in its capacity to implement class-bridging goals during a period when changes in women's public culture produced an unprecedented supply of talented women leaders, both middle-class and working-class, just when changes within men's public culture created a demand for women's talents and values.

Expressing what was good and right for the society as a whole, women's organizations became increasingly important as hubs that mediated diverse interests. Some scholarly interpretations of women's activism during this era credit it with inventing interest-group politics. Yet although women did invent the *methods* of interest-group politics as we know them in the late twentieth century, they thought of themselves as representing society more generally—often in explicit contrast to the self-interested politics pursued by their middle-class and working-class male contemporaries.[6] Florence Kelley's contribution to this process grew out of her capacity to envision not a single good or right but a set of conditions designed to empower groups she thought lacked the ability to empower themselves in public life. She imagined a more level playing field for a more pluralist society. In many ways, the broad strokes of her equalizing vision if not its every particular still inform our understanding of social justice.[7]

Although Kelley and her contemporaries did not themselves use the term, historians call the years between 1890 and 1920 the Progressive Era.[8] That crucial period in American history is still not well understood, partly because the centrality of women within it has not been fully explored, partly because the era has been studied in isolation from its roots in antebellum public culture. I take a long view by examining the development of women's public culture in the preceding six decades and providing a thick description of one aspect of women's public culture in the 1890s. Within this long view I rely on comparisons of American women activists with their English contemporaries to illuminate the particular qualities of American public life that nurtured women's public culture. Comparisons show that women's public culture was not a natural outcome of their gender identity but a consequence of particular social, political, and economic structures and values.

This book looks at Florence Kelley's early life, before she became a central player on the national stage of Progressive reform. In a subsequent volume, I will analyze her work as general secretary of the National Consumers' League from its founding in 1899 until her death in 1932. Here I consider the process by which Kelley's personal political identity took shape as she interacted with groups of extravagantly different political persuasions. Her experience highlights the subjectivity of social agency and the construction of historical agency within specific discourses and specific social positions, all of which were constantly changing.

Although I concentrate on public life, this book also contains a personal story—Florence Kelley's search for redemption through her quest for a meaningful place in human history. This search, which propelled her public life, reminds us that the history of civil society also embraces personal hopes and aspirations. The dramatic transformations in civil society during Kelley's lifetime were not simply the outcome of impersonal and abstract social and economic forces; they were also the contingent result of human agency and human struggle.

Acknowledgments

One of the most gratifying aspects of scholarly life is the nurturing networks of support that make it possible for authors to complete large projects like this book. I feel especially blessed in the help I have received from colleagues, friends, and family. Although I can mention only a few people here, many more have given assistance for which I am deeply grateful.

The painstaking efforts of archivists and librarians helped me locate materials I might otherwise have missed. Especially important in this regard were Eva Mosley and her staff at the Schlesinger Library; Archie Motley at the Chicago Historical Society; Mary Ann Bamberger at the University of Illinois, Chicago; archivists at the State Historical Society of Wisconsin, Columbia University, and the Sophia Smith Collection; the hard-working staff at the Manuscripts Division of the New York Public Library; archivists at the Manuscripts Division of the Library of Congress; and the Inter-Library Loan staff at SUNY-Binghamton. I am grateful to the Nicholas Kelley family for permission to quote from the Florence Kelley papers in the New York Public Library and at Columbia University.

Many generous colleagues read portions of the manuscript and gave me the benefit of their criticism. To them I am extremely grateful. Those who read and helped me shape the whole volume did more than any author has the right to ask for. I am especially indebted to Victoria Brown, Judith Coffin, Blanche Coll, Tom Dublin, William Forbath, Steven Fraser, George Frederickson, Estelle Freedman, Linda Gordon, Melanie Gustafson, Vivien Hart, Dolores Hayden, Daniel Walker Howe, James Patterson, Elisabeth Perry, Ruth Rosen, Nick Salvatore, Wendy Sarvasy, Mercedes Vilanova, Lynn Weiner, Gordon Wood, and Julia Wrigley. I thank Carol Elizabeth Adams, Karen Offen, Jean Quataert, Dorothee Schneider, and Anja Schüler for timely help with German history.

Eileen Boris, Alan Dawley, and Leon Fink provided valuable criticisms at the last stages of revision.

Since this is the first of two volumes and the research for both was done simultaneously, my debt to those who provided me with released time from teaching is especially large. I am grateful for a Rockefeller Foundation Humanities Fellowship in 1981–82, which launched this study. A summer fellowship at the Woodrow Wilson International Center for Scholars in 1982 allowed me to begin work at the Library of Congress, a Schlesinger Library Grant in 1982 brought me to that treasure trove of women's history, and a National Endowment for the Humanities Fellowship at the Newberry Library in 1982–83 connected me with the richness of Chicago's archives. A Grant-in-Aid from the American Council of Learned Societies supported the translation of many of Florence Kelley's German writings. A fellowship from the John Simon Guggenheim Foundation in 1985–86 and the aid of a Spencer Foundation Research Grant in 1986–87 at the Center for Advanced Study in the Behavioral and Social Sciences at Stanford University helped me finish research and begin to write. The manuscript for this volume was completed with the support of fellowships from the American Association of University Women in 1990–91 and the Woodrow Wilson International Center for Scholars in 1992–93.

For capable and careful research assistance I am obliged to many who lightened the drudgery of my labors over the years. The aid of Susan Popkin, the late Beth Weisz-Buck, Lynn Weiner, Amy Butler, and Jacqueline Braitman was especially crucial. I particularly thank Kathleen R. Babbitt, whose superlative scholarly standards have significantly enhanced this book.

I am grateful to Charles Grench of Yale University Press for reliable encouragement at every state of the book's production and to Sarah St. Onge for superbly rigorous copyediting.

Leonard Sklar and Susan Sklar Friedman, who grew to adulthood alongside this project, provided fortifying love for their often-preoccupied mother. Aryeh Friedman has helped me place my work in proper perspective, and Nevona Sklar Friedman has given me new reasons for caring about American history.

Part One
Beginnings

1

"The Good

Ship Democracy,"

1830–1860

Florence Kelley's most vivid early memory recalled the death of Abraham Lincoln in 1865, when she was five years old. Personal and public responses to this calamity fused in her mind. At the time visiting her maternal grandparents in Germantown, Pennsylvania, she was told: "My child, President Lincoln is dead. He was shot last night." Her grandfather seemed "chiseled in stone"; her grandmother "shattered." Silence engulfed the girl, her grandmother, and their carriage as they drove to her home in West Philadelphia later that day. "The sidewalks were empty. People were draping their doors with mourning, and shutters were closed as if Death had entered every home." They found her mother, Caroline Bonsall Kelley, "sewing deep mourning on the flag that had been so often raised to celebrate victories during the war." On that day, as on many others, her father, William Darrah Kelley, a leading Republican congressman, was away from home. He had gone several days before to participate in ceremonies celebrating the raising of "the flag of the Union over the ruins of Fort Sumter."[1] Caroline, Florence, and her older brother, Will Jr., coped without him.

As a child Florence Kelley learned that gender organized the fabric of life, on both routine and extraordinary days. Far more pervasive than mere ideology, assumptions about gender permeated family relationships, work, and public life, orchestrated the components of personal identity, and constructed the meaning of cultural symbols.[2] On the day of Lincoln's death as on others, gender melded with a multitude of other cultural and social meanings and behaviors to shape the world she knew.

Public life drew heavily on meanings and behaviors associated with the emerging mores of middle-class family life. As in the Kelley family at the time of Lincoln's death, middle-class women and men occupied different spaces within public culture, but they shared a common root of normative values that took middle-class family life as the ultimate measure of what was personally good and used this in determining what was socially just.

Two models of public activity informed Florence Kelley's childhood. One, exemplified by her father, embraced the official world of electoral politics with its array of governmental institutions and political parties. The other, symbolized by her maternal great-aunt, Sarah Pugh, encompassed women's organizations and the values that carried women into collective action. A sea change in public life between 1800 and 1860 had greatly empowered civil society—that large swath of activity between the economy and the state—and carried women into much greater prominence. Men's and women's public cultures developed as parallel entities; each could act independently, but each was further empowered through alliance with the other. Florence Kelley's generation eventually brought these two cultures into effective conjunction, thereby introducing important changes into American political life and the American state. Yet her generation's success in the Progressive Era would have been impossible without the dramatic development of a strong women's public culture in the antebellum era—a time dominated not so much by their mothers as by their grandmothers.

Two long-term trends within the seventeenth and eighteenth centuries came to fruition in the first half of the nineteenth century to produce an explosion of public activity. The spread of universal white male suffrage fueled the growth of male public culture, and sentiments and organizational strategies attached to evangelical religion activated new forms of public culture for northern white women. Together, between 1830 and 1860 they laid new foundations for American public life.[3]

The significance of these changes was especially great for Florence, who at an early age learned to invest public life with personal passion on the scale she first encountered at Lincoln's death. Through her father she came to know the hegemonic public culture of white men; through great-aunt Sarah Pugh she came to know a forceful oppositional public culture advanced by a small group of white women abolitionists. In the decades before her birth, these progenitors did much to construct the society she entered; during the Progressive Era she stood on what they built.

The dual tracks of William Kelley's politics—part opportunist, part idealist—began in his youth when he embraced both the individualistic values of the self-made man and a working boy's awareness of social justice. Because his own father, a jeweler and watchmaker, died in 1817, when William was only two years old, he was raised by his mother and left school at the age of eleven to become a wage earner. Kelley was descended from Scotch-Irish Protestants who settled in the Delaware River valley in the 1660s. His mother, Hannah Darrah, had been born into a prosperous farming family, her father having received a land grant of eight hundred acres in Bucks County, Pennsylvania, for his service in the Revolution. William's father, David Kelley, was the youngest child in a farming family whose father, respected and admired in his community, had served as a major in the Revolutionary War. William was born in 1815. Two years later, his mother's brother defaulted on a loan backed with the collateral of his father's shop. Stricken by the prospect of the seizure of his prosperous business by creditors, David Kelley fell dead in the street at the age of thirty-two. Hannah Kelley was left with four young children, no means of support, and a large debt to pay.[4]

In these trying circumstances, Hannah Kelley turned to a time-honored female occupation: she borrowed money, opened a boardinghouse, and successfully supported herself and her children for over thirty years. Part of the family folklore about her survival praised the female communal networks that saved her most treasured possessions from the auction held to pay her husband's creditors. A Quaker neighbor, Friend Scattergood, filled two baskets with Hannah's treasures and left before the bidding began, declaring, "It seems strange that Friend Hannah Kelley should not have returned [her] precious heirlooms." None of the creditors dared challenge her.[5]

Partly as a result of his mother's powerlessness before his father's creditors, partly out of respect for his mother's achievements, in the 1840s William Kelley supported Lucretia Mott's efforts to obtain the passage of laws protecting married women's property rights in Pennsylvania.[6] Later, in the 1870s and 1880s, Elizabeth Cady Stanton and Susan B. Anthony considered him one of their most reliable allies in support of woman suffrage.

William Kelley's support of married women's property laws was a small part of his larger mission of liberating the productive forces of his society from traditional fetters and constraints. For William Kelley between 1820 and 1860, civil society was shaped by ideas that equated the free association of people with the unleashing of economic productivity. This liberating "political economy" derived from the steady expansion of civil rights throughout Anglo-American society in the seventeenth and eighteenth centuries that endowed white men with free agency and provided liberty of person, speech, thought, and faith; the right to own property, make contracts, and engage in commerce; and (theoretically, at least) equal access to legal justice. These Enlightenment conventions replaced medieval guilds, estates, and other corporate institutions that bound individuals directly with the state. Civil society arose from the erosion of those corporate institutions and from the emergence of private groups that claimed a broad range of civil rights for individuals.[7] To defend these civil rights and this private activity, the designers of political institutions in the new American republic of the 1780s severely limited the powers of government.

Yet not all groups benefited equally from this unleashing of the powers of the individual. To preserve white male dominance within both family and public domains, civil rights were explicitly denied to married women and only episodically extended to free black men. White women and African-Americans of both sexes remained deeply embedded in feudal obligations. The standing of these groups in civil society could only be improved by positive governmental steps to include them in the nation's citizenry.

The changes in public life—and the social distinctions they embodied—deepened in the early nineteenth century, when universal white male suffrage (instituted by all state governments except Rhode Island by 1840) placed unprecedented political power in the hands of average men.[8] Although the limited power of government restricted the uses to which this new agency could be put, the appearance of popular political rights marked a historical turning point. Henceforth American civil life—always a contested terrain of social, political, and economic struggle—was at least nominally grounded in the belief that government existed to serve the people, not vice versa. Henceforth the struggle for dominance within civic life involved the key variable of a politically empowered white male populace that embraced more than property-owning men.

Yet the same soil that nurtured democratic trends in American politics also sustained the inequalities that flowed from American economic life. Expanding civil rights, limited government, and universal white male suffrage created a congenial environment for the growth of unregulated capitalism and its social analogue, laissez-faire individualism. These two potentialities in American life—democracy and capitalism—struggled for the allegiance of the nation's soul between 1830 and 1900, shaping the history of the American polity and of civil society.[9]

An explosive growth of voluntary associations ignited that struggle. Though grounded in individualism, democracy and capitalism could only flourish if society was more than an aggregate of individuals, if some institutions promoted concern for the welfare of the whole. Voluntary associations provided that cohesion. By balancing the centrifugal forces of individualism with the centripetal force of community life and social obligations, voluntary organizations became the chief means by which older values of social solidarity were expressed in the nation's civic life. Voluntary associations also gave groups excluded from electoral politics access to civil society.

William Kelley's career exemplified the power and plasticity of voluntary associations in shaping the new nation's public life. His first serious employment laid the foundation for his public leadership by tutoring him in the magical potency of language. Impatient to contribute to his family's welfare, in 1825 he worked as a copyreader in the printing business of the owner of the *Philadelphia Inquirer*. His job was to read aloud "with such distinctness as would satisfy a careful proof-reader" several volumes of history and "high class fiction." He later said that this work prompted his "intellectual awakening." It also taught him the trenchant use of language that secured his political career within the networks of communication that steadily expanded the range of American public life. Since his employer printed the journal of the recently established Franklin Institute, Kelley learned about diverse branches of technological innovation as well, which later lent authority to his views on American industrial development.[10]

Using his father's tools, which the law protected from creditors, he apprenticed with a Philadelphia jeweler and pursued the opportunities open to an upwardly mobile artisan. For seven years he lived with the jeweler's family, indulging his keen appetite for books in the evening by organizing the Youth's Library Company, an association of apprentice boys later called the West Philadelphia Institute. The society soon accumulated a lending library of several thousand volumes and sponsored an annual lecture series, for which William first spoke in public.[11]

Careful attention to the productive use of leisure time was a prominent characteristic of the artisan culture from which Kelley sprang. Valuing education as a means of sustaining personal independence in mind and work and viewing labor or "the producer" as the source of all wealth, that culture resisted the long hours that employers sought to impose. At the end of his apprenticeship in 1834, Kelley joined the nation's first general strike, uniting "with the journeymen of that and other trades in promoting the recognition of the ten-hour system."[12]

The reshaping of employer-employee relations by market values meant that wage earners lost many customary protections previously governing interactions among apprentices, journeymen, and masters. Instead, the work process was organized in ways that increased productivity and profits for masters, owners, or investors but also increased the arbitrary effects of the economic marketplace on skilled journeymen and reduced them to the status of day laborers.[13] The campaign for the ten-hour (and later the eight-hour) day exemplified the process by which workingmen sought to use their new civil rights to institute economic rights. After the economic right to form labor unions—itself highly contested—shorter hours became the single most important goal for organized labor during the nineteenth century. It expressed the economic belief that workers, being "producers," should share in the benefits made possible by industrialization, the political belief that popular sentiments should shape public policy, and the civic belief that leisure enhanced civic understanding. Leisure in this context became a unifying theme that combined economic, political, and civic rights.[14]

Highlighting the rising importance of workingmen in the American polity and their changing relations at work, the general strike's main success lay in obtaining legislation for a ten-hour day for those employed on municipal public works.[15] The strike's narrow gains showed the limited extent to which artisans could use political rights to advance their class interests. Political rights did not easily engender economic rights, partly because rights were conceived as existing independently of economic relationships, partly because American traditions of limited government discouraged the use of state power for social or economic purposes.

Labor leaders contributed to this trend because they experienced politics as a divisive rather than unifying force and steered clear of it. Internal dissension had splintered the Workingmen's Party of 1828 to 1832, and as a result the General Trades Union avoided affiliation with political parties altogether. Thus the spread of universal white male suffrage in the 1820s and 1830s actually deepened traditions of limited government. As a consequence, although many American workingmen exhibited intense class consciousness, the structures and values of American civic life encouraged other forms of political expression organized around neighborhoods, ethnicity, and voluntary associations. In England, by contrast, the exclusion of nonpropertied men from the suffrage forged solidarity among two generations of wage-earning men who agitated for the right to vote between 1830 and 1870. There class goals merged with political goals.[16]

William Kelley embodied the American disjuncture between class consciousness and political action. His entrance into politics was channeled by voluntary networks that undercut his commitment to labor activism and to an independent labor party. For example, the Presbyterian church, to which his Scotch-Irish background predisposed him, served in Philadelphia as elsewhere as a Democratic stronghold. There he heard stirring, if creed-bound, sermons on temperance and self-improvement, and he simultaneously enjoyed the opportunity to meet local leaders in the Democratic Party. Tall and slender, with finely chiseled features, while still an apprentice he joined the State Fencibles, a voluntary militia headed by Colonel James Page, Democratic Party chieftain and later postmaster of Philadelphia. When only seventeen, he became an active member of the Niagara Hose Company, one of many volunteer fire-fighting groups, which, bridging classes and organized along ethnic and political lines, functioned partly as a precinct headquarters, partly as a neighborhood gang.[17] With the exception of his church, these institutional and cultural portals to political life were emphatically male. Including the church, they were decisively voluntary — that is, outside official state structures.

Experiencing political life from the perspective of these institutions, Kelley developed a deep identification with that most conspicuous of voluntary organizations — the Democratic Party. In 1837 he marched with the Fencibles as they escorted Andrew Jackson and his supporters in a parade through Philadelphia to denounce the U.S. Bank and other emblems of government-begotten privilege for the rich. Like other recently enfranchised wage earners, young Kelley believed that limiting the power of government would curb the extent to which the wealthy could use the state as a lever for their own interests. Notoriously, the U.S. Bank represented such a lever, and when Kelley refused to sign a petition that his employers circulated for the bank's retention, he became unemployable in Philadelphia.[18]

In the summer of 1835, Kelley moved to Boston, where a friend found him work as a journeyman jeweler. There he pursued self-improvement at a higher level, amplified his understanding of party politics, and polished his rhetorical skills: "At a cost that even the laboring man did not feel, I found, night after night, week after week, in [Boston's] lyceums and lecture-rooms the means of intercourse with her Bancroft, her Brownson, her Everetts, her Channings, her Prescotts, her Emerson, and scores of other learned and as able, though perhaps less distinguished sons than these." He studied "the details of party organization" and, as he explained to his Philadelphia friend Henry Patterson in the summer of 1835, followed Pennsylvania politics, reading "1 Pennsylvanian, 1 Sentinel, and 3 Enquirers weekly." The opposite sex held little attraction. "I am getting into the habits of an inveterate bachelor," he wrote Patterson, "I scarcely look at the girls I meet."[19]

Bursting upon the Boston scene at the high-water mark of radical influence in the Massachusetts Democratic Party, William Kelley's first act of political leadership typified the opportunities for ambitious young men and the rhetorical blending of themes associated with democracy and productivity that dominated American civic life. During a pause between speakers at a Democratic Party rally, he jumped to the podium and, responding to the audience's murmured "Who is he?" declared: "I am an American citizen, a man who can earn his living by the sweat of his brow and the cunning of his good right hand—one who has come to this cradled temple of liberty to pledge himself to stem the tide of time on board the good ship Democracy, with her to swim or with her gloriously to sink." A metaphor for both the party and the nation, "the good ship Democracy" was also Kelley's own career vehicle. The national scope of the metaphor anchored the loyalty of the new citizens created through universal manhood suffrage and defined their hegemony within the new nation-state. He joined others in shifting the control of American governance away from traditional elites toward a new group of political professionals who rose to power in the new party system. Because the Democratic Party was expanding its electoral base and holding more mass meetings and conventions, men of Kelley's oratorical eloquence were especially welcome.[20]

Hearing him speak at a rally alongside Bancroft and Brownson, Kelley's former Philadelphia patron, Colonel James Page, invited the young orator to return to Philadelphia and study law under his direction. After passing his bar examination "with much credit" in April 1841, Kelley swiftly emerged as a local political leader. He proved a valuable advocate for the governor's election in 1844, and the next year, at the age of thirty, he was appointed Deputy Attorney General for Philadelphia. A year later he gained appointment to the Pennsylvania bench as an associate judge, entering that crucial branch of American government that adjudicated civil, political, and economic rights. In 1851 he won election to a ten-year term in the same position.[21]

Signifying the importance of family networks in civic life, in 1843 William Kelley married James Page's Scottish niece, Harriette Tennant. She joined the household he maintained with his mother, Hannah. Harriette gave birth to a daughter, Isabella, in 1845 but died following the birth of another daughter, Harriette, two years later. Soon thereafter Isabella also died. In 1850 William, Hannah, his young daughter Harriette, and his favorite sister, Martha, moved into the Elms, a spacious house outside of Philadelphia built to Kelley's specifications.[22]

Although William Kelley was known as Judge Kelley throughout the remainder of his career, the secret to his success lay less in his talents as a jurist than in his "unusual gifts as a popular orator." As the *Democratic Review* wrote in 1851, "To a tall and vigorous frame, he united an expressive and mobile play of features, and a voice of unusual depth and power." These gifts personalized his political image, bringing him "a popularity and influence seldom attained by one of his age." An 1842 newspaper story called him "the tribune of the people" for his passionate defense of hard currency. In keeping with his stance as the defender of working men, he endorsed equality as a national value: "Liberty is not the sole idea that possesses the American mind," for "to enjoy liberty, equality of rights must be established." [23]

William Kelley's popularity took shape against a background of social turbulence. Severe economic depression in 1837 fueled anti-Negro and anti-abolitionist mobs, which in 1838 burned to the ground a hall constructed for antislavery meetings. Black male suffrage was repealed in Pennsylvania that year. Violence accelerated in the mid-1840s when rapid economic expansion attracted large numbers of Irish immigrants fleeing the potato famine. In 1844 anti-Catholic mobs in Philadelphia killed and wounded scores of men, women, and children and burned two Catholic churches and several homes; it took more than five thousand militia men to restore order.[24] Kelley denounced this nativist violence, a stand that endeared him to the Catholic community within the Democratic Party and reinforced his reputation as a champion of the social underdog. During the 1840s and 1850s, however, his defense of the powerless led him away from his party and gradually molded him into one of Philadelphia's most outspoken abolitionists.

Beginning in the late 1840s, the effects of slavery within American political life required Judge Kelley to reconsider his political options. The expansion of slavery after 1848 into the western territories obtained from Mexico precipitated a national crisis that enlarged his view of the appropriate use of government's power to defend the rights of individuals—first and foremost "free" white workers but also ultimately free blacks. This crisis forced him to abandon his party's belief that "the best government governs least." He forged a synthesis of the political values of two localities—Boston, with its traditions of elite radicalism, and Philadelphia, with its customs of democratic solidarity. Thereafter Kelley not only broke with the tenets of limited government; he became one of the most effective advocates of a strong central state as the best means of promoting both commerce and social justice.[25]

The first sign of William Kelley's new political consciousness was his departure from the Presbyterian church in 1846 and his entry into the smaller, more elite, and more politically radical First Unitarian Church. Fostered by his years in Boston, where Unitarianism was the reigning belief system of the intellectual vanguard he revered, this shift in religious affiliation supplied a new moral foundation for his political vision. His new minister's oratory and the companionship he found at the church inspired Kelley to describe himself as one of many "young men of other congregations, freed from family restraint, who gather into our Church in the evening, to be warmed into hope and life by

William Darrah Kelley in midlife, ca. 1860. Courtesy of Rare Book and Manuscript Library, Columbia University.

the glowing truths that fall from our Pastor's lips." His fast friendship with his new minister, William Furness, a former Bostonian and committed abolitionist, and Unitarianism's belief in the primacy of individual conscience carried him into the growing abolitionist movement.[26]

Kelley explored alternatives to the Democratic Party, supporting the Free Soil ticket in 1848 and in 1851 running for the judgeship as an independent. As one of the city's most popular figures, he handily won the election, despite the vigorous opposition of the now-conservative Democratic Party. The Workingman's Republican Party, formed in 1851 by wage earners seeking to strengthen ten-hour legislation and consolidate city and suburban government, loyally supported his election, as did the opportunistic Whig Party and those within the nativist American Republican or Know-Nothing Party who had agreed on fusion with the Whigs. Democrats and die-hard nativists denounced Kelley as an abolitionist who would flood the city with cheap black labor and as a sympathizer with unnaturalized foreigners, especially English and German immigrants.[27]

In the years immediately following his 1851 election, Judge Kelley's antislavery commitment deepened. Like many other former Democrats in the North, he viewed the Kansas-Nebraska Act of 1854 as proof that the party was controlled by "the doctrine of Calhoun" and that he should "go forth to resist its great power for evil." When the Republican Party held its first Pennsylvania convention in 1855, Kelley helped organize a Republican Association in Philadelphia. The group called on the federal government to secure "Life, Liberty and Happiness to all men" by prohibiting slavery "in any of the Territories of the United States." After Charles Sumner of Massachusetts was beaten unconscious at his Senate desk by a member of Congress from South Carolina, Kelley denounced the act at a public meeting in his courtroom. At the Republican national convention in Chicago in 1860, he was one of the first to back Abraham Lincoln and joined the delegation that carried the news to the nominee in Springfield.[28]

This shift in his political affiliation potentially jeopardized William Kelley's reputation as an advocate of the interests of wage-earning men. Antagonism between abolitionists and wage earners increased in the 1850s, partly because workingmen feared unfair competition from slaves and former slaves, partly because most abolitionists supported the status quo between wage labor and capital. In a world witnessing the rapid erosion of traditional restraints on capital and the erection of very minimal protection for labor, abolitionists favored a "free market" and "free labor" restrained only by individual conscience. This attitude expanded the possibilities for capitalism at the same time that it condemned slavery, and many wage earners perceived it as a threat.[29]

To rectify this tilt away from his wage-earning constituency, Kelley increasingly drew his political metaphors from family life and spoke of the need for government to become more active—not only against slaveholders but also on behalf of the poor. He interpreted democracy and free labor in a Philadelphia speech in 1856: "Democracy believes not only in the rights of man to own himself but believes it to be the duty of government to protect the poor and the weak, and to secure to every child born into this beautiful world equal chances before the State and in society." This bold statement went to the heart of the conjunction between political and economic rights. Observing a widening gulf between classes, workingmen realized they could not hope to give their children "equal chances" with those of wealthier parents. Kelley emphasized that government could diminish their disadvantage: "While you are at labor in the workshop, do you not feel that, though you have to toil hard for a beggarly subsistence, your children, by the aid of our public schools and public libraries, shall stand the peers of the proudest in the land? . . . (Enthusiastic applause.) Yes, such feelings are in all your hearts." Hard toil "for a beggarly subsistence" could be countenanced if the state could redeem what the marketplace imperiled. Capitalism and democracy became compatible.[30]

Democracy, however, could never be compatible with slavery. In this same speech, Kelley dramatized the opposition between slave and free labor, not by contrasting work cultures, but by comparing the degradation of slave family life with the protective relationships formed among free families. Slave families were violated by the economic marketplace; free families were not. "The [slave] child may be torn from the mother's bosom as a blind pup is torn from its mother," he declared and asked, "Can the free laborer work in the midst of a system of that kind?"[31] This implicit call for the end of slavery did not champion the rights of slaves, but by taking free families as the measure of what was good, William Kelley found a way to attack slavery without threatening his constituency.

In 1854 Judge Kelley codified his political transformation by marrying Caroline Bartram Bonsall. The two met at Furness's Unitarian church. Caroline lived in Germantown with her adoptive parents, Isaac and Elizabeth Pugh, and Isaac's unmarried sister, Sarah Pugh, a leading abolitionist. Orphaned at the age of nine, Caroline was descended from John Bartram, the Quaker botanist who in 1742 had cofounded with Benjamin Franklin the American Philosophical Society. Taking up residence at the Elms, Caroline Kelley gave birth to eight children over the next sixteen years, Florence being the third in 1859.[32]

William Kelley's political transformation occurred as he witnessed the growing strength of a dissenting public culture among women in the antislavery movement. Like the male mainstream of civil society, women's public culture was not a monolithic entity but a field of discursive connections across many groups. Emerging within neighborhoods and villages, political ideologies and voluntary organizations, women's civic activism was never

Caroline Bonsall Kelley, ca. 1860. Courtesy of Nicholas Kelley Papers, Rare Books and Manuscripts Division, New York Public Library, Astor, Lenox and Tilden Foundations.

totally separate from the men with whom they shared those locations. Yet because white women did not possess the civil and political rights that delineated the public culture of white men, they pursued their own forms of gender-specific civil activism. Overwhelmingly, their equivalent of the male political parties were female voluntary associations, many of which arose from evangelical religion. The new voluntarist church could be as empowering for average white women as the new republican state was for average white men. When evangelical religion problematized many aspects of family life, ranging from mothers' influence on their children's salvation to the sexual double standard, it also multiplied women's opportunities for collective action. Drawing on the positive value romanticism attributed to "natural" feelings and relationships, evangelical religion gave women a central place in the symbiotic dramas of personal and social redemption. A wide variety of women began to define their own space, customs, and terms of action, achieving through collective action an unprecedented degree of female civic agency.[33]

Women's activities significantly expanded the space occupied by civil society between 1830 and 1860, not as much by the addition of their numbers to public life—traditional proscriptions against women's public activism and the material circumstances of women's lives kept their numbers small compared to men—as through the concentration within women's public culture of opposition to marketplace definitions of human values and relationships. The American Female Moral Reform Society's ferocious campaign against prostitution exemplified this matrix, as did the vigor of women's antislavery associations. Speaking for values other than those associated with profit or personal gain, women began to bridge social and racial differences. This, along with their claim to speak for the welfare of the entire society, carried their voices into the emerging discourse about the nation's future. They were inventing new traditions of women's participation in public life.[34]

Florence Kelley grew up within the most radical network in women's public culture—Garrisonian abolitionism. As represented by Sarah Pugh, that network lay outside the evangelical mainstream of women's public culture, and it fostered in young Florence an enduring commitment to the radical potential within women's activism.

The Germantown home where Pugh lived with her brother, Isaac, and his wife, Elizabeth, became Florence's second home. "Florrie," as she was called, remembered visits there as "the happiest days of my childhood." Isaac, Elizabeth, and Sarah Pugh inhabited an "ivy-clad, pebble-dashed, gable-roofed old house, on a slightly terraced hillside." At the foot of the hill was a goldfish pond. The Newfoundland dog, Hector, was one of her favorite companions. When Florrie contracted communicable diseases, such as scarlet fever in 1868, she stayed in Germantown for long periods to aid her convalescence and protect the other children. "Your darling Florrie is well and happy," Isaac wrote Caroline Kelley in 1866, adding that she had spent the night with friends.[35]

Isaac and Sarah Pugh, born in 1799 and 1800 respectively, were raised by their widowed mother, Catharine, after their father died at the age of thirty-six in 1803. Like William Kelley's mother, Hannah, Catharine Pugh turned to a traditional female occupation, dressmaking, to support herself and her children and, like Hannah, she relied on the help of female support networks. Forming a business with her unmarried sister, Phebe Jackson, Catharine financed a fine education for Isaac and Sarah, who both attended Westtown Boarding School, directed by the Philadelphia Yearly Meeting of Friends. Isaac became a successful paper merchant.[36]

Isaac's wife, Elizabeth Kay Pugh, was the daughter of a distinguished Unitarian minister. In 1794, a few years before Caroline's birth, the Kay family emigrated to the United States with the family of Joseph Priestley, eminent scientist and dissenting minister, whose church, house, and laboratory had been burned by a mob in Birmingham, England, in 1791 to protest his support of the French Revolution. Isaac and Elizabeth had no children of their own, but in addition to Caroline they adopted another daughter. "Never were father and mother more tenderly loved by children of their own flesh and blood than these," Florence Kelley later wrote. After completing her own schooling, Caroline taught youngsters in the Priestley and Kay homes.[37]

To Caroline and later to her daughter Florence, Aunt Sarah Pugh exemplified the possibility that women could become full-time reformers. Florence vividly remembered Sarah's dedicated correspondence with eminent British reformers:

> Scores of times I have heard her murmur to long-staying ladies calling upon our grandmother: "I am glad to have seen Thee; and now I have a little writing to do." No physician performing operations at fixed times in a hospital and keeping office hours day by day; no lawyer moving from office to court-room and back again; no teacher in school, was ever more methodically active than the silent little Quakeress who sat at least half of every day at her desk, in her room, writing letters to Cobden and Bright, John Stuart Mill, Lady Stanley of Alderley, and the Duchess of Sutherland, and later on for many years, to Mrs. Josephine Butler, of sainted memory, throughout her terribly painful crusade to abolish the Contagious Diseases Acts in England.

By the time she was fifteen, Florrie considered her aunt "conscience incarnate." [38]

Florence remembered Sarah as "small and slight of figure," wearing an "exceedingly fine, close-fitting cap of almost transparent net." As a "protest against the compulsory usage of long hair for women," she wore her hair bobbed. During Florence's childhood, Sarah Pugh regularly accompanied her dear friend Lucretia Mott when she spoke before women's rights conventions. Florence recalled the milder forms of protest that characterized their old age. Particularly amusing were the Sundays when Mott visited and the two friends sat knitting on the front porch "in protest against the prevailing rigid Sabbatarianism" of their neighbors. [39] This vignette captured the radical, oppositional quality of their brand of women's political activism.

Far from typical, Sarah Pugh's public life nevertheless offers a useful guide to some of the chief characteristics of women's public culture: its primary location in women's organizations; its reliance on the leadership of single women; its essentialist views of women as a homogeneous group; its use of religious justifications; and its difference from men's public culture. Although her advocacy of women's rights took her beyond the norms of most of her contemporaries, her efforts to integrate women's domestic and public lives, especially in fund-raising strategies, sounded more familiar notes.

Before 1800 and the explosive growth of civil society, groups of women meeting outside the controlling influence of ministers or husbands were almost nonexistent. An important exception were "women's meetings" within Quaker congregations, which traditionally gave women the power to discuss their own issues, select their own leaders, assemble with their own ministers (many of whom were women), discipline their own members, control their community's poor relief, and veto marriages they found inappropriate, as, for example, between elderly men and young women. Sarah Pugh and Lucretia Mott were deeply imbued with this tradition; indeed, Mott had become a Quaker minister in 1821 at the age of twenty-eight. Although decisions taken in women's meetings could be overruled by men's meetings, Mott thought that "imperfect as they are, [women's meetings] have their use in bringing our sex forward, exercising their talents, and preparing them for united action with men." In the 1820s and 1830s, this strategy of strength through separation was widely adopted by non-Quaker women for the first time in Pan-Protestant groups in which women began to act independently of ministerial direction.[40]

As an unmarried woman, Sarah Pugh bore a special relationship to the female public world. Since marriage rather than gender identity per se deprived women of civil rights, unmarried women retained privileges denied to their married sisters—privileges crucial to the success of women's associations, such as the ability to maintain bank accounts or enter into legal contracts. Married women often had other obligations; Pugh jokingly complained in 1846 that "several of our most efficient helpers [have] . . . gone into the service of the State, alias into the 'baby line.'" Pugh's status as a single woman helps explain why the Philadelphia Female Anti-Slavery Society (PFASS) elected her as its president for twenty-eight of its thirty-two years of existence between 1838 and 1870. Her Quaker identity also facilitated her prominence, for although PFASS attracted both Quaker and non-Quaker members, Quakers dominated among Philadelphia's antislavery women, just as they did among the city's antislavery men.[41]

Like most PFASS members and most members of other women's organizations, Sarah Pugh justified the society's existence not on the negative exclusionary grounds that women were prevented from joining the local men's antislavery organizations (for after 1838 they were not) but on the positive grounds of women's unique obligations for the welfare of others, especially the well-being of women and children. This vision of women's peculiar responsibilities promoted a rhetorical flattening of differences among women at the same time that it exhorted them to action. For example, an 1831 poem used the term *woman* to express a homogeneous view of women's public responsibility:

> Shall we behold, unheeding
> Life's holiest feelings crushed?
> When woman's heart is bleeding,
> Shall woman's voice be hushed?[42]

The prohibitions that "hushed" women's public voices made gender a more conscious feature of their identity—to friend and foe alike—than was the case in men's public culture. Although this gender consciousness ignored other components of women's identity, such as class and race, these elements also shaped women's public culture. Like that of men, women's public culture was constructed around shared debates as well as shared beliefs, and sharp disputes occurred sometimes, as in the case of divisions within the Boston Female Anti-Slavery Society over women's rights in 1839, which destroyed the organization and curtailed women's collective action.[43] Appeals to women as women deliberately ignored differences among women as a means of enhancing what was often an unstable solidarity.

As suggested in the phrase "life's holiest feelings," this gendered justification for women's public culture ultimately relied on moral and religious imperatives. The religious cast that pervaded women's collective action, even among Quakers, limited women's options in some ways because it differentiated women's groups from many of the civil organizations that fostered the careers of men like William Kelley. Yet this religious spirit also empowered women to resist traditional strictures against their participation in public life by allowing them to call on a higher authority to justify their breach of custom: their duty to God took precedence over their duty to man.[44]

For all these reasons, women's public culture was differently situated in American civil society and therefore could sometimes accomplish what men could not. For example, the Philadelphia Female Anti-Slavery Society was the first abolitionist organization in Pennsylvania to be composed of both white and black members.[45] "About one-tenth of our number were colored," Pugh wrote of the 1837 national convention of antislavery women, proud that women had a higher proportion of African-Americans at their conventions than men did. Moreover, the Philadelphia Female Anti-Slavery Society went beyond the nominal participation of black women to combat race prejudice in the North, something no group of white men attempted. When the 1838 national convention of antislavery women in Philadelphia insisted on including African-American women despite racist threats to disrupt the convention if they persisted, a howling mob of fifteen thousand men assaulted and burned to the ground the large hall in which they were meeting. According to the society's report, the women continued their proceedings "calmly and deliberately, while the shouts of an infuriated mob rose around the building, mingling with the speakers' voices, and sometimes overwhelming them; while stones and other missiles crashing through the windows imperiled the persons of many in the audience." Before the building was engulfed in flames, delegates left in a pattern that protected black women from the mob's fury, two white women walking arm in arm with each black woman. The next day, shaken and greatly reduced in numbers, women delegates sought refuge in Sarah Pugh's schoolroom. Advised to "separate ourselves into small companies, that we might not attract attention," some were nevertheless recognized. Women of the popular classes joined their assailants. One delegate reported, "As we passed through some lanes, several low-looking women, who I should think fit companions for the leaders of the mob, actually came out of their huts to leer at us; pointing the finger of scorn, distorting their faces to express contempt, and saying among other things which I could not understand, 'you had better stay at home, and mind your own business, than to come here making such a fuss.'" Meanwhile, "hundreds of infuriated men" still cruised the streets "hunting anti-slavery victims." [46]

The radical and extremely unpopular goal of immediate, uncompensated abolition made women's participation in Garrisonian antislavery unlike their experience in any other movement: it became a life-threatening commitment. While many aspects of Sarah Pugh's experience in that movement resembled women's public culture generally, other ingredients remained distinctive — most especially, the advocacy of women's equal right to serve as leaders within the movement. Partly because its program of immediate abolition posed a direct challenge to one of the most fundamental social structures in American society — racial slavery — the Garrisonian movement needed all the help it could recruit, and women rose rapidly within its ranks. In addition to forming their own anti-slavery organizations, women broke all social precedent by exercising leadership within predominantly male Garrisonian groups. Sarah Pugh and Lucretia Mott exemplified this when, with other women, they served on the executive committee of the Pennsylvania Anti-Slavery Society in the 1850s. [47]

In England, antislavery women came nowhere near such leadership positions. Why did they in the United States? The deeper entrenchment of slavery in the American economy, "like the roots of giant trees beneath the soil," in the words of one woman abolitionist, and the obvious inability of civil and political institutions to solve the growing conflict between free labor and slave labor systems meant that American abolitionists confronted much greater obstacles than was the case in England. Parliament outlawed slavery in British territories in 1833, but the much weaker American national government was incapable of so tidy a political resolution. Since American antislavery activists attacked a much more deeply embedded set of social problems than was the case in England, some — men and women alike — were willing to challenge traditional gender hierarchies within their own organization when those hierarchies were perceived as counterproductive. Encountering no life-threatening violence and denied access to leadership by male allies, with a few notable exceptions British women abolitionists did not evolve new views of sexual equality. British antislavery organizations remained overwhelmingly sex-segregated, and women were more auxiliaries than equals. [48]

When the World Anti-Slavery Convention brought together British and American abolitionists in London in 1840, no British women sought recognition as official delegates, but seven American women did, including Sarah Pugh and Lucretia Mott. The convention organizers refused to seat the American women, maintaining that "women thus sent by an entire nation are out of their place," and British women abolitionists condoned the exclusion. Lucretia Mott, shocked to find British women abolitionists fearful that "they might get 'out of their sphere'" should they even speak with the American women, was "much disappointed to find so little independent action on the part of [British] women." Pugh wrote a widely reprinted remonstrance against the exclusion of women delegates.[49]

Women's unprecedented rise to leadership within American Garrisonianism generated outrage—even, indeed especially, within antislavery ranks. Resistance to this furor in turn precipitated a separate women's rights movement. The year after she helped Elizabeth Cady Stanton organize the world's first women's rights convention in Seneca Falls, New York, Lucretia Mott expressed the ethics of that gathering in a sermon: "We deny that the present position of woman is her true sphere of usefulness; nor will she attain to this sphere, until the disabilities and disadvantages, religious, civil, and social, which impede her progress, are removed out of her way. These have enervated her mind and paralyzed her powers." Who knows, Mott asked, "but that if woman acted her part in governmental affairs, there might be an entire change in the turmoil of political life."[50] Mott was not only imagining new forms of public power for women; she was reflecting changes already under way in American civic life: by engaging in public debate and pursuing their own social agenda, antislavery women were behaving like citizens.

The most formal expression of women's growing power in civil society was the petition campaign that antislavery women joined during 1837 and 1838. Women inscribed two-thirds of the signatures on the four hundred petitions sent to Congress and state legislatures, urging the abolition of slavery in the District of Columbia and United States territories and calling for an end to the slave trade between states. Although Sarah Pugh's wealthy neighborhood produced few signatures, the public exercise seemed worthwhile. "In our aristocratic district we were generally civilly received and heard, and as civilly refused with few words," she wrote. Nevertheless, she had "many interesting conversations and opportunities for showing forth abolition truth."[51]

As was the case with other women's groups, women's antislavery activities overlapped with their domestic lives. Just as women's homes became political entry points during the petition campaign, dinners at James and Lucretia Mott's suburban residence, Roadside, offered spirited debate as well as traditional hospitality. In 1854, Sarah Pugh wrote to a friend: "At L. Mott's accidental dinner-party last week were present Griffith M. Cooper, of New York, a radical abolitionist, once a Friend, now an ultra-liberal; Mrs. [Ernestine] Rose, a Polish Jew, now an eloquent speaker on woman's rights and other ultraisms; Mrs. Townsend, a temperance lecturer; Sarah Grimké, a repentant slaveholder etc., etc.; Mr. Pelham, a Methodist slaveholder from Texas! . . . Have we not strange amalgamations?" After their marriage, Caroline and William Kelley joined the Motts' parlor mix. Two months before Florence's birth, Lucretia Mott wrote Caroline that "our friend Robert Dale Owen" would be visiting and "we should be pleased if Judge Kelly and thyself would accompany him to dine or take tea, or both." Rather than being a private sphere segregated from public pursuits, middle-class domestic life often integrated private and public activity.[52]

Antislavery women made their civic presence felt through consumer boycotts, which also combined the personal and the public. Although the term *boycott* was not coined until the 1880s, preferential purchasing was well known a generation earlier. A resolution drafted by Lucretia Mott and adopted at the 1837 National Convention of Anti-Slavery Women called for a boycott of slave-made commodities in terms that politicized everyday purchases.

> Resolved, That the support of the iniquitous system of slavery at the South is dependent on the co-operation of the North, by commerce and manufactures, as well as by the consumption of its products — therefore that, despising the gain of oppression we recommend to our friends, by a candid and prayerful examination of the subject, to ascertain if it be not a duty to cleanse our hands from this unrighteous participation, by no longer indulging in the luxuries which come through this polluted channel; and in the supply of the necessary articles of food and clothing, &c., that we "provide things honest in the sight of all men," by giving the preference to goods which come through requited labor.[53]

Although women did not always purchase their families' groceries and clothing, they could influence those purchases. A cycle of dynamic economic expansion in the northern states, under way since before 1800 but accelerating after 1830, produced stupendous growth in the market economy, increased productivity, accelerated the shift from indentured to free labor, and realigned classes to create a commercially oriented middle class alongside a wage-earning class. This economic transformation produced consumer goods on an unprecedented scale, attracting both middle-class and wage-earning purchasers. New forms of sentiment emerged to personalize and value goods for their own sake quite apart from the use they had. Antislavery women invested this nascent consumer consciousness with a new sense of social obligation.[54]

In 1838, Sarah Pugh joined the executive committee of the National Requited Labor Association, formed that year to promote "the duty of abstaining from the produce of slave labor." Mott served as the association's treasurer, and five of the eleven members of the executive committee were women. Philadelphia's black women also organized as consumers, forming the Colored Female Free Produce Society of Philadelphia at Bethel Church in January 1831. In 1829, James Mott opened Philadelphia's first free produce store, which until 1846 provided antislavery families with cotton and food goods untainted by slave labor. The store stocked "secrets"—brightly wrapped candies with mottoes—that were especially favored at children's birthday parties and improved the reader with inspiring couplets.

> If slavery comes by color, which God gave,
> Fashion may change, and you become the slave.[55]

In this way consumer consciousness built political consciousness.

Although the potential market for free produce was substantial, embracing more than half a million members of antislavery societies nationally, as well as Quakers and free blacks, the movement's myriad difficulties in obtaining and processing raw materials permitted the manufacture of only a fraction of the actual demand.[56] Nevertheless, free produce remained an ideal for thousands of women consumers before 1860. Later in the century, when consumer consciousness deepened, Florence Kelley mobilized consumers' political activism on a much broader scale.

After the Civil War, Sarah Pugh continued to shun products formerly made by slaves. Florence remembered asking, "Aunt Sarah, why does Thee never eat sugar? and why are Thy underclothes linen even in winter?" Explaining that cotton and sugar were grown by slaves, Pugh replied, "I decided many years ago never to use either, and to bring these facts to the attention of my friends." Not meaning to be impertinent, young Florence inquired further, "Aunt Sarah, does Thee really think any slaves were freed because Thee did not use sugar or cotton?" Her aunt's "perfectly tranquil" reply: "Dear child, I can never know that any slave was personally helped; but I had to live with my own conscience."[57]

Although many nineteenth-century social movements relied on women's fund-raising efforts, antislavery women went further than most in turning fund raising into a public festival. Through fund-raising fairs, women forged a more capacious community among abolitionists than political action alone could achieve. For almost thirty years, Sarah Pugh presided over the fair conducted by the Philadelphia Female Anti-Slavery Society at Christmastime in conjunction with the annual meeting of the Pennsylvania Anti-Slavery Society. Meetings to produce goods for fairs grew in size and number after 1837. When the "Fair Circle" met at the home of James and Lucretia Mott in 1853, about sixty were present at tea, forming a "brilliant scene" that grew even larger that evening when the gentlemen arrived. The fair became a statewide event in the 1840s and an international one in the 1850s. On September 12, 1859, the day that Florence Kelley was born,

Sarah Pugh wrote Richard D. Webb, a leading antislavery activist in Ireland, that "the working circles are busy in our country districts" preparing for the fair. That year, at what was called the Pennsylvania Anti-Slavery Fair and National Bazaar, contributions were received from as far away as London, Edinburgh, and Dublin.[58]

The fairs themselves became community rituals, as women's material culture built political culture. In the words of Mary Grew, a close friend of Sarah Pugh, they were like "Passover Festivals, whither 'our tribes went up' with gladness, and found refreshment and strength."[59] Samplers, stationery, pottery, and other handicrafts sold there carried the antislavery movement into the routines of daily life, blending domestic, religious, and civic life in ways that reflected the patterns of women's experience. The quotidian quality of women's domestic responsibilities fit well with a call for the practice of social justice in everyday life, but such a call could be profoundly radical because it held individuals responsible for the ethics of their social relationships.

Fairs became crucial moneymakers for the antislavery cause, the PFASS events alone realizing a profit of $28,025 over twenty-five years, most of which went to support the Pennsylvania and the American Anti-Slavery Societies. Since women's societies did not merely hand the money over but earmarked amounts for specific purposes, women actually shaped antislavery efforts. If power can be defined as the ability to control the distribution of social resources, these women certainly exercised it. The annual budget of the American Anti-Slavery Society in the mid-1850s reached six or seven thousand dollars, about eight hundred of which came from the Philadelphia female society alone.

Women's financial clout was one reason why five women, including Pugh and Mott, were elevated to the executive committee of the Pennsylvania Anti-Slavery Society in 1850 and why William Lloyd Garrison appointed Lucretia Mott and other women to the executive committee of the American Anti-Slavery Society in the 1840s.[60]

The growing public power of antislavery women combined with that of antislavery men to achieve what neither could have accomplished separately. Such results became dramatically evident in William Kelley's courtroom in the mid-1850s. "Our anti-slavery women were often at the courts," Lucretia Mott remembered. There they tried to prevent "the Slave Power in the form of United States officers and their ever ready minions" from overpowering what little protection the state of Pennsylvania could offer those who were claimed as slaves under the Fugitive Slave Act. On these occasions, women crossed the boundary between civil society and the state to become an explicit part of the law-enforcement process. They destabilized the courts' attempt to impart "a powerful aura of certainty" to what were in fact contingent identities and circumstances.[61]

Pennsylvania Anti-Slavery Society Executive Board, 1851. Courtesy of Sophia Smith Collection, Smith College. *Front row, seated from left:* Oliver Johnson, Margaret Jones (later Margaret Jones Burleigh), Benjamin Bacon, Robert Purvis, Lucretia Mott, James Mott. *Back row, left to right:* Mary Grew, E. M. Davis, Haworth Wetherald, Abby Kimber, J. Miller McKim, Sarah Pugh.

In 1855 Judge Kelley's court heard an infamous case involving a Virginia slaveholder who, then serving as minister to Nicaragua, was traveling by boat to New York via Philadelphia with three slaves—Jane Johnson and her two children. An activist in the Underground Railroad told Johnson that the laws of Pennsylvania emancipated all slaves brought into the state by their masters, and, the records of Philadelphia's Female Anti-Slavery Society reported, "she took possession of her own person and her own children." Johnson's former master succeeded in bringing her Underground Railroad protectors to trial for riot, assault, and battery, charging that Johnson and her children had been abducted. As the presiding judge, William Kelley had his hands full when, at great risk to her newly won freedom, Jane Johnson entered the courtroom to testify that she had left her master freely. Sarah Pugh, Lucretia Mott, and other members of the Female Anti-Slavery Society "attended her through that perilous scene," as did members of "the Vigilant Committee of Philadelphia," an African-American group that organized Underground Railroad rescues and often filled Philadelphia courtrooms as a means of protecting the interests of black defendants. Safeguarded in the courtroom, Johnson's freedom was confirmed "by the energy and skill of the presiding Judge," and, accompanied by Lucretia Mott, she was "driven rapidly away, under an armed guard," to Mott's home. There, "entering the front door, and quickly passing through the house," Jane Johnson was taken to a place of safety. Three years later, black women and white women remained prominent figures in the courthouse. From an African-American perspective, young Charlotte Forten wrote in her journal, "Last night the court sat for fourteen hours, the longest session that has ever been held in this city. Many ladies stayed during the entire night, among whom was the noble and venerable Lucretia Mott . . . whose 'very presence is a benediction!'" [62] Although lacking official authority, through collective action women brought their social authority to bear on public policy.

Women's antislavery networks resisted the hegemonic power of proslavery opinion through other public gestures. During John Brown's trial for treason against the commonwealth of Virginia as a result of his assault on the federal arsenal at Harpers Ferry with the goal of inciting slave insurrection, his wife, Mary, stayed at the home of Lucretia Mott. There William Kelley, Sarah Pugh, and others visited her. This display of support incensed most Philadelphians, but at Reverend Furness's Thanksgiving services many women parishioners "went to take Mrs. Brown by the hand, and by kind pressure or tender word expressed their sympathy." Sarah Pugh pronounced her "nerved for the trial." [63]

The presence of antislavery women at public rallies helped shape public opinion. On the day John Brown was hanged in December 1859, Pugh joined the Motts, Furness, William Kelley, and hundreds of others in a ceremony at National Hall. The *Philadelphia Evening Bulletin* reported that "the proportion of females present was large and they occupied front seats." Lucretia Mott spoke, and the *Bulletin* described her words as "not of the milk and water order." [64] The meeting ended with disruptions led by southern sympathizers.

The confrontation between Philadelphia's abolitionists and anti-abolitionists reached a peak in mid-December 1859 at a meeting organized by William Kelley at the Peoples Literary Institute. Kelley introduced the speaker, George Curtis, a noted Boston abolitionist, to the audience, half of whom were women. An angry mob threatened to stop the meeting, encouraged by James Page, Kelley's former mentor, who had declared "that the meetings of the abolitionists should be broken up by violence and the speakers hung on the spot." In the end, however, the mayor commanded the police to disperse the disrupters. [65]

The annual antislavery fair was in full swing that day, despite newspaper announcements inquiring whether readers would "suffer such a Fair to be held." Armed with a court order the next day, the mayor ordered the fair out of the hall it occupied. Sarah Pugh described to a friend the cool deliberations she and her colleagues conducted when, in the midst of the excitement generated by the presence of the sheriff and his men, they decided where to move the fair. The scene included "our interviews and discussions with trustees, lawyers, high-constables, and sheriffs; business meetings of the Fair Committee, all ladies, surrounded by gentlemen, who looked with wonder on the 'irrepressible women,' amazed to see them so 'plucky,' and declaring they would vote for them for the Legislature. Such were the comments that we afterwards heard had been made, while we were engaged in grave debate as to the best thing to be done under the circumstances. One spectator longed for the power of making a picture that would be historical." [66] In this case as in so many others, the vitality of women's public activism combined with the structures, values, and conflicts within civil society to draw women deeper into the American political process.

Although antislavery women occupied a narrow range of the political spectrum, Sarah Pugh and her associates nevertheless prefigured forms of women's public activity that spread more widely after the Civil War. By empowering voluntarism, American civil society also empowered women. Women's citizenship, no longer limited to their indirect power as the mothers of sons or to the occasional individual who raised her solitary voice, became a vital force in civil society as groups of women began to take collective action in public life.[67] Carried forward partly by the energy of female voluntary associations, partly by distinctive characteristics of the male-dominated polity, which invited the participation of voluntary groups in public life, and partly by national crisis in which men's and women's public cultures were enmeshed, Sarah Pugh's generation gave Florence Kelley's an impressive legacy of female social activism. Women abolitionists reshaped politics at the same time that they challenged and reconstructed definitions of womanhood. Though excluded from most civil and political rights, women were not merely passengers on the "good ship Democracy." They were an integral part of the crew.

2

"So Mature in Thought," *1859–1876*

Florence Kelley grew up on an isolated estate four miles as the crow flies west of Independence Hall; the Elms was so secluded during her early years that no one passed by between Thanksgiving and Easter.[1] This social solitude defined her childhood. Its effects were pervasive. Most obviously, it accentuated the terrible toll of infant mortality in her family and the burden of obligation these deaths placed on her young shoulders. A grim family struggle with infant and childhood illnesses haunted Florence's childhood. It tutored her in human loss and grief before she knew how to read and write and placed on her at an early age the survivor's heavy mantle of responsibility. Her youthful pictures reveal a child with mournful eyes and furrowed brow. In the long run, her childhood disciplined her to perceive and oppose the quotidian misery that her social system imposed on women and children. Eventually she converted her childhood sorrow into an adult capacity for rage and immoderate action; her travail helped her wage war against public policies that tolerated the loss of human life. In that war she took no prisoners.[2]

For almost twenty years, Caroline Kelley waged a desperate but losing battle against infant and childhood diseases, watching five of her eight children die before they were old enough to attend school. Although the exact causes of these deaths remain uncertain, the timing of the first three suggests summer diarrhea, the most common cause of infant death in mid-nineteenth-century America. During these months, infants and toddlers from even the most prosperous families became vulnerable to infection from contaminated food, milk, or water. By 1870 about one-third of all children in Philadelphia died before they reached age ten. Public health experts knew infant mortality was rising, but they could not reliably tell mothers how to keep children alive.[3]

The first of Caroline's losses occurred early in the autumn of 1859, just after Florence's birth, with the death of two-year-old Elizabeth Pugh Kelley. Another baby, Marian Bartram Kelley, died at eleven months in August 1863, when Florence was almost four. A third, Josephine Bartram Kelley, died at seven months, during Florence's sixth summer, in June 1865, two months after Lincoln's assassination. If any of these babies had been recently weaned, which was likely in the case of Marian, in view of her age, and Josephine, because she was a twin, her risk of acquiring the deadly diarrhea was even greater. Yet another infant, Caroline Lincoln Kelley, died at four months in February 1869, when Florence was nine. The final blow came in 1871 with the death of Anna Caroline Kelley, Josephine's twin, at the age of six, during Florence's twelfth year. No sisters escaped this cruel winnowing, but Florence's two brothers, William Darrah Kelley Jr., two years her elder, and the last Kelley baby, Albert Bartram Kelley, born in 1870, survived with her to raise children of their own.

Caroline's familiarity with loss led to entrenched sorrow rather than transcendence. Her grief was doubtlessly aggravated by her own childhood loss of her parents. Her brothers also became part of her chronicle of loss, when in 1850 Benjamin Bonsall died at the age of fifteen, and in 1870, William Bonsall died in the Kelley home of tuberculosis contracted in the Civil War. In her daughter's words, Caroline developed a "permanent terror of impending loss" and "a settled, gentle melancholy which she could only partly disguise." Caroline's letters made her suffering clear. Just before Florence's fourth birthday, she wrote William from the refuge of her girlhood home in Germantown about her reluctance to return to the Elms: "It is impossible to tell you how much I dread the thought of returning to those dreary chambers. They seem to me the abode of Death only. In other scenes I can think of my darling lost ones with something akin to hope and comfort, but there where I have suffered so much, grim Death and Desolation seem staring me in the face wherever I turn. I feel as if I could travel to the uttermost parts of the earth without pausing, provided my remaining children were about me." She found escape in dreams. When Florence was seven, Caroline wrote William, "I had a beautiful dream last night of traveling in England. I thought Mama and I were alone. . . . When I awoke I was so sorry and could barely make myself believe that I must return to dreary realities."⁴

Florence absorbed her mother's sorrow. During Florence's ninth year, in an effort to improve baby Caroline's health care, the family temporarily resided with friends in Philadelphia. There, "Florrie [was] taken out of herself almost unconsciously" by the companionship of other children, and found "amusement and strength in frequent walks," including trips to the library. As a special treat, she, brother Will, and sister Anna attended a minstrel show, but the baby's illness made it hard for Florence to enjoy herself. Afterward, Will told Caroline "that once, when Florrie's interest flagged, he saw the large tears slowly coursing down her cheeks, at the thought of the possible termination of the baby's illness." The hardest blow, however, was the death of six-year-old Anna, an event, Florence wrote in 1927, that "robbed the sunshine of its glory and created a shadow lasting to this present day."[5]

During her life and after her death, Anna's central place in the Kelley household was reflected in the family's correspondence, which referred to her in terms not applied to Florrie. "Fascinating Anna," "bright-eyed Anna," and other loving phrases testified to the child's unique place in the hearts of her parents and grandparents. A condolence letter from Elizabeth Pugh to Florence noted the family's expectation that Florrie would be of special value even if she could not take her sister's place. "You all lost a great treasure in losing your bright and beautiful sister," she wrote, adding that when a friend "asked for little Florrie. . . . I told him that you were not little Florrie but a dear good child and a great comfort to us all." Florence's great responsibilities to the living became an important part of her childhood identity. She quickly matured beyond her years. In 1870, at the age of eleven, as the oldest family member at home when William Bonsall died, she telegraphed Caroline and Will Jr. in New York and her father in Washington, D.C., earning her father's praise for her "womanly thoughtfulness," and the "grownup capacity" of her dispatches.[6]

Florence could not look to her mother for knowledge capable of sustaining youthful optimism. Instead, she turned to her maternal grandparents and great-aunt in German-town and to her father. William Kelley served as her chief intellectual and spiritual mentor. By the age of seven, she already identified strongly with him. "You have no idea how pleased she was at being told that she looked like you," Caroline wrote William of their daughter's reaction during social calls in 1867. "Everyone seemed struck with the resemblance and Florrie was highly gratified."[7]

Her harsh early lessons in infant mortality increased her receptivity to William Kelley's instructions about social injustice. Although by the time of Florence's birth he had become one of the wealthiest men in Philadelphia, William remained true to the republican principles of his youth and cultivated an active social conscience in his daughter. Since illness and her mother's fear of losing her prevented her from attending school, most of her early reading was done at her father's side. She recalled later that in her seventh year he tutored her in "a terrible little book with woodcuts of children no older than myself, balancing with their arms heavy loads of wet clay on their heads, in brickyards in England." She thought that the children "looked like little gnomes and trolls, with crooked legs, and splay frames." The book's text told her about the British reform tradition and the "hardships [children] were then suffering, nearly two decades after Lord Shaftesbury's bill to shorten the working hours of women and children in English factories had been enacted by Parliament."[8]

Through this book, William Kelley coached his daughter to sympathize with British working children and with "children in his own generation called 'bound' boys and 'bound' girls, who came from England under indenture to the people who brought them. They had to work long years without wages as household servants or unskilled farm help, to pay the costs of their journey to the land of the free." He described the plight of slave children, "who, born after I was and down to President Lincoln's Proclamation of Emancipation, had been sold away from their parents to grow up in distant states, far from their brothers and sisters." Florence so raptly absorbed his lessons that her mother and grandmother cautioned William against darkening her mind with "such dismal ideas." Her father "replied seriously that life can never be right for all the children until the cherished boys and girls are taught to know the facts in the lives of their less fortunate contemporaries." His instruction helped her understand a scene she passed on the streetcar when she briefly attended school in the late 1860s: "little skinny girls waiting on the sidewalk" in front of a "forbidding-looking brick building." These, she realized, were textile " 'hands' returning from their noon half-hour for dinner." [9]

William's influence loomed especially large because Florence attended school only briefly. Her susceptibility to infection and her mother's fear of losing her last surviving daughter kept Florence at home. Her longest uninterrupted attendance was "five or six months," beginning with her thirteenth birthday, at Miss Longstreth's school for girls in Philadelphia. Earlier she had attended "a delightful little school in Germantown" for a few weeks when she was eight, and shortly thereafter the Friends School of Philadelphia, but both stints were cut short by illness, first rheumatism, then scarlet fever. [10]

Correspondence between Caroline and William expressed a great concern over Florrie's health beginning with her fourth month of life, when they thought they detected a hearing problem. Home remedies for a variety of ills probably created their own complications. "Florrie complained very much of feeling badly, but I hope the treatment for worms may have a beneficial effect," Caroline wrote William in 1866. "If not, I shall have to see a physician." [11] Serious illness did not actually strike until her eighth and ninth years, but perhaps because of her parents' reaction, its effects lasted throughout her childhood and adolescence.

Recovering from an attack of infantile rheumatism sufficiently to attend drawing school in January 1868, Florrie received a letter from her mother during one of Caroline's trips to Washington laced with the anxiety that pervaded their relationship: "I am very anxious to know whether you went to drawing school yesterday. I said to Hannah as I left the door, that if it wasn't snowing you might go, but I did not think of rain, and when I saw the heavy rain after we left Philad. I felt afraid that your desire to go might compel you to do so. I hope you will write me a line at once, and tell whether you went and if so, whether you have taken cold. I will enclose an envelope, so that you need not be delayed. Put your note into it, never mind the mistakes, and give it to the post man as soon as you can." [12]

Beginning in her eighth year and lasting into college, chronic eyestrain was the cruelest effect of Florence's childhood illnesses. "Florrie is suffering a great deal with her eyes today," Caroline wrote William in 1868. Not well enough to leave home, the child wore a green shade over her eyes. Nevertheless, Florrie did not permit illness to deprive her of the pleasures of reading. "She waylaid the Dr. last week and begged permission to read a little by daylight, which he gave," Caroline continued. "At this moment, she is deep in the stories of Hans Christian Andersen." [13]

For most of her childhood, Florrie's schooling was limited to classes in music, drawing, and dancing. William thought that her native talents meant that she needed "less of the exacting details of education than most children." To Caroline, he exclaimed "What an admirable letter Florrie writes from one so young and whose health has kept her from school so long!" He constantly encouraged Florrie, partly as a way of prodding her older brother, Will, who was healthy but an indifferent scholar, to greater efforts in his schoolwork. Writing Will, he commented, "I cannot tell you or her how I admire her perseverance." [14]

Perhaps because they were so brief, Florrie's school experiences made a lasting impression. At Friends School in the late 1860s, she learned about two of Sarah Pugh's friends who taught in a freedmen's school on St. Helena Island off the coast of South Carolina. For that school, her teachers made frequent requests "for garments and books

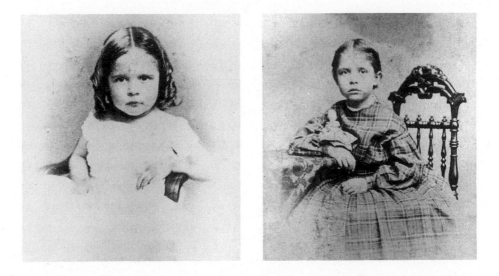

Florence Kelley as a child, ca. two, five, (previous page), seven, nine, and twelve years old. Courtesy of Nicholas Kelley Papers, Rare Books and Manuscripts Division, New York Public Library, Astor, Lenox and Tilden Foundations.

that *we liked* ourselves." Every Wednesday she participated in "the austere simplicity and peaceful quiet" of the school's Quaker religious services. So that her thoughts should not be distracted, before entering the meeting room Florrie was asked to leave with her teacher her only jewelry, a ring with "an almost invisible tiny diamond," which was duly returned at the close of the session. Otherwise, formal religious instruction was not a prominent feature of Florence Kelley's childhood. Although she attended the "children's festival" at Furness's Unitarian church on Easter, on most Sundays, since William was often in Washington, Caroline preferred to visit her parents in Germantown, and Florence attended Quaker Sunday School there. Outings into town or to the Pughs were major efforts in winter, however, so many sabbaths found Caroline and the children at home.[15]

Florence's voracious appetite for mental activity and her overdeveloped sense of duty drove her to excel at Miss Longstreth's. Her intellectual competitiveness elicited gentle warnings from William. "I have never entertained a doubt as to your assuming an honorable position at school, but let me warn you against being too ambitious," he wrote her. "Remember that if you succeed in getting at the head of your class there is no further promotion till the end of the term, though sickness or accident may put the best scholar down without fault on her part." Although this advice spoke to his daughter's unstable health, it ignored her desire to test herself against her peers. "I do not wish to discourage you," he concluded, "but to bring to your mind the vicissitudes that attend every stage in the life of an earnest or ambitious person."[16] Vicissitudes this child had aplenty. What she sought was a chance to express herself in a social context, however awkwardly.

Miss Longstreth's school was the best that Philadelphia had to offer young women of Florrie's social class. A Quaker institution founded in 1829, it emphasized moral responsibility as well as intellectual development. By the early 1870s the school had about a hundred pupils and six full-time teachers augmented by some thirty part-time instructors. In terms that suited Florence's need for self-direction, Mary Anna Longstreth taught her pupils how to acquire knowledge: "Learn thoroughly what you attempt to learn. . . . Investigate, compare, reflect; form habits of accuracy, attention and patient research; acquire the power of concentrating and controlling your thoughts. Do not be afraid of difficulties."[17] These were good mottoes for ambitious girls. When health considerations forced Florrie to withdraw from the school, she knew how to pursue her own intellectual path.

At first her parents did not encourage her studious bent. "She is very good and kind, but thoughtful beyond her years," Caroline commented to William in Florence's ninth year. "I am anxious to surround her with children." These sentiments were echoed by Elizabeth Pugh, who wrote William: "I agree with you entirely that she ought not to study so much this winter, but she is so mature in thought that she particularly requires the companionship of children—not to improve her mentally, but rather to make her keep to childish things and childish ways." "So mature in thought" that her mother and grandmother worried about her, Florrie nevertheless won her father's acceptance as a budding intellect when she was ten.[18]

Florence was "never willingly absent" from her father's study when he occupied it during congressional recesses, and beginning with her tenth birthday she inhabited the room in her own right. William Kelley had just returned home from a trip to California and Promontory Point, Utah, where, as a member of the Ways and Means Committee of the U.S. House of Representatives, he had witnessed the completion of the transcontinental railroad. On that "memorable birthday," he found her sitting on the study floor perusing *The Resources of California,* a folio-sized periodical he had carried home from his trip. Something about the sight moved him. As Florence remembered, "finding me absorbed in text as well as pictures, he welcomed me with enthusiasm into a companionship which has enriched my whole life." This event shifted the focus of the child's subjectivity from her mother's to her father's domestic space. Henceforth, she began "wholly without guidance, to read Father's library through, starting at the ceiling, at the southwest corner of the study and continuing the process whenever we were at home until, at the age of seventeen, I entered Cornell University." [19]

The seven years she spent in this enchanted room situated her in the world of male knowledge, male power, and male achievement. Here duty acquired a new meaning that fostered self-expression and even, occasionally, self-indulgence. "The top shelf was filled chiefly with modestly bound, small volumes of the Family Library," she recalled. "Though I understood almost nothing in these books of so-called Natural Science, and there were no illustrations to help, I did learn the names of Newton, Galileo, Giordano Bruno, Kepler, Copernicus, and a few other astronomers, chemists, and physicists whom I thereafter revered indiscriminately, classing them all with Dr. Priestley, who was a friend of Benjamin Franklin and . . . a hero of the family." Like young women of Sarah Pugh's generation, she read Walter Scott "in nine volumes of bad print," which "stood on a high shelf and was early reached." After two years of such reading, she began to explore the shelves of the Library of Congress. During family visits to Washington, which began for her in 1868, she read "Dickens and Thackeray, along with Miss Alcott and Horatio Alger." Back at home, she continued with the poetry of Shakespeare, Milton, Byron, and Goldsmith, as well as "the writings of President Madison, and the histories of Bancroft, Prescott and Francis Parkman." She was nearly fifteen when she arrived at "Emerson, Channing, Burke, Carlyle, Godwin, and Herbert Spencer." She later concluded that "only the circumstance that I was a very lonely child deeply ashamed of having no school experience . . . could have kept me at work six years (nearly seven) on this huge, indigestible, intellectual meal." [20]

Nurturing and constructing her spiritually as well as intellectually, her father's library offered an oasis in the desert of her mother's grief. There book learning conquered her home's chaotic clash between life and death. There she gained perspective on her childhood and gave birth to herself as an adolescent. More than a retreat, the library became a universe of her own making, confirming her existence within that wider world.[21]

Before her tenth birthday, Florence knew relatively little about her father's work or the enormous power he wielded. During those years she learned what she could from the irregular pulse of the household. Her recollection of "my colored mammy's ghost stories" shows that Caroline's practice of hiring free black servants to care for the children brought them into contact with African-American culture. Yet family correspondence revealed a rapid turnover among all the servants except George, Caroline's closest equivalent to a housekeeper, so this nursemaid did not become a fixture in Florrie's childhood. The replacement of servants was a constant problem that Caroline handled without much help from her husband. "I cannot counsel you about domestic affairs," he wrote her in 1871. Financially, the family was supported by rents collected from real estate William had acquired during his years as a judge. Ample as those properties were, however, rents often went unpaid, and Caroline had to adjust the household's expenditures. "I have been disappointed as to the rent coming in so that I can only give George $10.00 this evening," she wrote William in 1862. Caroline often purchased the family's provisions herself. "Only think, my marketing this morning cost me nearly $5.00," she wrote William in the midst of the Civil War. "Sometimes, I get quite discouraged." William's chief consolation was to supply instructions for how Will should help at home, telling Caroline, "May he be spared you long after I am gone hence." [22]

William could also be inaccessible to his daughter. Despite the intensity of their episodic contact, he was often irritable and aloof. Preoccupied by the Civil War and its aftermath, he carried his work home during congressional recesses. Even before the war, when he wrote Abraham Lincoln about the formation of his cabinet, he stole time to do so from his family: "It is Thanksgiving evening, the house is vocal with the laughter and shouts of children, from whom I have under an irresistible impulse, withdrawn myself to address you." In the late twentieth century he would have been called a workaholic. Caroline urged him to write letters to her because "my only consolation in your absence is, that you write so much more affectionately than you talk to me." As a family member, William Kelley was far from exemplary.[23]

His letters to Florence, though well-meaning and frequent, often accentuated the distance between them. Her domestic routines in Germantown and West Philadelphia were far removed from the public world he joined in the nation's capital. When he wrote her about the "splendid gaiety" of a "very brilliant affair" he had attended in honor of the "coming out" of a daughter of a member of the House, he widened the gap between his life and hers. As a city, Washington left much to be desired. Its few public buildings, such as the White House, the Treasury Building, and the Smithsonian, arose from fields that still retained their rural aspect. Nevertheless, to the imagination of the young girl in West Philadelphia, Washington seemed an enchanted metropolis.[24]

In her first decade of life, Florrie's main contact with public life was through fairs related to the war effort. "I think that song you bought Mama from the Fair is beautiful," she wrote her father at the age of six in 1865. "It is called, 'Shall we let our Soldiers perish?' Mama practiced it this morning." After her tenth birthday, however, William Kelley began to share his political life with his daughter. His letters contained fewer references to events of interest to a child and instead forwarded letters from prominent persons that he had recently answered and generally commented on the political news of the day. "I have been very busy. I am on two active committees and have been preparing a speech on San Domingo which I finished yesterday," he wrote her in 1871. By 1874 his accounts had become more detailed. "You will be glad to know I have just had a great triumph. My long pending financial resolution received a majority of 73 there having been but 82 votes cast against it. This was overwhelming." He confided in her: "You will be glad to know that my speech of Saturday is much commended and that I regard it as the most forcible and in some respects the most finished extended speech I ever made in the House. My homely opening and the denunciation of knowledge which follows it will amuse you. I hope to send you a pamphlet copy in about a week. Of course your eyes still give you pain but I hope they are better. Do not overtax them." On another occasion, he told Caroline that since Florrie was "fond of observing the verification of my predictions," she would want to read his recent speech in which he quoted "at length from a speech I had made in the 40th Congress more than seven years ago."[25]

Since they were often written during House debates, William's letters conveyed the immediacy of political power. "Nearly an hour of intense excitement has passed and I resume my pen to lay it down again I know not how soon," he wrote her during the debate on the Civil Rights Bill of 1875, adding later, "the vote is ordered and the pen must again be laid down. 3:40, The long struggle is over, the Civil Rights bill has passed." He also shared political strategy with her, writing later in 1875 that his reunion with her that weekend in Germantown would be delayed, since "if at all possible I will participate in the dedication of the new building of the West Philadelphia Institute. . . . As one of the principal founders it is fitting that I should be there. My political friends are also anxious that I shall show myself on the occasion." As she grew older and William took her more into his political confidence, she learned to associate his affection for her with his passion for politics. Politics became for her an arena imbued with the mystery of her father's love. It also became a realm of expert knowledge that she shared with her father. Day-to-day committee life in the House of Representatives, the relationship between local and national political action, and the voluntarist roots of American civic life all impinged on her everyday experience.[26]

William Kelley's career arched over his daughter's childhood in a pattern that soared to a peak around 1872 and then declined. Throughout his tenure as a congressman between 1860 and 1890, he was sustained by a loyal constituency of skilled workingmen in Pennsylvania's Fourth District, and he repaid their fidelity by backing policies beneficial to them. For his daughter, he set an example of passionate commitment to the notion that the growth and expansion of American democracy was compatible with the growth and expansion of industrial capitalism. Perhaps for that reason, he left a problematic legacy.[27]

During William Kelley's first six successful congressional terms between 1860 and 1872, he advocated one policy to smooth the conflicts between capitalism and democracy: protective tariffs for American industries. Tariffs would keep wages high at the same time they protected capital investment; the impoverishment of European working people would not happen in America.[28]

Yet protective tariffs required a larger dose of positive government than Kelley had ever previously endorsed. After losing his first run for Congress in 1856 on the Free Soil ticket, when he had championed free trade, and after observing the devastating effects of the 1857 depression on the state's iron industry, Kelley turned to his fellow Unitarian parishioner, Whig political economist Henry C. Carey, for advice. Noted for his moral approach to the nation's political economy and his advocacy of protective tariffs, for two years Carey tutored Kelley in the benefits and necessity of such governmental intervention, cloaking the cold industrial necessity of tariffs with the warm idealism of democratic social theory. By the time he ran for Congress as a Republican in 1860, he had become a thoroughgoing protectionist and confidently preached the compatibility of labor and capital and, with the zeal of a convert, pressed the tariff issue on every possible occasion. For example, he tried to recruit women's rights leader Caroline Dall to the cause, explaining to her in 1864, "Were I a woman . . . one who demanded . . . that my sex might be permanently blessed, I would clamor for a prohibitory tariff as a means of diversifying the industry of the country. It is only in semi-barbarous regions that women . . . follow the plow." Linked with another basic feature of Republican policy— western population growth fostered by the 1864 Homestead Act—tariffs nourished a vision of vastly expanded home markets, increased competition, lowered prices, and the transformation of producers into the double identity of producer-consumers. The chief alternative to this view, typified by cotton producers, called for the expansion of foreign markets through free trade.[29]

Kelley gained stature as a spokesman on fiscal and industrial matters in 1869 with his appointment to the House Committee on Ways and Means. His speeches extolled the harmony among democratic government, protective tariffs, and high wages. "To the existence of a Government resting upon the virtue and intelligence of the people [a protective tariff] is essential. . . . It is the duty of the Government to protect the laborers of the country in the receipt of such wages as will enable them to do this, the only means of keeping firm and unshaken the foundation upon which our republican institutions rest — intelligent popular opinion." Later critics, including his own daughter, argued that while protective tariffs increased wages, they also concentrated capital, drove small producers out of business, and placed great power in the hands of a few industrialists. But the expansive northern economy of the 1860s and 1870s obscured this dynamic.[30]

William Kelley's commitment to the welfare of working men and his willingness to use the power of the state to maintain their welfare made it easier for him to lead the Republican Party's effort to include former slaves in the American polity. The intractable problem of extending civil and political rights to freed slaves demanded an awareness of their needs and mandated new and imaginative uses of state power. These William Kelley readily supplied.

"I am very proud today to be known as a radical," he declared in 1866, reflecting the empowerment that flowed from the merger of party and state during the Civil War. In 1865 Kelley urged Congress to undertake two forms of radical reconstruction in the South. Economically, he sought the massive investment of northern capital, especially in Alabama's iron industry; politically, he promoted a new South controlled by a biracial Republican Party. To implement these policies he helped found the Philadelphia Union League, under whose auspices the development of a new economic and political order was launched in Alabama. "We are to shape the future," he said. "We cannot escape the duty; and 'conciliation, compromise and concession' are not the methods we are to use." [31]

William Kelley's leadership on black male suffrage was especially visible. The Thirteenth Amendment ended slavery in 1865; in 1868 the Fourteenth prohibited states from enacting legislation that deprived citizens of equal protection of the law. Yet without suffrage these amendments were more symbolic than real.[32]

Kelley first spoke on black voting rights in January 1865, five years before Congress passed the Fifteenth Amendment granting Negro suffrage, a few weeks before slavery was abolished, and three months before the end of the Civil War. His speech — laced with domestic images and advocating suffrage for all male citizens who could read the U.S.

Constitution—produced a "profound sensation" in the U.S. House of Representatives: "Let us conquer our prejudices. . . . Let us show the world that, inheriting the spirit of our forefathers, we regard Liberty as a right so universal and a blessing so grand that, while we are ready to surrender our all rather than yield it, we will guaranty it at whatever cost to the poorest child that breathes the air of our country." In the ensuing turmoil, all Reconstruction questions were tabled for two weeks, allowing Kelley's colleagues time to consider the explosive question of black voting rights. Ninety thousand copies of this speech were quickly printed and distributed by the friends of Negro suffrage. Five days later, Kelley was attacked and injured by a knife-wielding Louisiana congressman whose admission to the House of Representatives had been deferred because of Kelley's speech. Since few of his contemporaries could count on reelection as confidently as he and few could act so independently of white racism, only a small idealistic group voted for his suffrage proposal the summer of 1865.[33]

Traveling through the Deep South on a trip financed by the Union Republican Congressional Committee in 1867, Kelley spoke to large crowds of working people of both races, urging that the new Republican coalitions go beyond providing "all rights, privileges and amenities of citizenship" to "fellow citizens of African descent" by establishing free schools and maintaining a free press. Democracy was not sustained by free labor or abstract rights alone; it required citizens' full participation in civil society. His appeal met with a violent response in Mobile, Alabama, where a scuffle between hecklers and soldiers ended with gunfire directed at the podium, twenty persons wounded, and the deaths of two men, one black and one white.[34]

Kelley's vision of the political empowerment of former slaves hinged on his hope for the development of southern mineral resources. Alabama, he pleaded in Congress in 1868, was a state "in which gold, iron, copper, and various other metals are found along navigable streams and easily accessible for use." Yet this wealth "is paralyzed, and all that capacity to afford cheerful homes to millions of people is shut against the immigrant from Europe or the overcrowded cities of the East" because of Alabama's Democratic Party, which cared more about reasserting white rule than about economic development. In a speech delivered "to the Colored People in Charleston," Kelley argued that commercial development would promote social transformation: "There are Northerners who are prejudiced against you; but you can find the way to their hearts and consciences through their pockets. When they find that there are colored tradesmen who have money to spend, and colored farmers who want to buy goods of them, they will no longer call you Jack and Joe; they will begin to think that you are Mr. John Black and Mr. Joseph Brown." Observers noted that this passage elicited "great laughter" from the assembled freedmen.[35]

Yet William Kelley's respect for property rights and his trust in electoral rights prevented him from taking the crucial step advocated by his Pennsylvania colleague, Thaddeus Stevens, of confiscating the lands of disloyal southerners and redistributing them to former slaves. He thought civil institutions would evolve if northern capital flowed into the South. Kelley's vision foundered between 1868 and 1871 when northern finance capital joined with more conservative Republican Party members to oppose southern reconstruction and white "redeemers" murdered and intimidated black citizens. Republican concern for the stability of the national currency (given the enormous public debt inherited from the war) and the party's dislike of governmental regulation of property and class relations prevailed. The merger of state and party ended, setting the stage for white rule in the South and a return to limited government in the North. In Alabama, terrorists launched systematic assaults on Republican Party meetings; the biracial party waned and died.[36]

Too late, William Kelley advocated stronger government measures. After the Ku Klux Klan restored white rule through terrorism, he insisted: "A government that cannot protect the humblest man within its limits, that cannot snatch from oppression the feeblest woman or child, is not a government. It is wanting in the vital attributes of government. . . . Will [congressmen] never learn that the object of government is not to protect the strong, who can care for themselves, but to protect the weak, the ignorant, and those who are degraded because they have been made to suffer in the past?" He urged armed action against racist violence. "Do we live under a Government? Are we a civilized people? Because, if we are, and if we do live under a Government, the power to suppress outrages such as these is at our command, and the duty of doing it is laid upon us by a Power higher than a written constitution. Humanity implores, and the Father of man and God of justice commands us to put forth our powers." His appeal fell on deaf ears.[37]

Thereafter William Kelley's loving partnership with American politics began to dissolve. Although he subsequently enjoyed some major victories and never lost his solid working-class electoral base, he grew increasingly critical of his own party. Meanwhile, in 1874 Republican congressional hegemony was wrecked by Democratic victories, and in 1873 the Supreme Court affirmed the primacy of states' rights over the rights of individuals, effectively voiding the ability of the federal government to use the Fourteenth Amendment to protect freedmen from the Ku Klux Klan and other sources of violence.[38]

Much as the Reconstruction defeat must have reverberated in the Kelley household, in the late 1870s a more personal calamity surpassed it: William Kelley's disgrace in the Crédit Mobilier scandal. Like many of his congressional colleagues, he viewed railroads as essential vehicles of transcontinental national economic development. Closer to home, his tariff protection of the Pennsylvania iron and steel industries linked him with the health of the "iron horse." He, along with large majorities in Congress, supported legislation that allowed the Union Pacific and other railroad companies to reap huge profits from public lands and grow so dominant within the emerging national economy of the 1860s that they overwhelmed the capacity of the government to regulate them. One example of that process was the Crédit Mobilier scandal. During the electoral campaign of 1872, a Democratic newspaper in New York published an account, later sustained by congressional investigations, of the 1868 bribery of prominent Republicans, including Kelley, by Crédit Mobilier, a fiscal agent of the Union Pacific Railroad, in an effort to avoid investigations of its colossal profits.[39]

William Kelley had a cash-flow problem in the late 1860s that made him vulnerable to the approach of Massachusetts Congressman Oakes Ames. Ames and James Brooks, more deeply implicated in the scandal, were censured but not expelled from the House. Kelley avoided censure through a full disclosure of his affairs that painted "a life of self-denial . . . utterly inconsistent with venality." Defending himself on the floor of the House in the tones of Greek tragedy, he said that if censured, "I may and will teach the boy who bears my name when he shall meet any of you, to challenge you as to the blamelessness of my life among you. It shall be his privilege to ask . . . whether for the best twelve years of his life he did not place . . . before his associates in every walk of life the example of a life of labor and self-denial." He admitted that to forestall the loss of investments (through which he had hoped to provide "something for the support of my widow and children if I should be summoned hence") he had accepted collateral of $10,000 in railroad bonds that an unnamed friend put up for him. His health had been failing, he insisted, and thus it was not for himself that he pleaded, asking only that his colleagues give him "those privileges which are secured to the vagrant." His eloquence was successful; the motion to censure was tabled.[40]

The scandal had a direct impact on the Kelley family. During the Christmas holiday of 1872, Caroline could not "go into society" and retain her "equanimity." During the congressional hearings, William urged Caroline to tell Will "to keep a stiff upper lip and he will find that he may still pride himself on his father's integrity and the public recognition thereof." Perhaps because he was older or was presumed to take his father's public life as a model for his own, Will was the chief focus of Kelley's chagrin. Florence must also have smarted keenly from this taint on her father's name, but during the month-long investigation, William's letters home referred only to her convalescence from another eye-straining illness, visits from her friends, and her enjoyment of Miss Longstreth's school.[41]

During the March 1873 recess following the scandal, William Kelley took an extended trip to North Dakota, accompanied by Henry Carey and his daughter, Florence.

William Kelley Jr. and Florence Kelley, ca. 1872. Courtesy of Rare Book and Manuscript Library, Columbia University.

No longer comfortable in his party ranks, his alternatives were extremely limited, and, he wrote Elizabeth Cady Stanton, he felt "solitary and alone." The economic depression of the mid-1870s widened the gap between his own and his party's fiscal policies, and in 1875 he broke openly with the Republican Party, calling their programs "cruel and infamous" and likely to "concentrate in the hands of a few people all the property in the United States." His earlier vision lay in shambles; no longer did the nation's welfare seem sustained by industrial growth. He shared his political discontent with his daughter, writing her in January 1875, "You are right in thinking I am disgusted with the result of the financial question, and I may add that my disgust is intensified by the Presdts message of yesterday. Were the subject less grave I would regard this paper as ludicrously absurd." Florrie's replies to this and his other letters have not survived.[42]

Forced to choose between capital and labor, William Kelley chose labor. In 1875 he championed the Greenback-Labor movement by giving a keynote address at a Greenback convention in Detroit that united workingmen and entrepreneurs under the ancient banner of "producers." His statements on behalf of inflationary currency, the eight-hour day, and "fair American wages," as well as his denunciation of his party's policies prompted the *Cincinnati Daily Gazette* to accuse him of wishing "to set up a division of classes, to divide the laboring class from the rest, and to persuade working men that their interests [were] hostile to the rest." A Thomas Nast cartoon in New York's *Commercial and Financial Chronicle* depicted Kelley brandishing a "bullionist heart" on a spear, while words around his head declared, "Vive la Guillotine," "Tremble Tyrants," "The San Culottes are coming," and "More greenbacks or death." His inevitable break with manufacturers came that year, when the Pennsylvania Industrial League, terming Kelley's policies "revolutionary" and "unsound," urged industrialists not to support him. But, sustained by his constituents and by his seniority on the Ways and Means Committee, he regained his stature, chairing the committee in the early 1880s.[43]

During these turbulent years, Florence got to know her father better on long trips with him as he traveled on behalf of the Ways and Means Committee. These carried her out of his library and into stunningly direct confrontation with the bone and sinew of American economic development, giving her what she later called "national vistas, reaching far indeed beyond the Philadelphia of my childhood." In 1872 she accompanied her father, mother, and younger brother, Albert, to Denver, Salt Lake, Laramie, and Los Angeles. In Laramie, she rode "all over the range" with her father; "she rides as fearlessly as you and quite gracefully," William wrote home to Will Jr. Thereafter, at home and at college, Florence maintained her own saddle horse.[44]

In her letters to Isaac and Elizabeth Pugh, she exclaimed over sunsets "far beyond description," rocks "three to five hundred feet high," and her pleasure in gaining ten pounds. In Los Angeles, she witnessed "solemn ceremonies for the repose of the dead" among Chinese residents and visited a mission school for Chinese boys. One letter home concluded, "Papa thinks that this travelling will be worth very nearly a whole year's school to me, and I am *very nearly* of his opinion, although it robs me of the pleasant fall I had hoped to spend at the dear old place with you." Feeling the lack of formal schooling, however, she planned to devote "three hours every morning to study." The next year Florence accompanied her father and Henry Carey to the end of the railway line in Bismarck, North Dakota.[45]

The most important adventure with her father was more local. In 1871 the family spent the autumn in the Alleghenies "to give our mother a change of scene" after Anna's death.[46] There William introduced Florence to the romance of industrialization as manifested in the iron and steel industry. In her autobiography she depicted the event as a turning point in her life.

"Making Bessemer Steel at Pittsburgh: the Convertors at Work," *Harper's Weekly*, April 10, 1886.

William proposed that they witness the new Bessemer process through a nighttime visit to a nearby steel mill. She prepared for the trip by sleeping all day. She and William left their summer cottage around midnight. "It was nearly two o'clock in the morning, the first time I had ever consciously been awake at that hour, when the steel was turned out into the molds." She absorbed the "terrifying sight" of the "molten metal, white hot and fluid," pouring from the "monster" pear-shaped vessel into molds known as "pigs." The tension and human vulnerability of the moment remained vivid when she wrote about it half a century later: "No weirder scene could be conceived than the general dark interior and the locally blinding glare of the furnace that supplied heat for melting the iron ore. Then the moment of frightful suspense when if anything had gone wrong, several lives must inevitably have been lost." Before their visit, William had explained "how vast a step forward this invention was, substituting as it did the single procedure for the earlier usage of turning ore into iron first, and then as a second step, iron into steel." During the visit, he told her "how iron and steel were products of near-by coal and iron mines of Pennsylvania; how manganese, a Swedish product, was brought to this country because we had not yet discovered any in this hemisphere; and how immigrant laborers were sought like manganese; and how population and industry, thus stimulated, were increasing the greatness of this industrial Republic."[47] This memorable lesson in political economy brought her face to face with the might of industrial capitalism.

In more ways than one, the Bessemer process symbolized American industrial growth between 1870 and 1900. By making the production of steel possible on a vastly greater scale, the new Bessemer furnace hastened the nation's colossal industrial expansion. It also mechanized the work process in ways that stripped skilled workers of the control they had traditionally exercised over the production of iron, shifting it to management. In the United States, this meant that immigrant laborers—"sought like manganese"—were recruited to fill the expanding ranks of unskilled workers in the industry. These changes, in turn, meant that by the early 1890s Carnegie and other powerful steel magnates could ruthlessly crush efforts at unionization in the mills.[48]

Seen from her father's perspective in 1871, the Bessemer process heralded the dawn of a new, more intense phase of the industrial revolution. Yet, closer to the ground, Florence's viewpoint encompassed workers no one else noticed. Awed as she was by the pyrotechnic display, what interested her most was the "presence and activity of boys smaller than myself—and I was barely twelve years old—carrying heavy pails of water and tin dippers, from which the men drank eagerly." While everyone else watched the giant furnaces, her gaze followed the boys. The attitude of the adults dismissed them as unimportant, but for her they were a revelation. "The attention of all present was so concentrated on this industrial novelty that the little boys were no more important than so many grains of sand in the molds. For me, however, they were a living horror, and so remained." [49]

During the same vacation, she made another nocturnal visit to a glass factory near Pittsburgh. The ratio of children to men was much higher in the glass factories, where each blower had a "dog," as the boys were called. Crouched with his head close to the oven opening, the dog's job was to take "the blower's mold the instant the bottle or tumbler was removed from it, scrape it and replace it perfectly smooth and clean for the next bottle or tumbler which the blower was already shaping in his pipe." This experience confirmed her "astonished impression of the utter unimportance of children compared with products, in the minds of the people whom I was among." Her father's attitude made a deep impression. "Incredible as it seemed to me then, even my father's mind was completely preoccupied with technical and financial development of the great American industries." [50] This fiery immersion in her father's world posed a challenge: how could he offer an escape from the misery of her mother's world, if he endorsed a system that put young lives at risk?

At some point the two talked this matter through, and William Kelley tried to resolve this crucial question by encouraging his daughter to differentiate between the public mandate of his and her generations. His had built up "great industries in America so that more wealth could be produced for the whole people," he said, and the duty of hers "will be to see that the product is distributed justly. The same generation cannot do both." This distinction between her own and her father's generations made it possible for her to continue her affiliation with his world without denying the significance of her mother's sorrow. It embedded in her consciousness the notion that "the conservation of the human element was to remain a charge on the oncoming generation." [51] It also acquainted her with the personal and partial nature of all human knowledge.

During the 1870s, when Florence Kelley's relationship with her father gave her a front row seat in the theater of American politics, the drama included women. In part because of his family's relationship with Lucretia Mott, William Kelley served as the chief channel for woman suffrage petitions to the House of Representatives in the 1870s. Early in 1874, he introduced a request by Elizabeth Cady Stanton, Isabella Beecher Hooker, and Laura deForce Gordon to address the House "concerning the right of suffrage now withheld from half the citizens of the United States." A few years later, he described the same responsibilities to Florence in a letter replete with technicalities: "I . . . renewed my resolution for a hearing at the bar of the House and moved to suspend the rules. . . . I knew the effort was hopeless and feared that I could not command enough votes to make a record by ordering the Ayes and Nays, one fifth of the members present and voting.

The result was an agreeable surprise and the vote stood 107 for to 140 against." Even within his own family, William firmly defined the terms of the woman suffrage debate. "I do not wish you to make the acquaintance of either member of the firm of Woodhull and Claflin," he wrote Caroline in 1871, when those notorious free thinkers were visiting Lucretia Mott. "I have no sympathy with them." He admitted that at the last Republican convention, in a casual conversation with western women suffragists, he had "promised them all sorts of things," but his respect for the movement did not extend to its radical fringes occupied by Victoria Woodhull. "Do not go," he concluded. "But if Mrs. Mott or your Aunt Sarah should invite you to meet [Isabella Beecher Hooker] I think the occasion might interest you." [52]

Florence also made contact with the women's rights movement through Sarah Pugh. She "received from Aunt Sarah reprints of Mrs. Josephine Butler's addresses to the Queen, and to Parliament, for immediate abolition of segregation of women in lock hospitals in England and India." In 1866, Florence would have heard about her great aunt's trip south to the school where she had sent clothes and books. Traveling with her dear friend and cousin, Abby Kimber, to St. Helena, which they reached by row boat, Pugh visited "Miss Towne's and Miss Murray's 'Pennsylvania Freedmen's Relief School, No. 1'" where she found "over a hundred scholars, from six to twenty-six, both sexes, all shades of black, mostly dark; a number of married women." [53]

Between 1867 and 1876, years when Florence often visited Germantown, Sarah Pugh's reform activities focused on women's rights. Although she had not accompanied Lucretia Mott to the first women's rights convention in Seneca Falls, New York, in 1848, like Mott she considered herself a strong supporter of women's rights and a close friend of Elizabeth Cady Stanton. After a reunion with Stanton at a women's rights meeting in Germantown in 1867, Sarah described Stanton's reminiscences about "the days of her kittenhood" in London in 1840, where through her contact with Lucretia Mott she first became interested in women's rights. Sarah contrasted Stanton in those days with "her now beautiful silver hair" and "commanding presence, addressing an assembly with earnestness and ability." [54]

That year Sarah complained about lapses in her correspondence since she was "too busy" with "the 'Woman Question.'" Supporting the effort to link black suffrage and woman suffrage in the Kansas referendum of 1867, she wrote a friend that she believed "the field is 'wide unto the harvest' of equal rights for all irrespective of color or sex." After James Mott's death in 1868, she became Lucretia's traveling companion to women's rights conventions, making it possible for the aging progenitor of the movement to continue her public appearances. In January 1869 they attended a convention in Washington, D.C., and in May traveled for the same purpose to Boston. That year Pugh strongly endorsed Elizabeth Cady Stanton and Susan B. Anthony's paper, *The Revolution*, writing, "My heart is in this work for women, as the best work for humanity."[55]

Knowing both Lucy Stone and Elizabeth Cady Stanton, Pugh unsuccessfully tried to mediate a union between the two in 1869, the year they formed two competing organizations. Thereafter she attended meetings of both branches of the movement, feeling "I can work with all who are striving for the desired end."[56] She followed closely but did not attend speeches on behalf of woman's suffrage at hearings held by the House Judiciary Committee in 1871. She and Mott attended their last woman's rights convention at Rochester in July 1878, organized to celebrate the thirtieth anniversary of the original convention. They were seventy-eight and eighty-four years old, respectively.

Meanwhile, William Kelley drafted and nurtured through Congress a bill that allocated funds for the Centennial Celebration and International Exposition in Philadelphia in 1876. For him, the centennial provided a welcome opportunity to promote the virtues of his constituents. He argued that Philadelphia, "the cradle of liberty," was a logical place to celebrate the maturity of American society and culture, not only to show off its treasured Independence Hall but above all to demonstrate to the visiting peoples of Europe "the effect of free institutions upon the masses of the people" visible "in the homes of our working people."[57]

"The Centennial — Wall Paper Printing Press, Machinery Hall," *Harper's Weekly*, Dec. 23, 1876.

For his daughter, the fair was a many-faceted learning experience. Having just passed her entrance examinations to Cornell, Florence was only sixteen years old but she was ready for adulthood. When William sent her a printed guide to a forthcoming industrial exhibition in Vienna, she exclaimed, "How can I thank you for your valuable gift! I think it will just fill a vacancy which I have begun to feel." During the several visits she had already made to the Philadelphia fair, her questions were usually ignored. "If I ask an exhibitor a question about anything, except the jewelry in the Italian dept., he usually stares surprisedly at me, as though wondering what a girl of sixteen can possibly want to know, and answers in monosyllables with a bored air, or, which is still more discouraging, treats me as a Russian exhibitor does; saying to me 'I know nothing whatever about the subject' and then turning to an old gentleman near by volunteered a quantity of information on the very topic about which I had asked him, doing it in a way which made it impossible for me to stay and get the benefit of his explanations." Thinking that "a great many of the objects about which I want to learn something [will be] exhibited at Vienna and will therefore be mentioned in this report," she planned to use it as a guide to the Philadelphia exposition.[58]

This young woman was thirsting for knowledge. Her age and gender prevented her from gaining easy access to it, but she was determined to overcome those disadvantages. Finding one exhibit especially compelling, she solicited her father's interest by imagining his perspective on it: "What a country Russia must be! True, I do not know very much about its commercial importance (except that like our own country it exports wheat), but it seems to me that internal improvement is written everywhere in its exhibit." She concluded with an outright appeal for his attention and companionship on future visits to the fair. "How I wish we could study together in this great American kindergarten for children of a little larger growth! for I think there must be things here which will surprise you in spite of your knowledge of the relative industrial importance of the different countries."[59] Ambitious, intelligent, and extremely precocious, Florence Kelley shared her father's passion for the drama of industrial development. Yet she also had deep personal needs that were not being met.

That summer she visited the fair almost every day. Occasionally, she persuaded a friend to go with her, but friends rarely accompanied her twice, since she moved very slowly, "too interested in the things which might be useful to Father, who was too absorbed in the excitement of the campaign preceding the Hayes-Tilden presidential election to spend strength in visiting the Exposition."[60] With the fair as a fitting capstone on her youthful education in political economy, a tantalizing introduction to the wider world awaiting her, and a poignant reminder that she would have to make her own way in it, that autumn she put her childhood behind her and entered Cornell University.

3

"Equal
Intellectual Opportunity,"
1876–1882

Florence Kelley's peers thought of themselves as "the first generation of college-educated women." Their empowerment through higher education broke through the gendered divisions of knowledge that reinforced gendered divisions of labor and other gender hier- archies. Entry to higher education gave women access to a new plane of equality with men in civil society. Although women were denied many civil, political, and economic rights, by 1890 the effects of women's greater education became visible throughout public life as women individually and in groups assumed larger public responsibilities.[1]

Two changes in the 1860s and 1870s enabled white, middle-class women to attend col- lege in sufficient numbers to become a sociological phenomenon. Elite women's colleges, such as Vassar, Smith, and Wellesley, began accepting students between 1865 and 1875, providing equivalents to elite men's colleges, such as Harvard, Yale, and Princeton. And state universities, established through the allocation of public lands in the Morrill Act of 1862 and required to be "open for all," gradually made college educations accessible for the first time to large numbers of women in the nation's central and western states. By 1880 women, numbering forty thousand, constituted 33 percent of all enrolled students in higher education. Though a small percentage of all women, they exercised an influ- ence disproportionate to their numbers. Vida Scudder, a Smith graduate, summarized the results of this empowerment in 1890. "We stand here as a new Fact—new, to all intents and purposes, within the last quarter of a century. Our lives are in our hands."[2]

The generation of educated women that emerged in the United States in response to these opportunities had no equal in other industrializing nations. The contrast between women's access to higher education in England and the United States began in the first half of the nineteenth century, when the phenomenal growth in the demand for public school teachers across the new American continent feminized the teaching profession and inspired the founding of first-rate institutions of higher learning, such as Mount Holyoke, where women teachers could be trained. In England, where no equivalent geographic expansion occurred, common schools were not a major growth industry, and women teachers were much fewer in number. The closest equivalent to Mount Holyoke was Queen's College, founded in 1848 "to provide better education for governesses." English women's access to higher education relied on the efforts of feminists who established beachheads at older male universities — a much more difficult undertaking. Women were not admitted to German or French universities in significant numbers until well after 1900, reflecting the elite parameters of higher education in those countries as well as its gender limits.[3]

Thus Florence Kelley was part of an educational revolution that flowered in the United States in the 1870s but did not begin to have a comparable impact in England until at least a generation later. Beatrice Potter Webb, born in England in 1858 into circumstances that closely resembled those of Florence Kelley's childhood and who later pursued a parallel career in British social reform, sharply differed from Kelley in her educational options in 1876. While Kelley entered the collective living and learning experience of Cornell, Beatrice Potter, having intellectually surpassed what her governesses could offer, spent 1876 and 1877 following a self-designed course of reading reminiscent of Kelley's earlier reading of her father's library. Focusing on Herbert Spencer's *Social Statics* and *First Principles* along with the classics of Eastern religions, Webb did not personally suffer from the lack of formal schooling, but, unlike Florence Kelley, later in her career in the 1890s she could not rely on the grassroots support of large numbers of educated women contemporaries.[4]

After 1880 education became even more crucial for middle-class men and women concerned about the course of social change, for, lacking control of an economy dominated by industrial capitalists, unable to master chaotic urban growth, and frustrated by a polity dominated by party machines, their ability to influence public policy depended on their ability to process new forms of information, create new modes of communication, and devise new answers to social problems.[5] Much of this rising middle-class need was met by college-trained women.

Florence discovered Cornell's offer of "equal intellectual opportunity to women" in her fourteenth year, when she found a brochure with that message "in the otherwise empty waste basket in my father's study." That announcement heralded the admission of female students in 1873, four years after Cornell's founding. It fulfilled the wishes of the university's Quaker founder, Ezra Cornell, who wrote to his only granddaughter in 1867, "I want to have girls educated in the university, as well as boys, so that they may have the same opportunity to become wise and useful to society that the boys have." Cornell was an obvious choice for Florence Kelley. After a more systematic survey of her options, M. Carey Thomas, another talented young woman also born into a wealthy Pennsylvania Quaker family, wrote her favorite aunt on the brink of her own departure for Cornell in 1874, "I look forward to Cornell now, as that is the highest place open to ladies." At the end of her senior year, Thomas recorded in her journal, "I have graduated at a university. I have a degree that represents more than a Vassar one." [6]

Attracted to the notion of intellectual equality and perhaps to a university degree as well, Florence began to prepare herself for the Cornell entrance examination. The process brought her little satisfaction since no secondary school open to girls could provide her with the necessary skills in Latin, Greek, and other subjects. "My college preparation was in fact pure sham," she later wrote. "It was my grotesque experience to be prepared by tutors and governesses themselves not college bred." [7] Nevertheless, she passed the exams at the age of sixteen in June 1876, subject to conditions that required her to continue Latin, Greek, and mathematics during her freshman year.

The Elms did not easily relinquish its hold on her. From the time she began to prepare herself for Cornell and throughout her college years, her progress was marred by illnesses that threatened to reabsorb her into Caroline's realm of loss and regret. Responding to this possibility, Florence began to exert more authority over her own medical treatment even before she went to Ithaca. In January 1875 she protested against a physician's prescribed treatment, and her father came to her aid, writing, "I spoke to Dr. Starkey this morning about the effect the gas produced on you. He said you had better yield to the sleepiness as it exhibited a natural event, but if you think the gas is doing you harm do not take [it.]" Still ill that summer, Florence prescribed for herself more rest away from home. Caroline wrote Will Jr. from Nantucket, "Florrie is very unwilling to come [home] at present, believing that every day here is a positive gain. It would seem very strange to leave her, but I do not know what to do. . . . She has a great wish to stay another month." Florence stayed on alone. [8]

The stress of these illnesses was heightened by the publication in 1873 of Edward H. Clarke's *Sex in Education*, an attack on coeducation by a former professor at Harvard Medical School. Clarke claimed that girls were constitutionally unfit for coeducation because instruction in an educational regime designed for boys deprived girls of the energy they needed to sustain menstruation and other female physiological processes. Coeducation and schools for girls modeled on schools for boys were, Clarke wrote, "grounded upon the supposition that sustained regularity of action and attendance may be as safely required of a girl as of a boy; that there is no physical necessity for periodically relieving her from walking, standing, reciting, or studying." But, he insisted, "by deranging the tides of her organization," such "a regular, uninterrupted, and sustained course of work" diverted "blood from the reproductive apparatus to the head."[9] At best this stunted normal development; at worst it led to the insane asylum.

The scientific basis of Clarke's study was highly suspect, since it was limited to seven cases, including that of a fourteen-year-old Vassar student (which prompted the college's denial that it had ever admitted a student so young). Nevertheless the book's pseudoscientific tone appealed to many readers because it invoked one of the fundamental notions of Darwinian social theory—the creation of emphatic distinctions between men and women through the process of natural selection. This popular view held that evolution favored the development of strong, assertive men and maternal, passive women. The talents of men were tremendously varied, fitting them for a complex social world, but those of women were fundamentally alike, deriving from their biology. Coeducation, Clarke thought, "is intellectually a success, physically a failure."[10]

Clarke's volume was answered by a barrage of evidence to the contrary, including four books that defended women's right to higher education and refuted his contention that women's bodies could not bear the stress of mental exertion. Nevertheless, M. Carey Thomas later said that her generation of college women were haunted by the "clanging chains" of the gloomy specter of Clarke's book and did not themselves know "whether women's health could stand the strain of education."[11]

Florence Kelley ignored Clarke's crackpot warnings, but she took serious health precautions during her first semester. In addition to equal educational opportunities with men, Cornell offered her the chance to satisfy two urgent desires—to put her intelligence to use and to make friends. Thinking at first that her health forced her to choose between these, she put all her energy into academic pursuits. Her demanding weekly schedule consisted of twenty-two hours of classes in ancient and modern languages and mathematics. Wanting very badly to succeed academically, she wrote Caroline in October, "Give me a good long credit mark! I resisted the temptation to go to a German [cotillion] last night—the first of a series of Gymnasium germans to be given on Saturday evenings, the boys paying for the music one week, we the next." She realized she appeared a bit odd. "Of course, they will be great fun and it is considered a little peculiar not to take any part in them. They are the least objectionable things of the kind imaginable. Mrs. Kinney chaperones the girls and the dancing begins at 6:15 and the lights are out and even the most determined late-stayer is gone by ten o'clock." Even so, she thought it best to stay home. "With twenty-two hours of University work there is very little time left even on Saturday evening which I can afford to spend on anything but Latin and I should not feel justified (even by the training in small talk) in hurting my eyes by subjecting them to the lights of the gymnasium or in risking cold by running heated from the Gymnasium to the main hall along the piazza." Florence was learning to be her own mother.[12]

In spite of rigorous study she received only a "creditable" grade in German. "My shame, rage, and disgust ever since have been too great to be borne." Still, she hoped to "get into the honor section," where about twelve of the one hundred and fifty German students "choose their own professor, and their own books for the next term, and being relieved of the burden of the stupids, make much greater headway." Her commitment to Latin was just as keen. "If I only *could* describe my Latin lessons to you!!!! They are alternately delightful, and mortifying beyond measure, because for one I have plenty of time to prepare, for the next very little." Deliciously, her Latin achievements permitted her to patronize her older brother. "If only Will could share them with me I should have nothing more to desire, for I think he would now really enjoy the exquisite beauty of 'De Amiatia' and the quiet fun of Cicero's letters." [13]

Pictures of Florence during her Cornell years reveal a strong, handsome young woman, stately but intense in appearance, with deep, penetrating eyes, and full braids across the top of her head. Of classically statuesque proportions, she could have stepped out of a Winslow Homer painting. Deeply serious, she nevertheless looked like an appealing friend. As she became more confident about her academic progress, Cornell's social life claimed more of her attention. Indeed, her later memories recalled her freshman year as "one continued joy" since it not only gratified her thirst for learning but also "for young companionship." When William Kelley wrote her about "the exciting occasion" of observing in New Orleans the special commission that confirmed the outcome of the Tilden-Hayes election, she did not mind that none of her friends "was interested enough to listen to his letters." As she later wrote to a friend, she especially valued "the life at Sage College; the long, free talks with the women in the upper halls, the meals with the men and women students, and the recreations shared by the men and women and the younger professors." If forced to choose, she later thought, "I would give [up] the whole class-room work, and keep the University *life*." [14]

Though no one was required to live in the dormitory, Florence resided in Sage College with about seventy other young women. College authorities encouraged the women students "to share our half-empty dining room with men students, whom we were free to invite, six men and six girls to each table." After dinner, her table company moved to the gymnasium, where they danced to the accompaniment of a piano. Socializing resumed on Saturday, when there were no lectures and "nothing was farther from our minds than squandering a radiant autumn holiday in collateral reading." Having brought her horse Charlie and a small buggy to Ithaca, Florence and her friends took them on Saturday outings. "A group of friends, men and girls, after early breakfast [went] tramping five

Florence Kelley at Cornell. Courtesy of Nicholas Kelley Papers, Rare Books and Manuscripts Division, New York Public Library, Astor, Lenox and Tilden Foundations.

or six miles to a cider mill, or a gorge and waterfall, carrying in the phaeton lunch for all. Two or three rode together a mile or two, to a country road, then tied the horse to a fence and walked forward, the next comers taking their turn, until the last laggards arrived at the common meeting-ground. It was characteristic of the region that neither luncheon nor vehicle was ever interfered with." Gabrielle De Vaux Clements recalled that Florence's vitality pervaded their "intimate little circle" of men and women friends. "I should scarcely have thought of college without her influence and enthusiasm." Small wonder that romances blossomed and marriages ensued within this unchaperoned circle of friends.[15]

Kelley's friendships lifted her out of the morass of her mother's melancholy and drew her into visceral adventures that taught her how to have fun. Her female friends were especially important. One January afternoon she, Ruth Putnam, and another friend "donned our rubbers and leggings, our fur caps and capes, knit mittens, and having removed our dress skirts and having looped our overskirts high over our red skirts started forth equipped in most hygienic, delightful and picturesque style for a Saturday tramp." During this excursion, they "slid and tumbled along a half mile on top of the frozen stream." Later that "cold and exceedingly windy" night, Florence and her roommates gladly accepted a "summons to Miss Thomas's room" for "'conversatione' lasting from 9:30 p.m. of Jan. 20th to 8:30 a.m. Jan. 21st."[16]

In this group of friends, Florence found her first love — Margaret Hicks — whom she later remembered as "the beloved friend of my youth." The emotional environment in Sage Hall made it easy for young women to develop deep and meaningful homosocial relationships. Florence's love for Margaret exemplified the intimate friendships that were part of female college culture. Called "smashing," relationships in which young women courted each other and fell in love were closer than any permitted with male contemporaries. As was the case with Florence and Margaret, these devoted friendships often continued after college.[17]

When Florence arrived at Cornell, Margaret, two years older, was in the midst of a love affair with M. Carey Thomas, a senior. Their intimacy lasted from the fall of 1875 until June 1877. Thomas described its beginning in her journal: "Miss Hicks would come in her wrapper after I was in bed and we would read [Swinburne's "Atalanta in Calydon"] out loud and we learned several of the choruses. One night we had stopped reading later than usual and obeying a sudden impulse I turned to her and asked, 'Do you love me?' She threw her arms around me and whispered, 'I love you passionately.' She did not go home that night and we talked and talked. She told me she had been praying that I might care for her." Afterward they were inseparable, even though they often quarreled, and Thomas later worried that she should "have spent all that time in reading." Thomas, very

Group of Cornell students, including Margaret Hicks with hands resting on shoulders of
M. Carey Thomas. Courtesy of Nicholas Kelley Papers, Rare Books and Manuscripts Division,
New York Public Library, Astor, Lenox and Tilden Foundations.

selective in her associates, found "not the least bit of fastidiousness in Miss Hicks' nature. She likes everyone." Later Thomas recriminated that she felt "mastered" by the relationship. "I tell her she ought to be obliged to me. I taught her to love passionately and to be passionately angry. Neither of which she had experienced before." [18] After Thomas graduated in 1877, the relationship waned, and Margaret and Florence discovered each other. Until Margaret's early death in 1882, this friendship gave Kelley the beginnings of a new orientation toward female experience. Arm in arm with Margaret, she learned that love could create emotional patterns different from those that had dominated her family's life.

If Cornell suited Florence intellectually and emotionally, it also was appropriate socially, since the college placed relatively little emphasis on personal manners, compared to the "fashionable college society" that developed at women's colleges in the 1880s and 1890s. Like Mount Holyoke before it, Cornell attracted female students from the lower middle class as well as wealthier or elite young women like Thomas and Kelley. "The girls whom we see at the table are mostly as we expected: teachers and poor, struggling girls," Thomas wrote her parents. Living in a suite of three rooms and limiting her socializing to a small circle, Thomas disdained "the other girls in the Sage [who] were good enough students but not ladies." Thomas styled herself a lady and seemed to enjoy the formality of the women student's attire. "I have been to all my classes today. We go in our hats and gloves, just like a lecture." Florence was more casual about her appearance and gave her wardrobe minimal attention. "It is the custom for the girls who live anywhere near here to go home about this time and get their outfits somewhat freshened up," she wrote Caroline in October of her first semester, "a process of which I am rather in need inasmuch as going out in all weathers and writing a good deal as well as studying with one's arms on the table, a bad habit of mine which I think you may remember from the Miss Longstreth days, are not calculated to benefit clothing." Still, she thought she could get by with her "pretty black dress" and during the Christmas vacation would match her green silk skirt with a jacket to create a new suit. Although her room was not on the grand scale of Carey Thomas's, she wrote Caroline, "I like my room more and more; and when I get rocking chairs, table cover, pincushions, window curtains, books, pictures and book shelves (as I probably shall about graduating time) I shall consider myself quite satisfactorily placed." Still, she was conscious of living within a budget. "When the first of the month comes and with it the fresh installment of allowance," she wrote her mother, "I shall have clear accounts showing myself out of debt (except to you my most lenient creditor)." [19]

Illness forced Florence to remain "at home several weeks" the next fall, but she took the setback in stride. One of her father's acquaintances from a western trip also happened to be convalescing at the Elms. Mr. Livingston, an importer of fine laces, "was in constant contact with several foreign countries, making business journeys thither at what were then short intervals. His father had been a friend of Karl Marx." Florence's main interaction with this exotic guest was "to play third at dummy whist" and keep him "from going home before his cure was complete." Opening a new world to Florence, Livingston shared his "languid interest" in the remnants of the First International, whose headquarters had "transferred to Hoboken to save it from repression by European governments." Just before arriving in Philadelphia, "he had purchased, partly as curiosities, sample pamphlets printed in English on cheap paper in bad type, and bound in flaming paper covers." These Florence found as "startling" as her discovery years earlier of the reason Aunt Sarah ate no sugar and always wore linen. "Here were ideas and ideals undreamed of, and the headquarters of this world movement was as near as Hoboken!"[20]

During her next year and a half at Cornell, Florence began to see her studies in vocational terms. Tentative at first, she became as ambitious as any of her male peers. "I think I told you of my work," she wrote her father at the beginning of her third semester. "I suppose it will strike you as very school-girl-y. It comprises Latin, Italian, German, Early English, and lectures on the English and German Literatures, Roman History and Psychology." Nevertheless, she thought the courses were "fitting me for the work, which, with your concurrence, and help, I hope to do, if I ever, in the slow years, *do* grow into womanhood." When she passed five of her six examinations "with honor" that semester, she was "jubilant for several days." "My studies are exceedingly pleasant," she wrote Caroline at the beginning of her fourth semester. That spring she lavished energy on a Greek oration. "O, such an ordeal as I have been through this week!" she wrote home. After three weeks of "ruminating" on her subject, she finished "quite a good oration." "It was supposed to be the last lecture of Hypatia, an Alexandrian philosopher of the fourth century A.D., to her Greek pupils. It began with a graphic picture of the degradation to wh. the Greek race had fallen; then, picturing its glory eight hundred years before, claimed that it was not yet wholly base and painted a glorious future for mankind when the spirit of Phidias and Plato should revive." In the guise of a woman philosopher speaking for the welfare of Greek society, she practiced delivering her lecture twenty-one times "to myself, to Prof. Shackford, to the girls individually and collectively." When it came time to present the oration to the junior class "the boys all looked so interested that it was rather fun to do it." Later she heard that her oration was considered "better than any of the girls and among the best six of the boys'." Caroline and William did not need to be told that this triumph certified their daughter's skills in her father's field of rhetorical expertise.[21]

During her third and last year at Cornell, Florence's intellectual and social life gained new assurance and coherence as she started to specialize in social science. Her interest in history began to dominate. "I am heartily interested in my work this term," she wrote her father. Although she was still taking eight hours of Greek a week, her chief delight was the "wonderfully fine lectures on Modern European History from President White." Self-consciously her father's daughter, she criticized White for digressing "into discussions of monetary questions" that he knew little about but appreciated his specialized knowledge of the "Development of Rationalism in Europe." Even more rewarding were the fortnightly essays she was writing for the course. "The subjects for this term have been: 1. 'The Political Institutions of the Saxons in Germany.' 2. 'The Effect of the Norman Conquest on Anglo Saxon Institutions.' 3. 'Magna Carta; its Origin and Results.' 4. 'Growth of Parliament down to Henry VII' and 'Suspension of Parliament under the Tudors.' Next term we shall [do] seven more essays concerning American Constitutional History down to 1860." She thought these studies had clear vocational applications. "Isn't that good work for future editors, statesmen and lawyers? In reading for them we get a knowledge of the style and methods of all the best historians English and American." [22] Was she thinking of herself not only as an editor or a lawyer but also as a potential statesman? If so, she was obviously reaching beyond the possibilities open to her gender. But having found a field of study that excited her intellectually and including her male colleagues as well as herself in the sketch, she indulged in celebratory hyperbole. Part of her joy seems to have sprung from treading a path so close to her father's.

Henceforth social science became Florence Kelley's intellectual home. Andrew White at Cornell was the first to conceive of an inclusive department of social sciences, which he called the "Department of History, Political and Social Science." Columbia, Michigan, Johns Hopkins, and other universities promptly copied his innovation. Yet Cornell, like other American universities in the 1870s and early 1880s, actually offered very little training in the social sciences. Apart from history courses or the study of moral philosophy, students had to educate themselves, especially on the social issues of their own time. During Kelley's last term at Cornell, President White offered a lecture on Bismarck that was strongly influenced by his recent term as American ambassador to Berlin. There he learned to praise Bismarck and abhor Marx. "I do not know who would have been more astonished, Bismarck or Marx, at the picture of Socialism presented to our imagination!" Florence later recalled. She remembered him saying: "This class comes, I assume, from families whose heads are more or less responsible for carrying on the activities of the people of this state, the professions, agriculture, the industries, education, the press, transportation, and manufacture. Now if Socialism were introduced here, your fathers would be deprived of all that. It would all be handed over to the legislature at Albany." [23]

Although Cornell did not provide Florence with enduring tools of social analysis, it exposed her to the best that American universities had to offer and drew her into debates that resonated throughout her life. Above all, it served as a portal to the educated male world of public policy. For example, during her last term, Florence became the main force behind the founding of the Cornell Social Science Club. Her signature was the first to endorse the club's constitution, and, its only female member, she had "the honor to be secretary." "We students have formed a Social Science club which vows its intention of discussing 'all live questions social, moral and political,'" she wrote her father. "There are three or four professors who come very regularly; and, once in a while, take part in the debate. You would have been very much pleased, I think, with the rational tone of the whole performance." Kelley arranged for the club's first speaker, Mrs. Clara Neymann of New York City, who spoke on rationalism in Germany. Reflecting the spirit of social science in general and, in particular, the impact of Darwin's *Origin of Species,* published in 1859, the club's second meeting heard a member speak on the question: "Do the forms of animal life originate without the special interference of a Deity?" At subsequent meetings, members presented papers entitled "The True Spirit of Reform," "The Abolition of the Presidency," and "Economic Laws in the Organization of Society." Florence Kelley expressed her interest in nation-states by delivering a paper on national universities. Well launched, the club passed a resolution "that we the members of the Social Science Club feeling the necessity of scientific political education, throughout the country, express our regret at the lack of such instruction in Cornell University and hope it will be introduced as soon as possible." Florence was not able to attend this meeting, however, for she had fallen seriously ill.[24]

"The attack came on very suddenly, and seems to be going off as suddenly," Margaret Hicks wrote Caroline Kelley, explaining that Florence had seemed quite well when she left New York that morning. Margaret "felt troubled enough to insist on sleeping in her room," and "when the doctor came next morning, he looked very grave, and promised us a nurse at once."[25] William and Caroline immediately dispatched Will Jr. to monitor her condition. Though Florence did not fully recover, she completed the term, able to do her course work with Margaret Hicks's help and loath to exchange her life in Ithaca for another bout of illness at The Elms. Later diagnosed as diphtheria, Florence's illness finally forced her to go home in May. She blamed the severity of her illness on inadequate professional nursing. "Because the untrained local nurse was ignorant of the danger of overdosing and forgot the doctor's order to discontinue after ten days, I received large doses of brandy at two hours' intervals, from January to mid-May, following strychina, and other poisons. Three years out of college were the penalty paid for that illness and that untrained nurse."[26] She returned to Cornell only briefly in 1882 to take examinations and present her senior thesis.

Florence Kelley's premature departure could not destroy the great benefits of her three Cornell years. Female friendships lent strength to her gender identity. Competition with male peers erased self-doubts about her intellectual prowess. And her discovery of history and social science gave her a new route to public policy. She had the potential to extend paths blazed by her father and great-aunt without walking in their shadows.

When Florence returned to Philadelphia, Margaret Hicks came with her. As early as the previous February, William Kelley had appreciated "the effect of Miss Hicks' devotion to Florrie upon her studies" and agreed with Caroline that Margaret rather than Caroline should go with him and Florence to Europe that summer. In the meantime, he gratified Margaret's interests in architecture by sending her pictures of new public buildings in the nation's capital.[27]

To William, Caroline described a convalescent who took charge of her own recovery. "Florrie thinks she will go out on the piazza a little while, but not until noon, when she will be well wrapped up. She wishes me to tell you that she uses the gas daily, and attributes good effect to it, though she is still taking wine daily also." Her most important medicine, however, was the presence of Margaret Hicks. "Thank God for having given me such a friend," Florence wrote Margaret later. "Your unswerving generosity throughout our friendship, will alone suffice—should all things fail me—to maintain my faith in the Infinite Goodness." Ruth Putnam also visited for an extended period. During her stay, she, Florence, and Margaret took the buggy on an outing to the Chester County home of Mrs. Eliza Turner. (A leader in women's political culture in Philadelphia, Turner became a family friend after fund raising with William Kelley for the National Centennial Exhibition.) News of Florence's illness spread to the congressman's associates in Washington, one of whom wrote her hoping "to divert the thoughts of Miss Florence from her own condition" with news of her father's exploits on the floor of the House.[28]

To aid her recovery, William Kelley took his daughter to Europe in June, accompanied by Margaret and Will. The group toured Bruges, Brussels, Antwerp, Rotterdam, Amsterdam, and Berlin, where they met with President White of Cornell. "You will want to hear of Florrie," William wrote Caroline. "Her rapid improvement has surprised us all. She does not hesitate to demand rest whenever she feels fatigue so that I am not deceived as to her condition. She sleeps well and long, enjoys her food, is an eager sight seer, and enjoys Will's fun intensely." Florrie and Margaret toured cathedrals "for paintings" in England and France, visited schools in Switzerland, and, according to William, "saw much more of Europe than was expected when we landed." By August, William wrote that "Florrie's restoration appears to be perfect." Margaret proved to be an ideal companion. "Florrie could not have had a more useful or agreeable companion and her swift use of the pen has enabled her to render me many services." Florrie's strength and steadiness of nerve continued to improve. "Indeed she seems to be quite well." The group returned to Philadelphia in mid-September.[29]

Though apparently restored to health, Florence did not return to Cornell. Margaret and many of her close friends had left, and perhaps she feared the severity of the climate might cause a relapse. Very likely she also felt that she had little more to gain from another year in Ithaca—especially when her father held out the prospect of sponsoring her senior thesis research at the Library of Congress. From the fall of 1879 to the spring of 1882, this project dominated her life.[30]

Living with her father sporadically during those two and a half years in Washington, she did not devote all her time to research. Caroline often visited, and Florence was expected to accompany her on social calls. "We could not go out to make calls on account of the bad weather, and as we have a great many to make, we shall be very busy this week," Caroline wrote Will Jr. toward the end of one visit. Whether in Washington or Philadelphia, Florence often thought of Margaret. "I cannot help letting you know how constantly and freshly the thought of you comes to my mind," she wrote on one occasion.[31]

Left to her own devices without Caroline's presence, however, Florence walked daily between her boardinghouse and the Library of Congress, where she taught herself about the legal history of children in the past hundred years. Her readings focused on the legal treatment of poor children, illegitimate children, and wage-earning children and on child custody in divorce cases. Her thesis was titled "On Some Changes in the Legal Status of the Child since Blackstone"; this choice of subject, she said later, "followed naturally upon Father's years of effort to enlist me permanently in behalf of less fortunate children."[32]

Partly an introduction to a legal career, partly an apprenticeship in social legislation, the topic in her hands was not easily contained. It carried her beyond the legal status of children to include the rights of women, and their part in civic culture. In her essay, she adopted her father's view of the active state as the steward of social justice and her great-aunt's view of the moral responsibility of individuals. To these she added her own perspective on the place of women within civic society and highlighted women's abilities to shape public policy. "For me it was of incalculable importance," she later said of her thesis work.[33] Much of its significance lay in the way it caused her to come to terms with her legal identity as a woman and to explore the meaning of that identity within contemporary political culture.

In her interpretation, statute law since Blackstone had increasingly guarded "all children without reference to the family, diminishing paternal power, and making the child more and more nearly the ward of the State." Improvements in the status of illegitimate children were most notable in this regard, but all poor children benefited from compulsory education, child labor, and custody laws that considered the child's interests, not the father's, as paramount. By treating "the child's welfare as a direct object of legislation, apart from the family relation," she observed, "the strong arm of the law prove[d] itself tender and merciful." The child became "an individual, with a distinctive legal status" instead of merely being "an appendage" of the "absolute ownership of the father." [34] This recognition of the value of the individual differentiated the modern era from Blackstone's time.

By advocating the interests of children in opposition to male patriarchal authority, Kelley's essay viewed nineteenth-century legal history from a new perspective. Elizabeth Cady Stanton and Caroline Dall, among others, had criticized laws and legal traditions that buttressed patriarchy, but they had not recognized the steady stream of nineteenth-century social legislation as a force eroding patriarchy. While their advocacy of women's rights often adopted an adversarial stance toward the state, Kelley's noticed the importance of women's empowerment through the expansion of state authority—as experts, officials, or interested parties. In contrast to their usage, she never used the word *woman* to describe women collectively. Her intellectual roots lay in nineteenth-century history rather than in the eighteenth-century enlightenment; for her, the power of women derived from their part in the historical process, not from that abstract essence, *woman*. [35]

Her evidence came from state board of health reports, state education laws, state charity reports, as well as legal treatises. These documents showed "the superiority of the moral over the legal qualifications of the home in securing the child's welfare." Especially evident in changing divorce laws was "the growing value attached to human life and to human personality and the attendant respect for individuality in every form." With this consideration of the child's welfare, the "recognition of the child's need of legal power in the mother" grew, rendering obsolete Blackstone's dictum "that the mother as such, is entitled to no power, but only to reverence and respect." In her account of the social origins of changes in child custody laws, Kelley recognized what scholars today have identified as a central dynamic of nineteenth-century change—the growing moral power of women within middle-class family life—and, like recent historians, she understood that this change was propelled by larger cultural, social, economic, and political transformations. [36]

Kelley compared England and the United States to show "that the growth of care for the moral welfare of the child and the removal of the duty of education from the family to the State" correlated with the extension of suffrage. Expressing the state's self-interest, this correlation began in Massachusetts in the 1630s and persisted in the effort of American municipalities to provide schooling for immigrant children in the 1880s. In England, however, where male suffrage was still only partial in 1882, public schooling lagged, existing before that date only in the limited form of factory acts that extended traditional protections for "apprentices" by requiring half a day of school for child laborers. Thus the greater value placed on the duties of citizenship in American society was matched by the greater importance of education.[37]

"The influence of women . . . upon legislation affecting children" was yet another force behind the state's increasing intervention. The political process by which women and children were ceasing to be treated as patriarchal dependents and beginning to be viewed as individuals was one that women themselves were actively promoting. Although married women needed to be guarded by the state to protect them from patriarchal abuse, both they and single women became agents of change by promoting state guardianship of children. Kelley pointed to Mary Carpenter, who campaigned for free schools for poor children and generated British legislation for reformatories and industrial schools in the 1870s. In turn, the protectionist state created more opportunities for the influence of women. For example, the Massachusetts Infant Asylum placed children under "the legal custody of the women in charge," and some Massachusetts towns in 1879 began to reserve school board positions for women. Some women's voluntary associations, "chartered by law," aided in the enforcement of child labor laws and statutes that prohibited the sale of liquor and obscene literature to children. Weaving together the disparate strands of law and social movements, the individual, and the society, Kelley's thesis treated changes in the legal status of women and children as part of the same processes that invited the participation of women in civic life. Women, it seemed, could be equal partners in the construction of the "tender and merciful" state.[38]

This essay proved that Florence Kelley could excel at sustained and original research and writing. How did it fit into the intellectual and social context of male political culture in the early 1880s? Henry Adams's popular novel *Democracy* provided one answer. Published anonymously in 1880, his book idealized the humane and ethical effect of women in politics while it exposed the shabby dealings of politicians during the Grant administration. Yet the virtue of *Democracy*'s women came from their ability to transcend political life, not, as in Kelley's analysis, through their immersion in it.[39] If Adams was correct that American government was dominated by considerations of patronage, party, and personal gain, while women, the chief source of social morality, rose above politics, then there was little hope for Florence Kelley's view of an enlightened state working hand in hand with enlightened women. Kelley's essay, taking account of women's collective power in civic society, predicted a different outcome.

Florence Kelley loved her work and life in Washington. By 1880 the city, like the nation's economy, had undergone significant development. Although the Washington Monument was still not finished, Pennsylvania Avenue had emerged as a bustling commercial thoroughfare connecting the now-completed Capitol and the Executive Mansion. The train depot from which Florence arrived and departed occupied the present-day mall just west of the Capitol. Although the countryside lay only a few blocks in any direction from the city's center, the ongoing construction of large public buildings lent the city an aura of vitality and expectation.[40]

In an Easter poem written on her father's stationery from the Committee of Ways and Means, she expressed both her high spirits and her refusal to feel guilty for them.

> For one who will never be giddy and swear
> It is not outside of all reason
> To send at this time of devotion and prayer
> A card illustrating the season
> But for one who's as wicked and worldly as I
> To select a nice pious quotation
> Would a lack of consistency promptly imply
> And I don't care for that imputation.[41]

"Wicked and worldly," she returned to Ithaca in March 1882, presented her thesis, took examinations "in a multitude of subjects," and received her Cornell degree. Her thesis was one of nine receiving "Honorable Mention" at the Fourteenth Annual Commencement. The previous summer, during a visit with Margaret Hicks in Boston, the two friends had attended some of the first meetings of the New England branch of the Association of Collegiate Alumnae, forerunner of the American Association of University Women. Two years later, when the Cornell chapter of Phi Beta Kappa was formed, Kelley's strong academic record was rewarded with a membership key.[42]

Immediately on receiving her degree, Kelley "applied to the University of Pennsylvania for permission to enter for further study in advanced Greek." She probably selected this field of study in the hope that Professor Francis Jackson, a relative of her grandfather Isaac Pugh and dean of the classical department, would support her application even though women were not usually admitted. "After long failure of the faculty to respond," Judge Kelley formally requested the trustees to admit her. The university's response was both disappointing and insulting to a person of her talents and background: the son of William Furness, her father's close friend, replied that "the older he grew and the more he knew people, the lower his opinion of them became and the more abhorrent the thought of young men and women meeting in the classroom." So much for highly placed friends among Philadelphia's elite. Neither Kelley's Cornell degree nor her family's ties could overcome the obstacle of her gender.[43]

Just three years later, after administrative reorganizations that began in 1882, the University of Pennsylvania began to admit women to graduate study on an equal basis with men. Although by 1889 ten American institutions had granted doctorates to women, in 1882 only a few admitted women to graduate study, sometimes as "special students" who could not qualify for degrees. This problem was symptomatic of the predicament of early college graduates in the 1870s and 1880s: as the first generation with ready access to college, on graduation they inevitably encountered a world unprepared to utilize their talents. The most obvious option for Kelley and her contemporaries had been available to talented women for half a century — teaching. Of the seventy-five women who graduated from Cornell before 1883, forty-eight entered teaching; six of these obtained advanced degrees and taught at women's colleges. In this cohort, there were doctors and a dentist, but no lawyers. One classmate of Kelley's studied biology at the University of Pennsylvania and later taught at the Friends Select School in Philadelphia. Margaret Hicks studied architecture at Cornell during Kelley's last year there.[44]

With the exception of M. Carey Thomas, who became president of Bryn Mawr College in 1894, the closest that any of Kelley's Cornell female peers came to shaping public policy was by exerting leadership within the burgeoning world of women's reform associations. One member of the class of 1875 served as vice-president of the Illinois Woman's Exposition Board of the World's Columbian Exposition in Chicago and as secretary of the National Household Economic Association. An 1881 graduate served as secretary of the New York State Woman Suffrage Association and held "other offices in connection with reform organizations."[45]

Marriage and other forms of what Jane Addams later called "the family claim" were even more serious obstacles to professional careers for these early college graduates. Although a large proportion of educated, upper-middle-class women in Florence Kelley's generation postponed or avoided marriage, they were not free from the family claim. For both cultural and economic reasons, they found it difficult to establish the emotional and economic self-sufficiency that might have freed them from their large sense of family obligation. Kelley, like many other college women, returned home after graduation.[46]

For Florence, the family claim extended into public life. For example, when she attended a woman suffrage convention in Washington, it was as William's daughter, and when he failed to appear as one of the scheduled speakers, she was publicly as well as personally mortified. Susan B. Anthony added to her humiliation by announcing, "This is a new and painful illustration of the lack of respect for the vote even among men who are convinced advocates of suffrage." Identifying more with her father than Miss Anthony, Florence "went home with my heart in my shoes. I foresaw Father's indignation that, after a quarter century's active allegiance to a cause still sufficiently unpopular, he was ridiculed by the great leader whom he counted a friend. At breakfast the next morning I watched anxiously as he opened the paper. I had not courage to open it myself. Great was my bewilderment and relief to hear him laugh and say: 'The good old Major! I'm afraid I deserved that.'" [47] William's behavior sometimes tested his daughter's loyalty, but his example taught her how to negotiate the personal hazards of public life.

Although William Kelley could not get his daughter admitted to the University of Pennsylvania, he did arrange for her thesis to be published. "Mr. Porter is very anxious to read Florrie's thesis," he wrote Caroline in the summer of 1882. "He thinks that though it might be too technical for a Magazine it might do for a Review. Ask her to send it to me by express that he may read it." That August her thesis was published in a highbrow New York periodical on public affairs—the *International Review*. Prompted perhaps by Florence's presence in their city during her visit to Margaret Hicks, the *Boston Evening Transcript* commented on the publication of her thesis. The newspaper noted that she was the daughter of "the Hon. William D. Kelley of Pennsylvania," and praised her article for analyzing "the modifications wrought in the laws since the days of the great commentator . . . in an interesting style, and with all the conciseness, logic and accuracy in citation that characterize a trained writer on the history of law." The thesis was a source of pride to William Kelley. "He has a wonderful daughter," a congressional opponent said. "She is a person who will make her mark in the future." Another colleague congratulated him "on the possession of a daughter who could write the article he had read in the International." This first publication encouraged Florence to take her future seriously as a figure in the national polity, but it remained to be seen how she would evolve from a family possession to an independent person. [48]

4

"Brain Work Waiting for Women,"
1882–1884

Like higher education, social science served as another critical vehicle by which middle-class women expanded the ground they occupied within American civic life between 1860 and 1890. Social science offered tools of analysis that enhanced women's ability to investigate economic and social change, speak for the welfare of the whole society, devise policy initiatives, and oversee their implementation. Yet at the same time social science offered a new way for educated women to participate in civil society, it deepened women's gender identity in public life and attached their civic activism even more securely to gender-specific issues.

In the fall of 1882 Florence Kelley heralded the importance of women social scientists as molders of public policy. Her first writing after graduation, "Need Our Working Women Despair?" published in the *International Review,* addressed an arresting ethical question. She answered it by recommending female-specific sociology as an antidote for despair. Together, college-trained women and wage-earning women could produce new knowledge capable of enhancing the lives of both.

The gendered features of "humane" sociology justified and demanded women investigators, she wrote. "In the field of sociology there is brain work waiting for women which men cannot do." Referring perhaps to the likes of Mathew Carey, she argued, "While the science of man was a science of wealth, rest and self-interest there was slight inducement for women to touch it." However, the era of self-interest had passed. "The new social science has humane interest, and can never be complete without help from women." The new "science of human relations" must study people "as they exist, with patient care," but, she insisted, "exact tabulation of facts is the beginning only; afterward comes the work of interpretation. That can be complete only when accomplished by the whole human consciousness, i.e., by that two-fold nature, masculine and feminine, which expresses itself as a whole in human relations." Making a firm berth for herself among the generators of new knowledge, she emphasized that "any attempt made by a part of the race to explain phenomena produced by complementary beings must be inadequate." [1]

Kelley's formulation contained benefits and liabilities for the long-term interests of women. By insisting that sociology could never be complete without their contributions, she guaranteed a place for women in "the science of human relations." Yet this very guarantee accepted women's gendered responsibility for the welfare of others and their exclusion from other branches of social science. Her words reflected larger trends. Early social science was receptive to and shaped by women partly because it endorsed a relational ethics that many women reformers had historically found congenial, partly because it focused on the practical level of social reform. Yet as her ringing defense of women social scientists showed, the more the new field of social science incorporated women, the more it contained them in sex-segregated groups.[2]

Nevertheless, for the women and men who affiliated with it in the 1880s, social science supplied an empowering alternative vision of human nature and society that discarded the extreme individualism and laissez-faire views of Social Darwinism. Replacing eighteenth-century political economy, the new social science encouraged a scathingly negative critique of the ethical consequences of laissez-faire public policies. In an 1880 address to the American Social Science Association (ASSA), Franklin Sanborn, the association's founder and long-time president, condemned "the chimera of non-interference by government—the Franco-Brittanic specter of laissez-faire—which has been conjured up so many times to thwart wise statesmanship and decent public policy, in the ethical relations of government." [3] This moral tone in early social science buttressed values of community and a consciousness of collective life that had been weakened by the individualism of early industrial capitalism. In this project, the assistance of women was warmly welcomed, known as they were for their skills in meeting community needs.

Women were present at the birth of American social science; they came with the civic territory it embraced. Caroline Dall was a cofounder of the association in 1865, and other women were especially active in the ASSA's departments of education, public health, and social economy, which gave them clear but limited mandates for leadership. In the division of labor emerging in early social science, women were identified with social praxis—hands-on efforts—rather than the loftier realms of social theory. The departments of jurisprudence and finance, which generated endless amounts of social theory, were reserved for men. In 1887 Franklin Sanborn described the social economy division of the ASSA, which he headed, as "the feminine gender of Political Economy, and so, very receptive of particulars, but little capable of general and aggregate matters. . . . Social welfare, therefore, and not wealth in its wide and compound sense, is what we consider."[4]

Perhaps to escape these restrictions, women maintained their own social science associations at the same time that they participated in the American Social Science Association. In New York in the early 1870s they formed the New York City Sociology Club, the Women's Progressive Association, and the Ladies' Social Science Association (which Florence Kelley probably attended when it met in 1880 in the rooms of the New Century Club of Philadelphia). This social science strand of women's civic activity created an alternative channel for the expression of women's interests—one that ran parallel to women's rights or suffrage associations. At the first meeting of the Ladies' Social Science Association in 1869, Jane Croly's opening address urged women to see suffrage as one tool among many, declaring, "The ballot is at best only one agency; it cannot do everything. It does not do everything for men." Even more important, she said, were the "combined efforts of intelligent and active women in their own organizations to work for humanity."[5]

For Florence Kelley, as for many women of her generation, these organizations answered the question of "After college, what?" Notable among these groups were organizations concerned with the plight of working women. Since the 1830s, most prominently in the campaign against prostitution led by the American Female Moral Reform Society, middle-class women had addressed their version of the needs of women wage earners. Fair labor standards for women workers had been pursued by voluntary associations in New York since 1863, when the Working Women's Protective Union was founded to assist women who joined the labor force during the Civil War. Headed by a male board of directors and limiting itself to "employments other than household service," the union raised money from middle-class supporters to provide women free "legal protection from the frauds and impositions of unscrupulous employers." It also urged employers to increase wages and reduce hours, sought "new and appropriate spheres of labor in departments not ordinarily occupied by women," and maintained a registry of those seeking employment. In 1888 it administered an annual budget of more than seventeen thousand dollars, processed ten thousand job applicants, and prosecuted nearly five hundred cases of fraud against working women, involving a total of almost eight thousand dollars. During the 1880s, a decade of rapid increase in women's labor force participation and profound reorientation in women's public activism, middle-class women replaced middle-class men as the chief protectors of the welfare of wage-earning women.[6]

While the proportion of girls and women in the nation's paid labor force grew dramatically between 1870 and 1900, the 1870s and 1880s witnessed the most rapid growth.

Although women were excluded from most skilled work, their numbers increased in poorly paid unskilled jobs. Causes of this increase included the low wages of many adult men, which made them unable to provide for their families' needs; technological changes that reduced the skills required for many jobs; and the crowding of women into jobs in highly competitive, undercapitalized industries, such as garment making and box making, where firms survived by paying less than a living wage to their employees.[7]

Women and children worked for very low wages because they had no choice, but paltry as they were, these wages were larger relative to men's than they had ever been before. Wage-earning women in the 1880s could envision the possibility of being self-supporting, even if only for a few years before marriage. In the late 1880s approximately three-fourths of wage-earning women in the United States were younger than twenty-five and less than 5 percent were married, lending credence to the phrase "working girl." The vast majority of women left the paid labor force after marriage because their domestic labor for the social reproduction of their families was more valuable than the wages they could earn and because working-class culture defined respectability in terms of wives who did not work outside the home. Nevertheless, faced with the tantalizing possibility of improving their social options through a brief period of economic self-

Working Women's Protective Union: Hearing a complaint against a sewing machine operator. *Harper's Weekly*, Feb. 21, 1874. Courtesy of Library of Congress.

support, an increasing proportion of young single women in the 1870s and 1880s devoted their precious leisure hours to self-improvement.[8]

These trends were vividly borne out by the growing ranks of working women in Philadelphia. Between 1850 and 1880 the city's population doubled, but the number of adult women employed in industrial jobs more than tripled, rising from 15,620 to 51,033. Most of this increase was concentrated in textile and clothing production, where the numbers rose from 10,532 to 37,649. Large increases also occurred in the production of boots and shoes, paper, chemicals, food, machine tools, and hardware and in printing and publishing. Only New York, Boston, Baltimore, and New England textile towns attracted a larger proportion of wage-earning women.[9]

Kelley exemplified the emphatic middle-class response to these trends in her participation in Philadelphia's New Century Club. For her, this activity took the place of graduate study. Swallowing the injury of that rejection—for the time being—she turned the university's loss into the New Century Club's gain. Founded in 1877 by Eliza Sprout Turner, a close friend of the Kelley family who had entertained Florence and her friends at her country home in 1879, the New Century Club attracted Sarah Pugh's surviving colleagues from the antislavery movement but also drew a new generation of women into new forms of social activism. Whereas antebellum women's groups had revolved around a specific purpose or issue, postwar organizations offered their members a constantly expanding range of issues and efforts that filled the civil landscape between the economy and the state. The similarity between the two eras lay in their justification of women's activism as a form of social obligation, but now the obligation was imbued with national purpose.[10]

This expansion of the terrain of women's activism began during the Civil War with women's work for the United States Sanitary Commission. Modeled on the British Sanitary Commission, which Florence Nightingale energized during the Crimean War (1854–56), the American commission was, in the words of an 1863 fair brochure for the Boston Sanitary Commission, "the great artery which bears the people's love to the people's army." The commission, a quasi-public entity, drew heavily on the volunteer work of Northern women to fulfill the government's responsibility for the health and welfare of the Union soldiers and their dependents. Local women's associations served as powerful agents of nation-building. Mary Livermore estimated that the ten to twelve thousand women's aid societies affiliated with the U.S. Sanitary Commission "slew sectionalism at the outset, and overcame the difficulties of cooperative undertakings at the very start." In Philadelphia, in June 1864, the Great Central Sanitary Commission Fair organized by the Ladies Committee of the Commission raised more than a million dollars to aid the Union Army.[11]

After this wartime mobilization, women's organizations in the North displayed a new self-confidence, an impressive transregional scale, a generalized concern about all aspects of public life, and a new commitment to self-improvement. Beginning with Sorosis, founded in New York in 1868, the women's club movement quickly expanded throughout the northern states. In the words of one of its founders, that movement "proposed the inoculation of deeper and broader ideas among women, proposed to teach them to think for themselves, and get their opinions at first hand . . . to open out new avenues of employment to women, to make them less dependent and less burdensome, to lift them out of unwomanly self-distrust, disqualifying diffidence, into womanly self-respect and self-knowledge."[12] By entering into group life, the hope was, women would become more fully individuated as well as more socially effective.

Urban areas like Philadelphia, New York, Boston, and Chicago remained the most vital scenes of this shift in women's organizations, yet the single largest example of the new civic scope of women's activism, the Woman's Christian Temperance Union, reached rural as well as urban constituencies, North and South, East and West, black and white. Founded in the depression winter of 1873–74, the WCTU deepened and extended the moral reform movement of the antebellum era, while at the same time it adopted many of the women's rights views generated within the antislavery movement. Self-improvement became a vehicle not merely for aiding oneself or one's family but for changing society as a whole. The WCTU's militancy and confidence about reshaping the public world was evident in its goal "to make the whole world homelike." The union mobilized women to meet this goal by combining women's traditional moral concerns with scientific knowledge and modern methods of problem solving. For example, WCTU locals were spatially organized to conform with congressional districts, placing their membership in direct confrontation with male-dominated electoral politics. At their national convention in 1879, members endorsed woman suffrage as a means of implementing their goals—a strategy sustained by state unions in 1881. The organization rapidly became an umbrella for a wide range of social reforms. By 1896 twenty-five of its thirty-nine social action departments dealt wholly or mostly with nontemperance issues, such as child labor, working conditions for wage-earning women, and prison reform. In 1889 the union formally attributed intemperance to bad working conditions and long hours rather than to moral laxity. Ranging widely between the economy and the state, WCTU members viewed every public issue as a women's issue.[13]

Philadelphia's New Century Club exemplified this new expansive spirit in women's organizations. The club's motto, "Give her of the fruit of her hands" (Proverbs 31:31), expressed a new consciousness of the link between women's work and women's rights. For Eliza Turner and her associates, that link was strengthened after an instructive run-in with male community leaders in 1875 and 1876. The Women's Centennial Committee had raised $125,000 for Philadelphia's Centennial Exhibition with the understanding that part would go to a "Woman's Exhibit" in the fair's main building to display "the inventions and industries of the women of all nations." A separate women's exhibit was needed, the committee believed, "to give the mass of women, who were laboring by the needle and obtaining only a scanty subsistence, the opportunity to see what women were capable of attaining in other and higher branches of industry." Incredibly, the exhibition's board of finance accepted the women's money but then told them they had no room for a women's exhibit. Turner and her allies had no alternative but to raise another $30,000 for a separate building. They began the New Century Club keenly aware of the crucial importance of financial autonomy and determined to channel their resources to the needs of women.[14]

Florence Kelley first became active in the fall before her graduation, when, under the club's auspices, she launched evening classes for working girls and women. By early November the school was a smashing success with one hundred and twenty students and fifteen teachers. Kelley taught history. Other courses were offered in literature, French, German, drawing, physiology, oral reading, and bookkeeping. In February 1882, the school had to turn away applicants, and the curriculum expanded to include millinery, dressmaking, grammar, and cooking. Saturday evening lectures were also added on home nursing and child care; talks on hygiene were offered by a woman physician who also gave advice to individuals requesting it. This almost certainly included contraceptive information.[15]

At the beginning of the school's second year (when she could finally give it her full attention), Kelley chaired a group of teachers who formally established the New Century Working Women's Guild. This organization, which still remains vital in the 1990s, proved to be one of the most progressive societies for women in the United States in the 1880s. It provided a room for reading and social meetings and encouraged women to come together "for mutual help, enjoyment, and encouragement in high endeavor." Inviting to membership "any self-supporting woman, from whatever branch of industry, business, or any medical, scientific or artistic profession, and women interested in advancing the purposes of the Guild," the association quickly attracted more than five hundred members, with almost as many enrolled in day classes.[16] Day and evening classes filled to overflowing the rooms of the guild's rented downtown mansion.

In addition to teaching history, Florence Kelley also generated new forms of knowledge in other ways. In October 1882 she took up the key position of librarian, who was "empowered to make all selection of books, to appoint an Assistant and make all such arrangements concerning books and their distribution, as she may deem best." Not surprisingly, given Kelley's interests, the library that year consisted of "items of sociology of economic problems of the day." Guild account books show that Kelley brought in the organization's first contribution—$5.00 from Mrs. F. H. Jackson, wife of the Greek professor who had failed to aid her admission to the University of Pennsylvania. She also incurred the group's first expenditure, $10.83 for stationery, and probably also served on "a committee of ladies [who] sit twice a week to receive applicants who wish legal advice . . . [for] the collection of wages wrongfully withheld."[17]

In the midst of her guild activities in the fall of 1882, Florence Kelley wrote "Need Our Working Women Despair?" in response to an article entitled "Women's Work and Women's Wages," published in the *North American Review* that August. The author, Charles Wyllys Elliott, had been known to antebellum readers as a writer on domestic topics. Elliott decried the competition between women and men for jobs, the low wages that women inevitably received for their work, the workplace injuries they incurred, the growing number of women who did not marry, and the delusion that woman suffrage could improve women's lives. He implied that the economic self-sufficiency promoted by women's rights proponents was illusory.[18]

Kelley answered these charges much more cogently than they were posed. Situating herself in the civic terrain of women's activism with a range of vision that included economic conditions and the state's appropriate response to those conditions, her arguments justified the labor force participation of middle-class as well as working-class women and analyzed the bonds between the two groups. Using ideas deployed by advocates of working women since the 1830s, she emphasized that the "development of women's faculties" in "self-maintenance before marriage . . . insures helpful wifehood," helps women supply their own dowries, and protects them against the hazards of widowhood. In addition, she said, a growing number of women who were not marrying "must maintain themselves."

Fifty years earlier Catharine Beecher and others had urged the importance of women teachers in creating a coherent nation out of a population of migrants and immigrants; Florence Kelley echoed and amplified this call for utilization of the talents of middle-class women. Identifying herself as a "student of the census," she noted that the lives of all Americans, women included, had been changed by "millions of foreigners [who] have accepted the nation's invitation, and are helping us govern ourselves. If we are to assimilate these rulers to the spirit of our life, every energy of man and woman must be utilized." In this capacity, women were needed as teachers of a wide variety of skills, librarians, newspaper writers, city physicians, nurses, and charity workers and as chaplains, superintendents, and custodians of female charitable and reformatory institutions.[19]

Contrary to Elliott's assertion that the employment of women diminished the employment of men, Kelley argued that wage-earning women created more work for men; watchmakers, for example, had increased their production thanks to the growing number of working women requiring watches. Additionally, men were abandoning many fields of employment, such as retail sales, pursuing "more lucrative work created by steam and electricity in railroads and shipping."[20]

Her article included a significant section on women's industrial health. That topic posed knotty difficulties for women reformers of Kelley's generation. Decades of struggle by working women and men to limit the length of the working day through legislation had generated ample testimony about the harmful effects of exploitative working conditions (most especially the long working day from ten to fourteen hours), and opponents of women's participation in the paid labor force used these arguments to urge that women be eliminated from the industrial workplace altogether.[21] Kelley carefully associated herself with the view that the health of working women could be improved through education related to such matters as "physiology and hygiene" and through systematic changes in working conditions.

Kelley's views on this crucial social science topic were informed by Dr. Mary Putnam Jacobi's prize-winning 1876 study *The Question of Rest for Women during Menstruation*. The older sister of Florence's close friend Ruth Putnam, Mary Putnam obtained her M.D. degree from the Woman's Medical College of Pennsylvania in 1864 and by the early 1870s won recognition as the leading woman physician in the United States. Affiliated after 1873 with the Woman's Medical College of the New York Infirmary for Women and Children, that year she married Abraham Jacobi, one of the leading pediatricians in America, who had emigrated to the United States after being imprisoned in Germany during the 1848 revolution.[22]

Jacobi refuted Edward Clarke's conclusions about women's physiological limitations, basing her findings on the responses of two hundred and sixty-three women to a questionnaire. Although 46 percent of the respondents "suffer[ed] more or less at menstruation," the vast majority did not require rest, nor did they find mental activity debilitating. "Anatomical imperfections," not mental or physical activity, caused the extreme menstrual pain experienced by a minority. "In an immense majority of cases," Jacobi found that menstrual pain was tolerated "far better while the ordinary occupations are continued." Mental work could not disrupt physiological processes, she concluded, because "no really *mental* work will ever be performed at a time that the brain is really unable to perform it."[23]

While Jacobi's conclusions decisively championed the collegiate potential of young women, at the same time her study sustained the view that, because of their reproductive processes, women industrial workers merited special consideration from their employers. Spontaneous self-directed intellectual activity was not impeded by normal menstruation, but "work involving muscular effort and the strain of fixed attention" did become more difficult. Since almost half of her respondents did suffer menstrual pain, she concluded that "humanity dictates that rest from work during the period of pain be afforded whenever practicable" for those "engaged in industrial pursuits" or "under the command of an employer."[24]

The class facets of Jacobi's study neatly reversed those offered by Clarke. He had explained why "female operatives of all sorts are likely to suffer less, and actually do suffer less, from such persistent work, than female students; why Jane in the factory can work more steadily with the loom, than Jane in college with the dictionary; why the girl who makes the bed can safely work more steadily the whole year through, than her little mistress of sixteen who goes to school." Female operatives, according to Clarke, "have stronger bodies, a reproductive apparatus more normally constructed, and a catamenial function less readily disturbed by effort, than their student sisters." In apparent contradiction to these conclusions, however, Clarke lauded the recent passage of the Ten-Hour Act in England, which protected women against overwork, insisting that the law expressed agreement with his view "that the male and female organization are not identical." Thus Clarke wove class and gender biases into a cloth of his own convenience, urging protection of women in some cases and in others leaving them vulnerable to exploitation.[25]

Clarke's other critics did not completely ignore his contradictory evidence about working women, but it took Jacobi's careful research to show that the women whose reproductive processes merited social attention were not those studying to become ministers, doctors, or lawyers—women who would be competing with men of Clarke's social stratum—but women who were employed by such men.

In Kelley's first venture into print on behalf of working women, she defended their right to work for wages and at the same time scathingly censured their exploitation. The deliberately provocative words of her title, "Need Our Working Women Despair?" forced the reader to consider the question from the perspective of working women themselves. She offered practical, political solutions for the unethical exploitation working women experienced. First, she broadened the context of the debate to include men and called for the protection of all workers from industrial hazards. "Our industrial scorn of life's worth" was a major problem for women and men alike, she said. "Work not deadly in itself we make so by excess or mean economy. We injure women little more than men. The fluff of cotton mills is bad for human lungs, not women's lungs alone."[26]

Second, as a step toward that universal goal, she called upon middle-class women to use their political power to improve working conditions for laboring women. The nation's "defective legal provision" for the protection of workers she attributed to industrial "inexperience," compared to "England's older civilization," which "has been steadily framing laws in careful protection of women and girls in mills." She insisted, "Is not such need urgent here?" Pointing to the efforts of the workingman to obtain "short hours, fair wages and more healthful conditions of work . . . by his power of shaping legislatures," she noted that "from such self-help the working-woman is decisively shut off. She has absolutely no representation." Her essay advocated political rights among all women as a means of extending economic rights to working women. "Are American women blameless in shirking the responsibility of the ballot which alone can insure thorough legislative protection of working women?" she asked. "That is a question worth answering before we rest content with the sad assurance that 'it is almost certain that it is impossible' for working women to 'keep well.'" [27]

Her essay praised the work of middle-class women in the Women's Educational and Industrial Union in Boston, at Cooper Union in New York, and in the Working Women's Guild in Philadelphia, where "associations of ladies have been formed for the express purpose of securing the legal protection of working-women." By their mere existence, these organizations "have in a measure checked oppression," she postulated, "and prosecutions and convictions by them have destroyed a class of sewing-machine agents and sewing-contract men who lived by preying upon this worst-paid work." She believed that "the song of the shirt loses something of its tragedy when women begin to guard the sewing-girl's wages, provide safe boarding-houses for her, and wholesome evening recreations and summer country weeks." [28]

Addressing the political needs of workingwomen, middle-class women could provide "educative recreations" similar to those available to a workingman, who "can go to a library and forget the noise of his machine in reading or a quiet game, or he can enjoy the dignity of responsibility in discussing the coming election." In conclusion, she encouraged "humane companionship" between middle-class and working-class women. She suggested that "college-bred women" were well-suited for such companionship because "they are chiefly working-women, with quick sympathies." The future would tell "what may come of this new spirit that leads happy women to say, more than ever before, 'We that are strong, let us bear the infirmities of the weak,'" but until that time, she insisted, "surely our working-women need not despair." [29]

Buried in the ponderous pages of the *International Review*, Kelley's words did not reach many women's eyes, but for those who knew her they demonstrated a budding capacity for leadership. Her apprenticeship among Philadelphia's workingwomen released talents and passions worthy of the enormous transformation under way in women's public culture. She had become part of the process by which that culture was linking knowledge and obligation in new ways that brought the lives of middle-class and working-class women into intersection and significantly expanded the range of women's public concerns.

In the midst of her "work for humanity" in the Working Women's Guild, Florence Kelley's life changed suddenly and irrevocably. Her teaching "came to an abrupt end at Thanksgiving," she remembered, "when my older brother was ordered to the Riviera" to recover from bouts of blindness "and I was the only available person to go with him on four days' notice." Margaret Hicks, engaged to marry a Cornell classmate, wrote from Cambridge to thank Caroline for a wedding gift of "beautiful linen" and commented on Florence's departure: "Of course it is a great disappointment that Florence cannot be here, but so long as we know that she is happy in being of use to Will and to you all, we don't stop to think of our disappointment. I am sure that the change will be of benefit to Will, and Florence will enjoy going over the ground with him, too." To give his daughter an opportunity to benefit from her journey, William Kelley arranged for the secretary of state to provide her with a letter of introduction to "the French Minister of Instruction." The family envisioned the trip as a winter's jaunt; ultimately, however, Florence's European sojourn lasted four years. She departed as a dutiful daughter and sister committed to social reform. She returned as a wife, mother, and convert to Marxian socialism.[30]

"My brother William and I sailed in December, 1882, for the Riviera via Liverpool, London and Paris," she recalled. January discovered them in Paris and thereafter in Avignon, where they stayed until April, when they returned to Paris. Florence found the Avignon winter lonely "because so few people in the little Provençale city spoke French." In the midst of her "grim, grey experience," however, "one brilliant evening" stood out. Her Cornell acquaintance, M. Carey Thomas, stopped overnight at their hotel on her way to Italy. Having studied at Leipzig, Thomas had just completed a Ph.D. at the University of Zürich, Switzerland. Kelley found her "a most cheerful and stimulating companion." Through this chance contact, she learned that Zürich was the only European university willing to award graduate degrees to women. Study elsewhere was possible, including at Oxford or Cambridge, but it could not lead to a degree.[31]

In her memoirs Kelley called her brother's illness "temporary blindness," but in a more detailed account M. Carey Thomas described him to her mother as "a pill, a cad, everything dreadful as far as his appearance goes. I suppose he has gotten into this condition through dissipation and therefore she has never dared to leave him." Thomas added that William "was shot at in the street cars in Phila. by a labouring man some time ago, for a good reason I doubt not." Thomas regretted the dramatic decline in Florence's circumstances since their college days, for "she amounts to more than any of the other Cornell men or girls except my artist, Miss Clements" and "she has done a good deal of good in a philanthropic way . . . the legal thesis at Cornell was passed very highly." By contrast, her life with her brother in Avignon and Paris was abject in the extreme, since she "cannot leave him one moment while he is awake," and during his blind spells there was no one to whom she could turn. "There was no consul in the place, no doctor and all the people in the hotel think she is his mistress because it is unheard of in France or Italy for brothers and sisters to travel together," so they offered her no help. "I pitied her immensely," Thomas concluded. Florence's devoted care produced results. Months later in Paris, Thomas again encountered the pair, writing that Kelley "has never left her brother for one hour since we saw her in Avignon last January. She even sleeps in his room at night and now he looks perfectly well. It is impossible to believe he is the same man." [32]

Nursing ill relatives and friends was a central feature of female culture in the nineteenth century. Perhaps Kelley's receipt of such services from her family and friends made her more willing to bestow them. But if her Philadelphia experience had brought her the best that women's political culture had to offer, her travels with William schooled her in the way "the family claim" could absorb the lives of unmarried daughters. Even so, her exaggerated sense of obligation as her parents' only daughter meant that she committed herself to Will's cure as completely as she had given herself to building the Working Women's Guild.

In May 1883 Florence and Will met their mother and younger brother, Albert, then thirteen years old, in London. There she started a series of travel letters for the *New York Tribune*, an arrangement engineered by her father, whom the *Tribune* frequently interviewed. All but one of these letters remained unprinted or were not published under her name, but at the time they provided her with a welcome opportunity to combine her family responsibilities with her intellectual development. In spite of its difficulties, her European sojourn had left her looking "wonderfully well," Caroline thought. "I never saw her more blossoming. Her color, eyes, teeth and hair are beautiful, and she is delighted to have us with her." She still maintained the financial sobriety that characterized her college years. "Florrie's hat and coat are too shabby," Caroline wrote William, and she never "spends an unnecessary penny." [33]

In July Ruth Putnam joined the family, and she, Florence, and Albert visited the seacoast at Broadstairs in Kent, where Dickens wrote *Bleak House*. "We are thriving greatly," Florence wrote Caroline. "We came at once to the house . . . where we found a large room with *two* beds for Ruth and me, and a small pen for Bert, only two steps from ours." [34] Ruth ordered their meals, and their landlady cooked them. Florence pronounced herself "rested" but not yet "vigorous."

Though he joined his family in London that summer, William Kelley was beginning to suffer from the cancer that eventually took his life in 1890. In England and learning of his illness, Susan Anthony visited him. Florence remembered them as a pair of old campaigners: "He was lying on a couch, exhausted and wan, and Miss Anthony, wearing her famous Paisley shawl, sitting straight as a young birch tree, suggesting by her posture his affectionate nickname of the Major." Anthony found Florence "a most promising girl." [35]

When William recovered his strength, Florence accompanied him on an eye-opening tour of industrial centers in England and Wales. Setting out from Broadstairs, they visited South Wales, where "women and girls [worked at] the mouth of the coal pits, loading and hauling cars filled with coal" and performing other forms of unskilled labor, while "there was an immense number of men idle" and "the laboring population was little better than starving." [36] Then they "journeyed by train, by carriage and on foot in the Midland counties," visiting Birmingham, Manchester, and Sheffield. In nail-making towns they found much of the work done by women, again in circumstances that seemed to erode the welfare of all wage earners. Florence later believed the trip showed the need for protective labor legislation and the effects of "unrestrained capitalism." [37]

During this sojourn Florence Kelley explored the possibility of pursuing graduate study at Oxford University but then, finding "little offered to an American woman student," obtained her father's approval to follow M. Carey Thomas's example and enroll at the University of Zürich. Her care of Will deserved such a reward, and the rejection from the University of Pennsylvania still rankled. In her 1882 article on working women she had added a footnote castigating Harvard's President Eliot for announcing, "We have successfully resisted the admission of women," and she further noted that "the trustees of the University of Pennsylvania decided in November that women must buy admission to that ancient and conservative institution at a cost of $300,000," referring presumably to the figure set for fund raising to implement the university's decision to admit women.[38]

During her Oxford trip Florence lost the trunk containing her Cornell degree and was concerned that this might jeopardize or delay her admission to Zürich. However, on her arrival the Swiss dean told her: "You may listen and you may study. When you are ready, you may present yourself for examination. An American degree has no value." [39] Kelley listened and studied, but she never presented herself for a degree.

Caroline and Albert accompanied Florence to Zürich in September 1883. The trio's arrival was eased by Ruth Putnam, who engaged rooms for them in her boardinghouse and generally introduced them to the city. They had "a very pleasant parlor, with four windows, and a pretty outlook." Florence arranged for Albert to attend a local school. Zürich was full of Americans, whom they couldn't have avoided if they had wanted to, since, in Caroline's words, "in a small place we are thrown together and everyone seems drawn towards us." Florence appreciated the city's cultural attractions, especially the opera. "She greatly enjoys being so near everything," Caroline wrote William in December. "She can be at home and in bed in half an hour." [40]

Most of Florence's energy went into study. The daily routine included German lessons and recitations in the morning, work on German translations in the afternoon, lectures in the early evening, and, before supper, a visit to a reading room in the city offering papers and periodicals in English. She enrolled as a student of government (*Staatswissenschaft*), the only female student in that category until 1884–85, when she was joined by one Swiss woman. Three of the four courses for which she registered were taught by Professor Julius Platter, a Tyrolean who carried into the 1880s the revolutionary spirit that had characterized the university in the 1870s. Shunning the traditional approach to political economy as the study of laws, he instead focused on significant social questions about daily life. She attended his lectures on "the theory of national economy" (*Nationalöko-nomie*) and on "administration" (*Verwaltungslehre*) and participated in his seminar on "communist ideas and movements until 1848." On Wednesday she heard his lectures on modern history since 1852.[41]

Almost all of the small group of women at the university were studying medicine. The medical faculty in 1882–83 attracted seventeen women students, all foreigners, almost half from Russia, where women were denied admission to universities and professional schools. Only two came from the United States, where since the 1860s the Woman's Medical College of Pennsylvania and other female institutions had provided medical training for women. While the foreign colony of women in Zürich was dominated by Russians, their numbers were significantly fewer than they had been before 1873, since a Czarist edict forbade government employment to women who studied in Zürich after that date. Until then, and to some extent thereafter, Zürich was the most important foreign center for politically active Russian women, most of whom were born into gentry families, many of whom were able to travel only by arranging fictitious marriages with fellow students, and most of whom studied medicine as a means of reaching people outside their own class.[42]

Florence cultivated a set of friends that autumn who, according to her mother, made "very pleasant calls" at their hotel. "Her young friends are very attentive," she wrote William, "the girl students turning every pleasure that they can, the other sex being equally willing to supply us with books, and do anything to oblige. It is very pleasant to see her appreciated and admired." A succession of gaieties, including a ball at which she danced from eight o'clock until two, had left her "giddy."[43]

This bright world collapsed in mid-December when Florence learned of the death of Margaret Hicks. "The sad news from Karl threw me into a high fever which lasted one night . . . and alarmed good Dr. Heini a good deal," she wrote her father. "The next morning, however, after a night of mustard plasters on my feet and ice on my head, I was free from fever and only weak." The next day she sat up, and the day after she went for a short drive and walk. A week after the news she was able to sit two hours through dinner. Caroline wrote William that "the blow fell with awful suddenness upon dear Florrie. . . . We had vague fears about Margaret, but no one wrote anything definite, and we could only trust that all was going well. She had written her faithfully and had done all in her power to cheer her sick room. . . . Florrie's brave unselfish spirit keeps her up, but she is very much broken by this blow." In the care of a woman physician who put her on a diet in the hope of permanently ending her "lifelong dyspepsia," Florence wrote her father, "she forbade my reading heavy books or writing for a fortnight (so mother wrote the Xmas letter for the Tribune bless her!)" [44]

Not yet fully recovered from the shock of Margaret's death, Florence began receiving the attentions of Lazare Wischnewetzky, a Russian medical student. His first call occurred early on New Year's day, just after the Kelleys had successfully "banished" the Christmas tree through the window. She described him to her father as "a charming Russian gentleman who has been very kind in bringing me books on the National economy lectures that we both hear." At the university she had come to know him through rare books he had generously shared with her from a private library to which he had access. During his visit, "he was as well bred and friendly as usual, and spirited away all embarrassment over the by no means ugly disorder of the salon; and went away leaving us the pleasant conviction that our first caller was one whose acquaintance we shall value increasingly as the year wears on." Florence also received calls from her German tutor, a student himself, with "a huge frame and brightly-colored beard," who presented her with a New Year's gift of "a bundle of brochures on the Labor Question," and five American students, including her closest female friend in Zürich, Miss Dean, and her fiancé. Among this group Lazare Wischnewetzky was clearly the most interesting to Florence. [45]

Within Lazare's community of Russian student exiles, women were highly respected because radicalism required greater sacrifices from them. (Exile made it very difficult for them to reenter Russian society and to assume normal lives in the future.) Lazare's manners were impeccable, but his eagerness to share his intellectual enthusiasms with Florence and his view of her as an intellectual equal were even more affecting. Their shared admiration for Professor Platter forged a further bond between them. Florence presented Platter with a copy of her father's collected speeches and praised him in a letter to William: "What I would not give to have such a man in an American university! Just, candid, thoughtful, earnest, *learned*, enthusiastic." Her only regret was that "Mr. Wischnawisky [*sic*] and I are the only students upon whom his teaching takes a deep hold." She then dropped a telling notice of her interest in Wischnewetzky: "However, it would not be labor lost if the Russian were the only one." Her conclusion restored a more general tone: "I mean to make this year's teaching tell in my later work." [46]

Letters to Susan Anthony early in 1884 revealed the younger woman's mental state. Anthony appealed to her to stir her father and other congressmen "to go to work for Woman's Emancipation." Florence replied that this was "a double impossibility." First, her father had already proven his support "by presenting every suffrage resolution which has come up from the suffrage societies of Pennsylvania." Unhappily, he stood far in advance of his constituency on this question, since "neither the men nor the women of Pennsylvania support him to any helpful extent in carrying forward liberal measures for the Emancipation of Women." Second, her own future plans did not center on the suffrage movement. She strongly identified with women's rights issues, especially access to meaningful work and higher education. Reminding herself as well as Anthony, she added that she felt "humiliated that my country does not confer upon me a responsibility to which I feel myself adequate, just as I am mortified that the universities of America are closed to me." Nevertheless, she concluded, "When my student life is over, I shall give myself to work for the best interests of the working women of America, as my Father has given himself to work for the best interests of the country." In the meantime, mixing modesty with anger, she said she was "only a student not yet a teacher . . . accepting from this little Swiss canton instructions which the University of my own state, would on principle refuse me, if, in practice, it had such instruction to bestow." [47]

William Kelley wrote Caroline that he was glad "that dear Florrie shall remain abroad long enough to secure the long coveted degree." He was proud of her. His political acquaintances wished "to meet her whenever she may return to her country." For her part, Florence continued to be an excessively dutiful daughter, but Caroline seems to have feared that Florence's inordinate virtue was too good to be true, too good to last. "What a good girl she is!" Caroline wrote William during a trip to Italy with Florence and Bert, "and what a daughter and sister! Nothing she can think of is left undone and I depend upon her too much. I often feel afraid that I tax her more than is right." [48]

In the spring of 1884 Florence publicly expressed her deepening resentment over her exclusion from educational and professional opportunities in her own country. In May the *New York Tribune* printed a letter describing her conversations with two fellow students, Lizzie and Ella Sargent, daughters of the former U.S. minister to Switzerland, while traveling from Venice to Verona. Passing through Padua, "the conversation turned upon Portia, and drifted to Judge Ludlow's refusal to let Mrs. Kilgore practice law in Pennsylvania," referring to a woman who since 1870 had been struggling to practice law in the keystone state. "We all agreed that our position in respect to educational advantages is painfully like that of the negro at the close of the war," she wrote. "A few American institutions make us welcome; a few admit us, but would be thankful if we did not wish to come," she declared, "but more of the best universities still refuse to see the duty of fitting women for responsibilities which we must in consequence bear without being adequately fitted for them." By contrast, "Europe welcomes us, as she welcomed the negro, to much of the best that she has to give." [49]

Amid this unresolved anger, Florence Kelley took a leap of faith that carried her into a lifelong commitment to socialism. Feeling physically stronger than ever before in her life, she shifted her emotional center and her prodigious burden of personal obligation from her family to a social movement. The title of the portion of her autobiography that described this event, "My Novitiate," suggested a religious quest; she explained her acceptance of socialism in terms suitable for describing a religious conversion. "Coming to Zürich, the content of my mind was tinder awaiting a match," she said. Some of that tinder reached back into her childhood, including images of "the tragic oppression of the recently emancipated Negroes, by disfranchisement and lynching" and "pastyfaced little working children in jail-like textile mills in Manayunk, whom I saw in the streets year after year as I drove in the phaeton between my homes in West Philadelphia and German-town." Some came from her recent trip to England — "the pitiable toiling mothers in the chain-makers' cottages, and the diminutive men and women in the streets of the textile manufacturing cities of the Black Country." Zürich provided a solution for these "baffling, human problems." There, "among students from many lands, was the philosophy of Socialism, its assurance flooding the minds of youth and the wage-earners with hope that, within the inevitable development of modern industry, was the coming solution." [50]

This organic, historical theory of social change appealed to her intellectually, and the high-minded quality of socialist meetings appealed spiritually. Her first meeting marked a turning point. "It was in the old part of the city, on the second floor of a modest little eating-place permanently so clean that one could literally have eaten off the floor," she remembered. "As I took my seat I was so trembling with excitement that I grasped the sides of my chair and held them firmly," for Eduard Bernstein and other exiled leaders of the German Socialist Party were also present. "Here was I in the World of the Future!" Bernstein later confirmed her sense of religious awe, writing that the Zürich meetings "always struck me as resembling the meetings of the early Christians." In 1878 German antisocialist laws drove most leaders of the Social Democratic Party underground or into exile. London, where Karl Marx and Frederick Engels had resided since 1850, and Zürich, where many young leaders of socialism's second generation congregated, became their chief sanctuaries. An exile from her own society, Florence Kelley felt right at home among these banished leaders. [51]

The topic of her first socialist evening was Chancellor Bismarck's proposed high tariff for Germany. About twenty students "from about a dozen countries" and more than that number of "skilled wage-earners, men and women in the textile and railroad industries" filled the room. Having learned about tariffs as a girl, Florence was no stranger to the debate. "Before midnight every aspect of the tariff that I had ever heard or read of was presented," she recalled, "plus one which was utterly new to me." That one was argued by "a serious middle-aged Swiss railroad man" who urged the meeting to remember that "we are internationalists" and should know "the effect on the producers of raw silk in the Orient that the tariff would involve." Their livelihood would "have to be crowded down at least enough to meet the tariff charges in German custom houses." He asked: "Should we give our assent to this lowering of the standard of living of fellow workers on the other side of the globe?" In describing the meeting's effect on her, Florence reached beyond her father's image: "This might well have been a Quaker meeting. Here was the Golden Rule! Here was Grandaunt Sarah!"[52]

Perhaps because she had developed a strong social conscience but no explicit religious commitment, Florence's conversion to socialism was particularly deep and long-lasting. It filled an urgent need in her emotional life for a transcendent system of values capable of sustaining her demanding social conscience. Socialism also appealed because it offered a resolution to the conflict between her father's commitment to industrial growth and her own awareness of the human costs that growth incurred. The solution lay "within the inevitable development of modern industry" itself.

This conversion profoundly reorganized Florence Kelley's understanding of how her life converged with her times. Her adolescent exposure to steel-mill water boys and glass-blowers' "dogs," which simultaneously destabilized her view of her father's authority and situated her own knowledge at the margins of his ethical universe, aided her transition to this new world. Here her knowledge became central and her father's marginal. Social Democracy in Zürich allowed her to express a "divine discontent" with the rules of the capitalist social system and at the same time place herself in the vanguard of an unfolding future. Comfortingly, this fundamental intellectual shift did not require a change in her daily routine. After stirring meetings graced by the presence of Eduard Bernstein and Karl Kautsky, she returned home to Caroline and Albert.

Although the intensity of Kelley's response to socialism was exceptional, her attraction to its tenets was not. German thought exerted a deep and sustained impact on nineteenth-century American intellectual life, initially affecting theology and literature and, after 1870, social thought.[53] She joined others who since the 1830s had carried back to the United States from Germany organic views of society and history. German socialism allowed her and others of her generation to fuse redemptive notions about human society with systematic patterns within industrial capitalism. In this way, features of American religious teleology blended with scientific solutions for social problems.

One of the best examples of this process was Richard T. Ely. Returning to the United States in 1880 after four years of graduate study in Germany, he brought with him an outlook that combined religion, economics, and politics—believing that new economic circumstances dictated new social forms and new political action to preserve important moral values of an earlier way of life. During Kelley's years in Zürich, Ely's books, *French and German Socialism in Modern Times, Recent American Socialism,* and *The Labor Movement in America,* and many popular articles sympathetically interpreted socialism and trade unionism to middle-class readers and urged social activism on Protestant church-goers. He believed that his chief work as a social scientist was to influence public opinion so it in turn would influence public policy. As a professor of economics at Johns Hopkins University in Baltimore and as a lecturer in the Chautauqua movement, Ely did more than any other individual to advance the "new economics" of historical relativism and its corollary—the active intervention of "Science, the State and the Church" for "the amelioration of the laboring class."[54] Classical economics and its social policies of laissez-faire individualism were immoral and anarchistic, he thought; by promoting working-class misery they increased the likelihood of violent uprisings. Ely founded the American Economic Association in 1885 for the express purpose of discrediting Social Darwinist theories and laissez-faire public policies. At the AEA's founding he invoked religious values. "We wish to accomplish certain practical results in the social and financial world, and believing that our work lies in the direction of practical Christianity, we appeal to the church, the chief of the social forces in this country, to help us, to support us, and to make our work a complete success, which it can by no possibility be without her assistance."[55] Ely did not have women in mind, but his emphasis on "practical Christianity" inevitably encouraged women to join him. Early AEA members included about fifty-five women—slightly less than ten percent of the whole, but a much larger proportion than could be found in analogous professional organizations in law or the ministry.

For Kelley, as for Ely, the appeal of socialism arose partly from her inability to believe some inherited notions and partly from her desire to keep a warm faith in others. Socialism allowed her to shed the main principle of her father's career—that Americans could avoid the poverty of European working people by policies that kept wages high through protective tariffs—while at the same time it encouraged her to retain his faith in the ability of individuals to combine to shape their social environment and to use the state as a force for human betterment. She confronted her father with her new political outlook in a letter in June 1884. William Kelley rose to the occasion. The flood of foreign capital and labor entering the United States in the 1870s and 1880s had already invalidated protective tariffs in his eyes. He symbolically passed the torch to her by reading into the

Congressional Record extensive quotations from her letter, especially her argument that the eight-hour day was a more important means of aiding American workers than the maintenance of protective tariffs.

Introducing her as "a young lady, now in Europe, who bears my name," he quoted her compelling historical analysis of the changes in American relations between labor and capital. Before the Civil War, the interests of working people, in her words, "harmonized more or less with that of the American capitalist in general" because both groups "needed the industrial development of our resources, the development of capital in general." Then the Civil War brought northern capital and northern labor together against a common enemy. After the war came "a third form of forced identity of interest," she continued, "against the foreign capitalist and the foreign pauper." But this identity was rapidly "melting out of sight and existence under the influence of internal conflict." She thought she saw "better from this distance than I should if I were in the midst of it." Internal conflict—between American workingmen and "the labor of women and children," or between native-born workers and "imported contract laborers," or between all workers and an "ever-improving man-superseding machinery"—made tariffs irrelevant. Yet in order to clear itself of the free traders' claim that tariffs "work more in the interest of the American capitalist than the American laborer," she concluded, government policy must do what it could to support workingmen in their "growing struggle with American capital and American pauperism. . . . And the eight-hour law seems to me, from this point of view, not a possibility of the future but a need of to-day." [56]

Judge Kelley said that he agreed "with the conclusions of this young but profound student of political science" and ended his comments with a rousing call for a federal statute establishing an eight-hour day in the District and territories "with heavy penalties for its violation." He urged that "the safety of capital" in the United States was "not found in a standing army" but "in well-housed, sufficiently fed, reasonably well-educated, hopeful, and aspiring working people." Acknowledging that the word "socialism" had been "whispered" around him by members of both parties, he announced to his colleagues that if socialism meant the desire to achieve "the best possible conditions for our laborers, . . . I declare myself to be a socialist." He predicted that when lawmakers "shall fail to regard and provide for the social well-being of the laboring classes there will be an end to enlightened republican institutions." [57]

In "My Novitiate," Florence Kelley insisted that she never left her own culture. "My eager plunge into the enthusiasm of the new movement that was beginning to kindle throughout all Europe did not blind me to certain fundamental differences," she said. "Mine was after all an American background; those youthful years of talk with Father had whetted whatever discernment Nature had given me and those differences were to determine my later thinking." Yet if her political shift in Zürich conveyed continuity with some aspects of her political culture, it also expressed strenuous rebellion against it. And although her relationships with her parents seemed superficially untroubled by her conversion to socialism, that conversion offered her the chance to make a clean break with her past. On October 14, 1884, she acted on that opportunity and married Lazare Wischnewetzky.[58]

Part Two
Transitions

5

"To Act on This Belief,"
1884–1886

Lazare Wischnewetzky courted Florence so aggressively in the early months of 1884 that at first she thought him a nuisance. Caroline wrote Will Jr. in February, "Her adorer consumes rather more time than she thinks he is entitled to, but he does not see things precisely in that light. He is never so happy as when he can spend a quiet hour in her society, and he is so full of information, that one cannot be with him without learning something. Florrie has good reason to be satisfied with the attention she receives, both as to quantity and quality, but her only fear is, that he consumes too much time." Not long thereafter Florence wrote Lazare from Italy "that to stay in Europe and work at and for Socialism is utterly preposterous and out of the question" and that she could not possibly think of marrying him. Nonetheless, for reasons that remain unclear, she changed her mind. During an extended period in late May and early June when Caroline and Albert were absent from Zürich, following their doctor's orders to escape a contagious illness that especially affected children, Florence and Lazare were alone. When Caroline returned, the couple told her they intended to marry.[1]

Possibly to avoid complications with the university, Florence and Lazare kept their betrothal secret. Informed but not consulted, William Kelley tried to make the best of his daughter's breach of conventional family relations. "You were right. Your letter did 'bring' me 'surprise and pain.' During the three months you had the gravest question of your life under consideration, I might upon your suggestion of a mere possibility, have prepared myself for the result, and have felt at liberty to offer loving suggestions but as neither advice or consent have been invited, I will not thrust either upon you." Departing promptly for Europe to consult with Caroline, William added that he would not disclose her secret, "or speak of it until on my return I can hope to make our friends believe that I had been consulted."[2]

Caroline also tried to view events positively, writing in a letter to Will Jr., "I am satisfied that the two young people are calculated to make each other happy, and am not selfish enough to put my own loss into the balance, but I know she will be a treasure to any man." She added that "Florrie has a great deal on her mind at present" and hoped that Will would help his father absorb the news, since "however kindly he may look upon Florrie's decision and her plans, her letter cannot fail to give him a shock." Even she herself "who has been here to see that things were rapidly approaching a climax, did not feel prepared to see the young people married so soon." Nevertheless, she believed that their plans "have been thoroughly thought out." [3]

Pictures of Lazare Wischnewetzky reveal a large, handsome man, whose firmly-set jaw suggested a forceful personality. He was born in Taganrog, Russia, a Black Sea seaport four hundred miles east of Odessa.[4] Although none of the Kelley family mentioned it at the time, Wischnewetzky was Jewish.

In her description of her son-in-law, Caroline Kelley emphasized his moral qualities. "One thing I am perfectly sure of—Mr. Wischnewetzky is an upright man, a gentleman in every sense of the word, and his affection for Florrie is as sincere and deeply-*rooted* as any that ever existed in the heart of man. He is frank and truthful, and has no hidden motive. He is not looking for money or influence—has enough of both! I only mention these things because I have an opportunity to see him daily." She supported her daughter's right to choose a life partner. "Much as I would have liked to have Florrie near us, I dare not make any objection to that which is going to make her happiness for life—As Julia Durant said so long ago, 'He is not only her choice, but her affinity,' and Florrie's affinity would never be found a second time, and certainly her happiness is worth a sacrifice, when she has always been such a good, faithful daughter." Shortly thereafter, Florence fell ill but soon recovered and moved to a boarding place nearer the university and cheaper than the rooms she shared with her mother and brother.[5]

Excluded from the young couple's confidence and feeling the strain of keeping their plans secret, Caroline's tone grew disapproving that autumn. "I suppose Florrie has told you that the marriage will take place on the 15th," she told William. "I do not know any particulars. I thought Lazare would have learned them by this time, as he proposed to go to Geneva and make arrangements. As soon as I know anything more I will tell you. Sometimes I think I cannot stay here in this prying crowd, and, I assure you, have not much pleasure at present." Subsequent letters from 1884 between Caroline and William have not survived. Since this is the only gap in their lifelong correspondence, it almost certainly indicates that the letters were destroyed, probably because they expressed doubts about Wischnewetzky or concern about Florence's behavior.[6]

Even before her marriage, Florence began translating with Lazare the writings of leading socialists. Frances Mitchell, who visited Zürich in September, described their new life. "Florence and her betrothed met me at the station," Mitchell wrote. "They have my blessing. He is a noble fellow and very talented. I do not believe two people could be better suited to each other. Although he is studying medicine he is interested in the same subjects as F." The couple was busy "writing for the press. He translates Russian books into German, and Florence German into English." Since she did not speak Russian and he did not speak English, "their intercourse has been entirely in German." Frances thought that Florence spoke "with the greatest fluency." Around this time, Florence Kelley deepened her commitment to her new life by joining the German Social Democratic Party.[7]

Soon after their spare civil marriage ceremony, Florence and Lazare moved to Heidelberg, where he continued his medical studies. Feeling that her daughter still needed protection, Caroline followed with Albert and lived nearby. Perhaps Florence encouraged her, valuing the continuity Caroline represented in the midst of such abrupt change, especially since she became pregnant almost immediately after her marriage. In a letter to May Lewis, a Philadelphia friend active in the New Century Working Women's Guild, she described her quiet household routine. "My husband vanishes to his first clinic at nine and is gone three hours during which I translate or read for my degree. Then we have an hour among the English, American and German papers in the Museum. Then dinner at an admirable club in the neighborhood and a two hours chat or quiet reading time over our coffee, in our sunny study. Then come lectures from four until half past seven, during which I again translate or read for my degree. Then tea in the study and a long evening of reading aloud, rarely the theatre or a concert for we are happier together in our nook." Still, she cultivated her tie with Caroline. "Every day my Mother, who, with Albert, is in a German pension around two corners from me, comes to me or I go to her. Last night, a great exception—we were on-lookers at a carnival maskball in the museum until midnight."[8] In June the couple returned to Zürich, minus Caroline and Albert, who at last returned to Philadelphia.

Approaching childbirth, Florence wrote May Lewis that she had "not the slightest anxiety for the coming time. . . . We are back in the quiet lovely pension where I spent last year, have the same rooms which I had then and the same gentle friendly Swiss family who regard us as their youngest children and spoil us accordingly. We work, and walk, and debate, and make plans just as we did in our cozy Heidelberg life, with the difference that we have several friends here." She was particularly glad for the presence of an old Philadelphia friend. "I am greatly rejoiced at having Rachel Foster here, settled down for a long quiet study before resuming her active working in America." Foster was remedying her lack of understanding of economics, "having plunged boldly into social activity without the most superficial theoretical preparation." [9]

Pregnancy agreed with Florence. "I have been perfectly well ever since the middle of January, working six to eight hours daily at translation, dissertation and newspaper correspondence." Her hope for a baby boy was rewarded on July 12, 1885. Five months later, her study schedule still included reading American newspapers and "Political Economy in the evenings." Shortly before Christmas 1885, she wrote Caroline that she and Lazare had dismissed the baby's nurse two months before and had been "taking care of him ourselves." Nikolai, or "Ko," was "amazingly good" but needed "ten days of coddling" during a recent illness. "He has a high chair, stocking shoes, woollen diaper drawers, and little cream colored flannel dresses; and he looks like a little primrose." [10]

Perhaps to overcome the distance she had placed between herself and her family, Florence emphasized Ko's resemblance to his Philadelphia relatives. "His eyes are the color of yours and his skin such as Grandma describes yours as a young girl, creamy and rosy. He has two little lower teeth; and the hair which is only now beginning to come, is the color that Albert's was when he was a baby." During his illness she took special care with his diet (by this time he was no longer nursing). "He has gone through a course of milk and fennel tea, milk and rice water, milk alternating with Nestlemeal, and finally now drinks two liters of pure cows milk a day. . . . He says Mama, but only when he is hungry and sleepy and in despair generally." When his mother went downstairs to her midday meal, he slept "until three or four o'clock." Outdoors, Ko traveled in "a funny ark of a baby coach made of wicker, with four wheels, and with red curtains in front of the leather roof." Lazare returned to Heidelberg for several weeks, but she and Ko remained in Zürich because the doctor forbade a change in the baby's milk. Their one and only visit from "Madame Wischnewetzky" took place for a month that autumn. Florence wrote Caroline that her mother-in-law was "very gentle and lovely and devoted to the little boy," but "here she was far from well." [11]

Despite Florence's cheerful descriptions of her married life, photographs taken between 1884 and 1888 suggest another story (see pages 97–99). She appeared to possess all the confidence of her Cornell days in her first photograph with Lazare, taken around the time of their engagement and marriage, with Caroline and Albert. There Lazare exhibits more determination than geniality. Later, during her pregnancy, an air of anxiety supplanted her assurance, and his expression grew arrogant. Finally, after four years of marriage, she looked timorous and he downright menacing. The pictures imply that the marriage did not fulfill her early hopes. They also suggest that during these years of socialist conviction, her husband dominated her in ways that she could not have anticipated during their courtship. In marrying Lazare, Florence gambled that the alliance

clockwise from left: Caroline Bonsall Kelley, Lazare Wischnewetzky, Florence Kelley
Wischnewetzky, and Albert Kelley in Europe, fall 1884. Courtesy of Rare Book and Manuscript
Library, Columbia University.

Florence Kelley Wischnewetzky (pregnant) and Lazare Wischnewetzky in Europe, ca. 1885.
Courtesy of Rare Book and Manuscript Library, Columbia University.

Florence, Lazare, and Nicholas Wischnewetzky in New York, ca. 1888. John had been born a few months earlier, Margaret was almost one year old, and Nicholas was about three. Courtesy of Rare Book and Manuscript Library, Columbia University.

would free her from the oppressive responsibilities of her family of origin and at the same time help her express otherwise thwarted talent. Yet her chief model of male companionship, her father, predisposed her to select an impressive but self-centered mate.

Florence Kelley's marriage to Lazare Wischnewetzky fostered basic changes in her personal and political identity. By marrying Lazare, an extreme act itself for a young woman of her social origins, she began to construct a self capable of opposing the accepted rules of her parents' society. Now she could express the hostility to those rules that she had begun to accumulate in childhood. Thoughts and actions deemed taboo for the daughter of a leading American congressman became possible for the wife of a radical Russian physician. Because her marriage gave her cultural access to the world of European socialism, Florence Kelley Wischnewetzky could join that world in ways that Florence Kelley could not.

Under the guise of this new identity she began to explore the consequences of her conversion to socialism. Her family background, college education, and participation in early social science had equipped her to participate in public affairs through the aegis of women's social activism; now she could test her new moral authority and political understanding within the context of European socialism. Her new identity heightened her awareness of class as a fundamental category of oppression, but it posed new problems for her place within women's public culture.

No other American student who later emerged to prominence in the Progressive Era ventured so fully into European socialism; none left American political culture so far behind. Yet even as she moved away from her father's and great-aunt's values, she carried many of their basic tenets with her, particularly William Kelley's vision of an activist state, Sarah Pugh's efforts to integrate moral and market economies, their joint championship of working people, and their assumptions that they spoke for the national interest. In many ways her journey into European socialism was sustained, however invisibly at the time, as much by lifelines to her father's and her great-aunt's political traditions as by her marriage.

During this first year of marriage, Florence's main intellectual achievement was her translation of Frederick Engels's *Die Lage der arbeitenden Klasse in England, Nach eigener Anschauung und authentischen Quellen* (The condition of the working class in England, from personal observation and authentic sources). Published through her efforts in 1887, hers remained until 1958 the only English translation of this classic work and is today still the preferred scholarly version.[12] For her, the experience was supremely significant, since it supplied her with a belief system that helped her construct a historical understanding of her place in the political process and gave her a blueprint for combining class concerns with gender issues.

Frederick Engels, during his trip to New York, 1888. Courtesy of Nicholas Kelley Papers, Rare Books and Manuscripts Division, New York Public Library, Astor, Lenox and Tilden Foundations.

No evidence survives regarding Kelley's decision to begin the translation; presumably she settled on this work about the time of her marriage. When she approached Engels in 1884, his writings had established him (after the death of Karl Marx the year before) as the chief theoretician of German Social Democracy. After the failure of the revolution of 1848 forced both men to flee to England, Engels had supported Marx and his family. With the formation of the Socialist Workers' Party of Germany in 1869, Engels became the chief adviser of party leaders as diverse as Bebel, Bernstein, Braun, Liebknecht, and Kautsky. His greatest achievements, however, were his historical analyses of the development of industrial capitalism, and the most significant of these was *The Condition of the Working Class in England*, originally published in 1845. From this volume Karl Marx later developed his analysis of the relationship between capitalist development and working-class formation — of the creation of the proletariat through the mechanization of production and the inevitability of revolution as workers came together to live and work in larger groups, while capitalists remained captive to their own needs.[13]

Born into a wealthy German family of textile manufacturers, Engels was only twenty-four when he wrote *Die Lage* (as *The Condition* was known in German) — about the age of his translator forty years later. Rebelling against his father's intolerant piety and passion for profit, Engels attended philosophy lectures in Berlin during his military duty and studied Hegel and Feuerbach. There, through the Hegelian "communist rabbi" Moses Hess, he was introduced to the utopian socialism of Henri Saint-Simon, with its positive view of the potential of the industrial revolution. By 1842, when he went to Manchester to manage one of his father's firms, he had met Marx only briefly but already believed that economic factors were the basic cause of the struggle between different classes in society, that this struggle lay at the very root of political life, and that the political vanguard could be found in England, where industrial development had proceeded furthest. The author's purpose in writing *The Condition* was to explicate the future based on past and present conditions and to help both working-class and middle-class readers understand the reality of their opposing economic and political interests.[14] Empirical without being empiricist, his book linked a compelling method of analysis with a teleological vision of what should be.

For Florence Kelley, the book served as an ideal entry to a new system of thought, for alongside notions fresh to her, *The Condition* contained much that was familiar. Like her Cornell thesis, it relied on government reports and semiofficial writings, which, as suggested in the book's German subtitle, conveyed intimate details about its subject. In the longest chapter, "The Great Towns," Engels quoted articles by ministers and physicians and reports by government investigators, coroners, and police to reveal devastatingly inhumane conditions in which working-class families faced death by starvation, exposure, and disease. His pioneering description of the spatial distribution of working-class, middle-class and upper-class commercial sites and residences reinforced his magisterial view of the flow of human and material resources within the city's boundaries. His analysis carried Kelley further into a material understanding of the forces shaping human relationships and a concern with the effects of exploitation on the human body. Yet Engels was a moralist as well as a realist; his moral indignation matched that she had known in her father and great-aunt. Like them, he posited an ideal outcome of the process of historical change, one that dignified the individual, enshrined desires for freedom, and he believed humans could control the outcome of social change.[15]

Florence Kelley's conversion to German socialism heightened the tension between utopian idealism and hands-on practicality already present in her approach to social change. Engels confirmed both her irrepressible belief in a better tomorrow and her appreciation of the material dimensions of social change. Both children of Darwin's nineteenth century, they invested the patterns of material life with spiritual meaning.[16] In the long run, this tension between idealism and materialism proved creative for Kelley. In the short run, it turned her translation work into an adventure in self-improvement.

The Condition broke new ground by shifting the focus of industrialism's critics from the distribution of wealth to the conditions of production, particularly the labor of women and children; indeed, the chapter "Factory-Hands" focused almost exclusively on these workers. They made more obvious capitalism's ruthless treatment of workers as interchangeable parts. Like most of his contemporaries, Engels accepted sharp gender divisions of labor and viewed married women's factory work as a perversion of normal family life. "The employment of the wife dissolves the family utterly and of necessity, and this dissolution, in our present society, which is based upon the family, brings the most demoralizing consequences for parents as well as children." Drawing on parliamentary reports that had fostered early factory acts, accounts of agitation for the Ten-Hour Bill in the 1830s, and evidence of the need for further factory regulations, he leveled his most scathing criticism at the long working day, which could extend to more than thirteen hours. Long hours deprived workers of their health, making most men "unfit for work at forty years," produced crippling physical and mental effects on children, who were "sacrificed to the greed of an unfeeling bourgeoisie," and created serious deformities among women, visible in their greater difficulty in childbirth and greater vulnerability to miscarriage.[17]

Rather than calling for a return to traditional family relations, Engels used present circumstances to criticize the past. "If the reign of the wife over the husband, as inevitably brought about by the factory system, is inhuman, the pristine rule of the husband over the wife must have been inhuman too." If the contemporary family was being dissolved, "this dissolution merely shows that, at bottom, the binding tie of this family was not family affection, but private interest lurking under the cloak of a pretended community of possessions."[18] Engels made no specific proposals for future family relations.

Pointing to the ideological and partisan purposes that informed both sides of the debate over factory legislation, excoriating the inadequacies of enforcement, and envisioning revolution as the solution to social injustice, Engels's analysis posed serious difficulties for the position Kelley had taken in her 1882 defense of young, unmarried working women. In "Need Our Working Women Despair?" she had championed protective legislation as the cure for women's oppression in industry, assumed that such legislation could be adequately enforced, and postulated patronizing ties between (presumably older) middle-class women and (presumably younger) working-class girls as the remedy for social injustice. In 1885 Engels endorsed protective legislation for adult women, both married and unmarried: "That the working woman needs special protection against capitalist exploitation because of her special physiological functions seems obvious to me." He also condemned feminist opponents of labor legislation for women, saying that "the English women who championed the formal right of members of their sex to permit themselves to be as thoroughly exploited by the capitalists as the men are mostly, directly or indirectly, interested in the capitalist exploitation of both sexes."[19] Yet for him such legislation, valuable as it might be in the short run, was not a long-term remedy for the exploitation of working people — women or men. That remedy lay in the end of the system whereby most of the value produced by workers went to those who owned the machinery or means of production. By focusing on married women and by posing quite a different outcome to industrialization, Engels drew Kelley outside the assumptions of her father's polity and into remedies that treated men and women wage earners as suffering from the same systemic malady — capitalism.

One of capitalism's chief characteristics, unregulated competition, "undertaken not for the sake of supplying needs, but for profit," explained a great deal about the condition of working people. Competition goaded larger firms to swallow smaller ones, thereby transforming the independent artisan into a factory hand and a member of the propertyless proletariat. Competition led to periods of expansion in which reserve armies of unemployed were added to the labor force and then created economic slumps because of overproduction. Competition reduced society to a "battle of all against all" fought not only among the different classes of society but also "between the individual members of these classes."[20] Desperate poverty and opulent wealth could be traced to the same source. Gone forever from Florence Kelley's thinking was her father's belief in the cooperation of workers and employers through their shared identity as producers.

Similarly, *The Condition*'s teleology exploded notions of a unique American destiny. As the concentration of capital increased, so too, Engels argued, did the concentration of workers, and thus their ability to unite to defend their interests grew. The more workers were drawn away from agricultural labor and into factories, the more enlightened they became about their need to form their own protective associations. In this context, the future of the United States became not a theater for the unfolding of democracy and an expanded home market but a proving ground for the conflict between concentrated capital and enlightened workers.[21]

Where did middle-class women's public culture fit into this struggle? For Engels, bourgeois women were part of the problem, at best merely patching up damages inflicted by unrestricted competition, at worst, in their demands for individual rights, aligned with exploiters' demands for unfettered capitalism. The General Association of German Women had since 1865 advocated civil equality for women and in the 1880s broadened its agenda to address "the social question" through vocational education and employment agencies for women, but working women took an increasingly independent path, and by the late 1880s many rejected cooperation with middle-class women. Class differences between bourgeois and socialist women were exacerbated by the arbitrary enforcement of laws between 1850 and 1908 that prohibited women's participation in political organizations and laws between 1878 and 1890 that prohibited socialist organizations. Women's attendance at meetings sponsored by bourgeois political groups might be tolerated, but trade union or socialist meetings were routinely disrupted if women were present. This political climate amplified the commitment to class struggle of women intellectuals like Clara Zetkin, Kelley's closest equivalent. Alliances with bourgeois women required much more of a conscious crossing of class lines than was true in the United States and was usually characterized as regressive.[22] Forced to choose between her past allies in the United States and Engels, Kelley chose Engels.

In his book Engels fashioned a historical place for the likes of himself and Kelley that eased the anguish of her choice. Middle-class social critics and intellectuals could serve as agents of positive change by making the revolution less violent than it otherwise would be by helping wage earners rise above their personal bitterness and adopt the tenets of socialism. The revolution of the proletariat against the bourgeoisie was inevitable, but the extent of its "bloodshed, revenge, and savagery" would be reduced in proportion to workers' "comprehension of the social question"; thus writings like *The Condition* could shape the outcome of social struggle.[23] As Engels's translator, Kelley acquired a place in the evolving future—a place where she could use her inherited understanding of politics as an arena of moral struggle in which discourse could make all the difference. Engels's belief system allowed her to shed her reliance on middle-class dominance and express unremitting hostility toward capitalism, while at the same time it opened other forms of self-assertion and power.

In August 1884, Hermann Schlüter, publications manager of *Sozialdemokrat*, the official newspaper of German Social Democracy (edited by Eduard Bernstein and banned in Germany), conveyed Engels's permission for Florence Kelley Wischnewetzky to undertake the translation. After a "tedious illness" of three months and the move to Heidelberg, she began work in earnest, using the original 1845 German edition. She believed it "most important that the best of the german socialist literature should be made accessible to my countrymen in the near future" and wrote Engels that if this first translation should prove satisfactory, "I should go on with the work—with your permission—beginning with the Entwicklung des Sozialismus, taking next der Ursprung der Familie and so on, finishing with Dührings Umwälzung der Wissenschaft." Since the English translation of the first volume of Marx's *Capital* was nearing completion and since *The Condition* provided a good historical guide to the processes described in *Capital*, she thought that "it would be especially fortunate if 'die Lage' could appear not long after." Her goal, she said, "is to see such books as Gronlund's and Professor Ely's supplanted by scientific works." Kelley planned to offer her country a more "scientific" socialism — that is, to offer material rather than idealistic understandings of the direction of historical change.[24]

Kelley devoted herself to translating *The Condition* with the same intellectual passion she had brought to the books in her father's study. Her goal was nothing less than the transformation of the coming revolution in the United States. Letters to May Lewis chronicled her new convictions. She had no doubt about the direction of change. "Every American paper brings tidings of the coming revolution," she wrote May, "which you, who are long among the volcanoes, probably do not recognize as such, but which fill me with awe."[25]

Her reaction was commensurate with the everyday reality of industrial upheaval in the United States. She and Lazare were reading about "the revolutionary life of the working people on both continents, whose organs come to us in Russian, English, French, and German, weekly or monthly." One she might have read was *John Swinton's Paper*, an independent prolabor weekly whose pages glowed with the fires of labor protest sparked by capitalist oppression. "Today there is a rebellion of Capital against People as dangerous as the rebellion of Slavery against the Union," a front-page story declared on December 14, 1884. Two weeks later the paper reported "350,000 thrown out of work in manufacturing alone; fully two million now idle." Swinton editorialized that he "could not possibly print all the past weeks reports of wage-cutting and discharging of hands in scores of industries all over the country. They would overflow this paper." In mid-January, Florence would have read that state militia were called out in Iowa, Ohio, and Indiana. "Be Warned in Time; Foolish Work of Wage-Grinding Monopolists," Swinton's paper cautioned. Political solutions proved ineffective in this confrontation between capital and labor. "Capital Kicks Labor Out of Every Legislature" and "The Albany Quacks; Another Session of Legislative Tomfoolery; No Relief for the Factory Slaves; Nothing but Sham, Shame, and the 'Tramp Bill' — Political Capitalism," headlines declared in April 1885.[26]

These reports reflected phenomenal economic expansion in the United States during the early 1880s, which also precipitated economic dislocation and labor insurgency. Early in 1885 Kelley would have learned of *Bradstreet's* estimate that the American workforce grew by one-tenth between 1880 and 1882. The great majority of those new workers entered factories and other forms of industrial work that expanded across the landscape after 1880. By 1890 the average capital investment per worker was 50 percent greater than it had been in 1880. Industrial growth in the 1880s steadily carried the American economy into global preeminence. Steel production more than doubled in the four years after 1876, the first year when national statistics became available, moving from about 70 percent to 100 percent of English tonnage. By 1890 U.S. steel production had leapt to 3.4 times what it had been in 1880 and totaled about a third more than that of England. It doubled again in the 1890s, outpacing England's tonnage two and a quarter times by 1900 and almost equaling that of England and Germany combined. Between 1876 when Florence entered Cornell and 1884 when she married Lazare, the United States entered a trajectory of development that would soon make it the world's mightiest economy.[27]

From her retreat in Heidelberg, Florence monitored the social effects of that development, especially labor insurgency. Led first by the Knights of Labor and then by the new American Federation of Labor, labor protest crested on May 1, 1886, when 340,000 workers in twelve thousand factories across the country went on strike to demand the eight-hour day. Women occupied a central place in this insurgency, since the Knights of Labor defined "producers" to embrace not only industrial and craft workers but also shopkeepers, farmers, housewives, and even some professionals. The growth of the Knights in Philadelphia during 1883 and 1884 illuminated the crucial role women workers were playing in the new day dawning in Kelley's homeland. Sixty-five new local assemblies formed during those years, thirty-five of which sprang up in the woman-employing industries of shoes and textiles. Led by charismatic Mary Hanafin, women shoemakers responded decisively to the Knights' moralistic appeal in a militant strike in 1884. With the help of community supporters who repelled potential strikebreakers and

Eight-Hour Day Parade, Chicago. *Frank Leslie's Illustrated Newspaper*, September 16, 1882. Courtesy of Theodore F. Watts.

extended credit to families of strikers, female textile workers, who labored in the same factories as the "little skinny girls" that Florence saw on her way home from school in the late 1860s, maintained a five-month strike that ended in April 1885, and they remained militant throughout 1886.[28]

Yet in the face of economic depression and immigrant-fed surges in the labor force, wages fell and many strikes failed. These conditions led to the widespread use of a new tool for the advancement of labor's interests—the boycott. Labor papers described its rapid spread early in 1885: "A New Force in Hand; the Growing Power of the Boycott; A Formidable Weapon of Defense Against Blacklisting; Its Successful Use in Many Cases," *John Swinton's Paper* reported. For example, in Orange, New Jersey, brewers refused to furnish beer to saloon keepers who sold drinks to strikebreakers employed in a hat factory. Unions began to advertise boycotted products in labor papers. "Strikes and boycotts," emerged as a phrase describing labor's chief weapons.[29]

Florence Kelley responded to these harbingers of a new era by declaring her political independence in a series of articles published in the *Times–Philadelphia* in the spring and summer of 1885. She roundly attacked protective tariffs but praised forthcoming translations of Engels's *Condition* and Marx's *Capital*. These publications would refute "such patchwork compilations as Professor Ely's 'Modern Socialism,'" where Ely incorrectly wrote that socialists accepted "Bismarck's State Socialism." Kelley insisted that even "their worst enemies in Germany never accused" socialists of supporting Bismarck.[30]

To May Lewis, she expressed more personal complaints about the management of social change in the United States. "The letters of the men and women who ought to be guiding it to a peaceful solution show that their writings are all unconscious of the meaning of the times," she wrote. She and Lazare were not "friends of Most's or Rossa's or the other numerous cowards who preach bloodshed." The mightiest revolutions were peaceful ones, she insisted—"Socialism is not dynamite warfare." Yet she found the prospect of educating Americans about peaceful revolution daunting, because events revealed the political backwardness of workers in the United States compared to Germany. Although socialist meetings were outlawed in Germany, the fortunes of the Social Democratic Party expanded, and the number of socialist representatives (protected against prosecution by their Reichstag status) increased. By 1890, when laws against it dissolved, the SPD would become the largest political party in Germany. In 1885, Kelley contrasted that growth with conditions in the United States. "Whereas in Germany, six hundred thousand workingmen form a political party and elect four and twenty representatives to the Imperial Parliament—pledged to represent the interests of the workingmen of the nation," she wrote May in June, "our most intelligent organization, the Knights of Labor, are still back upon the primitive plan of development involved in a secret society, pass-words and all the nonsense involved therein." Thus there was "nothing iconoclastic" in her insistence that German economic writings were far in advance of those in the United States. "What consequence could be more natural than this?" Given the willingness of Americans to acknowledge German leadership in civil service reform and in university standards, she wondered why they objected to the superiority of "the German economic literature."[31]

With a sure but naive sense of her own contribution to the process of social change, she was "waiting impatiently for Dr. Aveling's translation of Marx, and my own trans-lation of Engels, to confront the Ely tribe and force them to stop their role of false prophets." If Ely and other German-trained Christian socialists "would use their knowl-edge of German for making honest translations they could enable their conscientious countrymen to bring their economic studies down to date, i.e. some twenty years further than the point which leading American publicists have reached at present." The timing was urgent, she thought, because "American industrial development strides onward with seven league boots and the blind continue to lead the blind, and to us it looks as though the ditch were not far off." Christian-socialist clergy earned a special rebuke. "Every minister arrives at social science via Theology and Philanthropy and it incenses me to hear one talking Politics or Political Economy."[32]

Florence defended herself against May's charge that she had "arrived at the last word upon the subject of Social Science," saying, "that would be a melancholy state of mind at twenty-five!" Yet the certainty of her bond with socialism carried her through a pas-sionate and thoroughgoing rejection of her father's example, especially his belief in the compatibility of democracy and capitalism. When May claimed that democratic gov-ernments made "different remedies necessary," she retorted: "I am perfectly convinced that the purer the democracy . . . the more speedy the development of capital and of the enslavement of labor, and the more inevitable the breakup of the capitalist form of production and of society."[33] Cutting closer to home, she complained that "ordi-nary, non-socialized workers let themselves be hoodwinked by Free Trade and Protection professional politicians."[34]

This path inevitably led to open conflict with her father. In December 1884, she withdrew from a project they had organized a year earlier that would have published letters they had written about working-class life during their tour of England. Her abrupt telegram to William stated: "Your published card just read. Posted card Sunday Phila. Press, Times, Record, Washington Republican, New York Nation, Evening Post, Boston Journal, Woman's Journal, Chicago Times, Tribune. . . Stop publication. Florence Kelley Wischnewetzky." As she explained to May, she "outgrew" the book when its printing

William Darrah Kelley, ca. 1885. Courtesy of Library of Congress.

was delayed for a year to coincide with her father's reelection campaign. "I found that it could be used for advocating Mr. Blaine and Protection and I believe in neither. I therefore wrote a final letter making clear the impossibility of any *thorough* improvement in the condition of the English people under our present system, and to point out the resemblance between our own workers' condition and theirs." The fact that her father "wanted the book for campaign purposes" made her all the more recalcitrant, for her political purposes were now in direct competition with his. Recognizing a good story, journalists exploited the father-daughter rift. Confiding in May, she blamed her father for the fact that "the whole American and Americo-European press has published a rumor that Lazare forbade me to publish the poor little book for fear of the Russian authorities (!) whence we became unhappy and I had left him to return to my family!" This quarrel with her father precipitated "profound unhappiness in [the] four months past." [35]

Despite William Kelley's public support of her socialist views, his career was too compromised by capitalist values to serve as a model for her own activism. Having learned well his lesson that politics were personal—equated with honor and with moral values—she felt her father's political transgressions all the more keenly. In a letter to Engels, she characterized her father as an example of how little enlightenment the "old parties offered the workers." "Fancy in a state so highly developed industrially as my native Pennsylvania, a constituency of working men electing for the fourteenth term, the twenty-eighth consecutive year of service, as their representative in Congress my father, whose sole wisdom is praise of the American protective tariff, and even now, when he admits in a tête-à-tête conversation that he no longer believes in the effectiveness of this panacea, the working men of his district [reelect him] by thousand majority every second year." Responding to May's contention that "the working man may improve his status in the United States" and that their own male relatives were proof, Florence replied that her own father "would never have become a member of Congress if he had stuck to his printing or his diamond setting; but he abandoned his craft and became a lawyer, i.e. entered the privileged class." Her brother, then assistant city solicitor, would never have

William Kelley Jr., ca. early 1880s. Courtesy of Nicholas Kelley Papers, Rare Books and Manuscripts Division, New York Public Library, Astor, Lenox and Tilden Foundations.

obtained that position "in a thousand years without the paternal name and fame." This was "not simply growling," she said, "I am looking at things as they are." [36]

Florence's break with her past and her family accelerated early in 1885, when Will told her that he was regularly receiving training in "Riot Drill" at the City Troop Armory, as she put it, "in order to be prepared to shoot down workmen in the expected riots." This she found deeply disturbing. In a letter to May Lewis in January, she explained that his news gave her an abrupt, personal understanding of the "mortal conflict that is inherent in the nature of the two classes." His letter destroyed her peace of mind, for all America "seems to be in the same sublime confusion of mind as Willy, while the causes which drive workmen into riots go mercilessly on." To her, Europe presented a striking contrast in consciousness: "All classes are conscious, and honorable men and women give their lives to [the] study of ways and means to a solution, and their sympathies are with the workers, not with paid armies who shoot them down." [37] Sometime between the summer of 1885 and the fall of 1886 Florence ceased to communicate with her Philadelphia family.

Through letters to May Lewis, Florence purged herself of past loyalties that inhibited her capacity for independent action. She was determined not to reproduce the social and political relationships that empowered her father and brother. The class privileges that once seemed appropriate now appeared malevolent, and she resolved to do without them. This decision strengthened her moral authority for the political long run, but it created abrasive stress in her family. While Caroline was still in Heidelberg, Will called Florence a "Nihilist," and she replied with such "terrible anger" that he thought her "demented." Her letter was "an insult to her right self," he wrote Caroline. Her language would be "anathema addressed to a dog" and revealed only "the weakness of the writer." "I realize the terrible pressure under which she is, and that her letters to Father and myself are her cries of pain. But has it not been self inflicted? Have not the Fates drawn her into the position in which she is susceptible of this suffering?" He thought that she did herself an injustice by claiming to disregard "family ties" and that her anger was "consuming her." Will wondered how she could accuse him of thinking only for himself, "when she has disregarded the happiness of all who love her, in taking her step." [38]

Apologizing for her seriousness, Florence observed to May, "I cannot write or talk of indifferent things." Despite her alienation from her family, she thought of herself as continuing their reform traditions of strong moral conscience and belief in the redeeming value of middle-class agitators. "If I am right, then the wrong to the working people, all the world over, is a question much graver than our slavery question was, as the working class is greater than the number of our slaves, [we are] bound to make restitution and to help them recover their own. . . . To act on this belief seems to me as imperative as the agitation for the freeing of the negroes seemed to the early anti-slavery workers.

And to ignore the question seems to me to be shirking the highest duty that our powers and education lay upon us." [39] William Kelley's daughter held capitalism to be as incompatible with democracy as he had once viewed slavery to be, and she was determined to act on that belief. Divergent as her future path might seem, it was shaped by her past attachments and privileges.

Florence Kelley's position as a publicist for "the German economic literature" strained her relationship with the political culture of American women. Yet she never stopped hoping that women's social activism in the United States would live up to its oppositional potential. It puzzled her profoundly, she wrote May in the summer of 1885, that none of the four major American women's journals carried "one single item concerning the strike of the girl carpet weavers in Yonkers," while "my German Workingman's Sheet published in N.Y., the *N.Y. Volkszeitung,* tells me that there are 2200 of these girls on strike since Feb. 11th, many of them now reduced to the verge of starvation or prostitution, and most of them more or less dependent upon the contributions of the organized workingmen." *John Swinton's Paper* noted: "Notwithstanding that the girls are carrying themselves with a jaunty air, they cannot live on that, and help is needed now more than ever." [40] Kelley thought that women of her own class appeared callous. "Now what *can* be the matter with the suffragists? Are they ignorant of the existence of the strike? and if so what a wretchedly narrow horizon they must have! Or are they afraid of the labor question? Or what other explanation is there?" She was sure that "if it were twenty-two hundred school teachers acting en masse, or twenty-two hundred property-holding women resisting the tax collector, there would be whole columns full of the occurrence." Yet the even more heroic deeds of "twenty-two hundred mill girls resisting starvation wages and the insults of a brutal overseer are not favored with a word." Instead, their fate was "left to the (fortunately efficient) tender mercies of the trades-union men to keep them from ruin of soul and body." [41] This was quite a different vision from the union of working-class and middle-class women that she had advanced in "Need Our Working Women Despair?"

Even so, she continued to reach out to women activists in the United States. During the final months of her pregnancy and her first months of motherhood in the spring and summer of 1885, she sent a barrage of letters to the major suffrage periodicals. These missives merged her previous experience in the Working Women's Guild with her new political identity. She worked like a missionary in women's civic culture, bringing the message and showing the way even though her would-be converts paid little heed.

"*We need a program,*" she emphasized in a letter to *The Woman's Tribune* of Nebraska. "Our platform of one plank, the ballot, is not enough. The maxim *Equality before the Law* is not enough, though it is good as far as it goes." Class had replaced gender and race as the nation's most onerous inequality, she insisted. At the end of the Civil War, "the inequality of the sexes was the greatest that there was, even outweighing the inequality between the Blacks and the Whites," she rashly asserted, but now greater inequalities had emerged. "At present the inequality of men among themselves is so frightful, that to make each woman (rich or poor) merely equal to the men of her family, or her class, is to leave the sum total of inequality now cursing society almost unchanged." The inequality between the "millionaire capitalist" and his employee "on the verge of starvation" was greater "than the difference between the millionaire and his wife, and the employee and his wife." The demands of the women's movement "must be more comprehensive" and embrace working women, or the movement will have "fallen behind the need of the times." [42]

Her letter to *The Woman's Tribune* cited examples of news about working women that should have appeared in the suffrage press but did not. "For instance the bill for prohibiting the manufacture of cigars in N.Y. tenement houses affecting chiefly women and children. The non-enforcement of the compulsory education act and the consequent employment of little girls in factories in Brooklyn, the strike of a thousand or more women and girls in the Yonkers carpet-mills; the bill for prohibiting the employment of children and restricting the mill hours of women in Michigan are all carefully registered or perhaps thoroughly discussed in my workingmen's organs." [43]

In a similar vein, she wrote to *The New Era,* a Chicago suffrage periodical, that movement conventions "discuss higher education and the laws affecting married women's property and the need of property-holding women getting school suffrage" but not the "immediate practical work in the interests of working-women," such as the eight-hour laws for the states of New York, Vermont, Connecticut, and Maine. This "one-sided" activity seemed to show "a want of sympathy with the hard-struggling thousands, who we, of all people, ought to represent, and defend and protect." [44]

Kelley's letter to *The Woman's Tribune* praised a petition "recently forwarded to the Imperial Parliament by three hundred and thirty workingwomen of Danzig" protesting a bill supported by Catholic conservatives "for restricting the work of women and children equally." There was much to be done to protect the workingwoman, the petition declared, but "to limit her in her work without granting her any compensation for her loss, is simply to make it harder for her to live honestly." Supporting their petition, a male representative from the German workingmen's party called for "the enforcement of the normal working day for all workers." Kelley thought that such representatives rendered German workingwomen far better off than their toiling sisters in America. Acknowledging that "The German women's movement did not exist among the 'comfortable class'" and that the movement in England sought the ballot only for "property holding women," she nonetheless insisted that the English movement never missed an opportunity to help workingwomen, for it always "watches new laws, [and] criticizes old ones." [45] Disregarding the frailty of her examples of class-bridging alliances among women in Germany and England, she seemed convinced that they could be effective in the United States.

Later that summer Kelley recommended to readers of *The Woman's Tribune, The New Era,* and other women's periodicals August Bebel's *Woman in the Past, Present and Future,* recently translated into English by "Dr. Adams Walther, a woman graduate of one of the Swiss Universities." The book was important, she said, because it "deals with the economic side of the woman question with a force and clearness which has hitherto been sadly wanting in our literature of the subject." Economic facts about women included "the growing number of women working at starvation wages; [and] the injury to both sexes and to the family wrought by women's underselling men in the labor market." Although she did not say so, one reason Kelley could recommend Bebel's book so enthusiastically was that, along with his economic analysis, he endorsed the political rights sought by bourgeois feminists and described the influence of woman's political participation as "ennobling." [46]

Important arbiters of respectable opinion in both men's and women's public cultures in the United States kept Kelley at a distance when she tried to reach a larger audience through her unpublished essay "American Women Students in Zürich." The essay "call[ed] attention to the culpable passivity of the so-called intelligent classes" and argued that "most philanthropic work" was a "vain struggle to patch and palliate an evil social system, so propping up what ought to be torn down and rebuilt." Yet in fragments of the article that appeared in a June letter to May, Kelley distinguished philanthropy from "active social work," such as May undertook at the Working Women's Guild, and praised social work as "an even more responsibility-involving task than mere pulpit preaching." To meet that responsibility she recommended the "systematic study of Social Science," beginning with Henry George's *Progress and Poverty* and Gronlund's *Cooperative Commonwealth,* though neither was "brilliant, profound or strictly scientific." [47]

The essay's wanderings charted the gulf Kelley had created between herself and her native civic culture. She first sent it to the *North American Review.* When they declined to publish it, she asked May to read it before the New Century Club, but the club also refused the piece a hearing, choosing instead a paper on woman suffrage. She accepted her defeat philosophically: "Times change! Three years ago the club would not let me talk suffrage; and now, to escape the labor question, it takes refuge behind the ballot! However, that is a very good and wholesome place for it to be in, and I am glad to have been instrumental in getting it there even for one afternoon." [48] George William Curtis, her father's friend and an editor at *Harper's,* also declined the piece, as did *Popular Science Monthly.*

Kelley's views were better received in Germany. She and Lazare had become part of the social scene among Social Democrats in Zürich and began to exercise influence. "Mrs. Wischnewetzky, and he too, have so many acquaintances and such a superior spiritual development," one friend noted. "Unfortunately, such simple, natural and honorable people [among] social democrats are uncommon." Mrs. Wischnewetzky moved from social to political influence in August of 1886 with a lengthy article entitled "Die Sozialdemokratie und die Frage der Frauenarbeit: Ein Beitrag zur Programmfrage" (Social Democracy and the question of women's work: A contribution to the platform question), which appeared anonymously in three issues of *Sozialdemokrat.* She also presented her ideas in a public lecture. The article and lecture placed her in a vanguard with few peers. At this time, women Social Democrats were just beginning to articulate a policy for German workingwomen; Clara Zetkin, living in exile in Paris, was emerging as the chief theoretician of the "Frauenfrage" (women question). Kelley joined the dialogue at an early, formative stage.[49]

Despite their obvious differences, Zetkin and Kelley Wischnewetzky had much in common. Born into a progressive, middle-class family, Clara Eissner was educated in the 1870s by a champion of women's rights in Leipzig, center of the nascent socialist movement. Her friendship with a community of emigré Russian students, especially Ossip Zetkin, Jewish and from Odessa, fostered her alliance with socialism. Alienated from her family and class, after residing briefly in Zürich in 1882 she joined Zetkin in Paris. Because German law deprived women who married aliens of their citizenship, they did not marry, but she bore two sons (1883 and 1885). The couple tried to support themselves by translating and by writing for periodicals like *Sozialdemokrat.* Ossip died in 1889 of spinal tuberculosis, and that year Clara Zetkin became the leading writer on women's issues within Democratic Socialism through her pamphlet *The Question of Women Workers and Women at the Present Time.* In 1891 she took charge of *Gleichheit* (Equality), the party's women's journal. Although they may never have met, Kelley and Zetkin almost surely knew about one another. In fact, it seems highly likely that Zetkin's romantic example of committing herself to a Russian and altering her class identity was urged on Kelley during Lazare's courtship.[50]

In the mid-1880s both Kelley and Zetkin were wrestling with the policy problem of whether workingwomen should be treated differently or the same as workingmen. Although Zetkin came to support special legislation for women, at this time she did not, insisting, "We demand no other type of protection than that which labor demands in general from the capitalists." Kelley sidestepped the question by aiming her remarks at another target—the party's policy, declared at the Gotha conference of 1875, of "prohibiting all women's labor which is detrimental to health and morality." Her translation of Engels' *Condition* made her acutely aware of the lack of agency he attributed to women. She sought to correct that perception. "We should erase that paragraph in our program which threatens a great number of women workers with unemployment and leaves them at the mercy of their class comrades," she boldly asserted. Buttressing her argument in a scholarly style with long excerpts from the writings of Marx, Engels, and Bebel, she urged an end to this policy, which, she believed, sought to eliminate unfair competition with male workers rather than to protect female workers. The party did not try to eliminate all work detrimental to men's health and morality; why do so for women? Domestic service, the occupation from which most prostitutes were recruited, clearly eroded women's morality, yet the party was not calling for the end of this chief source of women's employment. Rather, its ban applied to women industrial workers who competed with men. Poor relief remained the only alternative for such women—an option that improved neither their health nor their morality. Their removal from the labor force would prompt employers to substitute child workers or machines rather than make improvements for men. The burden of family life would become even more unbearable for fathers. "Under today's circumstances," she insisted, "it is mainly due to women's contributions that family life is maintained at all." Furthermore, "the possibility of an independent income provides proletarian women with an independent position vis-à-vis men" and saved them from the dependency that governed bourgeois marriage.[51]

Kelley offered an alternative that echoed her 1882 "Despair" article: "protective measures, which aim to preserve the working class in general, namely by reducing working hours, prohibition of Sunday and night labor, application of hygienic measures at work to protect the health of women and men workers, as well as special measures before, during and after confinement." Protecting her own place in the political economy, she warned against "the fatalist understanding that sufficiency in economic development will carry out the enlightenment of women" and called for "the propagation of enlightenment, organization, encouragement for solidarity and equality" among women workers.[52] With this volley against women's "class comrades," the obstreperous American added a new voice to German socialism. Her defense of the work of married women reflected her own marital status as well as her engagement in the "brain work" of Social Democracy.

Florence Kelley's correspondence with Engels between 1884 and 1886 documented her progress with the translation. He returned her first section in February, having "looked it over carefully, & entered some corrections & suggestions in pencil." Upon her request, he also provided translations for technical terms. Remaining close to his original, she retained the power of his prose. By June of 1885—just one month before she gave birth—she had completed the volume, except for "some of the English works quoted in the text," which she hoped he could supply in the original English.[53]

From the beginning of their collaboration, Engels made it clear that he relied on Kelley to arrange for the translation's publication. She turned first to G. P. Putnam, the father of Ruth Putnam; however, though she had characterized him to Engels as "an old friend of mine," he declined to publish the translation. He thought that "the factory acts, compulsory education, cooperation and trades unions organizations have done much to remove the evils" described in *The Condition* "and the new enfranchisement must do still more." Putnam's views were typical, she thought, of "all Americans almost without exception [who] regard America as exempt from the working of economic laws which, as they are perfectly willing to acknowledge, manifest themselves elsewhere." Criticisms similar to Putnam's would be preempted, she suggested to Engels, by a new preface.[54]

In a tribute to her belief in the importance of women's social activism as a vehicle for change, Kelley turned to her Philadelphia friend, Rachel Foster, then secretary of the National Woman Suffrage Association, to arrange for the American publication of Engels's book. In January 1886, she told Engels the good news that Foster, who recently had inherited a substantial sum of money, offered "to bear the expense" of its publication.

Rachel Foster Avery, Philadelphia, ca. 1887. Courtesy of Library of Congress.

For this service, Foster was listed on the copyright page as the book's sole copyright holder. Kelley assured Engels that Foster "will see to it that the book is placed in all the many libraries of [the National Woman Suffrage Association] and so within reach of a very large body of young workingwomen, teachers etc. as well as of the thousands of women for whom their movement has hitherto offered chiefly political interest." Engels gave no sign of being impressed by this opportunity to influence American women, nor did he respond enthusiastically to the news that "Miss Foster is ready . . . to go on publishing Socialist works as fast as I can translate them." While he said he learned "a good deal" working with her American English, he warned, "I cannot possibly always arrange to please everybody and to chime in with all arrangements made." [55]

In her search for a publisher, Rachel Foster forged an agreement with the executive committee of the Socialist Labor Party in New York, thereby irritating Engels, who learned of her efforts through the party's New York newspaper, *Der Sozialist*. "Neither Marx nor myself have ever committed the least act which might be interpreted into asking any Working Men's Organization to do us any personal favor," he complained to her. "I shall therefore be compelled to inform that Executive that this application was made strictly without my knowledge or authority." His translator replied that she had not known about Foster's actions and had not considered "what the bourgeoisie may think or say about it" but believed that there could be no question of a personal favor since they were charging her "quite as much as any bourgeois firm." [56]

Toward the end of Kelley's work on *The Condition*, epoch-making events in the United States beckoned her home. She and Engels were both elated over what seemed to be a historic insurgency of American workers. In Chicago in 1886 the world's first May Day parade attracted eighty thousand workers, who marched up Michigan Avenue. The colossal scale of this demonstration of strength was matched politically by independent labor tickets in 189 towns and cities in thirty-four of the thirty-eight states then in the union. [57]

Yet if this mass mobilization made the United States the most promising site for socialist transformation in the western world, that insurgency was quickly matched by a commensurate scale of repressive violence. Responding to a strike against the McCormick reaper factory and a citywide campaign for an eight-hour work day, labor groups in 1886 held a rally at Haymarket Square in downtown Chicago three days after the May Day parade. A bomb exploded there, killing one policeman and seriously wounding dozens of bystanders. Police shot into the crowd, killing at least four workers and injuring many others, including some policemen. Eventually six policemen died. A biased jury and judge summarily tried eight trade unionists, socialists, and anarchists, condemning seven to hanging and one to fifteen years' hard labor. The sentences of two of the condemned were later commuted to life imprisonment, one committed suicide, and four were executed.[58]

Rioting by workers and violence by police had been a growing feature of American labor conflicts since the great railroad strike of 1877, but the scale of labor mobilization in 1886, the apparently premeditated nature of the bombing, and the police fatalities were unprecedented. The stage was set for outbreaks of armed warfare between labor and capital during the next quarter century of American industrial development. Middle-class opinion split. And although some sought an alternative to violence, most supported the repressive measures.

For Engels, the Haymarket news was almost too good to be true. He wrote Kelley that "the breaking out of class war in America" had meaning for the whole world since the "bourgeois thought that America stood above class antagonisms and struggles" had now broken down. "I only wish Marx could have lived to see it!" He thought that "those wise Americans who think their country exempt from the consequences of fully expanded Capitalist production" should read about those consequences in the reports of the labor bureaus recently created in Massachusetts, New Jersey, and Pennsylvania.[59]

For Kelley, this watershed event opened endless vistas of translations. "The actions of the bourgeoisie arouse further the class consciousness of the workers, but it does not enlighten them as they need to be enlightened and I am convinced that much crude action and wasted energy might be spared if we could make the best of our literature available for them." She remained ready to translate *Origin of the Family, Private Property, and the State* that summer, reminding Engels in August that "the money for publishing whatever of yours or Marx' I may translate, is in readiness at any time." Expecting her second baby in November, she added that her "free time is rapidly passing" and that, since she would "be in America for a time," she could make better publishing arrangements than Miss Foster had done for *The Condition*.[60]

In a reply that boded ill for her long-term success as his translator, Engels responded that it would be "some time yet before the mass of the American working people will begin to read socialist literature." For the present "there is matter enough being provided." A translation of the recently published *Origin* would be missed "least of all" because Americans were not interested in theoretical works. Even though Engels subtitled *Origin* "*In the Light of the Researches of Lewis H. Morgan*" and believed he was interpreting the anthropologist's work on Native Americans from the perspective of Marx's writings, he responded coolly to Kelley's news in June that "a large section of the Suffrage Association in Iowa took for the subject of its discussions through the winter, Morgan's works, especially his Ancient Society." [61] Engels did not share Florence Kelley's

vision of an America transformed by his writings, and her reliance on the political culture of middle-class women only increased his skepticism. Nothing in his experience
prepared him to recognize the potential that Kelley saw in the mobilization of middle-
class women, and that, even more than her idealistic attitude toward his writings, created
a distance between them that was never overcome.

Kelley tried to reduce his reserve through a visit, writing that she hoped to have
the pleasure of calling on him that September when she and her family passed through
London on their way to New York. She persisted in her disagreement with his assessment of the American scene. After the publication of *Capital* and *The Condition,* "there
will be need of just such other smaller scientific works as *die Entwicklung, der Ursprung*
and others which are neither popular tracts for propaganda among the masses nor great
volumes a comprehension of which requires previous training, but compact and man-
ageable little books for young people of some general education but no specific training
in the direction of economic investigation." She told him that a large potential reader-
ship existed in the young people in the "scores and hundreds of little colleges" in the
United States.[62] Kelley's hopes of reaching a middle-class audience ran against the tide
of anti-anarchist and antisocialist hysteria then sweeping middle-class America in the
wake of the Haymarket massacre, but that was her vineyard, and she was determined to
cultivate it.

During her first two years of marriage, Florence Kelley Wischnewetzky disassoci-
ated herself from her father's political world and began to construct her own approach
to politics—one that emphasized rather than diminished class conflict. This required a
heroic effort on her part, personally and politically. Self-consciously locating herself and
her interpretive talents in the momentous rush of historical events, she invested a set of
new political beliefs with vibrant personal meaning. Ahead of her lay the task of locating
a political context where she could put those beliefs into action.

6

"Where Do
I Belong?"
1886–1888

When Florence, Lazare, and their young son, Nikolai, arrived in New York harbor in the fall of 1886, they entered a nation in the midst of industrial transformation and working-class political mobilization. In New York harbor, their ship would have passed the newly erected Statue of Liberty, whose dedication in October marked the beginning of a new era of massive immigration that fed the ever-expanding demand for more industrial workers. Although Florence and Lazare did not initially plan on remaining in the United States, the political opportunities there, combined with the birth of their second child in November (named Margaret after Margaret Hicks), delayed and ultimately scuttled their projected return to Europe. The growing family first settled into rooms at 3 Livingston Place, near Stuyvesant Square, Manhattan, and soon moved to 110 East 76th Street, where they lived for two years.

The young couple were befriended by Katharine and Friedrich Sorge, who had emigrated to the United States in 1852 and, living in Hoboken, represented the Marxist remnant of the First International. The only friend who had shared her previous life in Philadelphia was Helen Campbell, a member of the New Century Guild in 1883 and now a successful writer in New York about "the social question." In late October 1886 the *New York Tribune* began a series of articles by Campbell that soon became an influential book, *Prisoners of Poverty: Women Wage-Workers, Their Trades and Their Lives.* By December Kelley and Campbell were close friends—close enough for Campbell to lend Kelley seven hundred dollars, the equivalent of a year's income for a skilled worker. Campbell's financial success as a writer put her in a position to help Kelley, but to accept such a sizable loan the congressman's daughter must have been desperate. Lazare was unemployed, and Florence recovered slowly from Margaret's birth, five months after which, in May 1887, she was pregnant again, that child being born in January 1888. Deliberately avoiding her family, she could not turn to them for help. Campbell's loan sustained Florence and her two babies throughout 1887 while Lazare returned briefly to London for more medical training and then tried to establish a medical practice in Manhattan.[1]

Having solved her most pressing economic problem, Florence Kelley Wischnewetzky turned to the equally demanding task of establishing herself as a translator of German economic writings. First, she needed to locate an audience for those writings, and toward that end, she and Lazare joined the Socialist Labor Party (SLP). The leading socialist arm of the nation's labor movement, the SLP also served as a cultural extension of the German Social Democratic Party. It appeared to be the perfect bridge between Kelley's well-developed German connections and her entry into the American political landscape.

The Wischnewetzkys arrived in New York during a high point of popular political mobilization: Henry George's campaign for mayor of New York City. Like other panacea-based movements in the late nineteenth century, such as the Greenback move-

Katharine and Friedrich Sorge in Hoboken, ca. 1887. Courtesy of Nicholas Kelley Papers, Rare Books and Manuscripts Division, New York Public Library, Astor, Lenox and Tilden Foundations.

ment, George's appeal embodied the hope within republican ideology that if only the proper socioeconomic adjustments could be made, the rich potential of republicanism would be unleashed. Meanwhile, in actuality, machine politics and ward bosses were channeling the political energies of wave after wave of immigrants. An optimist might think it an opportune moment for Florence Kelley to assume the educator's role that she envisioned for herself. She was impressed with the "magnificence" of the campaign, "when George and the workingmen" held "eight meetings every night, indoors and out, with thousands of voters at each." Supported by a broad coalition of organized labor, immigrants, and reform-minded professionals behind the United Labor Party, George urged the redistribution of wealth through a tax on land. He received more than a third of the vote, outpolling the Republican candidate, Theodore Roosevelt, and depriving the Democratic victor of an electoral majority. Kelley enthusiastically wrote Engels that the campaign left a legacy in which "the work of separate political action and organization of the working class is going on throughout the country." [2]

These events highlighted the importance of her translation work. "Real enlightenment among the workers is so very limited," she wrote Engels, "and the literature available for meeting the present vast demand is so pitifully scanty (Gronlund, Ely!)." George's "*idée fixe*" of a tax on land blinded him to the significance of industrial workers, she felt. When given a copy of her translation of *The Condition*, George protested against its notion that "the history of the proletariat in England begins with the second half of the last century, with the invention of the steam engine and of machinery for working cotton." "No!" he insisted, "since land has been held as private property there have always been proletarians" — irking Kelley by "using the word as synonymous with *toiler* in general, or *poor man*" and remaining "utterly oblivious to the specific character of the proletariat." [3]

To remedy this ignorance, she urged Engels to complete a new preface for the English edition of *The Condition* to take account of "the massive political movement of the past three months" and to define "our position toward Mr. George." The timing was perfect. "All eyes are turned toward the writer's work of education; newspapers are being founded or enlarged, and the demand for literature and lectures cannot be met." Meanwhile, publication plans were proceeding smoothly. Rachel Foster remained loyal to the project, arranging "for an edition of five hundred to be placed in libraries, furnished to the press, etc." Cheap editions were being prepared, and "a very wide distribution seems to open before the book." [4] The success of Kelley's plans depended on the support and cooperation of the Socialist Labor Party. Without them, her voice and Engels's could not hope to be heard above the multitude contending for public attention. The party had newspapers, meeting halls, printing shops, and a loyal constituency at its command, all of which furnished the context she needed to promote "German economic literature." Yet this apparently fertile field turned barren at her approach. The Socialist Labor Party was not ready for Engels, let alone his disciple in the form of an aggressive Yankee woman. Almost immediately she and it fell into struggle over ideology and tactics.

Her most basic disagreement with the SLP arose from her interest in incorporating American-born and English-speaking members and the party's commitment to retaining its German character. In 1886 the SLP was at the high point of its membership, the great majority of which was German-speaking. Founded in 1876 at a convention in Philadelphia at the time of the Centennial Exhibition, the party's growth paralleled the rising insurgency among urban industrial workers, but in New York and other large cities German immigrants predominated. Hundreds of thousands had recently fled the repressive effects of the antisocialist law of 1878, and Germans ran the party nationally as well as locally. About a year after her arrival in New York, Kelley described to Engels "the lamentable course" of the national party congress in which the "good intentions" of the members led them to vote "English the language of the Congress"; when it became clear that "more than half the members understood no English," the proceedings shifted to German, and "the Anglo-Americans in order to be understood were forced to stumble along as well as they could in German." Party proceedings, printed exclusively in German until 1887, were not printed exclusively in English until 1900.[5]

This fundamental disagreement simmered while Kelley became embroiled in the party's internecine factional struggle between Lassalleans and trade unionists. She quickly learned that most members of the New York chapter remained loyal to the views of Ferdinand Lassalle, a leading German socialist who, having died in 1864 before the emergence of strong trade unions, argued that trade unions could never assume the leadership role within labor parties that Marx and Engels envisioned for them. Instead, Lassalle urged that workers pursue direct political action and use the state to establish workers' cooperatives. While Marxists and Lassalleans were partially reconciled in Germany in 1875, their differences remained unresolved among German-American socialists. As a result, the SLP maintained an aloof distance from organized labor, and Friedrich Sorge was almost alone in representing Marxian views within the party. Yet despite its Lassallean perspective, after Henry George purged socialists from his followers in 1887 the SLP also disdained American working-class political movements. Thus the pre-1890 party served its members primarily as a German cultural community.[6]

Engels criticized the inaction and isolation of the SLP in a letter to Kelley in December 1886. The Knights of Labor "ought not to be pooh-poohed from without but to be revolutionised from within," he said. "Many of the Germans there [in the United States] made a grievous mistake when they tried, in the face of a mighty and glorious movement not of their own creation, to make of their imported and not always understood theory a kind of *alleinseligmachendes* [the only true] *Dogma.*" Socialist theory, Engels insisted, "is not a dogma but the exposition of a process of evolution, and that process involves successive phases." No one could expect that the Americans "will start with the full consciousness of the theory worked out in older industrial countries." Rather, the SLP ought "to go in for any real general working-class movement, accept its actual starting point as such, and work it gradually up to the theoretical level." He thought that "a million or two of working men's votes next November for a bona fide working men's party is worth infinitely more at present than a hundred thousand votes for a doctrinally perfect platform."[7] This advice about the practical fundamentals of political action bolstered Kelley's decision to take on the SLP leadership and expand the party's political potential.

The party's future success in her view, and her own position within it, depended on its ability to advocate the "science" of Marx's *Capital* and Engels's *Condition of the Working Class in England*. Certain of her ideological superiority, Kelley approached her differences with the SLP as problems that could be solved through debate, and in her debut as an American socialist, she cleared the way for Marx and Engels by denouncing Lassallean views. Her 1887 article in *Workmen's Advocate* (later renamed *Workingmen's Advocate*), the chief English language newspaper of the American socialist movement, criticized a Lassallean Social Democrat, Johann Jacoby, and his 1870 speech, "The Object of the Labor Movement." "The spirit and traditions of the Jeffersonian Democracy still live in considerable part of the Laboring Class," she began, and building on those traditions, "our young Labor Party is now on the way towards becoming a great political party." But she criticized Jacoby's illusory hope "for a peaceful solution of the Labor Question on the part of the State and the Capitalist class," maintaining that the state became "year by year more completely the property, the willing tool" of the capitalist corporations and less capable of action in the interest of the people. Eight-hour laws remained unenforced, and child labor laws were "evaded for want of adequate inspection." Only through political action arising from the "Working Class" could the transition from "the Wage System to the Socialistic organization of society" be achieved. This salvo fired on behalf of the Marxist view of class struggle expressed more meteoric than lasting convictions on her part, but it reached its intended target, the SLP leadership.[8]

Their revenge was swift. When, to bolster her anti-Lassallean campaign, she circulated (without his permission) Engels's letter of December 28 and its derogatory comments about the isolation of the SLP, *Workmen's Advocate* deliberately misquoted the letter, making Engels sound ridiculous and stressing Kelley's breach of confidentiality. She indignantly objected. Engels was furious — as much with her as with them. She appealed to him for sympathy: Gronlund, a leading SLP member, was undercutting her effort to find a publisher for *The Condition,* and "instead of any kind of stimulus, encouragement, cheer, help, there is one miserable exasperation after the other." Meanwhile labor's political strength was waning as the United Labor Party headed toward "a complete split" into the new Federation of Organized Trades and Labor Unions on the one hand and the Knights of Labor on the other, both of which were attacking each other while conducting aggressive membership campaigns. As if to remind herself of the consolations in her personal life as well as to convey a personal greeting to Engels, she enclosed in her letter a "trifle" from "my boy's tree." [9]

A second controversy caught Kelley in the middle of sectarian cross fire that almost ended her relationship with Engels and ultimately terminated her affiliation with the SLP. In the spring of 1887, just as copies of *The Condition* were being bound, the intractable issue of party cooperation with the American labor movement reemerged. In London in 1884, Eleanor Marx, daughter of Karl Marx, had begun living with Edward Aveling and adopted his name even though they could not officially marry because he had not divorced his estranged wife. Engels, still financially supporting Eleanor and other members of Marx's family, had engaged Aveling to translate portions of *Capital.* Funded by the SLP's national executive committee, the couple undertook a fifteen-week tour of the United States that ended in New York in December 1886. At a mass meeting just before their return to London, Aveling championed an unpopular integrationist policy, declaring: "The best Knights of Labor come from the Socialists, and the best Socialists make the best Knights of Labor." He then emphatically reiterated the point during a meeting with the national executive committee. Perhaps for this reason, although it had honored all earlier requests, the committee refused to reimburse him for his last statement of expenses, claiming that it contained luxuries, such as flowers and cigarettes, that did not merit reimbursement and hinting that Aveling submitted expenses incurred by others. A week later the *New York Herald* carried a sensationalized report of the committee meeting, which omitted any mention of the dispute over the Knights of Labor and presented the financial squabble in terms designed to discredit the socialist movement in general and Eleanor Marx in particular. [10]

When this dispute first surfaced in January, Kelley accepted the SLP's version of Aveling's financial deceit and—possibly in the hope of restoring herself to the leadership's confidence, possibly because she herself did not trust Aveling—foolishly took it upon herself to warn Engels against him. The committee was about to issue "an official circular" exposing Aveling, she wrote, and she suggested that he warn Karl Kautsky to exclude Aveling from a joint publishing venture since "his name as one of the staff can only injure any organ." Engels was furious at her presumption and told her so. He had known and trusted Aveling for four years and felt like a father toward Eleanor, who was incapable of "swindling the working class." It was the executive committee, and not the bills, that were ridiculous, he wrote. As for warning Kautsky, "I feel certain you regretted having written this passage as soon as the letter had gone." Kelley initially sought the assistance of Friedrich Sorge as an intermediary to restore her relationship with Engels and later that spring sent Engels a lengthy apology.[11]

At this low point in their relationship, Engels denounced Mrs. Wischnewetzky and all her works in letters to Friedrich Sorge. The Wischnewetzkys "have behaved rather like Washragskys in the whole affair," he wrote upon learning that they "have been constrained to call [the executive committee] liars." Unfairly, insultingly, and irrationally, he said that his quarrel with her pleased him, "in so far as I now hope to be relieved of Mrs. W's harassing about translations. First of all, she translates like a factory, leaving the real work to me; second she neglected its publishing miserably, letting these louts get hold of it." A month later, however, he accepted her apology, noting that Sorge assured him that she and Lazare "have made all conceivable efforts to obtain justice for Aveling in the New York section." Engels wrote Sorge that he wanted to make the reconciliation "as easy for her as possible." But, he continued, in a penetrating description of her current circumstances, "she is awkward and, besides, a luckless person of the first water." Engels, who drew a substantial income from his father's estate, resided in an upper-middle-class neighborhood near Regents' Park and had no children, styled himself superior to Florence Kelley Wischnewetzky and felt no sympathy for the hard times that her own quite different life choices had induced.[12]

Skirmishes between Kelley and the SLP leadership broke into full-scale hostilities after the publication of Engels's English preface to *The Condition*. First conceived by Kelley, Engels's preface roundly praised the capacities of the American labor movement and chastised the German-American socialists. He began by noting the difference between American and European conditions. "On the more favored soil of America, where no medieval ruins bar the way, where history begins with the elements of modern bourgeois society as evolved in the seventeenth century," working-class consciousness ripened much more quickly. The Knights of Labor were "an immense amount of potential energy evolving slowly but surely into actual force" and "the only national bond" holding together "the whole class of American wage-workers." The American labor movement could benefit from the SLP's "intellectual and moral fruits of the forty years' struggle," but for this to occur, the party "will have to doff every remnant of their foreign garb. They will have to become out and out American," Engels insisted. "They cannot expect the Americans to come to them; they, the minority and the immigrants, must go to the Americans, who are the vast majority and the natives. And to do that, they must above all things learn English." This suited Florence Kelley Wischnewetzky perfectly.[13]

The executive committee responded by suspending her and Lazare's membership. "We've been suspended for a few days for *Majestätsbeleidigung* [insulting the crown]," Kelley wrote Engels, "and when the preface gets well into circulation we shall probably be suspended again for *Verbreitung verbotener Schriften* [distribution of prohibited writings]. The Executive does not like the preface and is burying it in impenetrable silence. The *Sozialist* never mentions the book except for purposes of misrepresentation." The precipitating cause of their suspension was Lazare's "handling the Executive Committee without gloves." She protested her innocence: "I was at home with the babies when the atrocity was said to have been committed." Later that summer the party permanently expelled the Wischnewetzkys for "incessant slander" against the national executive committee (*fortgesetzte Verleumdung des N.E.K.*).[14]

The momentum of Kelley's commitment to her translation work helped her toil on alone the spring, summer, and fall of 1887. Using a shop beyond party influence and with funding from Rachel Foster, she arranged the printing of twenty thousand copies of Engels's preface. She hoped the pamphlet would entice readers to purchase the book and believed it brought "the debate up at once to the level where it belongs"; she acknowledged, however, that "the circulation will be a source of some difficulty because we have to push the pamphlet ourselves, being unwilling to have anything to do with the wretched Executive."[15]

Predictably enough, the party ignored the publication of *The Condition* that April. "The book is out," Kelley wrote Engels. "I received the first half dozen copies yesterday." She assured him that her future translations of his work would be published by Lovell with the support of Rachel Foster and without any complicating arrangements with the party. Copies were sent to Karl Kautsky in London and friends in Zürich. In June she wrote that "the book is getting well noticed in the press—as one of the most dangerous publications of recent years!" Yet, except for paid advertisements, the socialist press was ignoring it. "The *Volkszeitung* has never mentioned the book," and the only labor paper to notice it was the *Leader*.[16] She admitted that this would not "contribute to the spread of the book among the working people" but still hoped that her own efforts at distribution, matched with Lovell's capacity to send "the book far and wide," could compensate for the party's neglect. Soon thereafter she sent Engels a packet of reviews and in August noted that "the pamphlet is finding satisfactory sale." Book agents were "ordering by hundreds," a thousand were in circulation within the party, and it would be sold at "all the great political meetings" during the fall political campaign.[17]

Rejected by her chosen political allies, uncertain of her support by women's organizations, the mother of two children, the oldest of whom had just turned two, and expecting a third baby that winter, during an August vacation in the "primitive seacoast village" of Gloucester, Massachusetts, Florence Kelley Wischnewetzky completed a personal-political trajectory launched in 1884.[18] She attacked the cornerstone of her father's career by translating Karl Marx's 1849 speech "Free Trade."

The translation occupied her throughout the fall. The subject was a critical one for the political development of the working class, she wrote Engels, since workingmen had been known to go through a whole campaign supporting a labor candidate only at the last moment to "vote for the regular bourgeois old party man because he happened to be a hotter protectionist." This had been true for generations, and she hoped to change it. She was giving the project "all the moments I can take from any daily hack work" and hoped that Engels would write a preface. Her own writing was done hurriedly, "in the intervals of daily drudgery," she told him, since most of the housework fell to her.[19]

Marx's argument was the antithesis of William Kelley's views, not only because Marx advocated free trade (it promoted more direct confrontation between the classes) but also because he relegated the whole tariff issue to an administrative question of little importance compared to the issue of worker exploitation through the extraction of surplus value from their labor. In a drubbing criticism of the American polity's fixation on the issue, Florence Kelley wrote Engels, "No one here seems to grasp the fact that Free Trade and Protection are really *Verwaltungsmassregeln* [administrative measures], and all the world treats them as fundamental questions of Social Science — Free Trade or Protectionist *Weltanschauung,* one might almost say, prevails from the professors and Congress to the least of the penny-a-liners." She was troubled, however, that some readers might not grasp the subtlety of Marx's argument. Some journalists, she feared, would tell working-men that "their own Marx thought Free Trade of such very subordinate importance, they might almost as well be protectionists outright," and she hoped Engels's preface would preempt such a possibility. "I have my own personal reasons for wishing the pamphlet perfectly unmistakable on the protectionist question," she said, "because the Republican protectionist press which is all at my father's beck and call will forthwith proclaim the fact that the daughter of the Apostle of Protection has come out in a pamphlet proving Free Trade rank Socialism and getting Marx himself as an authority." This ultimate challenge to her father's authority was published in the fall of 1888. Engels's preface concluded that "whether you try the Protectionist or the Free Trade plan will make no difference in the end," for both systems generated "a revolutionary class of laborers," who one day would "destroy the system itself."[20]

Kelley hoped that her translation of Marx's "Free Trade," would enlighten readers outside if not inside the SLP, but much of her political energy in the fall of 1887 was consumed in disputes with the "pitiful untrustworthy mediocrities" of the SLP's leadership. She issued statements and counterstatements and, with the help of Rachel Foster, circulars and countercirculars. Of course the party continued to neglect "the now accessible literature of scientific-materialistic criticism," preferring "confused stuff, calculated to do anything else rather than promote earnest thought among our Americans."[21]

That autumn she was swamped by the effort of distributing the pamphlet of *The Condition*'s preface. "The forty thousand copies are now in the market," she said, writing Engels from "the midst of the work of sending them, as we had many orders in advance from all parts of the country." The pamphlet's appearance was timely; Henry George had been revealed as a "wretched humbug," and "the class standpoint is *the* foreground now as it never was or could be before."[22] She had mailed pamphlets "to every American organization of workingmen of which I could find the address" and sent postal cards to agents and clubs. Significantly, she sent seven hundred copies "to the members of the National Collegiate Alumnae Association," which bore fruit "in orders for the book." By October she felt that the "success" of both the pamphlet and book was "most satisfactory."[23]

Florence Wischnewetzky never mentioned one crucial aspect of her struggle with the Socialist Labor Party—her identity as a woman. During this year of intense socialist activism, she was close to only one German socialist woman, Katharine Sorge, who was old enough to be her mother. She seemed unconcerned about and rarely came into contact with other women in the SLP, perhaps because those mostly German-born women did not participate as equals within the party. Instead, they served in an auxiliary capacity, organizing picnics and other community events for German-American socialist communities. When Eleanor Marx Aveling visited New York in 1886, women remained virtually invisible within party ranks, prompting her to urge them to participate within the larger party and bring their children to meetings if necessary. Women's rights were championed within the SLP briefly in 1888 and 1889 by Johanna Greie, a recent immigrant from Dresden inspired by August Bebel's *Women and Socialism*. Greie's 1888 essay in *Der Sozialist*, "Is It Necessary for Women to Organize Themselves?"—the only analysis of women's position within the SLP during Kelley's years in New York—argued against the party's hostility to women's wage labor and urged women to overcome their indifference to political activism. In a tour throughout the northeast that year Greie tried to create a national women's socialist organization, but in the hostile political climate of the late 1880s this proved impossible. Not until Social Democrats in Germany called for universal suffrage in 1891 were women energized within the SPD or the SLP. The activism sweeping native-born American women's organizations in the 1880s had no equivalent within the German-dominated socialist movement.[24]

Kelley's status as Engels's translator made her an exception to the general rule that discouraged women from participating in the Socialist Labor Party, but this did not exempt her from the prevailing prejudice against women. Engels himself expressed such prejudice openly in letters to Sorge during the Aveling affair, stereotyping her on the one hand as "a weak person, influenced by every gust of wind" and on the other hand believing that she was trying to "bamboozle me like a baby." On this and other occasions when she irritated him, Engels called her "Mother Wischnewetzky." He also made unwarranted assumptions about her contact with "gossipy German sisters." Such stereotyped views, shared by many German socialists in New York, stiffened resistance to Kelley's leadership.[25]

Although Kelley did not develop ties with her "German sisters," she did maintain contact with the public culture of native-born middle-class women. Responding to the pull of her class and culture, she believed in their significance within the American polity and in their capacity for regeneration. In a remarkable and passionate speech to the New York Association of Collegiate Alumnae in May 1887, just after her expulsion from the SLP, she reached out to them as if they were her chief constituency.[26] There, for the first time since her return to the United States, she used her own voice rather than Engels's, and her own historical understanding. There, though her ideas generated keen opposition, she was not ignored. Published later that year by the association as "The Need of Theoretical Preparation for Philanthropic Work," her talk expanded and revised the article she had asked May Lewis's help in publishing in 1886.

Kelley used the authority of her family background and personal experience to review three generations of women's philanthropic activity and point toward a new future. For "our grandmothers," she said, "before our system of production had developed to its present stage, when the contrasts of class were less sharply defined, philanthropic work was simple enough; neighborly help of those less comfortably placed, or, possibly, contribution to the maintenance of some one of a few charitable institutions."[27] For their mothers' generation, "there is simply the choice among the thousand and one forms of philanthropic activity approved by the class to which we belong." Yet their mothers had "lost step with the rapid march of industrial and social development that marks the last few years," she insisted, and "the thinking woman of our generation" faced much starker issues.

As she saw it, "the vital question is no longer between giving doles to street beggars on the one hand or supporting the associated charities on the other; or between the temperance, the white cross and the suffrage movements." Rather, she said, "the question that forces itself upon us, and imperatively demands an immediate answer, is this: In the great strife of classes, in the life and death struggle that is rending society to its foundations, where do I belong?" She followed this arresting question with a barrage of forceful corollaries that introduced a new discourse about charity workers and charity recipients. Having herself stepped outside the social and ideological matrix that maintained her own class in power, she now asked other middle-class women to follow her example and cease to reproduce their class relations. She prodded their consciences by articulating their doubts: "Shall I cast my lot with the oppressors, content to patch and darn, to piece and cobble at the worn and rotten fabric of a perishing society? Shall I spend my life in applying palliatives, in trying to make the intolerable endurable yet a little longer?" She questioned temperance work: "Shall I preach temperance to men whose homes are vile tenements, whose wives toil side by side with them because the father's wages no longer suffice to maintain the family? Men whose exhausted, ill-nourished frames demand stimulants because the wife has no time, strength, money with which to procure and prepare good and sufficient food?" She even questioned "social purity" reform: "Shall I preach chastity to homeless men, the hopeless discomfort of whose surroundings must concentrate their whole desire upon the gratification of animal passion, while want forces scores of thousands of women to sell themselves to the first-comer?" The biggest scourge—unemployment—she saved for last: "Shall I fritter away the days of my youth investigating the deservingness of this or that applicant for relief when the steady march of industrial development throws a million able-bodied workers out of employment, to tramp the country, seeking in vain a chance to earn their bread, until hundreds—aye, thousands—of them, broken, discouraged, demoralized, settle down into the life of the chronic pauper?" These questions were answered in thunder by another: "Shall I not rather make common cause with these, my brothers and my sisters, to make an end of such a system?"

This romantic picture of the future melded moral and economic images. The task of making clear to wage earners "the cause of the evils under which they, and with them, the whole of society suffer," she said, "is the true work for the elevation of the race, the true philanthropy." She asked her listeners "to cast our lot with the workers, to seek to understand the laws of social and industrial development, in the midst of which we live, to spread this enlightenment among the men and women destined to contribute to the change to a higher social order."

Florence Kelley Wischnewetzky was not the only person who could translate Engels, but she was the only middle-class woman who spoke to her peers in this way. How did they respond? Reactions to her oral presentation were not recorded, but when her essay was reprinted that summer in *The Christian Union*, the nation's leading advocate of moral activism on social questions, it inspired a sharp response. Vida Scudder, a Smith graduate who had recently returned to the United States after being converted to Christian social-

Vida Scudder, ca. 1890. Courtesy of Schlesinger Library, Radcliffe College.

ism during graduate study at Oxford University, took Kelley on. Scudder was developing plans for what later became a successful women's social settlement in Boston, and her lengthy letter to the editor of *The Christian Union* was competitive as well as defensive. She castigated those who "by their bitter invectives strive to widen the distance between classes." She attacked Kelley's "fundamental assumption" that the wealth of the upper classes caused the poverty of the laboring classes. Calling her "Madame Wischnewetzky" even though she was clearly identified as "Florence Kelley Wischnewetzky," Scudder insisted that her antagonist saw the upper class as "a small band of tyrannical and self-ish men, grinding into the dust, for the sake of personal gain, the helpless millions of the world's workers, and willing, at best, to palliate the resultant evils." These notions were especially inappropriate in the United States, she said, since "no sharp line between classes exists among us; the laborer of one generation is the merchant of the next." Noting that "the men most profoundly impressed today with a noble discontent are in the despised capitalist class," she insisted that "unconscious forces" rather than individuals were to blame for the "present social order, with its injustice, its suffering, and its sin." Chief among these forces was "the law of the survival of the fittest." But, Scudder argued further, these forces could be overcome by a spirit of Christian brotherhood, which took as its basic law "the protection of the weak." [28]

The Christian Union printed Kelley's reply that "the accumulation of capital is possible only out of the proceeds of unpaid labor. And until this proposition is disproved my charges against the capitalistic system stand valid." Replying to the editorial disclaimer that her article expressed "a bitterness of feeling which is the product of a very different social and industrial climate from our own," she likened herself to William Lloyd Garrison, whose "arraignment of negro slavery" was called "fanaticism" until slavery was swept away. "And we who find the evils of wage slavery as intolerable and far more universal than the evils of chattel slavery are in our turn held fanatics." [29] Significantly, both Kelley and Scudder assumed that women could rise above the limitations of their class perspective and shape social change through their public activism.

Gratified by the stir her essay caused, Kelley wrote Engels, "The editors received over eighty letters of inquiry and remonstrance and I was showered with books, pamphlets and letters from all parts of the country." She thought this response was "symptomatic of the interest felt among the . . . people of the middle class." By August, presumably with the financial support of Rachel Foster, she had reprints of the exchange available for mailing. She sent this reprint, accompanied by Engels's preface in both German and English, to members of the National Collegiate Alumnae Association, "scattered all over the union." They numbered "nearly a thousand members," she wrote Engels, so their pamphlets "will thus be brought into nearly every university in the country." [30] After her long sojourn outside the ranks of her class and culture, she had returned with a vivid message linking class and gender. And she had been heard.

In August 1887, Florence Kelley Wischnewetzky had been in the United States for almost a year without seeing or communicating with her mother or father. Her determined independence kept her free from the taint of her father's politics, distancing her from his compelling personality as well as from her mother's melancholy. Between 1884 and 1887 she had effectively replaced her father, both as intellectual mentor and champion of social change, with Lazare and Engels. This shift of allegiance helped her explore a universe of ideas that most of her American peers never knew existed. However, by the beginning of 1888, her relationship with Engels and her belief in the transforming power of "the literature of scientific-materialistic criticism" were running out of steam. At the same time, she seemed to have spent her hostility toward her family. A new era in her personal and political life began in December 1887 with the reconstruction of her relationship with William and Caroline Kelley.

In January 1888 William and Caroline visited their daughter in New York. Registering under assumed names in a hotel where they were not known, they tried to keep the reunion out of the newspapers, or, as William expressed it to Elizabeth Pugh, "to prevent those creatures who live by publishing and aggravating the sorrows and misery of families from rehashing the slanders poor Florence and her husband have been made to read or hear." Despite their previous alienation, William said, "a peace or truce has been patched up," and "affectionate intercourse [has] been resumed between our poor daughter and us." Though in an advanced stage of pregnancy, Florence then visited Philadelphia; the day after her return to New York, she wrote Caroline that she was "tired and stiff but very happy." She was "on duty" in her "exceedingly animated" nursery and was preparing a paper "for the Social Science Club meeting here tomorrow night." Lazare was "established as family doctor" with eight families on their street — "several of them wealthy American families through which he has already some Fifth Avenue cases." She joked that "a *confinement* is a 'resting spell' to be looked forward to with a sense of relief!" In conclusion she sent a "handshake" to Will and Bert.[31]

Another visit from her father two weeks later consolidated the reconciliation. "His visit was lovely," Florence wrote Caroline. "It did me infinite good; and Lazare enjoyed it no less than Father and I." She expressed thanks for various Christmas presents, especially a Bartram family genealogy, since Ko was "the man without a country *par excellence*," and it could not hurt him "to have seven grandfathers recorded in black and white." She described Ko's supreme delight with the tree, upon which she had spent the five dollars her father had given her for the children as well as two "unexpected cash fees for croup cases." She concluded by sending "my love to the boys." After John's birth, Caroline remained with the Wischnewetzkys until "Florrie began to improve decidedly" in late February. Will Jr. joined them for dinner on her last night in New York and helped his mother home. In March Florence said the baby was "thriving on Nestle food as a substitute for the model farm milk" that they were obliged to interrupt during severe winter snowstorms. Thanks to a generous gift from her father she was able to attend "the greatest luxury which New York could possibly have afforded me, namely an afternoon at the Metropolitan Opera House," her first "amuzement" in two years. His gift also bought her a box of wine "(which has done me visible good), [and] several long drives in the park while I was still weak." Possibly also because of a gift from her parents, that winter she employed two servants, one a "Yankee" school teacher, one "a bright Irish girl."[32]

Socially, however, the Wischnewetzkys remained isolated. Katharine and Friedrich Sorge, "acting as Godfather and Godmother," were the only friends invited to the "fine christening" at which Florence and Lazare named their third child "John Brown." Just before John's birth, his mother explored another political option — direct affiliation with organized labor. "We see a good deal of some of the more wide-awake, progressive and influential men among the English-speaking organizations (for instance Gompers, president of the Federation of Labor with its 600,000 members)," she wrote Engels in December 1887. An enduring connection with organized labor would have made eminent sense for her in England or Germany, but in the United States it did not. Gompers and the national AFL had just decided against forming a labor party. Rather, responding to the spectacle of massive internal dissension within the Henry George movement and the purging of its socialist members, Gompers led his movement into "pure and simple unionism," meaning that he pursued labor's goals through direct negotiation with employers rather than through politics and shunned involvement with third parties, especially the Socialist Labor Party.[33]

Gompers's shift away from politics recognized the inability of his skilled trades movement to defend working-class interests as a whole. Nationally and locally the AFL and its affiliates did pursue limited political action—their access to the ballot made it foolhardy for them to pass up the opportunity to elect representatives to Congress and state

Samuel Gompers, ca. 1890. Courtesy of the George Meany Memorial Archives.

legislatures who at least nominally supported their goals, and the American judiciary compelled them to struggle against repressive legal strategies, especially the antistrike injunction—but, beginning in the late 1880s, labor became more of an interest group and less of a vehicle for the welfare of society as a whole. At the local level, holistic views remained and would frequently unite with the moral imperatives that informed women's public culture, but labor was no longer a bandwagon at the head of the social justice parade.[34]

The AFL's retreat from politics cut off any alliance Florence Kelley Wischnewetzky might have forged with organized labor. She interpreted the retreat as a response to post-Haymarket repression. "The violence of the reaction among the workers themselves is surprising," she wrote Engels. At the recent annual convention of the newly formed American Federation of Labor, delegates voted in favor of maintaining taxes on cigars and equally frivolous matters, "but of the improvement of the Factory Acts, prohibition of the employment of children, etc. not one word could I find." She was amazed that "the Congress voted *against* the resumption of the Eight Hour Movement; *against* independent labor politics; and *against* a strike fund." Kelley knew that the 1885 New York Appeals Court decision *In Re Jacobs* helped explain Gompers's apolitical tilt. His fledgling federation had experienced gratifying political success in the New York state legislature in the early 1880s, obtaining the passage of laws that established a Bureau of Labor Statistics and prohibited the production of cigars in tenements. But after *Jacobs* overruled tenement legislation as unconstitutional, Gompers concluded that "the power of the courts to pass upon the constitutionality of the law so complicates reform by legislation as to seriously restrict the effectiveness of that method."[35]

Florence's biggest problem was Lazare. From May to September of 1888, she nursed him through a serious illness later diagnosed as rheumatic fever. She believed his symptoms were related to the "nervous despondency and years of sleeplessness which preceded it." Like William Kelley, Lazare was moody and irritable, but this breakdown went beyond anything known in the Kelley family, involving as it did "violent delirium" requiring regular morphine injections. "Embarrassed as they were, life was gloomy enough without this additional burden," Caroline wrote William about the couple's failing financial status, which preceded Lazare's illness. She hoped that "poor L. will come out of it, with his mind unimpaired." That July a series of loans and gifts from William and Caroline commenced with a spa vacation where Lazare was treated with daily baths and massage. "It is an unspeakable relief to be away from nurses, doctors and the sick room," Florence wrote Caroline. "If anything can cure my poor martyr it must be this vigorous treatment and the heavenly surroundings." Yet the Wischnewetzkys needed much more than a vacation. Florence and Lazare requested from William an immediate loan of $2,500, with other advances in the future, promising as security "a mortgage for $20,000 on the homestead of the elder Wischnewetzky, which was worth $40,000." The promised mortgage never arrived, however, and William could not advance the money without it. "I hope she pressures him on this point as persistently as she does me," William wrote his wife, regretting "in the embarrassed condition of my affairs," that he had already authorized his attorney to give her $1,500.[36]

In September 1888, Lazare was well enough to depart for Europe, where he spent most of the year visiting health resorts. Florence and the children moved to a less expensive apartment. That fall Kelley bade a painful farewell to Engels. Visiting the United States in September, Engels had initially asked Sorge to find out whether the Wischnewetzkys would be in New York during his visit, writing, "I shall see nobody else upon my arrival, for I do not want to fall into the hands of the Messrs. German Socialists." But he became ill during his trip, and just before his return to London wrote Kelley to express his "regret that unfortunate circumstances prevented me from seeing you more than once and but for a few moments." Her impassioned reply began, "I cannot imagine a keener disappointment than mine that you have left America without coming to see me." His staying for ten days within a two hours' ride and not seeing her was, she said, "a hurt to my feelings which cannot be made good and which there is no use in my trying to conceal. There is so much that I wanted to ask you about!" Engels defended himself against her implied charge of rudeness, writing Sorge, "Mother Wischnewetzky is very much hurt because I did not visit her." He assumed she was "hurt by a breach of etiquette and lack of gallantry towards ladies" and defensively added, "I do not allow the little women's rights ladies to demand gallantry from us; they want men's rights, they should also let themselves be treated as men. She will doubtless calm down." She sent him five hundred copies of the "Free Trade" pamphlet but otherwise did not write him for almost two years, ignoring his apology that he was "really too unwell, while in New York, to attempt an excursion of any kind."[37]

Florence Kelley's conversion to European socialism created a positive intellectual context for the reconstruction of her personal and political commitments. It gave her a new comprehension of the struggle between capital and labor and transformed her understanding of her own place in that struggle. Yet the ideas of Engels and Marx could not direct her to a viable political constituency in the United States. Her most rewarding skirmish had been with middle-class women. Even though they did not meet the theoretical requirement of helping the working class emancipate itself, she had begun a dialogue with them. On the rebound from the Socialist Labor Party but reconnected with her parents, she was giving the American civil landscape another look.

7

"If We Were Doing the Nation's Work," 1889–1891

Pushed by her frustrating conflict with the Socialist Labor Party and pulled by the restoration of her relationship with her father, Florence Kelley Wischnewetzky returned in 1888 to concerns that grew out of her Cornell thesis and her immersion in European socialism—the state's responsibility for the welfare of working women and children. More than any other topics, these invited the use of her specialized knowledge and held out the hope of translating that knowledge into power capable of affecting the lives of working people.

Her plan began with children. "I am working up the subject of Child Labor (and Compulsory Education) using statistics of State Bureaus, State Board of Education reports, census, Factory Inspectors' reports, etc.," she wrote Engels in March. First she expected to compile a book using "American official data" and later "a second volume based on European official data for comparison."[1] Although these books were never completed, between 1889 and 1891 her studies gave her a scholar's command of the topic.

Her first political success occurred with working women rather than with children, in Philadelphia rather than in New York. William Kelley's failing health brought her to the Elms for extended visits. On these occasions, she brought Ko, Margaret, and John with her and stayed long enough to get involved in fruitful work. Caroline and William doubtlessly enjoyed the opportunity to see their grandchildren, and their child tending gave Florence time to explore opportunities for usefulness in Philadelphia that often eluded her in New York.

In Philadelphia she found an able colleague in Leonora Barry, a former schoolteacher and factory hand who in 1886 had been appointed "general investigator" and national head of the women's division of the Knights of Labor. One of Barry's chief responsibilities as general investigator was to serve as a voluntary inspector of factories employing women. In that capacity she became increasingly aware that the worst conditions prevailed where she was denied entrance, that the Knights' voluntary efforts were insufficient, and that stricter state-enforced factory laws should be passed. With the precipitous decline in union membership, Barry came to rely even more strongly on factory legislation as a strategy for improving the lives of working women. Her 1888 annual report emphasized the youth and lack of education among women workers and the increasing numbers of immigrant women and children wage earners. Mechanizations, speedups, and starvation wages deprived women of the benefits of skilled work, intensified competition among them, and made union organizing extremely difficult.

In July 1888, in a measure designed to save money, Terence Powderly, head of the Knights, asked Barry to retire and disband the women's committee, which she did the next year. Barry expressed the ambivalence of working-class attitudes toward women's wage earning in her 1889 final annual report. First she paid homage to the patriarchal values that pervaded working-class culture: "I wish it was not necessary for women to learn any trade but that of domestic duties, as I believe it was intended that man should be the breadwinner." But, in a tribute to the talents of the women she had worked with in the Knights, she added that since present conditions made it impossible for men to be the sole breadwinners in their families, she "believe[d] that women should have every opportunity to become proficient in whatever vocation they choose or find themselves best fitted for." Nevertheless, she decried the tendency for women "who have steady employment, fairly good wages, and comfortable homes" to do nothing "to assist their less fortunate co-workers" because they hope "that in the near future marriage will lift them out of the industrial life to the quiet and comfort of a home."[2]

Kelley worked with Barry during the brief interval between her resignation from the Knights and Barry's marriage in 1890. The strength of the Knights was fading, carrying with it the high hopes of organizing women that the Knights had raised in 1886, when they had endorsed woman suffrage. Of 192 local assemblies consisting entirely of women affiliated with the Knights in 1886, by the end of 1889 only 15 women's assemblies remained, 2 in Philadelphia. Barry and Kelley temporarily joined forces with a combination of elite and working women to found the Philadelphia Working Women's Society, whose object was "to help women to form organizations for self-protection, enlightenment, mutual aid and benefit and for obtaining and enforcing legislation in the interests of the working class." Kelley was elected president. A forerunner of the Women's Trade Union League (established in New York in 1903) and very similar to the Women's Protective and Provident Committee founded in England in 1875, which evolved into the Women's Trade Union League in England, the society brought together "all those devoted to the cause of organization among wages-earning women, adopting a label, collecting statistics, publishing facts, furnishing information and advice." From its inception, the group focused on the enforcement of factory laws.[3]

Under the umbrella of the Philadelphia Working Women's Society, Barry drew on her contacts among working women and Kelley on hers among middle-class women in the Century Club. The Knights' chief political activist said that Kelley and the Working Women's Society were chiefly responsible for the passage of a pathbreaking bill in 1889 that not only regulated the employment of women and children but also required the state of Pennsylvania to hire two women factory inspectors—the first women to be employed in that capacity in the United States. The scale of this success is best seen in comparisons with other industrializing nations: no woman factory inspector had yet been appointed in Great Britain or in Germany, where factory inspection began.[4]

This success inspired even more remarkable achievements in New York. In July 1889 Kelley and Ida Van Etten, a socialist, incorporated the Working Women's Society of the City of New York, a spin-off of a larger group founded in 1886, the New York Working Women's Society. The *Advocate* reported that the goals of the new society were to "promote organization among women engaged in industrial pursuits, and to furnish indemnity to the members of said society, by payments of money collected by way of dues, against loss occasioned by sickness or lack of employment, and also in general to labor for improvement in the condition of all working women." Members of the society conducted a stunningly successful campaign for the hiring of women factory inspectors. As Kelley later wrote, "a small group of women from both the wealthy and influential class and the working class, . . . circulated petitions, composed resolutions." In 1889 and again in 1890 they brought "their proposal concerning the naming of women factory inspectorships to the legislature, philanthropic groups and unions." Responding to this pressure, in 1890 the New York legislature created eight new positions for women factory inspectors. Known as the Van Etten bill, it received the support of organized labor. In 1891 women in Massachusetts built on this achievement to became the third state to employ women factory inspectors.[5]

The reasoning behind the appointment of women factory inspectors was later articulated by Miss Margaret Finn, one of the first hired in New York. She said the appointment of women inspectors "did not seem unreasonable" in view of the great need for additional inspectors and "the large numbers of women and children employed in factories." The women's case "did not rest on the abstract justice of such representation of their sex." Rather, "it was confidently believed by the women, that women inspectors could accomplish certain ends that the male inspectors could not hope to accomplish." Women factory workers "would confide to women inspectors grievances relating to matters of propriety, that they would not tell to inspectors who are men." Thus women inspectors "would be able to regulate matters, that otherwise women employees would be obliged to suffer in silence." Finn thought the bill garnered "many and powerful friends" in Albany because this gender-specific argument was "urged in assemblies of women and women's clubs." Women of "social prominence" lobbied in the state capitol with working women "in season and out of season" until their "public presence was effectual." In the process, reform Governor Hill showed himself "generously disposed toward women as part of the body politic." [6]

Writing later about this campaign, Kelley emphasized the autonomy of the women's actions. "Their proposal to add women as officials in the office for factory inspection was made for humanitarian reasons: in no way did it belong to the goals of the general workers' movement, although it found support among the unions." Perhaps her attitude reflected the cold shoulder women seemed to be receiving from both the declining Knights and the emerging AFL. Certainly it revealed the surge of power that flowed through women's class-bridging organizations when they connected economic issues about women and children with the apparatus of the state.[7]

Who were these women of "social prominence," these "assemblies of women" who lobbied for women factory inspectors in the late 1880s and early 1890s? What had changed in women's activism and in civil society during Kelley's five-year foray into European socialism? New forms of knowledge and new methods for turning knowledge into power became visible in women's middle-class public culture in the 1880s. A new genre of writing drew readers into the personal testimonies of women victimized by poverty. And a new consumer consciousness sought to link knowledge about the way goods were produced to strategies designed to improve working conditions.

Helen Campbell was one of the many voices of the new era of reform struggling to be born in the 1880s. In an 1887 letter to Engels, Florence Kelley referred to "my friend Helen Campbell," saying she was "good and warm-hearted and gets at everything from the side of strongly human feeling." Her understanding of poverty was typically American, Kelley thought, since it came from "personal contact" rather than theoretical understanding. When Campbell traveled to Europe to gather material for a new book in 1889, she carried a card from Kelley to introduce her to Engels. The daughter of a New York attorney, Campbell was twenty years older than Kelley. After her marriage to a physician in 1861, she supported herself as a successful writer of children's fiction and books on household management while her husband served as a military surgeon. In the early 1870s she obtained a divorce and assumed her mother's maiden name. A decade later she began writing about poverty's blighting effect on the human spirit. Her 1887 book *Prisoners of Poverty: Women Wage-Workers, Their Trades and Their Lives*, helped focus "the social question" on working women. She joined the board of directors of the New York City Consumers' League when it was founded in 1891. That year the American Economic Association awarded a prize to her pathbreaking monograph "Women Wage-Earners," an expanded version of which was published with an introduction by Richard Ely in 1893.[8]

Campbell's writings exemplified the burgeoning literature that brought the voices of women wage earners to a middle-class audience. They also showed how trends in social science could dramatize the need for social action. Her 1882 book *The Problem of the Poor* first appeared serially in popular magazines. Among the earliest muckraking, it described her work at a city mission on New York's waterfront, where she encountered working women whose wages were too low to sustain a decent livelihood. She elaborated on this theme in *Prisoners of Poverty*. Vivid and sensationalist, Campbell's writings nevertheless embodied the new methods of social science, especially "social economy," drawing as they did on official reports, such as that of the New York Bureau of Statistics of Labor, and on the author's "minutest personal research into the conditions described." With the detail and empathy of fiction, *Prisoners of Poverty* focused on specific persons who worked in the city's needle trades or department stores but also stressed "that back of every individual case of wrong and oppression lies a deeper wrong and more systematized oppression."[9]

It is easy to imagine Florence Kelley responding warmly to Campbell's 1886 series in the *Tribune*, especially the first-person account of a bitter woman garment worker who worked at home: "I've worked eleven years. I've tried five trades with my needle and machine. My shortest day has been fourteen hours, for I had the children and they had to be fed. . . . It isn't work that I've any trouble in getting. It's wages." She described the steady decline in wages that accompanied the sharp rise in immigration in the 1880s. "Five years ago I could earn $1.50 a day, and we were comfortable. Then it began to go down, — $1.25, then $1.00. There it stopped awhile, and I got used to that, and could even get some remains of comfort out of it. I had to plan to the last half cent. We went cold often, but we were never hungry. But then it fell again, — to ninety cents, to eighty-five. For a year the best that I can do I have earned not over eighty cents a day, — sometimes only seventy-five." This woman was a candidate for violent action. "There's nothing left but men that live to grind the face of the poor; that chuckle when they find a new way of making a cent or two more a week out of starving women and children," she said. "I tell you I'm ready for murder when I think of these men. If there's no justice above, it isn't quite dead below." She warned that "if men with money will not heed, the men and the women without money will rise some day. How? I don't know. We've no time to plan, and we're too tired to think, but it's coming somehow." She was "not ashamed to say I'll join in if I live to see it come. It's a sea of tears that these men sail on. It's our life-blood they drink and our flesh that they eat. God help them if the storm comes, for there'll be no help in man." [10]

In response to such indictments, Campbell urged middle-class women to ask themselves probing personal questions: "What is the source of the income which gives me ease? Is it possible for me to reconstruct my own life in such fashion that it shall mean more direct and personal relation to the worker? How can I bring more simplicity, less conventionality, more truth and right living into home and every relation of life?" Encouraging readers to support the notion that all workers should earn enough "to make sharp want or eating care and perplexity impossible," her analysis traced such suffering to the business practices of the needle trades in which well-intentioned employers were forced either to give up business or adopt the hard-hearted practices of their competitors. [11]

Helen Campbell's popular writings represented traditions of social reform quite different from those of Engels, but nevertheless they expressed many of the same ideas: the inevitability of conflict between working people and their exploiters within the current construction of their social and economic relationships; ruthless and unregulated competition as the source of much human misery; and the need for middle-class people to understand their obligation to foster change.

Helen Campbell's impact on her contemporaries is hard to measure. More obvious was the effect of consumers' leagues that rewarded manufacturers who produced goods under safe and nonexploitative conditions. They too cast "the social question" in terms of working women. New York's equivalent to the New Century Working Women's Guild helped lay the foundation for the nascent consumers' movement. Partly through the work of Grace Dodge, a middle-class woman who encountered wage-earning women in her Sunday School classes, "Working Girls' Societies" blossomed in the early 1880s in New York City into a social movement that focused on wage earners' needs and desires for education. [12] Valuable as this educational work was, however, it did not bear directly on working conditions, it reproduced traditional power hierarchies between elite patrons and working-class petitioners, and it did not develop a moral critique of the economic marketplace.

More innovatively, a fresh understanding of the relationship between middle-class women consumers and working-class women producers began to evolve in 1886. That year, when Kelley wrote from Heidelberg to urge suffragists to aid women strikers, the New York Working Women's Society began to explore new strategies to improve their working conditions. One wage earner penned a novel appeal to middle-class women in *John Swinton's Paper:* "Ye maids and matrons of high station, living amid all the luxury that wealth can bestow, who tread on velvet or recline on satin, whose soft eyes rest on costly paintings and peachblow vases, whose mirrors reflect silks and laces given you by adoring husbands or fathers, do you realize that the money that bought them comes not out of the overflowing coffers of these same husbands and fathers, but out of the life of their employés? Do you realize that your houses are adorned at the expense of human souls?" "Help us, sisters!" this letter writer urged, asking women to "speak to your husbands and fathers." More practically, the letter concluded: "When you see the almost resistless advertisement of our great retail houses, with 'special sales at unheard of reductions,' think that the reduction does not affect the dealer or the manufacturer, but the women who stitch, stitch, stitch, all the weary day at reduced wages. Remember 'Special Sale' means starvation and Boycott the bargain counter." [13]

While the idea of influencing husbands and fathers posed too great a challenge to attract much support from middle-class women, consumer boycotts had greater possibilities for cross-class cooperation. As part of a larger expression of popular sentiment against sweatshop labor, in October 1888 the Working Women's Society organized a face-to-face meeting with the middle-class women who bought the goods they produced. About fifty middle-class women attended, almost certainly including Florence Kelley Wischnewetzky. [14]

In contrast to Boston, where the antisweatshop movement in 1891 succeeded in obtaining the passage of a state law prohibiting the production of goods by nonfamily groups in tenements, New York's antisweating movement was small, chastened by the 1885 appeals court annulment of a law prohibiting the production of cigars in tenements. Nevertheless, groups of working women began a new initiative in 1888. Leonora O'Reilly, a shirtmaker who later became a leader in the New York Women's Trade Union League, called upon Josephine Shaw Lowell, New York's most politically powerful woman, to help recruit middle-class attendance. Reporting on the meeting, the *New York Times* said that Ida Van Etten "made an eloquent appeal for help and sympathy from the wealthy and educated women of New-York for their toiling and down-trodden sisters" and described the work of the society. Two feather workers, a boxmaker, and Leonora O'Reilly gave the group "a clear idea of their life and labors." At the conclusion of the meeting, Reverend James Otis Huntington, Episcopalian founder of the Church Association for the Advancement of the Interests of Labor in 1877, exhorted the women "to feel it their personal duty to go on doing whatever and as much as they could to correct the social evil that permits their unfortunate sisters to be so frightfully overworked and badly paid." In response, some members of the audience "left their names and addresses, and expressed a willingness to answer any call upon them for the working girls' cause." [15]

Following up on this meeting, the consumers' league of New York became a formal organization two years later, after Alice Woodbridge, a department store clerk, asked Josephine Shaw Lowell's advice about the dissemination of a report that she and others had made of department store work. Because the report emphasized the impact of the work on their health, Lowell showed it to Dr. Mary Putnam Jacobi. Together they organized another public meeting of the Working Women's Society, which in turn called a mass meeting at Chickering Hall "under the auspices of many leading clergymen of various denominations and many prominent men and women."[16]

Woodbridge's charismatic presentation on that occasion was remembered many years later as the inspiration for the consumers' league movement. Her remarks emphasized the conflict between profits and morality. "She told them of the wearily long hours of work, of the lack of compensation for work done after the working day was supposed to be over; she described the unsanitary surroundings; she touched upon the pitifully young children who were sometimes employed at tasks far beyond their physical strength; she related how fidelity and length of service often met only the reward of dismissal; she told of the physical collapse of many girls after two years of steady work, because of the long hours of standing." In response, the "large, fashionable" audience passed resolutions calling on the Board of Health to remedy the bad sanitary conditions and on the legislature to limit the hours of saleswomen. The meeting resolved "that a committee be appointed to assist the Working Women's Society in making a list which shall keep shoppers informed of such shops as deal justly with their employees." In this way they hoped to "bring public opinion and public action to bear in favor of just employers, and also in favor of such employers as desire to be just, but are prevented by the stress of competition, from following their own sense of duty."[17]

As individuals middle-class women might be relatively cloistered, but collectively and in public they formed an imposing group and acquired a new and rewarding capacity to affect the course of public events. In the name of "their personal duty," they enlarged the boundaries of their own lives at the same time that they expanded the public space available to women. Well-established members of the middle class, they distinguished themselves from new entrants to that class and from lower-middle-class consumers by their willingness to pay more for well-made goods. Moreover, their goal of extending to wage earners some of the protections that they themselves enjoyed against the contingencies and perils of the marketplace was a satisfying way of projecting their own domestic security onto the larger society.[18]

The committee decided to form an association similar to one begun in London a few months earlier wherein consumers compiled a register similar to the list of fair houses published by trade unions. Such a register required systematic inquiry and constant updating, but it provided the means of "enlisting the sympathy and interest of the shopping public." In January 1891 the New York City Consumers' League was officially formed with Josephine Shaw Lowell as president and an exclusively female board of advisers and vice presidents. Eight years later several local consumer leagues united to form a National Consumers' League and hired Florence Kelley as general secretary, a post she held until her death in 1932.[19]

The consumers' league represented the newest phase in a long tradition wherein American social policy was initiated more by activists in voluntary associations than by legislators, civil servants, or organized labor. No one exemplified the new opportunities for middle-class women within that tradition better than Josephine Shaw Lowell. Her metamorphosis in the 1880s typified the growth of class-bridging sympathies within women's public culture and clarifies the motivation behind Florence Kelley's continued appeals to that culture. Fifteen years older than Florence Kelley, Josephine Shaw had not attended college. Daughter of a Boston abolitionist merchant, Josephine at the age of thirteen began to read widely in the library of George William Curtis, her politically powerful brother-in-law and mentor, who was a friend of William D. Kelley.[20] During the Civil War she worked with the New York Central Association of Relief, and after losing her well-born husband and her brother to heroic battlefield deaths, she became the

Josephine Shaw Lowell, 1880. Courtesy of Women's Rights Collection, Schlesinger Library, Radcliffe College.

epitome of patriotic widowhood. In 1876 she was the first woman appointed to the New York State Board of Charities. In 1881 her report on private charities in New York City led to the formation of the New York Charity Organization Society.

By the force of her personality and through extensive writings on public charities, Lowell set a new style in women's activism in the mid-1880s. Adopting rational and secular values more in keeping with Darwinian beliefs than the compassionate and religious values that had characterized women's participation in the antislavery movement, her views strongly resembled those of the men with whom she shared public responsibilities. A woman of Florence Kelley's sensibilities would have found almost all her ideas offensive. For example, as one of the most forceful advocates of "scientific charity," she drew a sharp distinction between public relief and old-fashioned charity, explaining in 1888, "Public relief must of necessity lack one of the requisites of charity, for the givers of it do not wish well to those who receive it." [21]

Like many women in elite, politically active families, Lowell took a vigorous interest in the mugwump movement that obtained the passage of the national Civil Service Act in 1883. After the failure of that act to have its desired effect, she wrote a Democratic friend in 1886 that she wished that all "decent people would come out of your disreputable party, as we have come out of our disreputable party, and let us all join to make a decent one of our own!" Lowell and other people "of intelligence and public spirit" hoped to reclaim the helm of government from political machines by requiring competitive examinations for all applicants for certain government positions. They imitated the English example where an educated elite—mainly Oxford and Cambridge University graduates—minimized the impact of broadened suffrage after 1867 by controlling government through civil service examinations biased in their favor. But this model of recapturing government through the rule of experts applied poorly to the United States, where access to higher education was much more democratic and the system of party patronage more entrenched. The mugwump movement failed utterly to end the abuse of public office that flourished during the Grant, Hayes, and Garfield administrations. The movement's first comedown occurred in the 1870s with the Port of New York. Highlighting the fiscal weakness of the national government, this port accounted for over 60 percent of the entire revenue of the federal government as late as 1918, making it the heart of the beast of political patronage and corruption. Despite the reformers' efforts, the port remained in the hands of "boodlers." [22]

This and other failures of civil service reform created grave problems for both Josephine Lowell's and Florence Kelley's visions of an enlightened state. Yet the limited effectiveness of civil service reform in the United States also created opportunities for groups of American women to take on tasks that in England fell to male civil servants.

"A Graduate" of the civil service examination for the New York police. *Harper's Weekly*,
January 16, 1886. Courtesy of Library of Congress.

And it placed middle-class women's organizations on the cutting edge of enlightened politics, since they viewed themselves and were viewed by others as uncorrupted political outsiders. For middle-class and elite male reformers, the failure of civil service reform had the consequence of drawing their energies into universities. In the United States, universities became the repository of the sociological and political expertise that in England flowed directly into government service.[23]

Despite Lowell's close involvement in male politics, she did not abandon women's public culture or its well-developed tradition of speaking for the welfare of women and children. She humorously expressed her consciousness of women's activism in a letter to her sister-in-law in 1881, which described a recent meeting attended by the "clergy," the "laity," and "the femality." Backed by the "femality," Lowell's investigations of the plight of women in state institutions led in 1885 to the establishment of the nation's first asylum for "feeble-minded" women and in 1886 to the creation of a state House of Refuge for Women that emphasized rehabilitation rather than punishment for women lawbreakers. Two years later she successfully campaigned for the placement of matrons in all New York police stations.[24]

In 1889 Lowell abruptly shifted her political allegiances. Possibly as a result of her contact with the Working Women's Society, she resigned from the State Board of Charities and devoted her energies henceforth to the working poor. "Five hundred thousand wage earners in this city, 200,000 of them women and 75,000 of those working under dreadful conditions or for starvation wages" seemed to her more important than the 25,000 dependents of the city's charities. She also altered her view of the causes of poverty. "If the working people had all they ought to have, we should not have the paupers and criminals," she wrote her widowed sister-in-law.[25]

This shift in Lowell's attitudes toward the poor symbolized the growing sophistication of many middle-class women in their approach to philanthropy as they became aware of the futility of charity and redirected their aim at the causes of poverty. The writings of Helen Campbell were one expression of that sophistication; the creation of the New York City Consumers' League was another.

Florence Kelley tried to channel this momentum in a long and comprehensive article "Our Toiling Children," published in 1889 in pamphlet form by the Woman's Temperance Publication Association in Chicago. This pamphlet carried her knowledge about child labor and her moral call to arms into the largest organization of women in American history. Translated and published in Karl Kautsky's *Die neue Zeit*, it also kept her reputation alive within the leadership of German Social Democracy.[26]

By 1890 the Woman's Christian Temperance Union embraced about three hundred and fifty thousand dues-paying members. Since 1878 the union had energetically campaigned to enfranchise women on school matters, and as most child labor laws took the form of compulsory schooling statutes, the WCTU was potentially the most powerful voice opposing child labor. Kelley gave them her best oratory, mixing technical policy points with words of moral outrage about the fate of individuals. "The child slave's life is cheap in Free America," she insisted. Reports from twenty-four states showed that most legislators tried "to appease the workers without depriving the employers of their supply of child slaves." The result, she said, "is a shameful collection of laws either incapable of enforcement or provided with every device for evasion." For example, in New Jersey and elsewhere "the factory inspector must prove an infringement of the law to be willful before the employer can be punished." A child recently killed in an industrial accident there "was as clearly murdered as any one who ever perished, [but] the employer, under the law of the state, cannot be punished beyond a fine of fifty dollars."[27]

Through their local organizations women could do much to change these unscrupulous conditions. Referring to the new consumer activism in New York, Kelley recommended that "the women of the nation, who are the buyers of the nation, unite with the wage-earners to control the conditions under which the things they purchase are produced." Women should "abstain from the purchase of goods in the manufacture of which child labor is employed" and, wherever they have the school vote, "use it for securing

more schools and better ones, and for the enforcement of the compulsory school laws."
Even where women had no vote, she said, "they can do as the Working Woman's Society
in New York has done with great success, organize the working women in Trades Associations, and petition the Legislature for the care of the children, by the appointment of
women inspectors." A profound social transition was under way, she wrote, "from the
control of production by irresponsible monopolists, to the order of social production,
conducted through the servants of the people, by the people, for the people." The violence or peacefulness of that change "will depend on the insight of the workers and the
women of the nation." Interestingly, Kelley did not urge women to act independently of
labor. Instead, she praised women who acted jointly with workingmen, as in the Woman's
Alliance of Illinois and Mrs. Leonora Barry of the Knights of Labor.[28]

Ultimately, Kelley's analysis held that "the capitalist system of production" and work
done "exclusively for exchange and profit" were responsible for child labor. Her class
analysis could not be more explicit. "Not until organized labor . . . wrests the means of
production from the service of the exploiting minority to the service of the now exploited
majority," she said, "need we look for any radical change in the conditions of life of the
child-workers of our tenement house population."[29] Her analysis of the causes of and
solutions for child labor had significantly widened since she had written on the topic in
1882. Then she had linked changing attitudes toward child labor with women's growing
influence in government. Now child labor served as a lever not only for women's activism
but for more general social transformation; it became a vehicle for addressing endemic
class injustice. Like other middle-class women, she was growing more knowledgeable
and more effective in her assault on unregulated capitalism.

Yet Kelley's caution about women's independent action immobilized her institutionally.
That caution arose from her Engelsian understanding of the importance of working-
class leadership in movements to improve working-class life, but it also flowed from her
experience with middle-class women. Though crucially important allies, middle-class
women could not be trusted as the chief architects of social reform. When she herself
was in charge, as was the case with the passage of women factory inspector legislation in
New York, women did fine on their own, but she could not count on other middle-class
women to do the right thing without her guidance or that of the labor movement. Their
views embraced too wide a political spectrum.

For example, in a symposium on child labor published in 1890 in the nation's newest
reform periodical, *The Arena*, Kelley advocated the most radical solutions, urging sweeping legislative remedies to prohibit the employment of boys and girls under eighteen
years of age. This plan required utopian resources: "abundant school accommodation; an

adequate teaching corps; truant officers and factory inspectors, both men and women, with sufficient salaries and travelling expenses, and finally good clothing, and books for such children as need them." [30] She did not say how these resources might be mobilized, but clearly she envisioned an activist state.

By contrast, her friend Helen Campbell participated in the symposium by rather vaguely urging readers to "reach one step farther" than the current campaign by the Children's Aid Society to rescue children from the slums "and rescue them with no less eagerness and determination from the factory." Even less helpfully, Jane Croly (writing under the pen name "Jeannie June"), cofounder in 1890 of the General Federation of Women's Clubs, said it was "a sad thing for the young child to be turned into the workshop instead of the school, but the workshop is better than the street." Blaming parents as the source of child labor, she evinced sharp hostility to working-class realities when she concluded: "The remnants of the primitive idea that men own women and children still linger in the minds of brutal and ignorant individuals, and summary methods are needed to dispel this idea." [31]

Here and there, the gulf between classes, if not between races, was bridged by shared goals that united producers and consumers, but the bridge was fragile. For all the optimism she had expressed in Germany about the potential for class-bridging action among American women, Florence Kelley grew steadily more pessimistic as she confronted the realities of American political life.

She brooded. In a short but hard-hitting 1890 essay, "Evils of Child Labor," she attacked the inadequacy of official efforts in New York City. "When 20,000 children actually applying for admission were turned away from the public schools last year, why should the sweeper's child apply?" Unlike "every city of Europe, outside of Russia," the New York School Board maintained "no registration of children," nor did it make a school census "to show where the children of compulsory school age may be found." The state had not found a way to inspire moral choices. Parents could not be blamed for evading the law and relying on the labor of their children, she said, particularly when "men and women are daily made to feel that the law is framed for their especial torment, and never for the protection of themselves or their belongings." Meanwhile, children's lives deteriorated spiritually as well as physically with "the criminal neglect of all that is sacred to the childhood of the working class." Yet Kelley suggested no long-term remedies, calling only for the continuance of "the Schools Conference," a body composed of delegates of labor organizations and school officials. [32]

Her single publication in 1891, "A Decade of Retrogression," might have been written upon her arrival in New York five years earlier, for it offered no solutions to social problems beyond those proposed by Marx and Engels. New Year's Eve, 1889, the last night of the decade, symbolized how poorly the nation functioned. It "found the city buried in stygian gloom, because the duty of lighting its streets is still a matter of private profit." Why? Because "the insolent corporation which fattens upon this franchise surrendered the privilege of murdering its linemen unpunished only when its poles were cut and its wires torn down." Such things would not happen "if we were doing the nation's work in an orderly manner," she lamented, but she did not say how her vision of "the nation's work" might be implemented.[33] No outlet seemed available for her deep sense of social obligation. Far from alone in her desire for systemic social change, she came into contact with others who were also trying to use new forms of knowledge and power to confront the nation's problems. Yet like the workingwomen's associations, these did not attract her as a spiritual home.

She kept a discreet distance from the most flamboyant social movement of the 1880s, Bellamy Nationalism. Inspired by the stupendous popularity of Edward Bellamy's 1888 utopian novel *Looking Backward, 2000–1887*, this briefly blossoming movement, like the enthusiastic response to Henry George's single-tax plan advanced in *Progress and Poverty* ten years earlier, showed that popular hopes for fundamental changes in the nation's social, political, and economic structures far outreached popular strategies for their realization. Envisioning a future society that nationalized the functions of production and distribution, the novel appealed to working-class as well as middle-class hopes, women as well as men. By 1891 over 160 Nationalist clubs had been formed throughout the United States, some of which consisted entirely of women. The movement attracted five thousand members in Boston, both middle class and working class, and a large following in New York.[34]

Unabashedly authoritarian in its vision and lacking any suggestions for steps that might be taken to improve present conditions, *Looking Backward* nevertheless provided its readers with a thoroughgoing critique of the inadequacies of laissez-faire social and economic thought. As the novel's protagonist had it explained to him, "Who is capable of self support? . . . There is no such thing in a civilized society as self-support. . . . Every man, however solitary may seem his occupation, is a member of a vast industrial partnership . . . . The necessity of mutual dependence should imply the duty and guarantee of mutual support; and that it did not in your day constitutes the essential cruelty and unreason of your system."[35]

All members of Bellamy's utopia received the same pay, no matter what their work or whether they worked. Women, like men, were "members of the industrial army" that produced and distributed the society's resources, leaving it "only when maternal duties claim[ed] them." Since the state provided enlightened child care and managed domestic work, women could return to work, serving "industrially some five or ten or fifteen years." Women did not perform the same work as men, however, "being inferior in strength and further disqualified industrially in special ways. . . . Under no circumstances is a woman permitted to follow any employment not perfectly adapted, both as to kind and degree of labor, to her sex." [36] Yet in spite of their physical and occupational differences from men, women had the same political and social rights. Most importantly, perhaps, as in Bebel's vision of the future in *Women Under Socialism,* women were not economically dependent on their husbands, and they married for love rather than for economic security.

Kelley's contact with Bellamy Nationalism was brief but timely. In *Workmen's Advocate* in March 1890, she criticized a *Nationalist* article that had branded New York State's new Factory Inspection Department "a genuine foot print of capitalism." Maintaining that such inspections should not be confused with Bellamy Nationalism or socialism, which would render such remedies unnecessary, she nevertheless insisted that "the existence of labor legislation and functionaries appointed for its enforcement indicates that the outrages of capital upon labor have already produced a revolt of labor, powerful enough to extort from reluctant law-givers certain palliative measures." For her, factory inspectors mattered. "The factory inspector of to-day, like the militiaman, is the child of the struggle of labor against capital. The factory inspector enforces the law for the worker against the capitalist. The militiaman shoots down the worker by command of the capitalist. It is characteristic of the present status of the forces engaged on each side, that there are hundreds of thousands of militia and less than fifty factory inspectors in the United States today." Like everything else "conceded to the workers under capitalism," the factory inspectorship "bears the trail of the serpent," she said, for the office was sometimes conferred as a bribe "to silence a too efficient labor agitator," or as a prize for a "party heeler," as was then "notoriously the case in New York State," or as a lever "for compelling employers to subscribe to campaign funds on condition of being unmolested," or a mere device for personal extortion for the individual inspector. Nevertheless, she encouraged Nationalists to "do all that lies in our power to obtain more straight labor legislation and better inspectors, both men and women, to enforce it," since (speaking in Bellamyesque terms) "their utility lies in their contributing, with the shortening of hours, the growth of organization and many other factors, to keep the adult in fighting trim." Factory inspectors also helped "check the devastation of childhood, which Capitalism unbridled is working upon the rising generation." [37]

Kelley devoted more energy to the emerging social settlement movement, but it too failed to lift her depression, perhaps because she identified that movement with Vida Scudder. Seeking to realize in action the ideals of Christian socialism, the settlement movement took hold in New York in 1889 when faculty and students affiliated with women's colleges imitated the English example of Toynbee Hall in East London and established a home for upper- and middle-class women in a poor neighborhood on New York's Lower East Side. The University Settlement on Rivington Street was an immediate success, receiving more than eighty applications for residence during its first year, 1890–91.[38]

Highlighting the value she placed on knowledge as a source of social change, that spring Florence Kelley Wischnewetzky ventured into the Lower East Side three times a week to lecture on economics to University Settlement residents. Her trips had the advantage of drawing her into immigrant neighborhoods, but she was not impressed with her middle-class audience. "It speaks ill for the scholarly atmosphere of several of our leading girls' colleges," she wrote Richard Ely, "that the 'settlers' are not only utterly blank concerning economics but have no habit of reading!" A month of "persistent sarcasms" during which she "jeered and scoffed at them" finally induced the young women to read the daily paper, to collect "$30.00 for the purchase of the nucleus of a library of economics," and to rearrange their "plan of daily work to include one hour of systematic reading." What must be the habits of mind "among the less earnest college girls," she wondered, since these were "not only brighter than the average of college graduates but earnest enough in their desire to help solve the social question to go and live in Rivington St. and work all the time among the denizens thereof!"[39]

Another group that failed to measure up to Kelley's standards were those who supposedly combined knowledge and power—state bureau of labor statistics officials. Testing her skills as a social analyst, she prepared a thorough critique of state reports on child labor for the Seventh Annual Convention of Commissioners of State Bureaus of Labor Statistics at Hartford, Connecticut, in June 1889. Although at the last minute she was unable to attend, her paper was read by the convention secretary. In this way she came to the attention of Carroll D. Wright, who as head of the Massachusetts Bureau of Labor Statistics between 1873 and 1884 almost single-handedly created the field of labor statistics in the United States and now as U.S. Commissioner of Labor Statistics led the way in collecting national statistics on wages, hours, and working conditions.[40]

Beginning with Massachusetts in 1869, organized labor successfully lobbied for state bureaus of labor statistics to offset the power of capital in state legislatures. Responding to labor insurgency between 1877 and 1886, twelve other states established similar bureaus. Such agencies sought to use statistics to disprove stereotypes about how economic realities reflected "the laws of nature," expose the profit motives and exploitative practices of capital, and establish a basis for favorable state intervention in capital-labor relations.[41] The problem with this plan was that although state legislatures—especially those with Democratic majorities—might be prolabor, they were also usually hostile to the extension of state authority. For example, the Pennsylvania State Board of Health was unsuccessful in its efforts in 1886 to appoint health officers as registrars of births, deaths, and diseases, concluding in its annual report that the legislature "evidently considered the public sentiment was not yet sufficiently advanced to sustain it in the creation of so large a number of salaried officers for an object which to many would appear purely theoretical." In this context of limited government, labor statistics fared slightly better than birth and death registration, but some regions remained happily backward in both respects. Nevertheless, the relative priority given to labor statistics demonstrated the urgency of the labor question in the United States and the emergence of positive government around it. In 1884, when Carroll D. Wright became the head of the newly created United States Bureau of Labor Statistics, similar labor agencies had not yet been created in Europe or England.[42]

Initially, state bureaus worked closely with organized labor, addressing such vital issues as company profit margins and fair wages for adult workers. But when these topics threatened to undercut the bureaus' tentative support in state legislatures, many of them changed their focus to child labor—a genuine grievance of organized labor but a less controversial target for bureau activism.[43]

Labor unions opposed child labor because child workers competed unfairly with adults, lowering wages and increasing hours, and because children were less easily unionized. The issue stood high on labor's legislative priorities, but it also typified the difficulty labor had in implementing political goals. Craft workers, such as shoemakers, eliminated child labor from their midst by threatening to strike if children were employed in their shops, but this option was not available to workers in less-organized trades, especially those employing large numbers of young women. Child labor thus tended to concentrate in those trades, requiring the coercive power of the state to dislodge it. Yet this coercion proved ineffective. Again and again, statutes passed to regulate child labor in New York were found of little value in practice because they could not be adequately enforced. Meanwhile, labor papers denounced the state's cotton mills for "grinding gold out of small human bones."[44]

In 1883–84, at the request of the Workingmen's Assembly, the newly founded New York Bureau of Labor Statistics had conducted an official inquiry into the obstacles blocking effective enforcement of child labor laws. First, the study concluded, the bureau's enforcement efforts were poorly funded and understaffed. The state's two inspectors were expected to investigate more than forty thousand manufacturing establishments; they found only 261 children in the 151 factories they visited—a lower proportion than had been identified by the 1880 federal census, where methods were anything but thorough. Second, working-class opinion was divided on the issue. When (as was often the case) male wage earners brought home less than the family needed to live on, most working-class families preferred to send children rather than mothers out to work. Except in those families lacking an adult male wage earner, mothers' domestic services and their income from boarders or industrial homework were considered more valuable to the family than what they could earn outside the home; fewer than 10 percent of wage-earning women were married. Children filled the gap, and families resented interference with that traditional practice, requiring the enforcers of child labor laws to challenge the customs of their own constituencies. Third, while child labor was an important priority among trade unionists, it was only one of many, usually trailing behind more pressing issues such as the eight-hour day and fair wages, and it threatened to absorb a disproportionate share of the bureaus' meager resources. Therefore, while state bureaus of labor statistics identified child labor as a significant focus of their activities, by the late 1880s their efforts to combat the problem had stalled.[45]

Around this time, middle-class reformers began to recognize that machine technology and its relentless division of labor had robbed work of its redemptive qualities—especially for children. While puritan views of children maintained that they needed discipline and external authority to overcome their inherently sinful natures, romantic notions after 1830 held that children needed loving nurture and education to develop their natural purity and God-given talents. Antebellum restrictions on working children were led primarily by educators, such as Horace Mann, whose attitudes reflected this altered view of children. In the 1880s the writings of G. Stanley Hall, one of the founders of the discipline of psychology, gave these views the imprimatur of modern science. Buttressing these changes in values, the shift in the location of children's work from the family farm to the urban factory and from parental to overseer's supervision heightened the degree to which children's factory labor became a positive evil rather than a positive good.

Typical of the new attitude among Kelley's contemporaries was that of Jacob Riis in *The Children of the Poor* (1892). Riis insisted that "the real reform of poverty and ignorance must begin with the children" and noted: "The trouble is not so much that the children have to work early as with the sort of work they have to do. It is, all of it, of a kind that leaves them, grown to manhood and womanhood, just where it found them, knowing no more, and therefore less, than when they began, and with the years that should have prepared them for life's work gone in hopeless and profitless drudgery." Lester Frank Ward stated the new attitude toward labor (for adults as well as children) most cogently, writing in 1886: "Though it may sound paradoxical, it is in leisure that the grandest work has always been performed, while from toil no great progressive consequences have ever flowed." Leisure engenders thought, "which toil never does," he said, and thought fostered the inventions that were transforming modern life. While these ideas reached native-born middle-class readers, changing Catholic attitudes reached immigrants through the *Rerum Novarum* Encyclical of Pope Leo XIII in 1891, which roundly condemned child labor. It took time for these attitudes to gain acceptance in American culture, but after 1870 the limitation of child labor was justified not only because it deprived children of schooling but also because it brutalized their sensibilities and bodies.[46]

Perhaps the best example of this new view of child labor was Charles Loring Brace's 1872 book *The Dangerous Classes of New York,* which argued that unless poor and neglected children had alternatives to the kinds of labor available to them, they would add to the city's already large lawless population. He advocated the wholesome labor of western farms, supported factory legislation that prohibited work by children under ten and required three months of schooling annually for wage-earning children aged ten to sixteen.[47] Brace supplied western farms with trainloads of orphans and children from destitute families. But his approach did not address the needs of thousands of children from the families of the working poor who toiled in the city's sweatshops, factories, and streets. For them, a new vision was needed of their right to the same opportunities for personal development as those enjoyed by middle-class children.

Kelley began to supply that vision in 1889. This reform field was ripe for harvesting, and she was ready to test her skills in it. In the spring of 1889 in published letters to newspaper editors she rebuked state officials for the inadequacy of their assault on child labor. And in Hartford in June she bearded the lions of labor law enforcement in their own den at the Annual Convention of Commissioners of State Bureaus of Labor Statistics.[48] Distinguishing herself from government officials, working-class parents, and middle-class philanthropists, she roundly criticized them all, beginning with state bureaus of labor statistics. She had, at last, found appropriate targets for her large store of hostility toward unregulated industry.

As in her association with the Socialist Labor Party, Kelley's interaction with labor bureau officials reflected the gender-related obstacles that confronted a lone woman reformer in the midst of men. Similar to women in the American Social Science Association twenty years earlier, she asserted her claim of equal expertise on a subject of special interest to women. Like Engels more than forty years earlier, she used the documents of bourgeois reform to demonstrate their own inadequacies and push for better results. And like her father throughout his career, she made sure that her efforts were accompanied by positive publicity.

New York and Hartford newspapers featured her in their preconvention coverage. The *Hartford Evening Post* thought that Mrs. Wischnewetzky might be "the chief attraction of the convention." The *Post* described her as "widely noted as the daughter of Pig Iron Kelley of Pennsylvania" and as one "who has devoted her life to social and industrial investigations." Exaggerating her qualifications, the paper said she was "the author of several important books and is thoroughly familiar with the difficulties surrounding the employment of children."[49]

Addressing the question, "Is child labor increasing or decreasing?" she first implicitly attacked the achievements of the bureaus by charging that child labor was increasing. She also criticized the methods by which their statistics were collected. Then, since her chief motivation in combating child labor was to defend the rights of children to leisure and education, not, as was the case with organized labor and state bureaus, to protect the jobs of adult men, she extended the definition of child labor to include workers under the age of sixteen, going beyond the usual limit of fourteen or less. Finally, since her views were anchored in children's rights rather than the welfare of the family economy, she noted how her goals were thwarted but not fundamentally compromised by the complicity of parents who evaded the law and sent their children to work. Therefore, unlike state labor commissioners, she did not shrink from enforcement strategies that took such complicity into account.

The U.S. census, the "census made by fifteen states, and reports of the twenty-one bureaus of labor statistics [were], statistically speaking, raw material," she said — "heart-rending, terrible, sensational," but, from the perspective of social science, "lamentably crude, insufficient, and misleading." She cited the example of Rhode Island, which merely gave the numbers of children gainfully employed, without mentioning that the numbers showed that child labor had increased by 25 percent in a period when the population as a whole had increased by only 10 percent. Such calculations were only "a dilettante's discovery," she said, but they deserved to be included in the official report.[50]

Kelley accompanied her attack with suggestions for future improvements. After showing that studies by a dozen bureaus had failed to measure change over time, she suggested that several state bureaus cooperatively investigate "one typical industry in which child labor is employed." Such an investigation of the silk industry, for example, could analyze the effect of various methods of enforcement to be found in various states, as well as the impact of French-Canadian immigrants, who were in Massachusetts and Connecticut but not in Pennsylvania or New Jersey. She also suggested cooperative, multistate studies of boys in mines in the midwestern, western, and southern states.[51]

Child labor ordinarily meant the labor of children under ten or thirteen, she acknowledged, but she defended her definition of child labor as "the wage-earning employment of children who have not yet passed the sixteenth birthday" on the grounds that "the child of prosperous property-holding parents is certainly regarded as a child and therefore ought not to earn its living at least until the completion of fifteen full years of the leisure of childhood." She claimed a "like measure of childhood for the little sons and daughters of the wages-earning class." [52]

The reception to Kelley's paper ranged from outrage to polite rejection. Willfully misconstruing her remarks, Mr. Bowditch of Rhode Island maintained that he did "not understand what the lady means by asserting that the report's treatment . . . is lacking in statistical detail." He and commissioners from Massachusetts, Missouri, and Nebraska pleaded that parents and mill managers colluded in overstating the ages of children. A Massachusetts commissioner disputed Kelley's suggestion of focusing on one industry, lamely concluding that "the facts brought out would be true only for the particular establishments or industry selected." Defending the traditional age limits, he said that employment of thirteen-year-olds was allowed only if children had twenty weeks of schooling per year. An Illinois Commissioner called her analysis "superficial" and, more to the point, said her suggestions would preempt "information concerning wages and the cost of living to adults, or the cost of production in manufacturers, or a record of strikes, or the statistics of debt, or of labor organizations, or of women at work." [53]

More conciliatory responses came from commissioners who knew Kelley. A New York delegate noted that "it is not a very pleasant task to criticize a lady at any time, and particularly so when the lady is absent" yet nevertheless insisted that "all that could be done was done" by the New York bureau, given their limited funding and the lack of parental cooperation. He also mentioned a topic familiar to her—the expected passage of a bill "providing for the appointment of eight or ten women inspectors" at the next legislative session. Carroll Wright concluded the session by expressing polite interest in Kelley's paper "and also in the position the distinguished essayist has taken in the public press relative to the work of the bureaus." He defended his belief that child labor was declining in Massachusetts but acknowledged that "the subject of child labor is so important that investigations should be made whenever it is possible." Wright kept his options open in his attitude toward this capable critic. Hers was a new voice in this male-dominated arena—that of an educated, middle-class woman who expected more of her government and knew how to ask for what she wanted. [54]

Despite her discontent, important ingredients in American life sustained Kelley's goal of a revitalized public conscience. One was the increasing significance of public opinion. British author James Bryce's influential 1888 book *The American Commonwealth* described the key role of public opinion in overcoming the inertia of the American political process. "There is an excessive friction in the American system, a waste of force in the strife of various bodies and persons created to check and balance one another," he said. "Power is so much subdivided that it is hard at a given moment to concentrate it for prompt and effective action." State legislatures, for example, were hampered by severe limitations, including sessions so short that proposed bills received only an average of twenty minutes of committee time. For Bryce, the antidote to this paralysis lay not with formal institutions of government but with mobilized public opinion. Effective governmental action, he thought, "happens only when a distinct majority of the people are so clearly of one mind that the several co-ordinate organs of government obey this majority."[55] During the 1880s and 1890s, middle-class women and men reformers like Florence Kelley, otherwise excluded from political power, more and more turned to public opinion as a way to express their opposition to the status quo.

She and they were also aided by the intellectual and theoretical foundations for positive state government lain in the early 1880s by such works as Lester Frank Ward's *Dynamic Sociology* (1883), which argued that society, a human creation, required human intervention. One reviewer of Ward's book noted that "the publicists tell us that we are governed too much, but the people are demanding more government, and in obedience to this demand, law-making bodies are rapidly extending the scope of law."[56]

Prompted perhaps by the proximity of her family during a Philadelphia visit, Kelley sought a rapprochement with the chief American advocate of positive government, Richard Ely. He had done his utmost to shape reformist public opinion through such pointed questions as: Has not "our State, unable to cope with great corporations . . . been too weak to be good?" Recognizing his significance if not his political sophistication, in 1888 she joined the American Economic Association; Ely remembered her as one of the "distinguished women" who attended early AEA meetings in Philadelphia. In 1890 she sought his help in locating "*American* data" about industrial illness, believing that "our whole method of production is so different from the European arrangements, that I cannot doubt that its effects upon the health must be very different." When he could not direct her beyond the two studies she already knew, she suggested he encourage Johns Hopkins medical students to write their theses on the subject.[57]

Despite her past scorn for Ely's writings, Kelley had a great deal in common with him. They had common ideological enemies, for example, in laissez-faire advocates like William Graham Sumner, a professor of political and social science at Yale who wrote in the 1880s: "The condition for the complete and regular action of the force of competition is liberty. Liberty means the security given to each man that, if he employs his energies to sustain the struggle on behalf of himself and those he cares for, he shall dispose of the product exclusively as he chooses." Sumner opposed as an interference with liberty the kind of social legislation that Ely and Kelley endorsed.[58]

Kelley engaged in a friendly correspondence with Ely in the spring of 1891. She promised to pass on his writings to "my 'settlers,'" even though she was not optimistic about the results.[59] "I find myself growing more radical as I grow older, in spite of a temperament anything but radical," she said. "The futility of palliative work and the comprehensive nature of the changes going on around us, impress me more from year to year." These, matched with "the state of intellectual unripeness in which these changes find us," alarmed her. Pervasive unripeness—"in all classes, rich and poor, wise and foolish, students and men of affairs"—meant that change was proceeding chaotically.[60] She felt sure that "the minority cannot go on forever exploiting the majority" but thought this could only be changed "by removing the means of production from the irresponsible few to the responsible servants of all."[61] At the age of thirty-two she felt as bleak as her prognosis for the nation's future.

When Kelley learned from Engels that autumn that her translation of *The Condition* was being published by an English firm, his seemed a voice from the past. She was glad that "the work of years ago is to come to life again after it seemed for so long a time to be consigned to oblivion," and in response to his inquiry about obtaining the copyright permission from Rachel Foster, she assured him that her own permission was sufficient. "She has directly confided to me all affairs concerning the book," Kelley brusquely replied, and, besides, "she has married, is Mrs. Rachel Foster Avery and too much absorbed in her two daughters to take much interest in Socialist propaganda."[62]

She went on to describe the pressure of her own domestic responsibilities. "We have had an atrocious time." After three years of "ceaseless struggle" to establish Lazare's institute of physical therapy, "we are hardly better off or more sure of the future than we were at the start. . . . We have been so absorbed in the struggle for existence for our children and the Institute that we could do little more than keep an eye upon the organs of the movement." This struggle doubtlessly contributed to her political depression. Nevertheless, she was loyal to Lazare and to her identity as Mrs. Wischnewetzky. Engels told her about his conflict with the English publisher, who tried to omit her "unpronounceable Russian name" because he feared it would injure the sale of the book, "as its bearer surely cannot be expected to know English!" She responded emphatically: "The omission of my name is out of the question of course—or any part of it! . . . Any change would be an infringement on the copyright."[63]

As the mother of three children, aged five, four, and three, Kelley relied on governesses and kindergartens to permit her to pursue social reform. "I have the paper to prepare for the Social Science Club meeting here tomorrow night; and as it is far from complete I must close, send the babies out and set about preparing it," she wrote Caroline in 1889. Some of her study of child labor could be done at home, but she also needed to engage in scholarly research that took her to libraries, social agencies, and government offices. Her loving references to Ko, Margaret, and John in her letters expressed her commitment to them as first priority, but she never thought that they kept her from social activism. In fact, she rather relished the chaotic domestic conditions they created. "The menagerie is exceedingly animated as both my small animals are squealing at the top of their lungs," she told Caroline. "However, they are well and happy and the happy tone in their voices makes up for the lack of musical quality." [64]

Although by 1889 Lazare had recovered his health, his medical practice failed to generate income, and Florence again was forced to appeal to her father for financial support. William Kelley tried to obtain an appointment for her with the federal census, and when that proved fruitless, he agreed to pay her rent but could not provide additional support. Lazare and Florence then entreated him to invest twenty thousand dollars in what later became "the Mechanico-Therapeutic and Orthopedic Zander Institute of the City of New York." Employing a technique developed in Stockholm and implemented elsewhere in Europe, Zander Institutes afforded "exercise by means of scientific apparatus." Since William Kelley was dying, his finances were being managed by his executor, William Nicholson; Florence shifted her appeal to him in December 1889. [65]

William Kelley died of cancer in his hotel room in Washington, D.C., on January 9, 1890, at the age of seventy-five, with his wife, sons, and sister at his side. Florence joined the family in Philadelphia and attended the funeral at the First Unitarian Church. Congressman Kelley's will left his estate to his executor in trust for Caroline, providing that upon her death its income should go to his children and grandchildren. In a codicil dated September 20 and witnessed November 14, 1889, he authorized his executor "in his discretion to advance unto my son-in-law Lazare Wischnewetzky M.D. such additional sum or sums of money as may be necessary to complete his purchase of the implements pertaining to the 'Zander system' under his contract with Dr. Zander and secure him the possession thereof in New York." The probate court's inventory of the estate appraised it at $35,419, three-fourths of which consisted of stocks in an iron company and a stove manufacturing company that employed Will Jr. Kelley had long ago sold the real estate holdings that had once made him a wealthy man, retaining only the Elms itself, the value of which had precipitously declined with the encroachment of working-class neighborhoods nearby. [66]

After William's death, Florence and Lazare engaged in a fierce struggle with Will Jr. and later with William Nicholson over the implementation of the codicil. William Kelley shortly before his death (or his executor shortly afterward) had advanced a large sum to Lazare. Will Jr. protested strenuously, and Florence fought back. Florence and Lazare's correspondence on the subject did not survive, but Will's did. "L. must have a low mind

"A mother's morning goodbye to her babe, Day Nursery of Grace Parish." *Frank Leslie's Illustrated Newspaper,* November 8, 1890. Courtesy of Library of Congress.

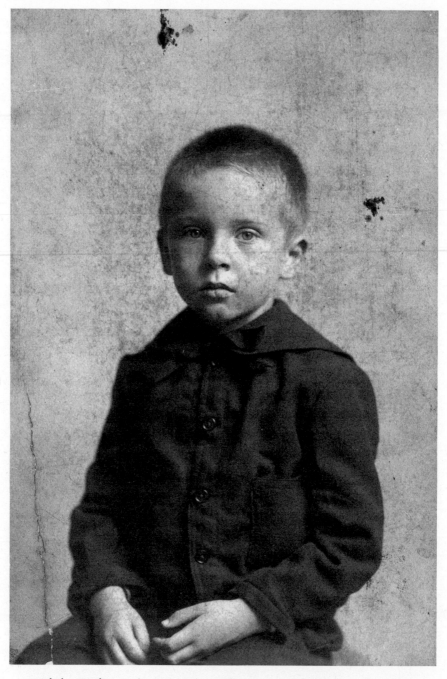

Nicholas Wischnewetzky, New York, ca. 1890. Courtesy of Nicholas Kelley Papers, Rare Books and Manuscripts Division, New York Public Library, Astor, Lenox and Tilden Foundations.

to be so suspicious and to use such vindictive language," he wrote Caroline. "F. ought to be ashamed to write to you in this way. She is as savage as the Tartar." From his perspective, Will was required to return twenty thousand dollars to the estate "because advances made to L. had made it necessary." When Nicholson decided not to advance Florence and Lazare more money, her brother wrote Caroline, "I never heard of such outrageous threats as F. makes. . . . Mr. N. must do as he sees his duty and such threats could avail nothing, if we [refuse] to interfere." [67] Although Florence invested in her husband's medical practice what she could wrest from her father's estate and although the Zander Institute did open in September 1890, her family finances remained desperately unstable. Lazare was more financially dependent on her than she on him.

According to his own later testimony, Lazare believed his marriage began to fail about 1889. "It was economy, economy most of the time," he was quoted as saying. Her "continual solicitude concerning the payment of our debts was extremely distressing to me." [68] He also became enraged when Florence spoke to the children or servants in English. By early January 1891, the couple's quarrels had erupted into physical violence. Florence later testified that Lazare struck her "in the face so as to disfigure her and cause her confinement to her room for two or three weeks." Lazare later admitted to using "vile" language but claimed that Florence had attacked him during a quarrel over her failure "to provide one of the ingredients of a Russian stew." [69] Florence said that he "used profane and indecent language" toward her in the presence of their children. When Florence showed "her blackened face" to his associate at the Zander Institute, and "asked his advice concerning a separation," he advised reconciliation, and she returned home.[70] Kelley tried to preserve the marriage, but economic pressures, cultural differences, and her own unwillingness (or inability) to tolerate Lazare's abuse continued to erode their partnership.

Just at this time Florence encountered a sad reminder of the gap between her own marriage and socialist ideals about family life. Richard Ely asked her to criticize his writings on socialism generally and on socialist views of marriage in particular. Warning him that "my friends think my criticisms more candid than kindly" and asking him "to make allowance for an inborn brusqueness which has brought me much trouble," she consented, replying thoughtfully to his suggestion that socialism did not threaten contemporary family life.[71] "If socialists may speak for socialism it certainly does entertain the notion that the family of today belongs to the industrial system of today, and that its economic foundation, i.e. the economic dependence of the wife upon the husband, passes away with the rest of the economic dependence of one person upon another." Hence, she concluded, "if you remove the economic dependence you do make love free." Utopian writers from Plato to Fourier and almost all socialist writers took this view, she said. "Morris, Marx and the Avelings are all explicit upon this point, and if they may be thought too strongly Marxist to represent English opinion fairly, there is George Bernard Shaw with his anti-Marxist Socialism and his anti-marriage-as-it-is-today novels." Most marriages had nothing in common with the socialist ideal, she added. "The duty of providing for her children makes life an endless petty economy for the average wife," who endures the yoke of marriage only "by reason of the sense of duty." [72] In his book Ely characterized Kelley's view as adhering "to a materialistic conception of history, which traces all social relations to economic conditions," but assured his readers that this was "no necessary part of socialism." [73]

On December 27, 1891, Florence Kelley's own sense of marital duty dissolved. That day Lazare hit her again, "spat in her face," and walked out the door. She gathered up Ko, Margaret, and John with a few belongings and took the train to Chicago, borrowing money for their fare from an English governess she knew.[74] Illinois's liberal divorce laws, the city's social ferment, and its distance from Lazare made Chicago an appealing haven. He returned home to find his family gone.

When Florence Kelley Wischnewetzky left New York, she carried with her a unique combination of professional and personal skills gained during her reform apprenticeship of almost ten years. She had established herself as a roving firebrand within the expanding ranks of bourgeois reform, but no platform seemed large enough to hold her. She had begun to work creatively within a set of gendered opportunities, but, trusting the social agendas of neither middle-class women nor government officials, her efforts lacked momentum. She could not gain a purchase on the process whereby she—a middle-class Yankee woman—could join the forces of light and cease to shore up the forces of darkness.

In ways that cannot be known, her personal life must have intensified her political pessimism. Lazare's violence, his illness, their financial anxieties, not to mention the demands of three young children, must have clouded her vision of the redeeming power of timely social action. Breaking first with her father, then with Frederick Engels, an important father figure, and finally with her husband, she emerged from more than two decades of intimacy with strong masculine personalities. In many ways, this tutelage had helped her escape more normative types of female cultural submission. Through William Kelley, Engels, and Lazare, she had entered into realms of experience customarily closed to women of her class and nativity. She had asked a great deal of these men, and in the end they all failed her. Now she was asking a great deal of herself.

Part Three
Agency

8

"A Colony of Efficient and Intelligent Women" in the Early 1890s

Although she managed to bring "two trunks of clothes," Florence Kelley Wischnewetzky and her children arrived in Chicago with very limited resources. Her first Chicago address was the Woman's Temple of the Woman's Christian Temperance Union. The recently constructed twelve-story building in downtown Chicago served the office and hotel needs of the union's national headquarters—a monument to its colossal success among midwestern women. There she sought the aid of Mary Allen West, who had worked with her on *Our Toiling Children* and, as editor of the WCTU's national newspaper, the *Union Signal,* might be expected to have more work to offer. West promptly directed her to Hull House.[1]

Leaving Ko, Margaret, and John behind in a WCTU nursery for working mothers, Kelley followed up on this lead before breakfast "on a snowy morning between Christmas 1891 and New Year's 1892." As she later remembered: "Reaching Hull-House that winter day was no small undertaking. The streets between car-track and curb were piled mountain high with coal-black frozen snow. The street cars, drawn by horses, were frequently blocked by a fallen horse harnessed to a heavily laden wagon. Whenever that happened, the long procession of vehicles stopped short until the horse was restored to its feet or, as sometimes occurred, was shot and lifted to the top of the snow, there to remain until the next thaw facilitated its removal." When she finally arrived at the settlement, another needy petitioner, Henry Standing Bear, a Kickapoo Indian, was waiting for the door to be opened. Jane Addams answered his summons, "holding on her left arm a singularly unattractive, fat, pudgy baby belonging to the cook, who was behindhand with breakfast." Miss Addams's movements were hindered "by a super-energetic kindergarten child, left by its mother while she went to a sweatshop for a bundle of cloaks to be finished." In Kelley, Addams quickly recognized an able coworker. The visitor felt instantly at home. "We were welcomed as though we had been invited. We stayed. Henry Standing Bear as helper to the engineer several months, when he returned to his tribe; and I as a resident seven happy, active years until May 1, 1899." These "seven happy, active years" relocated Florence Kelley within the public culture of middle-class American women and linked her with powerful new means of doing the nation's work.[2]

Hull House was founded in 1889 by Ellen Gates Starr and Jane Addams, who, having decided to form a settlement in Chicago modeled on Toynbee Hall in East London, searched for a location by accompanying truant officers, city missionaries, and news-paper reporters on their rounds.[3] They finally settled on a substantial middle-class house stranded in the midst of tenements in the Nineteenth Ward, a location sorely lacking in their forms of civic virtue.

The ward contained about fifty thousand souls of eighteen nationalities and "all pos-sible religious beliefs." "The streets are inexpressibly dirty," Addams wrote, "the number of schools inadequate, factory legislation unenforced, the street-lighting bad, the paving miserable and altogether lacking in the alleys and smaller streets, and the stables defy all laws of sanitation." Originally built to accommodate one family, each of the ward's small wooden houses was now occupied by several. Hundreds of dwellings remained unconnected with the street sewer; many had no water supply save a faucet in the back-yard. A constant flow of recent immigrants replaced those who managed to move to less desperate neighborhoods. The ward was home to two hundred and fifty-five saloons (one for every twenty-eight voters), the majority owned by wholesale liquor companies. Not counting many small Jewish synagogues, only seven churches and two missions graced the ward, all these small and struggling except two Catholic churches on the ward's boundaries. Seven Catholic schools accommodated 6,244 children, three Protes-tant schools cared for 141. Public schools attracted 2,957 students, but an equal number of children under the age of fourteen did not attend school, laboring instead in the ward's burgeoning sweatshops, hawking goods on the streets, or scavenging what they could from the neighborhood's prolific piles of refuse.[4]

The ward distilled the city's chaotic disregard for human life. By 1893 two people a day were being killed by trains plowing into unguarded crossings, and many more were injured, prompting a vision "of a city filling up with armless or legless people." Explo-sive prosperity overpowered concern about its costs. Vast quantities of raw materials flowed into the city by boat and rail, and recent migrants wrought goods from them that streamed into the nation's economy. Contemporary photographs of the Chicago skyline show clusters of buildings fifteen stories high, a dizzying new elevation that required electric lifts and dwarfed passersby. Enormous wealth, embodied in fantastic domestic castles lining Lake Shore Drive, contrasted grotesquely with clapboard tenements only

The Woman's Temple Building at the corner of La Salle and Monroe Streets, Chicago, 1890.
Courtesy of University of Illinois at Chicago.

Hull House as it looked when Florence Kelley arrived, 1891. Courtesy of University of Illinois at
Chicago, Special Collections, University Library, Jane Addams Memorial Collection.

Dead Horse with boys at play. The social geography of everyday life in a working-class
neighborhood in the urban North, ca. 1900. Courtesy of Library of Congress.

a few miles away that crowded whole families into a single room. Chicago's population
of some 1,100,000 made it the nation's second largest city in 1890, with foreign-born inhabitants totaling 450,666. Thousands of new arrivals each week brought that number
to 587,112 by 1900. In the decade between 1890 and 1900 the small African-American
population more than doubled, growing from about 14,000 to about 30,000 as a vanguard
of migrants from the south added a multiracial dimension to the city's multiethnic com-
plexion. Tens of thousands of white migrants from the nation's midwestern heartland
also poured into the city. This massive European and substantial native-born migration
produced ruinous social problems ranging from disease-ridden slums to violent confron-
tations between working people and the police. Chicago was, in other words, an ideal
habitat for Florence Kelley and her political agenda.[5]

In Chicago and other cities in the 1890s social settlements stepped into the breach
created by rapid urbanization on the one hand and traditions of limited government on
the other. Settlements grew in number from six in 1891 to seventy-four in 1897, over one
hundred in 1900, and four hundred by 1910. Many were affiliated with Protestant religious
denominations, an expression of the Social Gospel and the growing concern clergy and

Typical street in the Hull House neighborhood, ca. 1900. Courtesy of Prints and Photographs, Chicago Historical Society.

laity felt for their moral responsibility to the working poor. Nonsectarian women's settlements in New York, Boston, and Philadelphia attracted residents and financial support from women's colleges. Others, like Hull House, relied on local philanthropic support.[6]

Just as the Nineteenth was no ordinary Chicago ward, Hull House was no ordinary settlement. Before her snowy morning visit, Kelley had no reason to believe its residents had more to offer than Scudder's settlers in New York. Both institutions were quite new and experimental. However, she quickly discovered a place for herself that offered more than temporary shelter. "I have cast in my lot with Misses Addams and Starr for as long as they will have me," she wrote Engels after fourteen weeks' residence.[7] Almost immediately she recognized the power of the place to meet her needs. Behind that recognition lay her even more instantaneous trust of Jane Addams.

Like Florence Kelley, Jane Addams had devoted the past decade to a frustrating series of false starts and misadventures that mocked her earnest hope to engage in meaningful social service. She enrolled in medical school, traveled in Europe, and rejected a possible marriage. Through her friendship with Ellen Starr and their joint endeavor on Halsted Street, she had at last begun to construct a life she believed in. During the settlement's early years, Addams paid for emergency expenses like Florence Kelley's room and board out of her own pocket. In the three years before the Cornell graduate's arrival, she had spent over ten thousand dollars of her own money on the settlement—a small fortune at that time and a large portion of her family inheritance.[8] This fiscal autonomy gave Hull House its unique character, since unlike Vida Scudder's settlement in New York, which depended on donations from students and faculty at colleges, and unlike the many church-based settlements that sprang into existence in the 1890s, Hull House embodied the personal vision of its founder.

At the core of Addams's considerable genius lay a Darwinian belief in the vitality of the human species as expressed in working-class people and a determination to join these people, whatever the cost. When Florence Kelley arrived at her doorstep, the specifics of Addams's commitment were just emerging. She presented them publicly for the first time in a speech before the Chicago Woman's Club only days before Kelley's arrival. This talk, "The Outgrowths of Toynbee Hall," became the germ for her powerfully influential essay "The Subjective Necessity of Social Settlements," published in 1893. The basic idea of both speech and essay—social democracy—reverberated through the coming decades. "Democracy has made little attempt to assert itself in social affairs," she said, a situation "the more mortifying when we remember that social matters have always been largely under the control of women." Is it possible, she asked, "that with all our new advantage and liberty of action, women have failed to hear the great word of the century?"[9] Hull House was a response to this situation, "an effort to add the social function to democracy." Explicitly seeking to surpass the "best achievement thus far" in America—"the democratic ideal" expressed in the franchise—she wanted "to move beyond the position of its eighteenth-century leaders, who believed that political equality alone would secure all good to all men" and carry democracy into social relations—especially those between rich and poor, between native-born whites and blacks or immigrants. "We conscientiously followed the gift of the ballot hard upon the gift of freedom to the negro," Addams said, "but we are quite unmoved by the fact that he lives among us in a practical social ostracism." The same logic applied to Eastern European immigrants: "We hasten to give the franchise to the immigrant from a sense of justice, from a tradition that he ought to have it, while we dub him with epithets deriding his past life or present occupation, and feel no duty to invite him to our houses."[10] Hers was a radical vision of the expansion of civil society in which women could play a substantial role. Kelley fit into that vision quite nicely. Especially appealing from the newcomer's perspective, Addams had only begun to enact her social democracy project. Much of it remained to be defined.

By the time Kelley arrived, Addams was adept at solving the individual human problems that materialized on her doorstep. Kelley presented her with two: her need for useful employment and her need for a haven for the children. The first was more difficult. In consultation with Jane Addams, each resident determined her own employment. Kelley decided to organize a labor bureau that would train young immigrant women in domestic work at Hull House and then place them in well-to-do Chicago homes. Addams probably suggested the venture, and Kelley was in no position to decline. Following fast upon the heels of Addams's December talk at the Chicago Woman's Club, the head resident arranged for her new colleague to speak to the club less than a month after her arrival.[11] In her talk, "The Sweating System," Kelley appealed for financial support for the newly created Hull House bureau of labor for women.

This speaking debut in Chicago introduced Florence Kelley to one of the most influential groups of women in the United States. Their political power was substantial, and they had financial resources to match. Founded in 1876 as an activist alternative to the more literary Fortnightly Club, the Chicago Woman's Club inherited the public service orientation of local women who served on the U.S. Sanitary Commission. It attracted college-educated women, society leaders, professional and business women, as well as upper middle-class housewives and their daughters. One key to its success lay in its departmental form of organization, whereby each member channeled her efforts into one of four departments—home, education, philanthropy, and reform. This departmental structure imitated the extremely effective organizational framework of the WCTU.

The club's history of social activism began in 1877 when it helped form the Illinois Social Science Association. Under its motto "Nothing Human can be Alien to Us," club members in the early 1880s discussed such political questions as free trade, the eight-hour day, and Bismarck and his policy. By 1886 petitions "circulated under the patronage of the club" for such causes as state legislative bills to place the treatment of women in public institutions under the supervision of women and city council ordinances to place more women on the board of education. In response to the Avelings' tour of the United States in 1887, members debated socialism and the home. Two years later a club member led a class on the philosophy of government, and a member gave a speech entitled "The Influence and Results of Merely Palliative Measures of Reform."[12]

The groundwork had been well laid for Kelley during the two months preceding her talk, for in addition to Addams's discussion of social democracy, Jessie Lloyd had spoken on relative values, and "Miss Kenney of the Bindery Girls Union made reports of the wages of women in various trades and of the motives influencing the formation of trades-unions with some of the good resulting thereby." Advance newspaper publicity in the *Union Signal* billed Kelley as "a college graduate" and "an accomplished linguist," which would "enable her to instruct and assist the newly arrived candidate for the American labor market from whatever part of the world she may come." The story noted that

"Mrs. Kelley has given many years of careful attention to the study of social science, not only theoretically, but through wide travel and observation." Club members responded with a sizable donation.[13]

Kelley set up the bureau in a rented room in the mortuary next door to Hull House. An article in the *Union Signal* publicized the bureau's hope to establish "simple justice between woman and woman" by "induc[ing] employer and employed to agree upon a standard of hours and promote self respect." Employment offices run by men sometimes conducted "a most nefarious traffic in young girls," and this one protected women from that danger. Yet despite the fanfare accompanying its launching, the bureau did not attract job seekers. Manufacturing and commercial firms handled their own hiring, and women preferred these jobs to the domestic work that the bureau offered. Even so, this small office prevented its director from becoming a charity case during her first months in Chicago. It also gave her time to wage a court fight against Lazare, care for Ko, Margaret, and John, and explore the local political terrain. Moreover, the minimum demands of the labor bureau made it possible for her to enroll in law courses. Until she completed a law degree in June 1895, night classes at Northwestern University's downtown campus remained part of her weekly schedule.[14]

A bit stunned by her good fortune, the thirty-three-year-old mother wrote her own mother a summary of her circumstances around the time the bureau opened. "We are all well, and the chicks are happy. I have fifty dollars a month and my board and shall have more soon as I can collect my wits enough to write. I have charge of the Bureau of Labor of Hull House here and am working in the lines which I have always loved. I do not know what more to tell you except this, that in the few weeks of my stay here I have won for the children and myself many and dear friends whose generous hospitality astonishes me." She continued, "It is understood that I am to resume the maiden name, and that the children are to have it." She also changed John's middle name from Brown to Bartram. What must have been a hard decision now seemed easy. "I am better off than I have been since I landed in New York since I am now responsible *myself* for what I do." By joining a community of women, she achieved a new degree of personal autonomy.[15]

Addams helped Kelley with the urgent task of finding a home for the children. Hull House was not entirely suitable. The settlement maintained a kindergarten and nursery but had no provision for permanent nonadult residents, and the adjacent slums suffered high rates of infant and childhood mortality. Even more pressing, Lazare would be looking for the children, and Florence needed to place them beyond his reach. Addams suggested the home of Henry Demarest Lloyd, a frequent visitor at Hull House. Lloyd and his wife, Jessie Bross Lloyd, had just added a new children's wing to their home, Wayside, in the woods of Winnetka, about fifteen miles north of downtown Chicago, and their youngest child was about the same age as Ko. Kelley dispatched a request to Lloyd for an interview, introducing herself as an admirer of his writings and a friend of his sister, Caro. Consequently, she and her children formed ties with the Lloyd family that endured into the next generation.[16]

Kelley knew Lloyd as the author of *A Strike of Millionaires against Miners; or the Story of Spring Valley,* an 1890 book that depicted the suffering of families in northern Illinois when owners shut down mines rather than negotiate with workers. That book brought Lloyd to national prominence as a leading critic of "our bad wealth." Previously, as the financial editor of the *Chicago Tribune,* he had gained a reputation as the nation's premier antimonopoly journalist, calling for "a new democracy," and a "new religion" that would acknowledge the "humanity, brotherhood and divinity of every man." Just before the Haymarket Massacre, he had resigned from the *Tribune* to launch a new career as a full-time reformer. After he defended the innocence of anarchists accused of the Haymarket bomb throwing, polite Chicago society closed ranks to exclude him and Jessie. This deepened his commitment to reform, and after 1889 drew him closer to Addams and her remarkable crew. At dinnertime the Lloyd home often had the aura of a settlement. A visitor described their table as seating twenty to thirty people, "rich and poor, white and black, gentle and simple, college president and seamstress, artist and mechanic, divine and layman," all gathered "on the basis of liberty, fraternity, and equality." At his death in 1889 Jessie's father, a former lieutenant-governor of Illinois and publisher of the *Chicago Tribune,* left Jessie and the three Lloyd children an ample annual income. This fund also helped support Ko, Margaret, and John during Kelley's early years at Hull House, especially that first winter of 1892.[17]

Kelley visited her children as often as she could, but the separation pained her. "I miss the chicks with a perennial heartache," she wrote her mother. Winnetka could not be reached by streetcar, so she had to rely on private transportation to visit them. Sometimes news about them reached her through others. "Mrs. Lloyd saw Miss Addams and reported the chicks all right yesterday," she wrote Caroline in mid-March.[18] Reunions were bliss. "My exquisite bairns are enough to keep any one braced up and cheerful." She told their grandmother, "The children are so beautiful physically and so loving and frank, that I have never dreamed of anything like them."[19] Margaret, known affectionately as "Puss," was learning to sew "in a tentative way" with a thimble Caroline had sent. Whether at the Lloyd's or at Hull House, she gave special attention to Ko's intellectual and moral development. "Ko is learning to read. He goes at his primer as a hungry child does at a meal. He is a very intellectual boy. We are reading Joshua now, and his quotations are rich. He is well, growing, eats and sleeps well and enjoys the country thoroughly. I wish, however, that he had more of the happy go lucky disposition of the others."[20] She hoped to end the separation soon. "In the Autumn, I must have them within reach, in my own interests, though I really think they are far better off in the country."[21] Celara, "the faithful girl" who cared for the children in New York, had arrived with "a trunk of toys and clothes," so she urged Caroline not to worry.[22] All in all, she felt splendid. "I love Chicago, Hull House, my friends and my work."[23]

During the first five months after her arrival, Lazare tried to gain custody of the children. "Since Friday I have been in hiding," she wrote her mother in February. He came to the city with an attorney friend, and "they wanted to get habeas corpus writs and try the case at once." Nevertheless, she felt confident that his physical abuse of her made his case untenable. "There is no danger *now* . . . for my counsel has made it clear that I should ruin Dr. W. if I made merely the baldest statement of my reasons for my action."[24] She said that the "horrors" of her situation "settle down upon my spirits but only for a few moments at a time. Then I am all right again." She proposed that "when L. goes back to Russia" Caroline should come and live with her and the children in Chicago.[25]

Florence's struggle with Lazare elicited some penetrating self-criticism. She asked her mother to thank brother Will for helping with her legal costs "and tell him that I have at last resumed possession of my conscience which I handed over, seven years ago,

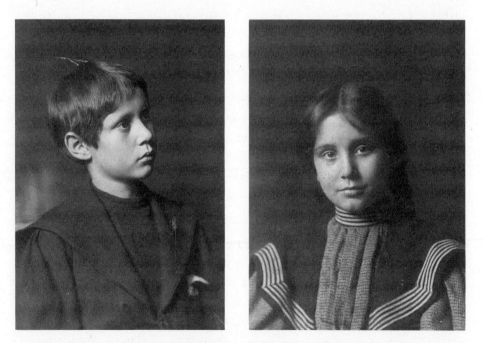

Nicholas Kelley, ca. 1892. Courtesy of Nicholas Kelley Papers, Rare Books and Manuscripts Division, New York Public Library, Astor, Lenox and Tilden Foundations.

Margaret Kelley in the mid-1890s. Courtesy of Nicholas Kelley Papers, Rare Books and Manuscripts Division, New York Public Library, Astor, Lenox and Tilden Foundations.

for 'safe' keeping." Now that she was away from Lazare and New York, she had "come to her senses *completely*." She urged Caroline not to worry. "Don't try to send me anything but as much kindly feeling as my years of cruel ingratitude may have left possible." Meanwhile, she was "living in real comfort in this beloved Hull House." [26] Caroline, Will, and Albert sent her money for lawyers' fees, which she repaid within a few months from her Hull House salary.

Just before the case went to court in March, Florence was gratified by Rachel Foster Avery's offer to testify on her behalf. Kelley's old friend lived in Chicago with her husband and three daughters. She remained a prominent suffragist and was then planning a meeting in Chicago of the International Council of Women. "I shall accept with vigor and she will [be] an invaluable witness," Florence wrote her mother. Other New York friends volunteered to provide monetary support "in case of illness or loss of work," and she felt "overwhelmed with the kindness which I find everywhere." [27]

On March 26, the *Chicago Tribune* carried an extensive report on the day-long court proceedings. Florence's testimony about why she came to Chicago "to make her way in the world for herself and for the sake of the three little ones" emphasized Lazare's abuse and his improvidence. "Her story of cruelty remained practically unshaken in spite of the long series of cross-questions directed against her by the doctor's attorney. She maintained that her literary ability, combined with the able ideas of sociology contributed by her husband, had furnished their means of support during their unromantic courtship and marriage in Switzerland. Afterwards the assistance gained from her father's estate, together with the business ability of borrowing money from friends, formed the family's income." Testifying on Lazare's behalf, the secretary of his institute told how Mrs. Wischnewetzky had sought his advice when her face was bruised. He described Lazare as "a nervous, demonstrative man, insistent upon his views and opinions but ready to take advice when the first burst of his passion had subsided." Lazare testified "that he had never struck her intentionally," though he admitted that "he became enraged when his wife conversed with the children and the servants in English." Not surprisingly, the court awarded custody to Kelley. Lazare pursued the case in New York, but, as Florence wrote her mother, "We are none of us in New York to suffer from the local press. The decision will infallibly go my way. And we are all well. And I have my lovely beautiful children." She urged her mother, "Do not worry about me! I have not been so well off in years!" [28]

She was especially grateful to the Lloyds. "Their warmth of heart and breadth of mind have made them seem like my own people. Their lives realize what L[azare]'s words used to picture to me years ago, when he seemed noble and full of righteous enthusiasm." The children loved the Lloyds, she continued, "and have more to thank them for than they will ever know." Suggesting that their Winnetka home was critical to her victory, she concluded, "it was the exquisite surroundings in which the Lloyds place them, which saved them for me at the trial." [29]

Thereafter Kelley adopted a radical view of marriage. To another woman reformer who inquired in 1894 about her views on the legalization of prostitution she wrote that prostitution "is the inevitable accompaniment of monogamy and that we shall never be rid of it until the relations of wife, spinster, and prostitute have become mere historical expressions . . . with the choice of motherhood and its responsibilities left absolutely with each woman." Assessing her position in the process of historical change, she continued, "Of course it is a long, long, look ahead to such a change. But the dissolution of the family is going on so fast, and the old vilification of the woman who asserts her claim to motherhood without the slavery of marriage is dying out so fast, that we shall doubt-less live to see a very widespread modification of public opinion upon the subject. . . . This, with the daily increasing economic self-dependence of women is greatly under-mining the status of marriage." By the end of May she had settled into a gratifying work routine. As she wrote Engels, "The Illinois courts have now finally awarded me the cus-tody of my three little children;—and I can begin once more to live and act somewhat methodically." [30]

Hull House and the Lloyds helped Florence Kelley knit together a new personal and political identity that confirmed both her visionary hopes and her capacity to handle the material details of social organizing. This congruence rekindled the glowing personality she had developed at Cornell and fused it with the combative self she had forged in Europe. It helped her integrate the contradictory impulses of her elite affiliation with power and her determination to change the balance of power in American society.

Her personality reflected this dualism. Her deep capacity for affection hid behind a gruff and demanding exterior. "Mrs. Kelley show[ed] a genial kindliness towards me that quite transforms her," one surprised Hull House visitor remarked. Alice Hamilton, who joined the settlement in 1897, described Kelley as a compellingly charismatic combina-tion of compassion and ferocity, a "vivid, colorful, rather frightening personality whom I came later to adore." She also remarked on Kelley's "bigness and manliness and warm heartedness." Kelley had at last found a setting capable of absorbing the contradictions of her forceful personality. [31]

Her new persona took shape in interaction with Jane Addams. In Addams she finally met a peer whose intellectual talents, spiritual depth, and commitment to social change matched her own. Born into an upper-middle-class family in Cedarville, Illinois, Addams was two years old when her mother died, which prompted a close relationship with her father, a flour-mill owner, banker, and political leader who served eight terms as a state senator in Illinois. Like William Kelley, John Addams was a founder of the Republican party and knew Abraham Lincoln. What Addams once said of herself could also be said of Kelley; both fathers "wrapped their little daughters in the large men's doublets, careless did they fit or no." Like Kelley, Addams benefited from women's increased access to higher education, graduating from Rockford Female Seminary in 1881 with one of the first Bachelor of Art's degrees awarded by that institution.[32]

Addams and Kelley took to each other straightaway. Nicholas Kelley said that "from the time my mother first went to Hull House until her death, more than forty years later, she looked upon Miss Addams as her dearest and most intimate friend. She loved Miss Addams and admired her and approved of her unreservedly." Julia Lathrop reported that Kelley and Addams "understood each other's powers" instantly and worked together in a "wonderfully effective way." Most observers noted their contrasting dispositions. "Miss Addams in grey—serene, dauntless . . . Mrs. Kelley, alight with the resurgent flame of her zeal." One who knew them both asked, "By what rare stroke of fortune were they brought together in the days when Chicago was a great focus of our mounting industrialism?"[33]

Their talents were remarkably complementary. Addams, the philosopher with a deep appreciation of the unity of life, was better able to construct a vehicle for expressing that unity in day-to-day living than she was capable of devising a diagram for charting the future. And Kelley, the politician with a thorough understanding of what the future should look like, was better able to invoke that future than to express it in her day-to-day existence. Addams taught Kelley how to live and have faith in an imperfect world, and Kelley taught Addams how to make demands on the future.

Yet more than their differences drew them together. Each had made a fundamental commitment to larger life forces, Kelley to the unfolding of historical change and Addams to what she once called "the impulse beating at the very source of our lives urging us to aid in the race progress."[34] Each understood society to be a process consisting of groups rather than a static contractual arrangement among individuals. Both nevertheless placed a high value on the individual and idealized the future for its ability to improve the lives of average people. Both believed that material changes could inspire spiritual changes. Expressing the nineteenth century's passion for organic, evolutionary notions of change, both knew that the future would evolve out of the present. Both therefore attributed an urgent importance to immediate action. Each found in society itself the answer to social dislocation and to her own alienation. Each sought to overcome that alienation by submerging herself in a larger whole.

Jane Addams, age thirty-five, ca. 1895. Courtesy of University of Illinois at Chicago, Special Collections, University Library, Jane Addams Memorial Collection.

Within a few days of her arrival, Kelley probably heard Addams relate a parable told by a member of the audience during the discussion after Addams's talk at the Chicago Woman's Club. As a girl "playing in her mother's garden," the woman recounted, she discovered "a small toad who seemed to her very forlorn and lonely" and some distance away "a large toad, also apparently without family and friends." With a heart "full of tender sympathy," the girl pushed the little toad into the company of the big toad and "to her inexpressible horror and surprise, the big toad opened his mouth and swallowed the little one." This, the clubwoman said, happened to those who lived "where they did not naturally belong." In reply Addams protested that that was exactly what Hull House residents wanted—"to be swallowed and digested, to disappear into the bulk of the people." [35] Like the small toad in the story, Addams and Kelley took transformation in their own lives to be a precondition for their inclusion in larger social realities. For both the price of participating in genuine social transformation was genuine personal metamorphosis.

Both shared a deeply moral commitment to social justice, Addams drawing on her vision of social democracy, Kelley on her understanding of Marxian socialism. Addams's instinct for peacemaking and conciliation made her see every side of social questions and feel compassion for all the actors, while Kelley's aggressive championing of the exploited usually dealt with stark contrasts between good and evil. Kelley expressed anger against the causes of social injustice; Addams demonstrated a tragic appreciation of and sympathy with suffering. Both were gifted speakers and writers, Addams coaxing others into her capacious vision, Kelley exhorting them to follow the logic of her social program.

Kelley's ardent and provocative personality kindled a fire within Addams's aloof self-possession, while the head resident's calm determination balanced the newcomer's volatility. Addams's nephew, Weber Linn, who came to live at Hull House in 1894, felt awed by the way Kelley "hurled the spears of her thought with such apparent carelessness of what breasts they pierced," but he nevertheless felt that she was "full of love." "[She was] the toughest customer in the reform riot, the finest rough-and-tumble fighter for the good life for others, that Hull House ever knew. Any weapon was a good weapon in her hand—evidence, argument, irony or invective." Addams's natural reserve placed her at the other end of the emotional spectrum. She was "firm beyond all imagining," Nicholas Kelley later said. "I never saw Miss Addams angry and never heard of her being angry. My mother once asked her how she could be so calm. Miss Addams replied that she had had a great struggle to master her temper when she was young." Ko thought her "humane, simple common sense" amounted in its effect to "imaginative genius." [36]

Addams was a person Kelley could learn from, a person she could love, yet she did not make the mistake of venerating her friend. She was the only resident who ever made fun of "Sister Jane." "Do you know what I would do if that woman calls you a saint again?" she once asked Addams. "I'd show her my teeth, and if that didn't convince her, I would bite her." Symbolizing their close relationship, Kelley sat beside Addams at the evening meal—an important daily ritual where Addams presided, distinguished guests were often present, and residents had an opportunity to discuss their varied activities.[37]

Jane Addams's personality and intelligence were the kernel around which the Hull House community took shape. One resident wrote that "Hull House was not an institution over which Miss Addams presided, it was Miss Addams around whom an institution insisted on clustering." Emily Balch, visitor to Hull House in 1895, a founder of Denison House in Boston, Wellesley faculty member, and the only other American woman besides Jane Addams to be awarded the Nobel Peace Prize, said that Addams "did not dominate the group. She, as it were, incorporated it and helped it to be itself." [38]

When Kelley arrived, in addition to seventy-five volunteers who conducted clubs or classes, the chief members of the Hull House community consisted of "fellow-founder" Ellen Gates Starr, formerly a teacher in a local academy for girls; Julia Lathrop, recently appointed county visitor for Cook County dependent families, who hailed from nearby Rockford; Jennie Dow, a nonresident volunteer who directed the kindergarten with "good sense and joyous good humor"; Anna Farnsworth, "an agreeable woman of leisure and means" who served as "hostess-on-call," answering the door "from breakfast until midnight seven days a week"; Mary Keyser, previously employed in Addams's sister's home, who supervised the settlement's household work; and Mary Kenney, who lived nearby with her mother whom she supported on her printer's wages of fourteen dollars a week. For Kelley, the most important of these companions were Julia Lathrop and Mary Kenney. In 1893 Lathrop was appointed to the Illinois Board of Charities, putting her in a position to reform the state's prisons, county farms and almshouses. Kenney had recently brought her union-organizing work "with self-supporting, wage-earning young women" under the aegis of the settlement.[39] In 1892 Samuel Gompers appointed her the first woman organizer for the AFL.

Addams, Lathrop, and Kelley were each about thirty years old. After completing college, each had spent nearly a decade seeking work commensurate with her talents. While Addams had studied and traveled, Lathrop worked in her father's law office. Now all three found that what others could not provide for them they could supply to one another— "dear friends," a livelihood, contact with the real world, and a chance to change it.

Kelley and her new colleagues seem never to have discussed the most fundamental aspect of their community—the fact that it only existed because each resident had decided not to marry or, in Kelley's case, had separated from her husband. For those who constituted the community's core—Addams, Starr, Lathrop, Kelley, and later Hamilton

—it would be hard to exaggerate the importance of their unmarried status as the key to their new standing as coresidents. Their silence on the topic only highlighted its significance. Each had broken the most compelling social rule regulating the lives of women of their class—the compulsion to marry. Indeed this rule might be called a "structural principle," so deeply was it implicated in the reproduction of their gender identity, their society, and its social relations. The chief means of enforcing that rule lay in the alternative to marriage: a lifetime of dependency on and service to married relatives. Addams and her colleagues broke precedent by transforming spinsterhood into a splendid self-sufficiency. They joined a small cohort who were reconstructing their gender identity by refusing to replicate their class identity through marriage. The settlement movement gave them the opportunity to destabilize both their class and their gender identities, one maneuver reinforcing the other, and to redefine the possibilities open to them as middle-class women. Since they each had decided not to marry (or, in Kelley's case, not to remain married) before they found each other, their appreciation of the settlement as a sanctuary was all the greater.[40]

Kelley's move to Hull House firmly situated her in a female environment. Jane Addams asserted her female identity by decorating Hull House as if it were her family home. "Probably no young matron ever placed her own things in her own house with more pleasure than that with which we first furnished Hull-House," she recalled, aim-

Ellen Gates Starr, ca. 1890. Courtesy of University of Illinois at Chicago, Special Collections, University Library, Jane Addams Memorial Collection.

Mary Kenney (later Mary Kenney O'Sullivan), ca. 1892. Courtesy of University of Illinois at Chicago, Special Collections, University Library, Jane Addams Memorial Collection.

Julia Lathrop, ca. 1892. Courtesy of University of Illinois at Chicago, Special Collections, University Library, Jane Addams Memorial Collection.

Dr. Alice Hamilton, ca. 1897. Courtesy of University of Illinois at Chicago, Special Collections, University Library, Jane Addams Memorial Collection.

ing for a style that combined Victorian furnishings from her Cedarville home with the simpler functional taste of John Ruskin and William Morris.[41] During the first year of their experiment, Starr and Addams occupied only the second floor and drawing room, but the following spring the owner gave them the entire house, rent free. High ceilings lent the rooms dignity, as did the carved marble fireplaces. Addams purchased a sixteen-foot table for the dining room, painted the walls and edges of the floor "a strong terra and cotta," and installed brass gas lights and a "handsome Wilton rug."[42]

The settlement expressed its female identity in a variety of ways, including residents' attention to problems related to children and women. Following their own judgment rather than the example of Toynbee Hall, Addams and Starr's first action at Hull House was to start a kindergarten and nursery. In a neighborhood in which one-third of the population was under the age of fourteen, the vicinity teemed with children and so did the settlement. As Kelley humorously put it, the house received "hordes of children, whose comings and goings it was far from easy to keep upon the agreeable footing of hosts and guests." Around the corner, a six-room house was rented for kindergarten and nursery work; a tiny cottage behind it served as a diet kitchen. As Addams wrote Mary Smith, the house and cottage regularly served as a shelter for women as well as children: "The nursery continues to be crammed to its utmost capacity and a good many forlorn

Hull House dining room, 1890s. Courtesy of University of Illinois at Chicago, Special Collections, University Library, Jane Addams Memorial Collection.

Hull House kindergarten, 1890s. Courtesy of University of Illinois at Chicago, Special Collections, University Library, Jane Addams Memorial Collection.

mothers and babies sleep there from time to time." Infants, toddlers, and kindergarten pupils arrived before dawn in winter, brought by working mothers on their way to their long days of ten to fourteen hours in factories or sweatshops. Kindergarten classes were held every weekday morning in the large drawing room; boys and girls clubs for older children met after school. Many took advantage of the lending library.[43]

In the afternoon, the drawing room was converted by the addition of a rug and chairs from kindergarten to meeting room for the Hull House Women's Club. At some club meetings, Dr. Leila Bedell, a homeopathic physician on the staff of the Chicago Hospital for Women and Children, discussed "physiology and hygiene" with club members and probably offered immigrant women a rare opportunity to discuss birth control techniques. In 1893 the settlement opened a public dispensary. Five bathtubs in the Hull House basement were the only washing facilities available to many of their neighbors. These also served as a *mikvah* for Jewish women or, as Florence Kelley put it, provided "the purification prescribed by their ritual." That service was replaced in 1892, when Hull House donated a nearby lot and the city allocated money for the construction of "seventeen shower baths, a swimming tank, and a tub."[44]

Before Kelley arrived, the settlement had expanded into a variety of rented spaces. The second floor of one nearby building served as a gymnasium, its ground floor as a coffeehouse. There, with its "generous fireplace," a newspaper story said, "you may obtain an excellent lunch at moderate cost. . . . While you are eating it you will see the neighborhood come in and purchase whole meals ready cooked to take home and heat over. Soups and stews, baked beans, oysters, bread, biscuits, cakes, and a variety of other things may be bought here cheaper and better than they themselves could prepare them." The coffeehouse served "an average of 250 meals daily" and furnished "noonday lunches to a number of women's clubs."[45]

Newspaper reporters noticed the settlement's feminine qualities. "One thing is clear to a visitor—that a man never started this enterprise, though men are now allowed to assist in conducting its activities. Everywhere the graceful hand and refined spirit, domestic instinct, artistic feeling and intuitive perception of woman are manifest." Hull House was not the only women's settlement that conveyed the feeling of a home. In the fall of 1892 in the United States there were two men's and three women's settlements. Vida Scudder commented on the source of major differences between them: "Put half a dozen young men together, and they instinctively evolve a club; put half a dozen young women together, and they as instinctively evolve a home." Women residents also spoke of the resemblance between settlements and their college dormitory experiences. "Upstairs in our rooms it seemed as if we were back in college again," one remarked. As at women's colleges, servants were hired for the tasks of cooking and heavy cleaning, but otherwise the housekeeping was cooperative. A Philadelphia settlement resident wrote,

"The house which we help to sweep and dust is far more ours than one which is left to the care of a maid." These continuities between home, college, and settlement drew women into reform work and smoothed their entrance into new forms of social action.[46]

Settlement living promoted intimate relationships among women residents. As a part of women's political culture, settlements recognized the special qualities of female identity, including the need for love unimpaired by repressive male dominance. Patriarchal values had been systematically eroded during the nineteenth century, and pre-Freudian sexual values did not discourage what came to be called "Boston marriages." Frances Willard, enormously powerful president of the WCTU in the 1880s and 1890s, lived openly with women partners and at the same time exemplified all that was desirable and honorable in American womanhood.[47] Women's settlements freed women to love other women, as sisters, as comrades, and as sexual partners.

Jane Addams's relationship with Mary Rozet Smith exemplified the lifelong loving partnerships that many women reformers developed with other women between 1890 and 1920, both within and outside the settlement movement. Hull House had grown out of Addams's close friendship with Ellen Gates Starr, and after the summer of 1892 it was sustained by her relationship with Mary Rozet Smith. "Tall, shy, fair, and eager," and ten years younger than Addams, Smith lived with her father, a wealthy manufacturer, a few miles away. Jennie Dow introduced Smith to the settlement, and Addams promptly assigned her to work with the boys' club.[48]

Smith arrived at the settlement at a time when Addams was beginning to recognize that she could not continue to pour her inheritance into its support. Such a policy had allowed her to shape the settlement according to her own wishes, but it also created large deficits. If she kept spending at the same rate, she would soon become dependent on the charity of other donors, a dismal prospect that would have deprived her of crucial discretionary power. She needed someone who could replace her as fairy godmother.

That someone was Mary Rozet Smith. In the fall of 1892 she began to share Addams's daily financial concerns, and by 1894 she had become the chief funder for the settlement's varied needs. Addams's love for Smith grew alongside her appreciation. Sharing the torrent of Addams's financial obligations, Smith soon became "the highest and clearest note in the music of Jane Addams's personal life." Very conscious that she was mixing her professional with her personal life, Addams wrote her, "It grieves me a little lest our friendship (wh.[ich] is really a very dear thing to me) should be jarred by all these money transactions." But the settlement setting encouraged such mixing, and for almost forty years the source of "delivering love" in Addams's life also helped her sort through Hull House accounts.[49]

Residents did not always reveal their deep feelings for one another. Alice Hamilton wrote her cousin that the presence of Jane Addams "still rattles me, indeed more so all the

Mary Rozet Smith, ca. 1892. Courtesy of University of Illinois at Chicago, Special Collections, University Library, Jane Addams Memorial Collection.

time, and I am at my very worst with her. I really am quite school-girly in my relations with her; it is a remnant of youth which surprises me. I know when she comes into the room. I have pangs of idiotic jealousy toward the residents whom she is intimate with. She is—well she is quite perfect and I don't in the least mind raving over her to you." Despite or perhaps because of these strong feelings, the emotional landscape at Hull House was more reserved than intimate. To other residents, Kelley was "Sister Kelley" or "Dearest F.K.," never Florence. Miss Addams and Miss Lathrop were almost never called Jane or Julia, even by their close friends, although Kelley occasionally took the liberty of calling Addams "gentle Jane," and both Mary Rozet Smith and Louise deKoven Bowen knew Addams as Jane.[50]

Addams prevented the atmosphere from becoming saccharine. Alice Hamilton described the relations among early Hull House residents as "almost entirely devoid of personal intimacy." It was not that Hull House was "bleak and business-like," as Hamilton once described settlements in New York but rather that Addams inspired a model of interaction that shunned the sentimentality and emotionality traditionally associated with women. "We knew each others' opinions and interests and work and we discussed them often and freely," Hamilton said, "but the atmosphere was impersonal, rather astonishingly so for a group composed chiefly of women." This gave each resident more psychological space and reduced the possibility of conflict. "I cannot imagine a diverse community in which there was less division or friction," one resident later said. "We did not behave like business partners trying to round the corners of each other's silences, or like huddled intellectuals, or like rasping literary groups, or even like those theological seminaries and college faculties whose members develop vested interests and are full of gossip and spite." Hull House residents did not mother one another. Hamilton commented, "[Addams] never tolerated the sort of protecting, interfering affection which is so lavishly offered to a woman of leadership and prominence. . . . She was impatient of solicitude, and her attitude brought about a wholesome, rather Spartan atmosphere." Consciousness of their public visibility may have prompted this behavior. One resident wrote about another settlement: "In a settlement we are so fond of our friends, so real a bond of sympathy exists between us, that we are apt to forget this, and to greet them on all occasions, as we should do in private." This, she said, "we should sedulously avoid," for "in a company of forty or upward it is practically impossible to be intimate enough with all to greet them in the same manner; and if we kiss one or two, will not the rest feel that we are making distinctions? or if strangers, will they not feel left out in the cold?" Hull House residents benefited from mutual support but were left free to pursue their own distinct goals — superb conditions for social innovation.[51]

Residing in this blend of home and social movement, Kelley described her Hull House colleagues to Engels as "a colony of efficient and intelligent women living in a working men's quarter with the house used for all sorts of purposes by about a thousand persons a week." She was "learning more in a week of the actual conditions of proletarian life in America than any previous year." One activity was "the formation of unions of which we have three, the cloak-makers, the shirt makers, and the book makers." She concluded on a note that mixed personal and professional perspectives. "I have found friends and an opportunity to work for the support of my little children; and I hope to be able to resume work among the wage earners."[52] She had finally found an environment capable of sustaining both her hunger for knowledge and her quest for the power to make a difference in the lives of working people.

With her passionate convictions and scorching wit, Florence Kelley made as immediate and vivid an impact on Hull House as it had on her. Julia Lathrop later said that her arrival "was timely and she helped from the first." Addams welcomed her influence as a guarantor of the settlement's seriousness of purpose. Kelley promptly reorganized Hull House priorities, supplying a rudder that firmly redirected the settlement's activities away from neighborly aid and toward larger issues in public policy. Earlier that year, returning home with Julia Lathrop after assisting at a difficult childbirth, Addams worried that the inexhaustible supply of local emergencies might deter them from undertaking more broadly effective measures and asked: "Why did we let ourselves be rushed into midwifery?" Kelley set a contrary example. One day when Ellen Starr departed to wash the corpse of a local child, she chided: "Sister Starr, if we [are to] bring about a change in this country peaceably, we've got to hustle. I believe it's a solemn duty to wash the dead, but it's mighty incidental!" Addams and Starr both benefited from their new friend's knack for making hard choices.[53]

Before long Kelley took a central place in the settlement's hectic routine, often filling in for Addams. "Mrs. Kelley seemed to be in charge," one visitor noted about a lecture in the gymnasium. "Poor tired Miss Addams came in towards the end." Addams's memory of those early years at Hull House was "blurred with fatigue" induced by "unending activity"; a trustworthy surrogate like Kelley seemed heaven-sent. Each morning "Sister Kelley" ate breakfast at the settlement's coffee shop, where she joined others in planning the day's strategies and responsibilities. Significantly, she also ridiculed into extinction the evening prayers and Bible readings that Addams and Starr led, often praying on their knees and holding hands. Even so, Starr still found Kelley irresistible, writing a cousin, "I roar, meditate profoundly, and do everything in between over her remarks."[54]

Kelley's compatibility with her Hull House colleagues had many sources, but one fundamental incentive lay in their effort to recast the relationship between middle-class women and working-class people. Jane Addams clarified that goal in the summer of 1892 with her lecture "The Subjective Necessity for Social Settlements." Read at a conference on applied ethics at Plymouth, Massachusetts, this essay articulated her new notion of "social democracy" and presented a fresh justification for women's social activism. Just when Florence Kelley was beginning to settle into life on Halsted Street, these ideas captured the imagination of the burgeoning settlement movement and catapulted Hull House into a position of national leadership in the newly consolidating ranks of social reformers.[55]

Addams cared about the human misery that poverty spawned, but she cared even more about her own spiritual authenticity. She spoke feelingly about her generation of young adults who "hear constantly of the great social mal-adjustment, but no way is provided for them to change it, and their uselessness hangs about them heavily." The plight of daughters received special treatment. They "are taught to be self-forgetting and self-sacrificing, to consider the good of the Whole before the good of the Ego," but "when all this information and culture show results, when the daughter comes back from college and begins to recognize her social claim to the 'submerged tenth,' and to evince a disposition to fulfil it, the family claim is strenuously asserted." Young women are told that they are "unjustified, ill-advised" to act on their beliefs, and "the girl loses something vital out of her life which she is entitled to." Addams recommended settlements both as a valid alternative to the "family claim" and as a strategy "to relieve, at the same time, the over-accumulation at one end of society and the destitution at the other."[56]

This merger of gender and class, and personal and social perspectives, could not fail to appeal strongly to Florence Kelley. In 1887 she had challenged middle-class women to view themselves as part of the social problem as well as part of its solution and ask themselves: "In the great strife of classes, in the life and death struggle that is rending society to its foundations, where do I belong?"[57] Addams's "Subjective Necessity" answered this question in ways that allowed middle-class women to recognize the problematic nature of their class identity without either abandoning it or submerging their efforts in working-class social movements—to recognize the worrisome relationship between capitalism and democracy without following Kelley's route into socialism.

Addams did not speak explicitly about one feature of settlement life that enhanced the "subjective necessity" of her work: the empowering experience of white middle-class women moving freely among exotic and alien cultures in ways that resembled travel abroad or work within the expanding missionary empires in Asia or Africa. Very few of their poor neighbors were native-born Americans who differed from them solely in terms of class. Neighborhood residents' Greek, Italian, Polish, and Russian cultures amplified the differences between them and settlement residents in ways that empowered the settlers racially and culturally as well as in terms of class. Working on the borders between their own white middle-class Protestant culture and the diverse cultures of their neighbors, they frequently experienced the best of both worlds, enjoying the superiority conferred by their cultural identity yet benefiting as well from the cultural values their neighbors assigned to their work. When an Italian workingman paid Addams's streetcar fare one day, and she asked the conductor if he knew to whom she was indebted, he roughly replied, "I cannot tell one dago from another when they are in a gang, but sure, any one of them would do it for you as quick as they would for the sisters."[58] In her own culture Addams could never have enjoyed the respect that Italians accorded to nuns, but on the streets of Chicago's Nineteenth Ward she often did.

On this cultural borderland, Addams discouraged traditional notions of charity. "I am always sorry to have Hull House regarded as philanthropy," she wrote in an 1892 companion essay, "The Objective Value of a Social Settlement." Although the settlement "has strong philanthropic tendencies and has several distinct charitable departments, which are conscientiously carried on," Addams thought it unfair "to apply the word philanthropic to the activities of the House as a whole." Instead, she believed herself to be exercising "the duties of good citizenship." This civic expression of moral obligation lay at the heart of Addams's achievement. A large concept capable of integrating diverse approaches to social change, "the duties of good citizenship" could embrace Florence Kelley's passionate materialism as well as the more traditional forms of social obligation expressed in meetings at the Chicago Woman's Club. "The duties of good citizenship" became more than a justification for women's public activism; it provided a public platform on which men and women stood as equals in shaping the nation's destiny.[59]

The settlement filled a crucial gap in civil society, she thought, because "the policy of the public authorities of never taking an initiative" was "fatal in a ward where there is no initiative among the citizens." Kelley agreed, noting that nowhere else is the individual "so left to himself" as in poverty-stricken urban neighborhoods "and nowhere does the devil clutch more voraciously after the hindmost." Thus "the playground, creche, kindergarten, college extension classes, popular lectures, political campaign meetings" and the settlement's thirty clubs created a badly needed focus for community among people who otherwise shared "only the narrowing experience of poverty and social disadvantage, [and] are farther held apart by differences of race, religion, traditions, manners and customs."[60]

Supporting trade unions for women was another means by which Hull House residents recast their relationship with working-class people. That work began with Mary Kenney in 1891, just before Florence Kelley arrived. Initially Kenney resisted her mother's suggestion that she attend a Friday evening concert at the settlement, and on her first visit Addams perceived her hostility. However, after Addams volunteered to help her union, Kenney looked around the drawing room and replied: "We haven't a good meeting place. We are meeting over a saloon on Clark Street and it is a dirty and noisy place, but we can't afford anything better." Henceforth Kenney's bookbinders and other women's unions met at Hull House. Kenney remembered that Addams also helped in other ways. "Miss Addams not only had the circulars distributed, but paid for them. She asked us how we wanted to have them worded. She climbed stairs, high and narrow. Many of the entrances were in back alleys. There were signs to 'Keep Out.' She managed to see the workers at their noon hour, and invited them to classes and meetings at Hull-House." Just a few days before Kelley's arrival at the settlement, Addams wrote Henry Demarest Lloyd, "Last week twenty more shirt-makers joined the union, so that we feel that they are well on their feet." A few days after Kelley's arrival, Addams asked Lloyd to help Mary Kenney establish a cooperative garment-making factory for her union. She hoped that Lloyd, Clarence Darrow, and Jenkin Lloyd Jones would contribute one hundred dollars each. English classes at the settlement offered important benefits to Kenney and other nascent labor leaders. As a delegate to the Chicago Trade and Labor Assembly, Kenney was asked "to draw up resolutions," but, having left school at the age of fourteen, she felt inadequate to the task. Hull House built her skills for those occasions.[61]

Directly connected to the settlement's union efforts was the Jane Club, a rented residence for about fifty self-supporting workingwomen established by Kenney and Addams in June 1892. The club emerged from discussions among striking shoe workers who noticed "that the strikers who had been most easily frightened, and therefore first to capitulate, were naturally those girls who were paying board and were afraid of being put out if they fell too far behind." One of four women living on her own in Chicago resided in a boardinghouse, but, as the club's treasurer told a reporter, members of the Jane Club felt especially fortunate. "There are a lot of successful working girls clubs in Chicago; lunch clubs, study clubs, boarding clubs and I don't know what all. But we are different from them all, in as much as we have no rules and no matron to order us around. We do as we please—in most things. Here every girl has a say in the affairs of the club." The connection between collective and individual autonomy among Jane Club dwellers mirrored that of Hull House residents.[62]

The settlement's ability to attract workingmen as well as workingwomen was particularly gratifying to Kelley. She wrote Henry Demarest Lloyd late in 1892: "We are getting a constantly improving body of men to make the house their headquarters, and now that the ground is actually broken and the foundation is laid for the [new] Coffee House and the lease secured for land for a great meeting hall, the nucleus cannot fail to grow into a larger mass of thinking, active workingmen." In keeping with that goal, the Hull House Men's Club was formed early in 1893, nominally "to arouse interest in athletic and other sports." Men were drawn to the settlement by ethnic social events as well as the talks at the Workingmen's Discussion Club. Thursday evenings were German nights, with reading, music, and cakes and ale. Saturday evenings were reserved for Italians, its organizer, Alessandro Valerio, being very successful at attracting all classes of his compatriots. The Workingmen's Discussion Club (later called the Working People's Social Science Club) attracted H. D. Lloyd and other prominent speakers on such topics as child labor, the eight-hour day, and labor unions. Kelley often presided.[63]

There was nothing genteel about their discussions. A visitor from France in the mid-1890s called it "a club where social science gladly uses the language of anarchy." The membership was cosmopolitan, she said, "plenty of those Russian Jews." Mme. Blanc was shocked at the "rage and rancor" that the working-class audience hurled at the evening's speaker, a University of Chicago professor, and was surprised that "Miss Addams allow[ed] her guests to be so ill treated." But she was impressed by the respect Addams elicited from the rough-and-ready men, who strictly observed the six-minute limit she suggested for the length of their remarks. Addams later acknowledged that "it was doubtless owing largely to this club that Hull House contracted its early reputation for radicalism."[64]

Noting the inclusion of men in the settlement's activities, a Chicago newspaper story commented on the difference between Hull House and women's charitable work: "This home is to differ from Young Women's Friendly Association, Young Woman's Christian Association and other organizations which aim to meet similar social needs, in that it will not confine its effects either to the young or the women only." In keeping with this goal of reaching all its neighbors, Hull House began to admit male residents in 1893. By 1894 the settlement accommodated sixteen residents, ten women and six men, the women domiciled in the original building and the men in the men's residence club. "The free association of men and women under the same roof" made it remarkable in Chicago's civil society.[65]

Revealingly, the presence of men did not threaten the hegemony of women residents. As Beatrice Webb drolly confided to her diary during her 1898 visit, "The residents consist in the main, of strong-minded energetic women, bustling about their various enterprises and professions, interspersed with earnest-faced self-subordinating and mild-mannered men who slide from room to room apologetically." Hull House impressed Webb as "one continuous intellectual and emotional ferment." [66]

Perhaps because the settlement embraced men in its mandate, wealthy Chicago men helped fund its expansion. The first structural addition, a two-story art gallery built adjacent to the original house, was donated by a powerful man in the world of Chicago art patronage. The first building added after Florence Kelley's arrival, which contained the new gymnasium and coffeehouse (both perceived as male-oriented spaces), was funded by a gift of fourteen thousand dollars from William Colvin and Allison Vincent Armour, whom the Chicago Post identified as "rich men," the latter associated with meatpacking. By early 1894 the settlement also embraced a cooperative residence for men, the Phalanx Club. In 1895, William Colvin paid for a third-story addition to the original Hull House building.[67]

German night at Hull House, 1894, clipping in Hull House Scrapbook.

Thoughtful men from all walks of life attended Hull House dinners. Weber Linn recalled that when Julia Lathrop and Florence Kelley were talking over dinner, "arguing some problem of correcting a social injustice, and disagreeing as they often did on the best method of procedure, it is doubtful if any better talk was to be heard anywhere. Prime ministers of Europe, philosophers of all doctrines, labor leaders and great capitalists . . . visited Hull House and dined there, and listened willingly to the odd half-reluctant meandering sentences of Miss Lathrop . . . and to the interrupting thrusts or the quick, close and yet sweeping logic of Mrs. Kelley, and were glad to be there." Addams grew adept at handling self-important or tiresome male visitors by assigning them to residents with a gift for listening. One short-term resident humorously described herself dealing with the responsibility of a gentleman who "was hardly seated before he was explaining the political situation to me, and telling me geographical and railway facts concerning the country. He took me under his wing of superior information at once, and poured mental food into my opened beak." [68]

Florence Kelley's decision to remain at Hull House in the 1890s (and subsequently to live at Lillian Wald's Henry Street Settlement after she returned to New York) was the same crucial life choice made by many other leading women reformers in the United States at the dawn of what came to be called the Progressive Era. Prominent women reformers who affiliated with the social settlement movement for much or most of their lives constituted a large proportion of the generation of leading women social activists born between 1860 and 1880.[69] By joining the settlement movement, unconventional and atypical Florence Kelley joined a strong social current. After 1900 this movement supplied vital leadership within middle-class women's organizations and helped channel women's grassroots activism in ways that shaped the outcome of Progressive reform and redefined the relationship between women citizens and their society. In the 1890s when Florence Kelley joined it, the social settlement movement was exceedingly diverse. Yet its chief features help us understand the new location she had acquired in American public life.

Men and women in the social settlement movement of the early 1890s were part of the just-emerging Social Gospel—a movement that deliberately blurred the lines between secular and religious concerns by emphasizing God's immanence in everyday life. Institutionally speaking, settlements descended from city missions that reached back to the evangelical heyday of the 1830s. New in the 1880s, however, was the secular tone of ministerial voices like Washington Gladden, pastor of the First Congregational Church of Columbus, Ohio, whose 1886 book *Applied Christianity* responded to the labor struggles of the late 1870s with a broad program of social reform, and of groups such as the Evangelical Alliance (1887) and the Church Association for the Advancement of the Interests of Labor (1887) that brought together clergy and laity concerned about "the social question." Laypeople like Henry George in *Progress and Poverty* (1881) and Richard Ely in *The Social Aspects of Christianity* (1889) blended spiritual yearnings with material analyses. Jane Addams added her own voice to this trend in 1892 by speaking for "the Christian movement toward Humanitarianism." Merging the sacred and the secular, religion and society, the Social Gospel empowered religion by fastening it to the whirligig of industrial development and empowered reformers by sanctioning their use of potent language and symbols. This fusion of sacred and secular world views in the social settlement movement made it possible for women of quite different mixtures of spiritual and political motivations, like Florence Kelley and Jane Addams, to labor together fruitfully.[70]

When Florence Kelley arrived at Hull House, however, the Social Gospel had barely begun. Addams referred to some clergymen who "were making heroic efforts to induce their churches to formally consider the labor situation," most of whom "failed to formulate the fervid desire for juster social conditions into anything more convincing than a literary statement." Not until November 1893, when a British proselytizer for the Social Gospel, William Stead, presented a riveting lecture series, "If Christ Came to Chicago," did the movement begin to achieve extensive support. Thus Hull House was as much the mother as the child of the Social Gospel.[71]

Settlements offered more to young women than to young men. "A College Settlement is supposed to be made up of 'emancipated women,'" a Philadelphia settler noted in 1894. Men had many other arenas in which to test their freedom and talents, but women had no better forum in which to explore the question, "After college, what?" Outsiders who viewed them collectively emphasized the moral and state-building components of their work. For example, Robert Woods, head resident of Boston's South End House and trained to be a minister, wrote of women settlers: "The reinforcement of the life of the home, the reconstruction of the neighborhood, the placing of people, particularly the young, in their normal moral setting in the scheme of social intercourse to which they belong,—this is the particular part of the building up of the State which is woman's peculiar privilege."[72] Woods highlighted the continuities between settlement work and women's past employments, but discontinuities were equally apparent. Settlements gave American Protestant women unprecedented opportunities to forge their own destinies at the same time that they reshaped urban neighborhood life. In the 1890s women residents had only begun to realize that by combining the security of a residential community with the activism of a social movement they had created a potent new source of power for women social reformers.

One telling difference between most male settlement leaders and the women settlers at Hull House lay in the different populations from which they were drawn. Both sexes were educated and middle-class, but men settlers consisted primarily of clergy and would-be clergy, while Hull House women were more politically motivated. Revealingly, Robert Woods of South End House in Boston received a regular salary, but no comparable woman leader did. Male settlement leaders were seeking alternatives to more routine religious careers. Like the women at Hull House, however, many women settlement leaders were pursuing alternatives to the political careers from which they were barred by reason of their gender. Many, like Kelley, grew up in politically active families and knew a great deal about the nuts and bolts of American public policy. Very few came from intensely religious families or had clergyman fathers; such daughters were more likely to be mustered into the missionary empires of American churches than into the settlement movement. Commenting on the "religious influence" in most settlements, a journalist observed that "it remained for the Misses Addams and Starr, the founders of Hull House, to undertake in the largest sense of the term the work of good neighboring." By welcoming politically motivated women, Hull House and other leading women's settlements became civic boats on the religious stream of the Social Gospel.[73]

A comparison of the relationship between leading British and American women reformers and their respective settlement movements illuminates the dynamic place American women settlers occupied in the American political process. Kelley once noted that "the divergences in social and economic conditions in England and America" were so great "that discussions of concrete evils and proposed remedies are commonly not equally applicable in both countries."[74] This was especially true of English and American settlement women, who faced different evils and sought different remedies.

Differences between the two movements began with sheer numbers. Observers in both countries remarked on "the large numbers of women workers" in the American settlements. "They are so much in the majority that the number of men is almost negligible," one British visitor wrote. By 1905 American women settlers outnumbered men by about four to one. Between 1886 and 1911 more than three-fourths of American settlement heads were women. This numerical dominance made it much easier for women to integrate men into space that they controlled. In England women were more often seen as marginal members of the male-dominated movement. Henrietta Barnett, wife of the founder of Toynbee Hall, said that Samuel Barnett "had nothing to do" with the women's settlement in Nelson Square, founded in the mid-1880s, except "his sympathy for whatever I was caring about."[75]

Britain's more activist state and effective civil service meant that British settlements became a training ground for "bright, young, reform-minded civil servants." As one of these later wrote, "Men who went into training under the Barnetts . . . could always be sure of government and municipal appointments." Thus Samuel Barnett, who was closely linked to traditional spheres of male influence, retained that connection by preserving "the settlement movement primarily for men." When the Barnetts visited Hull House in

1891, "they were much shocked that, in a new country with conditions still plastic and hopeful, so little attention had been paid to experiments and methods of amelioration which had already been tried" in England and looked in vain through the Hull House library "for blue books and governmental reports." Similarly, when Addams visited Toynbee Hall in the mid-1890s, she expressed surprise that "people take 'governing' so seriously, quite as a profession." [76]

In the United States, access to governmental influence flowed through the channels of party patronage rather than the civil service; thus ambitious young men seeking careers in government did not crowd women out of leadership positions in the American settlement movement. This made it possible for women's political culture to dominate the movement and use it to advance their dissenting traditions. Furthermore, American settlements were responding to a problem that their British equivalents confronted in a much milder form: the massive immigration of non-English-speaking people. Just as the nation's greater crisis over slavery elicited more innovative political participation among American women between 1830 and 1860, so too the colossal scale of immigration after 1880 created a more urgent and obvious need for their reform energy than was the case in England. In America, immigrants were not merely contributors to culture as they were in England; they were rapidly redefining it.

One measure of the effectiveness of American women's activism on this score can be found in the fear they inspired in immigrant newspaper editors. One Bohemian editor insisted in 1892: "When male America realizes that it is not strong enough to overpower the immigrant element, it calls upon the women for aid. It is for that reason we have such a large number of women's political organizations, whose sole aim is to agitate whenever and wherever possible against the immigrant." This keen sense of competition with women's political organizations had no equivalent among immigrants in England. While a significant number of Russian Jews settled in London's East End, the only reference to them in Henrietta Barnett's memoir of her husband's work was a passing notice of a "Minister of Reformed Synagogue in New York," who earned the compliment of being "the best Christian of the lot of us," despite his work with "ugly," "unkempt" Jews needing assistance in London courts. In her biography of her husband, Henrietta Barnett made no mention of these immigrants ever attending Toynbee Hall events. Instead, men's and women's social settlements in England focused their efforts on British-born members of the working class, work that lent itself more readily to class-based definitions and thus to male control. [77]

In the United States, where immigrants constituted the majority of nonagricultural wage earners, settlement work was by definition work with immigrants. As such, it placed greater demands on settlement residents and filled a more visible gap in the nation's social fabric. Florence Kelley reveled in the "Poles, Bohemians, Neapolitans,

Sicilians, and Russian Hebrews" of the Hull House neighborhood. By November 1892 she was teaching a night school with "sixty pupils, Greeks, French, Germans, Austrians, Poles, Russians, Bohemians." The vociferous "Russian Jews" who shocked Mme. Blanc were more than tolerated at Hull House; they were favored. Kelley wrote Engels that while she found "American and Irish American wages earners . . . the most shallow beings both in mind and heart that come in my way," to her "the most open minded workers" were "the Russian Hebrew Immigrants." [78]

Another difference in the two movements grew out of American political traditions. British and American settlements both tried to bridge dangerous and growing gaps between rich and poor, but Jane Addams and many of her colleagues at Hull House took on the added burden of extending the nation's democratic values. In her call for "social democracy," Addams situated the settlement movement in a political as well as a social vanguard. While Addams insisted that she was building democracy, Samuel Barnett believed he was aiding the poor. During a visit to England in 1896, Addams concluded, "The English Settlements are much more patronizing to their neighbors than we are." Anticipating a week's visit with Canon and Mrs. Barnett, she worried about how she would "get on in an 'ecclesiastical circle' and dread[ed] it a little." [79]

Divergent traditions of women's public activism created further differences in the opportunities open to settlement residents. Women's settlements in England remained loyal to middle-class philanthropic assumptions. Following Octavia Hill and her system of providing housing for the poor through a cadre of female, middle-class rent collectors, women's settlements remained closely aligned with the Charity Organization Society, which in turn was not far removed from punitive measures associated with the workhouse. On that topic a visitor to Hull House from the British Women's University Settlement, Helen Gow, engaged Addams in a short but illuminating debate. She thought that Addams's sympathy for the poor went too far. "In emphasizing the wide universal brotherliness and responsibility" Addams "seemed to break down the nucleus family obligations" and eliminate meaningful social hierarchies. Gow vigorously defended her settlement's practices. "I said we were landlords, we served police court notices, as Miss O. Hill's helpers." Addams replied that Hill "viewed everything too much from the landlord's point of view." The visitor explained that her "experience had lain more with resident landladies, and the suffering non-paying lodgers entailed on them, dragging them down to their own level by avoiding just debt." When Addams replied, "Oh! yes poor small landlords," Gow expressed disdain: "As if the smallness made the difference in principle." Such views undercut the ability of British women's settlements to forge cross-class alliances and generate new visions of social change. [80]

In England women's political action tended to be absorbed within the contours of class struggle rather than expressed autonomously. For example, there was no equivalent of the massive grassroots mobilizing of middle-class women that the WCTU accomplished in the United States in the 1880s and 1890s. Moreover, British women's public culture was hampered by a more limited access to higher education than was true in the United States. Reflecting the primacy of her class identity, Beatrice Webb signed an anti-woman suffrage petition circulated by Octavia Hill in 1889 and did not support woman suffrage until 1906.[81]

Perhaps the most revealing difference between the two movements was the degree to which each nation's leading women reformers affiliated with the social settlement movement between 1890 and 1915. In England, the settlement movement did not attract the most prominent women reformers, and perhaps for that reason it did not create a forum within which the leading forces in women's and men's middle-class public cultures interacted on a new plane of equality. By contrast, all the factors that reinforced women's dominance in the American settlement movement also attracted the lifelong commitment of the nation's most prominent women reformers. A British observer noted in 1898 that in the United States this "revolt of the daughters" was not, "as is generally the case here [in England], a fling, but the assumption of new and more worthy duties." While women in British settlements engaged in many activities that resembled those undertaken by their American peers, British women leaders equivalent to Addams, Kelley, and Lathrop worked not in settlements but in male-dominated movements, such as Fabian Socialism, the Liberal Party, and the Independent Labour Party. Indeed, with a few prominent exceptions, leading British reformers married politically active men. Thus although Beatrice Potter (later Beatrice Webb) visited Toynbee Hall frequently, knew the Barnetts well, and pursued a career as a social investigator and reformer, she never seriously considered joining the settlement movement.[82]

In the United States, cultural values and social structures took a different turn and posed different options, providing at least some women settlers with a relatively independent position within civil society where they could express and act upon their convictions about the national interest. They formed a vanguard capable of connecting economic and social issues in new ways. As Jane Addams put it in 1895, "The original residents came to Hull-House with a conviction that social intercourse could best express the growing sense of the economic unity of society. They wished the social spirit to be the undercurrent of the life of Hull-House, whatever direction the stream might take."[83] In this independent, female place on the unstable cultural boundary between native-born, middle-class women and mostly poor immigrants, Florence Kelley found a community of peers who buoyed her faith in the moment as well as in the future.

9

"To Speak as One Having Authority," 1892

Seeking more appropriate employment than the Hull House labor bureau, Kelley traveled to Madison to see Richard Ely in March 1892 to inquire about the possibility of a position at the University of Wisconsin. He told her "all the places were filled." On her return, she wrote Caroline, "Friends were all still up and my welcome was of the warmest." That affectionate greeting and Ely's rebuff epitomized the forces channeling her political energies. Jane Addams proved a far more effective patron than Ely. "Miss Addams is wirepulling with fair prospect of success for a position here in the bureau of labor statistics for me," she told Caroline. In late May her desire to "investigate the sweating system in Chicago with its attendant child labor" was rewarded with an appointment as a special agent of the Illinois Bureau of Labor Statistics.[1]

Florence Kelley's entry into this public office marked an important turning point in her career; she graduated from the apprentice to the journeyman stage of her reform work. The job symbolized her success at translating knowledge into power and power into state action. That dynamic relationship among knowledge, power, and state formation was already under way in Chicago when she arrived; Kelley herself did not invent it. However, gender, racial, and class divisions within the Chicago polity offered remarkable opportunities for her talents, and, making the most of them, she accelerated and focused the drive to empower certain forms of knowledge as the basis for state action.

Her chief vehicle for this project became the antisweating agitation that had mobilized middle-class and working-class activism in Chicago since 1888. Chicago was part of a national movement wherein trade unionists and middle-class reformers in large American cities joined public health officials in shaping a new consciousness of urban slums as a threat to public health and moved to regulate tenement sweatshops. In Boston the movement was dominated by men; in New York it took the shape of a consumers' movement. In Chicago, because of internal divisions within organized labor and the strength of women's class-bridging organizations, antisweating opened unprecedented opportunities for women's public leadership.[2]

Kelley's appointment to the Bureau of Labor Statistics of Illinois (BLSI) built on the accomplishments of twenty years of political mobilization among Chicago women around what were perceived as women's issues. Women's public culture gained a big boost in the early 1870s when several states passed laws declaring women eligible to serve on school boards. Illinois's 1873 law made possible the immediate election of eleven women county school superintendents. The school vote gave black women a new basis for neighborhood organization capable of drawing together diverse groups within the African-American community, including recent migrants from the south, but as a result of the exclusion of blacks from city and state politics, school votes did not become a springboard to larger political action. For white women, however, whose race gave them access to city hall and the state legislature, the school vote opened a wide range of possibilities.[3]

The experience of Corinne Brown, daughter of a stair builder, exemplified women's activism through the school vote. After working in Chicago schools as a teacher and principal for thirteen years, a talk at the Society for Ethical Culture in 1885 prompted her to retire and become a full-time reformer. Elected chair of the Ladies Federal Labor Union soon after its launching, she helped found the Illinois Woman's Alliance and led that group's efforts to enforce state and municipal compulsory education laws. Viewing her efforts as part of a class struggle, Brown attacked "the unscrupulous money-making greed of the Real Estate interests" that led them to block the creation of new schools in the city's densely populated center so that suburban lots where nearby schools were plentiful would increase in value. A prominent member of the Chicago Woman's Club, Brown was selected to represent the club at the founding meeting of the General Federation of Women's Clubs in New York in 1890.[4]

Because truancy laws were the chief means of regulating child labor, school matters drew Brown and other white women directly into labor issues (a natural extension of their interests since almost all child labor in the city was white, black children being largely excluded from industrial work). By far the most urgent of these issues in the late 1880s and early 1890s was the large number of women and children employed in the city's sweatshops. *Sweating* was a term invented in the 1840s to describe the practice whereby garment manufacturers contracted work to middlemen who hired their own workers. The word evoked the long hours, desperately low wages, and unhealthy and degrading tenement working conditions that characterized garment outwork. Like other features of Chicago's economy in the 1880s, sweatshops were spurred by massive immigration

Women voting at the municipal election, Boston, 1888. Courtesy of Library of Congress.

"Cheap Clothing—The Slaves of the 'Sweaters,'" *Harper's Weekly,* April 20, 1890. Courtesy of Library of Congress.

and easy access to a vast western market. Since garment making required little capital investment beyond the cost of rented sewing machines, the industry became highly competitive. Subcontractors who were themselves newly arrived immigrants could undercut the price of factory production; factory owners eliminated overhead costs by subcontracting all their work. Even women tailors who made clothes to order contracted work out to sweatshops. Labor organizers in the garment industry opposed contract outwork because it deskilled work, lowered wages throughout the industry, and made it difficult if not impossible to maintain unions.[5]

Elizabeth Morgan, British-born socialist and leading member of the Chicago Trade and Labor Assembly, and, like Corinne Brown, a founder of the Illinois Woman's Alliance, described what she found inside a typical sweatshop in 1891: "This place is a basement with an entrance so dark that we had to find our way in by the light of matches. There were no windows in the hallway and only two windows in the work room, which was about 10 by 17 feet. Lack of air, smell of lamps used by the pressers and stench of filth and refuse made this a most horrible hole. In this place 10 men, 4 girls and 2 little children not 10 years old were at work on pants and cloaks. The men work 14 to 16 hours per day, the girls and children 10 hours, Sunday included. Wages for men $6 to $9 per week, girls $1 to $4, children 80 cents." [6] Multiplied hundreds of times, these conditions created a growing blight in the city's poorer neighborhoods. To organized labor and middle-class observers alike, sweatshops represented the antithesis of nineteenth-century values about work. They inhibited rather than liberated society's productive forces; they fostered dependence rather than independence; they degraded rather than ennobled. Above all, they problematized the labor of children and young women.

Between 1870 and 1890 Chicago's garment industry and its accompanying sweatshops absorbed increasing numbers of women and children workers. The proportion of women in the industry doubled in the 1870s, rising from 16 to 34 percent. The actual number of women increased from fifty-five hundred — 46 percent of the total female work force in manufacturing in 1880 — to eight thousand by 1890, when 31 percent of Chicago's twenty-six thousand wage-earning women in manufacturing made garments, by far the single largest industrial occupation among women.[7]

Girls and young women surged into the expanding garment industry and other tenement occupations deemed "unskilled" because only a limited range of jobs were open to them. Gendered divisions of labor crowded women into a few job categories, leaving a far wider range available to men. Definitions of skilled versus nonskilled work focus on the degree to which workers are replaceable without extensive training. But the manual dexterity required of many jobs employing women — box, shoe, and garment making, for example — utilized skills that many girls learned at home. Girls and women were easily replaced and hence vulnerable to firing if they protested job conditions, not so much because they were unskilled as because scores of workers trained at home and limited to a few occupations were able to take over their jobs.[8]

Most white women tried to avoid the chief alternative to manufacturing work — domestic service — which required them to live with their employers, imposed even longer working hours, placed them under the close and constant surveillance of their employers, exposed them to sexual assault, and restricted their social lives. A well-informed woman journalist noted this preference in 1891: "Notwithstanding the hardships of factory life, the long hours, constant work, close, hot quarters, small wages, and the poor homes returned to at night, — and in spite of the fact that it is a poor house servant indeed who does not receive four dollars per week, have a pleasant room, as good fare as the family in which she lives, no expenses for washing, etc., still, good girls for general housework can with difficulty be obtained, while if the sign 'Girls Wanted' be placed in a factory window, hundreds will be refused employment."[9] Yet as more women joined the garment industry, the number of factory jobs decreased, and sweatshops grew.

While these changes progressed among working-class Chicagoans, changing patterns of domestic hygiene, particularly water filters and the siphon flush toilet, significantly reduced mortality within middle-class households. By the late 1880s middle-class women and men had become conscious of the threat that higher mortality rates in poorer neighborhoods posed to their own lower death rates, especially through the spread of epidemic disease. Chicago's first tenement and workshop inspection act was passed in 1879 in response to the revelation that garments were being produced in tenement rooms where men, women, and children lay sick with diphtheria, measles, smallpox, tuberculosis, and other diseases. Some of these illnesses could be carried on garments into their purchasers' homes, directly linking unseemly profit and hazardous goods. Enforcement languished, however, and sweatshops continued to multiply.[10]

Women emerged as the chief actors in a new enforcement campaign in 1888, when, in response to a crusading woman journalist's exposure of "City Slave Girls" in the garment industry, Elizabeth Morgan, Corinne Brown, and others organized the Illinois Woman's Alliance (IWA). United under the motto "Justice to Children, Loyalty to Women," the alliance brought together women members of the city's myriad clubs and organizations, some of which consisted entirely of women, such as the Chicago Woman's Club, and one of which was predominantly male—the Chicago Trade and Labor Assembly. The alliance's goals focused on political action. They sought "to prevent the moral, mental, and physical degradation of women and children as wage-workers by enforcing the factory ordinances and the compulsory education law" as well as "to secure the enactment of such new laws as may be found necessary." Perhaps most importantly, they aimed "to procure the appointment of women, responsible to this body, as inspectors of establishments where women and children are employed."[11]

Florence Kelley had written to congratulate the alliance on its founding in 1889. Her work along similar lines in workingwomen's societies in New York and Philadelphia was well enough known to alliance members to prompt them to read her letter aloud. A local labor paper reported that the "daughter of Congressman Kelley" declared that "there really should not be any American child under sixteen compelled to earn its bread" and that "the child labor question can be solved by legislation, backed by solid organization and by women cooperating with the labor organizations." She also urged "the formation of a national alliance of women which would furnish its label to all manufacturers of women's clothing" who would comply with its conditions (similar to the union label used by cigar makers) and whose members would "pledge themselves to buy no clothing which is not properly labeled."[12] This notion of a national organization orchestrating selective purchasing by women would dominate Kelley's life after 1899, but for the present it remained only a provocative blueprint.

During the three years between the alliance's founding and Kelley's arrival in Chicago, the Chicago Trade and Labor Assembly lost an important opportunity to shape the emerging antisweating crusade when it opposed the entry of women into public offices that emanated from the campaign. One of the chief actors in this drama was Elizabeth Morgan, who in 1888 helped found the Ladies Federal Labor Union, No. 2703, an early affiliate of the AFL that adopted the Knights of Labor principle of treating housewives as producers. Morgan represented both this union and the larger Trade and Labor Assembly in the Illinois Woman's Alliance.[13]

In the spring of 1889 the IWA obtained the board of education's agreement to appoint two women as school inspectors. One of these was to be a member of the Ladies Federal Union, the other from the Chicago Woman's Club. Surprisingly, Elizabeth Morgan and the other Trade and Labor Assembly representative in the alliance opposed such appointments. They told the assembly that they "refused to sign such petitions, as in their opinions such acts would create and encourage a class of office seekers within the organization and destroy the purpose for which the Alliance was formed" — namely, "to compel office holders to respect and enforce the law." The Trade and Labor Assembly endorsed their resolution that "everything possible should be done to check the movement after office that has so rapidly developed among the women, and which has received such influential encouragement from the politicians who have offices to give and appointments to make."[14] Women, it seemed, ran the danger of becoming part of the political establishment.

Nevertheless, the women's "movement after office" proved stronger than the assembly's ability to contain it. In July 1889 alliance activists succeeded in obtaining the city council's approval of the appointment of five women health inspectors to oversee conditions in sweatshops and factories. "They wear a star and are admitted everywhere," the IWA's annual report boasted. The women's victory followed hard on the heels of an unsuccessful petition by the Trade and Labor Assembly asking the mayor to issue inspector's badges to volunteers selected by the assembly to investigate factories and stores where women and children were employed.[15] Thus labor's endorsement of voluntarism was directly superseded by women's entry into public office.

After this triumph, the women became even more militant, assuming the social justice mantle of concern for working-class social welfare once worn by organized labor. That year alliance members confronted Chicago's board of education and the city council's finance committee with demands that they investigate the whereabouts of "30,000 children in Chicago not listed in school, shop or store" but shown to exist by the city's

Elizabeth J. Morgan. *Chicago Tribune*, April 5, 1892, 1.

census. They submitted a petition asking for the construction of thirty new schools and, five hundred strong, attended a city council meeting to demand the inclusion of a second woman on the school board. In June 1890, they obtained a municipal child labor ordinance prohibiting the employment of children under age fourteen, except for those obtaining special permission from the board of education. They also visited and criticized the maintenance of twenty-six public institutions, including police stations, which they called "festering nests for the incarceration of the poorer classes." In 1891 they sent a printed petition to the state legislature that began: "Although we, members of the I. W. A., are not voters under the laws of the State, yet we are vitally interested in all that concerns the welfare of the community. During the past few years we have been investigating and studying the administration of justice, and the management of public institutions as they affect women and children, and our experience makes it incumbent upon us to demand your consideration for the reforms as herein set forth." Even though their demands often met with "discourtesy and cigarsmoke," Corinne Brown and her colleagues kept up the pressure. Mary Livermore praised their aggressive stance in rhyme.

> For the cause that lacks assistance,
> Gainst the wrong that needs resistance,
> For the future in the distance,
> There's a woman's right to do!

In the fall of 1891, the alliance lobbied successfully for a municipal ordinance limiting the labor of children to eight hours a day.[16]

Why did Elizabeth Morgan and the Chicago Trade and Labor Assembly oppose the alliance's efforts to place women in public office? Just as women were moving toward public office, the assembly was turning away. Chicago labor leaders were skeptical about political solutions to social problems. And why not? They were painfully aware that they could not retain the loyalty of elected officials who came from their own ranks. In part, this was due to the ability of the Democratic and Republican parties to determine electoral outcomes. Chicago's legendary capacity for electoral fraud was well established by 1885, when a grand jury investigation revealed that only 7 of the city's 171 precincts did not show violations of election laws "at every step as the election progressed—fraud at the registration, fraud at the reception and at the counting of the ballots, and fraud at the final canvass of the returns." At stake in these elections was not good government versus bad government but which side would dispense city hall jobs and other party patronage. Political leaders in working-class neighborhoods were easily co-opted, ultimately remaining loyal to party officials responsible for their reelection rather than to their electoral constituency. Moreover, by one crucial measure—ethnic representation— city government was demonstrably democratic, making labor's task of offering an alternative much more difficult. Since aldermen were elected by wards, new ethnic groups, which clustered in specific neighborhoods, were quickly included on the city council; the first Italian was elected in 1885. Not being able to beat this system, William Pomeroy, president of the Waiters' Union, decided to join it. He and his union became a powerful extension of the Democratic Party and, though thoroughly compromised in their ability to work for the interests of labor, constantly threatened to take over the Trade and Labor Assembly itself. The assembly responded by opposing all office holding by its members, women included. In this context the labor movement fragmented and, as a labor editor put it, lost the "moral force which is the precursor to success in any movement." It also lost the chance to cooperate closely with the rising tide of women's activism.[17]

Still seeking to control the terms in which it participated in the city's antisweatshop movement, the Trade and Labor Assembly commissioned Elizabeth Morgan to conduct a sweatshop investigation in the summer of 1891. Although it documented shocking conditions, the report, published that October, offered a weak analysis of the causes creating sweatshops and proposed ineffective methods to eliminate them. Pointing to the "hordes of the offscouring of Southern Europe entering this country at the rate of half a million a year," particularly Russian Jewish immigrants, the study traced sweatshops to the unscrupulous among them who planted "in this free land the industrial conditions common under the despotic governments of Europe." The report's timid recommendations called for the implementation of existing sanitation ordinances and, doubting that this would be done by city officials, urged the Trade and Labor Assembly to create "a Bureau of Sanitation" of its own, "to which all violations of the health laws might be reported" and through which the assembly would issue pamphlets "to the general public instructing them in these matters."[18]

Mary Kenney, Hull House's semi-resident labor organizer, must have given Florence Kelley a vivid account of the corrosive internal divisions within the Trade and Labor Assembly, and her experiences almost certainly shaped Kelley's decision to steer clear of the labor establishment and commit herself to women's class-bridging activism. Just weeks after Kelley's arrival, Kenney's union got caught in a struggle between Thomas Morgan (British-born husband of Elizabeth) and W. C. Pomeroy, in which Elizabeth Morgan sided with her husband. Kenney challenged Elizabeth Morgan's credentials at an assembly meeting, accusing her "of having black balled members of the Shirt-makers union without cause" and having discouraged the shirt-makers' organization "because the young ladies were a lot of 'Pomeroy girls.'" Kenney's protégées surrounded Morgan, "and a wordy war ensued." One paper reported the meeting in purple prose: "In vain did the chairman rap for order and it seemed as though the pretty shirt-makers would be satisfied with nothing less than handfuls of hair, rivers of gore, and a storeful of disarranged female attire." Thereafter Kenney continued to object to Elizabeth Morgan's credentials. Samuel Gompers, drawn into the conflict, urged Morgan to cooperate with Kenney and, learning about Kenney's achievements with young workingwomen, appointed her as the first paid woman organizer for the AFL.[19]

By the time Florence Kelley emerged from her struggle with Lazare in May 1892, her political perspective was deeply rooted in women's public culture. The authority of the two male-dominated movements that had shaped her political framework between 1884 and 1892 — organized labor and organized socialism — had dissolved. To a considerable degree, her affiliation with women was a class-based affiliation with middle-class women, but that group's capacity to form meaningful coalitions with working-class women offered her a gratifying measure of class-bridging activism. To Engels she declared that "the best *visible* work is [being done] at the present moment by a lot of women who are organizing trades unions of men and women." Yet, distancing herself from his belief in trade unions as the mainstay of socialism, she added: "So far as my limited observation goes, I find more 'root and branch Socialism' among men and women of the prosperous class than I do among our native American and Irish American wages earners."[20]

Florence Kelley now considered herself a proponent of "English" socialism, meaning "the realization of socialism step by step, that as industry developed, the labor movement would develop, and through that force, laws would be enacted in the interests of labor." The core of Marx's account of capitalist exploitation—the extraction of profit in the form of surplus value from workers' labor and the chronic underpayment of workers in exchange for the value of their labor—remained vitally crucial to her thinking, but absent was the inevitability of revolution achieved through workers' consciousness of their oppression. This more gradual English socialism eroded the distinctions Kelley had previously taken such pains to maintain between her views and those of Christian socialists, Fabians, Bellamy Nationalists, and others who imagined a revitalized state as the key to a better future. By surrendering her ideological purity, she brought her own socialism into the mainstream of middle-class understanding. Policywise, *socialism* now meant an unspecific but significant extension of governmental authority into economic issues on behalf of working people. Feeling her way along this path uncharted in the writings of Engels or Marx, her ideas resembled those Eduard Bernstein would advocate in the late 1890s—socialism evolving within capitalism through the extension of economic rights that would gradually "transform the state in the direction of democracy." [21]

Ethically, however, socialism still signified a beloved community for Kelley—where human relations were valued above market relations. When questioned by her Hull House comrades about her affiliation with the Socialist Labor Party, she "lightly explained" that "she had been read out of the Socialist Party because the Russian and German Impossibilists suspected her fluent English." [22] Even so, she displayed her ongoing affiliation with German Social Democrats by posting on the Hull House bulletin board news of how socialists fared in German elections after the lifting of antisocialist laws.

Despite her avoidance of Chicago's labor establishment, Kelley did not cease working with men. Indeed, her new location at Hull House meant that her associates became more eclectic and her strategies more civic. Like Hull House itself, she became an integrative force within a wide range of coalitions of women and men, both middle-class and working-class. Instead of undermining capitalism by joining socialist groups or trade unions to burrow from within, she began to mobilize public support for a direct challenge to politics as usual. Kelley's leadership emerged in a series of mass meetings called by coalitions of middle-class reformers, clergy, trade-union leaders, and other critics of sweatshop labor. These gatherings gave her what none of those groups separately could: a public podium that reached both working-class and middle-class constituencies.

By early April and the first of these "monster meetings," Kelley had moved to the forefront of the antisweating campaign as leader of the Hull House efforts. She "galvanized us all into more intelligent interest in the industrial conditions around us," Addams later remembered.[23] Residents had "seen men, women and children trudging past with huge bundles of clothing," they had "read the Webbs [on sweating], but had done nothing about it until Mrs. Kelley came." At Hull House, Hamilton noted, "one got into the labor movement as a matter of course, without realizing how or when." Kelley was key in that regard. "It was impossible for the most sluggish to be with her and not catch fire." [24]

National and state legislators responded to antisweating campaigns by creating investigative commissions, and Hull House residents gave them an operational base in Chicago. Kelley wrote Engels with more excitement than she usually allowed herself to express to him, detailing the extent of the crisis. "Next week we are to take the initiative in the systematic endeavor to clean out the sweating dens. There is a fever heat of interest in that phase of the movement just at present: Senator Sherman Hoar is travelling about the country poking into the dens at night and unattended. The trades Assembly is paying the expenses of weekly mass meetings; and the sanitary authorities are emphasizing the impossibility of their coping, unaided, with the task allotted to them." As if to avoid being thought naive, she added, "So we may expect some more palliative measures pretty soon." [25]

The night after she wrote this letter, Kelley was the only woman on the podium at a "monster meeting" organized by Mary Kenney, chaired by the Reverend Jenkin Lloyd Jones, minister at All Souls' Unitarian Church, the most liberal pulpit in Chicago, and including Henry Demarest Lloyd as a speaker. As reported by the liberal *Chicago Times*, she "made the most sensational statement of the meeting." Although her allotted speaking time was only five minutes and Lloyd spoke for fifteen, the newspaper devoted twice as much space to her remarks as to Lloyd's. Kelley adroitly encouraged her listeners to become part of an aroused public opinion by quoting the words of the chief officer of the sanitary department, who, when confronted with his staff's malfeasance, told her: "We never do anything except what public opinion says we must. When it arises in its might and says go do this, we do it. Public opinion is not forcing us to the inspection of these so-called 'sweating dens.' We never get any communications about it, anyhow, except from cranks." [26] Passing this provocative challenge on to her audience, she deliberately subsumed all groups opposed to the sweating system—unions, clergymen, women clubmembers, and consumers—into "public opinion." This category had the virtue of civic inclusiveness; it consolidated her listeners into a coalition representing the welfare of the entire society rather than their specific interest groups, it embraced women and men as equals, and it defined a constituency Florence Kelley could lead.

Ten days later her speaking skills were even more evident as the only woman speaker at a "mass meeting of laboring folk" seeking to "abolish sweatshops." A prolabor newspaper said that hundreds attended—men "with Easter halos brushed onto their boots" and bright flowers in their buttonholes; women "in smart dresses" and "Easter bonnets." On the podium, Kelley joined Dr. Bayard Holmes, representing the city's medical opinion; Michael Britzius, a socialist from the Cigarmakers Union; Jesse Cox, a popular attorney; and Thomas Morgan, podium perennial representing the Chicago Trade and Labor Assembly. This friendly newspaper described Kelley as "a modest little woman in black, with a sweet pathetic voice, who had worked for years in London and New York, and she made the best speech of the lot. She was the noted Mrs. Kelly." The much more conservative *Chicago Tribune* described the meeting as "the Jewish branch of the Socialistic Labor party," and Kelley as "a bright little woman with a voice of wonderful sympathy" who spoke from experience. "Mrs. Florence Kelly described her visits to the sweat-shops in Chicago and other cities. Some of the children, all of whom were under 10 years old, only knew enough to say they were 14 when asked their age. . . . She told how the uniforms of soldiers, policemen, and postmen were made by sweaters, and related many pathetic incidents." The "noted" Mrs. Kelley had become a major attraction in the antisweating movement. The movement's combination of public speaking and street investigations unified her potentially contradictory strengths of idealistic vision and practical action. Day by day she grew more powerful.[27]

At these meetings, socialists seemed ineffective. She explained to Engels: "In the workingmen's meetings, Socialists are regarded as bores, nuisances and professional promoters of discord, not only between working men and capitalists, but especially among working men. And certainly the local Socialist agitators, Morgan and the Germans, faithfully earn the dislike with which they are regarded." In another letter, "the Irish American trades-unionists" earned her criticism, since they "seem never to read anything but a democratic or republican newspaper." Their obtuseness was partly due to the fact that "Chicago is 'booming' and everybody gets some share of the general prosperity and hopes for more next year." She hoped that "the more radical Irish-American leaders are turning towards the People's Party for the local Spring elections," but meanwhile "the Irish catholics 'run' the city government in the interest of the church and their own pockets, and the Trade and Labor Assembly is as corrupt and as stupid as the City Council."[28]

Children stood out as the most visible victims of this frustrating political setting. She had already measured the damage: "The municipal arrangements are so wretched that the filth and overcrowding are worse than I have seen outside of Naples and the East Side of New York. In the ward in which I live, the Nineteenth, with 7000 children of school age (6–14 inclusive), there are but 2579 school sittings and everything municipal is of the same sort." Municipal neglect made possible "child labor in most cruel forms and render[ed] the tenement house manufacture of clothing a deadly danger to the whole community."[29]

When she took up residence at Hull House, Florence Kelley shed her reliance on male mentors; Lloyd did not take the place of William Kelley, Lazare Wischnewetzky, or Frederick Engels. Lloyd did, however, quickly become a dear and trusted friend with whom she shared both her personal and professional lives. His biographer described him at the time he met Kelley as "slender, slightly above medium height, with a thoughtful, scholarly face, a mustache and wavy hair of iron gray, and bespectacled, kindly dark-blue eyes." Kelley wrote him an ebullient letter in June 1892, reporting good news on two basics—her children and her earnings—before discussing organizational strategies in the antisweating campaign. "The chicks are well and continue to like the quarters" at Hull House, she wrote, relieved to be reunited with them during the summer holiday. In the past month she had earned seventy-eight dollars as a special agent with the BLSI and twelve dollars for writings in the WCTU's *Union Signal*. "My current expenses are only $64.00 per month, so that I came out well ahead, so far."[30]

She easily shifted ground from the personal to the political. "Next as to the 'Cause,'" she continued, meaning the sweatshop campaign. "A lot of shops have moved into better quarters," thanks to the public pressure on the city's health department to enforce workshop health laws. But much remained to be done. The city's commercial leadership remained ignorant. She had obtained "a two hours interview with Marshall Fields a week ago. He says he cannot deprive worthy widows of the chance of working at home with their children! The only one I have yet found working for him, earned $9.37 in 13 weeks and we fed her children meanwhile!" The city's religious leadership lacked understanding. "On Monday morning I told 64 Congregational Ministers about our neighbours of the cloak trade," she continued. One minister was "woe begone" when she insisted that one of his prize parishioners was "a prop of the system." Six ministers then came to Hull House "to see for themselves," and Abraham Bisno steered them around the neighborhood. "When he finished they felt in their vest pockets for tips for him! He shrunk away from them, insulted beyond words."[31]

Kelley asked for Lloyd's advice about their next step. She had "gone through various states of minds" about reissuing her pamphlet on the sweating system in Chicago. "First, I wanted a new edition immediately. Then I wished to await the action of Mr. Ware [the City Health Commissioner]. Then I wanted an enlarged pamphlet. Now I want to wait, include Mr. Ware's data, the ordinances we spoke of, the latest enactments of Massachusetts and New York and make a rousing campaign document of it, for use when the legislature first meets." She believed they should act as the interface between the government and civil society. "Don't you think its just as well to let Mr. Ware investigate and the preachers preach, and then when their energies begin to flag, return to the charge ourselves, and make the proper authorities do some practical thing about it?" She was in no rush, since lawsuits filed by the Department of Health against violators of the city's health laws "seem to be slumbering over the summer holidays and my horizon continues serene and cheerful." [32]

The antisweating campaign exemplified the opportunities for Kelley's leadership that blossomed in Chicago's fluid political environment. Hull House served as the secure center from which she reached out to a variety of other groups and individuals. One of the most important of these was Abraham Bisno, the frustrated young union organizer in the women's clothing industry who came to work more closely with Kelley than with the Trade and Labor Assembly. He met her in the spring of 1892, after a long string of reversals. "We have fought and starved and struck and starved to little effect," he declared at an antisweatshop rally in May. "We struck in 1888, 1889, and 1890. Part of our people were jailed. We lost the strikes and resumed the eighteen-hour a day work at starvation wages." [33]

Sixty-five years later, Bisno still remembered Kelley vividly. He explained why he first sought her out: "In my reading about the labor movement, I ran across a book called Conditions of Working People by Frederick Engels, translated by a woman named Florence Kelley Wishnevitski." The book made a "great impression" as one of "the strongest indictments I had ever read against the present order of things." At Chicago's Lassalle Political and Educational Club, "Mrs. Wishnevitski, was spoken of as one of the greatest American socialists. It was said she was a Yankee from way back, that her father was the father of the system of protection in America, and that her father had also been a judge for a great many years. She belonged to the highest class of families in this country, and yet she had joined the Socialist Party and was held up as one of the great examples showing that the better class of people were with the socialists." He was told that "she had come to Chicago and was living in our immediate neighborhood, namely at a place called Hull House." [34]

Bisno recalled that Kelley spoke to him "about her great desire to participate in the activities of the labor movement," and he "invited her to address our meetings." She, in turn, introduced him "to other members of the Hull House group," including Jane Addams, whom he "found to be a person charged with moral and ethical principles." Bisno remembered the settlement very positively. "My acquaintance with the people at Hull House was an eye-opener to me. People who did not belong to our class took an interest in our lot in life. This was very new to me." He "appreciated cordially the nobility of their characters, [and] the integrity of their effort." Bisno became a Hull House regular, especially in the Working People's Social Science Club. [35]

He found Kelley enormously appealing. "The world of the rebel and the student was her world completely," he said. "Her criticism of the present order was sharp, bitter, vigorous, with a finely developed sense of humor always present, as well as enormous erudition." She was "well informed on political science, economic and industrial science, and also the natural sciences." Even so, she was easy to approach. "She talked with me as though I were her equal. The fact that she was a Yankee and I a Jew seemed to make no difference to her." He found her sympathy genuine. "When I described the poverty, suffering, and oppression of our people, she took a great deal of interest. She was very sensitive to suffering." She valued his union work and the sacrifices it entailed. "She believed most strongly in propaganda and education, considered herself a missionary for the cause in the labor movement, and offered herself in these efforts." In the mid-1890s, Bisno became one of Kelley's closest coworkers. He was one reason why she told Engels that "the most open minded workers" seemed to her "the Russian Hebrew immigrants." [36]

While drawn into union organizing with Bisno and Mary Kenney, through mass meetings, pulpit speaking, and a broad coalition of reform organizations, she became a voice that served no master but the public welfare. This stance made it possible for her to advocate an eclectic range of public actions, including the consumer boycott. "If the people would notify Marshall Field, Henry King, and others that they would buy from them no clothing made in sweatshops, the evil would be stopped," she insisted at a rally on May 8, 1892. That evening, services at Jenkin Lloyd Jones's church became a forum on the sweating system. The pastor said he "would rather see his child fade from sight under the treadmill of death known as the sweatmill sewing machine than to live and prosper on the profits of such an infamous system." Kelley, speaking from the pulpit, presented "many pathetic cases of little ones out of whom the life is being ground." She appealed to the women in the congregation to join a protest the following night led by the Woman's Alliance. Alliance members attended the city council meeting en masse and demanded that immediate action be taken to provide better school facilities in the Nineteenth Ward, where thousands of children lacked school places. [37]

The coherence and power of the Woman's Alliance was actually waning at this time, and more narrowly conceived civic groups were emerging to take its place. Early in 1892, the Municipal Order League, a spin-off of the Ladies Committee of the World's Fair Congress, was founded to seek ways to eliminate mounds of uncollected garbage that threatened public health, especially in poorer neighborhoods. The *Tribune* reported the group's activities through a fable that highlighted the governance vacuum that Chicago's women were filling: " 'Who will clean our streets?' asks the neat little housewife. 'I won't,' says the Mayor; 'I won't,' says the Council; 'I won't,' says the Commissioner of Public Works; 'I won't,' says the contractor, with his gang of intelligent Italians; 'I won't,' says the Inspector, who keeps tab on the intelligent Italian vote. 'Then I'll do it myself,' says the tidy little housewife." [38] Chicago offered women's organizations ideal conditions for expanding their power through civic action. Government and labor were stymied; women and children were suffering; and both working-class and middle-class families were potentially threatened by disease.

Kelley's praise for the power of consumers was timely. Recent court rulings had held secondary boycotts by unions to be criminal conspiracies that deprived entrepreneurs of their personal liberties, but judges could not stop individual consumers from using their purchasing power politically. At a mass rally in May, Ethelbert Stewart, a working-class protégé of Henry Demarest Lloyd then serving on the BLSI, was one of the most radical voices. Stewart believed that boycotts were "rapidly driving out tenement house cigars" and offered a way to "abolish the sweating system if we stand together and refuse to buy clothes made in those dens." He concluded, "Let us do it!" Although boycotters were initially male—"Keep the money of fair men moving only among fair men," a circular declared—clearly this was a field that could be cultivated by middle-class women. Stewart and Kelley were thinking along the same lines about different constituencies.[39]

In the spring of 1892, Stewart's endorsement probably aided Kelley's appointment as special agent of the BLSI. Like other state bureaus of labor statistics, Illinois's was distinctly a labor measure when it was established in 1879. The bureau's first achievement came in 1883, when it obtained legislation for the inspection of mines, achieving a major breakthrough in one of the state's most important industries. Kelley's appointment highlighted her investigative expertise. She was hired to research and write a two-part report on working women in Chicago and the sweatshop system in Chicago, which appeared in the bureau's seventh annual report.[40] The research was in progress when she joined the bureau, but she quickly imposed her views. Less than five months after her arrival in the city, she held an official position with considerable leverage for shaping public policy. New York was never like this.

Four days after her appointment, she proudly told Engels, "As you will see from the heading of this sheet, I have been made special agent for the Bureau." She enclosed a copy of the "schedule"—the form used to record data at the household and shop level. "For a full schedule, I receive the munificent compensation of fifty cents. This is piece work for the government with no regular salary. It remains to be seen how many I can fill in a month." She was expected to supervise "1000 schedules to be filled by 'sweaters victims' in the clothing trades. They are Poles, Bohemians, Neapolitans, Sicilians, and Russian Hebrews, almost excluding all other nationalities." The work consisted of "shop visitation followed by house to house visitation." She enjoyed these survey efforts and credited her success to her "polyglot acquisitions" and "living directly among the wage earners."[41]

That summer she had charge of Hull House. Misses Addams, Starr, and Lathrop had left, but since "the neighborhood takes no vacation," she had "an ample sufficiency of occupation," especially as Miss Farnsworth, who usually tended the door, lay "seriously ill," leaving that demanding task to Kelley.[42] Chicago was engulfed in record high temperatures and a typhoid epidemic, but Kelley thrived. She took an especially keen interest in the young people in her English classes. "Bessie Irahuisky comes two evenings a week to read English with me (and with a class of twelve of her compatriots). She is going to a Grammar School next year, living with her brother meanwhile. Pascha . . . with all her brothers and cousins are laboring through the third reader with me and when they have finished I mean to have them read William Morris' News from Nowhere and More's Utopia and then Engels Development of Socialism from a Utopia to a Science. They are really intellectual, the whole dozen, and it is delightful to teach them."[43]

Kelley's exploration of sweatshops for the Illinois bureau remained her most demanding work. She later testified that she investigated "between 900 and 1,000 places," making "a house to house canvass, from 9 o'clock in the morning until 7 at night." Ellen Starr described Sister Kelley's weariness. "Her feet are so swollen despite wearing extra large shoes that she sits with her feet in the washtub all the time she is not in the street." Starr told her the washtub "seemed to be her only dissipation," and Kelley said "it was the most expensive one she could afford." Supporting her children and their caretaker "takes all she can earn," Starr continued. "The poor lady is utterly destitute until she gets her next pay. She is wearing one green silk stocking and one blue one of former glory, and she has no car fare left." Still, Starr noted, Sister Kelley felt "awfully sorry for people who have no 'chicks.'" Starr hoped Kelley would teach her German, saying, "I intend to suck that orange to the extent of its juiciness and my capacity."[44]

While most of her visits with Ko, Margaret, and John occurred at the Lloyds, the children also visited Hull House. Yet her lack of privacy there meant those occasions could be stressful. Ko remembered a traumatic visit when his mother "was taking the three of us to see her tiny third-floor room, called the 'cell,' to read to us from Kipling, whose stories were new and exciting then." Their plans were ruined by a "scrub lady, who was drowning the floor [of her room] with dirty suds in the name of cleaning it." His disappointed mother reacted by unleashing a "storm of anger approaching a hurricane."[45]

In the fall and winter of 1892–93 Kelley set up her own apartment. "I have swarmed off from Hull House into a flat nearby with my mother and my bairns," she wrote Lloyd. The children attended local schools, and Caroline managed the household. Given the intensity of her daughter's schedule and the fragility of Caroline's emotions, this arrangement could only be temporary. "Don't let her be too much alone and get a chance to brood over the many disappointments of her life," brother Albert wrote in advance of

Caroline's arrival. "Mother must be kept cheerful." Yet the demands on Florence's time meant that Caroline was often left alone with the children. For their part, Ko, Margaret, and John seem to have missed Wayside. As Florence acknowledged to Lloyd, "I want very much to see Mrs. Lloyd, and the chicks beg me to take them to see 'the Lloyds' indiscriminately, but I seem to have no time for living of late." [46]

Ko later described the perilous pleasures of living in the Nineteenth Ward. At his "red-brick public school on Jackson Boulevard," he "heard children calling each other opprobrious names shocking to proper ears from Seventy-second Street in New York." Jackson Boulevard was then one of the very few asphalt streets in Chicago. "People drove on it in sleighs in winter. With the other fry I would run out among the sleighs and jump on the runners." Compared to going to Central Park "in spick-and-span clean clothes with a nurse who would not let us do anything for fear of soiling our clothes, this was a new and a better world." Of these years, he said, "I was blessed with the best bringing-up and educating of anybody that I have known of my time." [47]

Having her children beside her deepened Kelley's immersion in local conditions and lent weight to the conclusions she drew about social problems. "The wear and tear of living on the spot" was necessary, she wrote during her last year at Hull House, "if you are to speak as one having authority and not as the scribes in these matters of the common, daily life and experience." "You must suffer from the dirty streets, the universal ugliness, the lack of oxygen in the air you daily breathe, the endless struggle with soot and dust and insufficient water supply, the hanging from a strap of the overcrowded street car at the end of your day's work; you must send your children to the nearest wretchedly crowded school, and see them suffer the consequences." She described her demanding schedule to Lloyd in the fall of 1892. "I am teaching in the Polk Street Night School Monday to Friday evening inclusive." By day she had a new position as "temporary expert in the employ of the [U.S.] Department of Labor." In addition, she had accepted a batch of speaking engagements. "On Dec. 4 (Sunday), I go to Geneva, [Illinois], Dec. 11th to Madison to tout for Hull House under the auspices of Mr. Ely, and Dec. 17th and 18th to Oak Park to speak on Hull House and the Sweating System." [48]

Feeling her overcommitment, she declared, "Me Voilà! There is only a limited amount of me at best; and, such as it is, it works twelve hours on weekdays for 'grub and debts' and on Sundays it goes out of town to tell the outlying public how life looks in the nineteenth." To console her "small fry for the absences" she took them along. "Puss is going to Geneva and Ko to Madison with me." Her leadership in "the cause" necessarily suffered. "I don't see how I, personally, can agitate at all before Xmas." She urged Lloyd "to go ahead as if I were in New York, and if, later, I can lend a hand, so much the better." [49]

Perhaps because of the dangers of the city streets, perhaps because of Caroline's inability to run the household in her absence, and certainly because of the rigors of her own schedule, Kelley restored the children to the suburbs in the spring of 1893 as boarders with Anna Wright, the mother of Frank Lloyd Wright. Hull House colleagues compensated by making the children feel more at home during their visits. "Miss Starr has made Puss a white straw hat trimmed with poppies, and Puss, wearing her white dress with this hat, is a vision of beauty fit for the enjoyment of Gods and men," she told her mother, who had returned to Philadelphia.[50]

After completing her work for the BLSI, in the fall of 1892 Kelley tested her new civic stance by joining Corinne Brown in attacking Chicago's inadequate school facilities. With Brown she coauthored a hard-hitting report entitled "The Condition of the Public Schools of Chicago." They denounced the board of education and the city council for their neglect, backing their accusations with solid data, including "a table by wards showing that there are only nine wards in which the school sittings exceed the number of children, and these are where the wealthy live." The table depicted how many new school places were needed to accommodate children in each of the poor wards, concluding that 59,878 were needed throughout the city.[51]

Yet at the same time that Kelley was pursuing these civic opportunities, the labor question remained her first priority. In December 1892 she and others resigned from the Women's Committee on Labor Congresses, a subgroup associated with planning for the upcoming Chicago World's Fair, when the parent organization, the World's Fair Auxiliary, disapproved of their plans. She, Jane Addams, Julia Lathrop, Ellen Gates Starr, and other women in the group explained their resignation in words redolent of Kelley's style: "We believe that no adequate presentation of the labor question, which now agitates the entire civilized world, is contemplated by the controlling power of the auxiliary, and we are not willing to have any appearance of connection with what will be offered as a substitute for a real labor congress."[52]

Crucial differences between Florence Kelley's participation in women's public culture and Henry Demarest Lloyd's search for equivalents within men's public culture highlight the gendered construction of their political options and the greater opportunities open to women during this morning of the Progressive Era.

Lloyd was nine years older than Kelley and came of political age in the mugwump generation. Like Kelley, he was both intellectual and activist. The son of a Dutch Reform minister and a mother descended from a Huguenot family, Lloyd grew up in Illinois and New York City. After graduating from Columbia University and Columbia Law School, he plunged into political reform. His 1881 "Story of a Great Monopoly" in the *Atlantic*

Monthly so vividly exposed the methods of the Standard Oil Company that the issue went through seven printings, making him one of the first and most compelling muck-rakers. He criticized mugwump reform for wanting to make politics but not the economy unmercenary and called laissez-faire economic views "the irreligious, and I think un-scientific, doctrines which the Economists have put forward with such Calvinistic logic and cruelty." Emigrating to Chicago, he took a job at the *Chicago Tribune* and married Jessie Bross, the well-educated and warm-hearted daughter of the paper's publisher.[53]

Like Kelley, Lloyd saw himself as engaged in a national struggle for control of the social consequences of industrial growth. Like Richard Ely, he held a Germanic-Hegelian view of the state as the chief defender of civil, political, and economic rights. In a letter to Henry C. Adams after Haymarket in 1886, he declined to join the American Economic Association because he thought it mandated too little power to the state. He felt "firmly persuaded that the alternative before us is one of reform or Revolution; that is, we must either get redress for these 'wrongs' through the state or through anarchy." Meanwhile class war was proceeding apace. Courts were unable to resolve the conflict: "the court is an arena where as elsewhere the victory is to the strong and cunning." Instead, civil society was the means by which a new state would be created. An "umpire must be begotten out of the people of all classes, it must wield the power of the irresistible State, widened and strengthened to meet this crisis." Yet before this occurred, he thought that "the very *roots* of our notions about government, and about industrial relations, must be torn up." [54]

Like Florence Kelley, Lloyd underwent a personal epiphany that wedded him ever after to labor's side of the industrial struggle. His moment occurred on November 11, 1887, the day the Haymarket anarchists were hanged. Thereafter he saw labor's struggle in terms that equated contemporary class struggle with the crusade against slavery fifty years earlier. Like Florence Kelley Wischnewetzky before the Collegiate Alumnae Asso-ciation in May 1887, Lloyd challenged the post-Haymarket fear and loathing that his middle-class audience exhibited toward labor in an 1888 talk before Chicago's Ethical Culture Society, "The New Conscience or the Religion of Labor." Drawing on their presumed sympathy for the victorious antislavery campaign of their grandparents' era, he declared, "If labor is a commodity, the laborer is a commodity, and chattel-slavery still exists." Reprinted by the Knights of Labor and the *Illinois Staats-Zeitung*, Lloyd's speech deeply influenced Jane Addams's remarks before the Chicago Woman's Club just before Kelley's arrival at Hull House, and through it Lloyd quickly became a leading and favorite orator of the midwestern labor movement.[55] He praised labor's attempt to broaden "political freedom into industrial freedom" and thereby nurture "a new, better civilization"; in his eyes, labor was "the most religious movement of the day." In 1888 the

Knights of Labor convinced him to stand for Congress on the Union Labor Party ticket. When Kelley met him, Lloyd had just argued in *Strike of Millionaires against Miners* that "only a fool can suppose that the republic . . . will survive the continuance of such a system," in which the "captains of Industry" exercise arbitrary and socially abusive power.[56]

Lloyd knew about the writings of Marx through those of Gronlund, but his beliefs were rooted in the Emersonian tradition of anticlerical religious beliefs. He dedicated himself to a holy cause—the crusade to bring the golden rule to the "unevangelicized territory of trade, commerce, and industry"—which in a Darwinian way he felt would be a higher form of life and therefore destined to win. In the context of contemporary male political culture, Lloyd's views were somewhat utopian. His closest soul mates, Thomas Davidson and John Graham Brooks, were freelance intellectuals rather than men who worked chiefly within organizations.[57]

During Kelley's years in Chicago, Lloyd searched for an institutional setting commensurate with his politics. The power of mass meetings, such as those in which he participated with Kelley in the spring of 1892, was fleeting when unaligned with other organizations; apart from his own home, he had no equivalent to Hull House. He joined and often spoke before the Ethical Culture Society and the Sunset Club, the latter the city's chief forum for young business- and professional men to discuss current topics of local and national interest with labor leaders. Yet these clubs fell far short of matching his visionary hopes for American society.[58]

So too did the Chicago Civic Federation, founded in the fall of 1893 after William Stead's lecture series, "If Christ Came to Chicago." Pledged to improve "the material, social and moral conditions of our municipal life, whether through official or voluntary agency," the federation brought employers and labor organizers together and eventually became one of the city's most prominent agencies for social and political reform. Jane Addams was one of five founding members; women remained a strong presence within the federation, their effectiveness amplified by their own separate organizations. Yet because employers dominated the organization, Lloyd shunned it.[59]

Around 1890 Lloyd's quest for more ambitious forums than these middle-class organizations carried him into close association with Samuel Gompers and the AFL. Yet this alliance brought him little satisfaction. For example, in 1892, despite Lloyd's passionate pleas, Gompers refused to support the striking Carnegie steel workers at Homestead, Pennsylvania. Nevertheless, Lloyd's hopes for national regeneration had no better institutional vehicle. At the AFL's 1893 annual convention, he first articulated his vision of an "enlarged democracy" that united labor and reform on one platform and called for the abolition of "the social crime of enforced poverty and the dependence of any human being upon another for the necessaries of life."[60]

Henry Demarest Lloyd, Winnetka, at desk writing *Wealth against Commonwealth*, ca. 1893.
Courtesy of State Historical Society of Wisconsin, Madison.

Henry Demarest Lloyd's political beliefs were very similar to Florence Kelley's, but in the early 1890s the two reformers experienced quite different opportunities to translate their ideas into practical results. Kelley's relationship with women's public culture carried her into direct action; Lloyd's relationship with men's public culture muted his influence.

In keeping with the rising star of women's public activism, in the autumn of 1892 Florence Kelley accepted another public office. Carroll Wright asked her to direct the Chicago portion of a federal study of urban slums for the U.S. Department of Labor Statistics. She worked intensely on this project in the spring of 1893, her tabulations being published in 1894 in Wright's seventh special report, *The Slums of Baltimore, Chicago, New York, and Philadelphia*.[61] As a resident of a slum neighborhood and an able contributor to the work of the Illinois Bureau of Labor Statistics, she was an obvious choice.

A cadre of investigators arrived from Wright's bureau to work under her direction in May 1893. She and four government "schedule men" collected responses to sixty-four questions on printed schedules from "each house, tenement, and room" in the Nineteenth

Ward. This project produced data that Wright converted into scores of tables that drew on dozens of variables. Yet the information was best used by Hull House residents. There, under the guidance of Florence Kelley and Agnes Holbrook, a young settler, residents cooperated in compiling one of the most revealing social surveys of the Progressive Era. Extracting "the nationality of each individual, his wages when employed, and the number of weeks he was idle during the year beginning April 1, 1892," they then used color codes to translate the information onto public health maps that depicted each ward household.[62]

These maps utilized only two types of data—nationalities and wages—in conjunction with residential information. Yet because they displayed geographical patterns, they told more than any of Wright's charts. By defining spatial relationships among human groups, they vividly depicted social and economic relationships: the concentration of certain ethnic groups in certain blocks; the relationship between poverty and race; the distances between the isolated brothel district and the rest of the ward; the very poor who lived in crowded, airless rooms in the rear of tenements and those with more resources in the front; and the omniscient observer and the observed.[63]

Kelley's labors left her "hardworked and distracted as never before in my life." She wrote Caroline that "First Mr. Carroll D. Wright's right hand man came on to see why we did not get on faster, and he had scarcely left when the left hand man, so to speak, arrived and is here yet, driving 'for all he is worth.'" She "could not get off" during the past week and "had Ko with me here for ten days, but saw him very little while he was awake. Most of my views of him were while I was sleepless in the early morning hours."[64]

Sister Kelley and the settlement flourished in tandem. "The settlement has grown vastly," she continued to Caroline. "The playground and the project for baths now [consume] all the spare energies of everyone." The men's settlement consisted of "Mr. Arnold, Mr. Barnes, Mr. Learned, Mr. Bruce and two 'chumps.'" Significantly, she now occupied the house's premier study area on the ground floor off the parlor: "The octagon is my monopoly." The kindergarten had been "banished to the diet kitchen and still the house is as noisy as bedlam." She was noticed outside Chicago. When Caroline read about her in a Philadelphia newspaper, she wrote: "I wish I could see you read the paper and hear the applause of the friends and share the good time generally!" But, she added, "I must be satisfied with making my way in a manner that amazes even myself, and must not repine if many legitimate enjoyments go by the board."[65]

The reports on which Kelley worked for the Illinois Bureau of Labor Statistics did not bear her name as author; nevertheless, their chief characteristics closely reflected her interests. "Working Women in Chicago" investigated "the work, wages and welfare of 5,099 women and girls, employed in 95 establishments in 43 industries, and pursuing 474 different occupations." Kelley and other agents collected information from "pay-rolls and time-books" and by visits to workers at home. The latter "involved not only the finding of the homes, often widely and remotely separated, but the finding of the persons at home, and much subsequent explanation, suggestion and assistance." These home interviews verified the information acquired from employers about length of employment, weekly wages, annual incomes, and periods of unemployment. Interviews also asked about additional income, how income was spent, "age, nativity, conjugal condition and residence, health, years at school and at work, occupations of parents, and home surroundings." Like other studies promoted by Wright in the 1880s and 1890s, Kelley's constructed more reliable data than could be found in the census.[66]

Although the interviews taxed the memory "of the whole family," expense budgets were gathered from 2,819 out of 2,923 women and girls interviewed at home. Among the manufacturing operatives, 84 percent just covered their own expenses, including their contributions to their family's support; 15 percent acquired some savings; only 1 percent "failed to pay their way with the wages earned." Among office workers, 26 percent were able to save part of their earnings. Seventy-five percent of those working in shops and factories contributed all their wages "to the family fund."[67] Most of the 707 employees who did not live at home also contributed substantially to family members. For example, 36 daughters gave an average of $61 to their mothers out of their wages, which averaged $366 annually. Two-thirds of these women and girls employed dressmakers, spending an average of $12 annually. Only 52 spent money on entertainment, about $6 annually.[68]

Of those for whom personal data were collected (all employees in shops, factories, and offices), two-thirds were native-born, one-third foreign-born. Among the latter group, two-thirds came from the "old" immigration from northern and western Europe, and only one-third from Italy, Poland, Russia, Bohemia and other countries represented in the "new" immigration from southern and eastern Europe.[69]

Eighty-six percent of interviewed wage earners were under twenty-five years of age; 47 percent were under twenty; and 25 percent were younger than eighteen. Ninety-five percent were unmarried, 2 percent were married, and 3 percent widowed, and 95 percent lived either at home or with other families. Only 5 percent lived in boarding- or lodging houses. Similar statistics had been deduced by other studies of other cities, making it possible to conclude that "there is clearly small occasion for apprehension concerning the moral influence of industrial employment upon young women as a class."[70]

The study's most significant finding extended this family theme. Forty-eight percent of the large sample were "deprived of their natural protectors"—fathers and husbands. Therefore, their families "are all dependent upon them, in a greater degree than the families of those whose fathers or husbands are living and at work." [71] Thus though the great majority of these workers were under the age of twenty-five and less than 5 percent would remain in the paid labor force after marriage, the earnings of at least half possessed social significance beyond their contribution to their own support. [72]

By showing that not all families had male wage earners and that women were therefore in the labor force to stay, Kelley sought to show that, like men, women deserved wages sufficient to sustain themselves and their dependents. Her conclusion contrasted with that of labor advocates such as John Swinton, who claimed that one cause of low male wages was the presence of large numbers of women in the paid labor force and urged that working men get "the pay necessary for the support of their sisters, or daughters, or wives." [73]

This report's optimistic news about working girls and women contrasted with the bureau's sequel on sweating, which sounded a sharp alarm. When the focus shifted from women and girls in shops, factories, and offices to those in sweatshops, the evidence pointed toward legislative action. Kelley and other agents hunted down the offending workshops. "No suggestion nor rumor was unheeded," the report declared, "and every clue was diligently followed up in order to make the enumeration as complete and full as possible." These efforts disclosed 666 shops with nearly eleven thousand workers, three-fourths of whom were women and girls. Girls outnumbered women three to one because most sweated women worked at home as finishers rather than in the shop. [74]

The report identified three kinds of shops, known in the garment trade as "inside shops," "outside shops," and "home shops." The first of these were factories, where manufacturers dealt with employees through foremen and forewomen instead of contractors, "steam is provided for motive power, the sanitary ordinances are, in a measure, observed, and the establishments, being large and permanent, are known to the municipal authorities and are subject to inspection." Outside shops were smaller and run by subcontractors, relied on human-powered machines, and often eluded inspection. Home shops harbored the most captive labor force—often women with small children—who typically could not live on the wages they earned even though they worked long hours seven days a week. [75]

Shops were organized by ethnicity. Bohemians and Scandinavians constituted a majority of garment employees. Germans formed another 15, "Hebrews" 14, and Poles 12 percent of the total. Scandinavians ran the best shops, many of which used steam power and kept a ten-hour day. The worst conditions were experienced by Italian women who worked at home. They provided the most telling links between sweatshop production and communicable disease. [76]

The pressure of competition forced conscientious manufacturers either to contract work out or leave the business; thus the sweating system would continue to grow if left alone, the report insisted. "Any demand of the inside hands for increased wages or short-ened hours is promptly met by transfer of work from the inside shop to a sweater," Kelley said. Increasing numbers of manufacturers cut overhead costs, reduced the strength of unions, and shifted the burden of legal compliance onto contractors. This process de-graded workers from people to commodities: the shift from steam power to "leg power" in the operation of sewing machines left them exhausted at the end of the day; work was so minutely subdivided that no skills were required; shops changed location constantly to evade city health authorities; and "cooking, sleeping, sewing, and nursing of the sick" took place in the same room.[77]

Work discipline was more oppressive in sweatshops than in factories. In the best shops, employees were required to work for ten hours a day, six days a week; in the worst, they worked for sixteen hours (from 5 A.M. to 10 P.M.), seven days a week. Although workers were paid by the piece, each shop had its own rules requiring employees to perform stipulated amounts of work before they could leave for the day. Even the better shops "locked up" workers' hats and coats "from 8 A.M. to 6 P.M. to prevent their escape from full time." Finally, and perhaps most tellingly, wages had steadily declined, to the point where sweatshop workers had to appeal to charity to make ends meet. For example, payroll records showed that the wages of one woman who had earned $3.75 per week fell in successive weeks to $3.50, $3.00, $2.75, $2.50, $1.75, and $1.50. She worked a total of forty-six weeks in the year, earning an average of $2.72 a week.[78] This did not allow her to support herself, let alone aid her family.

Before suggesting remedies for these conditions, the report considered arguments advanced by supporters of the system who maintained "that the home finishing enables thrifty women to contribute to the support of their families, and widows to stay with their children while working for them and that the system thus utilizes an element of labor not otherwise available; in general that the small shop and the family group consti-tute a better industrial organism than the factory." To these arguments the report replied that "the total insufficiency of the earnings of widows and dependent women under this system does not commend it as a boon even to them." Despite their toil, sweated widows and children had to rely on charity. Although the report made no specific recommenda-tions for alternative means of support, such as widows' pensions, it declared in words that carried Kelley's voice: "The labor of such as these is not needed to perform the work of the world."[79]

The report recommended legislation requiring manufacturers to be licensed, the pro-hibition of garment manufacturing in tenements, regulation of the age when children could work, regulation of the hours that women and children could work, labels iden-tifying where garments were made, mechanical power in garment shops, and separate rooms for pressers and ironing. It argued that labor unions could not remedy sweat-shop workers' problems, for even though some of "the more intelligent and self-helpful in the garment trades" had formed unions, "differences of race, language and religion prove[d] an obstacle to the growth of organization." Going far beyond the recommenda-tions found in Elizabeth Morgan's 1891 report, Kelley's emphasized the need for "a rigid inspection service" that "shall not only enforce sanitary regulations, but also all laws relating to the employment of women and children." Law enforcement held the key to social melioration. "Mere enactments are idle in the face of a menace like this. The delin-quent must be confronted not only with the law on the statute book but the law-officer at his door." [80]

The Chicago Trade and Labor Assembly would never have recommended such an active role for the state, but Kelley viewed "the law-officer" at the door as salutary—partly because she saw herself in that role.[81] Her report eschewed the "sweet pathetic" voice of the April rallies, adopting instead the severe tones of state authority. Her firm stance was buttressed by groups of working-class and middle-class women who cooper-ated in the common goal of expanding state responsibility and power. Despite, or perhaps because of, their limited political rights, they viewed the expansion of state responsibility as a means of enhancing their own powers. By cooperating across class boundaries to achieve the complementary goals of social justice for working people and an expansion of women's public authority, women pursued their own class-specific and gender-specific goals with far more success than they could have achieved separately and more than the men of their respective classes could accomplish. In the process, they altered civil society and the terms on which public policy was negotiated.

Florence Kelley's remarkable access to the political mainstream widened still further in November 1892, with the election of one of the most radical governors and state legis-latures in Illinois history. In an unorthodox campaign led by German-born John Peter Altgeld, values usually limited to political mavericks like Abraham Bisno and Henry Demarest Lloyd gained wider currency. Expect the passage of "laws favorable to trades unions," the *Chicago Tribune* gloomily predicted. State labor leaders enumerated a list of three priorities—the elimination of convict-made products, "Pinkertonism," and sweat-shops. By far the most attainable of these goals, the end of sweatshops, appeared threat-ening enough to the *Tribune,* which predicted that no successful antisweating law could be passed because no law could be framed to eliminate "the middle man." [82]

Responding to Kelley's 1892 sweating report, the overwhelmingly Democratic and prolabor legislature appointed an investigative committee that held hearings in Chicago in mid-February 1893. On that occasion Abraham Bisno emphasized the convergence of moral and economic issues, analyzing how the sweating system undermined traditional negotiations that determined a just price for the work. "We immediately complain" when a sweater attaches a price of fifty cents "where the machine sewers believe that it is worth a dollar," Bisno said. When the contractor justifies low wages by saying, "'I only get so much from the factory,'" they go to the factory, where they are told: "'We don't know you people, we never saw you; we made no contract with you; you have nothing to do with us.'... nobody is responsible for the bad price." Bisno used moral terms to discredit the sweater: "The man that has the fox faculty, the man who is the shrewdest, the man that is without any moral scruples whatever, who has got the ability to grind women and children up to their utmost, and can hunt them out and find them—find the greenhorns that don't know anything, that is the man that survives in the sweating business and is the successful sweater. Others can't be." Amplifying this moral perspective, Bisno, Kelley, Elizabeth Morgan, and others also testified about the damaging effects of sweatshops on workers' health, beginning with wages too low to sustain life.[83]

Cooperating closely for the first and only time that February, Florence Kelley and Elizabeth Morgan guided the investigative committee members through some of the city's most offensive sweatshops. In shops where communicable disease had been found, some legislators waited outside in the gusty cold. All were appalled at the squalid conditions the tour revealed and grateful for the hospitable contrast Hull House offered. The residents used that opportunity to encourage legislative action. "I well recall," Jane Addams later wrote, "that on the Sunday the members of this commission came to dine at Hull House, our hopes ran high, and we believed that at last some of the worst ills under which our neighbors were suffering would be brought to an end."[84]

The commission received two legislative proposals—one from Elizabeth Morgan, one from Florence Kelley. Kelley's offered an ambitious expansion of state authority. Morgan's did not. Both banned the labor of children under fourteen, both regulated the labor of children aged fourteen to sixteen, and both outlawed the tenement production of garments for sale. But Kelley's went much further and prohibited the employment of women and minors under eighteen years of age "more than eight hours in any one day or forty-eight hours in any one week." Moreover, Kelley's provided for the creation of a state factory inspector's office, with a chief and assistant factory inspector and ten deputies "of whom five shall be women." Morgan's bill proposed enforcement through much more limited means—"sworn monthly statements from manufacturers and more conscientious reports by municipal health authorities."[85] Kelley's more ambitious program was just one example of what was becoming a trademark of her political activism: she pushed her advantage hard, using opportunities presented by one social problem as the occasion to gain ground on others, reaching always toward systemic rather than limited change.

Hull House served as an effective center for the drafting of Kelley's proposed bill. Bisno testified that "Mrs. Florence Kelly wrote that up with the advice of myself, Henry Lloyd and a number of prominent attorneys in Chicago." In his autobiography Bisno remembered that several Hull House regulars, including Bayard Holmes and Ellen Starr, formed a group "to engage in a campaign for legislation to abolish sweatshops, and to have a law passed prohibiting the employment of women more than eight hours a day." He remembered that it was "Mrs. Kelley, who with myself and Mr. Lloyd were the heart of the movement." [86]

Even though the Chicago Trade and Labor Assembly had not helped draft it, city and state labor leaders supported Kelley's bill as it made its way through the Illinois legislature. Unionized garment workers were especially supportive, since the bill advanced their goal of a shorter working day. Organized women and public opinion supported the bill as an expression of their opposition to child labor. Kelley and her colleagues at Hull House integrated these and other perspectives. As Jane Addams recalled, "Before the passage of the law could be secured, it was necessary to appeal to all elements of the community, and a little group of us addressed the open meetings of trades-unions and of benefit societies, church organizations, and social clubs literally every evening for three months." [87]

Newspaper accounts acknowledged Hull House leadership. One noted: "Judges, ministers, lawyers, progressive women and laboring men gathered to hear what Miss Addams, Mrs. Florence Kelley and the speakers they might select had to say of dens where human lives and clothing are both ground out in defiance of humanity and hygiene." Initially Addams disliked the term *lobbying* and still more the prospect, but she organized elite women to join in the effort. "We insisted that well-known Chicago women should accompany this first little group of settlement folk who with trade-unionists moved upon the state capitol in behalf of factory legislation." Not all were willing to join, however. Addams found that the General Federation of Women's Clubs was too "timid in regard to all legislation because it was anxious not to frighten its new membership," but some of Chicago's leading women activists, including Ellen Henrotin, who two years later became the federation's national president, enthusiastically worked for the bill.[88]

Anticipating the bill's passage in May 1893, Kelley looked forward to a phenomenal increase in her power. She wrote Caroline: "If our bill goes through, and it is nearly through now having passed the Senate and first reading in the House, I shall 'in all probability' be appointed Factory Inspector in July at $125.00 per month." The governor had offered the prospective job of chief factory inspector to Henry Demarest Lloyd, who in turn recommended Kelley. After the bill passed in June with surprisingly little opposition, Altgeld did appoint Kelley—a radical act in the eyes of some, but an appropriate one, since she had done so much to create the office. As Altgeld put it, "the sweatshop agitation was done by women." [89]

In Chicago Kelley joined class-bridging groups of women who, working in coalition with a broad political spectrum of men, achieved what men alone could not, and gender-specific legislation became a surrogate for class legislation. Emerging between the two key generations of male reformers—those allied with the mugwumps in the 1880s and those affiliated with the Progressive movement after 1900—Chicago women reformers in the 1890s symbolized the emergence of a crucial swing generation of women who set the style for a new reform movement—one that envisioned the state as a moral arbiter of social justice. [90]

10

"Useful
Employment,"
1893

Florence Kelley's new job as chief factory inspector of the state of Illinois gave her an unprecedented opportunity to expand governmental responsibility for social welfare. She had eleven deputies, five of whom were women, and an annual budget of twenty-eight thousand dollars. Nowhere else in the Western world was a woman trusted to enforce the labor legislation of a city, let alone of a large industrial region the size of Illinois.[1]

On a personal level, the job brought her financial security. "Governor Altgeld made my boy a good birthday present without knowing it," she wrote Lloyd, "when he mailed yesterday the commission which assures us four years of permanent useful employment." Professionally, she recognized the political challenge that lay ahead. "I only hope I may have the insight to make the most of the huge opportunity he has given me," she continued to Lloyd and asked for his help. "Any gray matter that you're willing to squander might be profitably employed by way of suggestions." A prominent liberal paper fully supported Kelley's appointment: "This lady needs no certificate of standing in Chicago. . . . Mrs. Kelly has during all her residence in this city devoted herself with rare talent and matchless enthusiasm to the amelioration of the condition of the working masses. An abler, fitter woman could not have been chosen for this untried field of labor."[2]

Nevertheless, her appointment generated protest. One of the most vehement appeared in the *Illinois Staats-Zeitung*. It called Kelley "an extremist socialist agitator who hardly differs from an anarchist" and claimed her "famous deceased father would have nothing to do with her." Kelley's reply was among her first official acts. In a letter to the *Staats-Zeitung* editor, she declared that her father "was much too courageous a man and too loving a father to let a difference of opinion about questions of political economy tarnish his relationship with one of his children." As for an attack on Altgeld for appointing her, she defended him by claiming "nothing political is involved." By this she meant "had he wanted to extend it for self-seeking reasons, he would have found a yes-person and politician, both of which I am not." [3]

The power of Kelley's office presented her with a great opportunity, but it also carried a great risk. She had used the powers of civil society to create new powers for the state. If she failed to use the state to make a difference in the lives of working people or to distinguish herself from the men she had criticized, the failure would be personal as well as professional. Could she reverse or at least offer significant resistance to the abuses of capitalism? Her hour of testing had come. At the age of thirty-four, she had a chance to justify the confidence others placed in her and to expand the power of the state to do good. For the first time, she controlled all four components of public policy: investigation, education, legislation, and enforcement. Prior to June 1893 she had demonstrated her skill at combining the first three tactics; now, with the backing of state authority, she could implement the full measure of her intentions.

Kelley's first step was a smart one: she located her office close to Hull House. Throughout her tenure as chief factory inspector she drew lavishly on the settlement's support. The second floor of a red brick building across the street from her "cell" became her second home. Addams welcomed this close affiliation with the factory inspector's office but noted that it came with a price. "The inception of the law had already become associated with Hull House, and when its ministration was also centered there, we inevitably received all the odium which these first efforts entailed." [4]

Just as important as Hull House support was the commitment of her deputies. Choosing them carefully, she picked Alzina Parsons Stevens as her chief assistant. Stevens had extensive experience in union organizing among women; in Toledo in the 1880s she rose to national prominence in the Knights of Labor. Moving to Chicago and becoming coeditor of the *Vanguard*, a weekly newspaper promoting economic and industrial reform under the motto "Marching Toward a Diviner Civilization," Stevens had worked with Clarence Darrow, Lloyd, and the Chicago Trade and Labor Assembly on the passage of the antisweatshop bill and served as a delegate to an antitrust convention Lloyd conducted in Chicago in the summer of 1893. During the year preceding her appointment as Kelley's chief assistant, Stevens had been a frequent participant in the Working People's Social Science Club at Hull House, and when she joined Kelley's staff, she moved into the settlement. "I hope to be a real help to her," she wrote Lloyd. Kelley appointed another Hull House regular, Abraham Bisno, as deputy inspector and reserved the services of Alexander Bruce, a lawyer friend of the settlement, and John Ela, an eminence in the Chicago bar, to prosecute legal cases. [5]

One of Kelley's favorite deputies, Fannie Jones, lived within a block of Hull House. She helped organize the Chicago Working Women's Council, which met monthly at Hull House. "Care for the interests of wage-earning women and children" was its object, and it advertised that "any complaints received will be carefully and thoroughly investigated and the name of the complainant not divulged if secrecy is desired."[6] Also appointed a deputy, Mary Kenney continued to live close to the settlement and probably worked closely with Fannie Jones.

In addition to Assistant Inspector Stevens, Fannie Jones, and Mary Kenney, three other women deputies—Mrs. Belle Powell, Mrs. Annie Burke, and Mrs. J. R. Powers—lived in Chicago, as did Abraham Bisno, Ewald Jensen, and John Merz. Two other deputies enforced the law outside Chicago, James Hickey in Austin (a Chicago suburb) and Joseph Ferris in Springfield. Their salaries equalled the wages of skilled workers, providing welcome economic security. Abraham Bisno, having married in 1892 and become a father, had found it almost impossible to support a family on what he earned as a union organizer. "Up to the time I became a factory inspector," he later wrote, "I had not earned enough to live on decently, went into debt, occasionally had to sponge on my friends, had period after period of unemployment, could not get a job even when there was work."[7]

During her tenure as factory inspector, Florence Kelley developed a reform strategy that characterized her work thereafter. Discerning the systemic interrelationships among diverse industrial conditions affecting working women and children (such as long hours, low wages, unsanitary conditions, rapid turnover, and weak unions), she focused her efforts on key ingredients that had the power to alter the whole setting. In this way, her reform efforts became less like a laundry list of needed changes and more like an engine, which, once started, generated other changes. This style distinguished her from organized labor in Illinois, which had not yet learned the benefits of selective lobbying and routinely submitted a long list of needs.[8]

The political environment in Chicago allowed Kelley to assault a key barrier to the improvement of working-class life—the length of the working day—and to use it as a lever for refashioning other working conditions. Having turned the issue of unsanitary sweatshop conditions into a beachhead for the eight-hour day through the 1893 law, Kelley quickly expanded and consolidated the territory under her control by soliciting a ruling from the Illinois attorney general that the child-labor and eight-hour provisions of the 1893 laws be applied to every factory and workshop in the state, not just those in tenements. His decision that key sections of the law were "general in their application" brought all Illinois manufacturing under Kelley's scrutiny.[9]

She and her staff pursued their goals with a fierce intensity, imbued with an awareness of their historical significance as agents of the state and their position in the vanguard of class struggle. Bisno's reminiscences captured their ardor. "When I was a deputy inspector I was fanatical almost to blindness with regard to the law. My impression is that Florence Kelley felt the same way I did. The same was true of most of the radical group with regard to factory inspection." Kelley exulted in a letter to Engels: "I find my work as inspector most interesting; and as Governor Altgeld places no restrictions whatever upon our freedom of speech, and the English etiquette of silence while in the civil service is unknown here, we are not hampered by our position, and three of my deputies and my assistant are outspoken Socialists and active in agitation." In this way, her office became a revolutionary stronghold. Her staff's "loyalty to one another and their teamwork" impressed Julia Lathrop. She attributed to Kelley's "warm-hearted humanity and dauntless spirit" her deputies' tendency to go beyond the requirements "set down in their instruction book." [10]

Jane Addams served as an antidote to their ferocity. Kelley needed help in selling to immigrant families the unpopular idea of limiting child labor, and Addams did all she could. "The sense that the passage of the child labor law would in many cases work hardship, was never absent from my mind during the earliest years of its operation," she later remembered. "I addressed as many mothers' meetings and clubs among working women as I could, in order to make clear the object of the law and the ultimate benefit to themselves as well as to their children." Just as important, Addams took practical steps to limit the law's deleterious effects by becoming one of the first to investigate the need for "widow's pensions." Kelley gave her "the names and addresses of all children under fourteen years of age who had been employed under the more lax old law and were now deprived of employment . . . whose mothers were widows." Addams then passed this information to Julia Lathrop, who, "in cooperation with the Bureau of Charities of Chicago," studied each case "with the utmost care." Families that needed the child's wages received financial help in the form of scholarships supplied by the Illinois Federation of Women's Clubs. Kelley thought that the relatively few numbers and small amount of money involved in this transaction showed "once for all how slight is the basis for the widely expressed fear lest hardship be inflicted far and wide by prolonging the period of childhood to the fourteenth birthday." [11] She took for granted the phenomenal network of women and women's organizations behind this maneuver.

The political setting of Florence Kelley's work magnified the intensity of her mission. John Altgeld implanted urgency from the start when, just before the passage of her bill as one of his first acts as governor, he issued pardons for the three anarchists still in prison as a result of the Haymarket trials. The pardons created a political uproar, pro-

John P. Altgeld, ca. 1893. Courtesy of Illinois State Historical Library, Springfield.

foundly alienating his middle-class supporters, and jeopardizing Kelley's reappointment by making Altgeld's reelection extremely unlikely.[12] Whatever she accomplished had to be done in four years.

Moreover, extraordinary national and international interest in Chicago lent weight to Kelley's work. Just as she took office, the city celebrated an epoch-making event — the Columbian Exposition, a world's fair celebrating four hundred years of contact between Europe and North America. During the seventeen years between the Philadelphia Centennial Exposition and this Chicago fair, she and the nation had matured in unexpected ways. Then she was a girl and the country still a collection of regions not yet recovered from civil war. Now she occupied one of the most powerful posts held by a woman in the industrial world, and the United States was challenging Germany and England for industrial supremacy. "All the world" came to Chicago in 1893. Turnstiles at the Columbian Exposition counted more than twenty-seven million visitors, vastly more than any previous fair, many from foreign countries. Emitting a constant fanfare for the "progress of human civilization," the fair created a raucous but earnest background for the state's first factory inspector.[13]

Kelley joined the midway throngs in the company of her children and thought the fairgrounds "by far the most beautiful thing I have ever beheld." On one visit she reached out to a figure from her past, probably from New York, who reminded her how much she had changed since coming to Chicago. "One afternoon I took Ko to the World's Fair, to hear Mr. Brodsky," she wrote Caroline. "He did not recognize me. I sent him my card and he came out after the concert was over and could scarcely believe his eyes. I looked so much stronger, healthier and happier than he had ever seen me."[14] Her new environment continued to heal as she began her second Chicago summer.

At the same time that the fair marked the city's emergence as a world-class metropolis, it also boosted the power of middle-class women's organizations. No Chicago resident and certainly not Florence Kelley could fail to notice the commanding position women held among the fair's organizers and at the numerous intellectual and cultural events it sponsored. "Notable in Chicago is the position taken by women," *Harper's* said. "It is in effect a new departure. It is said with some truth that it is a woman's fair." The Women's Building, planned by a group headed by Bertha Honoré Palmer, a wealthy Chicago hostess who made a hobby of social reform, greatly surpassed the achievements of the 1876 women's building in scale and elegance. Of more enduring importance, however, were the thirty congresses on themes of interest to women organized under the direction of Ellen Henrotin and the Woman's Branch of the World's Congress Auxiliary. Held in the newly constructed Memorial Art Palace (later the Chicago Art Institute), these congresses attracted participants from throughout the United States and the world. It would be hard to overestimate their effect on middle-class women's organizations. The WCTU sponsored a world meeting on temperance and an enormous "polyglot petition" that endorsed temperance in dozens of languages. The National Council of Jewish Women was founded there at the Jewish Women's Congress. The World's Congress of Representative Women, jointly organized by Elizabeth Cady Stanton and Susan B. Anthony, attracted over one hundred and fifty thousand people to a weeklong discussion of woman suffrage and women's rights.[15]

This strong manifestation of women's public culture included black women. In 1892, Ida B. Wells, Mississippi-born crusader against lynching, had settled in Chicago and organized the city's first black women's club, the Ida B. Wells Club. Author of the pamphlet *Southern Horrors: Lynch Law in All Its Phases* and organizer of the city's first kindergarten for black children, Wells justifiably protested against the fair's racism in a pamphlet, *The Reason Why the Colored American is Not in the Columbia Exposition.* As a leading black clubwoman, she likely would have attended the Congress of Representative Women. Two other prominent leaders of organized African-American women participated in the congress: Frances E. W. Harper, leader in the temperance movement, gave a speech entitled "Woman's Political Future," and Fannie Barrier Williams spoke to the congress in an address called "The Intellectual Progress and Present Status of the Colored Women of the United States since the Emancipation Proclamation." A member of Jenkin Lloyd Jones's church, Fannie B. Williams was also active in the Illinois Woman's Alliance. In 1891 she had raised money to establish a nurse training school for black women, and in 1893 she helped found the National League of Colored Women. In the fall of 1894 Ellen Henrotin and others nominated Williams for membership in the Chicago Woman's Club, and she was admitted a year later. Harper and Williams typified the mobilization of black women to improve their communities and challenge racist assumptions about black inferiority, especially in Chicago, New York, and other northern cities. Northern black women and white women did not often work together; the same racial divisions that characterized American society shaped women's activism. The World's Fair was a small and tentative exception to that rule.[16]

The General Federation of Women's Clubs, formed in 1890, held its first biennial meeting in conjunction with events at the fair, bringing together women from thirty-one states representing a membership of twenty thousand. Addressing that group, Ellen Henrotin struck a modern note: "The value of one person's mind or one person's work is steadily diminishing; it is the associate mind, the many hearts beating as one, that now move the world; and this is so well understood by women that they are rapidly learning what can be accomplished in economic, social and intellectual life by the power of an educated public opinion." *Inter Ocean* said that the meeting's agenda proved "that in the

Ellen Henrotin, 1894. Reprinted from Rev. John Henry Barrows, *The World's Parliament of Religions: An Illustrated and Popular Story of the World's First Parliament of Religions, Held in Chicago in Connection with The Columbian Exposition of 1893* (Chicago: Parliament Publishing Company, 1893), 63.

great domain of life, woman is coequal and coordinate with man." Florence Kelley was too busy with her own "coequal" work to participate extensively in these congresses, but she did present a paper, participate in a symposium at the Settlement Congress, and join Jane Addams in heading the reception committee at Hull House during the Congress on Moral and Social Reform. On these and other occasions, she would have noted how the congresses were enhancing women's public power.[17]

Another force focusing Kelley's ambitions was the most severe economic depression of the nineteenth century, which engulfed Chicago and the rest of the nation in the summer of 1893. After the New York Stock Exchange crashed on June 27, the economic disaster spread, its effects lasting for five years. In late August unemployed men rioted along the Chicago lakefront, and three hundred and fifty club-wielding policemen defended city hall from a crowd of thousands demanding jobs, food, and shelter. Kelley ventured among the barely subdued crowds when she attended a labor congress that Henry Demarest Lloyd organized in connection with the fair. When the congress shifted its venue out of solidarity with the unemployed, she and all her deputies joined a "great open air assembly" of unemployed people who "swelled to a surging torrent of humanity that filled Michigan avenue." That evening she spoke at a session on "the abolition of the sweating system."[18]

A month later she was a major speaker and presence at the Seventh National Convention of Factory Inspectors, which also met in Chicago. Addressing her fellow inspectors as their senior colleague, she used the occasion to proselytize for her pride and joy—Illinois's eight-hour law: "Not only does the new law provide for destroying infectious garments, for limiting the age of child workers and thoroughly inspecting home and shop and factory; it also limits to eight hours per day and forty-eight hours per week the working time of every female of whatever age in every factory and workshop in the state." This made it "a more searching law than adorns the statute books of any other State."[19]

Already, she said, the new law has produced "greater uniformity of work and rest insured to girls and women" by distributing work over the year. She hoped to end both the fourteen-hour day at midsummer and the "enforced idleness and privation at midwinter." Explaining why the Illinois hours law was more effective in combating sweatshops than "the tag and license provisions of the Massachusetts and New York laws," she argued that sweaters could not produce enough profit in eight hours to "make the shop pay." Profitable sweatshops, because of the small scale of their production and their reliance on human rather than mechanical power to operate sewing machines, required "the fourteen, sixteen, eighteen hours' day."[20] The enforcement of the eight-hour law would favor larger shops with power-driven machines and better working conditions, including easier access to union membership. As she explained on another occasion, "It is the belief of the sweaters' victims as well as of the inspectors, that a rigid enforcement of the eight-hour law within these shops will compel the sweaters to increase the number of employees, enlarge their shops, and so create groups numerically too strong to submit to conditions easily imposed upon ten or a dozen very poor people." [21]

Newspaper coverage of her talk emphasized that her strategy required her to work closely with unions to prevent the reduction of hours from becoming a reduction in pay. Even though her office was not yet prosecuting violators of the hours law, one of the largest firms in Chicago had "reduced the hours of the women and girls in its employ to eight per day, [and] at the same time reduc[ed] the pay of time hands $1 per week." She called on "the older trade unions and labor organizations of the city" to "take hold of this matter and assist in the work of [union] organization" to oppose such pay reductions. Unions had already been "invaluable aids in enforcing" the law, and she thought it "a matter of trade union principle for every union man and woman in Illinois to report at once every infraction of the law." [22]

Most of her work lay in educating both workers and employers. "Much explanation is needed everywhere before the affidavits required for children between fourteen and sixteen are made, filed, recorded on the work-room walls, registered in the office and deposited where the inspector can find them on demand," she noted. "Much argument and persuasion are requisite before the eight hours placards are duly posted, and often a factory must be watched for days before the firm decides that the inspector means what he says and the law must be obeyed." This coaxing was having good results. "There is now a large body of honorable employers who are complying with the law in good faith and a large and rapidly growing body of girls who not only obey the law and value it, but work as volunteers making known its provisions and urging upon all their acquaintances the duty of co-operation with the inspectors by insisting that the eight hours limit shall be observed." Her hopes were high. During the next generation, she forecast, "this law, which now commands so little attention, will unobtrusively fulfill its mission, checking the spread of disease, lengthening the childhood of the sons and daughters of the wage earners, prolonging the trade life of the girls and women, and paving the way for a shorter day of toil for men." All her audience may have "marvelled at the beauty of the World's Fair," but she predicted that "the people of Illinois of another generation, looking back from a happier day, will call this not the World's Fair year, but the first year of the Eight Hours Law of America." She had been in office for less than two months, but she delivered her message with the force of a seasoned commander. Responding to many questions, she spoke informally "at some length" after her talk. [23]

Kelley demanded a high level of expertise from her staff and constantly replaced unprofessional deputies. She provided "general rules for the guidance of inspectors" as well as "special instructions for individual inspectors" and permitted no laxity; when she doubted the accuracy of a deputy inspector's reports, she visited the factories herself. Asking Altgeld to dismiss a deputy, she said that his "inability to make a quick, effective survey of the premises, fill the schedule of inspection and leave, discredits the office and the statute in the eyes of business men." Inaccuracies in his reports rendered them useless "as statistics in the annual report" and as bases for prosecutions. She also fired women inspectors. One "failed in all directions," even having her son and daughter do inspections for her. "The usual standard of intelligence of deputy inspectors is far lower than in England or anywhere on the continent of Europe," she complained to Altgeld, urging that he help remedy that by appointing Dr. Josephine Milligan, "an efficient woman physician," to fill a vacancy on her staff.[24]

Readying herself and her staff to prosecute violators of the law, she was energized by the prospect, writing to Ely in August: "I think we must be doing fairly good work. We have had no prosecutions yet under the new law, of which I enclose a copy; but I am preparing for a long series of them to begin next week and continue for a month or more. Meanwhile the large manufacturers are obeying promptly and the little employers are bumptious just in proportion to the badness of their shops." She quickly organized support from other officials on the boards of health and education, who, she told Lloyd in October, were cooperating splendidly: "Out of sixty-five names of children sent to the Board of Education in our first month of notifying it when we turned children under 14 yrs. of age out of factories, twenty one were immediately returned to school and several others are known to be employed as nurse girls and cashgirls, i.e. in non-prohibited occupations. This is good co-operation." The medical profession was also supportive. Every child was required to bring a health certificate from a physician before being allowed to work. The law permitted her office to disqualify children under sixteen from future employment if their health seemed impaired. Industrial medicine had not yet been invented, but her work demonstrated the need for it. She told Ely, "We are weighing and measuring factory children at a great rate and shall publish photographs of deformed children found in the cutlery trade, where every boy yet found has shown the same deformity of the right shoulder and one youngster, having worked from his 11th birthday, is now, at 15, an actual monstrosity unfit for work for the rest of his life! I think the medical chapter of this report will start a new line of activity for medical men and factory inspector both." Her comments highlighted the new forms of knowledge, expertise, and power that took the corporal body as their touchstone, empowering statistical measures over impressions and surveyors over the surveyed. She was already collecting data for her annual report. Three newspapers could be counted on for helpful publicity.[25]

Steadfast support from the governor's office smoothed her path. "Governor Altgeld is doing everything in his power to back the law, and has authorized me to engage counsel for continuous prosecutions," she wrote Lloyd in October. She tested the prosecutorial waters first by enforcing the child labor and sanitary provisions of the law. The first case was tried on October 21, and by mid-November Kelley's staff was winning an average of one indictment a day. Some of the cases went to juries. "We won our first jury case last Tuesday," she wrote Altgeld in November, "and got a conviction of a 'sweater' employed by Beifeld and Co.—Joseph Beifeld being the treasurer of the Manufacturers' Association formed for the express purpose of defeating us in the courts. There was a certain pleasure in beating them at the first encounter." Beifeld was a powerful foe, but Kelley seemed unconcerned about the consequences. Her most immediate problem lay in the necessity of borrowing money from Jane Addams "with which to carry on the office," while she awaited travel and other reimbursements from Altgeld.[26]

Her court victories were especially sweet in light of the determined opposition of the Cook County district attorney. Kelley's first prosecution took her to his office. There she found "a brisk young politician with no interest whatever in the new law and less in the fate of the persons for whose benefit it existed." Her case involved "an eleven-years-old boy, illegally engaged to gild cheap picture frames by means of a poisonous fluid," who had lost the use of his right arm through paralysis. "The young official looked at me with impudent surprise and said in a tone of astonishment: 'Are you calculating on *my* taking this case?'" Kelley replied: "I thought you were the district attorney." "Well," he said, "suppose I am. You bring me this evidence this week against some little two-by-six cheap picture-frame maker, and how do I know you won't bring me a suit against Marshall Field next week? Don't count on me. I'm overloaded. I wouldn't reach the case inside of two years." Kelley later put a political spin on this story when she claimed that the encounter had prompted her to enter law school the following fall (in fact, she had been enrolled in night courses at Northwestern University Law School in downtown Chicago for almost a year).[27]

In writing the 1893 legislation, Kelley had taken care to provide for the power "to prosecute all violations . . . in any court of competent jurisdiction in this State," so she could sidestep the uncooperative district attorney. She put John Ela and Alexander Bruce in charge of prosecutions but oversaw them closely. In a typical court action that year, M. I. Fortsch, "who runs a sweat-shop in a basement" was prosecuted "for employing a girl 13 years old, one Mary Cyanowski, who testified through an interpreter that she could neither read nor write in any language." Her father, called to testify about his affidavit stating her age as fourteen, "made it clear that the affidavit was an afterthought, made to clear the boss."[28] The judge imposed the maximum fine on Fortsch, ten dollars and costs. Her staff also won cases against "custom tailors, who seem to think that they do not belong to the same class as the sweaters in the 'ready made' trade." [29]

"The new law is working wonderfully," Kelley declared in a newspaper interview in early November. "We have already cleared out most of the filthiest [sweatshops]." Former sweatshop workers helped by reporting violations. She boasted that the Illinois law forbidding child labor was "the most radical in the world, and a rigid inspection enables its enforcement," and she attributed it with doing "much to raise the intellectual, physical and moral standard of working children." Although inspectors were not yet enforcing the eight-hour law, she reported that its "observance is extending daily." [30]

By vigorously promoting union organizing, Bisno, Stevens, and other inspectors prepared for the day when they would enforce the hours law. Kelley herself focused on meetings with "laundry girls in which I am much interested" and hosted a party for "the Laundry Women's Association" at Hull House. Alzina Stevens, looked "distinctively good" to a Hull House visitor during the "annual party of her Women's Council of Union Delegates." This burst of activity did not pass unnoticed by the conservative *Chicago Tribune*. "Most of these inspectors are trying everywhere to organize unions among employés," the paper complained, "undertaking a general organization of unorganized labor in this city." The influential morning paper insisted that "it is not the business of any employé of the State to neglect his legitimate duty for the purpose of preaching 'organization,'" adding that "when they turn themselves into labor organizers then they go beyond all bounds." Seeking an explanation for this unconventional campaign, the *Tribune* reasoned that Altgeld was trying to build strength among Chicago voters, unable or unwilling to credit Kelley and her staff as its inspiration and not perceiving the connection between unionization and the enforcement of the hours law. [31]

At the same time as her staff fostered union organizing, Kelley boldly began to extend her power beyond the garment industry. In the fall of 1893 she hinted at such action in a newspaper interview. "After a little while, when the sweating system has been corrected, we will devote some of our time to trades that we have not been watching so closely. We do not wish any of the trades to think that our jurisdiction reaches only to the sweater shops. There are only twelve of us inspectors and there are 66,000 employers. For that reason we are going to enforce the laws rigidly in the courts." Chicago manufacturers immediately took note. Ignoring the state attorney general's earlier ruling, the *Tribune* declared, "It is stated on excellent authority that while the law limits the classes of establishments which should be looked after by these inspectors they are meddling with numerous other branches of labor, that they go into shops which they have no business to enter, and attempt to enforce there regulations which apply to other trades." This was "not lawful," the paper insisted. The inspectors "will have all they can do if they will attend to the special industries which they were expected to oversee." Judging by the complaints of her opposition, Florence Kelley was making a difference.[32]

Surveying the previous twelve months on New Year's Eve 1893, Kelley took time to count her blessings. She wrote Caroline: "I never before felt so imperatively the desire to write you at the end of the last day of the year. I think every month united me more tenderly with the loving heart that you kept so warm for me when I did not deserve it. It has been in every way, a good year for me, personally. Good health, good children, good work, good friends, and as much of your presence as it was at all reasonable to ask for. What more could a woman wish, who has survived the illusions of youth without bitterness." She was arranging a trip to "reconnoitre the situation of the clothing trades in New York City" but assured her mother that she could avoid any legal contest that Lazare might make for the children's custody. "I shall sleep in N. Jersey and any work will be in the obscure streets of the East Side of New York so that I have no fear of having any papers served upon me." She hoped to visit Caroline on her return trip. "Do not worry about me!" she wrote on another occasion. "I am well and *happy!* I shall always earn my way and I do not borrow trouble about the future at all. I live in the present." [33]

That present was preoccupied with the production of her first annual report. Like its successors, this report was an impressive credit to its scholar-activist author, exemplifying her commitment to crisp methods of inquiry as well as to effective political results. It organized information about inspections in the garment trades under the names of the contracting manufacturer and the deputy who inspected the shops. Shops that received contracts from more than one manufacturer were inspected and listed more than once. In this way, the report provided extensive data about 704 sweatshops employing 505 girls under sixteen years of age, 90 boys under sixteen, 3,617 women over sixteen, and 2,211 men over sixteen. The ratio of women and children to men was almost two to one. A typical analysis of each shop noted the subcontractor's name and address, described the room, sanitary conditions, type of power used, age and sex of the workers, and any action taken. Mary Kenney wrote of one establishment: "Shop is on second floor of rear building, low, stifling and dirty, reached by stairs used also by tenants; shut in on sides and in front by other buildings, and in rear having windows on alley where stable manure and other refuse are piled; closets [toilets] out of order; machines run by foot-power; contractor lives on premises; ordered to clean; employs 3 men, 5 women, 4 girls under 16 years." [34] In keeping with Kelley's determined extension of her authority beyond sweatshops, the report also noted the age and sex of 25,205 women and children and 42,876 men employed in 2,452 other workshops, the data organized by trade and specific location.

Readers could readily discern the situation of women and children workers in most of the city's workplaces. For example, the table entitled "Paper Boxes, Cases, etc.," showed that W. C. Ritchie was by far the largest of the nineteen employers in that category, with 58 girls under sixteen, 11 boys under sixteen, 217 women, and 64 men, a four-to-one ratio of women and children to men. Some trades, such as meatpacking, were even more uneven. The largest, Armour and Company, employed no girls or men, but 127 boys and 125 women. Three of the twenty-one meatpacking plants employed only children; six only boys and men. The trade as a whole employed 726 women and children and 597 men. The report's detailed analysis of the city showed that women and children constituted 37 percent of Chicago's industrial workforce and could be found in almost every occupation.[35]

In its interpretation of these statistics, this first report took every opportunity to justify the factory inspectors' powers. Injurious employment received special attention. One example focused on the employment of boys in tin can factories who worked in a crouching position on a shelf suspended between the first and second floor, their hands "bound up in cloths to prevent cutting, but in many cases these cloths were found to be saturated with blood." Another mentioned "boys slowly roasting before the ovens" of a cracker bakery, "in the midst of unguarded belting and shafting (a danger to health which men refuse to incur)." These and other harmful working conditions were investigated by "Dr. Josephine Milligan of Hull House" and Dr. Bayard Holmes, a Hull House supporter who taught at Chicago's College of Physicians and Surgeons and involved his students "in making measurements, tests, etc." Pointing to the tendency for some workshops to be lawful and some lawless, Kelley noted that "the prohibition of work for delicate children has been rarer in factories having good sanitary conditions, and known absolutely to obey the eight-hour section of the law, than in factories concerning which there was any doubt upon this point."[36]

Did children benefit from this systematic surveillance? Didn't they learn as much on the job as at school? Kelley referred to findings by Alzina Stevens to defend the removal of all children under fourteen and some under sixteen to schools: high illiteracy rates among working children; and high turnover rates on the job, which prevented them from acquiring technical training that might compensate for their loss of schooling. Stevens wrote that "our very thorough and complete system of handling the registers, records and affidavits, enables us to trace a child changing its place of work and also to note the number of changes in any one place." Inspection of a candy factory on August 22 and September 8, for example, found only one of sixty-three children still at work at the end of that two-week period. Others had drifted to other employment, having discovered the dead-end, negative features of their jobs and found situations they hoped might be better. This very instability saved them "from the specific poison of each trade," Kelley wrote, but it drew them into "a most demoralized and demoralizing condition," in which their employers exploited them to the fullest without giving them "a chance to learn a trade."[37]

The *First Annual Report* passionately vindicated the law's eight-hour clause. The author's own experience showed that prior to the law's enactment, students in her night school class had had to cease coming when "the candy factory in which they spent their days began to work overtime." They worked "from 7 A.M. to 9 P.M., with a half hour for dinner and no supper, a working week of eight-two hours." During the year of voluntary compliance with the law, however, "this factory worked eight hours," permitting its young employees to attend night school and allowing them and their mothers to sleep later in the morning. For working women in general the law provided "for more daily leisure and steadier work throughout the year," reducing unemployment since more were hired "during the busy season and fewer discharged in the dull one."[38]

In a special section above Kelley's name, the report provided an ambitious list of recommendations for future legislation. Demonstrating their feasibility, it quoted from the "labor laws of competing states"—Massachusetts, New York, New Jersey, and Ohio— each of which contained aspects of the recommendations, though none embodied all, and none reached as far as the Illinois eight-hour law. Some of her suggestions, however, were unique. For example, her reports repeatedly urged "that failure to supply adequate safeguards for life and limb in factories and workshops should be made a crime," something that no state had yet done. Many of Kelley's proposals also went beyond those endorsed by the Chicago Trade and Labor Assembly. For example, the assembly opposed the labor of children under fourteen, rather than sixteen, and did not support literacy requirements for child workers.[39]

Like each of Kelley's annual reports, her first served four purposes: it assembled information; it educated readers; it presented a future legislative agenda; and it described enforcement measures. Her goals were to investigate, educate, legislate, enforce. Together, these tactics built a new systematic framework for public policy initiatives in the emerging Progressive Era, one in which women experts, working closely with women trade unionists and middle-class club members, pursued what they considered "the advancement of humanity."[40]

Kelley's assault on sweatshops gained momentum during the deepening economic crisis of the fall of 1893. By September, seventy-four railroads had declared bankruptcy, and thousands of businesses followed. Desperate jobless people, mostly men, continued to pour into the city from the midwestern countryside. City hall corridors and stairways sheltered hundreds of homeless men each night, and the city hired thousands of additional laborers as a form of relief. The economic crisis followed Florence Kelley home at night, since "in that terrible winter after the World's Fair" Hull House became a shelter for homeless women. William Stead would visit late at night "wet and hungry" to drink hot chocolate and regale them with his latest discoveries among the city's down and out. "It takes something of an effort these hard times to keep up one's spirits, our neighbors are so forlorn and literally flock to the house for work," Addams wrote Mary Smith. The crisis prompted Addams to undertake "the most serious economic reading I have ever done," including "the tenets of socialism." [41]

In the first week of 1894, Kelley began to enforce the law's eight-hour provision. History beckoned. As her *First Annual Report* declared: "The Eight-hour section of the Illinois factory law is one link in a chain of measures which have been adopted during a long series of years in many countries and in several states of our union, all recognizing the principle involved in a restriction of the hours of work of women." Apart from the skilled trades, almost no reduction in hours had occurred in the 1880s, though improved mechanization and economies of scale meant that productivity soared. The AFL had vigorously promoted the eight-hour day between 1888 and 1891—resulting in shorter hours with no loss of pay for some of "labor's aristocracy"—but abandoned the project when strikes for shorter hours became less successful. In Germany, however, Social Democrats continued to champion the eight-hour day, which had been adopted in mines and among employees of the Prussian government. With the movement stalled in the United States but advancing elsewhere, Kelley put Illinois in the running for a historical breakthrough. Before the Illinois law, legislation for women in the United States had made only minimal contributions to hours reduction. Wisconsin passed an eight-hour law in 1867, but it went unenforced since the penalty applied only if an employer compelled a woman to exceed the legal limit. The nearest equivalent to the Illinois law was a recently passed New Jersey statute that limited women's work in manufacturing to fifty-five hours a week, essentially a ten-hour law providing for half a day on Saturday—not much of an advance over the Massachusetts ten-hour law for women passed in 1874.[42]

In an article for German Social Democrats, Kelley described her enforcement efforts. "Two facts characteristic of American conditions, namely the lack of compulsory school attendance and the ethnic mixture of the working class" made child labor regulations especially significant in the United States, she said. Except in Massachusetts, Connecticut, and New Jersey, school attendance was not enforced, so her efforts in Illinois made an important difference. Her group of inspectors was representative of the population, she thought. "Three are American-born with American parents, five have Irish parents, and one has German parents, while one has immigrated from Ireland, one from Sweden, and one from Russia, the last a Jew." The law's provision for an eight-hour day "caused a sensation," she acknowledged, and its enforcement posed a challenge.[43]

Fundamental to the vision of social justice one hundred years ago was the hope of redistributing two of the most important benefits of industrialization—leisure time and mass-produced commodities. Of all the shocking inequities industrialization produced in the 1890s, none was more grotesque than the contrast between those who toiled at repetitive, mind-deadening labor "the long day" of twelve, fourteen, or more hours, often not earning enough to provide for their basic needs, let alone to buy the commodities they made, and the wealthiest few who conspicuously consumed leisure and commodities. The redistribution of leisure, a radical goal in itself since it intervened in the relationship between workers and employers, was a key element in the rising standard of living among working people between 1880 and 1920 and a step toward the redistribution of wealth.[44]

Like other hours legislation, the Illinois law accepted the wage system and capital's control of the means of production but tried to negotiate less exploitative terms for workers, thereby redistributing leisure and material resources. Yet, however compatible these goals later became with American values of individualism and personal liberty, when Florence Kelley championed them in the 1890s, she drew on other values—traditional values of mutual responsibility and the welfare of society as a whole.

In January 1894 Kelley mailed an ultimatum to every Illinois manufacturer, announcing her intention to enforce "the law touching the hours of work of women and girls in factories and workshops in this state." Leaders in the eight-hour movement had for a decade argued that shorter hours would ease unemployment by making more work available to more people; Kelley tried to turn the depression into a force in her favor by emphasizing that effect. Through newspapers, she also warned employers who sought cheaper workers by firing men and hiring women that "in every case where future complaint is made [of hours violations], arrest and prosecution will follow." She specifically named "the great cloak manufactories of the city" where all employees were working from nine to twelve hours, "notwithstanding the fact that hundreds of competent cloakmakers have for months had nothing to do." With more than a bit of bravado, she claimed to feel "much encouraged in bringing suits, because we feel sure if they were appealed, our side would have a fair hearing."[45]

A conservative newspaper contradicted her optimism: "If she enforces the law or attempts to do so, a test case will be carried up, when, without doubt, the statute will be declared null and void by the higher court. . . . Mrs. Kelly might as well go into court now as to wait longer. The law is and will continue to be a dead letter. Its enforcement would be an outrage." This journalist knew that Illinois manufacturers had moved swiftly to oppose the new hours law in the courts. As early as August 1893 a group calling itself the

Illinois Manufacturers' Protective Association formed "for the purpose of co-operating to test the constitutionality of a recent act of the Legislature of this State limiting the hours of Female Labor." (At their second meeting, they adopted the more politically prudent name of Illinois Manufacturers' Association [IMA].) Led by prominent Chicago garment, shoe, and paper box manufacturers, including Joseph Beifeld, the IMA began to flex its muscles in February 1894, when Kelley began to prosecute all manufacturers and enforce the eight-hour law.[46]

That month the IMA claimed the support of one thousand employers, including "the largest employers of female labor in the state." They met weekly and authorized their "Directory" to spend "One Thousand Dollars for legal or other expenses." The IMA agreed to pay the expenses of any member who was "arrested for infraction of the eight hour female labor law." By May they had selected cases to defend before the Illinois Supreme Court and had spent over four thousand dollars on legal fees. Anticipating the manufacturers' success, hostile newspapers chided Kelley: "Mrs. Kelley augmented her own troubles. She was not satisfied with the size of her field, the sweatshops proper. . . . For this broad interpretation of the law Mrs. Kelley must have been profoundly thankful, but it will probably result in depriving her and her assistants of their good, fat jobs." Aided by the IMA, some manufacturers encouraged sweaters to disregard the law, promising to supply counsel for those arrested.[47]

Ominously, in January 1894 Kelley's office lost five child labor cases against a paper box manufacturer, W. C. Ritchie and Company. Levy Mayer, Ritchie's attorney and IMA secretary, assured her: "If you bring 10,000 cases one at a time we will be here to defend in all of them." Between January and May, her staff prosecuted nine violations of the eight-hour law for women, the first against W. E. Ritchie. All nine appealed. In May Kelley agreed to suspend further prosecutions until the Supreme Court ruled on the constitutionality of the hours law.[48]

The court heard the case deep in the southern region of the state in early May. "It was a big day at Mount Vernon," one newspaper noted. "Attracted by the brilliant array of Chicago lawyers, attorneys came in from miles around. The old court-room was jammed."[49] John Ela and Alexander Bruce officially authored the brief, but Kelley's scholar-activist mind and her experience with legal issues were evident in the structure of its argument.

The chief inspector and her coauthors had very little legal precedent on which to defend the 1893 law. The only hours law for women previously tested before a state supreme court was the Massachusetts 1874 statute, which generated almost no theoretical commentary. Ela and Bruce quoted from the Massachusetts decision upholding that law: "The law does not limit [a woman's] right to labor as many hours per day or per week as she may desire. It merely prohibits her being employed continuously in the same service more than a certain number of hours per day or week." This fragmentary logic was persuasive in Massachusetts in the mid-1870s because large numbers of textile workers—women and men—had formed unions that had been agitating for shorter hours since the 1840s, and factory owners had come to accept the inevitability of legislative action. Many large mills had already reduced hours and supported the law to prevent other mills from maintaining longer hours and undercutting their costs. In these circumstances the state's argument did not have to be watertight, so it evaded the question of whether government could deny workers the freedom to make any contract they wished with their employers.[50]

Kelley's brief had to do more. Her targets were tenement sweatshops, not large, highly capitalized textile mills that could pass on to consumers the costs associated with complying with regulation. Compared to them, sweatshops were inefficient; their profit margins depended on long hours as well as low wages, and hours laws could drive them out of business. Moreover, Illinois's law sought to protect unskilled rather than skilled and semiskilled textile workers. They did not live in company towns where large numbers worked in the same industry and sought the same remedies, and they could not be expected to grasp the long-term benefits of hours regulation when the short-term effects often diminished wages. Finally, the patriotic claim that regulation violated their own and their employees' economic rights sounded more believable when voiced by small businessmen instead of textile corporations.

Kelley needed new and irrefutable arguments. She sought them in women's reproductive lives. Legal precedent, social-justice ideas, epistemological beliefs, and Kelley's own political commitments overdetermined the shape of the arguments in her legal brief. With the issue of economic rights preempted by employers, it was hard for her and her colleagues to imagine alternatives to their focus on material conditions. The arguments they eventually settled on defined the terms of legislative action on behalf of women workers for decades to come.

Kelley and her associates built their case on three points. The first simply noted that Illinois regulated the work of men in a wide variety of occupations, ranging from miners to barbers. For example, laws setting aside Sunday as a day of rest upheld the government's "right to protect all persons from the physical and moral debasement which comes from uninterrupted labor." Law mattered, not only because it shaped material and economic relations, but because it constructed consciousness. As the outcome of struggles among competing groups, law championed different visions of social relations and social responsibilities.[51]

Yet laws for certain occupations and even Sunday blue laws for all occupations offered weak precedents for hours laws for women, and the brief moved quickly to another category of precedents: the regulation of women's factory work based on women's reproductive biology. First the brief noted that the employment of women in factories was limited by law in many states, among them, New York, Michigan, Minnesota, Massachusetts, Connecticut, Rhode Island, Pennsylvania and New Jersey. Then, making a synthetic leap that gathered all such laws under one heading, it declared that the "philosophy underlying these laws" was sustained by "medical investigations" conducted by state bureaus of labor statistics. These investigations showed "that the injury to a girl or a woman in her sexual functions" involved not only her own health and "the shortening of her own life and productive powers," but "the injury to society in the form of a physically and often mentally degenerate offspring, for whom society must afterwards care." Thus women deserved different treatment because the material consequences of their reproductive health had different and more extensive social significance.[52]

A third justification sought to buttress the second with facts about the effects of Illinois's hours law. The "long day" of more than eight hours deprived more women of their right to labor than did legislatively imposed short days, the brief argued. Shorter hours would enable more women to pursue wage work and to stay in the labor force longer. "All the scientific evidence" pointed in one direction: "that labor in factories more than eight hours a day deprives the average woman (to say nothing of girls and delicate women) of their health . . . so that in the end they are in fact *deprived* of labor by a long day; and obtain more labor, and the results of labor, by a short day." The brief also asserted that women's wages were higher in states with laws limiting their hours and denied that special laws for women gave men a competitive advantage or drove women out of the paid labor force.[53]

The brief's arguments about female reproduction rested on legal, social, and intellectual realities. Legally it was responding to traditions within Anglo-American law that since the 1840s had sustained the economic rights of employers more readily than those of employees. This bias in the free market system was especially evident in "freedom of contract" decisions, in which courts hesitated to rule against practices that benefited employers, such as payment in company scrip or employee responsibility for workplace injuries. Workers, courts often held, were free to contract their labor however they saw fit; if they were robbed or exploited, that was their choice. After 1880 this court-based defense of free enterprise was stronger in the United States than in England, where for many reasons—including the absence of a written constitution based on individual rights and the ability of Parliament to have the final say—abstract principles held less power. American beliefs in individual liberty and the power of courts to overturn statutes prevented many state legislatures from remedying class inequities directly.[54]

Between 1840 and 1870, after employers blocked the passage of more comprehensive statutes by claiming they violated workers' contract rights, working-class advocates of shorter-hour statutes in both countries invented the device that Kelley now used: hours legislation for women was enacted as a surrogate for laws for all workers. As she explained:

> It is much easier to find approval by appealing to the sympathy of the masses for the welfare of helpless working women and children than to find it by suggesting absolutely necessary measures to protect the lives, bodies and health of men, who are the fathers, husbands, and breadwinners of the same women and children. It is not easy to gain the sympathy of the whole population for these male workers, because it is assumed that they can protect themselves and that they can achieve what they need by virtue of their right to vote, without appealing to the support of public opinion.

Justified on the grounds that women's contract rights were already limited and on the basis of the state's police power to regulate matters of health and morals, this gendered strategy was understood to embrace men de facto. Even Kelley's critics agreed that where statutes reduced women's hours, they also reduced men's. "It is absurd to apply the eight-hour law to females in a factory where the males are permitted to work as long as they please," one said. "The two classes of work go hand in hand, and when you stop one you stop both." [55]

Another important goal of her legal strategy was to construct a judicial alternative to the property rights discourse that sustained laissez-faire capitalism. Property rights, which since the late eighteenth century had supplanted older conceptions of communal welfare and social responsibility, abstracted economic relationships out of their concrete material circumstances into a realm where social differences became irrelevant and the effects of the economic marketplace disappeared, where poverty and exploitation became personal misfortunes.[56] Rights discourse became a crucial tool for the maintenance of middle-class and capitalist dominance in social and economic relations. To revive older notions of communal responsibility that held individuals responsible for one another's welfare and permitted remedies for the causes of poverty, Kelley had to reintroduce material differences into her discourse. Since courts refused to recognize class as a valid basis for public policies, the differences deemed immutable between women and men provided the best terms for a materialist argument.

Material constraints lay all around her generation in the human and environmental changes wrought by machine production, and it set the terms within which social justice could be imagined. In Kelley's argument, women's bodies became a version of property that the state was obliged to protect. By being overworked, women's "lives are short-ened" and they were deprived of their labor.[57] Seen from this perspective, she was urging a new civil and economic right for women to be protected from abuse and ill health. The problem, from a contemporary judicial point of view and later from a feminist perspec-tive, was that she offered women no choice in the matter. The state defined and regulated abuse as well as its penalties. By offering women choices, the manufacturers spoke a language the courts respected.

The materialist bent in the state factory inspector's brief, however, offered the court a set of plausible new ideas. Conservatives as well as socialists had used gender to highlight capitalism's ruthless qualities. To treat women or children as extensions of machines or as interchangeable parts in machines or as commodities to be bought and sold offended a wide range of nineteenth-century beliefs. The most ancient of these was the patriar-chal notion that women and children had a higher obligation—service to husbands and fathers—than any they owed to an employer. Newer romantic notions about the sacred qualities of the human personality held family life, particularly the bond between mother and child, to be the defining difference between humans and other species, prompting conservatives as well as socialists to view the quality of family life as a fundamental measure of social well-being. Most compellingly, perhaps, Darwinian notions about the evolution of the species turned exploitation, something propertied classes could ignore, into degeneration, which they disregarded at their peril.[58]

To augment its notions of social justice, Kelley's generation drew on contemporary evolutionary thinking, in which real and imagined bodies on a scale of human develop-ment supplied a new secular guide to past and future human destinies. Carroll Wright expressed the late-nineteenth-century mixture of social justice and biological imperatives in 1895: "Shall society suffer that individuals may profit? Shall the next and succeed-ing generations be weakened morally and intellectually that estates may be enlarged?" Kelley's opponents denied the tangible causes and effects of exploitation; she amplified them. In that process, she constructed a contradictory legacy, for by measuring human welfare in corporeal terms, she built limits into the economic rights she sought to create. Yet in an unjust social system these differences offered the best route to a better world.[59]

Florence Kelley's personal experience reinforced her use of gender-driven legislation as a surrogate remedy for class exploitation. Since 1882 she had advocated legislative solutions for the problems facing working women. Through policies that treated women differently from men, she thought, the degradation and cheapening of the value of women's labor could be halted. She also knew that the legal history of hours laws for women predicted that courts would have a harder time rejecting a police-power argument based on gender than a social-justice argument based on class. From Engels himself she had learned that working conditions for women and children conveyed different meanings than those of men and revealed more of capitalism's capacity for inhumanity. For her, as for Engels, truth lay in organic structures rather than abstract hierarchies. The damage to human bodies mattered more than the free contract of the workplace. Biological ideas were simply another way of stating her 1884 vision that the solutions to industrialization's problems came from within industrialization itself: solutions for the problems of wage-earning women came from the material conditions of womanhood itself. Furthermore, at this crucial moment in her career, although her political vision was anchored in her understanding of class conflict, her political authority rested on women's institutions and women's issues. At various times in her life she had given priority to either gender-specific or class-specific measures. Now the two melded into one.

Kelley believed the ideas in her brief, but, just as important, she also thought they had the power to persuade the Illinois Supreme Court judges. As the biological link to the health of future generations, women constituted a category through which a seemingly callous judiciary could be cajoled into social responsibility. Her brief was part of an ongoing dialogue between advocates of social justice and defenders of the capitalist marketplace that resounded through the last third of the nineteenth century.[60] She said what she thought would convince the defenders of the unregulated marketplace of its destructive power. Democracy spoke to liberty, and, in this instance as in so many others, democracy's voice was gendered.

The defense of Illinois's law grew in importance after a Kansas eight-hour law for public employees, men and women, was declared unconstitutional in September 1893, a federal district judge having ruled it "a restraint on the liberty of action" and "in direct conflict with both the bill of rights of the state and with the fourteenth amendment of the federal constitution." By requiring an eight-hour day for women, which extended de facto to men, Illinois's law effectively equaled the most progressive hours law in the world—Australia's, which mandated an eight-hour day for both women and men. Relentlessly optimistic and perennially conscious of her place in history, Kelley told a newspaper reporter: "It only remains for the more conservative states to emulate the example of Australia and Illinois and to adopt the working week of forty-eight hours and the working day of eight hours." In another article, she was quoted as being pleased that "hours for men are also being reduced in shops where the men and women work independently."[61]

Hours laws fostered a more democratic distribution of the benefits of industrialization, sought to make producers into consumer-producers, and anticipated the growth of a new domestic market, but the movement had not imagined women as active agents in this process. A Democratic congressman from Chicago explained the goals of shorter hours in 1894: "When the hours of work are shortened, the laborer goes home with a long evening on his hands. He must have another suit of clothes to put on, another pair of boots, another hat, must have books or papers to read, or he must go for a walk, take his wife, thus increasing the consumption of products." Kelley added women to this vision. For younger unmarried wage-earning women, shorter hours would mean more time for night school, for improving their wardrobes, for friends, for courtship, for domestic responsibilities, for sleep. For married women workers, a shorter work day would create more time for their children, for their domestic responsibilities, and for their community organizations. For older married women who provided services for wage-earning family members, it would mean more sleep—since the hours gained usually fell in the morning—and more time for community organizations and self-improvement—since other family members would be more available to help with family life.[62]

Against this background of legal, economic, and ideological confrontation, a fierce struggle ensued for the loyalty of young women workers. Manufacturers who defended the piecework system called the eight-hour plan "ridiculously absurd," since the more hours women worked, the more they were paid. "When the harvest is ripe the reapers care nothing for hours except to fill them with industry so as to gather in as much as possible against the dull season that is to follow," one argued, applying an agrarian metaphor to this quintessentially urban issue. Organizers like Bisno retorted that the piece system did not necessarily motivate workers to labor longer hours. When they could, workers often negotiated a "just price" for piecework, thereby indirectly negotiating the "just price" for a day's work and the length of a working day.[63]

In late April Bisno and other garment organizers arranged a rally to defend the law. Middle-class and working-class supporters attended, and Ellen Henrotin spoke. Head of the women's congresses at the World's Fair, powerhouse within the Chicago Woman's Club, fluent writer and compelling speaker, Henrotin gave the law the imprimatur of a leader within women's public culture. This occasion marked her entry into a decade of progressive leadership within the women's club movement. She urged those in attendance "to agitate for shorter hours for women because it means in the end shorter hours for all workers, men and women." The Illinois law was crucial because it was testing "whether it is constitutional to restrict or limit a day's work by law." She denied that shorter hours led to reduced pay among pieceworkers: "The girls who do piece work have not had their earnings reduced by the shorter hours. They have found themselves able to accomplish as much work." However, she did acknowledge that " 'time' workers have suffered a slight reduction in pay" and urged workingwomen "to join labor unions," since this would help them avoid such reductions.[64]

Not wanting to compromise the objectivity of her office, Kelley did not speak at the rally, but she must have taken satisfaction in it, especially in Henry Demarest Lloyd's defense of the law as "evolutionary, not revolutionary. It follows logically and historically in the straight sequence of social development." He mocked "our great Chicago clothing manufacturers [who] say to their employes: 'You shall not have the shortening of hours in any way. You cannot have it by individual request; you cannot have it by union; you cannot have it by law.' " Manufacturers were not ignorant of the conditions in which their people worked. "So keen is their appreciation, on the contrary, of these conditions that business men go mad at the mere fear that they or their loved ones may descend into that inferno." Lloyd attributed the law's passage to "trades union leaders [who] raise[d] the people in mass-meetings" and guided investigators "through the baby farms of Chicago industry," and he promised that "the unions of Chicago are here to stay notwithstanding the war that is now being made upon them." So, too, "the anti-sweatshop law is here to stay." If the Illinois Supreme Court found the law unconstitutional, he passionately concluded, "we will change the form of the law. If that is not enough we will change the constitution." [65]

Support for the law by those it was designed to protect is difficult to gauge. Indirect evidence comes from an 1894 study by the Pennsylvania Bureau of Industrial Statistics, which asked more than two hundred women sales and clerical workers to state complaints about their jobs. The women objected to many features of their working conditions, including low wages, the lack of seats, and poorly ventilated toilets. But they lodged the largest number of complaints against the length of the working day and the requirement of Saturday hours. One woman bookkeeper said, "Working at night, as we are compelled to do, we are compelled to give up any thought of pleasure or recreation, as we do not feel like dressing and going out after such long hours of constant and exhausting work." [66] Historians analyzing this material concluded that the long day was a more acute problem for women because their family and home responsibilities pressed more urgently on their hours outside of the workplace than was the case with men. Young, unmarried women, as the great majority were, had to find time for these responsibilities and for their own social lives. Sales and clerical employees would have had more employment options than the sweatshop workers Kelley targeted, but their nonworking time would have held the same value. This would not necessarily translate into support for hours legislation, since the value of free time would be weighed against a possible reduction in wages, but the evidence does point to an important predisposition in favor the law's goals of reduced hours at the same pay.

Exemplifying this predisposition, all the women named in the Supreme Court appeal incurred their employers' ire by cooperating with the inspectors but nevertheless testified on behalf of the law. Lizzie Furlong, age twenty-seven, said that she worked nine and three-quarter hours a day, not counting time for lunch, at William Ritchie's box factory and hinted at coercion: "If a girl would not work up to those hours she might get a scolding," and "if she made a habit of not working those hours she would be discharged." [67] Others echoed her story.

Kelley had been careful to garner support from workingwomen when she first began to enforce the hours law in January. In a statement issued that month, the members of the Working Girls Eight Hour Club, meeting at Hull House, spoke for both men and women workers. They urged "patriotic citizens" to guarantee "that want shall not debase the manhood and womanhood of the sufferers by giving them only two alternatives—unlawful acquiescence with employers who demand a working day from ten to sixteen hours, or the acceptance of charity." Their resolutions acknowledged that shorter hours might prove inconvenient for employers and require "a sacrifice of wages on the part of some employes." Still, they stood willing to sacrifice "for their less fortunate [unemployed] sisters," believing that "in a period of distress the fortunate of all classes should be willing to help bear the general burden." [68]

Not all felt so magnanimous, however. When inspectors arrived at one firm, workers held an indignant meeting. "It is another case of women's injustices to women," a garment worker complained. "Before the women inspectors came to Mr. Palmer, every one was well paid and satisfied. . . . The firm is not to blame, they were forced to obey the inspectors. Formerly the girls worked nine and a half to ten hours, and made all the way from $9 to $10 a week. Now we can only work eight hours and our pay will be proportionately less." Just as bad, they no longer could compete with men on equal terms. "Now both men night workers and day workers can work as long as they want to, while we, whether the work be heavy or light, can only work eight hours. This in a busy season is worse than a hardship, and in the light season means little short of starvation." In another article, a woman protested, "There are 5,000 or 6,000 women in Chicago who earn their bread making cloaks. . . . Employers say that when business gets brisk eight hours a day will not fill their orders and that they will discharge the women and employ men who can work as long as necessary. The law is very unjust." Inevitably, employers zealously encouraged such opposition.[69]

By February the manufacturers had even gained supporters within the Illinois Woman's Alliance. Women shoemakers, who had carried out a successful strike a year earlier, "unanimously approved of the law," but when they appealed to the alliance to endorse the statute, members held it was "unjust" to deprive women "of the two extra hours a day permitted to the male operators." On the brink of its dissolution, the alliance was working more closely with the IMA than with the Ladies Federal Labor Union. Many middle-class leaders, especially Ellen Henrotin, did what they could to disavow the alliance vote, but support for the manufacturers' perspective among working- and middle-class women seriously challenged Kelley's claims to speak for the welfare of all women. Moreover, although Kelley had not relied on the support of the city's labor leaders, in February she appeared even more isolated when they began to speak openly of the law's demise. "The Supreme Court of the State of Illinois will undoubtedly repeal the law if asked to do so by men of money," one labor leader commented. They have repealed every law "designed for the benefit of the masses" and "will make short work of this one." [70]

In the spring of 1894 Florence Kelley occupied a vital position in the history of American social reform. But she was very vulnerable. Neither middle-class women's organizations nor mass meetings of grassroots supporters could help in this legal struggle. The decision rested with a court in a distant town that owed no allegiance to her or her constituents. Her official position made it possible for her to challenge the status quo, but it also removed her from the popular forces in which her power was rooted.

11

"The Power of a Few Enlightened Persons,"

1894–1896

Intellectually, Florence Kelley's work was anchored in a historical understanding of her place within the development of American capitalism. While she had discarded some aspects of Marxism, belief in her own significance as an interpreter and hence as a shaper of change remained secure. Knowledge was power. Using her knowledge and power she was determined to turn the state into a positive instrument in the lives of working people. While she awaited the Illinois Supreme Court's decision on the eight-hour law, her actions became more severe. The full use of her authority—both as a conscious agent of long-term change and as an enforcer of the law—required her to act without regard to short-term consequences.

While tension rose in the factory inspector's office over the outcome of the pending court decision, Kelley devised another way to end tenement sweatshops: by assaulting the special threat they posed to public health. Illinois's 1893 statute prohibited the production of garments in rooms used as dwellings but did not forbid garment work in tenement buildings. Kelley remained committed to the prohibition of all tenement work as the surest way to eliminate sweatshops. A smallpox outbreak offered her a timely opportunity to prove how all tenement production threatened the entire city. The contagion began in January and reached epidemic proportions by May, totaling 1,407 cases, most of which were concentrated in poor neighborhoods where sweatshops abounded. In February Kelley turned her own and her deputies' attention to the disease-infested neighborhoods. Smallpox became a lethal weapon in a sweatshop war she resolved to win.

Insisting on "the impossibility of guaranteeing safety for the purchasing public so long as tenement house manufacture is permitted," that month she launched a campaign

to burn all sweatshop clothing contaminated with smallpox. To 176 wholesalers and tailors "who control the garment trades in Chicago," she sent a circular warning that "a
rigid search of those districts in which clothing is manufactured" would be made and
"infectious goods" would be "immediately destroyed." [1]

This declaration of hostilities against sweatshop garments brought her into direct
conflict with the city health commissioner, Dr. Arthur Reynolds. Whereas she wanted to
burn contaminated goods, Reynolds insisted on the adequacy of fumigation, which he
promised his office would carry out but never documented. The germ theory of disease
was new to public health in the 1890s and only partially accepted; his inaction was prem-
ised on other explanations for the spread of the disease. Meanwhile, at the epidemic's
height that spring, when its center lay in the sweatshop district to the west of Hull House,
Kelley's staff counted as many as forty-seven cases in a single neighborhood in a single
day. Public health quarantine procedures permitted officials to remove smallpox victims
to a pesthouse, but families feared and resisted this cruel separation, especially when it
involved young children. Police were called in to assist health officials, and riots ensued.
Kelley drew an obvious conclusion—within families with even a single infected member
the spread of smallpox could not be stopped. "Many infants and little children we found
concealed on closet shelves, wrapped in bundles," to keep them "from being sent to the
dreaded hospital." However, the spread of the disease through infected garments could
be reduced. [2]

In early May Kelley warned the purchasing public through the daily papers of the
possibility of infection from tenement-made goods. A barrage of criticism of public
health officials sustained her position. One prolabor paper traced the progress of the
disease. "The lines radiating from the sweat shops enter every store where ready-made
clothing of all kinds is sold, and every home where ready-made clothing is bought. Each
one of these lines is a smooth path for the feet of the smallpox germ." Another paper
interviewed doctors who believed the city was not doing enough to combat the disease,
and yet another disputed Reynolds's belief that exposed garments could be disinfected
sufficiently. A week later, representatives of the state boards of health of Illinois, Michigan, Ohio, and Indiana, and of the United States Marine Hospital Service met in Chicago
and threatened to quarantine Chicago-made clothes if a lengthy set of regulations governing the sweatshops, factories and tenements was not followed. "If Dr. Reynolds is not
competent to handle this epidemic," said one visiting health board member, "we shall . . .
call upon the National Government to take hold of Chicago." Several papers called for
Reynolds's resignation. One declared: "He has proven himself utterly unprepared either
by mental equipment or by executive ability, by education or by prudence to be left in
charge of the sanitary work of Chicago." [3] Kelley's success seemed imminent.

At the height of this dispute, on May 12, Abraham Bisno supervised the burning of forty-three coats by agents of Reynolds's department, Kelley having notified the health official "that if these goods were not destroyed by 2 P.M. of the same day a petition in *mandamus* proceedings would be filed before the court closed." Clothing manufacturers evaded further burnings, however, and at the same time undercut Kelley's power by raising five thousand dollars to hire a special cadre of inspectors to guarantee consumers' safety. The group pledged that forty men would "at once make daily inspections of sweatshops" and all contaminated goods would "be turned over to the city health authorities for disinfection or destruction." [4]

Kelley fought back. To groups like the Society for Ethical Culture and the Central Council of the Chicago Civic Federation she predicted that smallpox cases among children who processed candy would spread the disease to consumers. She "would be tempted to resign her office at once," she said, if she ceased to believe she could abolish tenement sweatshops. The federation supported her claims that the city health department was concealing cases of smallpox "in order to cover up its inefficiency." A clothing store owner agreed that "so long as these so-called manufacturers give out clothing to be manufactured we will have the sweater and all the horrible consequences." Finally, Kelley stormed into the mayor's office, causing "a genuine stampede at the city hall," and insisted that "unless steps were taken immediately to quarantine the infected district," she would forward to the governor her official report "proving not only the prevalence of the epidemic in Chicago, but the utter imbecility of the department created to conserve the public health." [5] Despite all this, city officials retained the upper hand, especially after the private army of inspectors began assisting health department officers.

Ever the publicist, Kelley put a proposal to Altgeld. "For a little more than two months past, the State factory inspectors have worked almost exclusively in that tenement house section of this city where manufacture of clothing and the small-pox epidemic have been in progress together," she began. "The result of these inspections would make a most compelling document," she thought, since it would acquaint "the tax-paying and purchasing public with the real conditions and dangers of tenement house manufacture" and also form the basis for a campaign "with the next Assembly." [6] Altgeld approved, and she submitted a detailed account of her struggle with Reynolds in *First Special Report of the Factory Inspectors of Illinois, on Small-Pox in the Tenement House Sweat-Shops of Chicago, July 1, 1894.*

To Altgeld she confided her hope that the report would influence the Supreme Court justices in their forthcoming Ritchie decision at the least to preserve the prohibition against garment making in dwellings. "Shall I have copies of this ms. type-written and send them to the judges of the Supreme Court?" she asked. Reports of the court's thinking "which have leaked out so far, are rather harrowing." One rumor held that a judge had "sustained the law in all essential points." Another report thought the case had been "reassigned to Judge Bailey who is a partner . . . of Moran who was counsel for the mfrs. Ass'n and argued the case before the full bench, against the law." In any case, she thought that "the court is not unanimous and there is room for the smallpox report to do its work." She pointed out that Mrs. Stevens "typewrites well and quickly," so she could send out the copies right away.[7]

The *Tribune* characterized Kelley's July report as "a ferocious attack on the health authorities of Chicago." In case after case she documented the disappearance of goods from contaminated shops before her staff could seize them, the noncompliance of the health department with quarantine rules, and the ability of sweatshop subcontractors to conceal the presence of smallpox in family dwellings where garments were stored. "As there are in Chicago between 950 and 1000 licensed shops and about 25,000 other rooms in which garments are manufactured, it would be a hopeless task for any body of inspectors to attempt to enforce [quarantine] provisions in all of them," she concluded.[8] Only total prohibition of tenement garment making would help. "Miss Kelly's sensational report" elicited strong endorsements from the city's liberal papers, which called on the mayor to "bring the contumacious manufacturers about with a round turn" of "swift and stern repressive measures." One criticized manufacturers' "greed and contempt for public health," saying they had only themselves to blame if in the future they were "subjected to statutory regulations, which will either reduce their profits or drive them out of business altogether." Another paid tribute to "Miss Kelley" as "the only public official in the midst of us who exhibited competence during the small pox siege in Chicago. . . . We think it was by dint of her expostulations and threats that the municipal administration was brought finally to a realization of the dreadful condition which actually existed." Yet Commissioner Reynolds brushed off the controversy, saying he would "pay no attention to the report" and thought it "unnecessary" to say anything in reply to her statements.[9]

Florence Kelley lost this fight. Reynolds remained in office, and sweatshops stayed in tenements. Hedged in by the structural limits of her power, she had intensified her office's capacity for surveillance and discipline. In seeking to defeat one form of domination, she had done her best to establish another, becoming simultaneously a liberator and an oppressor. Yet hers was no mere exercise in dominance. Seeking to emancipate garment workers from sweatshop working conditions, she accepted the short-term cost of terrorizing tenement dwellers.[10]

That July Kelley's attention shifted to striking Pullman railcar makers and a sympathetic boycott by Chicago railway workers who refused to handle Pullman cars. The very night she put the finishing touches on her smallpox report, not far away a lawyer employed by U.S. Attorney General Richard Olney toiled all night on a new legal document, completed on July 2 and granted by a federal judge the next day, which permitted the federal government to use federal troops to suppress the strike.

Located at the intersection of several east-west and north-south railways, Chicago's 186 square miles contained over three thousand miles of tracks. These became the focus of a battle between railroad workers seeking a living wage and railroad owners asserting their right to control the terms of employment. In that contest, the antistrike injunction backed by federal and state militia proved crucial to the employers' victory. Based on the Sherman Anti-Trust Act passed by Congress in 1890 to limit the power of monopoly capitalism, this and future antistrike injunctions made it possible to declare strikers guilty of criminal conspiracy to restrict trade or the delivery of federal mail, thereby transforming struggles between labor and capital into conflicts between labor and government.[11]

"This event is an important epoch in America's political life," Kelley wrote in an 1894 article for a German Social Democratic periodical. She explained that railroads were crucial to the local and national economy because they held a monopoly on the transportation of goods. Therefore, "the traffic of America depends on the railway workers." The strike began among workers in the nearby company town of Pullman, Kelley reported, built as a monument to paternalist employment policies with company-owned housing as its chief attraction. Yet when wages were cut, workers found that they often had nothing left after rent was deducted from their pay. One skilled mechanic whose semimonthly pay totaled only $9.07 had only seven cents left. As he later recalled, "I would have to leave my work in the shop, go over to the bank and have an argument . . . to let me have money to live on, and sometimes I would get it and sometimes not. I have seen men with families of eight or nine children to support crying there because they got only three or four cents after paying their rent." The Pullman workforce was not unionized when strike plans began, but "they had joined the American Railway Union" two weeks before they struck.[12]

Kelley's narration focused on a figure who appealed strongly to her imagination. Eugene Debs, a former railway worker from Indiana and now head of the largest and fastest-growing union in the United States, the American Railway Union (ARU), had emerged as a charismatic leader only a few months earlier during a successful strike against the Great Northern Railroad in St. Paul, Minnesota. His new model of unionism strongly appealed to Kelley. "The union welcomed everyone who as a wage worker had some connection with the railway," she wrote, "including the laundresses who were cleaning the sheets of the sleeping compartments." She credited Debs with recognizing the need for a union that cut across craft divisions, embracing both skilled and unskilled

Eugene V. Debs, around 1900. Courtesy of the Texas Labor Archives, Special Collections Division, University of Texas at Arlington Libraries.

"The great railway strikes—the first meat train leaving the Chicago stock-yards under escort of
United States Cavalry, July 10, 1894." *Harper's Weekly,* July 28, 1894.

workers, women and men. Of the union's chief failing Kelley said: "Although the organization at their last annual meeting decided not to accept any negroes, it happened against
the will of Debs who emphasized that the race question was settled and one had to concentrate solely on the labor question." [13] Clearly the race question was far from settled,
but like Kelley and her settlement colleagues, Debs's attention was riveted on the white
labor force.

Kelley probably met Debs soon after he came to Chicago in mid-June, during the
strike's sixth week, for the first annual ARU convention. Debs actually cautioned ARU
members against endorsing the strike, but they, responding warmly to the pleas of Pullman workers and determined to resist the ruthless policies of their own employers,
voted to support a nationwide boycott of all Pullman sleeping cars. The boycott quickly
paralyzed the major western rail lines. In Chicago the General Managers' Association,
a combination of twenty-four railroad corporations, resolved to break the new union.
When neither the mayor nor the governor would agree to provide men to enforce the
antistrike injunction, two thousand federal troops entered the city on the night of July 3.
The next morning the association announced: "It has now become a fight between the
United States Government and the American Railway Union and we shall leave them to

fight it out." Like many supporters of the strikers, Kelley read the injunction "posted in the Rock Island yards." [14]

The injunction permitted the hiring of five thousand deputy marshals, many of whom were "thugs, drunkards, and other disreputable individuals." They occupied strategic points throughout the city by July 4, where their presence led to riots and bloodshed in encounters with strike supporters. Addams described "federal troops encamped about the post office." On July 6 seven hundred freight cars were burned, at least some at the hands of the peace-keeping forces. The next day troops fired into groups of protesting workers, killing and injuring dozens. Class war raged in Chicago for two more weeks. [15]

The *Tribune* instilled fear in its middle-class readers by portraying strikers as blood-thirsty anarchists opposed to the United States government. Even the wives and children of Pullman workers appeared menacing. Children were "steeped with the poisonous spirit of insurrection," the *Tribune* noted on July 9, and "holding their babies close for shields, the women still break past the patrol lines and go where no man dares to step." The Social Gospel was not strong enough among middle-class churchgoers to create a countervailing ethic. As Addams put it, "In the excitement following the Pullman strike Hull-House lost many friends." [16]

Kelley had begun to attend Chicago Civic Federation meetings that May, while Addams served on a conciliation board created by the federation and also visited strikers' homes. Addams hoped that discussions of the unfair rents could become the open-ing wedge for the arbitration of further grievances, even though Pullman refused to negotiate. In a talk before the Chicago Woman's Club, she tried to overcome her audi-ence's prejudices against the strikers by characterizing them as occupying the moral high ground. The Pullman workshops and dwellings were a "vast social operation," she said, managed "for the interests of the company owning the capital," rather than "the develop-ment of the workman thus socialized." Meanwhile, "the proletariat had learned . . . that 'the injury of one is the concern of all.'" Their watchwords were "brotherhood, sacrifice, the subordination of individual and trade interests to the good of the working class." She urged her listeners to join the "great accumulation of moral force" being "directed toward the emancipation of the wage-worker . . . as in another time it has made for the emancipation of the slave." [17]

Although middle-class support dissipated in the wake of violence, Kelley witnessed working-class sympathy deepening into a call for a general strike. "Cigarmakers, Jew-ish coatworkers, German printers, mattress workers, and workers of many other trades, which have nothing to do with the railway, stopped working and sent financial aid to the strike committee. . . . For the large mass of workers, the uprising in July meant a life and death struggle between the organized General Managers Association on the one side and the united workers on the other." Kelley's office did its part daily by filling out "age certificates for the fourteen year old girls and boys of those workers who are on the [Pullman] black list, so that their children, who have previously been going to school are allowed to support their families." [18]

"Almost every one on Halsted Street [was] wearing a white ribbon, the emblem of the strikers' side," Addams noted. "There had been nothing in my experience to reveal that distinct cleavage of society, which a general strike at least momentarily affords." Craft unionists made the cause their own. "A single Chicago association of printers alone gave $1000," Kelley said. This upsurge among his own affiliates brought Gompers to town, who declared that a general strike was "inexpedient, unwise and contrary to the best interests of the working people" and quashed the general strike movement in mid-July. Debs later blamed Gompers for the "brutal ferocity" with which the strike was broken. As one of the first signs of the strike's collapse, women scabs took jobs in the Pullman laundry in late July. Kelley tried to help the replaced workers by prosecuting the laundry for employing child labor, but the court ruled in the company's favor. Debs himself was arrested on July 10 on charges of conspiracy, his office ransacked and records confiscated. Out on bail by July 12, he was arrested again on July 17 on charges of contempt for violating the injunction. [19]

Alzina Stevens probably introduced Kelley to Debs. Alice Hamilton described Stevens as "one of the little group who used to stand by him during the hours of dark discouragement in the Pullman strike, keeping him from drowning his depression in drink, or when he could bear it no longer shielding him till he came back to himself." By mid-July Kelley was helping him in other ways. "Debs is in jail and his courage, while not failing, needs all the bracing it can get," she wrote Lloyd on July 18. The length of Debs's imprisonment might be "modified by the degree of public interest shown in the present injunction outrage," she thought. "Fancy an injunction that makes it a crime 'to attempt to induce by persuasion any person to refrain from handling a freight car'!" Anticipating Debs's arrest a few days earlier, she was trying to raise money for his bail but found this difficult since his arrest on June 10 had already required the posting of ten thousand dollars. Going first to a respectable banker who "indignantly repudiated the idea of associating his name in any way with the strike leader," she then approached others who evaded her less directly and finally got funds from "arch publicans and sinners" associated with the Democratic party.[20] Kelley also tried to arrange a cross-class "meeting of citizens of Chicago to protest against government by injunction and rifles," but among those she invited to speak, Professor Bemis of the University of Chicago did not reply, Frances Willard of the WCTU "wrote a characteristic evasion," Jane Addams could not leave her camp for Chicago children in Rockford, Mrs. Henrotin and others "thought it altogether wrong and injurious to have the meeting," Clarence Darrow justly withdrew "from the stage-defense," having "taken a very valuable active part in the work of the legal defense," and Lloyd himself was vacationing in Rhode Island with his family and Ko.[21]

Although the protest meeting for Debs never occurred, Kelley remained resolutely optimistic, convinced that "the strike has proved the long needed touchstone which finally separates the active elements of the two classes, the exploiting and the exploited."[22] She was frustrated that neither Debs nor Lloyd was exercising the kind of leadership the situation called for. Debs's influence, she told German readers, "as leader of the workers goes beyond the boundaries of the Railway Union and the number of followers is large." She described him as "not a member of the socialist movement. Although he is generally far more educated than his earlier co-workers, he lacks understanding of the historical labor movement." At the time she wrote, Debs was suffering a nervous breakdown, which she feared would end his influence. "Since the defeat of the strike he is suffering from a seemingly incurable disease damaging to his nerves which most probably will prevent him from continuing his role as leader of the workers." This saddened her, especially since the railway workers lacked "a strong program, a developed class consciousness, and comprehensive knowledge of economics."[23]

In June 1895 Debs began serving six months in a federal jail fifty miles from Chicago. He received many visitors, Florence Kelley probably among them. Later Debs credited his conversion to socialism during that imprisonment to the writings of Karl Kautsky, which came into his hands and "guided me into the socialist movement."[24] It seems likely that Kelley coached the imprisoned Debs about his place in history. Although years passed before he comfortably linked his own indigenous form of protest with the socialist movement, when he founded the American Socialist party in 1901, Florence Kelley was among the first to join.

Meanwhile, in the summer of 1894 Lloyd's distance from Chicago frustrated her. His absence was "a national calamity . . . now when the public mind is seething and the time is ripe for such far reaching action." She sent love "to Mrs. Lloyd and my boy and your boys" at the Lloyd vacation home but had no thoughts of joining them. "I have had moments of longing to get away from my slum and my drudgery," she confessed. "But I would not be out of Chicago today for a thousand dollars an hour."[25]

The Pullman conflict drew Kelley into the People's Party. This third-party insurgency had captured the governorships and legislative majorities in several states in the West, South, and Midwest, though its power was thin in Illinois. Frances Willard encouraged WCTU members to align with the party, and Henry Demarest Lloyd tried to construct a labor-farmer alliance. Speaking as the chief leader of the party in Chicago, Lloyd delivered a stirring address in October: "Our liberties and our wealth are from the people and by the people and both must be for the people. . . . The principles of liberty, equality, union, which rule in the industries we call government must rule in all industries. Business, property, capital, are also governments and must also rest on the consent of the governed." These sentiments and Lloyd's attack on monopolies in his monumental 1894 book *Wealth against Commonwealth* seemed to Kelley the noblest "since the days of struggle from 1850 to 1865." She believed his book launched "the beginning of a new era in our national life" and could well serve as the basis for a successful political campaign, and sure that "no one else can do so much good at this time," she urged him to run for Congress on the insurgent party ticket. In a letter to Jessie Lloyd, she insisted, "This is not wild personal enthusiasm. It is my honest conviction that it lies in the power of a few enlightened persons to use these last six years of our century for the work of peaceful transition. And the greatest contribution that one man can make, is to show what the disorder is and then take his part in changing that disorder by means of the machinery already at hand." Willard and Debs joined her in encouraging Lloyd's leadership, the latter writing him that "the People's Party will come into power with a resistless rush as did the Republican Party a little more than 30 years ago." But Lloyd felt more pessimistic. "In no event will the workingmen and farmers be allowed, no matter what their majority, to take control of the government," he wrote William Stead and replied to Kelley, "I am going to work harder than ever for radical social reform, and I think that is better than going to Congress to be beaten by the Sugar Mob." [26]

Radicals like Lloyd in the People's Party, outmaneuvered and outnumbered, conceded defeat in 1896, when the party supported the Democratic nominee for president, William Jennings Bryan. That reversal prompted a long heartfelt letter from Kelley to Lloyd about their political options. "The present Socialist organization in this country is a most undesirable one. The practice of expelling everyone who can speak English from the Socialist Labor Party, while not literally followed, is so nearly universal, that the party is very largely a bunch of greenhorns." But, she thought, "If there could be segregated from the Populist party a body, however small, of Socialists of American nationality and traditions, this seems to me worth a very great sacrifice indeed." Such a body could win followers, "but it had not occurred to me, until after my conversation with you last evening, that this *may* be the opportunity to obtain a nucleus of Americans to adopt that platform, yet who would never, of their own accord, enter the Socialist Labor Party as at present constituted. I am such an American. . . . I would make a good deal of sacrifice for the sake of working with a party of American Socialists." [27] Yet on this occasion, as in 1894, Lloyd could not be coaxed into political action, and Kelley herself, a disfranchised woman, did not feel up to the task of national political leadership.

Lloyd never did find a satisfying niche in American civil society. His foresight about the economic rights of working people made him a leading citizen of the English-speaking world, yet he never discovered an effective organizational vehicle for his ideas. His influence was widely felt, but not in an explicit or instrumental way. Perhaps for this reason he began to idealize the collective impact women were exercising on public policy. Men's public culture as Lloyd knew it was an array of large and small interest groups pitted against one another in a struggle for control of the twin temples of the economy and the state. Men's and women's groups both claimed to speak for the welfare of the whole society, but to Lloyd women better represented the needs of civil society and seemed better able to take action on behalf of the welfare of all. His hopes for women radiated from an 1894 article in which he dedicated his magnum opus, *Wealth against Commonwealth*, to women.

> It is in the womanhood of the world that are rising the great fountains of the enthusiasm and energy of the future. Through almost every page of his work the author was drawn on by the hope that some fact, some word, might kindle the mind of the woman who is to strike the keynote of the coming emancipation of the Commonwealth, and that out of our womanhood might come the wit, tenderness, and virtue to heal the question which has proved to be too big for the monopoly sex. To her who shall speak for this womanhood, this book was in spirit dedicated.[28]

Like many of his contemporaries, Lloyd yearned for a politics not dominated by the "monopoly sex."

Ko, Margaret, and John (nine, eight, and seven years old in 1894) saw their mother infrequently, since repeated exposure to smallpox kept her away from "the chicks" even more than usual. Yet despite this separation, painful both to her and to them, Kelley remained vitally involved with their welfare. To Lloyd, she expressed gratitude for "my boy's happy summer and present rubicund state" and asked Jessie to send some of Ko's possessions to Mrs. Wright's. Thereafter Ko spent every summer at the Lloyd's vacation home in Rhode Island. "The chicks are well and Mrs. Wright does not despair of Marnie's growing into a good and gentle woman," she noted that fall, referring to her most rebellious child. In September 1894 Margaret and John entered the Hillside Home School, run by sisters of Jenkin Lloyd Jones whom they called "Aunt Nell" and "Aunt Jennie." Ko remained with Mrs. Wright, and over the next few years Margaret and John frequently returned there for short visits.[29]

Kelley's biggest anxiety about the children focused on Lazare's continuing efforts to reclaim them. In the midst of her campaign against smallpox-contaminated garments in the summer of 1894, Addams wrote that she was "having an awful time just now with 'the Dr' who is prowling about the children constantly."[30] Yet her letters to the children never mentioned Lazare, nor did theirs to her.

Margaret and Ko blossomed into caretakers of their little brother. "John took sick with the tonsillitis this afternoon," Margaret wrote her mother from Hillside, "but I think he has not got them very badly and will be well in a day or two—please do not worry about him, because I did not tell you this to worry you or make you anxious, I told you because it seems deceitful not to tell you about everything—don't write to Aunt Nell, and make a big fuss about it because if you do I will get a fine long lecture—I will keep you well posted on his condition." Ko once wrote from Anna Wright's: "John has jus fallen down the stares but he did not hurt himself to speak of."[31]

The forced separation from her children and the risk she had incurred to her own and her deputies' lives, combined with the violent repression of the Pullman strikers and boycotters, put Florence Kelley in no mood to compromise on more mundane issues. Richard Ely found that out in July. Kelley had arranged for Ely to publish as part of his Library of Economics and Politics a collection of essays written by Hull House residents and maps that Kelley and Agnes Holbrook had devised from the data collected for Carroll Wright. To that volume she contributed an essay, "The Sweating-System," in which she summarized the results of one year's effort to enforce "the present Workshop and Factories Act"—"the reduction in number of the small children in shops; the partially successful separation of the homes from the shops; and the partially successful enforcement of the eight-hour day for the women and girls." These results were "not wholly unsatisfactory, in view of the fact that the law is not yet a year old," but Kelley emphasized that the act's "chief value lies in its use as a transition measure, paving the way for the abolition of tenement-house manufacture." With Alzina Stevens she also wrote a piece entitled "Wage-Earning Children." In quite a different tone, Jane Addams's essay—"The Settlement as a Factor in the Labor Movement"—described and defended the settlement's commitment to union organizing as part of the common cause of humanity. Speaking without Kelley's certitude, Addams argued against the division of society into "capitalists and proletarians," "exploiters and exploited": "Life itself teaches us nothing more inevitable than that right and wrong are most confusedly mixed; that the blackest wrong is by our side and within our own motives. . . . We cease to listen for the bugle note of victory our childish imagination anticipated, and learn that our finest victories are attained in the midst of self-distrust, and that the waving banner of triumph is sooner or later trailed to the dust by the weight of self-righteousness." Addams also wrote an introduction and provided an appendix describing the settlement's myriad activities. Essays by Julia Lathrop ("Cook County Charities") and Ellen Gates Starr

("Art and Labor") joined others by Hull House residents and close associates, including Charles Zeublin of the University of Chicago.[32]

In many ways the book's chief achievement lay in its spectacular color-coded maps depicting ethnicity and income on a household basis for the entire Nineteenth Ward. If social science replaced religion as the interpreter of moral priorities, Kelley's maps exemplified this substitution in special ways. Based on information gathered when Kelley worked for Carroll Wright, the maps were the American equivalent of Charles Booth's stunning "Descriptive Map of London Poverty," published with volume two of *Life and Labour of the People in London* in 1891. The Hull House maps covered a smaller area in greater detail—Booth's maps did not include ethnicity, and, relying on estimates by school board employees of the income level for each block, they contained no household level information. Like women's public culture itself, Kelley's maps were more interested in the social geography of everyday life than in large generalizations about the city's populace. Until the publication from 1909 to 1911 of the six volumes of the Pittsburgh Survey, the maps of *Hull House Maps and Papers* represented the state of the art of graphic social science analysis of urban, working-class life in the United States.[33]

Yet the maps were almost not published—at least they would not have been if Richard Ely had had his way. Kelley had no patience with Ely from the beginning of the project. She complained about an error introduced by the copyeditor that "places Mrs. Morgan under the leadership of Hull House, [which] would infuriate that irascible lady." Delays irritated her. In November, she told him she could have been paid "liberally and promptly" for her essay's publication elsewhere but had held back because Ely had told her "in May that the book would be in the market last September." She sent him three copies of her bibliography but received no assurance that it would appear with her article. So when Ely proposed abbreviating or eliminating the maps, she erupted. "This I positively decline to permit. The charts are mine to the extent that I not only furnished the data for them but hold the sole permission from the U.S. Department of Labor to publish them. I have never contemplated, and do not now contemplate, any form of publication except as two linen-backed maps or charts, folding in pockets in the cover of the book, similar to Mr. Booth's charts." If the publishers disagreed, she said, "it will be well to stop work at once."[34]

Jane Addams intervened to get the project back on track, explaining to Ely that Kelley's anger was sparked by "accumulated annoyances" from her work as factory inspector and assuring him that he would "have no further annoyance in regard to the book." A week later, after the page proofs had been returned to the publisher, Addams followed up with another soothing letter, saying that Kelley "seems to have fallen into a panic" and "to have written very hastily and unwisely. I am sure that you will recognize that her action was hasty and represented her alone. The residents as a whole have known nothing about it, and I assure you that we are all most grateful and appreciative of what you have done for us. I hope the book will justify your efforts." [35] Kelley may have upset Ely, but she got her way—the maps were published with linen backs in pockets in the book's cover. A cheaper edition was printed without linen backs, but there, too, the maps appeared in full.

That fall she concentrated on her official duties. "The law work goes well," she wrote to Jessie Lloyd in October. "I'm trying our own prosecutions and attending lectures and hope to be admitted to practice before the Supreme Court in July." She unrelentingly prosecuted employers of child labor, obtaining convictions against tailors, bakers, meatpackers, and makers of cigars, candy, shoes, pails, pickles, rattan items, electrical machinery, paper boxes, cutlery, baking powder, chemicals, sewing machines, and chairs. She lost her only prosecution of the adult hours law in December, when women workers in a watchmaking factory "testified that they were satisfied with the time and would consider it a hardship to have the law enforced" and IMA lawyers argued that the law was meant only for cigars and garment making. In this context, she tried to find consolation in her ability to harass meatpackers who violated the child labor law, they being among the largest, most dangerous, and therefore most pernicious employers in the city. She also took satisfaction in the scholarly aspects of her reports. "It is my ambition to make the most thoroughly specialized study of the statistics of child labor that has ever been made; and I am employing all the resources of my position to do this," she wrote to another woman reformer. [36]

Kelley had relatively little to cheer her on New Year's Eve 1894. The high hopes with which she began her responsibilities as chief factory inspector were much reduced. As was her custom, she spent the evening writing letters. In contrast to her pessimism of New Year's Eve 1889, however, these letters went beyond optimism to exaggerate her achievements. In a letter to Engels that might be seen as a last tribute to this father figure, she concealed the limitations of her work and her fears for the future. Instead, she described gains for the eight-hour day, which even if true at that moment were extremely fleeting. Ignoring her setbacks and making the most of her child labor convictions among meatpackers, she exclaimed, "We have at last won a victory for our 8 hours law. The Supreme Court has handed down no decision sustaining it, but the Stockyards magnates having been arrested until they are tired of it, have instituted the 8 hours day for 10,000 employees, men, women and children." If stockyards were implementing the eight-hour law, these gains were quickly reversed. More likely, in a vulnerable moment and based on fragmentary evidence, Kelley was expressing her hopes for the future—a pipe dream that warmed her approach to 1895 and the coming Supreme Court decision. In a similar vein she wrote Friedrich Sorge, "All big businessmen are either on bail because of legal proceedings against them, or they have accepted the eight-hour day." [37] Here again wishful thinking appealed more than the cold light of reality. Her letter to Engels read like a pep talk to herself. "We have 18 suits pending to enforce the 8 hours law, and we think we shall establish it permanently before Easter. It has been a painful struggle of eighteen months and the Supreme Court may annul the law. But I have great hopes that the popular interest may prove too strong." [38] Her hopes had outpaced the capacities of her office, but popular interest was a rock she relied on.

In the early months of 1895, still awaiting the Supreme Court decision, Kelley vented her frustration against her childhood horror—child labor in glassmaking—by launching a ferocious attack on the state's single largest employer of children, the Illinois Glass Company, in Alton, Illinois. In the state's southern reaches near St. Louis, the company employed more than seven hundred boys under sixteen, many of whom were recruited by exploitative "guardians" from orphan asylums in St. Louis. Since the speed of bottle production depended on the speed of the child "dogs" who fetched and carried for the glassblowers, the children were pushed to their utmost. "The sustained speed required of the children and the heated atmosphere render continuous trotting most exhausting," Kelley later remembered. An hour's steady trotting tired a healthy schoolboy, "but these little lads trotted hour after hour, day after day, month after month in the heat and dust." Of those who survived this process, "virtually none succeed in attaining the position and wages of a skilled glass-blower." Unions limited apprenticeship (beginning at age seventeen) to the blowers' own sons, who were never employed as dogs but attended school or worked "in some less destructive occupation than glass-bottle making." Chronic illness, frequent night work, serious burns, and illiteracy prevented these boys from being self-supporting in later life, ruining them "in body and mind before they entered upon the long adolescence known to happier children." Public relief agents contributed to the problem by refusing adequate aid to the female-headed families drawn to Alton by the opportunity to employ their boys—this despite the fact that "in no single case did the earnings of the little boys really support the family and relieve the community even immediately and temporarily of that burden." Although glassblowers belonged to a strong union, they cooperated with employers "to keep the children from receiving any adequate legislative protection." [39]

This campaign stood out in Ko's memory. "There might be week after week when she could not see us, for she was inspecting glass factories in southern Illinois, to find the little boys working at night." His mother determinedly disregarded the cost of this campaign—to herself or others. "Mrs. Florence Kelly . . . seems to be as arbitrary and unreasoning as any other woman with an alleged mission," a local newspaper wrote. "After agreeing with the officers of the glass work as to the course to be pursued and told . . . that it would take time to accomplish these things, she declared that she was tired of being fooled with and would bring suit at once and started uptown to do it. . . . Then look out for her ladyship." Jane Addams's nephew described Kelley during this period: "She drove through her duties as factory inspector with a dismaying energy and issued her orders with the same negligence of appearance that she showed in throwing her clothes on in the morning and like some daughter of Minerva and Mars sallying forth to war."[40]

Responding in kind, the Illinois Glass Company said "that if compelled to discharge the children it would close down all or part of its furnaces." This would throw a large number of men and boys "out of employment in the middle of winter" and let their families suffer. Not surprisingly, townspeople united behind the factory managers. Kelley took her case to Altgeld, who ordered a hearing. When factory managers said their child workers supported widows, the governor asked, "Why then [are] they paid such ridiculously low wages?" Ruling that "the law had to be respected even though it closed down every shop and factory in the state," the governor nevertheless negotiated a compromise in which "boys under twelve years of age" would be dismissed within a month and older boys at later intervals.[41]

Having won that battle, Kelley rented rooms in Springfield, where she spent the rest of the winter working on her third annual report, drafting improved child labor laws, and anticipating a negative decision by the Illinois Supreme Court on her cherished hours law. She lobbied aggressively for new child labor laws, but knowing she was pushing the legislature further and faster than it wanted to go, she asked middle-class allies to write a key member of the Illinois senate, "of course not referring to me, whose interest he probably already finds rather much." Appreciating the importance of his mother's work but asserting his claim on her attentions, Ko wrote: "I am glad that man is going to help you get what you want. When will you be home? Are you getting what you want?" Caroline did not help by writing, "I hope you are not breaking down under your mixed cares."[42]

On March 15, 1895, the decision finally arrived. In a unanimous opinion, the court found that the eight-hour law conflicted with the constitutional guarantee that "no person shall be deprived of life, liberty or property without due process of law" and that the "Legislature has no right to deprive one class of persons of privileges allowed to other persons under like conditions." The "mere fact of sex" did not justify the legislature's use of the state's police power to limit women's contractual rights "unless the courts are able to see that there is some fair and reasonable connection between such limitation and the public health, safety or welfare, proposed to be secured by it." The opinion was written by Benjamin Magruder, the same judge who penned the court's decision to uphold the murder conviction of the Haymarket anarchists in 1887.[43]

Just as Kelley used gender as a surrogate for class-based legislation, so the judges used gender to defend the class-based status quo. They buttressed their decision with the Fourteenth Amendment and a lengthy defense of women's rights. "As a citizen, woman has the right to acquire and possess property of every kind," they said. The decision cited the state's married women's property law of 1874 and a law passed in 1872 in support of Myra Bradwell's campaign to practice law in Illinois, which provided that "no person shall be precluded or debarred from any occupation, profession or employment (except military) on account of her sex." Their view of the primacy of rights over the primacy of health and their support for unregulated capitalism was graphically expressed in their opinion that "there can be no more justification for the prohibition of the prosecution of certain callings by women because the employment will prove hurtful to them than it would be for the State to prohibit men from working in white lead because they are apt to contract lead poisoning." This laissez-faire attitude toward workers' health made the American industrial workplace the most murderous in the western world during the nineteenth and twentieth centuries.[44]

Bipolar responses to the 1895 Illinois Supreme Court decision reflected class differences in the state's political landscape. Levy Mayer, speaking for the IMA, thought the ruling an appropriate correction of a legislature that had gone too far in regulating and controlling economic conditions. "Our lawmakers are too frequently influenced by public clamor and misdirected agitation for the cure of so-called social wrongs. . . . [The law] sprang from the needs of paternalism and socialism, neither of which has any place in this country." Almost as an afterthought, he added, "Woman is equal to man before the law and that her right to her labor, which constitutes her property, is as sacred and impregnable as is the similar right of man." One paper noted that "it was understood at the time of its passage that a similar measure regulating the number of hours men could be hired to work would follow on its heels." With this threat eliminated, the *Tribune* approvingly explained: "In far reaching result the decision is most important. It is the first decision in the United States against the eight-hour law and presents a new obstacle in the path of the movement for shorter hours." [45]

Members of the Chicago Trade and Labor Assembly objected: "No matter how carefully laws in the interest of labor might be drawn it seemed impossible to get anything on the statute books which the courts would not knock out when it came to a test." At a mass meeting to protest the decision the day after it was announced, a committee was appointed to carry its objections to the legislature, even though neither it nor the Illinois Federation of Labor had helped to defend the law. A prolabor newspaper noted: "There is a ghastly sort of irony in the attempt of the Supreme Court to explain or excuse its decision upon the plea that it is protecting the rights of weak individuals with labor to sell. . . . The disciples of laissez faire may find comfort in it if they will. People not of the doctrinaire type will discover that through it the way is opened to the most cruel oppression of people—men equally with women—who work for wages, to the depression of the standard of living and to the degeneration of the race." In his enormously influential 1894 book *If Christ Came to Chicago,* English Social Gospel leader William Stead anticipated the court's decision and offered comparative comments: "Legislative restrictions which even the most reactionary, hard-hearted capitalist in England admits to be indispensable for the protection of labor are unconstitutional according to the state of Illinois." He thought Illinois's "constitution makes a fetish of freedom of contract and immolates before this idol victims whom British law would have long since rescued." Stead concluded that "if the State of Illinois could be suddenly placed under the Acts of Parliament passed by the British legislature [the workingman and the workingwoman] would attain at one stroke almost all the reforms for which they are now clamoring in vain." [46]

Kelley blasted the decision in her third annual report. If the court had relied on the state constitution, that constitution could have been altered. But in basing its decision on the Fourteenth Amendment to the Constitution of the United States, the court defeated that remedy. As her father's daughter, she heaped scorn on the judges for using the amendment "passed to guarantee the negro from oppression" as "an insuperable obstacle to the protection of women and children." She felt certain the decision would not last. The observation of a few more years would convince "the medical profession, the philanthropists, and the educators" what factory workers and factory inspectors already knew: the length of the working day was "a life and death matter." Then it would be "possible to rescue the Fourteenth Amendment to the Constitution of the United States from the perverted application upon which this decision rests. We may hope that Ritchie v. The People will then be added to the reversed decisions in which the Supreme Court of Illinois is so rich." Unaware of the court's decision "overtaxed girls working in the sweated trades" continued to complain to her office about overtime work, signing their letters "Tired Girl" and "Victim," but, Kelley lamented, "there is now no power in any officer of the State to interfere in their behalf." [47]

In the immediate moment of mid-March 1895, however, Kelley turned from these feelings to concentrate on the legislative task at hand, claiming to be "rather elated than discouraged" since the decision explicitly left two vital aspects of the 1893 law intact: its prohibition of child labor and its provision for the enforcement of that prohibition. She was "urging the passage of two bills of wider scope than the act of two years ago," one of which required municipal boards of health to "destroy garments which the factory inspector shall find to have been made under unhealthy conditions." [48]

Ever vigilant, the IMA rented quarters in Springfield and actively lobbied against Kelley's new proposals. Railroads were exempted from an arbitration bill, the child labor bill died, and trusts were legalized. Fighting back, Kelley induced Altgeld to recall the legislature that summer to reconsider the child labor bill, but the Republican-dominated body denied her proposal. That fall Altgeld appointed a special legislative committee to "investigate the condition of child labor in the state," with special attention to the "greatest abuses in the stockyards," but that too was unproductive. During her last year in office Kelley vigorously prosecuted the child labor and home work provisions of the 1893 law. Her office successfully prosecuted 542 violations in 1895 and 520 in 1896. She made a difference throughout Illinois from Alton to Waukegan and produced model reports of her activities, but her power never reached beyond the limits set by the *Ritchie* decision.[49]

In February 1896, when she had not quite finished her third report, Florence wrote Caroline, "the 'heft' of it is off my shoulders and upon Mrs. Stevens, which is a relief to me and rather hard upon her." She mastered the art of the typewriter that year. "I think I have reached about the degree of skill which commands three dollars a week," she wrote in her first typed letter to Caroline. She had more time for Ko, Margaret, and John, who visited at Hull House many weekends. "The children have just started for school and Miss Addams and I, feeling a trifle exhausted by the exertion, have had an extra cup of coffee and begun the work of the day an hour earlier than usual." Now that they were older, the children often visited separately. Ko "very quietly" spent a week with her in June 1896. Other residents often cared for the children during their visits. "We are in town this morning," Margaret wrote, "and we are going to the field museum . . . with two of the Hull House residents, Miss Barnum and Miss Benedict." Kelley maintained close contact with her children's teachers, especially Ko's. "I think Ko ought to be promoted, and want to see his teacher and the Superintendent of schools," she told Caroline. "The little fellow's reports show that his work does not require enough exertion of him." A week later she wrote, "When he comes to town, I read aloud to him, and when he is alone he reads to himself, and when he can get the children to listen, he reads to them. He is really a student. He is in many ways like father but wholly without Father's irritability. I have great hopes of Ko's future. His teachers are all devoted to him." She thought "no child was ever such a hard worker." Early in 1897 she placed Ko in the Lewis Institute, where he did high school work. Margaret spent the school year of 1896–97 with Caroline in Philadelphia.[50]

Meanwhile her own social schedule remained active. A typical week found her dining with John Dewey, giving a public speech, or participating in a special dinner with distinguished guests at Hull House. Her fame spread to England. "I am anxious to hear more of Mrs. Kelly's work and of the Chicago Inspectorate," Gertrude Tuckwell, a contemporary active in the British Women's Trade Union League, wrote Addams. Sidney Webb wrote Kelley that he was "very glad to receive your Fourth Annual Report with its admirable record of good work under difficulties." On a visit to London, Addams noted that Lady Dilke was "much impressed with Mrs. Kelley's work." Addams asked Kelley to send her "a copy of the Eight Hour Law, and of the Supreme Court decision" for a British reformer to read. "He seemed so amazed that it should have been unconstitutional under the Illinois Constitution that I promised to procure a copy of the decision." [51]

Kelley, preferring local power to distant esteem, campaigned for Altgeld's reelection in the fall of 1896 as though she thought he could win. "We miss you very much in the campaign," she wrote Lloyd. "Things are badly muddled and Governor Altgeld's friends seem few, indeed, in this time of need." His only supporters seemed to be farmers, "silver populists and the straight trades-union vote." She allowed herself a moment of bitter reproach: "If the working people allow him to be defeated now, in the face of his record, surely they deserve to have no other friend until this generation dies out and another and better one takes its place." And she urged Lloyd to help. "I don't know whether you want Governor Altgeld reelected—everything is so confused this year that I don't feel certain of much in any direction! But if you do—he needs every bit of help, of every kind, that every friend can give him until election day." Lloyd wrote to a few friends but did not actively campaign. Three weeks before the election Kelley predicted its outcome to Lloyd, "I think the State is lost." In November the Republicans swept every major office, including the governor's.[52] What Kelley did not predict and perhaps refused to recognize was the effect of Altgeld's defeat on her own office. The preceding four years had brought her to the attention of the English-speaking reform world. She did not want to imagine that her time was up.

12

"Feeling

the Pinch,"

1897–1899

"I love her dearly and don't see how I can work without her if she is removed by governor Tanner," Florence Kelley said of Alzina Stevens when her assistant saved her "a tiresome trip" by going to Springfield to submit their fourth annual report and do some lobbying. To keep Kelley quiet while her successor was selected, the new governor assured her that she would not be dismissed as chief factory inspector. Yet at the same time he told the Illinois Glass Company at Alton to choose her replacement. That process took some months, but in August 1897 the company finally recommended a man who had been on their payroll for twenty-seven years.[1] The firing came as a shock to her. The thrust against her ambitions could not have gone deeper.

Florence Kelley's joblessness revealed the meager alternatives open to talented women reformers seeking professional work. "Nothing is so wretched as being without a regular salary," she felt, especially with three children to support. However, one thing was certain: Jane Addams did her utmost to help. On hearing the "sad news," Addams returned to Hull House from Rockford and immediately began "looking up various possible openings" but was "somewhat discouraged by the outlook."[2] Kelley went looking but came home "with a negative answer and quite discouraged." They saw Merritt Starr, prominent reform-minded Chicago attorney and editor of the *Annotated Statutes of Illinois*, but found "no opening." A week later the situation had grown desperate. "We are all much torn up because Sister Kelley has lost her place and put in all our spare time looking for a 'job,'" Addams wrote her sister.[3] The expense of the children's schooling weighed heavily. Addams urged Mary Smith to ask an acquaintance "if she would like to take a boy of ten to board" for ten to fifteen dollars a month. "It would be a great relief to have him in a cheaper place . . . whoever pays for him." That fall Kelley searched without success for an apartment where her costs would be less than those of boarding out the children.[4]

In the press of her financial need, she accepted evening work at the Crerar Library near downtown Chicago as assistant to the periodicals librarian. It underutilized her talents but brought in a weekly paycheck. Established with a $440,000 bequest in July 1894 and specializing in economic, scientific, and medical topics, the Crerar was a reference rather than a lending library. Kelley had used its space and drawn on its collection of printed governmental documents to write her annual reports. "Momma has had Three holidays from the Library," Margaret had written her Uncle Bert just before New Year's Eve 1894, when Kelley was writing her second report: "Christmas eve, Christmas night and Sunday night." Now a regular evening employee, Florence acknowledged the job's "drudgery" but thought it "fair to say that I do not know how else one could earn a salary with less disagreeable work."[5] Although most readers were businessmen or workers, she was glad that "a third of the visitors in the reference and reading rooms now are women. In the evenings and especially on Saturday afternoons the women students and teachers from the academies, the elementary and high schools stream into the library." The place became a refuge reminiscent of her father's library. "The Library is really a pleasure at present; cool, quiet, without hard work, and offering a marvellous abundance of books and reviews," she wrote Caroline in the summer of 1898.[6]

The job's chief drawback was her small salary, which did not meet her expenses. "Times are hard," she told her mother when forced to accept a check for Margaret's train-fare to Philadelphia. "Your generosity is most opportune." In July 1898 a long deferred "rise" in her salary from fifty to sixty dollars a month made "an incredible difference" in her accounts, but that September she was "down to my last shilling" and ashamed to borrow. In mid-month she wrote Caroline, "Never in the history of the world did a birthday present give more pleasure than yours to me, or come more thoroughly in the nick of time."[7]

Margaret, eleven years old in 1897, teased her mother "that if she [Margaret] had no fairy grandmother, she would be worse off than Cinderella ever was!" But Caroline's limited resources could not cover all of her granddaughter's expenses. Mary Rozet Smith paid Margaret's boarding school tuition in 1897–98 and 1898–99 "and will go on doing the same thing as many years as may be necessary," Florence reassured Caroline. "Mary Smith is so rich and so generous, and so fond of Margaret, that I do not feel at all embarrassed about accepting her kindness," though she would "not feel free to keep the child at so expensive a school year after year" if the tuition were draining Caroline's limited resources.[8]

Margaret began to develop expensive taste in clothes, which Caroline indulged, partly through her own sewing skills, partly by purchases made during her granddaughter's long summer visits. "It almost makes me cry when I look at the ruffles on Marmie's drawers, and think of your spending your precious eyes on such exquisite stitching," Florence protested, though she acknowledged in a later letter, "Margaret can have nothing done where the country-cousin method of dressmaking prevails." On her daughter's return in August 1898, Florence wrote, "The lady arrived in good order this morning; and is now engaged in unpacking the treasures which you have lavished upon her." Florence was grateful, but these expenditures made her uncomfortable. "The countless, nice lady-like things give me as much pleasure as they give her. Or rather, they would do so if I were not convinced that you are going without things which you ought to have." [9] She did not object to practical gifts. "Her trunk is so strong and well-made that it promises to last until she is an old lady." Thinking Margaret "as able as she is huge," Florence began to plan for her college preparation and made inquiries at Bryn Mawr. [10]

Caroline's attentions to Margaret somewhat displaced Florence as the central figure in her daughter's life. "It is a great pleasure to have her with me for a while," Florence wrote, "but I've almost come to look upon her as yours; and she calls me 'Grandma' in the most natural manner, identifying us quite naturally." [11] She accepted Margaret's chief flaw — "impatience" — as a "reminder of her father and grandfather." Yet Kelley had been less than candid with her daughter about Lazare's heritage. "Margaret is a handsome creature," Jane Addams wrote Mary Smith, "but her attitude when she found out her Semitic ancestry was pathetic, none the less so for its absurdity." [12]

As Ko, Margaret, and John grew older, they drew more heavily on the care of their mother's colleagues at Hull House. Alzina Stevens took Ko "one bright Sunday . . . on a long journey to the Northwest side to call upon Schwab, one of the three pardoned [Haymarket] defendants." Ko found him "a gentle-spoken, thin little cobbler, with rumpled black hair." Later Agnes Holbrook took Ko "to visit her family in Marengo, Iowa." [13] Addams and Smith assumed special responsibility for the children. From Hull House in September 1897 Addams sent "love and greetings to Margaret and Ko," who were with Mary Smith, and reported on John, who was staying with her. "John has gone to bed or would enclose remarks. He is perfectly obedient and as dear as he can be." Yet "the Chief," as Kelley sometimes called Addams, could not always meet the children's needs. "John and the little lady are clamoring to have me chaperon them some-where for a country vacation," Addams wrote Mary, "and I have weakly promised for next week unless I can find some-one else." [14]

Mary Smith also helped Kelley with Ko's boarding and tuition expenses at the Lewis Institute a few miles away. Addams and other Hull House residents helped furnish his room there. "Ko spent yesterday in putting his room in order, his 'buggery,' as I grieve to state that he calls it," Florence wrote Caroline, "and as Miss Addams gave him a very good large bureau and Miss Benedict bought him a pretty calendar and Miss Vernon a very nice easel-picture of Scott, he felt much encouraged." He was a "happy boy in possession" of "a nice book case . . . well-filled with good and well-bound books." Ko's behavior was monitored by many mothers. "I was inclined to less bicycle riding for him, but Miss Hamilton and the others insisted that it did him good," Addams wrote Kelley. When Mary Smith gave Florence a Christmas gift of one hundred dollars, she deposited it with her father's executor. "I am putting it beyond my reach," she declared to Caroline. It was an "immense comfort" to her to think that the money could start Ko "at college and keep him until he can get work or a scholarship to carry him through." [15]

Her favoritism for Ko went unconcealed. "Even the presence of the other two does not make up for his absence," she confided to Caroline. At summer's end in 1898 she felt "so hungry for the sight of Ko that I hardly know how to wait for his arrival." He reciprocated the next January, upon her return from a trip to New York. "Ko went off in high feather to school, so frankly pleased to have me at home again that it makes me sentimental." He spoiled her "with his prim and plentiful communications" and remained studious to a fault. "He is so ambitious and worries so over his work, that he is really hard to manage," she thought.[16] She intervened to encourage him to take "two hours of forge-work a day" at school—though he did "not do it very well"—rather than "third year English in which he would distinguish himself." Florence thought this "a distinct moral victory, for never did a professional beauty more enjoy 'showing off' than this little lad"; he "loves a high-honor as a racing-man loves a winning horse." She felt "very happy about his resolve, for a prig I do not wish my eldest son to remain." Altogether the children gave her enormous pleasure. "My chicks were a perfect picture show,—so well and rosy and handsome," she wrote Caroline just after Christmas 1898.[17]

Kelley's temporary unemployment gave her more time for Hull House duties. During the summer months when Addams and other residents departed, she often remained in charge. "Altogether the house is quiet and pleasant enough to make work very agreeable," she told Caroline in July 1898. "The shanty where the crèche used to be, is being torn down while I am writing, to make room for the new Jane Club, a beautiful four story club house," funded by Mary Smith. In the fall a constant stream of visitors poured through. "Two young lords, sons of Governors of New South Wales and New Zealand, dropped in to lunch and dinner," Kelley wrote her mother, "on their way to Oxford from their Pacific Ocean Provinces." There seemed to be "two currents of lordlings flowing round the world, one towards the East and the other towards the West, and when they meet they give each other letters of introduction insuring a square meal in Chicago!" Sidney and Beatrice Webb joined that flow, writing Kelley in 1897 to expect them a year hence on their return from Australia.[18]

In the mid-1890s Hull House residents had sustained Kelley in her public responsibilities. Now, at the end of the decade, they eased the pain of her separation from
those duties. Alice Hamilton, ten years younger than Kelley, professor of pathology at
the Women's Medical School of Northwestern University and, beginning in 1897, part of
the settlement's inner circle, spent her first evening at Hull House at a dinner with ex-
Governor Altgeld as the guest of honor. "I saw the admiration and appreciation with
which he, the defender of the Pullman strikers and the pardoner of the imprisoned anarchists, was greeted by Miss Addams, Mrs. Kelley, and Miss Lathrop. I listened while
Mrs. Kelley talked with him about her experience as Chief State Inspector of Factories
under his administration." Kelley could be cajoled into reminiscing. "A little group of us
residents used to wait for her return from the Crerar Library, where she was in charge
evenings, and bribe her with hot chocolate to talk to us. We had to be careful; foolish
questions, half-baked opinions, sentimental attitudes, met with no mercy at her hands.
We loved to hear her and the Scotch lawyer, Andrew Alexander Bruce, discuss the cases
they had had under the Altgeld administration."[19] These admiring residents gave her an
opportunity to relive the adventure of her recent past and in the process come to terms
with its conclusion.

Florence Kelley's identity as a mother heightened the emotional significance of her
struggle to locate meaningful, well-paying work. "I want first of all to take care of my
own bairns but at the same time I want to be able to do something for the bairns of
others," she wrote Alexander Bruce.[20] In some ways her situation resembled the circumstances in which she found herself in the late 1880s, but after five and a half years at Hull
House she had become a world-class reformer and expected more of her environment.
She now presumed her colleagues would help with child care; she had made unique
contributions to social science; she had set new standards in the enforcement of factory
legislation; and she occupied a prominent place within women's public culture. Yet without an institutional location through which she could continue to shape public policy,
these achievements could dissipate. Approaching her fortieth birthday, now more than
ever she needed meaningful work.

Florence Kelley's job crisis gave her a good opportunity to review her options in both
women's and men's public cultures. The relationship between these two was quite different from what it had been at the time of her graduation from Cornell fifteen years earlier.
The cascade of educated women produced by colleges and universities, the receptiveness
of social science to women's involvement, the vigorous mobilization of women's organizations on a national scale (including the suffrage movement), and the leadership of
women within the social settlement movement vastly increased the supply of publicly

active women throughout American society. Meanwhile, within men's political culture, the deepening power of urban political machines, the failure of civil service reform, the dominance of craft unions, the waning of broad-based unionism like the Knights of Labor, and organized labor's distrust of political solutions for workplace problems combined with trends within American society generally—especially the arrival of hundreds of thousands of "new" immigrants from southern and eastern Europe, the intensification of industrial growth, and the explosive expansion of urban areas—to create an urgent public demand for the skills white, middle-class women possessed and the agendas they represented. In the early 1880s politically active women's organizations had hardly ever overlapped with politically active men's groups, except within grassroots protests such as the Grange movement, and when they did, women occupied a distinctly secondary place in the political hierarchy. But changes under way in the 1890s had begun to alter that. Increasingly, women interacted with men on a new plane of equality and in some selected cases held power capable of overturning the male-dominated status quo. Florence Kelley's position as chief factory inspector exemplified these rare instances. Nevertheless, her search for work in 1897 and 1898 showed that the two gender-based public cultures were still more separate than equal.[21]

In that search, Kelley was not looking for work in the field of philanthropy. She had burned her bridges there by severely admonishing her audience in a talk on "The Working Child" at the 1896 convention of the National Conference of Charities and Correction. Opponents of child labor reform such as manufacturers' associations were "open to the charge of being somewhat sordid," she said, but they did no more harm than "the philanthropist who appears before the legislature, and in churches, and benevolent societies . . . always getting work for deserving little boys under the legal age." She characterized this pernicious do-gooder as a woman. "Not having had to support a family in her extreme youth, as the legislator had often had to do, she is far more relentless than he in her demand that the little boy shall do the Whole Duty of Man." She must have hoped that her searing criticism would help her listeners understand the "unmitigated evil of children's work," but she could not have expected any of that group to offer her meaningful work.[22]

Kelley first sought work through the growing commitment to reform in men's public culture. In June 1898 Congress funded the creation of an industrial commission to investigate the sources of and propose solutions for the nation's endemic violence between labor and capital. Alice Hamilton prodded Kelley into "asking a place on the commission." Believing the group should "have at least one person on it who really knows something of what it ought to do," Hamilton feared it would consist "entirely of innocuous old ladies of the male sex." Jane Addams wrote the secretary of treasury to recommend Kelley's appointment. He soon thereafter informed Kelley "that Mr. McKinley might be induced to consider the subject" of her appointment to the commission staff. Her salary would be $3,600 a year for two years.[23]

She and Addams promptly traveled to Washington to lobby for Kelley's appointment. "Mrs. Kelley and I had a famous interview with the President of the U.S.A. and find ourselves at home alternating between hope and fear," Addams wrote. Florence told Caroline that they "had a jolly little trip," the head resident paying both fares. "She cares so much to have the House represented on the Commission that I regard it as her trip as much as mine." McKinley "was very non-committal, but left us with just a ray of hope. He then expected to make the announcement of the appointments on Friday of this past week. But Friday has come and gone and the announcements are not yet made, and we are at a loss to know what he is going to do." She felt heartened because "he actually had tears in his eyes when he talked about Father," but she tried to repress her hope. "I suppose that is not difficult for him to accomplish; and may mean nothing at all." Hamilton felt ready to "expire of the suspense."[24]

That August Kelley could not help fantasizing about the possibilities of the commission job. "*If* B'rer McKinley should live up to his tears, I could visit you many times on my way to and from Washington," she wrote Caroline. Earlier, she had enlisted the support of her second most powerful ally, Ellen Henrotin, national president of the General Federation of Women's Clubs, writing Caroline in July, "I am just starting for a call upon Mrs. Henrotin, whom I am desirous of having address a letter to Mr. McK." She hoped "to have some really good news" for Caroline that week. Two weeks later she was still hopeful, taking no vacation "so that if B'rer McKinley *should* after all, appoint me, I could go to Washington for the necessary meetings without being docked in my library salary." The disappointing news finally arrived in September. "President McKinley has announced his appointments; and it is needless to say that I am not among them. Happily I never fix my mind upon the matter, but ask for the chance to do work for which I know I am fitted, and then, if I do not get it, there is no harm done. The Commission is a disgraceful one, and I shall probably live to thank my lucky star that I am not connected with it or responsible for its shams."[25] So much for a president's tears.

Six months later a similar opportunity appeared on her horizon: chief factory inspector of the state of New York. Theodore Roosevelt (TR), elected governor in 1898, had, as police commissioner of New York City, strenuously enforced laws regulating tenement workshops. Then and later he relied on the advice of Jacob Riis, the muckraking journalist who in 1890 exposed appalling tenement conditions in *How the Other Half Lives*. Early in 1899 Riis got Governor Roosevelt to back a bill that added fourteen paid workers to the factory inspector staff.[26]

Kelley openly campaigned for the job of chief inspector. "Nothing has seemed to me since I was twenty years old so great an opportunity for social usefulness as the position of Factory Inspector of New York State," she wrote Lillian Wald after visiting the influential head of the Henry Street Settlement on Manhattan's Lower East Side. Wald had dropped her other responsibilities to help her, and Kelley expressed her thanks for advancing "my old dream of enforcing the factory law in Manhattan." She returned home "with my wild hopes, and my new pocket-book, and a conscience burdened with wondering how long it might take you to pick up all the stitches I had caused you to drop." While in New York she had written a carefully crafted letter to the governor; back at Hull House she wrote Riis a second time and sent TR a copy of *Hull-House Maps and Papers.* Then she promised "to drop the matter and trust to Providence and Teddy's whims" but could not stop "thinking of it," since "Teddy's fearlessness to back up the Inspector makes it seem impossible that anyone else should have *that* opportunity." Her own qualifications were clear, she wrote Wald:

> You see there are so few people who know how to inspect inspectors! And that is what a Chief is for. It is not a question of caring, or meaning well, or sympathising with Labor (though I do that with all my heart). It is a question of knowing when a man is working honestly; and how to make the most of each one's qualities; and keeping track of what has been done, and of which industries are especially difficult, and all the technical points of keeping a staff going along uniformly attending to its duties without spurts or laggings. And that is what I had spent four years in learning when I was cut off in my prime!

In the same vein she wrote Henry Demarest Lloyd, "I have asked Governor Roosevelt to appoint me Chief Factory Inspector of New York. I am becoming a professional office-seeker. But it is only one kind of office I want; and I want it because, like my modest friend Mr. Bisno, I am persuaded that no one else now in the field would work so effectively against the sweating-system as I could with Teddy to back me in my enforcement of the law." [27]

As soon as Jane Addams's schedule permitted, she traveled to New York on Kelley's behalf. "Dearly Beloved," Kelley wrote Mary Smith, "Lady Jane is to see Teddy at his house on the 17th in New York. I have abandoned all hope because Teddy has not answered my letter or taken any notice of my existence." She hoped Addams could overcome his view expressed in a letter to Riis "that while *he* Teddy has no prejudices, the community would object to an Altgeld appointee." This Kelley thought a "polite and a tenable position." She only hoped that "the persuasive qualities of the Lady" would work a reversal. "I am so possessed by the magnitude of the opportunity that I can think of nothing else," she lamented, though she did have the presence of mind to add: "H.H. seems queer without you in reach. The Lady misses you more than the uninitiated would think she had time for." In New York Addams stayed with Wald and wrote her, about complications she encountered on her trip, "It will all [have] been worth it if Sister Kelley gets the appointment."[28]

Yet Kelley's appointment proved impossible for Roosevelt. In many ways, he resembled the rural Tories in England who spearheaded efforts to regulate industrial capitalism in the early nineteenth century, but he differed from them in one fatal regard: he owed his election to a Republican boss, Thomas C. Platt, and to upstate voters who responded to his "law and order" attacks on anarchists, immigrants, and criminals. "I am in favor of stamping out anarchy with a heavy hand," he said at one whistle-stop. Roosevelt concluded that he could not contradict himself by appointing a woman associated with the pardoner of the Haymarket anarchists. He frankly admitted to another lobbyist on Kelley's behalf that "the time was not ripe for the Governor of New York State to appoint a woman as factory inspector." Instead, he selected John Williams, an elevator operator in Albany who had energetically lobbied for the job, though he knew nothing about its responsibilities. TR told him to confer with Kelley. "She knows more about enforcing the factory law than any man I know of, and I want you to keep in touch with her." Oblivious to any error on his part, he told Kelley that he had asked Williams "to call on you."[29] This encounter with Roosevelt revealed that the emerging reform spirit within men's public culture was unlikely to replace women's autonomous institutions as the platform for her reform activism.

Appointive office was not all that men's public culture had to offer; Kelley's experience and qualifications also suited her for academic employment. But a university position seemed to lie beyond her reach. Her experience in social survey work, demonstrated in her government reports and the maps in *Hull-House Maps and Papers*, got her nowhere in academic social science. In 1892 Richard Ely had rebuffed her inquiry about work at the institution most open to her talents—the University of Wisconsin. In 1897, with substantial new credits to her name as a social researcher, she got no further. Ely's cold shoulder was partly due to Kelley's own demanding personality, but it also derived from the prejudice that excluded most women from academic life.[30]

Yet even more than this prejudice, the political climate within universities also prevented Kelley's career from taking an academic direction. Given her familiarity with European socialism, her commitment to social justice, and her ferocious temperament, she could never have survived the repressive political environment that dominated American campuses in this era. Henry Carter Adams at Cornell in 1886, Richard Ely at Wisconsin in 1894, Edward W. Bemis at the University of Chicago in 1894, John Commons at Syracuse University in 1899, and Albion Small at the University of Chicago in 1897 were all victims of political witch-hunting that reshaped academic social science in that decade. Richard Ely typified the accommodationist response to this throttling when he recanted his radicalism during a trial staged by the University of Wisconsin Board of Regents in 1894. He declared himself "a conservative rather than a radical," stated that the province of trade unions "must be a limited one," and withdrew from the American Institute of Christian Sociology. Ely described the forces behind his trial in a letter to Lloyd. "I have heard President Harper [of the University of Chicago] myself say before a considerable company something like this: 'The labor movement may be all right but we get our money from the capitalists and I am with the capitalists every time.'" Richard Ely did not again take part in labor reform activities until 1907, when he emerged as a founding member of the American Association for Labor Legislation and advocated the role of the neutral expert.[31]

These purges marked a fundamental watershed in the new social science disciplines. Early social science expressed beliefs in the sacred qualities of human relationships and communities. After 1900 "objectivity" and secular values that accommodated the needs of the marketplace replaced advocacy as the basic social science goal. The repression of those early visions eliminated or greatly reduced the ability of male social scientists to counter the growing hegemony of monopoly capitalism in American life and widened the distance between academic social science and women social reformers.[32]

Protected from these assaults by their political and economic autonomy, Hull House reformers applied social science techniques to social problems in ways that increasingly differentiated them from male academics, not so much in their methods as in their values and in the ways they harnessed social science methods to serve political goals. Addams insisted that Hull House residents lived in the Nineteeth Ward "not as students, but as citizens," and she "objected to the phrase 'sociological laboratory'" applied to the settlement, believing it "much more human and spontaneous than such a phrase connotes."[33]

These women knew the University of Chicago well. For example, they contributed repeatedly to Albion Small's newly founded *American Journal of Sociology*, Kelley placing articles in the second through fifth volumes, between 1896 and 1899. They knew Marion Talbot (dean of women and assistant professor of Sanitary Science in the Department of Social Science and Anthropology) and the university's growing coterie of talented graduate students, especially Sophonisba Breckinridge, who later codirected the university's School of Social Service Administration. But, relegated to the margins of academic life, full-time reformers like Addams and Kelley experienced more conflicts than continuities between their reform priorities and their academic encounters.[34]

In the summer of 1899 Addams and Kelley cotaught a lecture course at the University of Chicago that sent both into a tailspin. Addams found it excruciatingly difficult to meet the demands of Hull House life and prepare her lectures at the same time. "We are much as usual at H-H," she wrote Mary Smith. "Some days very wild as yesterday for instance a large reception to the woman's club, a poet to lunch, and down at the bottom of my mind the consciousness that my lectures were not being done." The deadline loomed. "Sister Kelley comes on the fourth of July and the next day the fight is on." The fight left them exhausted. "We are not doing very brilliantly with our lectures," Kelley wrote Wald. "The heat and the make-up of the audiences are agin us. And it is incredibly fatiguing. Alas! I wish our only audience were a friendly guide and a well-instructed resident of a sister settlement not likely to be fuddled by any error of ours." She was ill most of the time, "Not in bed, but going to the University on stimulants, and coming . . . to bed until the next lecture." [35] Their regular credit course was open to the public, so they could not predict whether their audiences had heard any preceding lecture. Kelley's last audience "consisted of thirty-eight persons, none of whom had ever attended before," making it impossible for her to "carry out her plan of giving for that lecture a hurried resumé of all the others." When the course ended they rejoiced greatly "over their liberty." Kelley thought Addams was "tired down to the very roots!" A sympathetic Hull House resident who thought the "lectures had disastrous effects on them both" said that Lady Jane "had bowel trouble added to lady-trouble" as the course concluded and that "Mrs. Kelley has not been herself at all—her lectures were not prepared carefully and she got perfectly miserable over them," ending the course "nervous and prostrated." [36]

Addams and Kelley were too unremittingly political to reside comfortably in academia, even in its public-minded periphery. True, Talbot, Breckinridge, and a host of other younger women embodied a professional approach to reform that incorporated many aspects of the political activism found at Hull House, and Addams and Kelley represented political strategies that encompassed many features of their professionalism; these women inhabited different points on a political-professional continuum rather than dichotomous worlds. Yet their dissimilarities loomed large enough to make the University of Chicago an unworkable option for Addams and Kelley. A letter to Kelley from Agnes Hamilton, Alice's cousin, captured the disdain Hull House residents often felt toward the university sociologists. As a student at Stanford, Agnes was "having such fun" reading "Small and Vincent's *Introduction to the Study of Society*. . . . They cite as the most flagrant example of oppression of the economically weak, whom do you think? The Landlord? The sweater or manufacturer? No, these are not even attended to. The arch oppressor is the pawn-broker! I long for some one to enjoy it with." [37]

Yet despite the unwelcoming academic climate in the United States, Florence Kelley found a ready and remunerative audience for her mixture of social science and reform perspectives in Germany, where Social Democrats had a better understanding of their place in history and where the state's central role in economic affairs was assumed. Beginning in 1898 she became a regular contributor to a prominent German journal devoted to the study of social legislation and social conditions, *Archiv für Soziale Gesetzgebung und Statistik* (Archive for social legislation and statistics). Founded in 1888, *Archiv* was established in Berlin by Heinrich Braun, who was part of a vital cluster of German reformers and intellectuals associated with the Social Democratic Party and—more than most American academic social scientists were able to do—linked empirical investigations of social conditions with political visions of social justice. He would have known Kelley through her 1889 article on child labor in Kautsky's *Die neue Zeit* and her 1894 German writings. Writer, publicist, and husband of one of Germany's leading feminists—Lily Braun—Braun rejected the class determinism of Marx and Engels, agreed with Eduard Bernstein's *Evolutionary Socialism* (1898), and promoted Lassallean notions of the reforming power of the state. In contrast with Kautsky's theoretical Marxian purity in *Die neue Zeit*, Braun wanted *Archiv* to apply Marxist ideas to practical problems and sought the widest possible range of contributors.[38] In 1897 he was Kelley's kind of socialist.

"I read with deep regret in the newspaper that you became a victim of the 'Spoils System,'" Braun wrote Kelley in that spring. "In the old as in the new world, and wherever social-political interest is lively, all will feel the loss of the best female Factory Inspector being torn out of her sphere of activity." He hoped she would soon find work appropriate to her talents and in the meantime warmly solicited her to make regular contributions to *Archiv*. She could name her price. He especially encouraged an article about the factory inspectorship in Illinois. In reply Kelley requested (and received) an honorarium of fifty dollars a month in exchange for original essays on "the social course of events in the States," critical reviews of "all remarkable social laws" together with their texts, and the activities of factory inspectors, bureaus of labor statistics, and strikes. Braun's letters always closed with greetings from his wife along with his own "friendly regards and deep respect."[39]

As a temporary transition between more meaningful jobs, the Crerar library served her well. But work for Braun was just as crucial; it regularly paid John's school fees, and it kept her intellectually active. "I send my German check to the school, every month, as soon as it comes," she wrote Caroline. "Although I have only eight [articles] a year, I find that I keep my eyes open and my ears sharpened for ideas much more acutely than I used to do; so the employment is really a healthful one."[40]

Kelley's lengthy scholarly articles for *Archiv für Soziale Gesetzgebung und Statistik* summarized her recent experience and allowed her to place herself in the unfolding future of American industrial democracy. All her *Archiv* writings viewed government as the key for unlocking systematic social improvements, and all synthesized ideas from men's and women's public culture. For example, her 1899 essay on the Italians of Chicago asked why the U.S. Bureau of Labor Statistics issued a special report on that group when they constituted only 6,773 of more than 1.8 million Chicago residents. The reason lay in the way Italians fueled anti-immigrant sentiment, she said, especially among trade unionists. But, Kelley argued, all the characteristics that turned Italians into targets for opponents of immigration—shabby dwellings, illiteracy, high infant mortality, their low rate of naturalization, and their use of the padrone labor system—could "be eradicated by a well-functioning city administration." Enlightened government could enforce existing housing, health, and school regulations and provide a rational labor policy. Unfortunately, "the city exercises no coercion on its inhabitants even when the public welfare would demand such coercion." While "Italians suffer more than anybody else from this policy of non-intervention," she thought, this was not reason enough to limit their immigration.[41]

One of her most intriguing *Archiv* articles paid tribute to female factory inspectors and interpreted their place in the emerging activist state. First employed in the United States seven years earlier, women inspectors numbered twenty-three in 1897. They showed "that all professions and occupations should be open to those who desire to pursue them." Working-class women proved to be the best female inspectors, Kelley thought, "particularly those who were suggested by the unions." They were used to working and had a strong interest "in protecting their fellow workers." She thought that women factory inspectors should "always wear the short, light, and comfortable cyclist suit during work. Women who can not part with corsets, high heels, the many petticoats and white gloves of our grandmothers, will of course not be able to keep up with" those "who wear the practical clothes of today's businesswoman." The scope of women inspectors' power varied. In Pennsylvania, women "perform all the functions of inspection," while in other states they checked "only the regulations having to do with women and children." Women factory inspectors were important to her chiefly because their reports were "used as sources" in talks that aroused interest and sympathy "in hundreds of women's clubs and scholarly institutions." Reports by women factory inspectors were "the best stimulus" of the interest of women of "the higher classes" in topics like "child labor, the sweatshop system, working hours for women and children, and other related topics," and this was "one of the most compelling reasons" for their appointment.[42]

Interestingly, she insisted that "the difference between men and women inspectors makes no difference in respect to the workers bringing complaints." If the inspector "pays attention to the details of the work, he soon usually succeeds in getting to the bottom of the matter. This is valid for men just as much as it is for women inspectors." Women and children "avoid speaking with a woman inspector just as much as with a man inspector," she said. "We are not a counseling but rather an executive authority." [43] Her commitment to gender-neutral expertise flowed from her hope for a joint political project in which men and women reformers worked together.

One article defined Kelley's sense of her place in the process of historical change through its focus on the state's growing social responsibility. "Drei Entscheidungen oberster Gerichte über den gesetzlichen Arbeitstag in den Vereinigten Staaten" (Three Supreme Court decisions concerning the legal limitation of the working day in the United States) stressed the significance of the U.S. Supreme Court's 1898 decision in *Holden v. Hardy*. That judgment upheld a Utah eight-hour law for miners on grounds that sustained the state's constitutional provisions that "eight hours shall constitute a working day in all workshops and enterprises operated by the state" and that the legislature should "pass laws in order to protect the health and the life of workers employed in factories, foundries and mines." That ruling, she felt certain, confirmed the Massachusetts law of 1874, over-ruled the Illinois 1895 decision, and extended legislative protections to include men. "The decision changes the foundation of the legislation that limits working time by no longer taking into consideration age and sex but the sanitary nature of the work in question and the effect it is likely to have on the organisms of men, women and children. It thus lays the foundation for a broader and more humane legislation than has been possible in this country up to now." *Holden v. Hardy* gave "an authoritative and liberal interpretation of the much disputed Fourteenth Amendment of the federal Constitution." She predicted that just as the eighteenth century unified the American colonies and the nineteenth century unified North and South, the new century would "regulate the working conditions uniformly in the entire republic according to the new, humane and enlightened decision of the federal Supreme Court." [44]

In a related article Kelley noted, however, that "it is also to be remembered that these things do not occur spontaneously; they are the fruits of long and patient labor." Adverse decisions in many states "have cumbered the earth with error, discouragement, apathy, if not actual antagonism, to this sane and hopeful, though slow and difficult, method of social amelioration." Describing her own labors, she concluded: "Years must be consumed in education and agitation before the fruits of this harvest of enlightened judicial interpretation can be fully reaped and enjoyed by the toilers throughout the United States. No time should be lost; the work should begin at once." [45]

If her forecast about the definitive effect of the Utah hours law of 1898 had been fulfilled, it would have altered Kelley's place in American history, though in unpredictable ways. On the one hand, her historical importance might have been reduced because there might have been less need for her to lead the judicial struggle she later waged on behalf of improved working conditions for women, children, and men. On the other hand her historical significance might have been heightened in a legal context more receptive to labor legislation. As it was, the *Holden v. Hardy* decision boosted her optimism at a critical low point in her reform morale.

Although she explored both appointive and academic possibilities in male public culture, Kelley could not expect to succeed in electoral politics. In that realm her stance remained adversarial. Expressing the growing maturity and power of women's public culture, as well as increased reform activity among upper-class and middle-class men, she joined with Addams in a Sisyphian effort to unseat their local ward boss and alderman, Johnny Powers, by far the most powerful member of the Chicago City Council. Inevitably, the settlement's attempts to improve living conditions in their neighborhood brought them into direct conflict with Powers. They wanted garbage collected, but he gave that job to cronies who "collected the money, but little of the garbage." They campaigned for more public schools, but Powers's support for a new parochial school stymied their efforts. They thought he was robbing the people by selling public transportation franchises to an exploitative monopolist, but he ignored their criticism. They viewed government as a public trust, but he saw it as a personal business. It galled them that in 1896, after almost ten years as a city alderman, he was reputed to be worth four hundred thousand dollars.[46]

Historians once believed that political bosses met the social welfare needs of urban immigrant constituencies, but recent scholarship challenges that assumption. While municipal governments did dispense most public welfare spending before 1930 and hundreds of patronage-based jobs were distributed according to party loyalty, taxes remained low and social services rudimentary. Partly because of a lack of imagination among party bosses and partly through the restraining influence of the tax-conscious middle class, urban political machines did not meet their constituencies' needs for positive government. They distributed food at Christmas and mediated between their constituencies and public relief and private charitable agencies. Sometimes they championed pure milk campaigns, supported woman suffrage, and welcomed the construction of new schools, but most were run by fiscal conservatives who, except in the business of getting votes, shunned policy innovations. Moreover, machine coalitions probably reinforced the power of capital by blocking working-class pressures that might have challenged employers' hegemony.[47]

The Hull House attack on Powers began in 1895 but reached a crescendo in 1898. "We expect to work until midnight every night," Alice Hamilton said just before the elections. Perhaps because the campaign carried women onto new political turf where they interacted as equals with men, Kelley cared passionately about the outcome. During the 1890s middle-class women had steadily increased their numbers in elected city and state offices for which women could vote, especially the Chicago School Board and the University of Illinois Board of Trustees. Paralleling their growing power as an independent political force that stood apart from the Republican and Democratic parties, women became increasingly effective in their ability to interact with men on both partisan and nonpartisan grounds. At the same time, Republican (though not Democratic) women began to present their own priorities and demands to party leaders.[48]

In this context, Johnny Powers's obstruction of Hull House goals grew less and less tolerable. He finally went too far in 1898 when, following Addams's success in getting the city's garbage-collecting jobs made into civil service appointments, he restored them to his patronage network by redefining administrative categories. The settlement declared war. In fact, this declaration was overdue, for male reformers in other wards had already launched successful assaults on the entrenched Democratic machine. "There was a strong movement throughout the city against the gang," Kelley said, and she longed to join it.[49]

The campaign highlighted the extent to which women reformers augmented their power by working with the wave of "good government" reform, which, fostered by the Chicago Civic Federation, strongly influenced middle-class male public culture in the middle and late 1890s. The federation drew together five "non-partisan" constituencies: education, commerce, labor, religion, and women—the last represented on its organizing committee by Jane Addams. "Improvement clubs" opposed to boss rule sprang up in many wards, including the Nineteenth, and in 1896 formed the Municipal Voters' League, a citywide group closely affiliated with the Civic Federation. Primarily devoted to good government, the coalition launched electoral campaigns against corrupt city alderman. Victories in the Seventeenth Ward, where Graham Taylor's settlement, Chicago Commons, campaigned successfully in 1896, were amplified by reform wins in the Twenty-second, Twenty-fourth, and Twenty-ninth Wards.[50] Yet none of these wards had taken on Johnny Powers, and no campaign was led by women. Moreover, excluded from city council suffrage and office, women had to rely on male supporters at every stage. Still, Hull House residents had always worked closely with men without being dominated by them, so their chances for success were good.

Florence Kelley was an energetic leader in the settlement's Nineteenth Ward Improvement Club, which led the local assault on Powers. Founded in March 1894 as a loose affiliate of the Chicago Civic Federation and aiming at the "municipal improvement of the neighborhood," the club consisted of roughly equal numbers of women and men, drawing heavily on the membership of other clubs affiliated with the settlement. In 1895, 1896, and 1898, the Improvement Club recruited electoral candidates from the Hull House Men's Club. Their candidate won in 1895, though he did not run against Powers; to the great disappointment of his Hull House supporters, he promptly joined the Powers machine. The 1896 and 1898 campaigns directly challenged Powers's seat, the second occurring just prior to the negotiation of lucrative fifty-year streetcar franchises.[51]

The settlement's campaigns attracted national publicity and garnered impressive support from popular reform figures such as Mayor Hazen Pingree of Detroit. The Nineteenth Ward Improvement Club had representatives in every precinct. Mary Kenney O'Sullivan returned from Boston to bolster the campaign's appeal to Catholic voters, and a nationally respected muckraking journalist arrived to report on events. "A boodle Alderman does not take money from the rich and give it to the poor," the Hull House candidate insisted in a public speech. "Rather, he takes money from the rich and in return gives them the power to rob the poor," exploitatively high streetcar fares being the best example. Influential middle-class men's groups, especially the Municipal Voters' League, lent support, as did "women's clubs, Italian clubs, Irish clubs, and Jewish clubs." Even so, these challenges failed—even more decisively in 1898 than in 1896. Indeed, in 1898, Powers declared total war: "Hull House will be driven from the ward, and its leaders will be forced to shut up shop," he threatened.[52]

The limitations of women's public culture were painfully apparent; Hull House residents and their supporters had been less successful than Graham Taylor's settlement in ousting the boodlers. Yet their efforts did not go totally unrewarded. Just after his victory, Powers withdrew his opposition to a Hull House plan for the expansion of a local public school. Kelley rejoiced that they finally "got the [City] Council to authorize the purchase of fifty feet of land" to expand a school to accommodate three to five hundred more children. She wrote Lloyd that it was "a distinct victory over Powers and the Jesuits, for they have fought this extension directly and indirectly for seven years."[53]

Addams and Kelley drew very different conclusions from this experience. Addams gained national renown with her explanation of Powers's appeal. "He is elected not because he is dishonest. He is elected because he is a friendly visitor," she said, emphasizing his power to deliver jobs and protect his constituency in time of need.[54] Her compassionate understanding of why working-class voters endorsed him, why they preferred his diamond stickpin to the working-class lunchpail of the settlement candidate, and why they found reformers lacking in concrete and human qualities expressed her belief in democratic social ethics. She could pursue social justice independently of campaigns for good government and, thinking Powers unbeatable for good reasons, decided to stop campaigning against him.

But for Florence Kelley, Powers remained the tool of monopolists and oppressors, a direct cause of the ward's high infant mortality rates, and the man who deprived children of seats in public schools. For her, the state was too central to social justice to surrender its control to exploiters. She insisted on renewed assaults. "Will Hull House accept defeat and withdraw from politics?" she asked in an otherwise loving 1898 tribute to the settlement. "That would be to accept the conventional ethics of too many existing powerful institutions . . . waxing fat while uttering sterile precepts not meant for application at election time." Rather than take this course, she declared, "it would be better to leave the field to the frank cynicism of the corporations who buy the Council and the voters, but at least do not pretend to inculcate ideals while they do it." Hull House could not "turn back" from its protest on behalf of municipal honesty. Kelley's greater commitment to this struggle derived partly from her greater zeal for conflict, partly from the greater hope she placed in governmental power, and partly from her opposition to municipal reform campaigns' becoming a male preserve. Finally, in the late 1890s, men's public culture was on the move, and she wanted women to be part of that action.[55]

Tellingly, however, these years of career drift carried her further into women's public culture. In February 1898 she took time to write a paper called "The Working Woman's Need of the Ballot," which was read at hearings on "the philosophy of the [woman suffrage] movement" conducted by a U.S. Senate Special Committee on Woman Suffrage. She argued that "no one needs all the powers of the fullest citizenship more urgently than the wage-earning woman," since she was "cut off from the protection awarded to her sisters abroad" but had no power "to defend her interests at the polls." This impaired her standing in the community and lowered "her value as a human being and consequently as a worker." As permanent and significant members of the labor force, women deserved better. If women could not defend themselves through their votes, at least they could receive the protection they needed. After the union of the two major national suffrage organizations in 1890, the American Woman Suffrage Association (Boston) and the National Woman Suffrage Association (New York) into the National American Woman Suffrage Association (New York and Boston), the suffrage movement began to modernize in the 1890s, and Florence Kelley began to make a place for herself within it.[56]

Her suffrage views were in keeping with a book she greatly admired: *Women and Economics: The Economic Factor between Men and Women as a Factor in Social Evolution* (1898), by Charlotte Perkins Stetson Gilman. Feminist writer and lecturer and daughter figure to Helen Campbell, Gilman spent three months at Hull House in 1895 and returned

Charlotte Perkins Gilman, ca. 1898. Courtesy of Brown Brothers, Sterling, Pennsylvania.

in the autumn of 1898. The visitor's personal life had made her notorious; Alice Hamilton described her as "the woman . . . who couldn't stand being married and so agreed with her husband to have a divorce and now is on excellent terms with her former husband and his present wife who takes care of [her] little girl." After some difficult years in the public limelight in California, Gilman was glad to be a "small fish in a large pond — well stocked with bigger ones." She thought "Jane Addams was a truly great woman" whose mind had "more 'floor space' in it than any other I have known. She could set a subject down, unprejudiced, and walk all around it, allowing fairly for every one's point of view." It was "meat and drink" to her "to be among people who *care*." [57]

The most important work of feminist theory in the emerging Progressive Era, Gilman's pathbreaking book made a vivid impact on Kelley and Addams. Addams called it a "masterpiece" and thought it put "perfectly clearly many things which I have been fumbling after." Kelley told Gilman it was "the first real substantial contribution made by a woman to the science of economics." On her job-seeking trip to Washington with Addams she "read it through on the way down and again, critically, on the way back." Addams had carried one of the settlement's two copies to Rockford and lent the other to Mary Smith, Kelley said, so "with our wonted frugality, the residents are waiting in rows for her to come back with it." [58]

Gilman's book drew on the iconoclastic sociological writings of Lester Ward, especially his 1888 article "Our Better Halves," which advanced a gynocentric view of human evolution in which women acted as the chief evolutionary force, and his book *Dynamic Sociology* (1883), which argued that human progress was achieved by the conscious mastery of society and nature, not by laissez-faire policies that favored the fittest. Employed in the Bureau of Statistics in Washington, D.C., Ward was part of a small but influential community of believers in the positive state who, escaping the repressions of university life, helped build that state, especially in its policies toward the natural environment. For Kelley's generation of reformers — men and women alike — Ward's writings in the 1880s provided an intellectual framework for the rejection of laissez-faire social Darwinism, one that reflected the growing importance of women in the processes of social change. Social reformers were for him a natural phenomenon that corrected society's inertia and its failure otherwise to respond to the need for change. Ward proudly described himself as having "roughly blocked out from the slab the statue which Gilman then refined with a fine-point chisel." [59]

Kelley found *Women and Economics* compelling because it viewed women's work as a lever with which women could gain greater participation in community life — provided their child care needs were met. "We are the only animal species in which the female depends on the male for food, the only animal species in which the sex-relation is also an economic relation," Gilman argued. "With us an entire sex lives in a relation of economic dependence." This "sexuo-economic" dependence greatly exaggerated and distorted women's sex-specific qualities, isolating them within their individual families, separating them from the richness of social life, and thereby retarded "human development." With work that allowed women to become economically independent this was changing, she argued, and she advocated the creation of cooperative housekeeping units that would allow women, like men, to have families and at the same time participate in the larger society. This conclusion rang true for Kelley. She promised, "It is going to be my most urgent duty (outside of earning shekels for my three open-billed robins) . . . to keep lending that book to women to read." [60]

Yet she had some telling criticisms. Gilman's view of women's economic independence focused primarily on middle-class women in professional or semiprofessional jobs, such as teaching or accounting. And her understanding of historical change relied heavily on vague but inevitable processes associated with human evolution. "It would strengthen the argument, to my way of thinking, if there were a little more admission that mere emergence [of working women] without accompanying transformations of the conditions of work, is not altogether beneficent or perhaps a very material gain, for the emergers at present," Kelley wrote. "Being one of the emergent, and feeling the pinch of the present maladministration of occupations, I would fain facilitate the process of transforming industry." If Gilman discussed the need for industrial transformation, Kelley thought she would be less vulnerable to criticism from women who defended their economic dependence on men by pointing to unsavory working conditions for women. Showing spirited hostility toward these middle-class nonworking women, Kelley added, "The non-emerging, self-excusing female cannot be deprived ruthlessly enough to suit me, of all arguments for self-defense in this discussion." [61] Despite these criticisms, however, *Women and Economics* reinforced Florence Kelley's commitment to women's public culture at a crucial juncture. Gilman's robust critique of gender inequality confirmed the former factory inspector's belief in the use of the state to improve working conditions for wage-earning women. And it deepened her willingness to incur the hostility of women as well as men.

Kelley had already found a new vehicle for her civic aspirations in the Illinois Consumers' League. The first department store opened in 1876, but not until the 1890s did the production of goods, their merchandising, and their marketing launch the consumer culture that came to dominate the twentieth century. Remarkably parallel to this trajectory, in the 1890s consumers' leagues emerged to channel consumer consciousness toward political action. In 1893, two years after the founding of the New York City Consumers' League, Kelley had first proposed the creation of an Illinois league in a talk before the

Chicago Association of Collegiate Alumnae. Initially nothing came of her exertions, but in 1896 a visit from John Graham Brooks of Boston seems to have renewed her commitment. Brooks, a former Unitarian minister, in 1894 authored "The Papal Encyclical upon the Labor Question," which applauded the church's view that wages "must be enough to support the wage earners in reasonable and frugal comfort." He lived at Hull House in 1896 while teaching a university extension course there on "Modern Socialism at Work." That year Kelley advocated "the starting of a consumers' league" that would endorse the production of "guaranteed garments"—clothes made in factories rather than tenements. Trying to get manufacturers to guarantee that their goods were made in factories and always anticipating the next step, she wrote Alice Hamilton, "The point is to clamor for a guarantee until some firm can be induced to give it and then use it as an entering wedge." To this end, she "was urging the starting of a consumers' league which should add to the functions of the New York one the demand for guaranteed garments." [62]

Her efforts paid off the next year, when the Chicago Association of Collegiate Alumnae organized a consumers' league within its membership. A committee began investigating conditions for department store clerks, and one ACA member took a job behind the counter to obtain firsthand information. To Chicago women's clubs the committee sent a circular on "Recommendations for Shopping" proposing guidelines for women

John Graham Brooks, ca. 1900. Courtesy of Schlesinger Library, Radcliffe College.

shoppers that would improve the Christmas holiday season for sales clerks. Kelley led this small group for two years; it was one of her "regular winter occupations" in 1898–99. She worked closely with three other Chicago women, including Ellen Henrotin. "We transacted a lot of Consumers' League business in the most agreeable way, in front of the open fire and over the lunch table," she said of one meeting.[63]

Florence Kelley's fireside alliance with Henrotin nurtured a bond that linked the enormous power of the General Federation of Women's Clubs with the consumer league movement. Ellen Henrotin, married to a prominent banker who later became president of the Chicago Stock Exchange, exemplified the substantial differences between women's and men's public cultures during the early years of Progressive reform, as well as the opportunities for innovative action women encountered and created. Born in 1847, Henrotin was twelve years older than Kelley. Her cosmopolitan education in schools in London, Paris, and Dresden may help explain the breadth of her political interests as well as her friendship with Kelley. As a result of her stupendous success as the chief organizer of the women's congresses at the 1893 Chicago World's Fair, she became president of the General Federation of Women's Clubs in 1894.

Just as Josephine Shaw Lowell rose to national prominence through the U.S. Sanitary Commission, so Henrotin did through the fair. Both were male-dominated organizations with clear internal divisions between male and female responsibilities that generated important new positions of public authority for women. Like Lowell, Henrotin promptly reinvested in women's separate institutions the power she accumulated in these male-dominated organizations. During Henrotin's four-year tenure as president of the federation (she was reelected in 1896), the number of local clubs more than doubled. To augment the power of local clubs, she fostered the creation of over twenty state federations and urged the establishment of national standing committees on industrial working conditions, national health, and the international arbitration movement. In this way she directed the path of what was to become one of the largest grassroots organizations of American women beyond the minimal goals of good government and civil service reform to the more challenging issues of social inequalities and social justice. "Departments of civics and social economics should be a part of all club work and study classes," she declared in 1895.[64]

Meanwhile, consumers' leagues grew in other cities. Aided by the New York City League, founded in 1891, women in Brooklyn and Philadelphia formed leagues in 1896, and John Brooks helped organize a Boston league in 1897. Each community's league built on existing women's organizations. Invitations to the founding meeting of the Boston league, for example, went to members of the Women's Educational and Industrial Union and the New England Women's Club.[65] Women constituted the great majority of those who responded, but liberal clergymen, male settlement heads, and academicians also attended. Structurally, therefore, consumers' leagues duplicated the relationship between women's and men's public cultures found at Hull House: influential male allies were added to a self-consciously female group in numbers too few to dominate but numerous enough to lend political clout.

League objectives noted the distinctive qualities of the new era at the same time that they drew on antislavery traditions. As Josephine Shaw Lowell, first president of the New York league, explained, "It was easy enough for the abolitionists to give up the use of sugar and cotton, because these were known to be slave-made, but the conditions of so-called free labor are more complicated, and in order to learn where and how the goods they desire to purchase are made, it is necessary to have concerted action." To meet this need the New York City league in 1891 devised a "White List" of department stores that met the "standard of a fair house" on wages, hours, physical conditions, management-employee relations, and child labor. Such a list required its own enforcement, and in 1897 the Massachusetts league inquired "whether the services of Mrs. Florence Kelley as inspector could be secured." [66]

Early in 1898, Kelley's position within this new national movement became even more prominent when it decided to support her long-standing proposal for a consumers' label as a way of identifying goods made under fair conditions. Imitating the use of union labels on goods produced in union shops (first introduced by cigarmakers in San Francisco in 1869), she proposed that the consumers' label be awarded to trade union shops that also met the league's other requirements, including standards of wages and hours. Her proposal sparked a sharp debate that eventually led to a decision by the Massachusetts league "to further the interests of the trade-union label by publishing details of its use, by investigating trades-union shops and by adopting trades-union standards of wages, without however requiring the trades-union label as requisite to the Consumers' League label." [67]

Highlighting the need for closer cooperation among the leagues, this debate led to the founding of the National Consumers' League (NCL) in New York in May 1898. Local leagues united "for the express purpose of offering a Consumers' League Label." They "closed like a fist to fight sweatshops" nationally, recognizing that local efforts could never succeed until all producers were "compelled to compete on a higher level." Kelley, representing Illinois at the founding national meeting, engaged in typical hyperbole by calling the Chicago league "the greatest consumers' league in existence" because it had forged an alliance with cigar workers to eliminate cigar making in tenements. At a mass meeting organized by the conference, she captivated her audience with descriptions of her antisweatshop campaigns in Chicago. On a more prosaic level, she joined Maud Nathan (president of the New York City League) and Katherine Coman (executive committee member of the Massachusetts league) in a committee of three to "investigate the work and expense necessary to introduce the [consumers'] label." [68] To monitor their white list, leagues had employed their own factory inspectors. The new label would require even more intense scrutiny of factory standards; for that purpose, the national league also required a paid staff position.

Josephine Shaw Lowell, Mary Putnam Jacobi, and Helen Campbell formed a committee to fill this new position. All three had personal relationships with Kelley — Lowell through George William Curtis's connection with William D. Kelley in the 1850s, Mary Jacobi through her sister's friendship with Florence at Cornell, and Helen Campbell through her friendship with Kelley ten years earlier. Moreover, as the former chief factory inspector of Illinois, Kelley had acquired a reputation that made her an obvious choice to enforce the league's factory standards. They picked her to be their "inspector and organizer." [69]

In January 1899 John Graham Brooks, president of the newly founded NCL, traveled to Chicago to urge Kelley to accept the NCL's offer to be their corresponding secretary with a salary of fifteen hundred dollars plus traveling and other expenses. "When one was face to face with him one felt his spirit and its eternal eagerness," a Brooks admirer said. As a Unitarian pastor in Brockton, Massachusetts, with a congregation that embraced both shoe factory workers and their employers, Brooks had created a group that discussed social and labor problems. Later he gave up his parish "to take up a ministry as wide as the English speaking world." He studied in Germany in 1882 and returned there in 1891 as an investigator for the U.S. Department of Labor to analyze German social security policy. More recently he had lectured on economics twice a week at Harvard University. Sharing Kelley's commitment to the process of collecting facts, presenting them to the public, and legislating change, Brooks presented the NCL's offer of the post of corresponding secretary in the most positive light.[70] Still hoping for the New York inspectorship, however, Kelley did not accept the league's offer until that option evaporated in mid-March.

Two weeks later she submitted an outline of action for the consumers' label to be considered at a special executive committee meeting. She proposed a plan that identified factories worthy of the label, designed the label, created a contract between manufacturers and the leagues, and devised "a well considered plan for advertising the label," since women who inquired for goods carrying the label would be their most effective promoters. Kelley's vision of the symbolic power of the consumers' label wedded the social and political potential of middle-class women's organizations with an emblem devised by the union movement. Her long search for a way to fuse the structures of women's grassroots power with the ideology of labor's quest for social justice seemed to be ending. The social and political power of this women's organization held out the hope that capitalism could be bent to become more compatible with democracy. The process of industrialization, urbanization, nationalization, and organization under way after 1870 may have had the effect of deepening both class and gender distinctions, but that same process had given rise to more, not less, independent public action by middle-class women.[71]

When Kelley accepted the NCL's offer in May, she acted against the advice of her closest friends, who thought she could find something better. "I have virtually accepted the position of Secretary to the National Consumers' League in spite of your advice and Miss Addams' and Miss Lathrop so I feel like a rash young thing rushing forth in the great world without the family blessing!" she wrote Wald.[72] She could not afford to refuse the offer. It doubled her income, placed her at the head of a potentially powerful vehicle for national as well as local legislative change, and gave her a great deal of autonomy in defining the organization's goals. Her acceptance finally created her own organizational habitat within women's public culture.

Yet despite all its many benefits, her new position also required her to move to New York. This meant leaving Hull House, and that she was extremely reluctant to do. She began work in New York on May 1 and initially found the change of pace exhilarating. "The change of work seems to be answering the same purpose as the regular rests might have done," she wrote Wald during her July lecture course, "for I came back to Hull House feeling fifteen years better and younger than when I left it two months ago." But the reality of her departure sank in that summer, draining her energy and, she wrote Wald, inducing "permanent nausea and sleeplessness." Addams told Mary Smith, "Sister Kelley has been miserable all summer." At summer's end, Margaret, John, and Julia Lathrop took her to the train, "the two ladies very solemn, and John cheered by the thought that he should see Buffalo Bill on the following day."[73]

For Ko, the shift was equally traumatic. "I am very sad today," he wrote his mother about separating from Alice Hamilton, with whom he had forged a deep bond of affection. "I don't believe I was ever sorry to go to [Sakonnet] before this year. I am now because I know that I shan't be coming back." From her perspective, Hamilton wrote Kelley, "I can't tell you how I felt when I said good-bye to [Ko]. One can say good-bye to grown people for a few years and feel that one will see them again, but Ko won't be Ko when I see him again. He stayed for my last lunch and risked being late to school, which pleased me immensely." Hamilton wished Kelley would "ring the bell just now and bring your milk bottle in and join in the talk. Then I would assure you that Ko went to bed early this evening and will be all rested by tomorrow." She knew that "the house

Hull-House Coffee-House receipts for rent and food, Florence Kelley and her children, 1899. Courtesy of Nicholas Kelley Papers, Rare Books and Manuscripts Division, The New York Public Library, Astor, Lenox and Tilden Foundations.

is going to be very empty soon and Miss Addams will have a lonely time of it." For her part, Addams relished her last days with Margaret. "Margaret and I spent two days at Winnetka last week and had a really charming visit," she wrote Kelley. Margaret was "gentle and responsive to every suggestion and talks about the fun of being at home again with absolute ardor." Having accompanied Margaret to the train, her heart "quite sank" as the youngster departed. "She has been charming and you would be touched by all the nice things people are saying about her. My heart swells with vicarious pride." [74]

"I have had blows before in connection with Hull House but nothing like this," Addams wrote Sister Kelley on another occasion, and Mary Smith added, "I have had many pangs for the dear presiding lady." Later that year Addams said, "I miss her amazingly although New York is the place for her, her eyes have the old fire when she thinks of it." To Kelley she wrote, "Hull House sometimes seems a howling wilderness without you." As for Kelley, when her name was removed from the list of residents in the *Hull-*

Florence Kelley after she became General Secretary of the National Consumers' League. Courtesy of National Consumers' League Records, Prints and Photographs, Library of Congress.

House Bulletin, she protested. Addams replied, "You overestimate the importance of the humble Bulletin," but she promised to restore Kelley's name, explaining that it was only removed to "stop people asking for her." Fourteen years later, in 1913, Addams wrote Kelley: "It is curious that I have never gotten used to you being away from [Hull House] even after all these years." [75]

That December Florence returned to Hull House to see her chicks. She and Ko had been living together in New York, but Margaret and John still attended school in Hillsdale. They enjoyed a blissful reunion in the familiar surroundings. She and Ko "were thirty hours on the train, but arrived by moonlight of the most gorgeous description," Kelley wrote Caroline. "We found the outer door open and the inner one ready for the latch key which Ko has carried all the years since he first came into residence." They were in bed by half past one. Later all four sat "around the library table with the sun shining in and the grate-fire glowing," conducting a "cross-fire of personal observations." [76] Kelley and her children never really left Hull House. Their years there shaped their relationships with one another for the rest of their lives. They faced a new future, but the shared experience of Hull House in the 1890s would always be with them.

At the end of the journeyman stage of her career, Florence Kelley could look back on seventeen years of wildly improbable changes in her political and personal identity: from dutiful daughter to rebellious mother, from innovative clubwoman to zealous socialist to social settlement reformer, from critic of labor statistics bureaus to special bureau agent, from advocate of labor's leadership on labor questions to advocate of women's leadership on labor questions, from agitator to factory inspector, from state official to voluntary society head.

Yet unifying themes ran through all these transformations. Each embodied her quest for new forms of social reproduction, both political and personal. For her the intersection of the personal and the political encapsulated the moment where individual agency interacted with social structure. As good Darwinists, Kelley and her generation knew that any lasting change had to be capable of reproducing itself, and that social reproduction began with the individual. Yet they also looked to the state as the most enduring progenitor of social justice, the most promising avenue to self-transcendence and permanence.

The personal changes in Florence Kelley's life between 1880 and 1900 reflected her impulse to encode social change in the intimate habits of everyday existence. In marrying Lazare Wischnewetzky and in joining Hull House, she poured the energy of her personal life into a new mold that matched the contours of her social vision. Her personal reconstruction was integral to her efforts at social reconstruction. From Engels she learned a truth later expressed in her measurement of the bodies of child laborers and her invasion of sweatshop homes: since the new order of industrial capitalism reconfigured personal as well as public life, any effort to challenge the hegemony of industrial capitalism had to do the same.

From childhood Florence Kelley had understood her identity in relationship to others. That relational reach in her life and work empowered her capacity to lead; the politics of her own location helped her to see that all identity was relational. Personal changes were never enough. Their significance lay in the ways they led to changes in group life, particularly changes in that highest expression of group life—the state. By 1899 Florence Kelley had established herself as a forceful agent of social change, and, no longer empowered by the state, she turned to the next best alternative: middle-class women activists in civil society. As the nineteenth gave way to the twentieth century, her destiny merged with theirs.

Abbreviations

Publications

AQ — *American Quarterly*
AHR — *American Historical Review*
FS — *Feminist Studies*
HEQ — *History of Education Quarterly*
HHM&P — [Residents of Hull House], *Hull House Maps and Papers*
ILWCH — *International Labor and Working Class History*
JAH — *Journal of American History*
JAP — *Jane Addams Papers*, Mary Lynn McCree Bryan, et al.
JPH — *Journal of Policy History*
JSP — *Journal of Social History*
LH — *Labor History*
NAW — James, James, and Boyer, *Notable American Women*
PMHB — *Pennsylvania Magazine of History and Biography*
RHR — *Radical History Review*

Archival Collections

CLMP — Consumers' League of Massachusetts Papers, Schlesinger Library, Cambridge
CPGC — Charlotte Perkins Gilman Collection, Schlesinger Library, Cambridge
CWCP — Chicago Woman's Club Papers, Chicago Historical Society
EGSP — Ellen Gates Starr Papers, Smith College, Northampton, Massachusetts

FASC — Friedrich A. Sorge Collection, New York Public Library
HDLP — Henry D. Lloyd Papers, State Historical Society of Wisconsin, Madison
HFP — Hamilton Family Papers, Schlesinger Library, Cambridge
HJGD — Helen J. Gow Diaries, Duke University, Durham, North Carolina
IMAP — Illinois Manufacturers' Association Papers, Chicago Historical Society
IISH — International Institute for Social History, Amsterdam
JAMC — Jane Addams Memorial Collection, University of Illinois, Chicago
JPAC — John Peter Altgeld Correspondence, Illinois State Archives, Springfield
KFP — Kelley Family Papers, Columbia University, New York
LDWP — Lillian D. Wald Papers, New York Public Library
MCTP — M. Carey Thomas Papers, Bryn Mawr College
NKP — Nicholas Kelley Papers, New York Public Library
NCGP — New Century Guild Papers, Historical Society of Pennsylvania
NCLR — National Consumers' League Records
PJA — Papers of Jane Addams, Swarthmore College Peace Collection
PSP — Papers of Sarah Pugh, Boston Public Library
RTEP — Richard T. Ely Papers, State Historical Society of Wisconsin, Madison

TEMC — Thomas and Elizabeth Morgan Collection, University of Illinois, Urbana

TRP — Theodore Roosevelt Papers, Library of Congress

WDKP — William D. Kelley Papers, Historical Society of Pennsylvania

People and Organizations

AASS — American Anti-Slavery Society

AEA — American Economic Association

AFL — American Federation of Labor

AH — Alice Hamilton

ASSA — American Social Science Association

BLSI — Bureau of Labor Statistics of Illinois

CAC — Citizen's Association of Chicago

CBK — Caroline Bartram Kelley

COS — Charity Organization Society

CWC — Chicago Woman's Club

EGS — Ellen Gates Starr

FK — Florence Kelley

FKW — Florence Kelley Wischnewetzky

GFWC — General Federation of Women's Clubs

GPO — U.S. Government Printing Office

HDL — Henry Demarest Lloyd

HJG — Helen J. Gow

IMA — Illinois Manufacturers' Association, Chicago Historical Society

IWA — Illinois Woman's Alliance

JA — Jane Addams

JPA — John Peter Altgeld

JSL — Josephine Shaw Lowell

LDW — Lillian D. Wald

MRS — Mary Rozet Smith

MTL — Mary [May] Thorne Lewis

NCL — National Consumers' League

NK — Nicholas Kelley

PFASS — Philadelphia Female Anti-Slavery Society

RTE — Richard T. Ely

SP — Sarah Pugh

SLP — Socialist Labor Party

TR — Theodore Roosevelt

USIC — United States Industrial Commission

WCTU — Woman's Christian Temperance Union

WDK — William Darrah Kelley

WDK Jr. — William Darrah Kelley Jr.

WPPC — Women's Protective and Provident Committee

Notes

Full citations are provided in the notes only for items not included in the bibliography. Dates are provided for all FK *writings at the first mention of each in the notes for every chapter.*

Preface

1. Bob Jessup provides a useful definition of *the state* as "a distinct ensemble of institutions and organizations whose socially accepted function is to define and enforce collectively binding decisions on the members of a society in the name of their common interest or general will." Bob Jessup, *State Theory: Putting the Capitalist State in Its Place* (University Park: Pennsylvania State University Press, 1990), 340. I find this definition useful because it incorporates political discourse, establishes a clear link with the wider society, and helps us distinguish between the state and government. It also highlights claims about the general will or common interest as a key feature of state systems, and differentiates the state from political domination or violent repression per se. This definition is compatible with a view of the state as relatively autonomous—that is, capable of serving interests other than those of one hegemonic group—while at the same time not a free-floating entity. By emphasizing the state's relationship to society, it highlights the state's importance as a process rather than a thing. See also Göran Therborn, *What Does the Ruling Class Do When It Rules? State Apparatuses and State Power under Feudalism, Capitalism*

and *Socialism* (London: NLB, 1978); and Giddens, *Constitution of Society.*

Analysts of political change tend to fall into two schools of interpretation. One sees the state, its organization and values, as the initiator of change; the other views social forces, their mobilization and beliefs, as the spark for political innovation. State-centered analyses include Amy Bridges, *The City in the Republic: Antebellum New York and the Origins of Machine Politics* (New York: Cambridge University Press, 1984); Ira Katznelson, *City Trenches: Urban Politics and the Patterning of Class in the United States* (New York: Pantheon Books, 1981); and Skowronek, *Building a New American State.* A good example of society-centered analysis, upon which many others are based, is E. P. Thompson, *The Making of the English Working Class* (1963; reprint, New York: Vintage, 1966). Women's history is overwhelmingly society-centered, since women's relationships with the state have usually been less direct than those of men.

2. Thomas Bender, "Wholes and Parts: The Need for Synthesis in American History," *JAH* 73 (June 1986): 126.

Antonio Gramsci defined civil society as "the ensemble of organisms called 'private'" (*Selections from the Prison Notebooks*, 12–13). Perry Anderson, *Considerations on Western Marxism* (London: NLB, 1976), 80, described this terrain as "a ramified network of cultural institutions—schools, churches, newspapers, parties, associations," which draw on "an ensemble of ideologies woven from the historical past and transmitted by intellectual groups auxiliary to the dominant class." This "stratified consensual structure" maintains the "hegemony" of the dominant class. For a summary of analyses and interpretations of Gramsci's view of civil society, see John Urry, *The Anatomy of Capitalist Societies: The Economy, Civil Society and the State* (London: Macmillan, 1981), 10–25; and Norberto Bobbio, "Gramsci and the Conception of Civil Society," in Mouffe, *Gramsci and Marxist Theory*, 21–47. For a theoretical discussion of culture studies, see Stuart Hall, "Cultural Studies: Two Paradigms," in Tony Bennett, Graham Martin, Colin Mercer, and Janet Woollacott, eds., *Culture, Ideology and Social Process: A Reader* (London: Open University Press, 1981), 19–38.

For Marx and Engels, "civil society" was the site of individualistic and capitalistic competition, not, as for Gramsci, the place where groups contended for political hegemony. See Bottomore et al., *Dictionary of Marxist Thought*, "civil society"; and David MacGregor, *Hegel, Marx, and the English State* (Boulder, Colo.: Westview, 1992), 54–88.

My view of public culture reaches beyond most definitions of political culture, in which "cultural" usually means "subjective." See, for example, Baker, *Affairs of Party*, 11–12.

3. The social theory of Jürgen Habermas, especially *The Theory of Communicative Action*, 2 vols. (Boston: Beacon, 1984, 1987) and *The Structural Transformation of the Public Sphere* have specifically addressed the consequences of the distinction between public and private for women. For critiques of Habermas, see Fraser, *Unruly Practices*, 113–43, and "Women, Welfare, and the Politics of Need Interpretation"; Craig Calhoun, introduction, in Calhoun, ed., *Habermas and the Public Sphere* (Cambridge, Mass.: MIT Press, 1992), 1–40; and Christopher H. Johnson, "Lifeworld, System and Communicative Action: The Habermasian Alternative in Social History," in Lenard R. Berlanstein, *Rethinking Labor History* (Urbana: University of Illinois Press, 1992), 55–89.

4. One of the best descriptions of female public culture is Temma Kaplan, "Female Consciousness and Collective Action: The Case of Barcelona, 1910–1918," *Signs: Journal of Women in Culture and Society* 7 (1982): 545–66. A helpful summary of cultural concepts in women's history is Scott, "Gender: A Useful Category of Historical Analysis." There Scott identified four features of gender analysis, each of which is pertinent to the study of women's public culture: normative concepts associated with gender; social institutions and their power to shape experience; symbols; and subjective consciousness. See also Denise Riley, *"Am I That Name?" Feminism and the Category of "Women" in History* (Minneapolis: University of Minnesota Press, 1988).

5. For a theoretical discussion of citizenship along these lines, see Chantal Mouffe, "Democratic Citizenship and Community," in Miami Theory Collective, eds., *Community at Loose Ends* (Minneapolis: University of Minnesota Press, 1991), 70–82.

6. For women and interest-group politics, see Baker, "Domestication of Politics." For an alternative explanation, see Sklar, "Historical Foundations of Women's Power."

7. See, for example, John Rawls, *A Theory of Justice* (Oxford: Oxford University Press, 1971).

8. The term *Progressive* comes from the group that splintered from the Republican Party in 1912 to form the Progressive Party. It came into use as an ideological label for reform-minded Wisconsin Republicans around 1906. See Thelan, *The New Citizenship*, 4. For the emergence of that movement from Populism, see Robert M. La Follette, *La Follette's Autobiography: A Personal Narrative of Political Experiences* (Madison: Robert M. La Follette, 1911), 18–49. Progressive Quakers in the 1830s first used the term to define a social group. See Albert John Wahl, "Congregational or Progressive Friends in the Pre-Civil-War Reform Movement" (Ph.D. diss., Temple University, 1951). As an interesting precursor of the term's use after 1900, the class of 1886 at Chautauqua called themselves "The Progressives." See Isabel B. Pedersen, "The Mosaics of the Hall of Philosophy," in n.a., *The Banners and Mosaics of Chautauqua, 1882–1992* (Chautauqua, N.Y.: Chautauqua Literary and Scientific Circle, [1993]), 32.

1. *"The Good Ship Democracy," 1830–1860*

1. Florence Kelley (hereafter FK), "My Philadelphia" (1926), 7. Kelley's autobiographical series of four articles has been reprinted in Sklar, *Autobiography of Florence Kelley;* and Leon Stein, *Fragments of Autobiography* (New York: Arno, 1974). Like most autobiographies, Kelley's was shaped to convey a particular message; far from a complete story, it stopped at 1894 and omitted what Kelley did not want others to know. Her text had two goals:

to invoke her native-born elite background as a defense against mid-1920s attacks on her as a foreign-bred socialist, and to advocate the renewal of the Sheppard-Towner bill and other Progressive legislation. Nevertheless, where its details are compatible with other sources, I have accepted the autobiography as accurate.

For more on contemporary rituals, see Anne C. Rose, *Victorian America and the Civil War* (Cambridge: Cambridge University Press, 1992); and Barry Schwartz, "Mourning and the Making of a Sacred Symbol: Durkheim and the Lincoln Assassination," *Social Forces* 70 (Dec. 1991): 343–64.

2. For the immanence of gender, see Scott, "Gender: A Useful Category of Historical Analysis."

3. See Williamson, *American Suffrage;* and Nathan O. Hatch, *The Democratization of American Christianity* (New Haven: Yale University Press, 1989). For the causal agency of families in the middling socioeconomic ranks, see Kathryn Kish Sklar, "The Schooling of Girls and Community Values in Massachusetts Towns, 1750–1820," *History of Education Quarterly* 33 (winter 1993): 511–42, and "Errata," *History of Education Quarterly* 34 (spring 1994): 69–71.

4. For more on William Kelley's family history, see L. P. Brockett, "Hon. William D. Kelley," *Men of Our Day* (Philadelphia: Ziegler, McCurdy and Co., 1868), 467. The best single source for Kelley genealogy is Greco, "William Darrah Kelley," 21–30. See also Kelley Family Records, Kelley Family Papers (hereafter KFP), reel 1, box 1.

The second *e* in Kelley's surname indicated his Protestant origins. Occasions when contemporaries omitted this *e* have not been marked with "sic."

5. FK, "My Philadelphia," 10. See Brockett, "William D. Kelley," 467.

6. See William Darrah Kelley (hereafter WDK), *An Address Delivered at the Democratic Town Meeting, in the State House Yard, July Fourth, 1841* (Philadelphia: Published by Request of the Meeting, 1841), 9; Ira V. Brown, *Pennsylvania Reformers: From Penn to Pinchot* (University Park: Pennsylvania State University, 1966), 18–19.

7. For political economy and the rise of civil society, see Bottomore et al., *Dictionary of Marxist Thought,* 375–78. For civil rights, see Marshall, *Citizenship and Social Class.*

8. Even after 1842, many states retained a poll tax that effectively excluded the very poor. See Williamson, *American Suffrage,* 242; and Robert J.

Steinfeld, "Property and Suffrage in the Early American Republic," *Stanford Law Review* 41 (Jan. 1989): 335–76. For the much slower expansion of British suffrage after 1867, see Eric J. Evans, *The Forging of the Modern State: Early Industrial Britain, 1783–1870* (London: Longman, 1983), 343–57.

9. Two historiographic schools of interpretation dominate writings about the early American republic—one emphasizing the emergence of procommercial Lockean individualism, the other focusing on traditional notions of community. For a discussion that synthesizes these seeming opposites, see Isaac Kramnick, *Republicanism and Bourgeois Radicalism: Political Ideology in Late Eighteenth-Century England and America* (Ithaca: Cornell University Press, 1990).

10. "William D. Kelley," *A Biographical Album of Prominent Pennsylvanians* (Philadelphia: American Biographical Publishing Company, 1888), 7–8. See also Bruce Sinclair, *Philadelphia's Philosopher Mechanics: A History of the Franklin Institute, 1824–1865* (Baltimore: Johns Hopkins University Press, 1974).

11. See anon., "Political Portraits with Pen and Pencil: William Darrah Kelley," *The United States Magazine and Democratic Review* 28 (June 1851): 553; "William D. Kelley," *Prominent Pennsylvanians,* 8; WDK to Henry S. Patterson, Boston, Aug. 23, 1835, KFP, box 5. Such institutes for young men derived from British predecessors. See A. E. Dobbs, *Education and Social Movements, 1700–1850* (London: Longmans, Green, 1919), 170–84.

12. WDK, "The Eight-Hour System: Letter to the Operatives in the Workshops and Factories of the Fourth Congressional District of Pennsylvania," in WDK, *Speeches, Addresses and Letters,* 278–79.

13. Conscious of this, shoemakers in a Philadelphia strike procession shouted, "We are all day laborers!" Laurie, *Working People of Philadelphia,* 86–87, 91. See also Roediger and Foner, *Our Own Time,* 13–16. Unskilled women textile workers also joined the strike. It was led by the nation's first association of trade unions, the General Trades' Union of the City and County of Philadelphia, formed in the spring of 1834.

14. The distinction among three types of rights comes from Marshall, *Citizenship and Social Class,* but for his third category, "social," I have substituted "economic." Artisan republicanism offers the best example of traditional notions of moral economy within male political culture. The key concept here was the fusion of individual energies with the

welfare of the whole society. See Sean Wilentz, *Chants Democratic: New York City and the Rise of the American Working Class, 1788–1850* (New York: Oxford University Press, 1985), 61–103; and Paul Goodman, "Moral Purpose and Republican Politics in Antebellum America, 1830–1860," *The Maryland Historian* 20 (fall / winter 1989): 5–39.

For the effects of changes in the work process before the advent of full factory production, see Laurie, *Working People of Philadelphia*, 3–32; Thomas Dublin, "Rural-Urban Migrants in Industrial New England: The Case of Lynn Massachusetts in the Mid-Nineteenth Century," *JAH* 73 (Dec. 1986): 623–44; and Wilentz, *Chants Democratic*, 191. For the moral dimensions of the ten-hour movement, see Murphy, *Ten Hours' Labor*. For the importance of the link between the ten-hour movement and new notions of citizenship, see Helen Sumner, "Citizenship," in Commons et al., *History of Labour*, 1:169–332; John Barkley Jentz, "Artisans, Evangelicals, and the City: A Social History of Abolition and Labor Reform in Jacksonian New York" (Ph.D. diss., City University of New York, 1977), 136–37 and passim; and Pole, *Pursuit of Equality*, 112–47. For an interpretation of the ten-hour day as an effort to rationalize work relations and reduce the arbitrary power of employers, see Christopher L. Tomlins, *Law, Labor, and Ideology in the Early American Republic* (Cambridge: Cambridge University Press, 1993), 329.

15. By *polity*, I mean civil society and government.

16. More a social and intellectual than a political movement, the Workingmen's Party was upon its collapse absorbed into the reform wing of the Democratic Party, leaving a continuing vacuum on the political left. That vacuum persisted alongside the consolidation of the dual political party system in the late 1820s and early 1830s. One of the best summaries of the often-confusing history of the workingmen's parties is Amy Bridges, "Becoming American: The Working Classes in the United States before the Civil War," in Katznelson and Zolberg, eds., *Working Class Formation*, 157–96. See also Amy Bridges, *The City in the Republic: Antebellum New York and the Origins of Machine Politics* (New York: Cambridge University Press, 1984); Wilentz, *Chants Democratic*, 212–16; and William A. Sullivan, "Did Labor Support Andrew Jackson?" *Political Science Quarterly* 62 (1947): 569–80. Sullivan, "Philadelphia Labor During the Jacksonian Era," *Pennsylvania History* 15 (Oct.

1948): 305–320, pointed out that *The Working Man's Advocate* and other Philadelphia labor newspapers entered the political arena to advocate the passage of legislation for free tax-supported public schools, the abolition of imprisonment for debt, and the ten-hour day—all of which were soon supported by the Democratic Party.

Selig Perlman, *A Theory of the Labor Movement* (New York: MacMillan, 1928), 167, was the first to note the negative effects of the ballot on American working-class political consciousness. See also Ira Katznelson, *City Trenches: Urban Politics and the Patterning of Class in the United States* (New York: Pantheon Books, 1981), 18; Stephen Thernstrom, *Poverty and Progress: Social Mobility in a Nineteenth Century City* (Cambridge: Harvard University Press, 1964), 57–79; Alan Dawley, *Class and Community: The Industrial Revolution in Lynn* (Cambridge: Harvard University Press, 1976), 194–219; Iver Bernstein, "Expanding the Boundaries of the Political: Workers and Political Change in the Nineteenth Century," *ILWCH* 32 (fall 1987): 59–75; and Richard Oestreicher, "Urban Working-Class Political Behavior and Theories of American Electoral Politics, 1870–1940," *JAH* 74 (March 1988): 1257–86. For the British contrary example, see Maureen Tomison, *The English Sickness: The Rise of Trade Union Political Power* (London: Tom Stacey, 1972); James Vernon, *Politics and the People: A Study in English Political Culture, c. 1815–1867* (Cambridge: Cambridge University Press, 1993); George J. Barnsby, *The Working Class Movement in the Black Country, 1750–1867* (Wolverhampton, England: Integrated Publishing Services, 1977); and Maurice Cowling, *1867: Disraeli, Gladstone, and Revolution* (Cambridge: Cambridge University Press, 1967).

17. See "William D. Kelley," *Prominent Pennsylvanians*, 8. For the importance of links between religious and political affiliation, see Kelley, *The Cultural Pattern in American Politics;* Richard Jensen, "Religious and Occupational Roots of Party Identification," *Civil War History* 16 (1970): 325–43; Baker, *Affairs of Party;* Anne Norton, *Alternative Americas: A Reading of Antebellum Political Culture* (Chicago: University of Chicago Press, 1986); and Daniel Walker Howe, "Religion and Politics in the Antebellum North," in Mark Noll, ed., *Religion and American Politics from the Colonial Period to the 1980s* (New York: Oxford University Press, 1990), 121–45. Later, Kelley became a patron of

the Fencibles. As late as 1877, he introduced them to the president of the United States in the inaugural parade. Thomas S. Lanard, *One Hundred Years with the State Fencibles* (Philadelphia: Nields, 1913), 175, 199, 260. See also Bruce Laurie, "Fire Companies and Gangs in Southwark: The 1840s," in Allen F. Davis and Mark H. Haller, eds., *The Peoples of Philadelphia: A History of Ethnic Groups and Lower-Class Life, 1790–1940* (Philadelphia: Temple University Press, 1973), 71–88; and Laurie, *Working People of Philadelphia*, 36–37.

18. See Brockett, "William D. Kelley," 496; Greco, "William Darrah Kelley," 42. For the importance of political parades, see Susan G. Davis, *Parades and Power: Street Theatre in Nineteenth-Century Philadelphia* (Berkeley: University of California Press, 1986). For the looming physical presence of the U.S. Bank in Philadelphia, see Deborah C. Andrews, "Bank Buildings in Nineteenth-Century Philadelphia," in William W. Cutler and Howard Gillette, *The Divided Metropolis: Social and Spatial Dimensions of Philadelphia, 1880–1975* (Westport: Greenwood, 1980), 64–65. See also Louis Hartz, *Economic Policy and Democratic Thought: Pennsylvania, 1776–1860* (Cambridge: Harvard University Press, 1948); and Edward Pessen, "*Should* Labor Have Supported Jackson?; Or Questions the Quantitative Studies Do Not Answer," *LH* 5 (summer 1972): 427–37, reprinted in Daniel J. Leab, ed., *The Labor History Reader* (Urbana: University of Illinois Press, 1985), 96–106.

19. *Congressional Globe*, 38th Cong., 1st sess., Feb. 23, 1864, 773; WDK to Henry S. Patterson, Aug. 23, 1835. Kelley's work on a set of gold cups for the imam of Muscat earned his firm a gold medal. See "Political Portraits with Pen and Pencil," 555. For more on the 1835 gubernatorial race, see Charles McCool Snyder, *The Jacksonian Heritage: Pennsylvania Politics, 1833–1848* (Harrisburg: Pennsylvania Historical and Museum Commission, 1958), 54–67. Kelley's political passions were partly kindled by local conditions in Massachusetts and Pennsylvania. Party structures were just beginning to assume a modern form, integrating political life at the municipal, state, and federal levels and heightening the competition between Whigs and Democrats. In Boston the Whigs won this competition, but in Philadelphia, perhaps because politics was indirectly fueled by an insurgent labor movement, Democrats dominated. See Ronald P. Formisano, "Boston, 1800–1840: From Deferential-Participant to Party Politics," in Formisano and

Constance K. Burns, eds., *Boston 1700–1980: The Evolution of Urban Politics* (Westport: Greenwood, 1984), 50–51. As late as 1845 Kelley was still in touch with George Bancroft, writing him that year about a U.S. Supreme Court recommendation he wished Bancroft to forward to the president (WDK to George Bancroft, Dec. 6, 1845, Massachusetts Historical Society).

20. Mr. Cameron of Pennsylvania, *Memorial Addresses on the Life and Character of William D. Kelley. Delivered in the House of Representatives and in the Senate*, 51st Cong., 1st sess., misc. doc. no. 229, 1890, 71. Kelley's leap onto the platform was typical of the rough-and-tumble methods of Jacksonian politics. For more on this electoral culture, see Ronald P. Formisano, *The Transformation of Political Culture: Massachusetts Parties, 1790–1840s* (New York: Oxford University Press, 1983), esp. 257–61; Arthur M. Schlesinger Jr., *Age of Jackson* (Boston: Little, Brown, 1945), 144–76; and Snyder, *Jacksonian Heritage*, 20. For the ongoing egalitarianism of the Democratic Party in the 1840s, see John Ashworth, "*Agrarians*" and "*Aristocrats*": *Party Political Ideology in the United States, 1837–1846* (Cambridge: Cambridge University Press, 1987), 7–51. For the emergence of this new political class, see Sean Wilentz, "Society, Politics, and the Market Revolution, 1815–1848," in Eric Foner, ed., *The New American History* (Philadelphia: Temple University Press, 1990), 51–71.

21. For Kelley's decision to study law, see Greco, "William Darrah Kelley," 168–89. Law was a major route of upward mobility in antebellum America, since common sense went a long way toward meeting the technical demands for admission to the bar, and attorneys' work brought them into contact with business opportunities. See Maxwell Bloomfield, *American Lawyers in a Changing Society, 1776–1876* (Cambridge: Harvard University Press, 1976), 145–52.

For Kelley's move to the bench, see WDK to Martha Kelley, Philadelphia, April 18, 1841, William D. Kelley Papers (henceforward WDKP); Brockett, "William D. Kelley," 497. In addition to the usual powers of a county court, Kelley's court also held equity powers "of the highest character, and an exclusive criminal jurisdiction" ("Political Portraits with Pen and Pencil," 557). Laurie, *Working People of Philadelphia*, 195–97, contains the most complete account of the election of 1851. See also Gary B. Nash, "The Philadelphia Bench and Bar, 1800–1861," *Comparative Studies in Society and History* 7 (1964–65): 203–220. Nash notes (215) that the most frequent religious affiliation among Philadelphia judges was Presbyterian.

22. See Greco, "William Darrah Kelley," 114.

23. "Political Portraits with Pen and Pencil," 557; WDK, *An Address . . . 1841*, 15. For the importance of oratory in American politics, see Howe, *The Political Culture of the American Whigs*, esp. 281, where Lincoln is described as "a man whose power over others derived from his power over words." See also Kenneth Cmiel, *Democratic Eloquence: The Fight over Popular Speech in Nineteenth-Century America* (New York: Morrow, 1990). A later estimate of WDK described his rhetorical powers in relationship to other skills: "He is singularly equipped for responsible leadership. It is not often that you find a combination of high oratorical powers and innate capacity for investigation and study. The declaimer is too frequently a mere rhetorician; but in the case of Judge Kelley you realize unusual speaking capacity, admirable manners, a rich melodious voice, an imposing presence, and an aptitude for statistics and for details, with an insatiate desire to trace every proposition to its sources" (John W. Forney, *Anecdotes of Public Men* [New York: Harper and Bros., 1881], 2:376). See also "Political Portraits with Pen and Pencil," 556. Kelley's interest in a political rather than a judicial career is reflected in his absence from the list of judicial reformers studied by Allen Steinberg in *The Transformation of Criminal Justice: Philadelphia, 1800–1880* (Chapel Hill: University of North Carolina Press, 1989).

24. See Elizabeth M. Geffen, "Violence in Philadelphia in the 1840s and 1850s," *Pennsylvania History* 36 (Oct. 1969), 381–410; Sam Bass Warner Jr., *The Private City: Philadelphia in Three Periods of Its Growth* (Philadelphia: University of Pennsylvania Press, 1968), 125–57; Diane Lindstrom, *Economic Development in the Philadelphia Region, 1810–1850* (New York: Columbia University Press, 1978), 184. Greater upward and downward social mobility doubtless contributed to the social dislocation of the decades after 1830. See Stuart Blumin, "Mobility and Change in Ante-bellum Philadelphia," in Stephan Thernstrom and Richard Sennett, eds., *Nineteenth-Century Cities: Essays in the New Urban History* (New Haven: Yale University Press, 1969), 165–208.

25. For the uses of national power before and during the Civil War, see Louis S. Gerteis, *Morality and Utility in American Antislavery Reform* (Chapel

Hill: University of North Carolina Press, 1987), 86–129.

26. *Proceedings of the Regular Autumnal Convention of Unitarian Christians: Held in Philadelphia, 28th September, 1846*, 6, quoted in Elizabeth M. Geffen, *Philadelphia Unitarianism, 1796–1861* (Philadelphia: University of Pennsylvania Press, 1961), 219. Kelley's timing was perfect, since his Unitarian membership came shortly after the Wilmot Proviso was introduced into Congress in 1846 by a Pennsylvania Democrat who proposed the prohibition of slavery in all territories that might be acquired from Mexico. Although never enacted, the proviso raised the curtain on the sectional drama of the next twenty years, for it was the first time that congressional votes split along sectional divisions of North and South rather than along familiar party lines. See, for example, David M. Potter, *The Impending Crisis, 1848–1861* (New York: Harper and Row, 1976), 18–23. For Unitarian politics, see Daniel Walker Howe, *The Unitarian Conscience* (Cambridge: Harvard University Press, 1970), esp. 211–26. For more on the ethnoreligious connections with politics in this era, see Howe, *The Political Culture of the American Whigs*, esp. 150–80.

27. See Laurie, *Working People of Philadelphia*, 195–97.

28. WDK, *Replies of the Hon. William D. Kelley to George Northrop, Esq., in the Joint Debate in the Fourth Congressional District* (Philadelphia: Collins, 1864), 7; Greco, "William Darrah Kelley," 229, quoting from the constitution of the association. Kelley's first judicial actions favoring the antislavery cause came in 1851, when he successfully defended Quakers and free blacks accused of murdering a slave owner in the Christiana Riot. See Jonathan Katz, *Resistance at Christiana: The Fugitive Slave Rebellion, Christiana, Pennsylvania, September 11, 1851, A Documentary Account* (New York: Crowell, 1834), 203. For the political context of Kelley's actions, see Eric Foner, *Free Soil, Free Labor, Free Men: The Ideology of the Republican Party before the Civil War* (New York: Oxford University Press, 1970), 103–48; Richard H. Sewell, *Ballots for Freedom: Antislavery Politics in the United States, 1837–1860* (New York: Oxford University Press, 1976); William E. Gienapp, *The Origins of the Republican Party, 1852–1856* (New York: Oxford University Press, 1987); and William E. Gienapp, "'Politics Seem to Enter into Everything': Political Culture in the North, 1840–1860," in Gienapp, Thomas B. Alexander, Michael F. Holt, Stephen E.

Maizlich, and Joel H. Silbey, *Essays on American Antebellum Politics, 1840–1860* (Arlington: Texas A and M University Press, 1982), 14–69.

29. See Bernard Mandel, *Labor: Free and Slave: Workingmen and the Anti-Slavery Movement in the United States* (New York: Associated Authors, 1955); and John Ashworth, "The Relationship between Capitalism and Humanitarianism," *AHR* 92 (Oct. 1987): 813–28. David B. Davis and Alan Dawley have argued that abolitionism drew attention away from injustices associated with northern wage labor and confirmed the hegemony of the emerging capitalist order (Davis, *The Problem of Slavery in the Age of Revolution* [Ithaca: Cornell University Press, 1975], 347–61; and Dawley, *Class and Community: The Industrial Revolution in Lynn* [Cambridge: Harvard University Press, 1976], 196 and 238–39). Eric Foner criticized these interpretations in "Abolitionism and the Labor Movement in Antebellum America," in Christine Bolt and Seymour Drescher, eds., *Anti-Slavery, Religion, and Reform: Essays in Memory of Roger Anstey* (Folkestone, Kent, England: Wm. Dawson and Sons, 1980), pointing out that mill owners did not oppose slavery and that the abolitionist movement provided political language and organizational training for social critics throughout the second half of the nineteenth century. Significantly, in the election of 1856 Kelley refused the support of the nativist Know-Nothing Party (Greco, "William Darrah Kelley," 235). See also Tyler Anbinder, *Nativism and Slavery: The Northern Know Nothings and the Politics of the 1850s* (New York: Oxford University Press, 1992).

30. "An Address Delivered by Hon. William D. Kelley at Girard Avenue above Eleventh St., Philadelphia, October 3rd, 1856," *Philadelphia Morning Times*, 1856, 3; "An Address Delivered by the Hon. William D. Kelley at Spring Garden Hall, Philadelphia, on September 9, 1856," *Philadelphia Morning Times*, 1856, 9.

31. *Address . . . at Spring Garden*, 11. William Dusinberre noted William Kelley's strategy of "imaginatively describing slavery in terms of the lives of white men" in *Civil War Issues in Philadelphia, 1856–1865* (Philadelphia: University of Philadelphia Press, 1965), 35. David Brion Davis has pointed out that "what distinguished slavery in much of the pre-modern world was not its antithesis to free labor but its antithesis to the normal network of kinship ties of dependency, protection, obligation, and privilege, ties which easily served as

a model for non-kinship forms of patronage, clientage, and voluntary servitude. The archetypal slave was an outsider, torn from his protective family matrix" ("Slavery and 'Progress,'" in Christine Bolt and Seymour Drescher, eds., *Anti-Slavery, Religion, and Reform: Essays in Memory of Roger Anstey* [Folkestone, Kent, England: Wm. Dawson and Sons, 1980], 358). See also Jonathan A. Glickstein, *Concepts of Free Labor in Antebellum America* (New Haven: Yale University Press, 1991); Christopher Clark, *The Roots of Rural Capitalism: Western Massachusetts, 1780–1860* (Ithaca: Cornell University Press, 1990); and Robert J. Steinfeld, *The Invention of Free Labor: The Employment Relation in English and American Law and Culture, 1350–1870* (Chapel Hill: University of North Carolina Press, 1991).

32. See Kelley Family Records, KFP. Family records do not reveal for whom Florence might have been named. After Florence Nightingale became a popular heroine during the Crimean War in 1854–55, the name became more fashionable. FK never used her middle name, Molthrop, and family papers do not clarify its origins. No official notice of her birth survives; birth certificates were not issued by Pennsylvania until 1860. For Bartram, see Christopher Hobbs, "The Medical Botany of John Bartram," *American Institute of the History of Pharmacy* 33, no. 4 (1991): 181–89.

Caroline Bartram Bonsall, born in 1829, was the great-granddaughter of John Bartram's eldest daughter, Mary. Bartram's grandfather had settled in Chester County in 1682, responding to the opportunity William Penn provided that year by founding a colony for Quakers and other persecuted sects. Mary Bartram married Benjamin Bonsall in 1755. Her only son, James, was the father of Caroline's father, Henry L. Bonsall, who was born in 1807 and married Hannah Wentz in 1822. See Kelley Family Records, 1746–1890, KFP, reel 1, box 1; and FK, "My Philadelphia," 52–53. Henry Bonsall was a retail merchant well liked by his clientele. Unfortunately for him and his three children, however, his wife Hannah died in 1833. Even more unfortunately for the children, Henry died five years later. Close friends and neighbors Isaac and Elizabeth Pugh adopted nine-year-old Caroline; her two brothers found homes elsewhere. See FK, "My Philadelphia," 53. Henry Bonsall's identity as a merchant is revealed in a fragment of a letter Caroline wrote sometime around 1846, probably to her adoptive parents, n.d., n.p., no addressee, box 6, Kelley Family Records, KFP.

33. Religious voluntarism arose in part from the "disestablishment of religious institutions, beginning with Virginia in 1776, which rescinded laws requiring households to pay taxes for ministers' salaries. Nowhere else in the western world were clergy so dependent on the voluntary contributions of their parishioners, and nowhere else could churchgoers so easily withhold financial support from ministers they disliked. In response, some white clergymen cultivated the support of their female congregants and replaced traditional misogynist views of women with glowing assertions of women's capabilities, particularly as evidenced in their voluntary associations. See William G. McLoughlin, *New England Dissent, 1630–1833: The Baptists and the Separation of Church and State*, 2 vols. (Cambridge: Harvard University Press, 1971); and Rhys Isaac, *The Transformation of Virginia, 1740–1790* (Chapel Hill: University of North Carolina Press, 1982).

The influence of evangelical religion on African-American women was not so visible, since the church offered a unique opportunity for African-American male leadership that ministers defended against the authority of laywomen. Nevertheless, religious institutions and groups provided black women with crucial avenues to social power. See Jualynne Dodson, "Nineteenth-Century A. M. E. Preaching Women: Cutting Edge of Women's Inclusion in Church Polity," in Hilah F. Thomas and Rosemary Skinner Keller, eds., *Women in New Worlds: Historical Perspectives on the Wesleyan Tradition* (Nashville: Abingdon, 1981), 276–92, reprinted in Darlene Clark Hine, Elsa Barkley Brown, Tiffany R. L. Patterson, and Lillian S. Williams, eds., *Black Women in United States History* (New York: Carlson, 1990), 1:333–49; and Jean McMahon Humez, ed., *Gifts of Power: The Writings of Rebecca Jackson, Black Visionary, Shaker Eldress* ([Amherst]: University of Massachusetts Press, 1981).

34. In its crusade against prostitution and the sexual double standard, the American Female Moral Reform Society boasted almost five hundred local branches and published the nation's most widely read evangelical newspaper. These evangelical women were not dichotomous with women abolitionists, but they did occupy different points on the spectrum of women's activism. See Smith-Rosenberg, "Beauty, the Beast and the Militant Woman: A Case Study in Sex Roles and Social Stress in Jacksonian America," *AQ* 23 (Oct. 1971): 562–84; Barbara Berg, *The Remembered Gate: Origins of American Feminism: The Woman and the City, 1800–1860* (New York: Oxford University Press, 1978); Kathryn Kish Sklar, *Catharine Beecher: A Study in American Domesticity* (New Haven: Yale University Press, 1973), 63–100; and Nancy A. Hewitt, *Women's Activism and Social Change: Rochester, New York, 1822–1872* (Ithaca: Cornell University Press, 1984). A good example of the effects of evangelicism on men's political activism is Robert H. Abzug, *Passionate Liberator: Theodore Dwight Weld and the Dilemma of Reform* (New York: Oxford University Press, 1980). Examples of how women's organizations used moral imperatives to speak for the welfare of the whole society even though they represented distinct social groups can be found throughout Hewitt, *Women's Activism and Social Change*. See also Eric Hobsbawm, "Inventing Traditions," in Hobsbawm and Terence Ranger, eds., *The Invention of Tradition* (Cambridge: Cambridge University Press, 1983), 1–14.

35. FK, "My Philadelphia," 54; Isaac Pugh to Caroline Bonsall Kelley (hereafter CBK), Germantown, Oct. 29, 1866, FK Papers, CBK, Correspondence with Foster-Grandparents, Isaac and Elizabeth Pugh, Nicholas Kelley Papers (hereafter NKP). Recovering from a lengthy illness in Germantown, Florrie wrote her father in January 1869, "I am a great deal better and com[e] downstairs to all my meals and Grandma says I like mutton and chops and everything else that is good" (FK to WDK, Germantown, Jan. 12, 1869, NKP).

36. See *Memorial of Sarah Pugh*, 9–10.

37. FK, "My Philadelphia," 52–53. For more on Joseph Priestley, see Anne Holt, *A Life of Joseph Priestley* (London: Oxford University Press, 1931), 145–78; and E. F. Smith, *Priestly in America, 1794–1804* (Philadelphia: Blakiston, 1920). The "Girls' Studies" department of Caroline's school was described in Helen G. Hole, *Westtown Through the Years: 1799–1942* (Westtown, Penn.: Westtown Alumni Association, 1942), 100–101.

38. FK, "My Philadelphia," 54. In the mid-1860s Sarah Pugh maintained her own home in Philadelphia and took in boarders. Caroline described her finances: "Aunt Sarah is here for a couple of days. She would stay longer but is anxious to see about her money matters. It is pleasant to think that she has some to invest once more. [The income] of

her house and that of the family promise to make her quite comfortable. It seems only right that she should have what she earned by honest labor in her early years, but I was very much afraid she would not recover anything" (CBK to WDK, Germantown, April 26, 1864, CBK to WDK, 1860–1888, KFP, reel 1, box 2). Single women only rarely managed to maintain their own homes, and the achievement was highly valued. See Susan B. Anthony, "Homes of Single Women" (Oct. 1877), reprinted in Ellen Carol DuBois, ed., *Elizabeth Cady Stanton and Susan B. Anthony: Correspondence, Writings, Speeches* (New York: Schocken Books, 1981), 146–51.

39. FK, "My Philadelphia," 54.

40. Lucretia Mott to Abby Kelley, May 1839, quoted in Margaret H. Bacon, "Quaker Women and the Charge of Separatism," *Quaker History* 69 (spring 1980): 25. In 1853 and until her efforts were successful in 1877, Mott challenged the right of men's meetings to override decisions made by women's meetings. See also Jean Soderlund, "Women's Authority in Pennsylvania and New Jersey Quaker Meetings, 1680–1760," *William and Mary Quarterly,* 3rd series, 44 (Oct. 1987): 722–47.

The leadership of Lucretia Mott in the antislavery movement and Susan B. Anthony in the women's rights movement was no accident; they expressed a tradition of women's autonomous activism generated within Quakerism. See Nancy Hewitt, "Feminist Friends: Agrarian Quakers and the Emergence of Women's Rights in America," *FS* 12 (spring 1986): 27–50; Carol Stoneburner, "Drawing a Profile of American Female Public Friends as Shapers of Human Space" and "Time Line of American Female Public Friends, 1650–1950," in Carol Stoneburner and John Stoneburner, eds., *The Influence of Quaker Women in American History: Biographical Studies* (Lewiston, N.Y.: Edwin Mellen, 1986), 1–56 and 413–78. For the Quaker influence on antislavery women, see Blanche Glassman Hersh, "To Make the World Better: Protestant Women in the Abolitionist Movement," in Richard L. Greaves, *Triumph over Silence: Women in Protestant History* (Westport: Greenwood, 1985), 173–202; Janis Calvo, "Quaker Women Ministers in Nineteenth Century America," *Quaker History* 63, no. 2 (1974): 75–93; and Margaret Hope Bacon, *Mothers of Feminism: The Story of Quaker Women in America* (New York: Harper and Row, 1986). For women ministers in other denominations, see Louis Billington, "'Female Laborers in the Church': Women Preachers in the Northeastern

United States, 1790–1840," *JAH* 19 (Dec. 1985): 369–94. For an example of the functions of women's meetings in the Society of Friends, see n.a., *Rules of Discipline of the Yearly Meeting of Friends, Held in Philadelphia* (Philadelphia: Kimber, Conrad, 1806). For an overview of women's separate organizations, see Anne Firor Scott, *Natural Allies: Women's Associations in American History* (Urbana: University of Illinois Press, 1991), 11–57.

41. SP to Elizabeth Pease, Philadelphia, Jan. 20, 1846, Papers of Sarah Pugh (hereafter PSP). The best history of PFASS is Caroline Luverne Williams, "Religion, Race, and Gender in Antebellum American Radicalism: The Philadelphia Female Anti-Slavery Society, 1833–1870" (Ph.D. diss., UCLA, 1991). See also Ira V. Brown, "Cradle of Feminism: The Philadelphia Female Anti-Slavery Society, 1833–1840," *PMHB* 102 (April 1978): 143–66. I am indebted to Carolyn Williams for this computation of Sarah Pugh's tenure as president of PFASS. The number of PFASS members is difficult to determine since it was not recorded in their annual reports. Their *Fourth Annual Report* (1838, 4), mentioned forty new members, an addition "greatly exceeding the average increase of any of the preceding years of the Society's existence." The older Pennsylvania Abolition Society, established in 1775, did not admit female members and did not endorse the two keystones of the Garrisonian movement — immediate and unconditional abolition. For more on antislavery activism among the Quakers, see Jean R. Soderlund, *Quakers and Slavery: A Divided Spirit* (Princeton: Princeton University Press, 1985).

42. Elizabeth Chandler, quoted in Milton Meltzer and Patricia Holland, eds., *Lydia Maria Child, Selected Letters, 1817–1880* (Amherst, Mass.: University of Massachusetts Press, 1982), 41. See also Lydia Maria Child to the Boston Female Anti-Slavery Society, Oct.–Nov. 1835. For the construction of gender consciousness as a precondition for women's public activism, see Nancy F. Cott, *The Bonds of Womanhood: "Women's Sphere" in New England, 1780–1835* (New Haven: Yale University Press, 1977).

43. See, for example, Debra Gold Hansen, *Strained Sisterhood: Gender and Class in the Boston Female Anti-Slavery Society* (Amherst: University of Massachusetts, 1993).

44. For the pervasive influence of religion, even within the women's rights movement, see Nancy Gale Isenberg, "'Coequality of the Sexes': The Feminist Discourse of the Antebellum Women's

Rights Movement in America" (Ph.D. diss., University of Wisconsin, 1990).

45. See Williams, "Religion, Race, and Gender," 11. The older, non-Garrisonian Pennsylvania Abolition Society was open to whites only. Two years after the PFASS was founded, an interracial male organization, the Young Men's Anti-Slavery Society of Philadelphia, was started in 1836. In 1837 the Pennsylvania Anti-Slavery Society, which included both races and sexes, was established. The first female antislavery societies were African-American, founded in 1832 in Salem, Massachusetts, and Rochester, New York. See Dorothy Sterling, ed., *Black Women in the Nineteenth Century* (New York: Norton, 1984), 113–19. Not all female antislavery societies were as radical as the PFASS. See Amy Swerdlow, "Abolition's Conservative Sisters: The Ladies' New York City Anti-Slavery Societies, 1834–1840," in Jean Fagan Yellin and John C. Van Horne, eds., *The Abolitionist Sisterhood: Women's Political Culture in Antebellum America* (Ithaca: Cornell University Press, 1994). See also Terborg-Penn, "Discrimination against Afro-American Women," 18; Julie Winch, *Philadelphia's Black Elite: Activism, Accommodation, and the Struggle for Autonomy, 1787–1848* (Philadelphia: Temple University Press, 1988), 86; Benjamin Quarles, *Black Abolitionists* (New York: Oxford University Press, 1969), 27–30, 178–80; Janice Sumler Lewis, "The Fortens of Philadelphia: An Afro-American Family and Nineteenth-Century Reform" (Ph.D. diss., Georgetown University, 1978); Emma J. Lapsansky, "Feminism, Freedom, and Community: Charlotte Forten and Women Activists in Nineteenth-Century Philadelphia," *PMHB* 113 (Jan. 1989): 3–19; and Jean Fagan Yellin, *Women and Sisters: The Antislavery Feminists in American Culture* (New Haven: Yale University Press, 1989), 58–59.

46. *Memorial of Sarah Pugh*, 18; PFASS, *Thirty-Sixth Annual Report*, 1870, 11–12; Laura H. Lovell, *Report of a Delegate to the Anti-Slavery Convention of American Women, Held in Philadelphia, May 1838, Including an Account of Other Meetings Held in Pennsylvania Hall, and of the Riot: Addressed to the Fall River Female Anti-Slavery Society* (Boston: Knapp, 1838), 21; and *History of Pennsylvania Hall, Which Was Destroyed by a Mob, on the 17th of May, 1838* (Philadelphia: Merrihew and Gunn, 1838), 135. See also Ira Brown, "Racism and Sexism: The Case of Pennsylvania Hall," *Phylon* 37 (June 1976): 126–36; and Anna Davis Hallowell, ed., *James and Lucretia Mott, Life and Letters*

(Boston: Houghton Mifflin, 1884), 128–33, which includes a description of threats to the Mott home, which at that time was in the city. For an analysis of the leading citizens involved in such riots, see Leonard L. Richards, *"Gentlemen of Property and Standing": Anti-Abolition Mobs in Jacksonian America* (New York: Oxford University Press, 1970), 3, 43, 156. A conservative but telling description of the event and its alliance of white and black women is in Nicholas B. Wainwright, ed., *A Philadelphia Perspective: The Diary of Sidney George Fisher Covering the Years 1834–1871* (Philadelphia: Historical Society of Pennsylvania, 1967), 49: "Black & white men & women sat promiscuously together, & walked about arm in arm. Such are the excesses of enthusiasm." The founding meeting of the National Requited Labor Association was being held at Pennsylvania Hall at the same time as the convention of antislavery women. See Ruth Ketring Nuermberger, *The Free Produce Movement: A Quaker Protest Against Slavery* (Durham: Duke University Press, 1942), 24.

47. See Kathryn Kish Sklar, " 'Women Who Speak for an Entire Nation': American and British Women Compared at the World Anti-Slavery Convention, London, 1840," in Yellin and Van Horne, *The Abolitionist Sisterhood.*

48. Letter by Maria Chapman quoted in Anna M. Stoddart, *Elizabeth Pease Nichol* (London: Dent, 1899), 63. See Sklar, " 'Women Who Speak' "; and Bolt, *Women's Movements*, 68–69. For a parallel among Chartists, see Jutta Schwarzkopf, *Women in the Chartist Movement* (New York: St. Martin's, 1991), 246.

49. Mary Howitt, [London, June 1840], quoted in Margaret Howitt, ed., *Mary Howitt, An Autobiography* (London: W. Isbister, 1889), 1:291–92; Frederick B. Tolles, "Slavery and 'The Woman Question': Lucretia Mott's Diary of Her Visit to Great Britain to Attend the World's Anti-Slavery Convention of 1840," *Journal of the Friends Historical Society*, supplement no. 23 (Haverford, Pa.: Friends' Historical Association, 1952), 23, 49. See also Sarah Pugh to Elizabeth Pease, Philadelphia, Nov. 16, 1840, PSP, 44. Opposition to women antislavery speakers in mixed groups persisted in England during the late 1850s. See Ruth Bogin, "Sarah Parker Remond: Black Abolitionist from Salem," *Essex Institute Historical Collections*, 110 (April 1974), 137. The example of the American women had an effect, however, as Sarah Pugh wrote to friends, "The women there [at the convention] with but few ex-

ceptions, were not prepared to take our position, though they thanked us most heartily for coming; they would not have been admitted even as visitors had we not come,—now they say, this privilege will not again be withheld, and they consider it a step gained" (*Memorial of Sarah Pugh*, 27). An exception to the rule of caution among British women was Elizabeth Pease of Edinburgh, Pugh's frequent correspondent after 1840 and the most influential woman in British antislavery circles. Pease wrote on July 17, 1840, about the convention: "I regretted it deeply & several of us mourned over our utter inability to help it" (Clare Taylor, ed., *British and American Abolitionists: An Episode in Transatlantic Understanding* [Edinburgh: Edinburgh University Press, 1974], 102).

50. Dana Greene, ed., *Lucretia Mott: Her Complete Speeches and Sermons* (New York: Edwin Mellen, 1980,) 148 and 156.

51. *Memorial of Sarah Pugh*, 22. PFASS joined with the Pittsburgh female antislavery society to carry the petition movement into every county in Pennsylvania. The campaign significantly escalated the terms of the debate over slavery because, following the passage of the "Gag Act," it enlarged the debate to include issues of free speech. See Gerda Lerner, "The Political Activities of Anti-Slavery Women," in *The Majority Finds Its Past* (New York: Oxford University Press, 1979, 115). For more on the petition campaign, see Lerner, "Political Activities"; Judith Wellman, "Women and Radical Reform in Antebellum Upstate New York: A Profile of Grassroots Female Abolitionists," in Mabel E. Deutrich and Virginia C. Purdy, eds., *Clio Was a Woman: Studies in the History of American Women* (Washington, D.C.: Howard University Press, 1980); Magdol, "A Window on the Abolitionist Constituency"; and Nancy Hewitt, "The Social Origins of Women's Antislavery Politics in Western New York," both in Alan M. Kraut, ed., *Crusaders and Compromisers: Essays on the Relationship of the Antislavery Struggle to the Antebellum Party System* (Westport: Greenwood, 1983). Baptist, Congregationalist, Presbyterian, and Quaker congregations were more sympathetic to petitioning by and among women than were Methodists or Episcopalians. See Edward Magdol, *The Antislavery Rank and File: A Social Profile of the Abolitionists' Constituency* (Westport: Greenwood, 1986).

52. *Memorial of Sarah Pugh*, 90; Lucretia Mott to CBK, [Philadelphia], July 16, 1859, KFP, box 1.

53. *Turning the World Upside Down: The Anti-Slavery Convention of American Women, Held in New York City, May 9–12, 1837* (1837; reprint, New York: Feminist, 1987), 19. Women's power as consumers was consciously developed by the PFASS. In 1834 the society urged its members to remember "that the refusal to purchase or use the products of slave labour is one of the most efficient means of abolishing slavery" (PFASS minutes, January 14, 1834, cited in Williams, "Religion, Race, and Gender," 190). Thomas Haskell has argued that antislavery moral values were shaped by capitalist market processes that brought greater numbers of people indirectly into contact with others, making it possible for them to be imaginatively concerned about strangers ("Capitalism and the Origins of the Humanitarian Sensibility," parts 1 and 2, *AHR* 90 [April 1985]: 339–61 and 547–66). For a penetrating review of recent scholarship on this topic, see Thomas C. Holt, "Review Essay: Explaining Abolition," *JSH* 24 (winter 1990), 371–78. See also Charles Sellers, *The Market Revolution in Jacksonian America, 1815–1846* (New York: Oxford University Press, 1991), 396–427.

54. See Stuart M. Blumin, *The Emergence of the Middle Class: Social Experience in the American City, 1760–1900* (Cambridge: Cambridge University Press, 1989), 138–91.

55. Nuermberger, *Free Produce Movement*, 25; and Hallowell, *James and Lucretia Mott*, 88. See Norman B. Wilkinson, "The Philadelphia Free Produce Attack Upon Slavery," *PMHB* 66 (July 1942): 294–313. For the Colored Female Free Produce Society, see Quarles, *Black Abolitionists*, 74. These organizations were an extension of the Quaker free produce movement, especially its local predecessors—the Female Association for Promoting the Manufacture and Use of Free Cotton and the Free Produce Society of Pennsylvania. For more on the Mott's store, see Nuermberger, *Free Produce Movement*, 22, 119. Mott sold the store around 1830 to the woman who maintained it until 1846.

56. Nuermberger located twenty-six free produce societies in the United States between 1826 and 1856, *Free Produce Movement*, 58.

57. FK, "My Philadelphia," 54.

58. PFASS, *Third Annual Report*, 1837; Sarah Pugh to Richard Webb, Sept. 12, 1859, PSP. See also PFASS, *Thirty-Sixth Annual Report*, 870, 22–23, and *Twenty-Fourth and Twenty-Fifth Annual Report*, 1859, 19; and Orwin Rush, "Lucretia Mott and the Pennsylvania Antislavery Fairs," *Bulletin of Friends Historical Associations* 36 (autumn 1946): 63–76. The first antislavery fair was organized in Boston in 1834 by Lydia Maria Child. It received

handicrafts from numerous women's antislavery societies in New England and netted $300. See Keith Melder, *The Beginnings of Sisterhood: The American Woman's Rights Movement, 1800–1850* (New York: Schocken Books, 1977), 70. The apex of this activity was reached in 1853, when $2,673 was realized. The budget of 1859 was typical, with $925 donated to the Pennsylvania society for various purposes, $700 to the national, and $155 to support *The Anti-Slavery Standard* and other abolitionist periodicals (PFASS, *Thirty-Sixth Annual Report,* 1870, 22, and *Twenty-Sixth Annual Report,* 1860, 24). For the budget of the American Anti-Slavery Society (hereafter AASS), see Merton L. Dillon, *The Abolitionists: The Growth of a Dissenting Minority* (DeKalb: Northern Illinois University Press, 1974), 213. Fairs conducted by the Boston Female Anti-Slavery Society were even more successful. Pugh noted that her colleagues there raised $3,000 in 1845 (SP to Elizabeth Pease, Philadelphia, Jan. 20, 1846).

In the late 1830s, only eight or ten had attended the Pennsylvania circle. Sarah Pugh remembered that they "repaired to a school-room because it was central, each with her supper of nuts and cakes brought in pocket, eaten at twilight while we walked in the yard—then a few more hours' work by the glimmer of candles" (*Memorial of Sarah Pugh,* 86). See also Rush, "Lucretia Mott," 63–76. For antislavery activism among women in the Pennsylvania countryside, see Joan M. Jensen, *Loosening the Bonds: Mid-Atlantic Farm Women, 1750–1850* (New Haven: Yale University Press, 1986), 181–204.

59. Mary Grew, "Annals of Women's Anti-Slavery Societies," in AASS, *Proceedings of the American Anti-Slavery Society at Its Third Decade* (New York: American A.S. Society, 1854), 128, quoted in Ronald G. Walters, *The Antislavery Appeal: American Abolitionism after 1830* (Baltimore: Johns Hopkins University Press, 1976), 24. See also Ira V. Brown, *Mary Grew: Abolitionist and Feminist, 1813–1896* (Selinsgrove, Pa.: Susquehanna University Press, 1991).

60. See Sklar, "Women Who Speak." *Webster's Tenth New Collegiate Dictionary* defines power as "possession of control, authority, or influence over others;" "ability to act or produce an effect;" "physical might." Historically the power of women is more appropriately defined as the ability to control the distribution of social resources.

61. Hallowell, *James and Lucretia Mott,* 388 and 356; Tomlins, *Law, Labor, and Ideology,* 297.

Pennsylvania courts had historically been friendly to women who came before the bench. See G. S. Rowe, "The Role of Courthouses in the Lives of Eighteenth-Century Pennsylvania Women," *The Western Pennsylvania Historical Magazine* 68, no. 1 (Jan. 1985): 5–23.

62. PFASS, *Thirty-Sixth Annual Report,* 1870, 17–18; Hallowell, *James and Lucretia Mott,* 355–57; and Ray Allen Billington, ed., *The Journal of Charlotte Forten: A Free Negro in the Slave Era* (New York: Norton, 1953), 127. See also William Still, *The Underground Railroad* (Philadelphia: People's Publishing Co., 1871), 86–97; and Julie Winch, "Philadelphia and the Other Underground Railroad," *PMHB* 111 (Jan. 1987): 3–26. For the Vigilant Committee of Philadelphia, see Nick Salvatore, *Amos Webber: The Making of an African-American* (New York: Random House, forthcoming), ch. 4.

63. *Memorial of Sarah Pugh,* 93–94. A summary of this event can be found in Potter, *Impending Crisis,* 356–84. The most complete discussion of Mary Brown is Daniel Rosenberg, "Mary Brown: From Harpers Ferry to California," occasional paper no. 17 (New York: The American Institute for Marxist Studies, 1975). Benjamin Quarles, ed., *Blacks on John Brown* (Urbana: University of Illinois Press, 1972), 16–19, contains a letter to Mary Brown from black women in New York City.

64. *Philadelphia Evening Bulletin,* Dec. 2, 1859, 1. For more on Mott's sermons, see Greene, *Lucretia Mott.*

65. Nicholas B. Wainwright, ed., *A Philadelphia Perspective,* 340–41; PFASS, *Twenty-Sixth Annual Report,* 1860, 19; Hallowell, *James and Lucretia Mott,* 393. Curtis's lecture on that occasion has been reprinted in Charles Eliot Norton, ed., *Orations and Addresses of George William Curtis* (New York: Harper and Bros., 1894), 1:61–94. See also Edward Cary, *George William Curtis* (Boston: Houghton Mifflin, 1894), 127–129. Dusinberre described how the mayor maintained order: "He arrayed fifty policemen in front of the platform, scattered another fifty through the audience, massed 400 more at the rear and outside, and himself sat on the stage as a symbol of municipal authority" (*Civil War Issues in Philadelphia,* 90).

66. PFASS, *Twenty-Sixth Annual Report,* 1860, 16–19; *Memorial of Sarah Pugh,* 95–96.

67. For a discussion of citizenship as a bounded and ordered rather than universal and equal concept, see Carole Pateman, *The Sexual Contract* (Stanford: Stanford University Press, 1988).

2. So Mature in Thought, 1859–1876

1. FK, "My Philadelphia" (1926), 51. Appropriately enough the dwelling was later converted to a hospital for women and children. In 1990 the site occupied an empty lot at Forty-First and Parrish Streets. Like most rural households, the Kelleys maintained a calf and milk-producing cow. FK to WDK, Philadelphia, Dec. 2, 1865, NKP.

2. For a historical treatment of this theme, see Carol Zisowitz Stearns and Peter N. Stearns, *Anger: The Struggle for Emotional Control in America's History* (Chicago: University of Chicago, 1986).

3. The deaths of the Kelley children were recorded in Family Record, Nicholas Kelley Unsorted, NKP. For infant mortality, see Rose A. Cheney, "Seasonal Aspects of Infant and Childhood Mortality: Philadelphia, 1865–1920," *Journal of Interdisciplinary History* 14 (winter 1984): 561–85. See also R. Schofield, D. Reher, and A. Bideau, eds., *The Decline of Mortality in Europe* (Oxford: Oxford University Press, 1991), 16; and James C. Riley, "Insects and the European Mortality Decline," *AHR* 91 (Oct. 1986): 833–58. For the rise in mortality, see Meckel, *Save the Babies;* and Steckel, "Health and Mortality of Women and Children." Steckel notes that in the mid-nineteenth century "socioeconomic characteristics of the household influenced health less than found in modern data" (345). American infant mortality rates remained high across class in 1900. See also Condran, Williams, and Cheney, "Decline in Mortality in Philadelphia"; Virginia A. Metaxas Quiroga, *Poor Mothers and Babies: A Social History of Childbirth and Child Care Hospitals in Nineteenth-Century New York City* (New York: Garland, 1989); and Preston and Haines, *Fatal Years.* The first publication to introduce to American mothers Pasteur's success in retarding disease in milk by boiling it was Abraham Jacobi and Mary Jacobi, *Infant Diet* (New York: Putnam and Sons, 1874). For the growing importance of mothers' health responsibilities in the nineteenth century, see Dye and Smith, "Mother Love and Infant Death"; Ann Douglas, "Heaven Our Home: Consolation Literature in the Northern United States, 1830–1880," in David E. Stannard, *Death in America* (Philadelphia: University of Pennsylvania Press, 1979), 49–68; and Wendy Simonds and Barbara Katz Rothman, *Centuries of Solace: Expressions of Maternal Grief in Popular Literature* (Philadelphia: Temple University Press, 1992). Perhaps in an effort to replace these dying infants,

Caroline gave birth to a greater number of babies than did most of her contemporaries. For contemporary fertility rates, see Sklar, "Victorian Women and Domestic Life."

4. FK, "My Philadelphia," 11; CBK to WDK, [Germantown], Sept. 9, 1863, WDKP; and CBK to WDK, Feb. 25, 1868, WDKP. The death of Benjamin Bonsall is recorded in Family Record, Nicholas Kelley Unsorted, NKP. William's death is described in FK, "My Philadelphia," 11.

The ongoing effects of her children's deaths were apparent in Caroline's later correspondence. For example, in 1894 she wrote Florence, "We have had a very happy Christmas. I have not enjoyed one so much since I lost dear little Anna. The very name of the day has always been painful to me, since that bright, lovely one in 1870—the last one that she spent with us" (CBK to FK, Philadelphia, Dec. 25, 1894, both held by FK's grandniece, Jane Holland, of Gainesville, Florida).

5. CBK to WDK, Philadelphia, Feb. 26, 1869, KFP, reel 1, box 2; FK, "My Philadelphia," 11. Baby Caroline died that February.

6. Elizabeth Pugh to FK, Willow Ave., Sept. 3, 1871, NKP, box 66; WDK to FK, Washington, [D.C.], Jan. 18, 1870, KFP, reel 4, box 5.

7. CBK to WDK, Feb. 20, 1867, WDKP.

8. FK, "My Philadelphia," 9. For a similar woodcut, see frontispiece in George Smith, *The Cry of the Children from the Brickyards of England: A Statement and Appeal, with Remedy* (London: Simpkin, Marshall, 1871).

William Kelley acquired rental property at such a rapid rate in the 1850s that by 1860 his holdings were valued at $100,000, putting him in the top 1.3 percent of people in Philadelphia with some personal property and the top 0.2 percent of all households in census samples taken by the Philadelphia Social History Project. By 1870 his wealth had declined slightly, but he nevertheless remained in the top 6.3 percent of all sampled individuals and the top 13 percent of persons with some personal property. These statistics are from United States Census, manuscript for Sixth Precinct, Twenty-fourth Ward, Philadelphia County, June 7, 1860, 47; and manuscript for District 79 of Philadelphia County, June 7, 1870, 34. I am grateful to Walter Licht and Margaret David for their research on William Kelley in U.S. census records and to Thomas Dublin for his analysis of WDK's relative standing in the census sample.

9. FK, "My Philadelphia," 9, 56.

10. FK, "My Philadelphia," 54. For Longstreth, see Helen W. Ludlow, *Memoir of Mary Anna Longstreth by an Old Pupil* (Philadelphia: J. B. Lippincott Co., 1886).

11. CBK to WDK, Jan. 19, 1866, WDKP. See also WDK to CBK, Washington, [D.C.], Jan. 16, 1860, Florence Kelley Papers: WDK Letters to his wife, NKP.

12. CBK to FK, Washington, [D.C.], Jan. 30, 1868, CBK to WDK, 1860–1888, KFP, reel 1, box 2.

13. CBK to WDK, July 1, 1868, WDKP.

14. WDK to CBK, Washington, [D.C.], April 5, 1869, WDKP; WDK to CBK, Washington, [D.C.], March 12, 1871 (second of two letters written to her on that day), KFP, reel 4, box 5; WDK to WDK Jr., Washington, [D.C.], Dec. 2, 1869, KFP.

15. FK, "My Philadelphia," 55. CBK to WDK, Philadelphia, March 29, 1869, CBK to WDK, 1860–1888, KFP, reel 1, box 2. For the Sunday visits to Germantown, see WDK to CBK, Washington, [D.C.], Feb. 28, 1871, KFP, reel 4, box 5; WDK to FK, Washington, [D.C.], Feb. 23, 1868, WDKP.

16. WDK to FK, Washington, [D.C.], April 15, 1871, WDKP.

17. Ludlow, *Memoir of Mary Anna Longstreth,* 159. The school closed in 1877.

18. CBK to WDK, West Philadelphia, July 7, 1868, KFP, reel 1, box 2; Elizabeth Pugh to WDK, n.p., n.d., NKP (letter is on the back of FK to WDK, Germantown, Jan. 12, 1869).

19. FK, "My Philadelphia," 8–9. *The Resources of California* was a monthly periodical that Wentworth and Boruck began publishing in San Francisco in September 1870. Surviving at the Library of Congress is *Resources of California* 2, no. 11 (Aug. 1873). For an illustration of and commentary on WDK, see "House Committee on Ways and Means," *Harper's Weekly* 31 (May 26, 1888): 386–88. Caroline Kelley also used the family library, particularly as a place from which she wrote William, as a cool retreat on hot summer days (CBK to WDK, July 7, 1868).

20. FK, "My Philadelphia," 53. For more on the early reading of Progressive Era women reformers, see Barbara Sicherman, "Sense and Sensibility: A Case Study of Women's Reading in Late-Victorian America," in Cathy N. Davidson, *Reading in America* (Baltimore: Johns Hopkins University Press, 1989), 201–25; and Kate Flint, *The Woman Reader, 1837–1914* (New York: Oxford University Press, 1993).

21. For a useful analysis of the social construction of experience, see Joan W. Scott, "Experience," in Judith Butler and Joan W. Scott, *Feminists Theorize the Political* (New York: Routledge, 1992), 22–40.

22. FK, "My Philadelphia," 5; WDK to CBK, Washington, [D.C.], March 16 and March 17, 1871, KFP, box 5; CBK to WDK, Philadelphia, Feb. 29, 1862, WDKP; WDK to CBK, March 16 and March 17, 1871.

23. WDK to Abraham Lincoln, Philadelphia, Nov. 29, 1860, Abraham Lincoln Papers, Library of Congress; CBK to WDK, Philadelphia, Oct. 27, 1856, NKP. WDK's irritability was mentioned in FK to CBK, 247 West Polk St., Feb. 10, 1896, KFP: "He [FK's son, Nicholas] is in many ways like father but wholly without Father's irritability."

24. WDK to FK, Washington, [D.C.], Jan 13, 1869, NKP, box 66. For more on Washington at that time, see Reps, *Washington on View.*

25. FK to WDK, North Philadelphia, Dec. 2, 1865, NKP; WDK to FK, Jan. 22, 1871, WDKP; WDK to FK, Washington, [D.C.], Jan. 12, 1874, NKP; WDK to CBK, Washington, [D.C.], Feb. 14, 1875, NKP. The fair Florrie mentions was probably sponsored by the U.S. Sanitary Commission. See Darney, "Women and World's Fairs," 25.

26. WDK to FK, [Washington, D.C.], Feb. 5, 1875, WDKP; WDK to FK, Washington, [D.C.], June 1, 1875, WDKP. For voluntarist traditions, see also Pole, *Pursuit of Equality,* 177–200.

27. For information about WDK's District 4, see Stanley B. Parsons, William W. Beach, and Michael J. Dubin, *United States Congressional Districts and Data, 1843–1883* (Westport, Conn.: Greenwood, 1986), 81, 133, 207. Between 1863 and 1875, District 4 grew in population from 93,082 to 141,519. Kelley's constituency during these years was about 2 percent black, and 25 percent foreign-born, including about 5 percent born in Germany and about 15 percent born in Ireland.

28. See Malcolm Rogers Eiselen, *The Rise of Pennsylvania Protectionism* (Philadelphia: Porcupine, 1974), 257–66. For the effects of protective tariffs on the development of the American iron and steel industries, see Peter Temin, *Iron and Steel in Nineteenth-Century America: An Economic Inquiry* (Cambridge: MIT Press, 1964). The tariff issue was heaven-sent to the new Republican Party, or the Peoples' Party, as they called themselves in the late 1850s. It gave them an issue that appealed to all classes, an effective weapon for attacking the Democrats, and a means of forging unity within their own untested ranks. Most importantly, in the nation's last election before plunging into Civil War

over the expansion of slavery in the West, the tariff issue permitted Republican candidates to avoid that disruptive topic in districts that could not be carried on the slavery issue alone.

29. WDK to Caroline Dall, House of Representatives, June 12, 1864, Massachusetts Historical Society. See also Dall, *The College, the Market and the Court;* and Gary Sue Goodman, " 'All about me forgotten': The Education of Caroline Healey Dall (1822–1912)" (Ph.D. diss, Stanford University, 1987). It was this pitch of enthusiasm that created the label by which he became known to his contemporaries and future generations of American schoolchildren — "Pig Iron" Kelley. Regrettably for his historical reputation, the nickname conveyed a crass self-interest that none of Judge Kelley's contemporaries associated with him. To them he was often naive but never crude. "As a fighter he was fair and manly, and as a friend he was loyal and constant," one wrote (WDK obituary, *Harper's Weekly* 34 [Jan. 18, 1890], 52). The nickname, which began to be used in 1869, seems to have arisen from WDK's advocacy of protectionism on the Ways and Means Committee, beginning in 1869.

For Kelley and Carey, see Greco, "William Darrah Kelley," 245–52. Responding to the effects of widespread unemployment, traditionally Democratic iron and manufacturing districts abandoned their party wholesale because of the tariff issue in the elections of 1858. See also Eiselen, *Rise of Pennsylvania Protectionism*, 244–48, 250, 272–73; Howe, *Political Culture of the American Whigs*, 108–22; Bruce Collins, "Federal Power and Economic Policy: Henry Carey and the 1850s," in Jeffreys-Jones and Collins, *Growth of Federal Power*, 36–48; and Joseph Dorfman, *The Economic Mind in American Civilization, 1606–1865* (New York: Viking, 1946), 2:789–805; and Paul K. Conkin, *Prophets of Prosperity: America's First Political Economists* (Bloomington: Indiana University Press, 1980), 261–307. A sensitive exploration of the relationship between state building and the defense of capitalism in Britain could apply to the United States of 1870 — Philip Corrigan and Derek Sayer, *The Great Arch: English State Formation as Cultural Revolution* (Oxford: Blackwell, 1985). Except for his support of protective tariffs, Carey was an economic individualist; for example, he opposed the regulation of factories.

30. WDK, "Should Congress Compel American Laborers to Work for Lower Wages?" *Congressional Record*, 42nd Cong., 2nd sess., March 16, 1872, 1752–56. For Kelley's power on the committee from 1869 to 1889, see Donald R. Kennon and Rebecca M. Rogers, *United States House of Representatives, The Committee on Ways and Means: A Bicentennial History, 1789–1989* (Washington, D.C.: GPO, [1989]), 185, 187, 208. See also Charles H. Stewart, *Budget Reform Politics: The Design of the Appropriations Process in the House of Representatives, 1865–1921* (Cambridge: Cambridge University Press, 1989). For the timing of capital concentration in Pennsylvania, see David Montgomery, "Radical Republicanism in Pennsylvania, 1866–1873," *PMHB* 85 (1961): 439–57, reprinted in James Mohr, ed., *Radical Republicans in the North: State Politics During Reconstruction* (Baltimore: Johns Hopkins University Press, 1975), 50–65. For an example of capital concentration in the West, see W. Turrentine Jackson, *The Enterprising Scott: Investors in the American West after 1873* (Edinburgh: Edinburgh University Press, 1968). For the all-important concentration of northern capital in the South, see Bensel, *Yankee Leviathan*, 303–65.

31. WDK, *The Dangers and Duties of the Hour: An Address delivered at Concert Hall, Philadelphia, March 15, 1866* (Washington, D.C.: n.p., 1866), 10; WDK, *Congressional Globe*, 38th Cong., 2nd sess., Jan. 16, 1865, 290. Kelley's March 15 speech warned against a possible military dictatorship by the "reactionary" president, Andrew Johnson. See also *Chronicles of the Union League of Philadelphia, 1862–1902* (Philadelphia: Union League, 1902), 402. Kelley's reputation as a radical was buttressed by his vigorous support for the recruitment of black troops into the Union ranks. See WDK, "Arming the Negroes" (a speech delivered in the House), *Congressional Globe*, 37th Cong., 3rd sess., Jan. 29, 1863, 606–7. Speaking on this issue on July 6, 1863, Kelley became the first elected official in Philadelphia to join black leaders in addressing a predominantly black audience (Nicklas, "William Kelley," 115; and Brown, "William D. Kelley," 316–29). Two years after helping to found the Philadelphia Union League, Kelley took important initiatives in shaping the Second Reconstruction Bill, which was vetoed by President Johnson. See William R. Brock, *An American Crisis: Congress and Reconstruction, 1865–1867* (New York: St. Martin's, 1963), 204.

32. Eric Foner, *Nothing But Freedom: Emancipation and Its Legacy* (Baton Rouge: Louisiana State University Press, 1983), concluded (46), "Nowhere else did blacks achieve a comparable degree of political influence after the end of slavery." For the

significance of the expansion of federal powers during and after the Civil War, see Michael Kammen, *A Machine That Would Go of Itself: The Constitution in American Culture* (New York: Knopf, 1986), 140–41.

33. *Congressional Globe*, 38th Cong., 2nd sess., Jan. 18, 1865, 289. The pamphlet was entitled *Remarks of Hon. William D. Kelley, of Pennsylvania, in Support of His Proposed Amendment to the Bill to Guarantee to Certain States whose Governments Have Been Usurped or Overthrown, a Republican Form of Government, Delivered in the House of Representatives, Jan. 16, 1865* (New York: Loyal Publication Society, 1865). George Sterns, the pamphlet's editor, told Charles Sumner he planned to print a total of five hundred thousand copies. See also Wendell Phillips and Frederick Douglass, *Equality of All Men Before the Law, Claimed and Defended* (Boston: Press of Geo. C. Rand and Avery, 1865); and James M. McPherson, *The Struggle for Equality: Abolitionists and the Negro in the Civil War and Reconstruction* (Princeton: Princeton University Press, 1964), 319. David Donald analyzed the roll call vote on the motion to table further discussion of Reconstruction in *The Politics of Reconstruction, 1863–1867* (Baton Rouge: Louisiana State University Press, 1955), 85–90. See also Alfred Alvins, ed., *The Reconstruction Amendments' Debates: The Legislative History and Contemporary Debates in Congress on the Thirteenth, Fourteenth, and Fifteenth Amendments* (Richmond: Virginia Commission on Constitutional Government, 1967).

As an entering wedge for his suffrage proposal, Kelley had in the previous December introduced a bill providing for Negro suffrage in the District of Columbia. Since the Constitution gave Congress jurisdiction over voting rights in the District, this bill gave radicals the opportunity to discuss black suffrage independently of the issue of the constitutional jurisdiction of the states over voting rights within their boundaries. Nicklas, "William Kelley," 169–74; and William Gillette, *The Right to Vote: Politics and the Passage of the Fifteenth Amendment* (Baltimore: Johns Hopkins University Press, 1965), 29.

In 1868, Kelley supported the following wording: "No state shall deny to or exclude from the exercise of any of the rights or privileges of an elector to any citizen of the United States by reason of race or color." The amendment as adopted in 1870 read: "The right of citizens of the United States to vote shall not be denied or abridged by the United States or by any State on account of race, color, or previous condition of servitude." This wording omitted the reference to male voters that in 1868 had become part of the Fourteenth Amendment and justifiably angered woman suffragists. Some woman suffragists, especially Elizabeth Cady Stanton and Susan B. Anthony, lobbied for phrasing that would include women in the Fifteenth Amendment. See Mari Jo Buhle and Paul Buhle, *The Concise History of Woman Suffrage: Selections from the Class Work of Stanton, Anthony, Gage and Harper* (Urbana: University of Illinois Press, 1978), 257–68; Dubois, "Taking the Law," 19–40; Ellen Carol DuBois, *Feminism and Suffrage: The Emergence of an Independent Women's Movement in America, 1848–1869* (Ithaca: Cornell University Press, 1978); Lorini, "Public Rituals"; and Israel Kugler, *From Ladies to Women: The Organized Struggle for Woman's Rights in the Reconstruction Era* (Westport: Greenwood, 1987).

34. Nicklas, "William Kelley," 233–35. See Sarah Wiggins, "The Pig Iron Kelley Riot in Mobile, May 14, 1867," *The Alabama Review* 23 (Jan. 1970): 45–55. For verbal attacks on Kelley's racial egalitarianism by northerners as well as southerners, see Forrest G. Wood, *Black Scare: The Racist Response to Emancipation and Reconstruction* (Berkeley: University of California Press, 1970), 45, 48–49, 73, 79. See also Michael W. Fitzgerald, *The Union League Movement in the Deep South: Politics and Agricultural Change During Reconstruction* (Baton Rouge: Louisiana State University Press, 1989), 245.

35. *Congressional Globe*, 40th Cong., 1st sess., March 26, 1868, 2141; reprinted in Lydia Maria Child, ed., *The Freedmen's Book* (Boston: Ticknor and Fields, 1865), 261–63, Kelley's speech was a popular text in schools where former slaves learned to read in the 1860s.

36. For Kelley's views on reconstructing the South, see Richard H. Abbott, *The Republican Party and the South, 1855–1877* (Chapel Hill: University of North Carolina, 1986), 88. Historians' earlier skeptical interpretations of the radical Republicans have given way to studies that emphasize the limitations of Republican ideology, which prevented the radicals from extending material aid through property grants and dispatching troops to protect black suffrage. See especially Foner, *Reconstruction*. In "Negro Suffrage and Republican Politics: The Problem of Motivation in Reconstruction Historiography," *Journal of Southern History* 38 (Aug. 1967): 303–30, LaWanda and John H. Cox criticized the notion that Kelley and other radicals were opportunists, concluding that they displayed "a

genuine concern for the equal status of the Negro" (328). Criticism of the limitations of the radicals' measures can be found in Patrick W. Riddleberger, "The Radicals' Abandonment of the Negro during Reconstruction," *Journal of Negro History* 45 (April 1960): 88–102. For the radical nature of the shift in state-federal relations created by the Thirteenth and Fourteenth Amendments, see Robert J. Kaczorowski, "To Begin the Nation Anew: Congress, Citizenship, and Civil Rights after the Civil War," *AHR* 92 (Feb. 1987): 45–68.

The best discussions of the economic context of Kelley's radicalism are Montgomery, *Beyond Equality*, and Montgomery, "Radical Republicanism in Pennsylvania, 1866–1873." He emphasizes that the firms with which WDK and others were aligned before 1873 were relatively small and did not represent the same interests as the monopolies owned by Andrew Carnegie and John D. Rockefeller. Radical policies were eventually defeated by these commercial interests after they began to control industrial growth in the 1870s. Kelley and other radicals demonstrated their prolabor bias by supporting the 1868 federal eight-hour law. See also David Roediger, "Ira Steward and the Anti-Slavery Origins of American Eight-Hour Theory," *LH* 27 (summer 1986): 410–26; and Michael Les Benedict, *A Compromise of Principle: Congressional Republicans and Reconstruction, 1863–1869* (New York: Norton, 1974), 42–55.

Given the relative newness of Republican political organization, combined with the trying conditions under which they came to power, most of their attention and resources remained concentrated on winning elections in the Northeast, Midwest, and West. See Abbott, *Republican Party and the South*. For terrorist violence against the Republican Party, see George C. Rable, *But There Was No Peace: The Role of Violence in the Politics of Reconstruction* (Athens: University of Georgia Press, 1984). Nevertheless, Republicans continued to advocate more positive government than Democrats. See Salisbury, "The Republican Party and Positive Government," 15–34.

37. WDK, "The Enforcement of the Fourteenth Amendment Essential to the Prosperity of the South," U.S. House of Representatives, *Congressional Globe*, 42nd Cong., sess. 1, March 29, 1871, 339–40. WDK's votes before 1869 can be viewed in comparison with his colleagues in Glenn M. Linden, *Politics or Principle: Congressional Voting on the Civil War Amendments and Pro-Negro Mea-*

sures, 1838–69 (Seattle: University of Washington Press, 1976).

38. For the Slaughterhouse decision of 1873, see Robert J. Kaczorowski, *The Nationalization of Civil Rights: Constitutional Theory and Practice in a Racist Society, 1866–1883* (New York: Garland, 1987), 253–334. For the reinstitution of decentralized government, see Kaczorowski, *The Politics of Judicial Interpretation: The Federal Courts, Department of Justice and Civil Rights, 1866–1876* (New York: Oceana Publications, 1985), 199–227.

39. Crédit Mobilier, a construction company that contracted for work on the Union Pacific Railroad, was controlled by key Union Pacific stockholders. To prevent a congressional investigation of their financial practices, these insiders had sold Crédit Mobilier stock at a discount to several members of Congress. A full report on the scandal appeared in *Scribner's Monthly Magazine* 7 (March 1874): 546–57. Another account of the scandal can be found in *The Nation*, no. 399 (Jan. 30, 1873): 127–29. See also Mark Wahlgren Summers, *The Era of Good Stealings* (New York: Oxford University Press, 1993), 231–37. For other radicals involved in the scandal, see Hans L. Trefousse, *The Radical Republicans: Lincoln's Vanguard for Racial Justice* (New York: Knopf, 1969), 463. WDK's early endorsement of the Union Pacific is described in Leonard P. Curry, *Blueprint for Modern America: Nonmilitary Legislation of the First Civil War Congress* (Nashville: Vanderbilt University Press, 1968), 120. For the impact of railroads on American political institutions in this era, see Farnham, "The Weakened Spring of Government"; Skowronek, *Building A New American State*, 121–62; Berk, "Adversarial by Design"; and Mark W. Summers, *Railroads, Reconstruction, and the Gospel of Prosperity: Aid under the Radical Republicans, 1865–1877* (Princeton: Princeton University Press, 1984), 98–117. See also Nelson Trottman, *History of the Union Pacific: A Financial and Economic Survey* (New York: Ronald, 1923), 30–54.

40. WDK to CBK, Washington, [D.C.], Feb. 21, 1873, WDKP; *Congressional Globe*, 42nd Cong. 3rd sess., Feb. 27, 1873, 1840. See also WDK's testimony to the investigating committee, *Reports of Committees of the House of Representatives for the Third Session of the Forty-Second Congress, 1872–73*, 197–204. Kelley later claimed that his reputation as one of "the poorer but influential members of the House" inspired Ames to draw him into the scheme in December 1867. Ames offered to invest $1,000 of his own funds in the Union Pacific and

to provide Kelley with the earnings. Kelley later accepted $329 on this basis, followed by a loan of $1,000 to be repaid out of future dividends, even though he did not own the stock. *Scribner's* said Kelley "early [became] frightened" and returned the stock. Before 1873 WDK's official misconduct was limited to showing undue consideration for the interests of his financial backers. Most particularly, in January 1872 he was extremely inept as the floor manager of a coinage bill, partly because he sought to advance the federal purchase of nickel produced by fellow Philadelphian Joseph Wharton (Walter T. K. Nugent, *The Money Question During Reconstruction* [New York: Norton, 1967], 86). In an 1875 letter to Caroline, Kelley described one aspect of his financial difficulties: "During our trip to the Pacific coast in 1869, he [Ames] learned of my pecuniary entrapment and offered me [illegible] which I then declined; but the 19th of April 1871, I borrowed from him $3720 with which to meet an exigency and avoid a destructive sacrifice of property. At the end of the year, I paid the interest $223.20 and we never referred to the subject again, till the 2nd of this month when to his apparent surprise I handed him a check for $4341.24 in full payment and interest" (WDK to CBK, Feb. 14, 1875).

41. WDK to CBK, Washington, [D.C.], Jan. 9, 1873, Feb. 23, 1873, and Feb. 2, 1873, WDKP. See also WDK to CBK, Washington, [D.C.], Jan. 31, 1873, and Feb. 24, 1873, WDKP.

42. WDK to Elizabeth Cady Stanton, Dec. 13, 1872, quoted in Nicklas, "William Kelley," 320 (since the time of Nicklas's research, this letter has disappeared from the WDKP); *New York Times*, Aug. 28, 1875, quoted in Nicklas, "William Kelley," 375; WDK to FK, Washington, [D.C.], Jan. 15, 1875, WDKP, box 2.

43. Quoted in Irwin Unger, *The Greenback Era: A Social and Political History of American Finance, 1865–1879* (Princeton: Princeton University Press, 1967), 278–79, 284, 344. The cartoon (printed July 31, 1875) is reprinted in Morton Keller, *The Art and Politics of Thomas Nast* (New York: Oxford University Press, 1968), 249. The alliance between radical Republicans and organized labor on the question of soft money is analyzed in Montgomery, *Beyond Equality*, 425–47. However, the Greenback-Labor party had little impact in Pennsylvania. See Ralph R. Ricker, "The Greenback-Labor Movement in Pennsylvania" (Ph.D. diss., Pennsylvania State University, 1955), 38. For WDK's tenure as chair of the Ways and Means Committee, see Kennon and Rogers, *The Committee on Ways and Means*, 187.

Kelley's championship of labor was doubtlessly influenced by the mobilization of labor in Philadelphia during those years. See Greenberg, "Strikes, Organizing and Change," 363–407. Kelley's disaffection with the Republican Party while remaining within it can be seen as a reflection of the enormous power of parties in American political life: it was the only game in town. On this point, see McCormick, *Party Period and Public Policy*, 229.

44. FK, "My Philadelphia," 9; WDK to WDK Jr., Laramie, Oct. 17, 1872, WDKP. See FK, "When Co-education Was Young" (1927), 561. The earliest reference to Florence's visits to Washington is in WDK to FK, Feb. 23, 1868.

45. FK to Isaac Pugh, Colorado Springs, July 21, [1872], NKP; FK to Isaac and Elizabeth Pugh, Pico House, Los Angeles, Aug. 7, 1872, NKP; FK to Isaac and Elizabeth Pugh, Aug. 7, 1872. For Florence's trip, see FK, "My Philadelphia," 57.

46. FK, "My Philadelphia," 55.

47. FK, "My Philadelphia," 56–57. FK might have known of Rebecca Harding Davis's anonymously published "Life in the Iron Mills," *Atlantic Monthly* (April 1861): 430–51, which fictionalized the visit of an upper-class group to a Wheeling, West Virginia, mill. Harding's stern realism championed workers in ways that the young Florence would have appreciated ten years later. See Rebecca Harding Davis, *Life in the Iron Mills, with a Biographical Interpretation by Tillie Olsen* (New York: Feminist, 1972); and "Rebecca Harding Davis" in *NAW*.

48. The best description of this process is Paul Krause, *The Battle for Homestead, 1880–1892: Politics, Culture, and Steel* (Pittsburgh: University of Pittsburgh Press, 1992), 81–266. For a discussion of the need for American industrial technology to emphasize unskilled work to match its immigrant labor pool, see John McDermott, "History in the Present: Contemporary Debates about Capitalism," *Science and Society* 56 (fall 1992): 291–323.

49. FK, "My Philadelphia," 56–57. Skilled steel workers and some laborers were organized into the Sons of Vulcan, which in 1867 negotiated a sliding-scale wage agreement that maintained industrial peace until 1874, so the presence of children was apparently accepted by the union. See George Swetnam, "Labor-Management Relations in Pennsylvania's Steel Industry, 1800–1959," *The Western Pennsylvania Historical Magazine* 62 (Oct. 1979): 326. The first Bessemer steel works in Pennsylvania was built in 1867; by 1876, the state contained five more. So the plant Kelley visited was quite new (William T. Hogan, *Economic History of the Iron and*

Steel Industry in the United States [Lexington, Mass: Lexington Books, 1971], 1:31–36).

50. FK, "My Philadelphia," 56–57.

51. Ibid., 8 and 57. This quote from William Kelley and his interpretation of the relationship between his generation and his daughter's appeared first in John Commons, "Tariff Revision and Protection for American Labor," *Annals of the American Academy* 32 (July–Dec. 1908): 51–56.

52. Resolution reprinted in *Congressional Globe*, 42nd Cong., 2nd sess., 973, Feb. 12, 1872; WDK to FK, Jan. 14, 1877, WDKP; WDK to CBK, Washington, [D.C.], March 19, 1871, KFP, reel 4, box 5. Born to a poor frontier family, Victoria Woodhull and her sister, Tennessee Claflin, joined the suffrage movement in January 1871. That year Victoria spoke before the Judiciary Committee of the House of Representatives urging Congress to legalize woman suffrage under the Fourteenth Amendment. This brought her to the attention of Stanton and other leaders of the National Woman Suffrage Association, founded two years earlier, who were meeting in Washington. Stanton and Anthony befriended the sisters despite their disreputable past selling patent medicine and dabbling with spiritualism and their financial speculation funded by Cornelius Vanderbilt. In 1870 the sisters began to publish *Woodhull and Claflin's Weekly*, which endorsed free love and legalized prostitution along with a variety of other radicalisms. Their journal published the Communist Manifesto for the first time in English in the United States in 1871. See "Victoria Woodhull," *NAW*.

53. FK, "My Philadelphia," 54; *Memorial of Sarah Pugh*, 113. See also Jacqueline Jones, *Soldiers of Light and Love: Northern Teachers and Georgia Blacks, 1856–1873* (Chapel Hill: University of North Carolina Press, 1980); and Allis Wolfe, "Women Who Dared: Northern Teachers of the Southern Freedmen, 1862–1872" (Ph.D. diss., City University of New York, 1982). For an analysis of Josephine Butler's campaign against the British government's authoritarian methods of combating disease in prostitutes, see Judith R. Walkowitz, *Prostitution and Victorian Society: Women, Class, and the State* (Cambridge: Cambridge University Press, 1980). Although Butler was not a Quaker, the majority of those on her organization's executive board were Friends (*Prostitution and Victorian Society*, 122). Sarah Pugh joined Philadelphia's Moral Education Society in 1876 and contributed to local campaigns against prostitution (*Memorial of Sarah Pugh*, 127–28).

54. Sarah Pugh to Richard Webb, Germantown, Feb. 5, 1867, PSP.

55. *Memorial of Sarah Pugh*, 115; Sarah Pugh to E. P. Nichol, Germantown, April 15, 1867, PSP; *Memorial of Sarah Pugh*, 116–17.

56. *Memorial of Sarah Pugh*, 120.

57. WDK, "Centennial Celebration and International Exposition," *Speeches*, 425. For a discussion of working-class "respectable" culture and home ownership in Philadelphia, see Fones-Wolf, *Trade Union Gospel*, 24–25. For the centennial fair in context, see John D. Bergamini, *The Hundredth Year: The United States in 1876* (New York: G. P. Putnam's, 1976).

58. FK to WDK, Germantown, July 29, 1876, FK Papers, WDK Letters from His Daughter, 1865–1888, NKP.

59. Ibid. William Kelley encouraged his daughter to benefit from the fair as early as June 1875, when he wrote her in response to her description of an early exhibition: "The method with [which] you studied the exhibition was admirable. All excellence is comparative and can only be judged by comparisons such as you made of the porcelain work of exhibiting nations. They who study the exhibition thoroughly as your method will derive most instruction from it." Florence's first published writing may have been on the 1875 exhibition, for, in the only reference to it, William continued, "Save the copy of your article that [I] may read it, which I will do with interest. Did you write over your full name?" (WDK to FK, June 1, 1875).

60. FK, "When Co-education Was Young," 559.

3. Equal Intellectual Opportunity, 1876–1882

1. Women first gained access to higher education in the 1830s, but FK's generation was the first to do so in large numbers. See Solomon, *Educated Women*, 43–62; Woody, *History of Women's Education*, 2:179–303; Horowitz, *Alma Mater*. The single greatest distinction between suffragists and antisuffragists became the extent of their education. See Joyce Follet, "Gender and Community: Kenosha, Wisconsin, 1835–1913" (Ph.D. diss., University of Wisconsin, 1991), ch. 6. For a full treatment of the significance of women's equal access to education, see Gerda Lerner, *The Creation of Feminist Consciousness: From the Middle Ages to Eighteen-seventy* (New York: Oxford University Press, 1993).

2. Scudder, "Relation of College Women,"
2–3. Public universities accepting women by 1870
were: Iowa (1855), Wisconsin (1867), Kansas, Indiana, Minnesota (1869), Missouri, Michigan and
California (1870) (Solomon, *Educated Women*, 53).
For an overview of land-grant institutions, see
Roger L. Williams, *The Origins of Federal Support
for Higher Education: George W. Atherton and the
Land-Grant College Movement* (University Park:
Pennsylvania State University Press, 1991); and
Mary Wright Sewall, "Coeducation in Secondary
Schools and Colleges," *The Arena* 17 (April 1897):
767–75. The significance of higher education for
Kelley's generation of reformers is analyzed in Fitzpatrick, *Endless Crusade*. By 1870 almost a third of
all American colleges and universities open to men
also accepted women, enrolling eleven thousand
female students, 21 percent of the total number.
By 1890 nearly 36 percent of all American undergraduates were female, a total of fifty-six thousand.
Admittedly many of these women pursued sex-segregated studies, especially teacher education, but
even so their presence on campus made coeducation and college-trained women distinct realities
in middle-class American life by the time Florence
Kelley graduated from Cornell in 1882 (Newcomer,
Century of Higher Education, 37 and 46). See also
Goldin, "Meaning of College." For the desire for
college educations among the generation born
in the 1860s and 1870s, see Antler, *The Educated
Woman*, 22–135; and Rebecca A. Martusewicz,
"The Will to Reason: An Archaeology of Womanhood and Education, 1880–1920" (Ph.D. diss.,
University of Rochester, 1988). For the education
of non–college-bound girls, see Rury, *Education
and Women's Work*. For the delayed effects of this
change in the southeast, see Deborah A. Hall,
"'Coming of Age' in the Progressive Era: The
Role of Southern Women's Higher Education between 1900 and 1917" (D.Ed. diss., University of
Kentucky, 1991); and Audrey Thomas McCluskey,
"Mary McLeod Bethune and the Education of Black
Girls in the South, 1904–1923" (Ph.D. diss., Indiana
University, 1991).

3. George Ramanes, "Founding of Queens College," in Dale Spender, ed., *The Education Papers:
Women's Quest for Equality in Britain, 1850–1912*
(New York: Routledge and Kegan Paul, 1987), 32–
33. See Kathryn Kish Sklar, "The Founding of
Mount Holyoke College," in Carol Ruth Berkin
and Mary Beth Norton, eds., *Women of America: A
History* (Boston: Houghton Mifflin, 1979), 177–201;
and Sklar, *Catharine Beecher: A Study in American

Domesticity (New Haven: Yale University Press,
1973). See also Malcolm Seaborne, "Early Theories
of Teacher Education," *British Journal of Educational Studies* 22 (Oct. 1974): 325–39, in which the
possibility of women teachers is not mentioned
during the first half of the nineteenth century.
Butler, in *Education and Employment of Women*,
also based her argument for improvements in the
higher education of women on their work as governesses. See also Vicinus, *Independent Women*,
24; and Joyce Senders Pedersen, "Schoolmistresses and Headmistresses: Elites and Education
in Nineteenth-Century England," *Journal of British
Studies* 15 (1975): 135–62.

Parliamentary testimony about the condition of
female education in England in 1867–68 by Frances
Mary Buss, founder of the North London Collegiate School for Ladies, is reprinted in Hellerstein,
Hume, and Offen, eds., *Victorian Women*, 76–80;
and Gordon, *Gender and Higher Education*. For protests against the lack of higher education for British
middle-class girls, see Maria Gurney, "Are We to
Have Education for Our Middle-Class Girls" (1872)
and others in Spender, *Education Papers*, 186–98.
Secondary schools designed for upper-middle-class daughters did develop between 1850 and 1900,
sustained not by the motivation to provide teachers but by "those professional groups and wealthy
businessmen who aspired towards a new standard
of 'gentility' which would differentiate them from
the bulk of the middle class" (Carol Dyhouse,
*Girls Growing Up in Late Victorian and Edwardian
England* [London: Routledge and Kegan Paul,
1981], 5). The number of publicly funded grammar
schools for girls increased between 1869 and 1874
under the Endowed Schools Act, but growth diminished thereafter. See Sheila Fletcher, *Feminists
and Bureaucrats: A Study in the Development of
Girls' Education in the Nineteenth Century* (Cambridge: Cambridge University Press, 1980). For
an example of the feminist activity behind Newnham and Girton Colleges after 1860, see Andrew
Rosen, "Emily Davies and the Women's Movement, 1862–1867," *Journal of British Studies* 19 (fall
1979), 101–21. For Europe, see Joanne Schneider,
"Volksschullehrerinnen: Bavarian Women Defining
Themselves through their Profession," in Geoffrey
Cocks and Konrad H. Jarausch, *German Professions,
1800–1950* (New York: Oxford University Press,
1990); James C. Albisetti, *Schooling German Girls
and Women: Secondary and Higher Education in the
Nineteenth Century* (Princeton: Princeton University
Press, 1988); Karen Offen, "The Second Sex and

the Baccalauréat in Republican France, 1880–1924," *French Historical Studies* 13 (fall 1983): 252–86; Jo Burr Margadant, *Madame le Professeur: Women Educators in the Third Republic* (Princeton: Princeton University Press, 1990); and James C. Albisetti, "American Women's Colleges through European Eyes, 1865–1914," *HEQ* 32 (winter 1992): 439–58.

4. A few British women first had access to higher education equal to that of men in 1869, with the admission of thirteen students to Girton College, then in Hitchin, Hertfordshire, five of whom proceeded to the second year. In 1871 five female students under the supervision of a mistress formed the nucleus of what later became Newnham College, Cambridge. Girton's fifteen students moved to Cambridge in 1873. Not until 1881 were these colleges officially recognized by the university, and until the 1890s their students numbered only a handful. For an example of the feminist activity behind Newnham and Girton Colleges after 1860, see Andrew Rosen, "Emily Davies and the Women's Movement, 1862–1867," *Journal of British Studies* 19 (fall 1979): 101–21. Two residence halls for women opened at Oxford in 1879 and slowly grew into colleges during the 1880s and 1890s. In London, Bedford College, a struggling institution founded in 1849 as an alternative to Queen's College, became affiliated with the University of London in 1878, when the university began to grant degrees to women. Women began to attend colleges in significant numbers in the 1890s. By 1897 almost eight hundred women students were enrolled, half at institutions in Cambridge and Oxford, half in London. See Barbara Stephen, *Girton College, 1869–1932* (Cambridge: Cambridge University Press, 1933), 24 and 44–75; and Vicinus, *Independent Women*, 124–27. See also Rita McWilliams-Tullberg, *Women at Cambridge: A Men's University—Though of a Mixed Type* (London: Gollancz, 1975). For Webb, see Deborah Epstein Nord, *The Apprenticeship of Beatrice Webb* (Amherst: University of Massachusetts Press, 1985), 39–42; and Jane Lewis, *Women and Social Action in Victorian and Edwardian England* (London: Elgar, 1991), 83–121.

5. See, for example, Wiebe, *Search for Order*.

6. FK, "When Co-education Was Young" (Feb. 1927), 557; Ezra Cornell to his granddaughter, Feb. 17, 1867, quoted in Waterman Thomas Hewett, *Cornell University: A History* (New York: University Publishing Society, 1905), 1:255; M. Carey Thomas to Aunt Hannah, Atlantic City, Sept. 8, 1874, in Dobkin, *Making of a Feminist*, 94, 116. See also Barbara Sicherman, "Reading and Am-

bition: M. Carey Thomas and Female Heroism," *AQ* 45 (March 1993): 73–103. William Kelley knew Andrew White, the university's president. The institution's Quaker affiliations had already attracted other friends of her family. For example, Sarah Pugh attended Cornell's graduation ceremonies in 1877 (*Memorial of Sarah Pugh*, 129). Florence was probably familiar with Caroline Dall's view of the significance of coeducation. A recent book had reprinted her lecture series delivered in Boston between 1859 and 1862. It was dedicated to Lucretia Mott and provided a sweeping critique of women's economic and social status: "We claim for women a share of the [educational] opportunities offered to men, because we believe that they will never be thoroughly taught until they are taught at the same time and in the same classes" (Dall, *The College, the Market and the Court*, 8).

For Kelley, one set of alternatives to Cornell included small coeducational colleges with antislavery or Quaker ties, such as Oberlin in Ohio, which had been admitting women since 1836, or Swarthmore, founded by Hicksite Quakers in Pennsylvania in 1864. However, the religious bent of these institutions probably deterred her. Also academically excellent though too religious was Mount Holyoke, founded in Massachusetts in 1837 and serving for decades thereafter as a rigorous training ground for women missionaries and the wives of missionaries, as well as for schoolteachers. Another set of options were the new women's institutions, such as Vassar College, which began to receive students in 1865, or the fine seminaries patterned after Mount Holyoke, such as Jane Addams's alma mater, Rockford Seminary, in Illinois. Bryn Mawr did not open until 1884, the "Harvard Annex," which later became Radcliffe, was not incorporated until 1882, and Barnard became part of Columbia University in 1889. See Solomon, *Educated Women*, 43–55.

7. FK, "When Co-education Was Young," 557.

8. WDK to FK, Jan. 15, 1875, WDKP; CBK to WDK Jr., Nantucket, Aug. 6, 1875, KFP, reel 1, box 2. The gas WDK mentioned was probably nitrous oxide, which was used for medical therapeutics, including hysteria, as well as serving as an anesthetic. See J. J. Colton, *The Physiological Action of Nitrous Oxide Gas, as Shown by Experiments upon Man and the Lower Animals, Together with Suggestions as to Its Safety, Uses, and Abuses* (Philadelphia: Samuel S. White, 1871). I am grateful to Charles Rosenberg for providing me with this clarification of FK's treatment.

9. Clarke, *Sex in Education*, 125–26.

10. Clarke, *Sex in Education*, 144. For descriptions of the medical and intellectual context of Clarke's book, see Walsh, *Doctors Wanted*, 124–32; Rosalind Rosenberg, *Beyond Separate Spheres: Intellectual Roots of Modern Feminism* (New Haven: Yale University Press, 1982), 5–27; and Fish, "The Struggle over Women's Education," 263–76. See also Elaine Showalter and English Showalter, "Victorian Women and Menstruation," in Martha Vicinus, ed., *Suffer and Be Still: Women in the Victorian Age* (Bloomington: Indiana University Press, 1973), 38–44; Janice Trecker, "Sex, Science, and Education," *AQ* 26 (Oct. 1974): 352–66; and Vern Bullough and Martha Voght, "Women, Menstruation, and Nineteenth-Century Medicine," in Judith Walzer Leavitt, ed., *Women and Health in America: Historical Readings* (Madison: University of Wisconsin Press, 1984).

11. Thomas, "Present Tendencies," 68. The four books were Howe, *Sex and Education;* Anna C. Brackett, *The Education of American Girls* (New York: n.p., 1874); Eliza Bisbee Duffy, *No Sex in Education: Or, An Equal Chance for Both Girls and Boys* (Philadelphia: Stoddart, 1874); and Comfort and Comfort, *Woman's Education and Woman's Health*. Contemporary writings on the debate over women's education can also be found in Louise Michele Newman, ed., *Men's Ideas/Women's Realities: Popular Science, 1870–1915* (New York: Pergamon, 1985), 54–104. An analysis of the campaign against women's education by *Popular Science Monthly* can be found in Zschoche, " 'Preserving Eden,' " 49–76. Rosalind Rosenberg noted in *Beyond Separate Spheres*, 10, that Clarke's biography in *The National Cyclopaedia of American Biography* (New York: James T. White, 1940) reveals that he left Harvard in his junior year because of weak health that hindered his studies for years thereafter. President White of Cornell was quoted at a meeting of the Chicago Woman's Club as thinking that the statistics given against Clarke, "especially from the President of Oberlin and the lady students themselves at the Michigan University, seem to show that the health of young women in colleges is quite as good as out of it" (minutes, Chicago Woman's Club Papers, Dec. 21, 1876, Chicago Historical Society). Charles Darwin's *The Descent of Man and Selection in Relation to Sex* (London: J. Murray, 1871) heightened this debate by emphasizing "difference in the mental powers of the two sexes." See Bell and Offen, *Women, the Family, and Freedom*, 1:408–11.

12. FK to CBK, Ithaca, Oct. 29, 1876, KFP, reel 1,

box 2. For FK's course load, see FK, "When Co-education Was Young;" and "Register of the Studies of Florence Kelley," Deceased Alumni Records, Cornell University Library. Webster's *Third New International Dictionary, Unabridged* defines a "german cotillion" as "a dance consisting of capriciously involved figures intermingled with waltzes."

13. FK to CBK, Oct. 29, 1876. At the age of sixteen, Florence had begun to tutor her older brother. His lack of interest in intellectual activity prompted his father to write her then: "I charged him with doing himself injustice in not maintaining among his fellows the mark nature assigned him. If he will work efficiently with you and your mother he will soon retrieve the past" (WDK to FK, Washington, April 15, 1871, WDKP).

14. FK, "When Co-education Was Young," 559; FK to Marion Talbot, Chicago, Oct. 12, 1896, Marion Talbot Papers, University of Chicago, box 2, folder 1. Coeducation was not a lark for all women students. "It is a fiery ordeal to educate a lady by coeducation," M. Carey Thomas wrote in her journal in 1877. Her parents forbade the kind of companionship Kelley developed with male peers, and perhaps for this reason Thomas reacted more negatively to their dominance on the campus: "There is nothing disagreeable here about the men except that they collect by fifty's on the steps of the different buildings and to pass between them into the lecture rooms is quite an ordeal. They stare so— usually I find myself perfectly crimson by the time I am past them" (M. Carey Thomas to her father and mother, Cornell, [1875], in Dobkin, *Making of a Feminist*, 103, 121). After 1885 coeducation became less freewheeling at Cornell. In part, this was due to declining enrollments, both female and male, which the administration sought to overcome by providing increased chaperonage and academic distinctions between male and female students. See Conable, *Women at Cornell*, 98–134. For the return of women's colleges to more domestic ideals than those that shaped the early years of women's higher education, see Frankfort, *Collegiate Women*.

15. FK, "When Co-education Was Young," 561; Clements to Nicholas Kelley, July 28, 1932, KFP. Kelley's closest male friend at Cornell seems to have been Archer Randolph, who attended the University of Pennsylvania Medical School and died in 1888. See FK, "When Co-education Was Young," 561. References to Randolph can be found in FK to Margaret Hicks, [Philadelphia], April 13, 1881, KFP, box 6, and Deceased Alumni Records, Cornell University Library.

16. FK to CBK, [Ithaca], n.d. [Jan. 1877], WDKP.

17. FK, "When Co-education Was Young," 602. Margaret Hicks, whose father died in 1858 when she was two years old, was raised by her widowed mother, Mary Dana Hicks, a descendant of Richard Dana, who settled in Cambridge, Massachusetts, in 1640. Mary Hicks forged a career in art education, employing Froebel's notions of a child-centered curriculum. In 1900 she married Louis Prang, who had emigrated from Germany after the aborted revolution of 1848. See "Mary Amelia Dana Hicks Prang," in *NAW*. Around 1900 Mary Hicks became one of Florence Kelley's closest personal friends.

For "smashing," see Horowitz, *Alma Mater*, 65–68; Solomon, *Educated Women*, 99–100; and Sahli, "Smashing." Occasionally, schoolgirl crushes led to lifelong homoerotic relationships; often, they preceded traditional marriage. For the female-specific values they embodied, see Carroll Smith-Rosenberg, "The Female World of Love and Ritual: Relations between Women in Nineteenth-Century America," *Signs: A Journal of Women in Culture and Society* 1 (autumn 1975): 1–29.

18. Excerpts from the June 12, 1877, entry of M. Carey Thomas's journal, in Dobkin, *Making of a Feminist*, 119.

19. Dobkin, *Making of a Feminist*, 103, 117; FK to CBK, Oct. 29, 1876. The social origins of college women in this era are discussed in Solomon, *Educated Women*, 62–77. Living arrangements and female culture at women's colleges are analyzed in Horowitz.

20. FK, "My Novitiate" (April 1927), 35. For the First International, see chapter 6, note 1, below. FK corresponded with Livingston, telling her mother, "I had written Mr. L. so hastily that I feared I had hurt his feelings. I need have no qualms of conscience on that score for he seems as impervious as the rest of his sex; and Friday brought a long amusing letter. . . . I really do not see now, how I can do otherwise than let him write as he pleases, unless I quarrel with him openly which I am very far from intending to do. Besides, his letters are very amusing" (FK to CBK, Ithaca, March 23, 1878, KFP, reel 1, box 2).

21. FK to WDK, Ithaca, Nov. 3, 1877, NKP, box 66; FK to CBK, [Ithaca], n.d. [Jan. 1878], Misc. to and from Family, WDKP; FK to CBK, March 23, 1878. FK followed a "Literature" course of study, which required Latin in the first year, substituted German for Greek, and demanded less of mathematics and the natural and physical sciences and "more of the modern languages, history, literature, social

and political science." A contemporary brochure described the literature program as "well suited to those wishing to take up the study of the law and especially to those who aim to work on public opinion through the press, in the lecture room, or in politics, in the best sense. In view of its adaptation to these latter purposes, it has sometimes been incorrectly referred to as the 'Journalistic Course.' " She also pursued the "Arts Course," which required "ancient languages" and was designed "for those intending to enter the ministry and for many of those looking forward to the legal profession." Its requirements were similar to those for the literature course. During her fourth semester, she studied "French, German, Latin, Anglo-Saxon, Solid Geometry . . . [and] Rhetoric." See *The Cornell University: What It Is and What It Is Not* (Ithaca: Cornell University Press, 1872), 6–9.

22. FK to WDK, Ithaca, Dec. 2, 1878, NKP.

23. FK, "My Novitiate," 35. See Anna Haddow, *Political Science in American Colleges and Universities, 1636–1900*, ed. William Anderson (New York: Appleton-Century, 1939; reprint, New York: Octagon, 1969). The first sociology course in the United States was taught by William Graham Sumner at Yale in 1876, the second by Frank B. Sanborn at Cornell in 1884, after Kelley had graduated (Albion Small, "Fifty Years of Sociology in the United States [1865–1915]," *American Journal of Sociology* 21 [May 1916]: 721–864). During Kelley's years as a student, Cornell's offerings in social science were bolstered by occasional lectures by Goldwin Smith, a retired Oxford University professor of history, who opposed both the admission of women to Cornell and woman suffrage. See Conable, *Women at Cornell*, 65–80; Goldwin Smith, "Woman Suffrage," in *Essays on Questions of the Day: Political and Social* (New York: Macmillan, 1894), 197–238; Elisabeth Wallace, *Goldwin Smith: Victorian Liberal* (Toronto: University of Toronto Press, 1957), 48–49. For the establishment of the social science disciplines in the United States, see Ross, *Origins of American Social Science*, 53–97. For social science instruction, see Paul Buck, ed., *Social Sciences at Harvard, 1860–1920* (Cambridge: Harvard University Press, 1965), 18–27 and 93–94; and Robert L. Church, "Economists as Experts: The Rise of an Academic Profession in the United States, 1870–1920," in Lawrence Stone, ed., *The University in Society* (Princeton: Princeton University Press, 1974), 2:571–609. One of the earliest American proponents of social science was Henry C. Carey, William Kelley's friend, who, like Herbert Spencer,

tried to take economics in a sociological direction. See his *Principles of Social Science*, 3 vols. (Philadelphia: J. B. Lippincott, 1858.)

24. FK to WDK, Dec. 2, 1878; Social Science Club Records, Jan. 29, 1879, Cornell University Library. For the club's first speaker, see Social Science Club Records, Oct. 30, 1878. After speaking for the club, Mrs. Newmann was listed as a cospeaker with Florence Kelley and others at mass meetings on behalf of woman suffrage in 1911 and 1912 who "addressed the Germans" (Ida Husted Harper, *The History of Woman Suffrage* [New York: National American Woman Suffrage Association], 6:702). At later club meetings that year, members discussed socialism and heard papers with titles such as "The Injustice in the Relations of Profits and Wages," "The Theory of Government," "The Development of the Scientific View of Nature," "Our System of Election and its Influence on the Form of Our Government," "The Submission of the Laws to the People for Consideration before Their final Adoption," "The Duty of the Country in the Protection of Forests," and "The Referendum." After getting the society off to an excellent start, these student papers gave way in 1879 and 1880 to lectures by faculty, including Professor Henry Carter Adams, who addressed "The Irish Land Question."

25. Margaret Hicks to CBK, [Ithaca], Jan. 13, 1879, KFP, reel 1, box 2.

26. FK, "When Co-education Was Young," 600. See also WDK to CBK, Washington, Jan. 14 and Jan. 19, 1879, KFP, reel 4, box 5. An earlier bout with diphtheria in 1872 should have provided Florence with immunity. See Elizabeth Pugh to FK, Willow Glen, Feb. 15, 1872, NKP: "I shall not be so afraid to have you now that you have had Diphtheria."

27. WDK to CBK, Washington, D.C., Feb. 23, 1879, WDKP.

28. CBK to WDK, Philadelphia, KFP, April 12, 1879, reel 1, box 2; FK to Margaret Hicks, [Philadelphia], April 13, 1881, KFP, box 6; William L. Morris to CBK, Washington, D.C., April 17, 1879, WDKP. For Putnam's visit, see WDK to CBK, April 29 and May 1, 1879, WDKP.

29. WDK to CBK, Brussels, June 24, 1879, KFP, reel 4, box 5; WDK to CBK, June 18 and July 27, 1879, WDKP; WDK to CBK, Paris, Aug. 13, 1879, WDKP. The meeting with White was anticipated in WDK to CBK, Washington, D.C., May 3, 1879, WDKP.

30. Family letters do not mention the details of her work at the Library of Congress. During these years, WDK's power in Congress was restored through his appointment as chairman of the House

Ways and Means Committee, from 1881 to 1883. See Donald R. Kennon and Rebecca M. Rogers, *United States House of Representatives, The Committee on Ways and Means: A Bicentennial History, 1789–1989* (Washington, D.C.: GPO, [1989]), 187.

31. CBK to WDK Jr., Washington, Feb. 14 and 17, 1882, KFP, reel 1, box 2; FK to Margaret Hicks, [Philadelphia], April 13, 1881, KFP, box 6.

32. FK, "My Novitiate," 32. For FK's research at the Library of Congress, see CBK to WDK Jr., Washington, Feb. 14 and 17, 1882, KFP, reel 1, box 2. William Kelley continued to share his political triumphs with his daughter: "I will ask that a copy of the *Protectionist* of Saturday with a full report of my Brooklyn address be sent to Florrie with whom I discussed some of my points in advance," he wrote Caroline (WDK to CBK, Washington, Feb. 1, 1882, KFP, reel 4, box 5). Kelley's influence as a mentor in his daughter's education conforms to a pattern of mentoring in her generation (by fathers and others) studied by Lagemann in *A Generation of Women*. For an analysis of Kelley's overemphasis on her father's influence, see Rebecca Louise Sherrick, "Their Fathers' Daughters: The Autobiographies of Jane Addams and Florence Kelley," *American Studies* (spring 1986), 39–53. Unfortunately, Sherrick's discussion is weakened by factual errors. For example, Kelley's autobiography was not written at "midlife" but between the ages of sixty-seven and sixty-eight.

33. FK, "My Novitiate," 32.

34. FK, "Changes in the Legal Status of the Child" (Aug. 1882), 84, 95, 91, 84.

35. For a view of earlier family law, see Daniel Walker Howe, "The Social Science of Horace Bushnell," *JAH* 70, 2 (Sept. 1983): 305–22. For the English example of changes in child custody, see Bell and Offen, *Women, the Family, and Freedom*, 2:161–63. For Cady Stanton's views, see DuBois, *Elizabeth Cady Stanton*. Kelley was doubtlessly also influenced by Caroline H. Dall, and her book, *The College, the Market and the Court*. FK's vision of the links between public policy and women's activism was also shaped by her participation in the New Century Club in Philadelphia, described in chapter 4 below. For an assessment of Kelley's originality, see Grossberg, *Governing the Hearth*. Grossberg concluded (298) that Kelley's essay was a harbinger of the approaching Progressive Era. Ignoring her gendered approach to her topic, he contends that her essay "reveal[ed] the reformers' incompatible objectives: trying to preserve republican individualism and economic liberalism,

while creating a more cooperative community and active state."

36. FK, "Changes in the Legal Status of the Child," 86, 19, 97. Her essay drew on evidence ranging chronologically from the Elizabethan Poor Law to 1881 reports by Massachusetts state agencies. One of her most important sources was "Legal Rights of Children," *Circulars of the Bureau of Education*, no. 3 (Washington: GPO, 1880), 141–236.

37. FK, "Changes in the Legal Status of the Child," 95, 88. Modern support for Kelley's interpretation of the effects of suffrage emphasizes the corporate nature of Puritanism rather than suffrage per se. See James Axtell, *The School Upon a Hill: Education and Society in Colonial New England* (New Haven: Yale University Press, 1974), 5–50, for the enforcement of New England school laws.

In England as well as in the United States, church- or charity-sponsored schools were important antecedents of public systems. Nevertheless, Kelley's analysis is sustained by J. S. Hurt, *Elementary Schooling and the Working Classes, 1860–1918* (London: Routledge and Kegan Paul, 1979), 1. The Elementary Education Act of 1870 gave a great boost to public education by requiring some schooling for all children, not only the small numbers affected by the factory acts. See also O. Jocelyn Dunlop and Richard D. Denman, *English Apprenticeship and Child Labour: A History* (New York: Macmillan, 1912), 261–95; and Henry Pelling, *America and the British Left: From Bright to Bevan* (London: Black, 1956), 30–34.

38. FK, "Changes in the Legal Status of the Child," 97, 87, 96, and 95. For Mary Carpenter, see Jane Rendall, *Origins of Modern Feminism: Women in Britain, France, and the United States, 1780–1860* (London: Macmillan, 1985), 265–70; Mary Carpenter, *Reformatory Schools* (London: C. Gilpin, 1851); and Joseph Estlin Carpenter, *The Life and Work of Mary Carpenter* (London: Macmillan and Co., 1879). Carpenter's fame was reinforced in the United States by a visit she made in 1873 to Boston and other cities. "The impression of her teaching and example will be long felt," declared the *Journal of Social Science* (5 [1873]: 6).

39. [Henry Adams], *Democracy* (New York: Holt, 1880).

40. See Reps, *Washington on View*, 194–200.

41. Poem in FK's handwriting, [1882], WDKP.

42. FK, "When Co-education Was Young," 562. For Kelley's honorable mention, see the Cornell University Register, 1882/83, Cornell University Library. For Kelley and Hicks in Boston, see FK,

"When Co-education Was Young," 563. Margaret Hicks was listed as a delegate to the 1881 founding meeting, Kelley as a member in 1884 (American Association of University Women Papers, Washington, D.C., reel one).

43. FK, "When Co-education Was Young," 562.

44. For the changes in the University of Pennsylvania's admission policy, see Edward Potts Cheyney, *History of the University, 1740–1940* (Philadelphia: University of Pennsylvania Press, 1940), 297–306. For women in graduate study, see Margaret W. Rossiter, "Doctorates for American Women, 1868–1907," *HEQ* 22 (summer 1982): 160. In 1877 Boston University became the first to award a doctorate to a woman. Institutions that granted doctorates to women before 1890 were Syracuse University (seven); Boston University (four); College of Wooster (four); Cornell University (two); The University of Michigan (two); Smith College (two); and four others that awarded one each. Biographies of early Cornell women graduates in *A Tribute to Henry W. Sage from the Women Graduates of Cornell University* (Ithaca: Andrus and Church, 1895), show that in the class of 1875 Julia Thomas studied at Leipzig, Germany, and became a professor of Greek at Wellesley College in the 1890s; M. Carey Thomas, class of 1877, studied at Leipzig and Zürich and became a professor of literature (and later president) at Bryn Mawr College; Mary Roberts, class of 1880, studied at Cornell and became an instructor in history and economics at Wellesley and Stanford; Alice Goddard, class of 1881, studied at Zürich and Cambridge universities and became an associate professor of Classics at the Woman's College of Baltimore; Emily Gregory, also class of 1881, studied at Zürich and became a professor of botany at Barnard College; Alfreda Withington studied at Cornell and in Europe, received an M.D. from the Woman's Medical College of the New York Infirmary and became an instructor in physiology at the college. Margaret Hicks completed a bachelor's degree in architecture in 1880 after graduating from Cornell in 1878.

45. *A Tribute to Henry W. Sage*, n.p.

46. Addams, *Twenty Years at Hull House*, 119. Addams's views on this subject were first published in "A New Impulse to An Old Gospel," *Forum* 14 (November 1892): 345–58; and "The College Woman and the Family Claim," *Chicago Commons* 4 (Sept. 1898): 3–7. For a discussion of this theme among early Wellesley graduates, see Joyce Antler, "'After College What?': New Graduates and the Family Claim," *AQ* 32 (fall 1980): 409–34. The high

point of public consciousness of the gap between women's access to college educations and their ability to put that education to some use developed in the 1890s with such publications as Charlotte Porter, "After Graduation, What?" *Outlook* 48 (Nov. 18, 1893): 892–93; and Helen Ekin Starrett, *After College, What? For Girls* (New York: T. Y. Crowell, 1896).

Despite the seeming inevitability of marriage and childbirth for many college graduates, their falling fertility rates prompted much contemporary commentary. An average of 50 percent of college-educated women did not marry (see Solomon, *Educated Women*, 120; and Rota, "Between 'True Women' and 'New Women,'" 285). This percentage was considerably higher than that for the female population as a whole, although there, too, record numbers (higher than in the late twentieth century) never married. The proportion of never married native-born Massachusetts women between the ages of thirty-five and forty-four was 25.6 percent for a cohort born in 1870. See Peter Uhlenberg, "A Study of Cohort Life Cycles: Cohorts of Native-Born Massachusetts Women, 1830–1920," in Maris A. Vinovskis, ed., *Studies in American Historical Demography* (New York: Academic, 1979), 420.

47. FK, "My Novitiate," 31.

48. WDK to CBK, Washington, July 4, 1882, KFP, reel 4, box 5; "Children, Legally Considered," *Boston Evening Transcript*, Sept. 7, 1882, NKP, box 63; Sophonisba Breckinridge at Memorial Services for Mrs. Florence Kelley and Miss Julia C. Lathrop, Hull House, Chicago, May 6, 1932, Anita McCormick Blaine Papers, Madison, 32; WDK to CBK, Washington, Dec. 4, 1882, KFP, reel 4, box 5. Kelley's thesis was printed in *The International Review* (Aug. 1882).

4. Brain Work Waiting for Women, 1882–1884

1. FK, "Need Our Working Women Despair?" (Nov. 1882), 521.

2. The most complete discussion of female social science activity before 1890 is Leach, *True Love and Perfect Union*. For the period after 1890, see Fitzpatrick, *Endless Crusade*.

3. Franklin B. Sanborn, "Social Sciences, Their Growth and Future," *Journal of Social Science* 23 (Sept. 1886): 10. See Haskell, *Emergence of Pro-*

fessional Social Science, 136; and Ross, *Origins of American Social Science*, 63.

4. Franklin B. Sanborn, "Address of the Chairman of the Department," *Journal of Social Science* 23 (Nov. 1887): 21. For the founding of the ASSA, see Brock, *Investigation and Responsibility*, 37–39; and O'Keefe, "Bond of Perfection," 93–101. Women were also important as publicists. In 1881, as general secretary of the ASSA, Franklin Sanborn summarized the "three-fold aspect of social science in America" as "The Educational Work of Social Science; Its Administrative Work; [and] Its Work of Agitation and Indoctrination" and pointed to "agitation and indoctrination" carried on "by persons who at other times are engaged in the practical administration of public charities, reformatories, and prisons" (Sanborn, "Three-Fold Aspect of Social Science," 33).

The activism of women in early American social science paralleled that of British women, who also carved out a place for themselves in the study of society on the basis of their gender-specific expertise. See Cobbe, "Social Science Congresses." There (94) she quoted an address by Lord Shaftesbury that commented on "the value and peculiar nature of the assistance" given by women to social science. "Men may do what must be done on a large scale; but, the instant the work becomes individual, and personal, the instant it requires tact and feeling, from that instant it passes into the hands of women. It is essentially their province, in which may be exercised all their moral powers, and all their intellectual faculties. It will give them their full share in the vast operations the world is yet to see." See also Barbara Caine, *Victorian Feminists* (Oxford: Oxford University Press, 1992), 103–49; and Eileen Yeo's forthcoming book, *Social Science, Class and Gender in Britain, 1789–1914* (London: Virago).

5. Quoted in Leach, *True Love and Perfect Union*, 185. During the 1870s and 1880s the Ladies' Social Science Association also convened as "the Woman's Congress" and launched the development of the American Association of University Women (*True Love and Perfect Union*, 86, 185, 317 passim). For FK's participation in the Ladies' Social Science Association, see FK, "When Co-education Was Young" (Feb. 1927), 563.

6. See the Working-Women's Protective Union, *Fifth Annual Report* (New York: Gray and Green, 1868), 2. The union's annual reports from 1868 to 1894 are at the New York Public Library. See also Ginzberg, *Women and the Work of Benevolence*, 131–211; Walter I. Trattner, "Louisa Lee Schuyler and

the Founding of the State Charities Aid Association," *The New-York Historical Society Quarterly* 51 (July 1967): 233–48; and Cumbler, "Politics of Charity." For the dilemma of women college graduates, see Joyce Antler, "'After College, What?': New Graduates and the Family Claim," *AQ* 32 (fall 1980), 409–34; Antler, *The Educated Woman*, 136–201; and Linda W. Rosenzweig, "'The Anchor of My Life': Middle-Class American Mothers and College-Educated Daughters, 1880–1920," *JSH* 25 (fall 1991), 5–25. For the cross-class aspects of women's antebellum activism, see Benson, "Business Heads." For an early failed effort at cross-class organization, the Working Women's Association of 1868, see Ellen Carol DuBois, *Feminism and Suffrage: The Emergence of an Independent Women's Movement in America, 1848–1869* (Ithaca: Cornell University Press, 1978), 138–53. In the 1880s Grace Dodge founded working girls' clubs in New York, "feeling the desire for increased knowledge among self-respecting women." See Abbie Graham, *Grace H. Dodge: Merchant of Dreams* (New York: Woman's, 1926), 66–98; and Katz, "Grace Hoadley Dodge." Dodge was recruited into social activism by Louisa Schuyler, leader of the New York Sanitary Commission.

7. Alba Edwards, *Comparative Occupational Statistics for the U.S., 1870–1940* (Washington: GPO, 1943), 91–92, 99. See also Brown, "Working-Women of New York"; and Kessler-Harris, *A Woman's Wage*. However, a substantial portion of women's income-producing activity escaped the attention of the census. For a discussion of that issue, see Nancy Folbre, "Women's Informal Market Work in Massachusetts, 1875–1920," *Social Science History* 17 (spring 1993): 135–60.

8. U.S. Commissioner of Labor, *Fourth Annual Report, Working Women in Large Cities* (Washington, D.C.: GPO, 1889), 62–64. Claudia Goldin, *Understanding the Gender Gap: An Economic History of American Women* (New York: Oxford University Press, 1990), 62. Between 1820 and 1860 average female earnings rose from about one-third to about 45 percent of average male earnings. By the mid-1880s that ratio rose to about 58 percent, a level that, with the exception of the Great Depression of the 1930s, remained fairly constant for the next hundred years. Although women employed in manufacturing in 1880 were paid about the same proportion of male earnings as women working in manufacturing in 1980, the purchasing power of both men's and women's wages was vastly greater

in 1980 than in 1880, when both men and women earned relatively low wages.

9. See Laurie and Schmitz, "Manufacture and Productivity," 47, 521.

10. For the visit with Turner, see CBK to WDK, Philadelphia, April 12, 1879, KFP, reel 1, box 2. Turner was also a founding member of the Pennsylvania Woman Suffrage Association in 1869. See Ira V. Brown, *Mary Grew: Abolitionist and Feminist (1813–1896)* (Selinsgrove, Pa.: Susquehanna University Press, 1991), 175–76.

11. Wormeley, "The Sanitary Commission;" Livermore, "Coöperative Womanhood," 285. For more on the Sanitary Commission, see Attie, "'A Swindling Concern'"; Ginzberg, *Women and the Work of Benevolence*, 133–73; Parrish, "The Western Sanitary Commission"; George M. Frederickson, *The Inner Civil War: Northern Intellectuals and the Crisis of the Union* (New York: Harper and Row, 1965), 102–5; and Peter Dobkin Hall, *The Organization of American Culture, 1700–1900: Private Institutions, Elites, and the Origins of American Nationality* (New York: New York University Press, 1982), 226–27. Women of the Northwest Sanitary Commission in Chicago raised more than $75,000 in five days. Fairs elsewhere were equally successful, raising more than $250,000 in Cincinnati, $50,000 in Boston, and in New York and Brooklyn more than $1,300,000. The combined efforts of these fairs contributed more than $5,000,000 in twelve months to the Union war effort. The success of the Philadelphia fund-raising was based in part on the strategy—devised initially in 1865 by a great-granddaughter of Benjamin Franklin as a proposal for improved street cleaning and later implemented in the city's Charity Organization Society—of dividing the city into small neighborhoods, with a person in each who reported to a larger board. For more on the fairs, see Darney, "Women and World's Fairs," 4–8, 17; and Attie, "'A Swindling Concern," 301–6.

12. Croly, *History of the Woman's Club Movement*, 21. See also Blair, *Clubwoman as Feminist*, 15–38. For the derivation of the name "Sorosis," see Croly, *History*, 16, 18. Plans for secular self-improvement also inspired the founding of the New England Woman's Club in 1868, the Chicago Woman's Club in 1876, and sixty-five others, which united with Sorosis in 1890 to form the General Federation of Women's Clubs (Croly, *History*, 88.)

13. Quoted in Buhle, *Women and American Socialism*, 65. The WCTU declared this goal in 1884 in the minutes of its eleventh annual meeting. See

also Leeman, *"Do Everything" Reform;* and Bordin, *Woman and Temperance,* 52, 62, 89, 92–118. By its tenth anniversary in 1884 the union was organized in every state and territory at the state level and at the county level in over half the counties in the United States, with 150,000 dues-paying members by 1890. For the explosion of female religious leadership that matched this outburst of lay activity, see Janette Hassey, *No Time for Silence: Evangelical Women in Public Ministry around the Turn of the Century* (Grand Rapids, Mich.: Academie Books, 1986).

14. Darney, "Women and World's Fairs," 20–27. Turner read a paper on women's clubs at the centennial's Women's Congress and edited the fair's all-woman newspaper, *New Century for Women.* For the New Century Club's motto, see [New Century Guild], *One Hundredth Anniversary,* 14, 26.

15. Although in "My Novitiate" (April 1927), Kelley wrote (32) that she began teaching workingwomen in the fall after graduation, the records of the New Century Club show that it was the year before; for this and more on the school, see [New Century Guild], *One Hundredth Anniversary,* 27–28. For more on the club, see Campbell, *Women Wage-Earners,* 240–45. Many of the club's leaders, including Eliza Sproat Turner, were also leaders in the Philadelphia Society for Organizing Charity, founded in 1878, which sought to rationalize and strengthen voluntary philanthropy to make it a viable alternative to public relief and to increase the importance of women in the administration of social welfare. For the social movement of which this school was part, see Priscilla Murolo, "Working Girls' Clubs, 1884–1928: Class and Gender on the Common Ground of Womanhood" (Ph.D. diss., Yale University, 1992). See also Rauch, "Unfriendly Visitors."

16. [New Century Guild], *One Hundredth Anniversary,* 30.

17. New Century Working Women's Guild, minutes, Oct. 19, 1882, New Century Guild Papers (hereafter NCGP), Philadelphia; bound vol., Treasurer's Report, 1882, New Century Working Women's Guild, NCGP; bound vol., "Evening Classes and Office Accounts, Dec. 1, 1882 to Feb. 8, 1889," 1, NCGP. For legal aid offered by the club, see also *Journal of Women's Work,* published every four weeks by the New Century Guild of Working Women from 1887 to 1913, vol. 1, no. 1 (Dec. 10, 1887). The importance of the library was stressed in one of the earliest historical accounts of the guild, an undated newspaper clipping from around 1894,

which quoted Mrs. Turner, "Once established, the first thing the Guild started out to accomplish was to provide itself with a library" (scrapbook of clippings, NCGP). Most of the guild's financing came from contributions rather than dues. In 1884, for example, the executive board received $11.30 in dues and $266 in contributions and maintained a balance on hand of $1,561, most of which came from past contributions. Reflecting their interest in social science, the library's first magazine subscription was to *Popular Science Monthly* (Year Books, New Century Guild, 1885–1908, Executive Board report, 1884, 8, NCGP). Internal evidence indicates that legal assistance was one of the earliest dimensions of guild activities. I am grateful to Marie Kitzmiller, president of the New Century Guild in 1986, for aiding my access to these records before they were donated to the Historical Society of Pennsylvania.

18. See "Charles Wyllys Elliott" in Rossiter Johnson, ed., *The Twentieth Century Biographical Dictionary of Notable Americans* (Boston: Biographical Society, 1904). Julia Ward Howe also replied to Elliott's article: "The Industrial Value of Woman."

19. FK, "Need Our Working Women Despair?" 518–19.

20. Ibid., 519–20.

21. For a contemporary combination of the views that sought to limit women's employment and those that sought to improve it through better working conditions, see Ames, *Sex in Industry.* See also Sklar, " 'The Greater Part of the Petitioners.' "

22. See "Mary Putnam Jacobi," in *NAW;* and Arno Herzig, *Abraham Jacobi: Die Entwicklung zum sozialistischen und revolutionären Demokraten: Briefe, Dokumente, Pressartikel (1848–1853)* (Minden: Mindener Beiträge, 1980).

23. Mary Putnam Jacobi, *The Question of Rest for Women during Menstruation* (New York: Putnam, 1877), 225, 226, and 231. Jacobi's methods and her receipt in 1876 of the annual Boylston Medical Prize awarded by Harvard Medical School are described in Walsh, *Doctors Wanted,* 130. For an assessment of Jacobi's pioneering place in twentieth-century writings on menstruation, see Fausto-Sterling, *Myths of Gender.* See also Morantz, "Feminism, Professionalism, and Germs"; and Wright, "Health Statistics of Female College Graduates." For the best treatment of working-class women in a book opposing Clarke, see Comfort and Comfort, *Woman's Education and Woman's Health,* 122–24.

24. Jacobi, *Question of Rest,* 232.

25. Clarke, *Sex in Education,* 131–34, 159–60.

26. FK, "Need Our Working Women Despair?" 523.

27. Ibid., 523–24.

28. Ibid., 526. The "Song of the Shirt" refers to a genre of protest engendered by the long hours and low wages of women seamstresses, which began with a poem of that title published in 1843. See Edelstein, "They Sang 'The Song of the Shirt.'"

29. FK, "Need Our Working Women Despair?" 523–27.

30. Margaret Hicks to CBK, [Cambridge, Mass.], Dec. 14, 1882, KFP, reel 1, box 2; WDK to CBK, Dec. 11, 1882, WDKP. The classmate Hicks married was Karl Volkman, later head of the Volkman school (FK, "When Co-education Was Young," 561).

31. FK, "When Co-Education Was Young," 562. See also M. Carey Thomas to her mother, London, Jan. 13, [1883], and [Paris, April 1883], M. Carey Thomas Papers (hereafter MCTP), Bryn Mawr. For the itinerary, see WDK to CBK, Washington, Jan. 21, 1883, WDKP. For women at Oxford and Cambridge, see Rita McWilliams-Tullberg, "Women and Degrees at Cambridge University, 1862–1897," in Martha Vicinus, ed., *A Widening Sphere: Changing Roles of Victorian Women* (Bloomington: Indiana University Press, 1977), 117–45; and Susan J. Leonardi, *Dangerous by Degrees: Women at Oxford and the Somerville College Novelists* (New Brunswick: Rutgers University Press, 1989).

32. M. Carey Thomas to her mother, Jan. 13, [1883], and [April 1883]. William Kelley described Florence's assistance of her brother to the editor of *The International Review:* "My daughter is now crossing the ocean in care of her stricken brother whose restoration to health depends in obtaining a completeness of nervous and mental repose which could not be hoped for at home" (WDK to Mr. Handy, Washington, Dec. 11, 1882, WDKP, box 2).

33. CBK to WDK, May 4, 1883, KFP. Under the editorship of Horace Greeley, the *New York Tribune* was an aggressively Republican paper. Caroline wrote Will Jr., that "[Florrie] felt very much like giving up writing for the Tribune, and had written [them] saying so, but she suddenly made up her mind to continue a little while at least and she has just read aloud to me a letter which I think surpasses all that she has sent for some time" (CBK to WDK Jr., Feb. 24, 1884, letter in the possession of Jane Holland, Kelley's niece, to whom I am grateful for permission to quote from it). Later Florence and her father discussed the publication of her letters in a book. She wrote him, "It will be a crude little

book; but if it can be published in very cheap form it may fall into hands in which it will not be less useful for its crudity. But I do not wish to publish it unless Mr. Houghton feels sure that it will pay for itself. I am glad Captain Lemon likes the idea" (FK to WDK, Zürich, Jan. 2, 1884, KFP, reel 1, box 2).

34. FK to CBK, Broadstairs, July 8, 1883, KFP, reel 1, box 2. The emphasis suggests that on other occasions she and Ruth slept in one bed. The location of Broadstairs comes from an interview with WDK in the *New York Tribune,* Oct. 28, 1883, 3, col. 1.

35. FK, "My Novitiate," 31. For Anthony's opinion of FK, see Susan B. Anthony Diary, June 15, 1883, Library of Congress (or Patricia Holland and Ann Gordon, eds., *The Papers of Elizabeth Cady Stanton and Susan B. Anthony,* series 3, reel 22, #0979).

36. WDK interview, *New York Tribune,* Oct. 28, 1883. See also Angela V. John, *By the Sweat of Their Brow: Women Workers at Victorian Coal Mines* (London: Routledge and Kegan Paul, 1984); and Jane Mark-Lawson and Anne Witz, "From 'Family Labour' to 'Family Wage'? The Cast of Women's Labour in Nineteenth-Century Coalmining," *Social History* 13 (May 1988): 151–74.

37. WDK to CBK, [England], Aug. 28, 1883, WDKP; FK, "My Novitiate," 32–33. Kelley recalled the injustice of England's compulsory school laws, which required school attendance but did not provide free schools. When families failed to send their children because they could not pay the fees, the courts ordered mothers imprisoned rather than fathers, since women worked for lower wages and so the loss to the family would be less.

38. FK, "Need Our Working Women Despair?" 525.

39. FK, "My Novitiate," 33.

40. CBK to WDK, Zürich, Oct. 19, 1883, WDKP; CBK to WDK, Zürich, Dec. 14, 1883, NKP. For Putnam's help in Zürich, see CBK to WDK, Zürich, Oct. 7, 1883, NKP.

41. For FK's routine, see CBK to WDK, Zürich, Jan. 20, 1884, NKP. For more on The University of Zürich, see Ernst Gagliardi, Hans Nabholz, and Jean Strohl, *Die Universität Zürich, 1833–1933, und Ihre Vorläufer* (Zürich: Verlag der Erziehungsdirection, 1938), 658 and 831. See also n.a., *Das Frauenstudium an den Schweizer Hochschulen* (Zürich: Rascher, 1928), 49, which mentions FK. For FK's courses with Platter, see Register of Feepayers, UU 24.21.S.190, Universität Zürich. In the spring of 1884 she enrolled in Professor Platter's courses

on "theory of constitutional law" and "political economy of governmental practice" and attended lectures by others on "foundations of the philosophy of law" and "general constitutional law."

42. For the composition of the student body, see the Register of Feepayers, Universität Zürich. There were forty-one foreign students among the one hundred and sixty-three male medical students. For women's medical institutions, see Walsh, *Doctors Wanted;* and Regina Morantz-Sanchez, *Sympathy and Science: Women Physicians in American Medicine* (New York: Oxford University Press, 1985). 69. For the Russian colony in Zürich, see Richard Stites, *The Women's Liberation Movement in Russia: Feminism, Nihilism, and Bolshevism, 1860– 1930* (Princeton: Princeton University Press, 1978), 131–138; Barbara Alpern Engel and Clifford N. Rosenthal, eds., *Five Sisters: Women Against the Tsar: The Memoirs of Five Revolutionaries, of the 1870s* (New York: Knopf, 1975), xxiii–xxiv, 4–26; J. M. Meijer, *Knowledge and Revolution: The Russian Colony in Zürich, 1870–1873: A Contribution to the Study of Russian Populism* (Assen, The Netherlands: Van Gorcum, 1955), 131–39; Johanson, *Women's Struggle for Higher Education in Russia*, 8–53; and Thomas N. Bonner, "Pioneering in Women's Medical Education in the Swiss Universities, 1864–1914," *Gesnerus: Swiss Journal of the History of Medicine and Sciences* 45 (1988): 461–473.

43. CBK to WDK, Jan. 20, 1884; CBK to WDK, Zürich, Dec. 3, 1883, Jane Holland private collection, Gainesville, Florida.

44. FK to WDK, Jan. 2, 1884; CBK to WDK, Zürich, Dec. 23, 1883, KFP, reel 1, box 2. The cause of Margaret's death was never stated.

45. FK to WDK, Jan. 2, 1884. Wischnewetzky was pronounced Vish-ne-VET-sky.

46. FK to WDK, Jan. 2, 1884.

47. FK to Susan B. Anthony, Jan. 21, 1884, NKP, box 62.

48. WDK to CBK, Washington, Jan. 7, 1884, KFP, reel 4, box 5; CBK to WDK, Florence, Italy, March 25, 1884, KFP, reel 1, box 2.

49. FK, [no title], *New York Tribune*, May 28, 1884, 4, 5. Kilgore was first refused admission to the bar by the Pennsylvania Supreme Court in 1870; in 1871 she was denied admission to the University of Pennsylvania Law School. She eventually obtained a law degree from Penn in 1883 and, after being admitted to practice before the state Orphans' Court in 1883, she was admitted to the Courts of Common Pleas in 1884 and the state supreme court in 1886. See Lelia Robinson, "Women Lawyers in the United States," *Green Bag* 2 (1890): 10, 28; and Robert R. Bell, *The Philadelphia Lawyer: A History, 1735–1945* (Selinsgrove, Pa.: Susquehanna University Press, 1992), 164–65.

50. FK, "My Novitiate," 34–35.

51. FK, "My Novitiate," 35; Eduard Bernstein, *My Years of Exile: Reminiscences of a Socialist* (New York: Harcourt, Brace and Howe, 1921), 97. Bernstein became known as an advocate of socialism within capitalism. See Peter Gay, *The Dilemma of Democratic Socialism: Eduard Bernstein's Challenge to Marx* (New York: Columbia University Press, 1952), 28–46; and Pierson, *Marxist Intellectuals.*

52. FK, "My Novitiate," 35.

53. See Carl Diehl, *Americans and German Scholarship, 1770–1870* (New Haven: Yale University Press, 1978); and Jürgen Herbst, *The German Historical School in American Scholarship: A Study in the Transfer of Culture* (Ithaca: Cornell University Press, 1965), 1–22. See also Joseph Dorfman, "The Role of the German Historical School in American Economic Thought," *The American Economic Review* 45 (May 1955): 17–39. For an overview of students abroad in the 1880s, see Stokes, "American Progressives and the European Left," 5–28.

54. Ely, *Recent American Socialism*, 71–72. See Rader, *The Academic Mind and Reform*, 28–82. Raised in a Presbyterian manse in upstate New York, Ely considered it "a matter of course that I should go abroad to study, preferably to Germany" when he received a fellowship for graduate study in 1876 (Ely, *Ground Under Our Feet*, 36). See also Kloppenberg, *Uncertain Victory*, 207–208; and Lowe, "Richard T. Ely." He studied with professors who were "very sympathetic to the aspirations of the workingman" and viewed economics as "the study of man in society in terms of its historical growth" (Ely, *Ground Under Our Feet*, 44). Yet in contrast to Kelley's affiliation with exiled activists, Ely associated with the professorial socialists who helped Bismarck forge social legislation designed to undercut the appeal of socialism. German thought was dominated by Hegelian views of modern civil society (which Marx continued) as the site of crass materialism, modern property relations, and egotism. See "Civil Society," in Bottomore et al., *Dictionary of Marxist Thought*, 72–74. Ely was attracted to the Hegelian "German doctrine that the state protects freedom against attacks from society" (Richard T. Ely to Henry Demarest Lloyd, Madison, Wisconsin, June 3, 1895, Henry D. Lloyd Papers). While governmental policy might be corrupt or flawed and civil society might consist of

self-serving individuals, in Ely's view, the state itself remained uncorrupted, and its potential for the defense of freedom undiminished.

Ely provided a very credible summary of Marx's writings in *French and German Socialism,* quoting favorable comments about Marx from both German and American sources and explaining the connection between Marx's theory of surplus value and the movement to reduce the length of the working day (170–182). See also Dombrowski, *Early Days of Christian Socialism,* 50–59; and Frederick, *Knights of the Golden Rule,* 14–15.

Important male contemporaries who also studied in Germany included Henry Carter Adams, W. E. B. Du Bois, and Albion Small. Adams studied in Berlin and Bonn and worked with the chief of the Prussian Statistical Bureau. Thereafter he advocated the intervention of the state in capital-labor relations through government regulation. When these ideas drove him out of Cornell, he found a safe haven at the University of Michigan until his death in 1921. See John A. DeBrizzi, *Ideology and the Rise of Labor Theory in America* (Westport: Greenwood, 1983), 50–51. W. E. B. Du Bois returned to the United States in the 1890s with an expanded understanding of the organization of race and class in social structures. See W. E. B. Du Bois, *Dusk of Dawn: An Essay toward an Autobiography of a Race Concept* (New York: Harcourt, Brace, and World, 1940), 42–48. Albion Small, founder of sociology at the University of Chicago, also studied with Du Bois's mentor, Gustav Schmoller. For Small, see Ross, *Origins of American Social Science,* 122–38.

55. Quoted in Dombrowski, *Early Days of Christian Socialism,* 51. See also John R. Everett, *Religion in Economics: A Study of John Bates Clark, Richard T. Ely, Simon N. Patten* (New York: King's Crown, 1946); and Ross, "Socialism and American Liberalism," 5–80. Ely modeled the goals of the American Economic Association upon those of the *Verein für Sozialpolitik* in Germany. See Watkins, "The Professors and the Unions," 105; Eugen von Phillipovitch, "The Verein für Sozialpolitik," *Quarterly Journal of Economics* 5 (Jan. 1891): 220–37; and Irmela Gorges, "The Social Survey in Germany before 1933," in Bulmer, Bales, and Sklar, *The Social Survey,* 316–39. Interestingly enough, women protested against institutional sex segregation at AEA conventions; in the 1880s they boycotted a separate reception arranged for female members when they were excluded from the association's main reception. See Ely, *Ground Under Our Feet,* 147; *Publications of the American Economic Association,*

vol. 1, *Constitution, By-Laws and Resolutions of the American Economic Association, with List of Officers and Members of the American Economic Association. Supplement* (Baltimore: Guggenheimer, Weil, 1889), 27.

56. WDK, *Congressional Record,* 48th Cong., 1st sess., June 3, 1884, 4774.

57. WDK, *Congressional Record,* 48th Cong., 1st sess., June 19, 1884, 5354–55.

58. FK, "My Novitiate," 35. October 12, 1884, was mentioned inaccurately as the date of their marriage in FK to Nicholas Kelley (hereafter NK), New York, June 19, 1908, NKP. October 14 is confirmed on their marriage certificate at Zivilstandsamt, Abteilung Geburten, Stadthaus, Zürich.

5. To Act on This Belief, 1884–1886

1. CBK to WDK Jr., Feb. 24, 1884, Jane K. Holland private collection, quoted in Katherine K. Holland, "Daddy's Girl: A Family Biography of Florence Kelley" (senior thesis, Amherst College, 1980), 30; FK to Mary Thorne Lewis [May Lewis] (hereafter MTL), Heidelberg, March 19, 1885, NKP, box 63, quoted in Blumberg, *Florence Kelley,* 45. Henceforward, when Blumberg brought a source to my attention, I cite her book; however, in all cases I have consulted the original. Since in many cases I use more of the source, my pagination sometimes differs. Occasionally, I disagree with Blumberg's interpretation of the source and draw different conclusions from the same document.

Uneasy at the time, Caroline wrote to William from Interlaken: "I have never felt quite right since Florrie went back to Zurich 15 days after we were banished, but I did not like to oppose it too much, because she would have been so unhappy. I thought it could do no good to tell you, as it would only make you anxious. She is very well, and bright and exceedingly busy. We saw her very little last week at Gersau because she went up into the woods to study, but it was pleasant to have her at meals, and a little while in the evenings" (CBK to WDK, Interlaken, May 29, 1884, KFP, reel 1, box 2).

2. WDK to FK, Washington, June 18, 1884, WDKP, box 4.

3. CBK to WDK Jr., [Zürich, June 1884], KFP, reel 1, box 2.

4. Student Register, University of Zürich.

5. CBK to WDK Jr., [June 1884]. For FK's move, see CBK to WDK Jr., n.d., [June 1884], KFP.

6. CBK to WDK, [Zürich, Sept.–Oct. 1884], NKP. One measure of the gossip her situation generated was an 1892 letter by Florence's contemporary Isabel Howland, who wrote to her aunt in Boston about what Alice Ames asserted was "the real cause" of Florence's alienation from her father. "Judge Kelley himself told Mrs. Ames that Wischniewietsky [*sic*] wanted Florence to live with him without being married and he had gained her consent, having won her over to his radical views. Judge Kelley found it out and positively insisted upon the marriage being performed, which displeased both the young people" (Isabel Howland to Emily Howland, Boston, March 29, 1892, Emily Howland Papers, Collection #2681, Cornell University Library). Unlike German law, American citizenship law at this time did not deprive of their citizenship women who married aliens. An 1855 law gave American citizenship automatically to women who married American citizens or whose husbands became American citizens. A 1907 law declared that "any woman who marries a foreigner shall take the national of her husband." In 1922 women's citizenship became independent from marriage in the Married Women's Independent Citizenship Act. See Lemons, *The Woman Citizen*, 64–65; and Virginia Sapiro, "Women, Citizenship, and Nationality: Immigration and Naturalization Policies in the United States," *Politics and Society* 13, no. 1 (1984): 1–26. See also Candice Dawn Bredbenner, "Toward Independent Citizenship: Married Women's Nationality Rights in the United States" (Ph.D. diss., University of Virginia, 1990).

7. Frances Mitchell to her sister, Zürich, Sept. 28, 1884, Froelicher Collection, Baltimore. For Kelley's joining the German Social Democratic Party, see FK to Carrie Chapman Catt, New York City, June 4, 1927, "Florence Kelley—General Correspondence," National American Woman Suffrage Association Papers, reel 11. Catt had given Kelley the opportunity to deny right-wing charges about her European socialist past, and Kelley refused to do so, replying, "The Socialist Party when I joined it in Switzerland in 1884, was a revolutionary party, and I made no mental reservations in joining it."

8. Florence Kelley Wischnewetzky (hereafter FKW) to MTL, Heidelberg, Feb. 12, 1885, NKP. May Lewis is listed as a founding member of the guild in a newspaper clipping from ca. 1894 in a guild scrapbook. Her father, Enoch Lewis, was listed first among the guild's male advisory board. The 1884 and 1885 Philadelphia city directories listed him as a "purchasing agent."

Although Kelley called herself Florence Kelley Wischnewetzky during the seven years of her marriage, I will also refer to her as Kelley. In print she hyphenated her name on only one occasion (in "White Child Slavery" [Dec. 1890]).

9. FKW to MTL, Zürich, June 10, 1885, NKP.

10. Ibid.; FKW to CBK, Zürich, Dec. 16, 1885, "FK Letters to CBK, 1876–1904," KFP, reel 1, box 2. In 1892, when he was six, Kelley changed her son's name to Nicholas. Florence's letter to Caroline related events of the past three months, showing that she had not written her mother during that time.

11. FKW to CBK, Dec. 16, 1885.

12. Kelley's translation was entitled *The Condition of the Working Class in England in 1844* (New York: John W. Lovell, 1887). Since Engels read and revised Kelley's translation, hers was the authorized version. It was reprinted in London in 1892 and appears in *Karl Marx, Frederick Engels, Collected Works* (New York: International Publishers, 1975), 4:295–596. Eric Hobsbawm chose Kelley's translation for a (frequently reprinted) edition of *The Condition* (London: Granada, 1969), for which he wrote the introduction. Hobsbawm's introduction and FK's translation are also available from Academy Chicago (1984). The competing translation of 1958 is by W. O. Henderson and W. H. Chaloner (Stanford University Press). Some sources spell Engels's first name "Friedrich"; he himself preferred "Frederick." In citations, I have retained the spellings that appear in the various works; otherwise, I spell his name "Frederick."

13. The Socialist Workers' Party of Germany (*Sozialistische Arbeiterpartei Deutschlands*), outlawed because of its avowed socialism, was the predecessor of the German Social Democratic Party, formed in 1891. For Engels in his political context, see Hunley, *Life and Thought of Friedrich Engels;* and Steenson, *After Marx, Before Lenin*. The best summary of the influence of Marxist writings in 1885 is Bottomore, *Sociology and Socialism*, 41–43. See also Bottomore et al., *Dictionary of Marxist Thought*, "Engels." The centrality of *The Condition* to Marx's writings is discussed in Hunley, *Life and Thought of Friedrich Engels;* Jones, "Engels and the History of Marxism," 316; Terrell Carver, *Marx and Engels: The Intellectual Relationship* (Bloomington: Indiana University Press, 1983), 50; and John M. Sherwood, "Engels, Marx, Malthus, and the Machine," *AHR* 90 (Oct. 1985): 837–65. Marx's *Capital* also relied heavily on official governmental reports. See Robert Paul Wolff, *Understanding Marx: A*

Reconstruction and Critique of Capital (Princeton: Princeton University Press, 1984).

14. For other French influences on German socialism, see Maurice Mandelbaum, *History, Man and Reason: A Study in Nineteenth-Century Thought* (Baltimore: Johns Hopkins University Press, 1971). For Engels's motivation in writing *The Condition*, see his preface to the first German edition of 1845, reprinted in Henderson and Chaloner, 3–5. Henderson and Chaloner also reprinted the preface to the American edition of 1887 and the preface to the English edition of 1892, most of the second having been originally published as an appendix to the 1887 American edition.

15. Engels chose to drop the subtitle from the first English edition. Engels relied on Mary Burns, a young woman in her twenties who had worked in a Manchester factory, to introduce him to proletarian circles in Manchester. In this way he met Chartist leaders who helped him gather material for his study. Mary Burns became Engels's common law wife. See Hunley, *Life and Thought of Frederick Engels*, 16. Henderson and Chaloner list sources quoted by Engels in their edition of *The Condition*, appendix 4, 372–74. The factory reports on which Engels relied have been the subject of much scholarly debate. See David MacGregor, *Hegel, Marx, and the English State* (Boulder, Colo.: Westview, 1992), 218–52; P. W. J. Bartrip, "The Evolution of Regulatory Style in the Nineteenth-century British Factory Inspectorate," *International Journal of the Sociology of Law* 8 (1980), 175–86; and Robert Gray, "The Languages of Factory Reform in Britain, c. 1830–1860," in Patrick Joyce, ed., *The Historical Meanings of Work* (Cambridge: Cambridge University Press, 1987), 143–79. For the spatial aspect of the book, see Ira Katznelson, *Marxism and the City* (Oxford: Oxford University Press, 1992), 143–56.

While Engels exaggerated the bucolic qualities of preindustrial life and the demonic effects of machinery, so too did most critics of early industrialization. Despite Engels's tendency to overstatement, scholars today recognize *The Condition* as a work of original and pathbreaking scholarship. For scholarly commentary on *The Condition*, see Eric Wolf, "The Peasant War in Germany: Friedrich Engels as Social Historian," *Science and Society* 51 (spring 1987): 82–92; Stephen Marcus, *Engels, Manchester, and the Working Class* (New York: Random House, 1974); Alan J. Kidd and K. W. Roberts, eds., *City, Class and Culture: Studies of Social Policy and Cultural Production in Victorian Manchester* (Manchester: Manchester University Press, 1985);

Gary S. Messinger, *Manchester in the Victorian Age: The Half-Known City* (Manchester: Manchester University Press, 1985); and Roy Whitfield, *Frederick Engels in Manchester: The Search for a Shadow* (Manchester: Manchester Free, 1988). For a fictional treatment of Manchester using some of Engels's themes, see Elizabeth Gaskell, *Mary Barton: A Tale of Manchester Life* (London: Chapman and Hall, 1848; reprint, New York: Norton, 1958). For Engels's idealist bent, see Cornell West, *The Ethical Dimensions of Marxist Thought* (New York: Monthly Review Press, 1991), 102–16; John Ehrenberg, *The Dictatorship of the Proletariat: Marxism's Theory of Social Democracy* (New York: Routledge, 1992), 179–88; and Jennifer Ring, *Modern Political Theory and Contemporary Feminism: A Dialectical Analysis* (Albany: State University of New York Press, 1991), 151–86.

16. The link between socialism and Darwinism is studied in Pittenger, *American Socialists*.

17. Engels, *The Condition*, 172, 179, 187, 189. This and all subsequent references to *The Condition* are to the Granada edition introduced by Hobsbawm.

18. Ibid., 174. A fine summary of historians' views of Marx and Engels's writings about women is Benenson, "Victorian Sexual Ideology." See also Nancy Folbre, "Socialism, Feminist and Scientific," in Marianne A. Ferber and Julie A. Nelson, eds., *Beyond Economic Man: Feminist Theory and Economics* (Chicago: University of Chicago, 1993), 94–110.

19. FE to Gertrud Guillaume-Schack, [London, July 5, 1885], *Karl Marx–Friedrich Engels Werke* (Berlin: Dietz Verlag, 1958–68), 36:341. His letter continued: "I admit that I am more interested in the capitalist exploitation of both sexes, than in the absolute formal equality of the sexes during the last years of the capitalist mode of production. It is my conviction that real equality of women and men can come true only when the exploitation of either by capital has been abolished and private housework has been transformed into a public industry" (quoted in Kenneth Lapides, *Marx and Engels on the Trade Unions* [New York: Praeger, 1987], 131–32).

20. Engels, *The Condition*, 108.

21. See ibid., 54–56, 239–66.

22. Ute Gerhard, *Unerhört: Die Geschichte der deutschen Frauenbewegung* (Reinbek: Rowohlt, 1990), 68. See also Herrad-Ulrike Bussemer, *Frauenemanzipation und Bildungsbürgertum: Sozialgeschichte der Frauenbewegung in der Reichgründungszeit* (Weinheim: Beltz, 1985), ff. 191. For the effect of Engels's *Origin of the Family, Private Property, and the State* on Clara Zetkin, see Honey-

cutt, "Clara Zetkin," 73–80. See also Clara Zetkin, "Proletarische und bürgerliche Frauenbewegung," *Gleichheit* 10 (Nov. 21, 1900): 186; and Honeycutt, "Socialism and Feminism in Imperial Germany." Richard Evans, *The Feminist Movement in Germany, 1894–1933* (Beverly Hills: Sage, 1976), 72–73, 87, 93, argued that these laws made the German women's movement more conservative. Quataert, *Reluctant Feminists,* discusses the conflict between Zetkin and Lily Braun over the extent to which Social Democratic women should cooperate with bourgeois feminists (107–36). Antisocialist laws (1878–1890) banned "associations with the purpose of overthrowing the existing state and social order by working for social democratic, socialist or communist ideas" (Michael Schneider, *A Brief History of the German Trade Unions* [Bonn: Dietz, 1989], 51). Until 1908 socialist meetings with women in attendance could be broken up with the pretense of enforcing laws prohibiting women's political participation, and women's organizations could be disbanded for sending delegates to Socialist Party conventions. After the passage of the antisocialist laws, Engels and Marx sent a joint letter to the leaders of the German Social Democratic Party warning against cooperation with bourgeois organizations: "We cannot therefore associate ourselves with people who openly state that the workers are too uneducated to emancipate themselves and must be freed from above by philanthropic big bourgeois and petty bourgeois . . . for which purpose the working class must place itself under the leadership of 'educated and propertied' bourgeois, who alone possess the 'time and opportunity' to acquaint themselves with what is good for the workers" (quoted in Yvonne Kapp, *Eleanor Marx* [New York: Pantheon, 1972], 1:208).

23. Engels, *The Condition,* 117, 321, passim. Engels also thought that such writings could create a meeting ground for the proletariat and "the better elements of the bourgeoisie" (321–22).

24. FKW to FE, Heidelberg, Dec. 5, 1884, International Institute for Social History (hereafter IISH): FKW to FE, Heidelberg, Feb. 6, 1885, IISH. Portions of many of FKW's letters to FE were printed in Blumberg, "Dear 'Mr. Engels'"; however, since I often quote different portions of the letters, I cite the original archive.

For Kelley's interest in translating more of FE, see FE to FKW, Feb. 25, 1886, quoted in *Karl Marx, Friedrich Engels Gesamtausgabe* (Berlin: Dietz Verlag, 1988), sect. 1, 27:1077 . Kelley actually translated none of these. *Entwicklung des Sozia-*

lismus von der Utopie zur Wissenschaft (Zurich: Schweizerische genossenschaftdruckerei, 1882) was translated by Edward Aveling as *Socialism: Utopian and Scientific* (London: Swan Sonnenschein; and New York: Scribner's, 1892). This work consisted of three chapters from *Herrn Eugen Dührings Umwälzung der Wissenschaft* (Leipzig, 1878), the entirety of which was translated and published as *Anti-Dühring: Herr Eugen Dühring's Revolution in Science* (Moscow: Foreign Languages Publishing House, 1962). *Der Ursprung der Familie, des Privatigentums und des Staats: Im Anschluss an Lewis H. Morgan's Forschungen* (Zürich: Verlag der Volksbuchhandlung, 1884) was translated by Ernest Untermann as *Origin of the Family, Private Property and the State* (Chicago: Charles H. Kerr, 1902). See Hal Draper, *The Marx-Engels Register: A Complete Bibliography of Marx and Engels' Individual Writings* (New York: Schocken, 1985).

Lawrence Gronlund, a Danish immigrant who had studied law in Germany, worked as an attorney in Chicago in the 1870s. His extremely popular 1884 book, *Cooperative Commonwealth,* was the first full statement of modern socialism published in the United States. This and his later writings interpreted socialism in a religious light, viewing moral questions of public policy as more important than economic issues. For more, see Bliss, *Encyclopedia of Social Reform,* "Lawrence Gronlund," 674; and Pittenger, *American Socialists,* 43–63. For Richard Ely and many of his academic contemporaries, "professorial socialism" led to Christian Socialism. See Ely, *French and German Socialism,* 245.

25. FKW to MTL, Heidelberg, Jan. 4, 1885, NKP.

26. FKW to MTL, Feb. 12, 1885. *John Swinton's Paper* (1883–86), edited by journalist and labor leader Swinton, tried to focus the political goals of workingmen. See Bliss, *New Encyclopedia of Social Reform,* 1184; Swinton, *A Momentous Question;* and Sender Garlin, *Three American Radicals: John Swinton, Crusading Editor; Charles P. Steinmetz, Scientist and Socialist; William Dean Howells and the Haymarket Era* (Boulder, Colo.: Westview, 1991). Other American labor papers that Kelley might have been reading would have reflected the same events.

27. For the growth of the workforce, see *Bradstreet's,* Dec. 10, 1884, quoted by Selig Perlman, "Upheaval and Reorganisation," in Commons et al., *History of Labour,* 2:358. For the average capital investment, see U.S. Census, *Compendium* (Washington, D.C.: GPO, 1890), pt. 3, 672–85. For U.S.

steel production, see Brian R. Mitchell, *European Historical Statistics, 1750–1975* (New York: Facts on File, 1980), 420; and *Historical Statistics of the United States: Colonial Times to 1970* (Washington, D.C.: GPO, 1975), 694. What was true for steel was also true for dozens of other commodities, including those traditionally employing women and children, such as textiles, garments, or shoes. With the exception of Chinese laborers employed on western railroad construction, most of the labor force needed for this vast industrial expansion was met by European immigrants. For the transition around 1880 of immigrants from western Europe to immigrants from eastern and southern Europe, see Richard A. Easterlin, "Immigration: Economic and Social Characteristics," in Stephan Thernstrom, ed., *Harvard Encyclopedia of American Ethnic Groups* (Cambridge: Harvard University Press, 1980), 476–86.

28. See Perlman, "Upheaval and Reorganization," 356–394; Goldberg, "Strikes, Organizing, and Change," 170–231; Fink, "Uses of Political Power," 113; Fones-Wolf, *Trade Union Gospel*, 87; John B. Andrews and W. D. P. Bliss, *Report on Condition of Woman and Child Wage-Earners in the United States*, vol. 10, *History of Women in Trade Unions* (Washington: GPO, 1911), 113–32; and "Leonora Barry," in *NAW*. Susan Levine characterizes the "labor feminism" of the Knights of Labor as insisting "upon full equality with men, including equal pay, equal rights within the organization, and equal respect for their productive work whether in the home or in the factory." Lady Knights agreed with other nineteenth-century feminists who "believed in a particularly feminine sensibility, one that upheld the values of hearth and home and that could at the same time infuse the public world with a more moral, humane, and cooperative character." Like many other nineteenth-century reformers, the Knights believed that women's proper place was in the home. "Although the Knights accepted women's wage work as unavoidable under present circumstances, they hoped that in the cooperative commonwealth women would no longer need to venture into the labor marketplace." But as producers in the home they would have equal rights with other producers. See Levine, *Labor's True Woman*, 86, 121, 135. For differences between women in the suffrage movement and women in the Knights of Labor in the 1880s, see ibid., 103–27.

29. *John Swinton's Paper*, Jan. 25 and April 5, 1885. For advertisements, see any issue of the paper after November 1, 1885. For a discussion of "strikes and boycotts," see March 20, 1887.

30. FK, "Socialism in Germany" (June 1885).

31. FKW to MTL, Jan. 4, 1885, Feb. 12, 1885, and June 10, 1885. Johann Most (1846–1906), a communist anarchist and a believer in propaganda by deed, was expelled from Germany for political reasons. He emigrated to London and in 1882 to the United States, where he became a leader of the International Working People's Association. See Frederic Trautmann, *The Voice of Terror: A Biography of Johann Most* (Westport, Conn.: Greenwood, 1980). Jeremiah O'Donovan Rossa was a leading supporter of Irish independence. For more on the debate between anarchism and socialism in the United States in the mid-1880s, see Sidney Fine, ed., "The Ely-Labadie Letters," *Michigan History* 36, no. 1 (March 1952): 1–32. For the SDP, See Steenson, *Karl Kautsky*, 83. The Knights of Labor had actually shed its secrecy in 1882. See Powderly, "Organization of Labor," 118–26.

32. FKW to MTL, March 19, 1885.

33. FKW to MTL, June 10, 1885, and Jan. 4, 1885.

34. FKW to MTL, March 19, 1885.

35. FKW to WDK, Heidelberg, Feb. 1885, KFP, box 7; FKW to MTL, March 19, 1885. Presumably the book was to resemble an earlier prototype: William D. Kelley, *Letters from Europe: Six Letters Written to the Philadelphia Times During the Summer of 1879* (Philadelphia: Porter and Coates, [1879]), which introduced American readers to Dühring, Bismarck, and Cernuschi.

36. FKW to FE, Zürich, June 9, 1886, IISH; FKW to MTL, March 19, 1885. WDK Jr.'s political career was short-lived. By 1887 he had joined a stove-making firm in Chattanooga, Tennessee, where he married and settled permanently.

37. FKW to MTL, Jan. 4, 1885. Will Jr. had been active with the state militia since 1877. That year he wrote his father about his duty at Altoona during the national strike of railroad workers: "The men who had preceded us at Tyrone refused to obey orders and yielded to the strikers, we were left alone with only the officers of the other companies. The strikers were good-natured & joked with everybody though they are heavily armed & determined. They offer to feed us & send us home, but will not let us go to Pittsburgh" (WDK Jr., to WDK, Altoona, Pa., July 22, 1877, box 5, "WDK Jr. Letters to WDK," KFP). See also Joseph J. Holmes, "The National Guard of Pennsylvania: Policemen of Industry, 1865–1905" (Ph.D. diss., University of Connecticut, 1971). Eventually President Hayes

employed federal troops recently removed from the South to put down the railroad workers' uprising. See Robert V. Bruce, *1877: Year of Violence* (New York: Quadrangle, 1970); and J. T. Headley, *Pen and Pencil Sketches of the Great Riots* (New York: E. B. Treat, 1877), 369–96. "Riot drills," viewed as provocative by workers, sometimes themselves produced riots. See "Those 'Riot Drills'—Interference with a Riot Drill of the Militia in Providence," *John Swinton's Paper*, June 15, 1884.

38. WDK Jr. to CBK, [Philadelphia], Feb. 27, 1885, NKP. Will added: "I do not speak of her except when questioned and then only pleasantly of course."

39. FKW to MTL, March 19, 1885.

40. FKW to MTL, Zürich, June 22, 1885, NKP; "The Women's Fight for Life; the Long Strike at Yonkers," *John Swinton's Paper*, May 24, 1885.

41. FKW to MTL, June 22, 1885. The strike is described in Levine, *Labor's True Woman*, 90–96. In May and June the strikers became a cause célèbre within the labor movement, appearing weekly at meetings of the Central Labor Union of New York City.

42. FKW, "Correspondence" (Sept. 1885), 1. The paper's masthead carried the motto "Equality before the Law." For the larger context of suffrage periodicals, see Linda C. Steiner, "The Women's Suffrage Press, 1850–1900: A Cultural Analysis" (Ph.D. diss., University of Illinois, 1979), 262–71.

43. FKW, "Correspondence," 1.

44. FKW, "Letters From the People" (May 1885), 150–51. See also Steiner, "Women's Suffrage Press," 268–71. *The New Era* is described and FKW's letters are extensively quoted in Buechler, *Transformation of the Woman Suffrage Movement*, 133–35.

45. FKW, "Movement among German Workingwomen" (May 1885), 7, 3. While the petition opposed the regulation of women's hours, as distinct from hours for all workers, it supported "the need of safeguards against accidents and preventable disease, the appointment of women overseers in factories, the arrangement of separate washing and dressing rooms and other measures equally practicable and beneficent." The close correlation between the women's petition and the views of men representing working people in parliament suggests an agreement between them to oppose the regulation of hours for women in order to enhance support for the regulation of hours for both men and women. Recent scholarship in German women's history reveals that socialists and other allies of working women supported sex-specific

legislation for women by 1890. See Quataert, *Reluctant Feminists*, 39–45; and Franzoi, *At the Very Least She Pays the Rent*, 60–65.

46. FKW, "Letter from Germany" (July 1885), 1; FKW, "Letters from the People" (July 1885), 215–16. See August Bebel, *Women in the Past, Present and Future*, trans. Dr. H. B. Adams Chapman Walther (New York: John Lovell, [ca. 1884]). Though himself a Social Democrat, Bebel's analysis was not explicitly Marxist, and although he claimed a connection between socialism and women's emancipation, none actually emerged from his argument. That connection had only just been made in Engels's *Der Ursprung der Familie* (1884). The original title of Bebel's book, *Die Frau und der Sozialismus* (1878) had caused it to be banned, so he had issued a new edition with a new title in 1883: *Die Frau in der Vergangenheit, Gegenwart und Zukunft*. Ninth and subsequent editions after 1890 once more assumed the title *Women and Socialism*, which after 1910 was translated as *Women under Socialism*. See Francis L. Carsten, *August Bebel und die Organisation der Massen* (Berlin: Siedler Verlag, 1991); Ursula Herrmann and Volker Emmrich, *August Bebel: Eine Biographie* (Berlin: Dietz Verlag, 1989); and Lewis A. Coser, introduction to *Women Under Socialism*, by August Bebel, trans. Daniel DeLeon (New York: New York Labor News Press, 1904; reprint, New York: Schocken, 1971); and Honeycutt, "Clara Zetkin," 53–56. John Lovell Company subsequently published FK's translation of Engels's *Condition*.

47. FKW to MTL, Jan. 4, 1885, and June 10, 1885.

48. FKW to MTL, March 19, 1885.

49. Gertrud Guillaume-Schack to FE, Zürich, Aug. 16, 1886, Marx-Engels-Nachlass L 2055, IISH. For a translation, see "Social Democracy and the Question of Women's Work," reprinted in Sklar, Schüler, and Strasser, *A Transatlantic Dialogue*. FK's authorship of the article and her public lecture are mentioned in the letter cited above. Other internal evidence, including references to the American suffrage movement, also point to FK's authorship. I am grateful to Ursula Herrmann of Berlin for bringing my attention to this article and to Guillaume-Schack's letter. See Ursula Herrmann, "Engels' Schrift 'Der Ursprung der Familie, des Privateigentums und des Staats' in der deutschen Sozialdemokratie 1884 bis 1885," *Marx-Engels Jahrbuch* (Berlin: Dietz Verlag, 1987) 10:65–102, which cites the letter referring to Kelley's authorship of the essay. Prior to Herrmann's article, scholars had attributed this article to Clara Zetkin. *Der Sozial-*

demokrat was edited by Eduard Bernstein during most of the 1880s, and it is possible that he solicited Kelley's article.

50. See Honeycutt, "Clara Zetkin," 30–117; Quataert, *Reluctant Feminists*, 65–73; Thönnessen, *Emancipation of Women*, 43–49; Clara Zetkin, *Die Arbeiterinnen- und Frauenfrage der Gegenwart* (Berlin: Volks Tribüne, 1889). See also Luise Dornemann, *Clara Zetkin: Leben und Wirken* (Berlin: Dietz Verlag, 1973); Ann Taylor Allen, *Feminism and Motherhood in Germany, 1800–1914* (New Brunswick: Rutgers University Press, 1991), 135–48; and Carole E. Adams, "Pre-World War Socialist Feminism in Germany: Homo Economicus," in Barbara Caine, E. A. Grosz, and Marie de Lepervanche, eds., *Crossing Boundaries: Feminisms and the Critique of Knowledges* (Sydney: Allen and Unwin, 1988), 147–56. Zetkin's middle-class origins were commonplace among German Social Democratic leaders. Marx, Engels, August Bebel, Heinrich Braun, Lily Braun, Johann Dietz, Karl Kautsky, Rosa Luxemburg, and others shared Florence Kelley's class background. Surplus value was a theme in their personal as well as in their intellectual lives. Engels noted the importance of an independent income when he lamented that, among the younger generation, "Kautsky, the only one who studies industriously, must write in order to live, and can therefore certainly produce nothing" (FE to August Bebel, April 30, 1883, quoted in Steenson, *Karl Kautsky*, 48).

51. Clara Zetkin, "Speech at the International Workers' Congress, Paris, July 19, 1889," reprinted in Philip Foner, ed., *Clara Zetkin, Selected Writings* (New York: International Publishers, 1984), 45–50, 49; [FKW], "Die Sozialdemokratie" (Aug. 11, 1886). Ute Frevert, *Frauengeschichte: Zwischen Bürgerlicher Verbesserung und Neuer Weiblichkeit* (Frankfurt: Suhrkamp, 1986), 86–87, showed on the basis of 1885 data that while domestic service did produce the largest number of prostitutes, their numbers were proportionate to the high percentage (about one-third) of women wage earners in domestic service.

52. [FKW], "Die Sozialdemokratie" (Aug. 11, 1886).

53. FE to FKW, 122 Regents Park Road, London, Feb. 4, 1885, Friedrich A. Sorge Collection (hereafter FASC); FKW to FE, Zürich, June 16, 1885, IISH. When Engels could not locate the original English for some of his quotations, with the exception of a ballad, which was omitted, she retranslated them back into English, adding a translator's note at the back of the book that enumerated each retranslated item. She asked Engels to "determine the title of the translation" (FKW to FE, Zürich, Dec. 28, 1885, IISH). The ballad comes at the end of the "Factory-Hands" chapter and has been restored in Hobsbawm's edition. All the original English passages were restored in the Henderson and Chaloner translation, with an appendix that criticizes her rendering of these English documents.

In an introduction to their translation, Henderson and Chaloner justified their efforts by disparaging Kelley's. Trying to discredit her by referring to her only as "Mrs. Wischnewetzky" and without mentioning her family or educational background, they claimed that her translation was "little more than a word-for-word transcript of the original into another language" and that "the book as Engels wrote it is full of lively and vigorous passages which have been translated in a very pedestrian fashion" (xx–xxi n. 2). However, a comparison of her translation and theirs to the original German shows that Henderson and Chaloner often interpreted the text in unwarranted ways, sometimes through wordy additions in mid-twentieth-century prose that fell far short of the vigor of the mid-nineteenth-century original, sometimes through reductions that lost the original meaning. Kelley's close attention to the original captured more of its nuance. These differences are evident in the chapter titles. Engels's title "Resultate," Kelley called "Results," but Henderson and Chaloner translated it as "Results of Industrialization." For Engels's title "Die einzelnen Arbeitszweige: Die Fabrikarbeiter im engeren Sinne," Kelley used "Single Branches of Industry. Factory-Hands," and they called it "The Proletariat." The next chapter's title "Die uebringen Arbeitszweige," Kelley translated as "The Remaining Branches of Industry," and they called it "The Proletariat (continued)."

Kelley's translation can be compared with the original and the 1958 translation in the following passage from the beginning of the second chapter, "The Industrial Proletariat."

Engels:

> *Die Reihenfolge, nach der wir die verschiedenen Sektionen des Proletariats zu betrachten haben, ergibt sich von selbst aus der vorhergehenden Geschichte seiner Entstehung. Die ersten Proletarier gehörten der Industrie an und wurden direkt durch sie erzeugt; die industriellen Arbeiter, diejenigen, die sich mit der Verarbeitung von Rohstoffen beschaeftigen, werden also zunächst unsere Aufmerksamkeit in Anspruch nehmen. Die Erzeugung*

*des industriellen Materials, der Roh- und Brenn-
stoffe selbst, wurde erst infolge des industriellen
Umschwungs bedeutend und konnte so ein neues
Proletariat hervorbringen: die Arbeiter in den
Kohlengruben und Metallbergwerken.*

Florence Kelley Wischnewetzky:

The order of our investigation of the different sections of the proletariat follows naturally
from the foregoing history of its rise. The first
proletarians were connected with manufacture,
were engendered by it, and accordingly, those
employed in manufacture, in the working up
of raw materials, will first claim our attention.
The production of raw materials and of fuel for
manufacture attained importance only in consequence of industrial change, and engendered a
new proletariat, the coal and metal miners.

Henderson and Chaloner:

We propose to discuss in detail the characteristics of the various sections of the English
working classes. The arrangement of our material
follows naturally from the history of the working
classes that we have just sketched, and we will
discuss each group in turn. The first members
of the proletariat are the product of changes
in manufacturing and these are the industrial
workers engaged in working up raw materials.
We shall consider this group first of all. Secondly
we shall examine the workers engaged in the
production of raw materials and fuel. This section of the proletariat increased in importance at
a rather later stage. It includes coal miners and
miners of metal ores.

In *Engels, Manchester, and the Working Class*
(New York: Random House, 1974), Steven Marcus
also disparaged Kelley's translation and provided
his own translations of passages that he analyzed.
Marcus said he tried to recapture the original's
"semi-Hegelianisms," but his translations differed
from Kelley's only in very minor ways (xi–xiii).

54. FKW to FE, Feb. 6, 1885, and Dec. 28, 1885.
For Engels's reliance on Kelley, see FE to FKW, Lon-
don, Feb. 10, 1885, FASC (cited in Blumberg, *Florence
Kelley*, 49). (Most but not all of Engels's letters to
FK have been printed in [Trachtenberg], *Letters to
Americans*. The one dated Feb. 10 from Engels to
Kelley appears on 144–45.) In FKW to FE, Dec. 5,
1884, Kelley responded to Engels's willingness to
write an English preface for the American condition

"only on condition of my first finding a publisher."

55. FKW to FE, Zürich, Jan. 10, 1886, IISH; FE to
FKW, London, Feb. 3, 1886, FASC (printed in [Tracht-
enberg], *Letters to Americans*, 149). Kelley referred
to her efforts with publishers in FKW to FE, Zürich,
Feb. 6, [1886], IISH. In FK to CBK, Dec. 16, 1885,
she had written that Rachel Foster's mother had
died, leaving her "a hundred thousand dollars." For
Foster's central role in the contemporary suffrage
movement, see "Rachel G. Foster Avery," in *NAW*.
Born in 1858 and raised as a Quaker in Philadelphia,
she was elected corresponding secretary of the
National Woman Suffrage Association in 1880. In
1883 she became Susan B. Anthony's "dear adopted
niece," scheduling her travels, writing on the history of the suffrage movement, and financing much
of Anthony's participation in the movement.

56. FE to FKW, Feb. 25, 1886; FKW to FE, Zürich,
March 1, 1886, IISH.

57. See Perlman, "Upheaval and Reorganiza-
tion," 356–94; Fink, "Uses of Political Power";
Laslett, "Haymarket, Henry George, and the
Labor Upsurge," 74. See also Fink, *Workingmen's
Democracy;* Schneirov, "The Knights of Labor";
and Dieter Schuster, *Zur Geschichte des 1. Mai in
Deutschland* (Düsseldorf: DGB, 1991).

58. See Paul Avrich, *The Haymarket Tragedy*
(Princeton: Princeton University Press, 1984), 197–
214, 260–93. See also Wheelock, "Urban Protestant
Reactions"; Jeremy Brecher, *Strike!* (Boston: South
End, 1972), 25–52; Bruce Christopher Nelson, "Cul-
ture and Conspiracy: A Social History of Chicago
Anarchism, 1870–1900" (Ph.D. diss., Northern Illi-
nois University, 1986); and Keil, "The Impact of
Haymarket."

59. FE to FKW, [London], June 3, 1886, FASC
(printed in [Trachtenberg], *Letters to Americans*,
157–58), and June 7, 1886, FASC.

60. FKW to FE, June 9, 1886, and Zürich, Aug. 4,
1886, IISH.

61. FE to FKW, Eastbourne, Aug. 13, 1886, FASC;
FKW to FE, June 9, 1886.

62. FKW to FE, Zürich, Aug. 26, 1886, IISH.

6. Where Do I Belong? 1886–1888

1. FKW's second letter to Engels mentioned "our
good friends the Sorges" (FKW to FE, 110 E. 76th
St., New York City, Jan. 8, 1887, IISH). Kelley must
have discussed with the Sorges the pamphlets that
Mr. Livingston carried to her Philadelphia home in

1877. The Socialist International traced its ancestry to the International Workingmen's Association, founded in 1864 in London by Karl Marx and Frederick Engels. It dissolved in 1876 in Philadelphia. As socialist parties gained strength in various European countries, they revived their organization as the Second International, founded in 1889 in Paris. This collapsed during World War I. In 1919 the Socialist International was again revived, although the communists split away and founded the Third International, later known as the Comintern. See Bottomore et al., *Dictionary of Marxist Thought.*

Helen Campbell was listed as a member of the New Century Guild in 1883 in bound vol., "Evening Classes and Office Accounts, Dec. 1, 1882 to Feb. 8, 1889," NCGP). FK to Helen Campbell, Boston, Feb. 20, 1911, NKP, acknowledged "the receipt of seven hundred twenty dollars, from Florence Kelley, as payment in full of the sum of seven hundred dollars lent her in December, 1886, and twenty dollars initial payment of accrued interest at six percent per annum." For more on Campbell, see chapter 7 below. For the income of skilled workers, see FK's analysis of 1889 family budgets in Wright, *Seventh Special Report,* 460–501.

2. FKW to FE, 3 Livingston Place, [New York City], Dec. 10, 1886, IISH. George's popularity was partly due to his endorsement of unregulated economic competition. In that sense he resembled earlier advocates of laissez-faire who criticized monopolies and governmentally based favoritism. See Commons et al., *History of Labour,* 2:446–54; Foner and Chamberlin, *Sorge's Labor Movement,* 218–24; and Thomas, *Alternative America,* 223–29. Although organized labor initiated this political movement, SLP representatives were among the delegates who founded the United Labor Party. See Samuel Gompers, *Seventy Years of Life and Labor* (New York: Dutton, 1925), 1:312; and Howard H. Quint, *Forging of American Socialism* (Columbia: University of South Carolina Press, 1953), 37–44. Lillie Devereau Blake, president of the New York Woman Suffrage Association, endorsed George because his platform advocated equal pay for "equal work without distinction of sex" (quoted in Sally Roesch Wagner, *A Time of Protest: Suffragists Challenge the Republic: 1870–1887* [Yankton, S.D.: Sky Carrier, 1992], 103). William Kelley's opinion of Henry George has not survived. See also Frank C. Genovese, "Henry George and Organized Labor," *American Journal of Economics and Sociology* 50 (Jan. 1991): 113–27; and Michael Silagi, "Henry

George and Europe," *American Journal of Economics and Sociology* 52 (Jan. 1993): 119–27.

3. FKW to FE, Dec. 10, 1886.

4. Ibid.

5. FKW to FE, 110 E. 76th St., New York City, Oct. 7, 1887, IISH. For socialism versus "laborism" in the early SLP, see Commons et al., *History of Labour,* 2:270–71, 288; Quint, *Forging of American Socialism,* 16. See also Dirk Hoerder, "German Working-Class Radicalism in the United States from the 1870s to World War I," in Hoerder, ed., *"Struggle a Hard Battle": Essays on Working-Class Immigrants* (DeKalb: Northern Illinois University Press, 1986). For the development of New York City's German community, see Dorothee Schneider, *Trade Unions and Community: The German Working Class in New York City, 1870–1900* (Urbana: University of Illinois Press, 1994). For more on the German language press, see Herbert Gutman, "Alarm: Chicago and New York, 1884–1889," in Joseph Conlin, ed., *The American Radical Press, 1880–1960* (Westport, Conn.: Greenwood, 1974), 2:380–86; Dirk Hoerder and Christiane Harzig, eds., *The Immigrant Labor Press in North America, 1840s–1970s: An Annotated Bibliography,* 3 vols. (Westport, Conn.: Greenwood, 1987); Carol Poore, *German-American Socialist Literature, 1865–1900* (Bern: Peter Lang, 1982).

6. For Ferdinand Lassalle, see Bottomore et al., *Dictionary of Marxist Thought,* 273–74; Miller and Potthoff, *History of German Social Democracy;* and Steenson, *After Marx, Before Lenin,* 55–59. For the conflict between Lassallean and Marxian views in the United States, see Johnson, *Marxism in United States History,* 18–20; Tomlins, *The State and the Unions,* 52–57; and Foner and Chamberlin, *Sorge's Labor Movement.* The best discussion of Sorge's stance is in Herreshoff, *American Disciples,* 56–59, 72–82, 90–105. See also Kenneth Lapides, *Marx and Engels on the Trade Unions* (New York: Praeger, 1987), 135–44. The absence of SLP commitment to the publications of Marx and Engels is evident, though not commented on, in Philip S. Foner, "The Writings of Marx and Engels in the United States," *Nature, Society and Thought* 2 (1989): 97–119, 217–51. For more on the SLP in the late 1880s, see Morris Hillquit, *History of Socialism in the United States* (New York: Funk and Wagnalls, 1910), 254–57; Paul Buhle, "Socialist Labor Party," in Mari Jo Buhle, Paul Buhle, and George Georgakas, eds., *Encyclopedia of the American Left* (New York: Garland, 1990); and Girard and Perry, *The Socialist Labor Party,* 10–12. The SLP changed substantially soon after

Kelley's departure. See Perrier, "The Socialists and the Working Class," 485–511.

7. FE to FK, Dec. 28, 1886, FASC, quoted in Lapides, *Marx and Engels*, 139–40.

8. *Workmen's Advocate*, Feb. 5, 1887, noted in Blumberg, *Florence Kelley*, 64. FKW's translation of Jacoby's speech was published serially in *Workmen's Advocate* between January 22 and Feb. 19, 1887. For more on the speech, see Edmund Silberner, *Johann Jacoby: Politiker und Mensch* (Bonn–Bad Godesberg: Verlag Neue Gesellschaft, 1976), 407–11.

9. FKW to FE, Jan. 8, 1887. For the misquotation, see FKW, "In Defense of Engels" (Jan. 1887), 4. The misquoted letter was printed in [Trachtenberg], *Letters to Americans*, 165–67, and in Lapides, *Marx and Engels*, 139–40. Engels's response to her was harsh: "As to the distorted passage from my letter . . . it is no use for Rosenberg & Co. to saddle Aveling with it. The passage . . . occurred in my letter to you and in no *other letter*. So you will know who is responsible for this indiscretion and for putting this nonsense into my mouth." (FE to FKW, London, Feb. 9, 1887, FASC, quoted in [Trachtenberg], *Letters to Americans*, 169).

The Federation of Organized Trades and Labor Unions became the American Federation of Labor of Trades and Labor Unions in December 1886, later shortened to the American Federation of Labor. Here I will refer to the organization as the AFL. For the struggle between the AFL and the Knights of Labor in 1886, see Commons et al., *History of Labour*, 2:396–413.

10. *New Yorker Volkszeitung*, Dec. 22, 1886, quoted in Blumberg, *Florence Kelley*, 68. The most extended treatment of the Aveling controversy can be found in Yvonne Kapp, *Eleanor Marx* (New York: Pantheon, 1976), 2:116–22, 166–91; see esp. 171–73 for the *Herald* article.

11. FE to FKW, Feb. 9, 1887. FK's letter to Engels on the topic of Aveling has not survived, but its contents can be deduced from his response. For Kelley's apology, see FKW to FE, n.p. [New York], May 2, 1887, IISH. For a more complete account of Kelley's role in the Aveling affair, see Blumberg, *Florence Kelley*, 67–74. Many people did not trust Aveling; eventually he deserted Eleanor Marx, and she committed suicide. See Kapp, *Eleanor Marx*, 2:680–95. Editor of *Die neue Zeit*, Karl Kautsky was seen within the party to be the leading Marxist thinker of the Second International between 1889 and 1914 and a crucially important member of the second generation of Marxists. From 1885 to 1890 he lived in London and worked closely with Engels,

translating Marx's *Poverty of Philosophy*. Kelley's letters to Engels always asked him to remember her to Mrs. Kautsky, who worked for him. For more on Kautsky, see John H. Kautsky, ed., *Karl Kautsky and the Social Science of Classical Marxism* (Kinderhook, N.Y.: Brill, 1990); and Bottomore et al., *Dictionary of Marxist Thought*, 248–49.

12. FE to Friedrich Sorge, London, April 9, 1887, quoted in [Trachtenberg], *Letters to Americans*, 182; FE to FKW, London, May 7, 1887, FASC, in *Letters to Americans*, 187; and FE to Sorge, London, May 7, 1887, *Letters to Americans*, 186. Other evidence indicates that Engels realized that Kelley was better than most translators. For example, he wrote Sorge in 1886 that he was "glad that the gentlemen over there [in the United States] do not translate anything of mine; it would turn out beautifully. Their German is enough, and then their English!" (FE to Friedrich Sorge, London, April 29, 1886, in *Letters to Americans*, 154). Engels's confidence in Kelley was suggested by his recommendation that she translate Marx's pamphlet, *Wage Labor and Capital* (FE to FKW, London, Feb. 25, 1886, FASC, in *Letters to Americans*, 150–51). However, Engels judged Kelley fiercely in a later letter to Sorge. "Her last long letter on the Aveling affair can be characterized by one word alone: filth" (FE to Sorge, London, April 23, 1887, in *Letters to Americans*, 183–84).

Engels's London address was 122 Regent's Park Road. See Asa Briggs, *Marx in London* (London: British Broadcasting Company, 1982), 75.

13. FE, preface to *The Condition of the Working Class*, i–vi. The preface also appears in the Henderson and Chaloner edition, 352–59, and in the Moscow edition (Progress Publishers, 1973), 16–24. Engels also published the preface separately as "The Labour Movement in America" in the *Sozialdemokrat* (June 10 and 17, 1887) and in French in the *Socialiste* (July 9, 16, and 23). Kelley interacted with Engels as a critic as well as a translator. She did not hesitate to recommend revisions, saying on one occasion that there was an "apparent contradiction" in his discussion of party platforms, and he should review his comments on that subject (FKW to FE, 110 E. 76th St., New York, April 26, 1887, IISH).

14. FKW to FE, April 26, 1887; *Der Sozialist*, Aug. 27, 1887. *Majestätsbeleidigung* and *Verbreitung verbotener Schriften* were the crimes of which socialist leaders in general and Eduard Bernstein in particular were accused in Germany, both during and after the antisocialist laws. A more complete account of Kelley's struggles with the SLP can be found in Blumberg, *Florence Kelley*, 59–88. By

December Kelley conceded victory to the New York leadership. Withdrawing from a debate with the *New Yorker Volkszeitung* over their obligation to promote English editions of socialist writings, she decided to "let the thing go without farther dispute" (FKW to FE, 110 E. 76th St., Dec. 29, 1887, IISH). The next March an investigating committee appointed by the national convention recommended the Wischnewetzkys' reinstatement, but the New York executive committee appealed that decision to the local membership, who decided against reinstatement. See FKW to FE, Gloucester, Mass., Aug. 28, 1887, IISH; and FKW to FE, 110 E. 76th St., March 11, 1888, and March 29, 1888, IISH. Engels wrote to Sorge: "If the whole German Socialist Labor Party went to pieces . . . it would be a gain, but we can hardly expect anything as good as that" (FE to Sorge, Feb. 8, 1890, [Trachtenberg], *Letters to Americans*, 224).

15. FKW to FE, April 26, 1887. When Kelley printed his preface separately as a pamphlet, Engels kept the Aveling controversy alive by adding a footnote to the first page, denouncing "the miserable slanderous accusations . . . which the Executive Committee of the American Socialist Labour Party was unscrupulous enough to circulate about Edward Aveling" (FE, *The Labor Movement in America*, 1).

Engels was angry when Kelley arranged for Alexander Jonas, editor of the *New Yorker Volkszeitung*, to translate the preface from English to German and publish it. He wrote Sorge, "I cannot put up with any outsider's translation of my English writings into German, and especially such a translation, which is full of mistakes and misunderstands the most important points" (FE to Sorge, April 23, 1887, 183–84).

16. FKW to FE, New York City, April 26, 1887; FKW to FE, 110 E. 76th St., New York City, June 16, 1887, IISH. For the recipients of copies, see FKW to FE, 110 E. 76th St., New York City, June 6, 1887, IISH. Later Kelley summarized the annoyances surrounding the publication: "After Miss Foster had paid the S.L.P. Exec. Com. $500.00 to issue the book and they had squandered the money,—the unbound sheets were given to John W. Lovell to bind, sell, and re-imburse himself out of sales. He mismanaged the book and soon failed. So Miss Foster never got back a penny of the $500.00 and, after all these years, I am still trying to get a first accounting from Mr. Lovell's successor; who has recently been advertising the book and pushing it vigorously" (FKW to FE, Zander Institute, 246

25th St., N.Y., Oct. 13, 1891, IISH). The *Leader* was edited by socialist Sergius Shevitch. See Stuart B. Kaufman, Peter J. Albert, Elizabeth A. Fones-Wolf, Dolores E. Janiewski, David E. Carl, Dorothee Schneider, and Grace Palladino, eds., *The Samuel Gompers Papers*, vol. 1, *The Making of a Union Leader* (Chicago: University of Illinois Press, 1986), 430.

17. FKW to FE, June 6, 1887; June 16, 1887; and Aug. 28, 1887. In her August letter, she described the boycott of the pamphlet: "After boycotting the book as far as they dare, Volkz. and Socz. are pursuing the same policy" with regard to "the pamphlet." In her translator's note, FK touted *The Condition* as "the best introduction to the study of Marx."

18. FKW to FE, Aug. 28, 1887.

19. FKW to FE, Dec. 29, 1887, and Aug. 28, 1887. William Kelley's response to his daughter's translation went unrecorded.

20. FKW to FE, 110 E. 76th St., New York City, Oct. 24, 1887, IISH; FE, preface to *Free Trade*, by Karl Marx (1888), 24.

21. FKW to FE, Aug. 28, 1887, and Dec. 29, 1887. The circulars addressed the Aveling affair, the deceit of the executive committee, the mismanagement of the Labor News Company, and the poor editorial judgment of *Der Sozialist*. Kelley prepared for a showdown at the party's national convention that fall and naively hoped that Engels could and would help by "dealing a decisively final blow to the whole clique at the Congress, securing the N.Y. section a thorough snubbing from the Party throughout the land" (FKW to FE, Aug. 28, 1887).

22. FKW to FE, 110 E. 76th St., [fall 1887], IISH; FKW to FE, Aug. 28, 1887. For accounts of the expulsion of socialists from the Henry George movement, see Gompers, *Seventy Years*, 1:322; and Foner and Chamberlin, *Sorge's Labor Movement*, 223–24.

23. FKW to FE, Oct. 7, 1887.

24. See Buhle, *Women and American Socialism*, 26–40, 125; and Kapp, *Eleanor Marx*, 2:167. See also the Avelings' review of Bebel: Edward Aveling and Eleanor Marx Aveling, *The Woman Question* (London: Swan Sonnenschein, 1886); 1–6. For Greie's essay, see *Der Sozialist*, Jan. 14., 1888. For the preservation of traditional gender and family relations among German immigrant women, see Seifert, "The Portrayal of Women"; and Ruth Seifert, "Women's Pages in the German American Radical Press, 1900–1914: The Debate on Socialism, Emancipation, and the Suffrage," in Elliott Shore, Ken Fones-Wolf, and James P. Danky, *The German-*

American Radical Press: The Shaping of a Left Political Culture, 1850–1940 (Urbana: University of Illinois Press, 1992).

25. FE to Sorge, April 23, 1887, and London, May 4, 1887, quoted in [Trachtenberg], *Letters to Americans,* 185–86. Prejudice against Yankee women within the SLP began with the First International's quarrel with spiritualists-suffragists-freethinkers Victoria Woodhull and Tennessee Claflin, who led the American contingent within Section Twelve of the International Workingmen's Association in New York. Woodhull was expelled from the International in 1872. See Herreshoff, *American Disciples,* 84–93.

26. Rachel Foster probably arranged for FK's appearance before the New York Association of Collegiate Alumnae.

27. All quotations in the following discussion are from FK, "Need of Theoretical Preparation" (1887), 15–26 (reprinted in Sklar, *Autobiography of Florence Kelley,* 91–104). More typical of her peers was Helen Backus's essay, which praised "the intelligent exercise of moral and mental power" in such activities as reformed designs for tenement houses, The New York Health Protective Association, and sanitary science clubs, all of which were shaped by women. See Helen Hiscock Backus, "The Need and the Opportunity for College-Trained Women in Philanthropic Work," in Backus, *The Need and the Opportunity for College-Trained Women,* 1–14.

28. Vida D. Scudder, "A Protest," *The Christian Union* 35 (June 16, 1887): 16. (*The Christian Union* changed its name to *The Outlook* in 1893 and became a leading advocate of Progressive reform.) See also Scudder, "Relation of College Women to Social Need," 1–16; and Scudder, *Socialism and Character* (Boston: Houghton Mifflin, 1912). In the fall of 1887 Scudder began a forty-year teaching career at Wellesley. After 1900 she exchanged her Christian Socialism for Christian Marxism. See Arthur Mann's chapter on Vida Scudder in *Yankee Reformers in the Urban Age: Social Reform in Boston, 1880–1900* (Chicago: University of Chicago Press, 1954), 201–228; Frederick, *Knights of the Golden Rule,* 113–40; and "Vida Dutton Scudder," in *NAW.*

29. FKW, "A Reply" (June 23, 1887), 27.

30. FKW to FE, Aug. 28, 1887. No copies of the pamphlet version remain.

31. WDK to Elizabeth Pugh, Washington, Dec. 20, 1887, WDKP; FK to CBK, New York City, Dec. 20, 1887, KFP, reel 1, box 2.

32. FK to CBK, 110 E. 76th St., Dec. 29, 1887, KFP, reel 1, box 2; CBK to WDK, Philadelphia, Feb. 24,

1888, WDKP; FK to WDK, N. Y., March 20, 1888, NKP. For the servants, see FK to CBK, Dec. 29, 1887.

33. FKW to FE, March 29, 1888, and Dec. 29, 1887. John's name was later changed to John Bartram.

Historians have recently corrected the view that Samuel Gompers's "pure and simple unionism" avoided politics altogether. A summary of Gompers's avoidance of politics appears in Louis S. Reed, *The Labor Philosophy of Samuel Gompers* (New York: Columbia University Press, 1930). In the past decade, three modifications of that view have emerged. First, Gompers's predecessors also had difficulty pursuing labor's goals in the political domain. Fink in *Workingmen's Democracy* demonstrated the political activism of the Knights before 1890 but also explained why the Knights' own antistate beliefs undercut their effectiveness. Second, Tomlins in *The State and the Unions* analyzed the AFL's effort to stabilize labor-management relations by attributing legal status to trade agreements, which effort, however, took place on the margins rather than in the center of governmental action. Third, Forbath in *Law and the Shaping of the American Labor Movement* and Mink in *Old Labor and New Immigrants* analyzed labor's lobbying activities in opposition to labor injunctions and to unregulated immigration, efforts designed to end governmental actions deemed to hamper labor rather than actions seeking to use governmental power for positive goals, such as hours or wage legislation.

34. See Leon Fink, "Labor, Liberty, and the Law: Trade Unionism and the Problem of the American Constitutional Order," *JAH* 74 (Dec. 1987): 904–25; Gary Marks, *Unions in Politics: Britain, Germany, and the United States in the Nineteenth and Early Twentieth Centuries* (Princeton: Princeton University Press, 1989); Richard Oestreicher, "Urban Working-Class Political Behavior and Theories of American Electoral Politics, 1870–1940," *JAH* 74 (March 1988): 1257–86; and David Scobey, "Boycotting the Politics Factory: Labor Radicalism and the New York City Mayoral Election of 1884," *RHR* 28–30 (1984): 280–325.

35. FKW to FE, Dec. 29, 1887; Gompers, *Seventy Years,* 1:194. The best treatment of *In Re Jacobs* is Boris, *Home to Work.* The correlation between strong courts and a weak labor movement is analyzed in Hattam, *Labor Visions and State Power.* See also Eileen Boris, "'A Man's Dwelling House Is His Castle': Tenement House Cigarmaking and the Judicial Imperative," in Ava Baron, ed., *Work En-*

gendered: Towards a New History of American Labor (Ithaca: Cornell University Press, 1991), 114–41; *A Verbatim Report of the Discussion on the Political Programme, at the Denver Convention of the American Federation of Labor, 1894* (New York: Freytag, 1895); Henry Howard Quint, *The Forging of American Socialism: Origins of the Modern Movement* (Columbia: University of South Carolina Press, 1973), 32–71; Fink, "Labor, Liberty, and the Law"; Friedman, "The Working Class and the Welfare State"; and Benjamin R. Twiss, *Lawyers and the Constitution: How Laissez Faire Came to the Supreme Court* (Princeton: Princeton University Press, 1942), 93–109.

36. FK to CBK, May 24, 1888, New York, KFP, reel 1, box 2; CBK to WDK, May 25, 1888, KFP, reel 1, box 2; FK to CBK, Sharon Springs, July 4, [1888], KFP, reel 1, box 2; WDK to CBK, Washington, July 2, 1888, WDKP. For the identification of Lazare's illness as rheumatic fever, see FKW to FE, Oct. 13, 1891. Caroline noted to William that Florence "never dwells upon her own state, but it cannot be otherwise than injurious if not dangerous, for her to be obliged to rub or lift, or even *stand*, about the patient" (CBK to WDK, May 25, 1888).

37. FE to Sorge, London, July 11, 1888, quoted in [Trachtenberg], *Letters to Americans*, 201; FE to FKW, Sept. 18, 1888, in *Letters to Americans*, 205; FKW to FE, Sept. 20, 1888, IISH (Florence also noted in this letter Lazare's departure for Europe); and FE to Sorge, London, Jan. 12, 1889, in *Letters to Americans*, 209.

7. If We Were Doing the Nation's Work, 1889–1891

1. FKW to FE, 110 E. 76th St., New York City, March 29, 1888, IISH.

2. Knights of Labor, General Assembly, *Proceedings*, 1889, reprinted in Mary Blewett, *We Will Rise in Our Might: Workingwomen's Voices from Nineteenth-Century New England* (Ithaca: Cornell University Press, 1991), 175–76; and Levine, *Labor's True Woman*, 139–40. For Barry's dismissal, see Leonora Barry to Charles Lichtman, July 1888, quoted in S. Levine, *Labor's True Woman*, 184. See also John B. Andrews and W. D. P. Bliss, *Report on Condition of Woman and Child Wage-Earners in the United States*, vol. 10, *History of Women in Trade Unions* (Washington, D.C.: GPO, 1911), 113–32; "Leonora Barry," in *NAW;* and Schofield, "The Rise of the Pig-Headed Girl," ch. 3.

3. "A Workingwomen's Society of Philadelphia," unidentified newsclipping [March 1889], Thomas and Elizabeth Morgan Collection (hereafter TEMC), vol. 2, reel 6. After her marriage, Barry left the labor movement, and as Mrs. Barry-Lake or "Mother Lake," she became active in Catholic charities, temperance, and the woman suffrage movement.

For women's assemblies affiliated with the Knights, see Andrews and Bliss, *History of Women in Trade Unions*, 129–31. In Virginia, Arkansas, Florida, and North Carolina, some assemblies consisted entirely of African-American women. Women also joined locals with men in the Knights. The Women's Protective and Provident Committee (WPPC) was founded by Emma Paterson, who at the age of sixteen was plunged from middle-class to working-class circumstances when her father died. Its primary purpose was to assist women in forming trade unions, but its most important campaign was for women factory inspectors. See "Emma Anne Paterson," in Olive Banks, *The Biographical Dictionary of British Feminists*, vol. 1, *1800–1930* (New York: New York University Press, 1985), 156–57; and Morris, *Women Workers and the Sweated Trades*, 112–34.

4. See Goldberg, "Strikes, Organizing, and Change," 396. The earliest history of women factory inspectors is FK, "Die weibliche Fabrikinspektion" (Women factory inspectors) (1897), 128–42, 130. That essay is reprinted in Sklar, Schüler, and Strasser, *A Transatlantic Dialogue*. The first printed discussion of women factory inspectors was by a Pennsylvania inspector, Mrs. M. B. McEnery, "Factory Inspection," in *Fourth Annual Convention of the International Association of Inspectors of Factories and Workshops of North America* (Boston: Wright and Potter, 1890), 41–43. The most complete analysis is Edith Reeves and Caroline Manning, "The Standing of Massachusetts in the Administration of Labor Legislation," in Kingsbury, *Labor Laws and Their Enforcement*, 221–308. See also J. Lynn Barnard, *Factory Legislation in Pennsylvania: Its History and Administration* (Philadelphia: Winston, 1907), 56; Mary Drake McFeely, *Lady Inspectors: The Campaign for a Better Workplace, 1893–1921* (Oxford: Blackwell, 1988); Lee Holcombe, *Victorian Ladies at Work: Middle-Class Working Women in England and Wales, 1850–1914* (Hamden, Conn.: Archon, 1973), 170–71; and Quataert, "A Source Analysis in German Women's History."

5. *Workmen's Advocate*, July 6, 1889; FK, "Die weibliche Fabrikinspektion," 130 (see also 131). A

speech by Van Etten published by the AFL in 1891 insisted that "inhumanly long hours of labor and starvation wages are the rule with the great majority of working-women." She urged the passage of sixty-hour week legislation out of "regard for the future of the race" and the formation of "separate [union] organizations for women" because "many subjects which are of vital importance to them as workers are of only secondary interest to men" (Van Etten, *Condition of Women Workers*, 7, 15). Later in the decade the Ladies' Health Protective Association of New York expanded the number of inspectors to fifteen and the number of women inspectors to ten (*Report of the Second National Convention of the Woman's Health Protective Associations of the United States* [Philadelphia: n.p., 1897], 38).

6. Margaret Finn, untitled paper, *Seventh Annual Convention of the International Association of Factory Inspectors of North America, Chicago, Sept. 19–22, 1893* (Cleveland: Forest City, 1893), 13–17.

7. FK, "Die weibliche Fabrikinspektion," 130. Sarah Deutsch first used the term "class bridging" in her insightful article about women's public culture in Boston, "Learning to Talk More Like a Man," which focuses primarily on the years after 1900.

8. FKW to FE, New York, Dec. 29, 1887, IISH. The best biographical treatment is still "Helen Stuart Campbell," in *NAW*.

9. Campbell, *Prisoners of Poverty*, 10, 66. Campbell also wrote financially successful novels on the theme of poverty among women workers: *Mrs. Herndon's Income* (Boston: Roberts Bros., 1886) and *Miss Melinda's Opportunity* (Boston: Roberts Bros., 1886). Walter Fuller Taylor concluded in *The Economic Novel in America* (Chapel Hill: University of North Carolina Press, 1942) that "between 1870 and 1901, some two hundred and fifty volumes of economic fiction—mostly novels—were published in the United States" and that they created "a well-defined, clearly recognizable literary movement—a movement whose influence was felt intermittently throughout that generation, but whose chief concentration was reached between 1888 and 1897" (59). Many of the novels he lists were written by women. Another example was Elizabeth Stuart Phelps's *The Silent Partner* (Boston: Osgood, 1871), which utilized the reports of the Massachusetts Bureau of Labor Statistics. See Nancy Lynn Webb, "Form and Ideology: An Examination of Factory Novels by Women in Late Nineteenth-Century America" (Ph.D. diss., Northern Illinois University,

1986); and Laura Hapke, "The American Working Girl and the New York Tenement Tale of the 1890s," *Journal of American Culture* 15 (summer 1992): 43–50. For muckraking, see Ellen F. Fitzpatrick, *Muckraking: Three Landmark Articles* (Boston: St. Martin's, Bedford Books, 1994). See also Bremner, *From the Depths*, 86–107.

10. Campbell, *Prisoners of Poverty*, 53–54.

11. Ibid., 255–57. Implicitly Campbell also criticized the practice of paying lower wages to women because they were assumed to be supported by the larger wages paid to men.

12. See Abbie Graham, *Grace H. Dodge: A Biography* (New York: Woman's, 1926), 66–72, 94–95; Joanne Reitano, "Working Girls Unite," *AQ* 36 (spring 1984): 112–34; and Stanley, *Clubs for Working Girls*. Beginning in 1881 the WCTU also had an active "Young Women's Branch" that preceded the YWCA's work along these lines in the early 1890s. See Frances W. Graham, *Sixty Years of Action: A History of Sixty Years' Work of the Woman's Christian Temperance Union of the State of New York* (Lockport, N.Y.: n.p., [1934]), 67.

13. "A Working Woman," *John Swinton's Paper*, June 27, 1886.

14. The October meeting occurred just a few weeks after Engels's disturbing visit to New York. For a brief summary of the event, see Alice Henry, *Women and the Labor Movement* (New York: George Doran, 1923; reprint, New York: Arno, 1971), 55. The goals of the Working Women's Society were described in their 1892 *Annual Report:* "to found trades organizations in trades where they do not exist, and to encourage and assist existing labor organizations to the end of increasing wages and shortening hours." Henry and subsequent scholars have been unable to find manuscript records pertaining to the Working Women's Society. See Alice Henry to John B. Andrews, Chicago, March 30, 1915, American Association for Labor Legislation Papers, Cornell University. The society eventually evolved into the New York Women's Trade Union League. See Dye, *As Equals and as Sisters*, 10–11.

15. *New York Times*, Oct. 10, 1888, quoted in Blumberg, *Florence Kelley*, 102. For more on Huntington and this meeting, see Griffin, "Christian Socialism." For Josephine Shaw Lowell (hereafter JSL), see Stewart, *Philanthropic Work of Josephine Shaw Lowell;* "Josephine Shaw Lowell," in *NAW;* and Joan Waugh, "Sentimental Reformer: Josephine Shaw Lowell and the Rise and Fall of Scientific Charity" (Ph.D. diss., UCLA, 1992). For

Lowell as a mentor of other women reformers, especially Maud Nathan and the New York Consumer's League, see Lagemann, *A Generation of Women*, 46–51, 76–77. Van Etten's political views about women were summarized in a report about her talk before the New York Nationalist Club Number 3 (see *Workmen's Advocate*, Dec. 27, 1890).

16. Nathan, *Story of an Epoch-Making Movement*, 21. The definition of the word *consumer* as one who uses up something and reduces its exchange value, in contrast to *producer*, was just coming into being. See Raymond Williams, *Keywords: A Vocabulary of Culture and Society* (New York: Oxford University Press, 1976), 68–70.

17. Ibid., 20, 22. Extracts from Woodbridge's report are printed as appendix A of *Story*, 129.

18. See Kathryn Kish Sklar, "Two Political Cultures in the Progressive Era: The National Consumers' League and the American Association for Labor Legislation, in Linda Kerber, Alice Kessler-Harris, and Kathryn Kish Sklar, eds., *U.S. History as Women's History* (Chapel Hill: University of North Carolina Press, 1995).

19. Although originally known as the New York City Consumers' League, the group changed its name to the New York Consumers' League in 1898, when the national league was formed and each municipal league was deemed a subgroup of its state league. For this and dates of other leagues, see Nathan, *Story of an Epoch-Making Movement*, 23, 25–30, 67–68, 132, and 138–222. For FK's tenure as general secretary of the National Consumer's League, see Goldmark, *Impatient Crusader;* Kathryn Kish Sklar, *Florence Kelley and Progressive Reform* (New Haven: Yale University Press, forthcoming); and Louis Athey, "The Consumers' League and Social Reform, 1890–1923" (Ph.D. diss., University of Delaware, 1965). Interestingly enough, the London League, which collapsed soon after its formation, did not try to appeal primarily to women. See Nathan, *Story of an Epoch-Making Movement*, 130–31.

20. Curtis warmly endorsed women's political activism in an 1858 speech, insisting that "the sphere of the family is not the sole sphere either of men or women. They are not only parents, they are human beings, with genius, talents, aspiration, ambition. They are also members of the State, and. . . . they are equally concerned in its welfare" (Charles Eliot Norton, ed., *Orations and Addresses of George William Curtis* [New York: Harper and Bros., 1894], 1:230).

21. JSL, "Our Duties in Connection with Charity and Relief-giving" (1883), in Stewart, *Philanthropic Work*, 152. See also "Duties of Friendly Visitors" (1883), in ibid., 142–50. Lowell's enormously influential book *Public Relief and Private Charity* (New York: Putnam, 1884) advocated that the public should "refuse to support any except those whom it can control." See also JSL, "Women in Philanthropy—Charity," in Annie Nathan Meyer, ed., *Woman's Work in America* (New York: Holt, 1891), 323–45; and Barry J. Kaplan, "Reformers and Charity: The Abolition of Public Outdoor Relief in New York City, 1870–1898," *Social Service Review* (June 1978): 202–14.

22. JSL to Mrs. Charles Fairchild, Southampton, July 17, 1886, Fairchild Papers, box 1 #134, New-York Historical Society; JSL, "Civil Service Reform and Public Charity," in Stewart, *Philanthropic Work*, 499. The Independent Republican, or mugwump, movement was distinctly unfriendly to women's political participation. See Sproat, *"The Best Men,"* 252–53; and Stewart, Philanthropic Work, 189. See also Thomas E. Rush, *The Port of New York* (New York: Doubleday, 1920), 46; and Skowronek, *Building a New American State*, 61. Historian Morton Keller called civil service reform in the 1870s "giddily inadequate" to its purpose (*Affairs of State*, 272–75, 313–14). "Boodler" was a term used to describe political bosses who engaged in graft. See "Report of Delegates to the Women's Alliance," *Chicago Record*, Nov. 16, 1889, TEMC.

23. The Pendleton Civil Service Act provided for competitive examinations for all applicants for certain specified positions on a list that could easily be expanded. Promotion was to be on the basis of merit and competition. William Kelley supported the reform, though not arduously. See Hoogenboom, *Outlawing the Spoils*, 42, 217. For the British model that American reformers tried to imitate, see Eaton (the chief author of the Pendleton Act), *Civil Service in Great Britain;* and Noel Gilroy Annan, "The Intellectual Aristocracy," in John Harold Plumb, ed., *Studies in Social History: A Tribute to G. M. Trevelyan* (London: Longmans, Green, 1955), 241–87.

24. JSL to Annie [Mrs. Robert Gould Shaw], Oct. 30, 1881, in Stewart, *Philanthropic Work*, 127. For Lowell's other achievements, see ibid., 61, 89–90, 103–4, 320–33; and Elizabeth K. Hartley, "Social Work and Social Reform: Selected Women Social Workers and Child Welfare Reforms, 1877–1932" (D.S.W., University of Pennsylvania, 1985), 63–153.

The large proportion of women managing charitable institutions helped anchor Lowell in women's perspectives. For example, by 1886 women made up 173 out of a total of 487 delegates to the National Conference of Charities and Correction. See *Proceedings of the National Conference of Charities and Corrections at the Twenty-third Annual Session Held in the City of Grand Rapids, Michigan, 1896* (Boston: George H. Ellis, 1896), 444–49.

25. JSL to Annie [Mrs. Robert Gould Shaw], May 19, 1889, quoted in Stewart, *Philanthropic Work*, 358–59. In 1895 JSL publicly affiliated with labor in its struggle with capital, declaring that "the laborers are the people . . . and their interests, therefore . . . are the important interests" (JSL, "Discussion of 'Settlement Work,'" *Charities Review* [June 1895]: 465, quoted in Carson, *Settlement Folk*, 84). For more on this shift, see Alice Henry, "Life and Letters of Josephine Shaw Lowell," *Life and Labor* (July 1914): 196–200. For Shaw's earlier work, see also Paul T. Ringenbach, *Tramps and Reformers, 1873–1916: The Discovery of Unemployment in New York* (Westport, Conn.: Greenwood, 1973).

26. The Woman's Temperance press published three weekly papers, the largest with a circulation of over ninety thousand, and many books by well-known authors. See Livermore, "Coöperative Womanhood," 289.

Kautsky's biographer described Marx and Darwin as the twin pillars of *Die neue Zeit*. Through the journal Kautsky wanted "to popularize knowledge, to enlighten the workers," and to strengthen the radical, Marxian side of the Social Democratic Party (Steenson, *Karl Kautsky*, 52).

27. FKW, *Our Toiling Children* (1889), 35–36. Jeremy Atack and Fred Bateman, "Whom Did Protective Legislation Protect? Evidence from 1880," Working Paper no. 33 (Washington, D.C.: National Bureau of Economic Research, 1991), 26, concluded through a sample of the 1880 census that children constituted more than 5 percent of the industrial labor force. Among the earliest articles on child labor in middle-class magazines was Julia A. Holmes, "Children Who Work," *Scribner's* 1 (April 1871): 609–11. See also Clare de Graffenried, "Child Labor," in *Publications of the American Economic Association* (Baltimore: AEA, 1890), 5:71–149; and William Willoughby, "Child Labor," in ibid, 5:5–70. For the weakness of child labor laws in Massachusetts, see Kingsbury, *Labor Laws and Their Enforcement*, 159–219.

28. FKW, *Our Toiling Children*, 37.

29. Ibid., 25.

30. FK-W, "White Child Slavery" (Dec. 1890).

31. Helen Campbell in "White Child Slavery: A Symposium," *The Arena* 1 (Dec. 1890): 589–91; [Jane Croly] in ibid., 598. See also "Jane Cunningham Croly," in *NAW*. Campbell pointed out that the 1880 census statistic of 1,118,356 gainfully employed children between ten and fifteen years of age showed an increase in child labor of 50 percent, whereas the population in that age category grew only 20 percent.

32. FKW, "Evils of Child Labor" (March 1, 1890), 84.

33. FKW, "A Decade of Retrogression" (1891), 371, 370. In 1890 New York City had thirty-two utility companies, with six power lines running down Broadway. See the cartoon "The Electrical Situation," *Harper's Weekly* 33 (Dec. 21, 1889): 1019.

34. See Edward Bellamy, *Looking Backward, 2000–1887* (New York: Ticknor, 1887; reprint, New York: Random House, 1917). Buhle, *Women and American Socialism*, 77–79, 100, described the book's forceful appeal to women, including Jane Cunningham Croly, founder of New York's first women's club, Sorosis, and the inspiration behind the formation of the General Federation of Women's Clubs in 1890. For a critical analysis of Bellamy Nationalism, see Arthur Lipow, *Authoritarian Socialism in America* (Berkeley: University of California Press, 1982).

35. Bellamy, *Looking Backward*, 104–5.

36. Ibid., 210.

37. FK, "A Foot Print in New York" (March 15, 1890).

38. For settlements, see chapter 8 of this volume. Jane Robbins mentions FK taking "a resident off to Albany to oppose child labor" ("The First Year at the Settlement," *The Survey* 27 [Feb. 24, 1912]: 1802). Robbins noted (in what FK would have called an understatement): "We had no idea at first that a public career was looming up before any of us."

39. FKW to Richard T. Ely (hereafter RTE), New York, n.d. [1891], Richard T. Ely Papers (hereafter RTEP), box 3, folder 7. The names of residents who heard Kelley at the College Settlement in 1890–91 are listed in *Second Annual Report of the College Settlements Association for the Year 1891* (New York: Brown and Wilson, 1892), 19.

40. See FKW, "Child Labor" (1890). Kelley's absence was probably caused by the demands of family life.

41. Brock, *Investigation and Responsibility*, 179. See also Fones-Wolf, "Class, Professionalism and

the Early Bureaus"; and Campbell, "Labor Bureaus and Their Work in Relation to Women," in *Women Wage-Earners*, 111–25. After Massachusetts, other states forming bureaus of labor statistics were Pennsylvania (1872); Connecticut (1873); Kentucky (1876); Ohio (1877); New Jersey (1878); Illinois, Indiana, and Missouri (1879); California, Michigan, New York, and Wisconsin (1883); Iowa and Maryland (1884); and Kansas (1885). Terence V. Powderly of the Knights of Labor devoted an entire chapter of his autobiography to bureaus of labor statistics, believing that they could "ascertain beyond the shadow of a doubt what the earnings of labor and capital are in order that justice may be done to both" (*Thirty Years of Labor, 1859–1889* [Columbus, Ohio: Excelsior Publishing, 1890], 306).

42. Quoted in Brock, *Investigation and Responsibility*, 55. The origins of state bureaus of labor statistics are delineated in ibid., 148–185. See also Wright, *Industrial Evolution*, 68–78; Leiby, *Carroll Wright and Labor Reform*, 76–94; and Wendell D. McDonald, "The Early History of Labor Statistics in the United States," *LH* 13 (spring 1972): 267–78. Analogous agencies came into being in Europe and England in the 1890s. See Furner, "Knowing Capitalism," 247. Other studies of the bureaus include Fones-Wolf, "Class, Professionalism and the Early Bureaus"; Charles Pidgin, *History of the Bureau of Statistics of Labor of Massachusetts and of Labor Legislation in That State from 1833 to 1867* (Boston: Wright and Potter, 1876); Richard Mayo Smith, "American Labor Statistics," *Political Science Quarterly* 1 (1886): 45–83; Carroll D. Wright, "The Growth and Purposes of Bureaus of Statistics of Labor," *Journal of Social Science* 25 (Dec. 1888): 1–86; Willoughby, "Child Labor"; Ewan Clague, *The Bureau of Labor Statistics* (New York: Praeger, 1968), 3–12; Gustavus Weber, *The Bureau of Labor Statistics, United States Department of Labor: Its History, Activities, and Organization*, Bulletin of the U.S. Bureau of Labor Statistics, no. 319 (Washington: GPO., 1922).

43. Fones-Wolf, "Class, Professionalism and the Early Bureaus"; Carroll Wright, U.S. Bureau of Labor, "The Value and Influence of Labor Statistics," *The Engineering Magazine* 4 (Nov. 1893): 137.

44. "Hells Mills at Cohoes," *John Swinton's Paper*, March 28, 1886. Historians have recognized two reasons for the decline of child labor: legislation and long-term declines in the supply and demand. For arguments linking the latter causes with the growth of consciousness of surplus and leisure in the United States, see Daniel T. Rodgers,

The Work Ethic in Industrial America, 1850–1920 (Chicago: University of Chicago Press, 1974), 133–34; Rosenzweig, *Eight Hours for What We Will;* and Behlmer, *Child Abuse and Moral Reform.*

45. The U.S. Census of 1870 had been the first to report on child labor, so the census of 1880 provided the first indication as to whether child labor had increased. For the inefficacy of inspection, see Felt, *Hostages of Fortune*, 14. Educational reformers first initiated compulsory education laws, beginning with Massachusetts in 1852 and followed by many northern states in the 1860s and 1870s. Child labor legislation was initially passed as a means of enforcing compulsory education laws. After 1883, however, this relationship was reversed, and compulsory education laws became a means of reinforcing child labor laws. For a negative assessment of the impact of compulsory legislation, see Eisenberg, "Compulsory Attendance Legislation in America." Dann, " 'Little Citizens,' " 90–94, describes organized labor's backing of and the difficulty of enforcing New York's child labor law of 1886. A complete summary of child labor legislation before 1890 appears in Foner and Chamberlin, *Sorge's Labor Movement*, 196. See also F. J. Stimson, *Handbook to the Labor Law of the United States* (New York: Scribner's, 1896), 74–75; Willoughby, "Child Labor"; Ensign, *Compulsory School Attendance;* Felt, *Hostages of Fortune*, 1–37; Elizabeth Brandeis, "Child Labor Legislation," in Commons, Lescohier, and Brandeis, *History of Labor*, 3:403–20; Gewen, "Intellectual Foundations of the Child Labor Reform Movement," 212–16; and Lewis Solomon and William Landes, "Compulsory Schooling Legislation: An Economic Analysis of Law and Social Change in the Nineteenth Century," *Journal of Economic History* 32 (March 1972): 54–91.

Carroll Wright exemplified this policy stagnation. As late as 1893, Wright justified the existence of state labor bureaus on the basis of what they had done to reduce child labor alone, but his own activism on the subject ended as early as 1878, when he declared himself "unconvinced that factory labor is severe or injurious to any considerable extent to children over ten years of age working on half-time" (Massachusetts Bureau of Statistics of Labor, *Ninth Annual Report* [Boston, 1878], quoted in Barry Hewen, "The Intellectual Foundations of the Child Labor Reform Movement" [Ph.D. diss., Harvard University, 1972], 254). Yet the half-time system was never adopted in the United States, primarily because half-time schools were not supported by parents or educators, who saw them as unfortunate declensions and second-class aberrations within the American traditions of public schooling.

Wright's view echoed the contemporary status quo of the half-time system in England. After 1870 organized labor supported an arrangement in which children under the age of fourteen worked for six-and-a-half hours a day and attended school for three hours, and further reform efforts proved unavailing. See Edmund Frow and Ruth Frow, *A Survey of the Half-Time System in Education* (Manchester: E. J. Morten, 1970), 17–23. Even Karl Marx tacitly approved of the half-time system, writing in *Critique of the Gotha Programme* (1875) that "an early combination of productive labour with education is one of the most potent means for the transformation of present day society" (quoted in Hugh Cunningham, *The Children of the Poor: Representations of Childhood since the Seventeenth Century* [Oxford: Blackwell, 1991], 170). The legal provisions on education in the Factory Act of 1844 remained virtually the same until they were replaced by the 1918 Education Act. See Jocelyn Dunlop, *English Apprenticeship and Child Labour: A History* (New York: Macmillan, 1912), 311–33; and Eric J. Evans, *The Forging of the Modern State: Early Industrial Britain, 1783–1870* (London: Longmans, 1983), 385–88.

46. Riis, *Children of the Poor*, 144; Lester Frank Ward, "Broadening the Way to Success," *Forum* 2 (Dec. 1886): 246. See also Mary Jo Maynes, "The Contours of Childhood: Demography, Strategy, and Mythology of Childhood in French and German Lower-Class Autobiographies," in John R. Gillis, Louise A. Tilly, and David Levine, eds., *The European Experience of Declining Fertility, 1850–1970: The Quiet Revolution* (Cambridge: Blackwell, 1992), 101–26; Dorothy Ross, *G. Stanley Hall: The Psychologist as Prophet* (Chicago: University of Chicago Press, 1972), 104–33; Selwyn K. Troen, "The Discovery of the Adolescent by American Educational Reformers, 1900–1920: An Economic Perspective," in Lawrence Stone, ed., *Schooling and Society: Studies in the History of Education* (Baltimore: Johns Hopkins University Press, 1976), 239–51; and Vincent A. McQuade, *The American Catholic Attitude on Child Labor Since 1891* (Washington, D.C.: Catholic University of America, 1938). For the moral meaning attached to drudge work for children in the antebellum era, see Jonathan A. Glickstein, *Concepts of Free Labor in Antebellum America* (New Haven: Yale University Press, 1991), 187–259.

Riis began his book with a political point: "The problem of the children is the problem of the State. As we mould the children of the toiling masses in our cities, so we shape the destiny of the State which they will rule in their turn, taking the reins from our hands" (*Children of the Poor*, 1).

47. See Brace, *The Dangerous Classes of New York*, 222–33, 246–70, 353–65.

48. Kelley's paper and responses to it were not printed in the official proceedings. An unusual preface to the proceedings stated: "The Secretary feels chagrined to be compelled to omit the valuable paper read by him at the Convention prepared by Mrs. Florence Kelley Wischnewetzky. This paper was borrowed from the Secretary by several of the visitors in attendance upon the Convention, and one of them failed to return it. The most diligent search has been made for it, but it has been fruitless. A request was also made for a copy of it, but this could not be had. It is with keen regret the Secretary is thus obliged to omit it from these proceedings. Remarks made upon the paper by various members of the Convention are of course omitted" (*Proceedings at the Seventh Annual Session of the National Convention of Chiefs and Commissioners of the Various Bureaus of Statistics of Labor in the United States* [Des Moines: Iowa Printing Co., 1889]; later called *Proceedings of the Association of Officials of Bureau of Labor Statistics of America*). Kelley's paper and replies to it were nonetheless printed in the *Fifth Annual Report of the Bureau of Labor Statistics of the State of Connecticut* (1890), 43–55.

49. *Hartford Evening Post*, June 25, 1889, quoted in Blumberg, *Florence Kelley*, 104. Kelley's criticisms were also reported in "Labor Statisticians in Council," *The Christian Union* 40 (July 4, 1889): 7. There she was described as asserting "that in most states the word of the parent as to the age of the child worker is accepted as conclusive, even though the size of the child would indicate falsehood in the parent's statement; but in Wisconsin, whose factory laws give more power to the inspectors than even in Massachusetts, the inspectors can order any child to leave the factory whose appearance indicates under age."

50. FKW, "Child Labor" (1890), 44. Supporting Kelley's view of child labor as increasing was Willoughby's 1890 study, "Child Labor." He criticized the U.S. censuses of 1870, 1880, and 1890 for underrepresenting the number of working children, since they did not include those who "helped" their parents in sweatshops and elsewhere. Dann concluded that "the year 1890 appears to be a peak point in

the percent of children among workers in non-agricultural occupations" (" 'Little Citizens,' " 94).

51. FKW, "Child Labor," 43–45. Felt, *Hostages of Fortune,* 17–37, supports Kelley's analysis of the inadequacies of statistics and the need for better studies.

52. FKW, "Child Labor," 43.

53. Ibid., 45, 47, 52. The commissioner from Missouri noted that "as long as the wages of the head of the family fall as short of supporting the family as recent investigations show," parents will lie about their children's age, and employers will hire them (51). Birth registration, fines, and increased bureau funding were proposed as remedies. Connecticut's representative added that since many mill-working children came from French-Canadian families, "the father exercises his legal right to the services of his children till they are twenty-one," and when younger children are dismissed, the entire family departs, "seeking occupation in some mill, where the labor of the younger children could be utilized" (55). Only the Wisconsin representative claimed perfect enforcement in his state (50). The Massachusetts commissioner insisted that only the federal census could determine whether child labor was increasing or diminishing and that the state boards could not be condemned for being unable to accomplish what was beyond their scope. He criticized Kelley for overlooking a recent Massachusetts report on data from the 1885 census, which, when compared to the 1875 census, supported Carroll Wright's contention that child labor had decreased (46–49).

54. Ibid., 49, 52–54.

55. James Bryce, *The American Commonwealth* (London: Macmillan, 1891), 1:295–96.

56. Clipping in the Lester Ward Papers, cited in Brock, *Investigation and Responsibility,* 43.

57. RTE, "Co-operation in Literature and the State," in William E. Barns, ed., *The Labor Problem: Plain Questions and Practical Answers* (New York: Harper and Bros., 1886), 16; RTE, *Ground Under Our Feet,* 147; FK to RTE, New York, n.d. [1890], RTEP, box 3, folder 7. Arguing against the tendency for organized labor and reformers generally in the United States to settle on panaceas, Ely continued in "Co-operation in Literature and the State": "Co-operation is a good thing; arbitration is a good thing; profit sharing is a good thing; but let us remember amid all this discussion that every hope of a permanent reform in industrial and social life must be illusory unless it has a firm foundation in a lasting State reformation" (16). See also John

Rutherford Everett, *Religion in Economics: A Study of John Bates Clark, Richard T. Ely, Simon N. Patten* (New York: King's Crown, 1946); and Ross, "Socialism and American Liberalism." Ely remembered Kelley being at the first annual meeting of the AEA in 1886, but her inclusion in the membership after the 1888 meeting makes this date her most likely initial participation in the association. For the date of Kelley's membership, see *Publications of the American Economic Association,* vol. 1, *Constitution, By-Laws and Resolutions of the American Economic Association, with List of Officers and Members of the American Economic Association. Supplement* (Baltimore: Guggenheimer, Weil, 1889), 27.

Kelley thought American methods of production were less regulated than was the case in Europe. She anticipated that "In Europe the investigations in connection with compulsory insurance are destined to throw a flood of light upon the health of the different sections of the working class within the next few years. But we have apparently no source of authoritative information" (FK to RTE, n.d. [1890]).

58. William Graham Sumner, "The Challenge of Facts," in Albert Galloway Keller and Maurice R. Davie, eds., *Essays of William Graham Sumner* (New Haven: Yale University Press, 1911; reprint, Archon Books, 1969), 2:93. Sumner's essay, originally titled "Socialism," was first published in *Scribners* 16 (1878): 887–93. See also Sumner's essay "State Interference," *North American Review* 145 (Aug. 1887): 136–49. Sumner's pessimism limited his popular appeal. See Robert Green McCloskey, *American Conservatism in the Age of Enterprise: A Study of William Graham Sumner, Stephen J. Field and Andrew Carnegie* (Cambridge: Harvard University Press, 1951); and Bannister, *Social Darwinism,* 97–163.

59. FKW to RTE, n.d. [1891].

60. FKW to RTE, n.d. [ca. 1890, letter A], RTEP.

61. FKW to RTE, n.d. [ca. 1890, letter B], RTEP.

62. FKW to FE, New York, Oct. 13, and Nov. 25, 1891, IISH.

63. FKW to FE, Oct. 13, 1891; FE to FKW, London, Jan. 28, 1892, NKP; FKW to FE, New York, Dec. 1, 1891, IISH. Engels's November letter to which Kelley was responding has not survived, but he repeated the publisher's objections in January.

64. FKW to CBK, New York City, Dec. 20, 1889, KFP. The kindergarten movement began in Germany and in the 1870s was adopted in the United States, where it was supported by both socialists and middle-class women. See Alan R. Pence,

"Preschool Programs of the Nineteenth Century: Towards a History of Preschool Child Care in America" (Ph.D. diss., University of Oregon, 1980), 118–41; and Ann Taylor Allen, "Gardens of Children, Gardens of God: Kindergartens and Day-Care Centers in Nineteenth Century Germany," *Journal of Social History* 19 (spring 1986): 433–50.

65. FK to WDK, New York, Dec. 11, 1889, NKP; "The Mechanico-Therapeutic and Orthopedic Zander Institute of the City of New York," undated pamphlet, NKP. For William Kelley's financial help, see WDK to FK, Philadelphia, Sept. 9, 1889, WDKP. Lazare Wischnewetzky was not listed in the medical registers of New York, New Jersey, or Connecticut (1887–1890) or in Polk's *Medical and Surgical Directory of the United States* (1886 and 1890), indicating that his medical standing was unsustained by a state license.

66. Last Will and Testament of Hon. William D. Kelley, filed Jan. 14, 1890, Register of Wills of the City and County of Philadelphia, Historical Society of Pennsylvania, microfilm, 148, 537–39. No evidence bearing on Florence Kelley's reaction to her father's death has survived. After a memorial service in the House of Representatives, his body was conveyed to Philadelphia by a special train, which also carried family members and close friends. He was interred in the family plot that also held the remains of his mother, father, sister, first wife, and their children. In February Caroline transferred the graves of their five daughters to this family plot. See Permits for Internment, records maintained at Laurel Hill Cemetery.

67. WDK Jr. to CBK, The Perry Stove Manufacturing Company, South Pittsburg, Tennessee, March 5, March 8, and March 18, 1890, box 5, KFP.

68. *Chicago Tribune*, March 26, 1892, 9. The news story reported the trial wherein Lazare tried to obtain custody of the children. When the coverage reached Florence's social set, it caused quite a stir. Isabel Howland wrote her aunt Emily Howland in Boston referring to a clipping that mentioned "his ill treatment of her, beating, throwing bottles at her, &c." Friends of Florence, she said, "all feel very sorry for her though none of them had wanted her to marry him." She also mentioned that a friend who visited Florence recently "said that Lazari [*sic*] seemed cross to Florence." See Isabel Howland to Emily Howland, Boston, March 29, 1892, Emily Howland Papers, Collection #2681, Cornell University Library.

69. Cook County Divorce Proceedings, July 15, 1900, NKP; *Chicago Tribune*, March 26, 1892, 9.

70. Ibid.

71. FKW to RTE, n.d. [ca. 1890, letter B].

72. FKW to RTE, New York, April 23, 1891, RTEP, box 3, folder 11.

73. RTE, *Socialism: An Examination of Its Nature, Its Strength and Its Weakness, with Suggestions for Social Reform* (New York: Crowell, 1894), 48–49.

74. Cook County Divorce Proceedings. For Florence's flight, see FK to CBK, Hull House, Feb. 24, 1892, NKP.

8. A Colony of Efficient and Intelligent Women in the Early 1890s

1. FK to CBK, Hull House, Feb. 24, 1892, NKP. For the Woman's Temple, see "Matilda Bradley Carse," in *NAW;* and Bordin, *Woman and Temperance,* 145–47. NK later wrote that his mother "became a resident at Hull House almost at once after we came to Chicago" (NK, "Early Days at Hull House," 424–29). FK to Henry Demarest Lloyd (hereafter HDL), Jan. 4, 1892, Henry Demarest Lloyd Papers (hereafter HDLP), gives "Miss West's" as a return address. That address, 161 LaSalle, was listed in the *Chicago City Directory* for 1891 as belonging to the W.T. [Woman's Temperance] Publishing Association. West, a professional journalist who had been president of the Illinois WCTU, became editor of the *Union Signal* in 1885 (Bordin, *Woman and Temperance,* 91). On the basis of oral interviews with Florence Kelley, Josephine Goldmark, *Impatient Crusader,* 22, stated that Kelley "turned first to Frances Willard's organization, the Woman's Christian Temperance Union, but it had nothing to offer her."

2. FK, "I Go to Work" (June 1927), 271. Addams seems not to have heard of Kelley before her arrival at Hull House.

3. Addams (hereafter JA) began mobilizing support for her project in May 1889, when Ellen Henrotin, an influential member of the Chicago Woman's Club, "gave a reception to about thirty young ladies," during which Addams "indoctrinated them in regard to the scheme" (JA to Anna Haldeman Addams, Chicago, May 9, 1889, Jane Addams Memorial Collection (hereafter JAMC) (and *JAP,* reel 2, #1064).

JA has not received the attention she deserves as one of the most significant shapers of American democracy during a major historical watershed. *The Young Jane Addams,* Victoria Bissell Brown's forthcoming biography of JA's life before 1895, will help remedy this. Most useful are Christopher Lasch, *The New Radicalism in America, 1889–1963* (New York: Knopf, 1965), 3–37; Davis, *American Heroine;* Anne F. Scott, introduction to JA, *Democracy and Social Ethics;* "Jane Addams," in *NAW;* Farrell, *Beloved Lady;* Jill Conway, "Women Reformers and American Culture, 1870–1930," *Journal of Social History* 5 (Winter 1971), 164–82). Deegan, *Jane Addams and the Men of the Chicago School;* and Christopher Lasch, ed., *The Social Thought of Jane Addams* (Indianapolis: Bobbs-Merrill, 1965).

4. FK, "Hull House," 65; JA, *Twenty Years at Hull House,* 91; and JA, "Objective Value of a Social Settlement," 31–32. For demographic information about the Nineteenth Ward, see Department of the Interior, Census Office, *Compendium of the Eleventh Census: 1890. Part 1. Population* (Washington: GPO, 1892), 438–39. Addams and Starr named the settlement after the original builder of the house in the 1850s. For more on Starr, see Jennifer Lynne Bosch, "The Life of Ellen Gates Starr, 1859–1940" (Ph.D. diss., Miami University, 1990). Religious affiliation in Chicago was 68 percent Catholic, 30 percent Protestant, and 2 percent Jewish. See Bruce Nelson, "Revival and Upheaval: Religion, Irreligion, and Chicago's Working Class in 1886," *JSH* 25 (winter 1991): 234. For more on the Chicago urban context, see Harold M. Mayer and Richard C. Wade, *Chicago: Growth of a Metropolis* (Chicago: University of Chicago Press, 1969), 160, 262.

5. William Cronon, *Nature's Metropolis: Chicago and the Great West* (New York: Norton, 1991), 373–74, quoted in Garry Wills, "Chicago Underground," *New York Review of Books,* Oct. 21, 1993, 15. Whereas in the 1870s three of every five migrants into Chicago had been native-born, in the 1880s two of every three new arrivals were foreign-born. Between 1870 and 1890 the U.S. population rose from 38.5 to 62.6 million. The state of Illinois grew from a population of 2.5 million in 1870 to 3.8 million in 1890, making it the third most populous state in the union. In 1890 almost half of the state's population was of foreign parentage. See Census Office, *Eleventh Census,* 2, 4, 69, 434–5, 438–9; and Department of the Interior, Census Office, *Twelfth Census of the United States, taken in the Year 1900. Population. Part I* (Washington: GPO, 1902), 651. Chicago led a statewide economic shift from agriculture to manufacturing, in which the capital invested in Illinois manufacturing establishments increased from $140.6 million in 1880 to $502 million in 1890. See Ernest L. Bogart and Charles M. Thompson, *The Centennial History of Illinois,* vol. 4, *The Industrial State, 1870–1893* (Chicago: McClurg, 1922), 505.

6. For the settlement movement, see Davis, *Spearheads for Reform,* 12; and Robert A. Woods and Albert J. Kennedy, eds., *Handbook of Settlements* (New York: Russell Sage Foundation, 1911; reprint, New York: Arno, 1970), vi. To some degree, settlements took on the character of their city's social services. Thus in Cincinnati settlements were closely associated with churches, in New Haven with case-work methods, and in Boston with educational clubs. Chicago and New York, containing the greatest variety of social service systems, offered the greatest opportunities for innovation.

For the strength of college ties when Kelley joined the movement, see *Second Annual Report of the College Settlements Association for the Year 1891* (New York: Brown and Wilson, 1892). Most early women's settlements called themselves college settlements, but Addams termed Hull House a social settlement. See also Vida D. Scudder, "College Settlements and College Women," *Outlook* 70 (April 19, 1902): 973; and Solomon, *Educated Women,* 109–10, 165, 236.

7. FK to FE, Hull House, April 7, 1892, IISH.

8. Finances are analyzed in Sklar, "Who Funded Hull House?" 96. Kelley paid no room or board until September 1892. See also Louise Knight, "Jane Addams Manages Hull House: A Study of an Early Nonprofit," *Nonprofit Management and Leadership* 2 (winter 1991): 125–41.

9. JA, "Outgrowths of Toynbee Hall," typed manuscript, [1891], Papers of Jane Addams (hereafter PJA) (and *JAP,* reel 46, #0480).

Essentially a religious institution, Toynbee Hall was designed to fill the gap between the practical assistance offered to the poor by government and the spiritual encouragement offered by religious missions. It gave young men at Oxford and Cambridge Universities the opportunity to live in a working-class neighborhood and learn firsthand about conditions there, while at the same time they tried to represent important cultural values to the poor.

10. JA, "Subjective Necessity," 1–3. For JA's interaction with African-Americans after 1900, see Lasch-Quinn, *Black Neighbors,* 14–15.

11. For Kelley's talk, see Chicago Woman's Club (hereafter CWC) minutes, Jan. 25, 1892, Chicago Woman's Club Papers (CWCP). In 1895 members changed the organization's name from the Chicago *Women's* Club to the Chicago *Woman's* Club, but both usages were common in both periods of time.

12. See CWC minutes, March 3, 1886; Chicago Woman's Club Annual Report, March 2, 1887; minutes, May 1, 1887, CWCP; "Child of His Brain: Altgeld Helped to Prepare the Educational Bill," *Chicago Tribune*, Nov. 7, 1892, 1. The club grew from a membership of twenty-one in 1876 to sixty-four in 1880. Spurred perhaps by their participation in the Illinois Woman's Alliance, the activism of club members grew stronger in 1890, when they expanded their already large kindergarten; protested the "dismissal of all the women employees in the Internal Revenue Office in Chicago"; collected "names of persons to serve on the Board of the Illinois Industrial School" (which was built entirely from funds raised by the club); called for volunteers to visit tenements "to look after their sanitary condition and to see to the enforcement of the laws"; and supported "an attempt to secure legislation which shall improve the condition of the Public Charitable Institutions of Cook County by placing them in the hands of a properly constituted Board of Trustees." In 1891, the club drafted Illinois's first compulsory education law, and the next year they spent one thousand dollars to enforce it. Nevertheless, Kelley doubtlessly found much to criticize in the membership's social understanding. For example, she took exception to a member who, in a speech called "The Very Poor of Chicago," suggested "that the poor liked to herd together" (CWC minutes, April 6, 1892).

13. [FK], "Household Labor" (1892), in Hull House Scrapbook I [1889–1897], 11, JAMC (and *JAP*, reel 81, addendum reel 10). All references to Hull House scrapbooks come from this location in the microfilm. Pagination in the scrapbooks is erratic; where it occurs in the original, it is provided. For the donation, see CWC minutes, March 23, 1892, CWCP. Hull House records show that the settlement received $350 for the labor bureau and spent $420. See also Sklar, "Who Funded Hull House?" 98–99. In 1889, the Chicago Woman's Club had eagerly recruited JA's membership and treated her as a distinguished addition to their ranks. Addams received "invitations from all sides" before Hull House opened, and she thought "it must be [due to] the 'Women's Club' people" (JA to Mary Addams Linn, Feb. 26, 1889, quoted in Lana Ruegamer, " 'The Paradise of Exceptional Women': Chicago Women Reformers, 1863–1893" [Ph.D. diss., Indiana University, 1982], 184). See also Henriette Greenebaum Frank and Amalie Hofer Jerome, *Annals of the Chicago Woman's Club for the First Forty Years of Its*

Organization (Chicago: Chicago Woman's Club, 1916). For the Fortnightly Club, see Muriel Beadle, *The Fortnightly of Chicago: The City and Its Women, 1873–1973* (Chicago: Regnery, 1973); and Martin, *The Sound of Our Own Voices*, 117–18. For a post-1900 contrast between women's and men's political cultures in Chicago, see Flanagan, "Gender and Urban Political Reform."

14. [FK], "Household Labor"; and "Hull House Bureau: Intelligence Office Added to this Worthy Institution," *Chicago Post*, Jan. 23, 1892, Hull House Scrapbook I, 14. For the bureau's relative lack of success, see FK, "I Go to Work," 272. For the importance of employment bureaus in general to Progressive Era reformers, see Grace Abbott, "The Chicago Employment Agency and the Immigrant Worker," *American Journal of Sociology* 14 (Nov. 1908): 289–305; and Frances Kellor's attack on corrupt employment agencies after 1900 in Fitzpatrick, *Endless Crusade*, 312–36. For Kelley's law studies, see Northwestern University, *Catalogue, 1891–92* (Chicago: Northwestern University, 1891), 201; "Northwestern University Thirty-Seventh Annual Commencement, June 13, 1895" [program], Northwestern University Archives.

15. FK to CBK, Feb. 24, 1892. In 1855 Lucy Stone was the first to retain her maiden name but call herself "Mrs." See "Lucy Stone," in *NAW*. See also Susan J. Kupper, *Surnames for Women: A Decision-Making Guide* (Jefferson, N.C.: McFarland, 1990), 9–21.

16. FK to HDL, Jan. 4, 1892. FK may have met Caro Lloyd in Europe. Compelling parallels between the two women emerged in a letter Lloyd's father wrote to Henry Demarest Lloyd in 1894. Caro and her husband, Lothorp, then in the United States, were planning to return to Europe. "We should discourage her return to Paris—There she is regarded as a Pariah & is classed with the Proletariats. In fact she seems to have imbibed through Lothorp the spirit of this class & rather accepts that position. If she goes back there, it will simply be to act as the servant and supporter of her husband. Her faithfulness may under certain circumstances be admirable. But it is misplaced & inconsistent. . . . Let [Lothorp] abandon all quixotic schemes of revolutionizing the governments of Europe & the world" (Aaron Lloyd to HDL, Belleville, N.J., Aug. 17, 1894, HDLP). Later Caro wrote a loving biography of her brother (see bibliography).

Like the Motts' Roadside in the 1840s, Wayside was a social crossroads for reformers, and Addams knew it well. See Stephen Beal, *Wayside, The*

Henry Demarest Lloyd House in Winnetka, Illinois (Chicago: Landmarks Preservation Service, 1977); and Clarence E. Glick, "Winnetka: A Study of a Residential Suburban Community" (M.A. thesis, University of Chicago, 1928). Lloyd regularly participated in the Workingmen's Discussion Club at Hull House. See JA, *Twenty Years*, 283.

17. NK, "Early Days at Hull House," 428; Destler, *Henry Demarest Lloyd*, 187, 431. On its title page, Lloyd called *A Strike of Millionaires* " 'Our Bad Wealth' Series, No. 1" and quoted Emerson: "It is high time OUR BAD WEALTH came to an end." In 1892 Henry D. Lloyd was writing his classic study of American monopolies, *Wealth against Commonwealth*. See Digby-Junger, "The Gilded Age Journalist." Responding to the request of the local Knights of Labor, child labor was one of the first topics Lloyd wrote on as a free-lance reformer. For the legacy, see Destler, *Henry Demarest Lloyd*, 218. For William Bross, see John James Pauly Jr., "The City Builders: Chicago Businessmen and Their Changing Ethos, 1871–1909" (Ph.D. diss. University of Illinois, 1979), 69–84.

Before they went to boarding school, Kelley's children also lived with Anna Lloyd Wright, mother of Frank Lloyd Wright and sister of Chicago's liberal Unitarian minister, Jenkin Lloyd Jones. For Anna Wright's contribution to early childhood learning, see Jeanne S. Rubin, "The Froebel-Wright Kindergarten Connection: A New Perspective," *Journal of the Society of Architectural Historians* 48 (March 1989): 24–37.

18. FK to CBK, Chicago, March 16, 1892, NKP. In a later letter, she wrote Caroline, "I was with the chicks on Decoration Day and the older ones went for an hour to the Village school for the patriotic exercises" (FK to CBK, fragment [June 1892], NKP). The first electric trolley line between Winnetka and Chicago opened in 1899. See Michael Ebner, *Creating Chicago's North Shore* (Port Washington, N.Y.: Kennikat, 1977).

19. [FK to CBK], fragment, n.d. [1892], NKP.

20. FK to CBK, Hull House, May 24, 1892, NKP.

21. [FK to CBK], another fragment, n.d. [1892], NKP.

22. FK to CBK, Feb. 24, 1892. This was the only time FK mentioned Celara, who may have lived with the children at the Lloyd's that winter.

23. FK to CBK, March 16, 1892.

24. FK to CBK, Feb. 24, 1892.

25. [FK to CBK], fragment, n.d., NKP.

26. FK to CBK, Feb. 24, 1892. Florence's regret remained keen two years later when Elizabeth Pugh

was dying. "Your letters about Grandma made me very sad," she wrote. "I have a very strong sense that I have never made her any adequate acknowledgement of her goodness to me when I was a child. I do love her very much and it was an irreparable part of the blight of those unhappy years which made me write her letters that could never be explained away or forgotten" (FK to CBK, State of Illinois, Office of Factory Inspector, Feb. 10, 189[4], NKP). These letters to Pugh have not survived, but they apparently resembled those Kelley wrote to May Lewis from Heidelberg.

27. FK to CBK, Feb. 24, 1892.

28. *Chicago Tribune*, March 26, 1892, 9; FK to CBK, May 24, 1892. How Kelley's "literary ability" made financial contributions to her household in Switzerland is unclear. She earned small amounts writing for American periodicals, but her translation of Engels paid nothing until the book was published and very little then.

29. FK to CBK, May 24, 1892.

30. FK to "Miss Williams," State of Illinois, Office of Factory Inspector, Chicago, Nov. 18, 1894, Consumers' League of Massachusetts Papers (hereafter CLMP). FK to FE, Hull House, May 27, 1892, IISH. Kelley petitioned only for custody, not divorce, at this time; she was not divorced until 1900. For child custody, see Mary Ann Mason, *From Father's Property to Children's Rights: The History of Child Custody in the United States* (New York: Columbia University Press, 1994). For contemporary divorce, see U.S. Department of Commerce and Labor, *Marriage and Divorce, 1867–1906* (Washington: GPO, 1909; reprint, New York: Arno, 1978); Glenda Riley, *Divorce: An American Tradition* (New York: Oxford University Press, 1991); and Johannes Stuart, "A Study of Divorce in Cook County" (Ph.D. diss., University of Chicago, 1931).

31. Helen J. Gow (hereafter HJG), April 11, 1897, and April 17, 1897, Helen J. Gow Diaries (hereafter HJGD), vol. 3; Hamilton, *Exploring the Dangerous Trades*, 55; Alice Hamilton (hereafter AH) to Agnes Hamilton, Hull House, Wed. evening [March 30, 1898], quoted in Sicherman, *Alice Hamilton*, 113. I am grateful to Lucy Knight for calling the Gow diaries to my attention and sharing her transcription of them.

32. "Memorial Services for Mrs. Florence Kelley, Miss Julia C. Lathrop, Hull House, Chicago, May 6, 1932," typed transcript, 20–21, Anita McCormick Blaine Papers, State Historical Society of Wisconsin, Madison. Addams drew the quote from Elizabeth Barrett Browning and included it in

Twenty Years, 22. For similarities in FK's and JA's family backgrounds, see Sherrick, "Private Visions, Public Lives"; and Rebecca Louise Sherrick, "Their Fathers' Daughters: The Autobiographies of Jane Addams and Florence Kelley," *American Studies* (spring 1986), 39–53. For Addams's degrees, see JA, *Twenty Years,* 63.

The emphasis the settlement movement placed on educational background put Florence Kelley at an advantage, for her schooling at Cornell and Zürich equalled or exceeded that of any other leader in the movement, woman or man. Since daughters of the so-called leisured class rarely attended college before 1920, they generally did not become leaders in the settlement movement. See Rousmaniere, "Cultural Hybrid in the Slums"; and Scudder, "College Settlements," 975.

33. Quoted in Linn, *Jane Addams,* 138; quoted in JA, *My Friend, Julia Lathrop,* 77; Paul Kellogg, "Twice Twenty Years at Hull-House," *The Survey* 64 (June 15, 1930): 265–67.

34. JA, "Subjective Necessity," 22. Their greatest difference was on the question of relative values. Addams said that she easily understood the oppressive character of the "industrial capitalist" but could not agree with "the proposition that the social relation thus established proceeds to create principles, ideas and categories as merely historical and transitory products" (JA, *Twenty Years,* 186).

35. JA, *Twenty Years,* 308–9.

36. Linn, *Jane Addams,* 138; NK, "Early Days at Hull House," 426.

37. Linn, *Jane Addams,* 139. For the ritual of the evening meal, see HJG, April 26, 1897, HJGD, vol. 3.

38. Francis Hackett, "Hull House—A Souvenir," *The Survey* 54 (June 1, 1925): 275–80, 277; Mercedes Randall, ed., *Beyond Nationalism: The Social Thought of Emily Greene Balch* (New York: Twayne, 1972), 212.

39. FK, "I Go to Work," 271.

40. For structural principles, see Giddens, *Constitution of Society,* 16–22. Other single women, such as Mary Rozet Smith (hereafter MRS), while never residents, found a focus for their lives in Hull House. Some married women, such as Louise DeKoven Bowen, also became central members of the Hull House community even though they were not residents. See n. 46, ch. 3.

41. JA, *Twenty Years,* 94. See also NK, "Early Days at Hull House," 426; and Eileen Boris, *Art and Labor: Ruskin, Morris, and the Craftsman Ideal in America* (Philadelphia: Temple University Press, 1986).

42. Mary Lynn McCree, "The First Year of Hull-House, 1889–1890, in Letters by Jane Addams and Ellen Gates Starr," *Chicago History* 1 (fall 1970): 108. Hamilton described the newly constructed dining room that served the settlement after 1897 in *Exploring the Dangerous Trades,* 68.

43. FK, "Hull House" (July 1898), 555; JA to MRS, Hull House, Aug. 26, 1893, PJA (and *JAP,* reel 2, #1844). For the juvenile population of Chicago, Census Office, *Eleventh Census,* 262–63. For Hull House's physical structure, see Horowitz, "Hull-House as Women's Space"; Guy Szuberla, "Three Chicago Settlements: Their Architectural Form and Social Meaning," *Journal of the Illinois State Historical Society* 70 (May 1977): 114–29; Horowitz, "Varieties of Cultural Experience"; and Horowitz, *Culture and the City,* 126–44.

44. "Two Women's Work: The Misses Addams and Starr Astonish the West Siders," *Chicago Tribune,* May 19, 1890, Hull House Scrapbook I, 2 (reprinted in Mary Lynn McCree Bryan and Allen F. Davis, eds., *One Hundred Years at Hull House* [Bloomington: Indiana University Press, 1990], 18); FK, "Hull House," 554; JA, "Hull-House: A Social Settlement," in *HHM&P,* 219. See also George Rosen, "Public Health: Then and Now," *American Journal of Public Health* 61 (Aug. 1971): 1620–37; and Marilyn Thornton Williams, *Washing "The Great Unwashed": Public Baths in Urban America, 1840–1920* (Columbus: Ohio State University Press, 1991), 82–95. Dr. Bedell had been president of the Chicago Woman's Club in 1885–86. After 1907 Rachelle Yarros pursued this health work at Hull House more systematically. See "Rachelle Yarros," in *NAW.*

45. "Hull-House Kitchen Will Provide a Great Boon to Many," *Chicago Herald,* Aug. 12, 1893, Hull House Scrapbook I, 45; Alzina Parsons Stevens, "Life in a Social Settlement—Hull House, Chicago," *Self Culture* 9 (March–Aug. 1899): 43.

46. Unidentified newsclipping, "What Two Women Did, Their Practical Work to Elevate the Poor of Chicago," Aug. 3, 1891, Hull House Scrapbook I, 9; Vida Scudder, "The Place of College Settlements," *The Andover Review* 18 (Oct. 1892): 341; Jane Robbins, "The First Year at the College Settlement," *The Survey* 27 (Feb. 24, 1912): 1800–02; Woods, "Life in a College Settlement," 41. For more on cooperative housekeeping at Hull House and other women settlements, see Dolores Hayden, *The Grand Domestic Revolution: A History of Feminist Designs for American Homes, Neighborhoods, and*

Cities (Cambridge: MIT Press, 1981), 162–67; and "Katharine Pearson Woods," in *NAW.*

47. See Ruth Bordin, *Frances Willard: A Biography* (Chapel Hill: University of North Carolina Press, 1986), especially indexed references to Anna Gordon and Lady Somerset.

48. Linn, *Jane Addams,* 147. Duos of women were important agents of innovation in American public life throughout the nineteenth century (Angelina and Sarah Grimké; Elizabeth Cady Stanton and Susan B. Anthony, for example). But the same-sex partnerships of the Progressive Era brought this personal and public support system to a new level. Unfortunately, no systematic study exists of the effects of this system on women's participation in Progressive reform. For a late example of one relationship, see Susan Ware, *Partner and I: Molly Dewson, Feminism and New Deal Politics* (New Haven: Yale University Press, 1987). For an account of women partners that does not ask questions about the partnerships' collective impact on public life, see Patricia Franzen, "Spinsters and Lesbians: Autonomous Women and the Institution of Heterosexuality, 1890–1920 and 1940–1980" (Ph.D. diss., University of New Mexico, 1990), 166–69. In addition to Jane Addams and Mary Rozet Smith, examples of enduring partnerships maintained by Progressive Era women reformers include: Vida Scudder and Helena Dudley; Molly Dewson and Polly Porter; Josephine Baker and Florence Laighton; Martha May Eliot and Ethel Durham; Frieda Miller and Pauline Newman; Mary Elisabeth Dreier and Frances Kellor; Mary Parker Follett and Isobel Briggs. See their biographies in *NAW.*

Middle-class resources were crucial to the privacy on which "Boston marriages" were constructed. One important reason for the evolution of "butch-femme" roles among working-class women-oriented women was the tradition of "passing." Two women could not earn enough to support the privacy they desired, but a woman passing as a man could earn a man's wage and thereby support their privacy. See John D'Emilio and Estelle B. Freedman, *Intimate Matters: A History of Sexuality in America* (New York: Harper and Row, 1988), 191–92.

Historians are currently debating two definitions of *lesbian.* Leila Rupp, "Women Alone Stir My Imagination: Lesbianism and the Cultural Tradition," *Signs* 4 (summer 1979): 719–20, argued that women-oriented, homosocial women should be considered lesbians whether or not the relationship can be documented to be sexual. More recently, Elizabeth Lapovsky Kennedy and Madeline D.

Davis, *Boots of Leather, Slippers of Gold: The History of a Lesbian Community* (New York: Routledge, 1993), 6–7, argued that sexuality was central to lesbian identity, and the term should only be used to embrace that meaning. The term *lesbian* only came into widespread use among women-oriented women in the 1960s; whether it should be applied to women who did not themselves use it is also debated among historians. My own view is that since Mary Smith was viewed by close contemporaries (like Florence Kelley) as the "dearly beloved" partner of Jane Addams—in every way the equivalent of her spouse—and since Addams often slept at Smith's house and they were perceived as homosocial intimates, their relationship would in today's society be called lesbian. However, the anachronistic ring of the term when applied to the 1890s, together with the indirect nature of evidence about their sexual relationship, leads me to prefer the term *homoerotic.* See also Blanche Wiesen Cook, "Female Support Networks and Political Activism: Lillian Wald, Crystal Eastman, Emma Goldman," in Nancy F. Cott and Elizabeth H. Pleck, eds., *A Heritage of Her Own: Toward a New Social History of American Women* (New York: Simon and Schuster, 1979); Maglin, "Vida to Florence"; Judith Schwarz, "*Yellow Clover:* Katharine Lee Bates and Katharine Coman," *Frontiers* 4 (spring 1979), 59–67; Anna Mary Wells, *Miss Marks and Miss Woolley* (Boston: Houghton Mifflin, 1978). For the end of nineteenth-century acceptance of "Boston marriages," see Christine Simmons, "Companionate Marriage and the Lesbian Threat," *Frontiers* 4 (spring 1979): 54–59, reprinted in Kathryn Kish Sklar and Thomas Dublin, eds., *Women and Power in American History* (Englewood Cliffs: Prentice-Hall, 1991), 2:183–94. For a review of recent historiography on homosexuality from a deconstructionist perspective, see the introduction to Domna C. Stanton, ed., *Discourses of Sexuality: From Aristotle to AIDS* (Ann Arbor: University of Michigan Press, 1992), 1–46.

49. Linn, *Jane Addams,* 147; JA to MRS, Hull House, [1894], PJA (and *JAP,* reel 2, #1482); JA, untitled poem, quoted in Linn, *Jane Addams,* 290. Soon after Florence Kelley arrived, Starr left on a trip to England and Venice, where she came to terms with the personal and professional loss of her partnership with Addams. Kelley might have been unaware of the drama behind her departure: "Miss Starr starts tomorrow . . . and I shall be of real use during her absence apart from my own work" (FK to CBK, March 16, 1892). See also Sklar, "Who Funded Hull House?" 100–104. Smith lived

with her parents until her mother died around 1900 (personal correspondence with Mary Lynn McCree Bryan, June 17, 1988). A young immigrant woman who taught a course at Hull House in the 1890s left a vivid description of Mary Smith's presence at the settlement: "Although I had very little contact with Mary Rozet Smith, her beauty and charm would pass a current of joy through me every time she passed me. All the gifts of nature and material wealth had been bestowed on this woman. Yet she was simple in her dignity. She was Jane Addams's closest friend, and Miss Addams spent as much time as she could spare from her work at the home of Miss Smith, on the Near North Side of Chicago" (Polacheck, *I Came a Stranger*, 100).

50. AH to Agnes Hamilton, Hull House, Oct. 13, 1897, quoted in Sicherman, *Alice Hamilton*, 116; NK, "Early Days at Hull House," 426. AH's cousin, Agnes Hamilton, commented revealingly on name usage in a letter to Kelley: "I quoted 'Mrs. Kelley' to crush some one the other day, and she said, 'Florence Kelley?' I inquired if she knew you. Only by reputation, she said—but to her you were *Florence Kelley* just as Miss Anthony is *Susan B.* Do you remember how the latter lady called you *Florence?*" (Agnes Hamilton to FK, n.p., Jan. 17, 1895, KFP).

51. AH to Agnes Hamilton, Fort Wayne, Nov. 26, 1898, quoted in Sicherman, *Alice Hamilton*, 127; Hackett, "Hull House," 176 (Hackett went on to speculate that harmony was achieved partly through the "probation," which "did result in a real selection," since "thorny people were not admitted"); AH, *Exploring the Dangerous Trades*, 61; Woods, "Life in a College Settlement," 65. The New York settlements to which Hamilton referred were the University and Rivington Street settlements, the former a men's, the latter a women's settlement.

52. FK to FE, April 7, 1892.

53. Obituary of FK by Julia Lathrop, first published in *The Survey* 67 (March 15, 1932): 677, and quoted in JA, *My Friend, Julia Lathrop*, 129; JA, *My Friend, Julia Lathrop*, 53; Ellen Gates Starr (hereafter EGS) to Mary Blaisdell, Chicago, July 25, 1892, Ellen Gates Starr Papers (hereafter EGSP), box 1.

54. HJG, April 9, 1897, HJGD, vol. 3; JA, *Twenty Years*, 147; EGS to Mary Allen, Oct. 14, [1892], EGSP, box 7. Edward Burchard remembered the prayer meetings ceasing with FK's arrival (Edward Buchard to EGS, Chicago, Jan. 16, 1938, EGSP, box 11).

Helen Gow thought Hull House residents were "tired weary-looking women," but that Addams was "tired looking beyond all the tired Settlement

workers I have seen." Once, she said, Addams "came in looking scarcely alive—I have never seen one so death-like moving about" (HJG, April 11, 1897, and April 17, 1897, HJGD, vol. 3).

55. See JA, "Subjective Necessity," 14–15, 22. See also Kathryn Kish Sklar, "Jane Addams, 'The Subjective Necessity for Social Settlements,' " in David Nasaw, ed., *The Course of United States History* (Chicago: Dorsey, 1987), 2:135–40. Present at the conference were Julia Lathrop and other women from Chicago, as well as a large contingent of settlement leaders from New York and Boston, including Vida Scudder, Helena Dudley, Katharine Coman, and Emily Balch, and two leading men in social statistics, Franklin Sanborn and Carroll Wright.

56. JA, "Subjective Necessity," 22.

57. FK, "Need of Theoretical Preparation" (1887), 18 (reprinted in Sklar, *Autobiography of Florence Kelley*, 94).

58. JA, *Twenty Years*, 84–85.

59. JA, "Objective Value of a Social Settlement," 55–56.

60. Ibid., 29; FK, "Hull House," 551, 557.

61. Mary Kenney, autobiographical manuscript, Schlesinger Library, quoted in Davis and McCree, *Eighty Years at Hull House*, 34–35; JA to HDL, Dec. 15, 1891, HDLP; Mary Kenney, quoted in Davis and McCree, *Eighty Years at Hull House*, 35. For Addams's proposition regarding the factory, see JA to HDL, Jan. 2, 1892, HDLP.

62. JA, *Twenty Years*, 136; "The Jane Club: Working Girls Live Cheaply and Pleasantly on the Cooperative Plan," *Inter Ocean*, July 1892, Hull House Scrapbook I, 15. For more on the Jane Club and an analysis of the options of wage-earning women in boarding houses, see Joanne J. Meyerowitz, "Sexual Geography and Gender Economy: The Furnished Room Districts of Chicago, 1890–1930," *Gender and History* 2 (autumn 1990): 274–96; and Meyerowitz, *Women Adrift*, 71, 96–98. See also Weiner, " 'Our Sisters' Keepers' "; and Harriet Fayes, "Housing of Single Women," *Municipal Affairs* 3 (1899): 95–107.

63. FK to HDL, 327 W. Harrison St., Nov. 28, 1892, HDLP; unidentified newsclipping, "Hull House Men's Club Organized," [Jan. 1893], Hull House Scrapbook I, 27. For the schedule of social events, see "A Home on Halsted Street," unidentified newsclipping, July 11, 1889, Hull House Scrapbook I, 1; and "Two Women's Work."

64. Marie Thérèse Blanc, *The Condition of Woman in the United States* (Boston: Roberts Bros.,

1895), 74–82; JA, *Twenty Years*, 183. Addams continued, "And yet as I recall the members of this early club, even those who talked the most and the least rationally, seem to me to have been particularly kindly and 'safe.'" She remembered Mme. Blanc's visit: "I recall a brilliant Frenchwoman who was filled with amazement because one of the shabbiest men reflected a reading of Schopenhauer" (*Twenty Years*, 182).

65. "A Home on Halsted Street," unidentified newsclipping [July 1889], Hull House Scrapbook I; HDL, quoted in Lloyd, *Henry Demarest Lloyd*, 2:301. Although at many other settlements the head resident assigned duties to residents and prohibited work outside the settlement, Hull House affiliates were free to pursue their own projects related to other aspects of city life. Charged a minimal fee for room and board, residents were accepted after a brief probationary period provided they promised to remain at least six months. Eight short-term residents were present in 1893.

66. David A. Shannon, ed., *Beatrice Webb's American Diary, 1898* (Madison: University of Wisconsin Press, 1963), 108.

67. "Another Praiseworthy Gift," *Chicago Post*, Dec. 27, 1892, Hull House Scrapbook I, 46. For the art gallery, see Linn, *Jane Addams*, 75, 122. JA built a public library branch and space for clubs and classes into the gallery (see *Chicago Tribune*, June 21, 1891, Hull House Scrapbook I). For the expansion of Hull House, see Davis and McCree, *Eighty Years at Hull House*, 22; "A Day in Altruria: A Visit to Hull House in Chicago," *The Chronicle* (Feb. 4, 1894), Hull House Scrapbook I, 47; "Hull House: A Social Settlement," *The Confection Baker and American Caterer* (July 1894), 8–9, Hull House Scrapbook I, 53; and "Plans for the Poor: Hull House and Groceries," unidentified newsclipping, Sept. 6, 1894, Hull House Scrapbook I, 50. Addams rejected what she considered "tainted money," especially when it came from "a man who was notorious for underpaying the girls in his establishment and concerning whom there were even darker stories" (JA, *Twenty Years*, 138).

68. Linn, *Jane Addams*, 140; HJG, April 1, 1897, HJGD, vol. 3. Discussions were even more electric at the house meetings that only residents attended.

69. Such a list of white women would include, in addition to those already mentioned, Grace Abbott, Emily Balch, Gertrude Barnum, Katharine Bates, Sophonisba Breckinridge, Helen Campbell, Katharine Bement Davis, Lavinia Dock, Crystal Eastman, Charlotte Perkins Gilman, Alice Henry, Mary White Ovington, Mary McDowell, Leonora O'Reilly, Jane Robbins, Mary Kingsbury Simkhovitch, Emma Woerishoffer, Rachelle Yarros, and Maud Younger. Many others could be added. This group was compiled from the classified index "Settlement House Leaders," in *NAW*, vol. 3, and "Settlements," in Barbara Sicherman and Carol Hurd Green, eds., *Notable American Women, the Modern Period: A Biographical Dictionary* (Cambridge: Harvard University Press, 1980). See also appendix 2 in Fastenau, "Maternal Government." The White Rose Mission, founded in 1897 in New York City, became the first settlement for blacks. See Cash, "Radicals or Realists," 717. For differences that emerged between white and black settlement women after 1897, see Gordon, "Black and White Visions of Welfare."

70. JA, "Subjective Necessity," 22. This interpretation draws on Fox, "Culture of Liberal Protestant Progressivism." In New York, the Social Gospel movement started between 1886 and 1889 with the efforts of Walter Rauschenbusch, recently returned from study in Germany, where he became persuaded that religion begins in individual experience not theological concepts. See Kloppenberg, *Uncertain Victory*, 208–9. See also White and Hopkins, *The Social Gospel;* Crunden, *Ministers of Reform;* Christopher Lasch, "Religious Contributions to Social Movements: Walter Rauschenbusch, the Social Gospel and Its Critics," *Journal of Religious Ethics* 18 (1990): 7–25; John Patrick McDowell, *The Social Gospel in the South: The Woman's Home Mission Movement in the Methodist Episcopal Church, South, 1886–1939* (Baton Rouge: Louisiana State University Press, 1982); Luker, *Social Gospel in Black and White;* Frederick, *Knights of the Golden Rule*, 141–83; Paul A. Carter, *The Spiritual Crisis of the Gilded Age* (DeKalb: Northern Illinois University Press, 1971); and Herbert G. Gutman, "Protestantism and the American Labor Movement: The Christian Spirit in the Gilded Age," in Gutman, *Work, Culture, and Society*, esp. 79–117. Gutman argued that working-class and middle-class Social Gospel movements were parallel rather than intersecting, but at Hull House and elsewhere in women's public culture the two did intersect. Writings about English and European Christian socialism are abundant. See especially Peter d'A. Jones, *The Christian Socialist Revival, 1877–1914: Religion, Class, and Social Conscience in Late-Victorian England* (Princeton: Princeton University Press, 1968).

71. JA, *Twenty Years,* 190. See Stead, *If Christ Came to Chicago,* 15.

72. Woods, "Life in a College Settlement" (Jan. 1894), 41; Robert A. Woods, "The Advantages of Settlement Work for Women," in Perkins, *Vocations for the Trained Woman,* 56. Woods attended Andover Theological Seminary, the fountainhead of Social Gospel theological training. See Davis, *Spearheads for Reform,* 28; and Edward S. Shapiro, "Robert A. Woods and the Settlement House Impulse," *Social Service Review* 52 (June 1978), 215–26. Woods also conceded women's dominance of the movement when he referred to settlement men as "a group of exquisites" (Robert A. Woods, "University Settlement," *Andover Review* 17 (Oct. 1892): 9, quoted in Reinders, "Toynbee Hall," 45).

73. "The Mission of Hull-House," *Review of Reviews* (1896), Hull House Scrapbook, Addendum [1890–1906], n.p. For salaries of settlement leaders, see AH to Agnes Hamilton, [March 30, 1898]. For women's reasons for joining the settlement movement, see Sklar, "Hull House as a Community of Women," 663.

Of the forty settlements founded in Chicago between 1889 and 1910, two were sponsored by Catholics, three by Jews, and two by universities. The first settlement for African-Americans was founded in 1908. The only settlement that served a predominately white, native-born neighborhood was The Forward Movement, which in 1896 left its initial sponsor of the Methodist Episcopal Church and became nonsectarian. Settlements whose chief purpose was to proselytize and gain converts did not last more than a few years. For the settlements founded during Kelley's years in Chicago, see Woods and Kennedy, *Handbook of Settlements,* 37–80, 311–12. The national settlement scene during Kelley's years at Hull House was captured in an 1896 survey by Julia Lathrop to which twenty-seven of the forty-four settlements replied: Julia Lathrop, "What the Settlement Work Stands For," in Isabel C. Barrows, ed., *A Report of the National Conference of Charities and Correction, 1896* (Boston: Ellis, 1896), 106–10, 166–76.

74. FK, "Towards Social Reform," review of a book by that title by Canon and Mrs. Barnett, *The Survey* 23 (Feb. 24, 1910): 711–12. See also Reinders, "Toynbee Hall."

75. Emil Muensterberg, "Impressions of American Charity: Settlements," *Charity and the Commons* 17 (Sept. 17, 1907): 711; Percy Alden, "American Settlements," in M. A. Reason, ed., *University and Social Settlements* (London: Methuen, 1898), 138;

and Henrietta Octavia Barnett, *Canon Barnett, His Life, Work, and Friends* (Boston: Houghton Mifflin, 1919), 2:32.

Fastenau "Maternal Government," 4, calculated the following statistics from Woods and Kennedy, *Handbook of Settlements.* Seventy-two percent of those settlements providing information about their founders' gender were established by women; 86 percent of the headworkers between 1886 and 1911 were women; 73 percent of the residents and 81 percent of the nonresident volunteers were women; and of the 244 providing information about the sex of their residents, 53 percent had only women residents, and in another 33 percent the majority of the residents were women. For a brief comparison of women in British and American settlements see Bolt, *Women's Movements,* 216–23. The first American settlement, Neighborhood Guild, was founded by Stanton Coit in New York in 1886, but it collapsed when he moved to England in 1887. In 1891 Neighborhood Guild was reorganized and renamed University Settlement. See Kraus, *Settlement House Movement,* 46–72; and Bliss, *Encyclopedia of Social Reform,* s.v. "Settlements (Social, University, College, and Church),'' 1106–9. Complete records of the undertakings and fundings of the women's college settlements after 1890 are in the annual reports of the College Settlements Association, available on microfilm from the Social Welfare Archives, University of Minnesota, Minneapolis.

The best statistical depiction of English settlements, men's, women's, and mixed, is the table in Werner Picht, *Toynbee Hall and the Settlement Movement* (London: G. Bell and Sons, 1916), 100–101. In London before 1900 the only nonreligious women's equivalent to Toynbee Hall was the Women's University Settlement, Southwark, founded in 1887. Picht noted the "peculiar position" of most women's settlements, "which stand in entire dependence on the clergy (as in the Roman Catholic Women's Settlements) or form a branch of a Men's Settlement (e.g., St. Margaret's House and St. Mildred's House in connection with Oxford House)" (103). British women's settlements are studied in Seth D. Koven, *Culture and Poverty: The London Settlement House Movement, 1870 to 1914* (New York: Routledge, 1994); Jane Lewis, *Women and Social Action in Victorian and Edwardian England* (Stanford: Stanford University Press, 1991), 24–82; Jane Lewis, "Gender, the Family and Women's Agency in the Building of 'Welfare States': The British Case," *Social History* 19 (Jan. 1994): 37–56; Julia Parker, *Women and Welfare: Ten*

Victorian Women in Public Social Service (London: Macmillan, 1988); and Seth Koven, "Borderlands: Women, Voluntary Action, and Child Welfare in Britain, 1840 to 1914," in Koven and Michel, *Mothers of a New World*, 94–135.

Reflecting the difficulty with which he accepted women leaders in the settlement movement, Samuel Barnett called Jane Addams "the greatest man in America" (Barnett, *Canon Barnett*, 2:31). Barnett deliberately excluded women from residence in Toynbee Hall, fearing that if women were admitted they would dominate (see 2:51). Henrietta Barnett's own influence had more to do with domestic than political economy; her most influential publication was *The Making of the Home: A Reading Book of Domestic Economy for School and Home Use* (London: Cassell, 1885). The most complete study of Toynbee Hall is Emily K. Abel, "Canon Barnett and the First Thirty Years of Toynbee Hall" (Ph.D. diss., Queen Mary College, University of London, 1969). See also Seth Koven, "Henrietta Barnett, 1851–1936: The (Auto)biography of a Late Victorian Marriage," in Susan Pederson and Peter Mandler, eds., *After the Victorians: Private Conscience and Public Duty in Modern Britain. Essays in Memory of John Clive* (London: Routledge, 1993), 30–53.

76. Standish Meacham, *Toynbee Hall and Social Reform, 1880–1914: The Search for Community* (New Haven: Yale University Press, 1987), 85; George Lansbury, *My Life* (London: Constable, 1928), 130, quoted in Vicinus, *Independent Women*, 215; Barnett, *Canon Barnett*, 51; JA, *Twenty Years*, 292; JA to EGS, London, June 27, 1896, EGSP (and *JAP*, reel 3, #0403). Richard Ely's founding in 1893 of the American Institute of Christian Sociology—which he saw as "a civil academy to do somewhat for the civil service that which West Point and Annapolis do for the military"—was an attempt to remedy the lack of training for "governing" in American settlements (RTE to Albert Shaw, Jan. 25, 1892, quoted in Watkins, "The Professors and the Unions," 149). For more on the U.S.–British comparison, see Levine, *Poverty and Society*, esp. 120–29. For comparisons with the German settlement movement and German civil service, see Christoph Sachsse, *Mütterlichkeit als Beruf: Sozialarbeit Sozialreform und Frauenbewegung, 1871–1929* (Frankfurt: Suhrkamp, 1986), 125–38; and Jane Caplan, "Profession as Vocation: The German Civil Service," in Geoffrey Cocks and Konrad H. Jarausch, eds., *German Professions, 1800–1950* (New York: Oxford University Press, 1990), 163–82.

77. "What Awaits Us?" *Svornost*, March 10, 1892, the Chicago Foreign Language Press Survey, Chicago Public Library; Barnett, *Canon Barnett*, 2:65. In "Outgrowths of Toynbee Hall," 13, Jane Addams declared that "Hull House found no precedent at Toynbee Hall for dealing with this foreign life." See also J. A. R. Pimlott, *Toynbee Hall: Fifty Years of Social Progress, 1884–1934* (London: Dent, 1935), who explained: "The constant influx into Whitechapel of Jews from the Continent and from other parts of London displaced the Gentiles, and by the end of the century the district had become predominantly Jewish. . . . Efficient agencies belonging to the Jewish faith provided for most of the social needs of the poor Jew. One consequence was a widening in the geographical scope of the activities of Toynbee Hall [i.e., beyond Whitechapel]" (91). As a Christian clergyman Barnett considered Jews outside his ministry. See also Emily K. Abel, "Middle-Class Culture for the Urban Poor: The Educational Thought of Samuel Barnett," *Social Service Review* 52 (Dec. 1978): 596–620.

78. FK to FE, May 27, 1892; Hull House, Nov. 27, 1892, IISH; and April 7, 1892. White, "Social Settlements and Immigrant Neighbors," 57, noted that Jane Addams did not think that homogeneous beliefs would eventually develop out of the diversified immigrant population but envisioned a sense of community based on an acceptance of difference. For a positive autobiographical immigrant account of Hull House in the 1890s, see Polacheck, *I Came a Stranger*. For a negative assessment of the interaction between immigrants and Hull House residents, see Rivka Lissak, *Pluralism and Progressives: Hull House and the New Immigrants, 1890–1919* (Chicago: University of Chicago Press, 1989). Lissak argues that Russian Jews and Italians frequented Hull House only before they formed their own community halls. Nevertheless, she noted that "Jewish radical and trade union leaders maintained close relations with Hull House" (93). See also a review of Lissak by Rudolph Vecoli, *Journal of American Ethnic History* (fall 1991): 103–6. For another negative assessment of JA, see Alun Munslow, *Discourse and Culture: The Creation of America, 1870–1920* (London: Routledge, 1992). We have very few studies of Chicago immigrant women from the perspective of their communities. An exception is Christiane Harzig, *Familie, Arbeit und Weibliche Öffentlichkeit in einer Einwanderungsstadt: Deutschamericanerinnen in Chicago um die Jahrhundertwende* (St. Katharinen, [Germany]: Scripta Mercaturae Verlag, 1991).

79. JA to John Weber Addams, London, June 1, 1896, PJA (and *JAP*, reel 3, #233). For Addams's unfavorable characterizations of charity, see JA, "Hull House, Chicago: An Effort toward Social Democracy," *Forum* 14 (Oct. 1892): 227–41; and *Democracy and Social Ethics*, 168–71.

80. HJG, April 11, 1897, HJGD, vol. 3. For Octavia Hill's close association with the Charity Organization Society (hereafter COS), see C. Edmund Maurice, *Life of Octavia Hill as Told in Her Letters* (London: Macmillan, 1913); William Thompson Hill, *Octavia Hill: Pioneer of the National Trust and Housing Reformer* (London: Hutchinson, 1956), 82–92; and Anthony S. Wohl, *The Eternal Slum: Housing and Social Policy in Victorian London* (Montreal: McGill–Queen's University Press, 1977). For relative lack of success in the United States of Octavia Hill's approach, see John Sutherland, "The Origins of Philadelphia's Octavia Hill Association: Social Reform in the 'Contented' City," *PMHB* 99 (Jan. 1975): 20–44; "Ellen Collins" and "Emily Wayland Dinwiddie," in *NAW*; and Louis Albert Banks, *White Slaves or the Oppression of the Worthy Poor* (Boston: Lee and Shepard, 1893), 201, where the author urges "conscientious landlordism."

For the importance of the class orientation of the COS in British women's settlements, see Margaret A. Sewell and Eleanor G. Powell, "Women's Settlements in England," in Reason, *University and Social Settlements*, 92. See also Vicinus, *Independent Women*, 216–18, 224–31, 243–44. One woman resident's dislike of the "stony-hearted, cold-blooded" attitude of COS methods used in her settlement can be found in A. L. Hodson, *Letters from a Settlement* (London: Arnold, 1909), 178–88.

This difference with Hull House was more of a spectrum than a dichotomy. In 1897 Hull House organized a study class for "friendly visitors," before which Florence Kelley spoke on March 9. The class studied "various methods of out-door and in-door relief and visit[ed] county and city institutions." All interested in charity organization and in friendly visiting were "cordially invited to become members" (*Hull-House Bulletin*, March 1, 1897, in Hull House Scrapbook III. Almost certainly Julia Lathrop took responsibility for the group. But this aspect of Hull House work never attained a large significance for residents. For the COS in Chicago, see Kusmer, "Functions of Organized Charity."

81. See ch. 3 above; and Sklar, "Historical Foundations of Women's Power." For Webb, see Margaret Cole, *Beatrice Webb* (New York: Harcourt, Brace, 1946), 34, 128; and Barbara Caine,

"Beatrice Webb and the 'Woman Question'," *History Workshop Journal* 16 (autumn 1982): 23–43. For a discussion of the relative uniqueness of each national polity, see Michael Kammen, "The Problem of American Exceptionalism: A Reconsideration," *AQ* 45 (March 1993): 1–43; and Geoffrey Finlayson, *Citizen, State and Social Welfare in Britain, 1830–1990* (New York: Oxford University Press, 1994).

82. J. Ramsey MacDonald, "American Social Settlements," *Commons* 2 (Feb. 1898): 4–6, quoted in Reinders, "Toynbee Hall," 45. See also Kalberg, "The Commitment to Career Reform." Beatice Potter spent a great deal of time and energy anguishing over her choice of a marriage partner, finally settling on Sidney Webb. Within this partnership, she advanced her career as a social investigator and reformer and worked within the context of Fabian Socialism rather than within women's public culture. See Lewis, *Women and Social Action*, 83–145; Jeanne MacKenzie, *A Victorian Courtship: The Story of Beatrice Potter and Sidney Webb* (London: Weidenfeld and Nicolson, 1979); Deborah Epstein Nord, *The Apprenticeship of Beatrice Webb* (Amherst: University of Massachusetts Press, 1985); and Carole Seymour-Jones, *Beatrice Webb: Woman of Conflict* (London: Allison and Busby, 1992).

83. JA, "Hull-House: A Social Settlement," 207–8.

9. To Speak as One Having Authority, 1892

1. FK to CBK, Chicago, March 16, 1892, NKP.

2. For the antisweating movement in Boston and New York, see Boris, *Home to Work*. Contemporary writings on urban slums include government publications, such as Massachusetts Board of Health "The Homes of the Poor in Our Cities," *Public Documents of Massachusetts* 4, no. 31 (1873): 396–411; and reformer's accounts, particularly those of Jacob A. Riis — *How the Other Half Lives* (1890), *The Children of the Poor* (1892), *Ten Years' War: An Account of the Battle with the Slums* (Boston: Houghton Mifflin, 1900).

3. For school suffrage, see "Suffrage Gained" index entries in Elizabeth Cady Stanton, Susan B. Anthony, and Matilda Joslyn Gage, *History of Woman Suffrage*, vol. 3, *1876–1885* (Rochester, N.Y.: Susan B. Anthony, 1886; reprint, Salem, N.H.: AYER, 1985), 1009; and Woody, *History of Women's Education*, 1:515–17; 2:108, 459–60. For the equivalent importance of school board suffrage in

England, see Patricia Hollis, *Ladies Elect: Women in English Local Government, 1865–1914* (Oxford: Oxford University Press, 1987), 71–194.

4. "Danger from Sweat Shops: Miss Kelly's Views—Woman's Alliance on Overcrowded Schools," unidentified newsclipping, [Nov. 1892], TEMC, vol. 2, misfiled with 1889 clippings). Brown also led alliance protest against police harassment and extortion of prostitutes ("Working for the Unfortunate," May 1890, unidentified newsclipping, TEMC, vol. 2). For Brown, see newsclipping, Sept. 2, 1894, TEMC, vol. 2.; minutes, CWC, May 7, 1890. In 1898 Brown was appointed head of the Committee on Industrial Conditions Affecting Women and Children of the General Federation of Women's Clubs. See Mary I. Wood, *The History of the General Federation of Women's Clubs* (New York: General Federation of Women's Clubs, 1912), 120. Elizabeth Morgan also organized support for the enforcement of the compulsory school attendance law by gathering clothing for more than three hundred fifty children. See Hannah Morgan to Mr. Zimmerman, n.d., Chicago Trade and Labor Assembly Papers, Chicago Historical Society.

5. On wages declining nationwide as a proportion of the value of the product in the 1880s, see Stanley Lebergott, *The Americans: An Economic Record* (New York: Norton, 1984), 378. For sweating, see Charles Booth, "Sweating," in Booth, *Life and Labour of the People in London* (London: Williams and Norgate, 1891; reprint, New York: Augustus M. Kelley, 1969), 4:328–47. See also N. N. Feltes, "Misery or the Production of Misery: Defining Sweated Labour in 1890," *Social History* 17 (Oct. 1992): 441–52; Bliss, *Encyclopedia of Social Reform*, 1299; James A. Schmiechen, *Sweated Industries and Sweated Labor: The London Clothing Trades, 1860–1914* (Urbana: University of Illinois, 1984); Robert McIntosh, "Sweated Labour: Female Needleworkers in Industrializing Canada," *Labour/Le Travail* 32 (fall 1993): 105–38; Morris, *Women Workers and the Sweated Trades;* Eileen Boris, "Crafts Shop vs. Sweatshop," *Journal of Design History* 2 (fall 1989): 175–92; and Stansell, "The Origins of the Sweatshop." Sweating is, of course, still a reality. See Fiona Wilson, *Sweaters: Gender, Class and Workshop-based Industry in Mexico* (New York: St. Martin's, 1991).

6. Chicago Trade and Labor Assembly, *The New Slavery*, 19. Morgan replaced Elizabeth Rodgers as Chicago's most eminent woman organizer. See "Elizabeth Flynn Rodgers," in *NAW;* and Scharnau, "Elizabeth Morgan."

7. Schneirov, "The Knights of Labor," 457–58. For the numbers of women working in industry and, in particular, making garments, see United States Census Office, *Compendium of the Tenth Census,* vol. 2 (Washington, D.C.: GPO, 1883), 1046–51; United States Census Office, *Report on the Manufacturing Industries in the United States at the Eleventh Census: 1890*, pt. 2 (Washington: GPO, 1895), 130–45.

8. See Anne Phillips and Barbara Taylor, "Sex and Skill: Notes towards a Feminist Economics," *Feminist Review* 6 (1980): 79–88.

9. Katherine A. Jones, "Working Girls of Chicago: Their Wages, Their Homes, and Their Summer Outings," *Review of Reviews* (Sept. 1891): 168–72. This crowding of women into a few available occupations could create desperation among those unable to find what they felt was suitable employment—a desperation best expressed in literature. See Laura Hapke, *Tales of the Working Girl: Wage-Earning Women in American Literature, 1890–1925* (New York: Twayne, 1992).

10. For the public effects of innovations in domestic hygiene, see Tomes, "The Private Side of Public Health," 509–39. City government provided some services on a scale unprecedented in Europe—such as paved streets and electric lights—but paid inadequate attention to other municipal responsibilities. Sometimes this was because its ambition outreached its technical skills, as was the case with the city's water supply, which was chronically tainted with waste. Profiteering went hand in hand with most public services. Private transportation monopolies garnered fabulous wealth but paid the city minuscule amounts for their franchises. Services that involved little profit, such as garbage collection, were often ineffective. Where regulation was essential to profit making, as in the case of the Chicago stock market, it was not left to the city but was privately enforced by the Chicago Board of Trade. Where city health regulations impeded profit, as was the case in the garment industry, officials looked the other way. See Pierce, *History of Chicago*, 216–18 and 309–13; Lurie, *Chicago Board of Trade;* Harold L. Platt, *The Electric City: Energy and Growth of the Chicago Area, 1880–1930* (Chicago: University of Chicago Press, 1991); and Teaford, *The Unheralded Triumph.* Germ theory was introduced into public health in the 1890s. See James H. Cassedy, "The Flamboyant Colonel Waring: An Anti-Contagionist Holds the American Stage in the Age of Pasteur and Koch," *Bulletin of the History of Medicine* 36 (March–April 1962): 163–76. The contagious qualities of tuberculosis were

not yet recognized, but the disease was understood as life threatening to workers made vulnerable by long hours, low wages, and unsanitary working and living conditions. Chicago Department of Health annual reports show that the Chicago Department of Health expanded its activities around 1876. In 1879 the first tenement inspection act was passed but not enforced. In 1880 a second tenement and workshop inspection act was passed, buttressed the next year by added enforcement powers.

11. Unidentified newsclipping, [Nov.] 1888, TEMC, box 4, vol. 2. In some documents the alliance called itself the Illinois Woman's Alliance, in some the Illinois Women's Alliance. Since the majority of references seem to use the former, I have adopted that nomenclature, except in direct quotations to the contrary. The alliance's motto appeared in *Inter Ocean*, Nov. 2, 1889, TEMC; women inspectors were mentioned in the *Chicago Tribune*, July 26, 1889, TEMC. Stories by Nell Nelson appeared in the *Chicago Times*, a prolabor paper, and were later reprinted as a book whose title captured the sensationalism attached to sweatshop labor: *The White Slave Girls of Chicago*. Women garment workers called a meeting attended by representatives of twenty-six women's organizations on October 5, 1888. The next day a committee chosen by that group sent a circular to "seventy women's societies, about eighty churches, and a few labor organizations" (unidentified newsclipping, Oct. 24, 1888, TEMC, vol. 2). A movement by women for women at the peak of its influence in 1890, the alliance embraced an impressively wide range of middle- and working-class women. See Sklar, "Hull House," 666. The most complete account of the alliance is Tax, *The Rising of the Women*, 65–93; and Scharnau, "Elizabeth Morgan."

12. Kelley's work in Philadelphia was described in unidentified newsclipping, [March 1889], TEMC, vol. 2, reel 6; her letter was quoted in "Work for the Women," unidentified newsclipping, [Nov. 1888], TEMC, vol. 2.

13. For the Knights' inclusion of housewives as producers, see Levine, *Labor's True Woman*, 108–9.

14. Unidentified newsclipping [Spring 1889], TEMC, vol. 2. Assembly leaders said they had seen "union after union" brought under political control, and as a result, "the factory, workshop and tenement house ordinance was dead, and every pretense of inspection made in its name was farce." The assembly also opposed women school inspectors being given free trolley passes (unidentified newsclipping, April 8, 1889, TEMC, vol. 2).

15. Quoted in Livermore, "Coöperative Womanhood," 291. For the city council's decision to appoint women inspectors, see "Women as Officials," unidentified newsclipping, July 26, 1889, TEMC, vol. 2.

Clarence Darrow of the city council's "Law Department" told an alliance committee "that there were no legal obstacles in the way of securing an ordinance under which they could do what they wished to in the interest of working women and children in the city." There was strong opposition to the idea on the council, "but women were on hand to combat it, and they were successful in finding gentlemanly champions, who worked to help them gain their point." See "Another Victory," unidentified newsclipping, Aug. [3], 1889, TEMC, vol. 2. For the Trade and Labor Assembly's petition, see unidentified newsclipping, Jan. 1890, TEMC, vol. 2. Another brief struggle ensued over the mayor's effort to appoint needy widows on whose loyalty he could rely, but by January 1890, city hall had yielded to the women's pressure and accepted their nominees. Alliance nominees included highly qualified women physicians, who "will not be so hampered by the necessities of life as to be subservient to political factions for their positions" ("Women Want War," unidentified newsclipping, Oct. 28, 1889, TEMC, vol. 2).

16. "Women Want War"; IWA Annual Report, Feb. 1898, quoted in Livermore, "Coöperative Womanhood," 291 (Livermore also reviewed the IWA's achievements); copy of 1891 petition, TEMC, vol. 2; "Working to Help Society," unidentified newsclipping, Nov. 15, 1890, TEMC; newsclipping, Nov. 22, 1891, TEMC, folder 9, reprinted in Livermore, "Coöperative Womanhood," 291 (see also Joseph Dana Miller, "The New Woman in Office," *Godey's Magazine* 132 [Jan. 1896]). For the June 1890 ordinance, see "Journal of the Proceedings of the City Council of the City of Chicago, Illinois," June 9, 1890, Municipal Reference Library, Chicago; Livermore, "Coöperative Womanhood," 205. Chicago's equivalent of the Charity Organization Society was the Chicago Relief and Aid Society, which was controlled by men. During the 1880s and 1890s women slowly but surely gained power in the administration of both public and private charity. See Brown, *History of Public Assistance in Chicago*, 120–21; John Albert Mayer, "Private Charities in Chicago from 1871 to 1915" (Ph.D. diss., University of Minnesota, 1978), 69–116; and McCarthy, *Noblesse Oblige*.

17. Pierce, *History of Chicago*, 3:360; *Rights of Labor*, Dec. 17, 1892, quoted in Richard Schneirov, "From Political Collective Bargaining to Private Collective Bargaining" (paper presented at American Historical Association, 1991), 19–20. For fraud, see Pierce, *History of Chicago*, 3:361. The Chicago labor movement fragmented into four groups, the German socialist Central Labor Union, the Building Trades Council, the Knights of Labor District Assemblies, and the Trade and Labor Assembly. See Staley, *History*, 84–99. This disunity further discouraged the labor movement from attempting to achieve its goals through political action. Pomeroy's gang was finally ousted in 1895. See John H. Keiser, *Building for the Centuries: Illinois, 1865 to 1898* (Urbana: University of Illinois Press, 1977), 250.

Since the Germans who dominated the traditional skilled crafts joined more traditional trade unions rather than the Knights of Labor, they had not participated in the local political activism that characterized the Knights during their heyday in the mid-1880s. Collective political activity grew even more remote with the emergence of the AFL in the aftermath of Haymarket in 1887. See Schneirov, "Political Cultures and the Role of the State"; Schneirov, "The Knights of Labor," 346, 453–54; and John B. Jentz, "Artisan Culture and the Organization of Chicago's German Workers in the Gilded Age, 1860–1890," *Amerikastudien/American Studies* 29 (1984): 133–48. In other American cities, labor initiatives sometimes led to public office. See Herbert G. Gutman, "Joseph P. McDonnell and the Workers' Struggle in Paterson, New Jersey," in Gutman, *Power and Culture: Essays on the American Working Class* (New York: Pantheon, 1987), 92–116.

18. Chicago Trade and Labor Assembly, *The New Slavery*, 23, 14, 19.

19. "War of Words between Women," unidentified newsclipping, Jan. 18, 1892, TEMC, vol. 6. For Kenney's appointment to the AFL, see Samuel Gompers to Mrs. T. J. Morgan, New York, Nov. 25, 1892, TEMC, folder #46. The struggle between Morgan and Pomeroy expressed the paradigm within American labor between political action on a socialist platform and "pure and simple unionism." Like other features of Chicago labor relations, it erupted at national AFL conventions. See J. F. Finn, "AF of L Leaders and the Question of Politics in the Early 1890s," *Journal of American Studies* 7 (1973): 243–323.

20. FK to FE, Hull House, May 27, 1892, and Nov. 27, 1892, IISH. One example of middle-class socialism was Charles Kerr's publishing company. In 1893 Kerr, son of a classics professor at the University of Wisconsin, reorganized the firm from a Unitarian religious press into a cooperative socialist enterprise. See Susan Curtis Mernitz, "The Religious Foundations of America's Oldest Socialist Press: A Centennial Note on the Charles H. Kerr Publishing Company," *Labour/Le Travail* 19 (spring 1987): 133–37.

21. Bisno, *Union Pioneer*, 116; Eduard Bernstein, quoted in Bottomore et al., *Dictionary of Marxist Thought*, 49.

22. JA, *Twenty Years*, 196.

23. "To Wipe Away the Evil: Bricklayers' Hall Speakers Denounce the Sweating System," *Chicago Times*, April 9, 1892; JA, *My Friend, Julia Lathrop*, 116.

24. AH, *Exploring the Dangerous Trades*, 62, 61. Contemporary works by Beatrice Potter (later Beatrice Webb) that Addams might have read include Beatrice Potter, "The Tailoring Trade," in Charles Booth, ed., *East London* (London: Williams and Northgate, 1889), pt. 2, ch. 3; and Beatrice Potter, "The Lords and the Sweating System," *Nineteenth Century* 27 (June 1890): 885–905.

25. FK to FE, [Hull House], April 7, 1892, IISH. Sherman Hoar of Massachusetts was not a senator but a member of the House of Representatives. The investigative commissions' hearings were dominated by manufacturers, although Elizabeth Morgan, who had sent a copy of her report to the committee, Abraham Bisno, an organizer from the Cloak Makers Union, and a few garment workers also testified. See U.S. House of Representatives, *Report of the Committee on Manufactures of the Sweating System*, report no. 2309 (Washington: GPO, 1893), 92–95.

26. "To Wipe away the Evil."

27. *Chicago Herald*, April 18, 1892, newsclipping, TEMC, vol. 6; *Chicago Tribune*, April 18, 1892, 10. Bayard Holmes (1852–1924) was Chicago's most eminent physician. At the height of his career in 1892, he was professor of surgery at the Postgraduate Medical School of Chicago, professor of surgical pathology and bacteriology at the University of Illinois College of Medicine, and attending surgeon at the Cook County Hospital. In 1895 he was socialist candidate for mayor of Chicago. Dumas Malone, ed., *Dictionary of American Biography* (New York: Charles Scribner's Sons, 1932). Although he affiliated closely with Hull House, city directories show that he lived elsewhere.

28. FK to FE, Nov. 27, 1892, and April 7, 1892.

Kelley's negative view of the Irish was prompted in part by the greater entrenchment of that ethnic group in machine politics. Being less skilled than many other mid-nineteenth-century immigrants, the Irish relied more heavily than most on patronage politics for work. See Steven P. Erie, *Rainbow's End: Irish-Americans and the Dilemmas of Urban Machine Politics, 1840–1985* (Berkeley: University of California Press, 1988), 64.

29. FK to FE, May 27, 1892. One notable inadequacy in the administration of the city's justice was the failure of public agencies to enforce the municipal child labor law, passed in 1889. The printed statute, which can be found in TEMC, vol. 6, prohibited employers from "knowingly" hiring children under fifteen years of age and limited children's work to eight hours between 7 A.M. and 6 P.M. But employers could always claim that they did not know their workers were under fifteen, and inspectors had no way to verify how many hours children worked.

30. Destler, *Henry Demarest Lloyd*, 263–64; FK to HDL, State of Illinois Bureau of Labor Statistics, June 30, 1892, HDLP. Henceforth, the children called Hull House home, though they spent most of their time elsewhere (see, for example, Margaret Kelley to Albert Kelley, Hull House, n.d. [1898], KFP: "We came home from Hillside last Thursday"). Kelley's detailed account of her financial circumstances may have been prompted by an offer from Lloyd to lend her money to help support the children during the summer.

31. FK to HDL, June 30, 1892.

32. Ibid.

33. *Chicago Tribune*, May 9, 1892, 6.

34. Bisno, *Union Pioneer*, 115–16. See also Carsel, *A History of the Chicago Ladies' Garment Workers' Union*, 28; and Young-soo Bae, "Men's Clothing Workers in Chicago, 1871–1929: Ethnicity, Class, and a Labor Union" (Ph.D. diss., Harvard University, 1989), 11–129.

35. Bisno, *Union Pioneer*, 116–19. Bisno's description of one discussion resembled that of Mme. Blanc (see ch. 8 and n. 64 there). At a talk by "one of the great preachers of the Episcopalian Church," whose "indictment of the order of things was as vigorous as that of any socialist" but who urged his listeners to place their hope in God, Bisno "denounced this doctrine as a hypocritical shield to protect the interests of the clergy who were in league with the capitalists to benefit by the unequal distribution of wealth [and] the oppression of labor." Some in the audience "thought I had made a

very ill-bred attack on a man who was the guest of the house, and that I should have been more gentle and less personal in my talk." When he asked Miss Starr's opinion, she replied: "Our meetings are free, and it is our intent that everybody attending should speak his mind honestly and freely" (Bisno, *Union Pioneer*, 120).

36. Ibid., 116–17; FK to FE, April 7, 1892. Specifically, Bisno said that Kelley was "in favor of labor legislation limiting the hours of labor, insuring conscientious work in the factories, prohibiting the employment of children, limiting the hours for the employment of women and younger people, establishing municipal ownership of transportation, of our light and telephone systems, of our water works, in extending the function of a municipality by way of playgrounds, parks, and the extending of our school system, giving working men's children the benefit of an education equal to that of the best in the country."

37. "Denounced from the Pulpit: All Souls' Church Congregation Hears of the Sweating System," *Chicago Tribune*, May 9, 1892, 6. For insight into the close alliance between progressive clergy and the labor movement in this period, see Clark D. Halker, *For Democracy, Workers, and God: Labor Song-Poems and Labor Protests, 1865–95* (Urbana: University of Illinois Press, 1991). See also Lloyd Wendt and Herman Kogan, *Give the Lady What She Wants!: The Story of Marshall Field and Company* (South Bend, Ind.: And Books, 1952); and Robert W. Twyman, "History of Marshall Field and Company, 1865–1906" (Ph.D. diss., University of Chicago, 1950).

38. "For Clean Streets: Chicago Women Prepare to Fight a Great Nuisance," *Chicago Tribune*, March 19, 1892, 9. In May the Municipal Order League issued a report that attacked the negligence of public authorities in every city ward. See "Why Filth Abounds: Revelations in Reference to Streets and Alleys: Women Use Their Eyes: An Investigation by the Municipal Order League: Reports of the Members: How Careless City Employes Neglect Their Labors," *Chicago Tribune*, May 21, 1892, NKP. That summer Florence Kelley participated in the league's work with a report on "West Side Streets and Alleys," which pointed out that in "all the great cities of the United States . . . where the people who live are prosperous," the streets are "comparatively clean and well-paved," and where "dwellers are poor and lack influence," they are "neglected and ill-paved" ("Only One Safe Way," *Chicago Tribune*, July 3, 1892, 19). For a summary of these trends,

see Mary E. Mumford, "The Place of Women in Municipal Reform," *Outlook* 31, (March 1894): 587–88, who declared: "[Women] have made themselves wholesomely respected and feared by men who had defied the orders of the law and the petitions of the people."

39. "Scored by Speakers," *Chicago Tribune*, May 9, 1892, 6; circular from ca. 1890, quoted in Forbath, *Law and the Shaping of the American Labor Movement*, 83. See also Hurvitz, "American Labor Law"; and Wright, *Industrial Evolution*, 318–20. Stewart eventually served as U.S. commissioner of labor between 1920 and 1932. See Chester McArthur Destler, "A Coffin Worker and the Labor Problem: Ethelbert Stewart and Henry Demarest Lloyd," *LH* 11 (summer 1971): 409–32; and "Ethelbert R. Stewart," in "Biographical Sketches of Commissioners of the BLS," *Monthly Labor Review* 78 (Jan. 1955): 49. Stewart helped Addams's ongoing but unsuccessful efforts to establish a cooperative garment factory. See JA to HDL, Hull House, Dec. 26, 1892, HDLP.

The "White List" of the New York Consumers' League (see ch. 12 below) was designed precisely to avoid the legal problems associated with black lists. See the testimony of Josephine Shaw Lowell in "Report and Testimony Taken before the Special Committee of the Assembly Appointed to Investigate the Condition of Female Labor in the City of New York," *Documents of the Assembly of the State of New York, One Hundred and Nineteenth Session, 1896* (New York: Wynkoop Hallenbeck Crawford, 1896), vol. 23, no. 97, 73. For the illegality of boycotts, see Daniel Robinson Ernst, "The Lawyers and the Labor Trust: A History of the American Anti-Boycott Association, 1902–1919" (Ph.D. diss., Princeton University, 1989), 11–46.

40. See BLSI, "Working Women in Chicago" and "The Sweating System in Chicago" (1893). For the history of the Illinois bureau, see BLSI, introduction to *Eighth Biennial Report, 1894* (Springfield: Hartman, State Printer, 1896), 3–7; and Earl R. Beckner, *A History of Labor Legislation in Illinois* (Chicago: University of Chicago Press, 1929), 488–91. For bureau publications, see Carroll D. Wright, ed., *Index of All Reports Issued by Bureaus of Labor Statistics in the United States Prior to March 1, 1902* (Washington, D.C.: U.S. Department of Labor, 1902; reprint, Westport, Conn: Greenwood, 1976).

41. FK to FE, May 27, 1892.

42. FK to HDL, 327 W. Harrison St., Nov. 28, 1892, HDLP.

43. FK to FE, Nov. 27, 1892. Kelley thought that "it would be hard to duplicate this prosperous, polyglot workingmen's school" outside of Chicago.

44. Illinois Senate and House of Representatives, *Report and Findings of the Joint Committee* (1893), 12; EGS to Mary Blaisdell, Chicago, July 25, 1892, EGSP, quoted in Carrell, "Reflections in a Mirror," 203.

45. NK, "Early Days at Hull House," 427.

46. Albert Kelley to FK, Philadelphia, Sept. 12, 1892, "Albert Kelley letters to Florence Kelley," KFP, box 2; FK to HDL, Nov. 28, 1892.

47. NK, "Early Days at Hull House," 424–25.

48. FK, "Hull House" (July 1898), 550; FK to HDL, Nov. 28, 1892.

49. FK to HDL, Nov. 28, 1892.

50. FK to CBK, Hull House, May 27, 1893, NKP.

51. "Danger from Sweat Shops." Unidentified clipping [late 1892] *TEMC*, vol. 2; misfiled with 1889 clippings. Copies of the report have not survived.

52. "Resigns in a Body: Action of the Auxiliary Women's Labor Committee," *Chicago Tribune*, Dec. 29, 1892, 9.

53. HDL to William Salter, Winnetka, Oct. 30, 1885, HDLP. See Henry Demarest Lloyd, "Story of a Great Monopoly," *Atlantic Monthly* 47 (March 1881): 317–24. The article has been reprinted in Ray Ginger, ed., *The Nationalizing of American Life* (New York: Macmillan, 1965), 31–41.

54. HDL to Henry C. Adams, Winnetka, Dec. 6, 1886, HDLP.

55. HDL, "The New Conscience," *North American Review* 147 (Sept. 1888): 331.

56. An 1889 speech quoted in Destler, *Henry Demarest Lloyd*, 224–25; HDL, *Strike of Millionaires*, 214.

57. JA, "Brief Address" (eulogy of HDL), *Programme of Memorial Exercises for Henry Demarest Lloyd* (Chicago, [1903]), Chicago Historical Society, 16. For Marx, see Lloyd, *Henry Demarest Lloyd*, 1:121.

58. For the Ethical Culture Society, see Howard B. Radest, *Toward Common Ground: The Story of the Ethical Societies in the United States* (New York: Frederick Ungar, 1969), 61–70. For the Sunset Club, see Ernest Ludlow Bogart and Charles Manfred Thompson, *The Centennial History of Illinois*, vol. 4, *The Industrial State, 1870–1893* (Chicago: McClurg, 1922), 208. Lloyd also joined the Chicago Club, the Chicago Literary Club, and the Press Club. For a list of women's and men's reform organizations in Chicago, although many

were founded after 1900, see Diner, *A City and Its Universities,* appendix 2, 191–94.

59. Stead, *If Christ Came to Chicago,* 15. For HDL's alienation from the Chicago Civic Federation, see Destler, *Henry Demarest Lloyd,* 351. The federation later became the model for the National Civic Federation. See Marguerite Green, *The National Civic Federation,* 1–12. See also Smith, "When Stead Came to Chicago"; Douglas Sutherland, *Fifty Years on the Civic Front: A History of the Civic Federation's Dynamic Activities* (Chicago: The Civic Federation, 1943); and Albion W. Small, "The Civic Federation of Chicago, a Study in Social Dynamics," *American Journal of Sociology* 1 (July 1895): 79–103. See also Civic Federation of Chicago, minutes, 1893–1897, Chicago Civic Federation Papers, Chicago Historical Society.

60. HDL, *The Safety of the Future Lies in Organized Labor* (Chicago: American Federation of Labor, 1893), 8. For the Carnegie steel workers' strike, see HDL to Samuel Gompers, Little Compton, Rhode Island, July 15, 1892, HDLP.

61. See Wright, *Seventh Special Report,* 460–501. For a review of the completed study, see "Live in the Slums," *Chicago Tribune,* July 28, 1894, 9.

62. Agnes Sinclair Holbrook, "Map Notes and Comments," in *HHM&P,* 7. Holbrook noted that in many cases reports obtained from one person as to wages and unemployed seasons were corroborated by statements from other workers at the same trades and occupations ("Map Notes," *HHM&P,* 11–12).

63. Kelley and Holbrook also collected data for an unemployment map, but none was ever produced. See ibid., 7. For more on this publication, see ch. 11 below and Sklar, "Hull-House Maps and Papers." Holbrook paid tribute to Kelley's supervision of the map-making process and the older woman's "experience in similar investigation and long residence in the neighborhood," which enabled her "to get at all particulars with more accuracy than could have attended the most conscientious efforts of a novice" (Holbrook, "Map Notes," 12).

64. FK to CBK, May 27, 1893.

65. Ibid.

66. BLSI, "Working Women in Chicago," xi, xiii, and xxxvii. Although Kelley's authorship of the reports was filtered through the bureau's staff, especially through Carroll Wright, her own views were apparent in a later newspaper interview. See "Fair Wage Earners," *Inter Ocean,* Aug. 31, 1896, TEMC, folder #10. For the gender bias in Wright's own work, see Anderson, "The History of Women and

the History of Statistics," 28. Commons commented on Wright's repression of "individual initiative" among his subordinates (*Myself: The Autobiography of John R. Commons* [Madison: University of Wisconsin Press, 1964], 93).

67. BLSI, "Working Women in Chicago," xxv and xxxvii.

68. See ibid., xxxiii and xxxv. The small sums spent on entertainment support Kathy Peiss's interpretation of women's dependency on male "treating" for commercial entertainment in *Cheap Amusements: Working Women and Leisure in Turn-of-the Century New York* (Philadelphia: Temple University Press, 1986).

69. BLSI, "Working Women in Chicago," xliv.

70. Ibid., xliii.

71. Ibid., xlvi. Of the absent male wage earners, 96 percent were fathers, and only 4 percent were husbands; 69 percent had died, 9 percent had abandoned their families, 8 percent were chronically unemployed, and another 13 percent were either elderly, invalids, or had remained in Europe.

72. See ibid., xxvii. Although it pertains primarily to a later period, see also Kessler-Harris, *A Woman's Wage.*

73. John Swinton, *Striking for Life: Labor's Side of the Labor Question: The Right of the Workingman to a Fair Living* (n.p.: American Publishing, 1894), 63. See also Samuel Gompers, "A Minimum Living Wage," *American Federationist* (April 1898): 25–30. Although historians now refer to this male claim for higher wages as the "family wage," Swinton and his contemporaries did not use that term. Instead they called for a "living wage" and defined it as enabling male workers to support their families. See also May, "Bread before Roses"; and Glickman, "A Living Wage." The views in Kelley's report were in keeping with those of another associate of Carroll Wright, Clare deGraffenried, in "The Needs of Self-Supporting Women," in *Johns Hopkins University Studies in Historical and Political Science* (Baltimore: Johns Hopkins University, 1890), 3:4–86. See also Lala Carr Steelman, "Mary Clare de Graffenried: The Saga of a Crusader for Social Reform," in *Studies in the History of the South, 1875–1922* (Greenville, N.C.: East Carolina College, 1966), 53–83.

74. BLSI, "The Sweating System in Chicago," 374.

75. Ibid., 360–63.

76. One example was a mother "at work on silk-faced summer jackets for ladies," whose child was "sick with scarlet fever" (ibid., 380). For the

importance of ethnicity in Chicago's labor force and the political balkanization it induced, see Eric L. Hirsch, *Urban Revolt: Ethnic Politics in the Nineteenth-Century Chicago Labor Movement* (Berkeley: University of California, 1990). Nevertheless, Kelley did not advocate immigration restriction as a solution to the sweating problem. "Nobody seriously believes that in order to boost a few debased trades, it is necessary to close the ports of America to immigrants who escape from religious persecution [Russian and Polish Jews] or from the poverty of Sicily and Calabria" (FK, "Das Sweating-system" [1898], 232).

77. FK, "The Sweating-System" (1895) 28; BLSI, "The Sweating System in Chicago," 361–62.

78. BLSI, "The Sweating System in Chicago," 393. See ibid., 384. Kelley's 1892 study of single women employed in nonsweatshop manufacturing in Chicago revealed that 53 percent of her sample of 4,526 employees earned between four and seven dollars per week. These women were largely unskilled or semiskilled and held jobs such as dippers in candy factories, worker in broom factories, and cracker packers in bakeries. Another 23 percent of the sample, semiskilled women workers, earned between seven and ten dollars weekly, working, for example, as quality inspectors in corset and cloak factories or as bookkeepers in book binderies. See BLSI, "Working Women in Chicago," xiv, 8, 11, 21, 24, 31, 36.

79. Ibid., 400–401.

80. Ibid., 398, 402.

81. As early as 1885 the male leadership of the Trade and Labor Assembly opposed legislative solutions for the chief problem plaguing women's work—long hours—saying they feared this would throw some women out of work. The assembly amended the bill to apply only to children. See Schneirov and Suhrbur, *Union Brotherhood*, 21–43, 58–59.

82. "Look to Lawmakers," *Chicago Tribune,* Nov. 14, 1892, 7; "The Demands of Illinois Labor," *Chicago Tribune,* Dec. 21, 1892, 12; and "A Compulsory Eight-Hour Law Impossible," *Chicago Tribune,* Jan. 5, 1893, 4. By January a state legislator made news with his proposal of an eight-hour law for "all mechanical trades, arts, and employments," provoking an outburst of opposition from the *Tribune,* which appealed to women to resist the law since it would drastically shorten their servants' workdays. The movement toward radical legislative solutions for Chicago's labor problems would never grow so strong as to reach the servant population.

83. Illinois Senate and House of Representatives, *Report and Findings of the Joint Committee,* 139–40, 147–50, 236–37, 242.

84. JA, *Twenty Years,* 201. For the diverse reactions of immigrant children to schooling, see Selma Berrol, "Immigrant Children at School, 1880–1940: A Child's Eye View," in Elliott West and Paula Petrik, eds., *Small Worlds: Children and Adolescents in America, 1850–1950* (Lawrence: University of Kansas, 1992), 42–60. On child labor, see ibid., ch. 7.

85. *Report and Findings of the Joint Committee,* 139–40, 148–50.

86. Bisno, in ibid., 239; Bisno, *Union Pioneer,* 122–23. Almost certainly included among the attorneys helping with the drafting of the proposal was Clarence Darrow, who participated actively in lobbying for the legislation. For Darrow's participation, see Alzina Stevens to HDL, May 30, 1893, HDLP. Bisno also noted other goals written into the legislative proposals: "prohibiting the employment of children under fourteen, registering all under sixteen, and to expose to the public the unsanitary conditions of the tailor shops and to protest against low wages, long hours, and oppressive conditions as experienced by the people of all varieties in the clothing industry" (Bisno, *Union Pioneer,* 122–23).

87. JA, *Twenty Years,* 201. For the garment workers' support, see Bisno, *Union Pioneer,* 148. "The Trade and Labor Assembly resolution on the passage of our bill . . . will of course be forwarded to the legislators by trusty hands," Alzina Stevens wrote to Henry Demarest Lloyd on May 30, 1893. Stevens urged Clarence Darrow to lobby for the bill in Springfield, but he said "what he can do must be done from here [Chicago]" (Stevens to HDL, Chicago, June 7, 1893, HDLP). See also Destler, *Henry Demarest Lloyd,* 255.

88. "To Abolish Sweatshops: Mass-Meeting of Citizens Resolves for the Sulzer Bill," unidentified newsclipping, n.d. [ca. 1893], Hull House Scrapbook I [1889–97], 70, JAMC (and *JAP,* reel 81, addendum reel 10); JA, *Twenty Years,* 202. See also Carsel, *A History of the Chicago Ladies' Garment Workers' Union,* 28–31. See "Ellen Martin Henrotin," in *NAW.*

89. FK to CBK, May 27, 1893; "Sweat Shops Are Included: Attorney General Moloney Defines the Rights of Factory Inspectors," *Inter Ocean,* Aug. 1, 1893.

90. Wiebe discusses the two generations of male reformers in *Search for Order,* 172.

10. Useful Employment, 1893

1. "An Act to regulate the manufacture of clothing, wearing apparel and other articles in this State, and to provide for the appointment of State inspectors to enforce the same, and to make an appropriation therefor" is reprinted in [FK], *Second Annual Report* (1895), 8–9. For the funding level of Kelley's office, see [FK], *Third Annual Report* (1896), 136. The next woman to hold such power was Frances Perkins, when in 1919 Governor Al Smith appointed her a member of the New York State Industrial Commission, where she took charge of the Bureau of Mediation and Arbitration, reorganized the factory inspection division, and went into the field to settle strikes. See "Frances Perkins," in Barbara Sicherman and Carol Hurd Green, eds., *Notable American Women, the Modern Period: A Biographical Dictionary* (Cambridge: Harvard University Press, 1980).

2. FK to HDL, U.S. Department of Labor, July 13, 1893, HDLP; "Sweat Shops Are Included," *Inter Ocean*, Aug. 1, 1893, NKP.

3. "Gemeinheit gegen eine brave Frau," *Illinois Staats-Zeitung*, July 22, 1893, NKP.

4. JA, *Twenty Years*, 206–7. See also Sklar, "Hull House." For Kelley's new quarters, see JA to MRS, Hull House, Aug. 26, 1893, PJA (and *JAP*, reel 2, #1462–64). The Chicago City Directory of 1897 shows that on the eve of her departure from office, Kelley shifted her staff's location to Blue Island Avenue.

5. Alzina Stevens to HDL, Chicago, July 25, 1893, HDLP. Stevens also retained a residence not far from the Hull House neighborhood. See Alzina Stevens to HDL, Chicago, May 22, May 30, June 7, 1893, HDLP. Stevens was born into a middle-class Maine family but became a wage earner at the age of thirteen when her father died. The loss of her right index finger in a textile mill provided her with a constant reminder of the need for labor reform. Stevens was divorced. As an organizer of women in the Knights of Labor, Stevens said that "working men and women are beginning to understand each other . . . that women have ceased, as a rule, to cut under men in prices for their labor, and that they have done it in just the proportion men have opened their trades unions and labor organizations to them, and said: 'Come in and help us,' instead of the old growl of 'get out of *my* place'" ("The Woman Question," *John Swinton's Paper*, Feb. 21, 1886). The fullest treatment of Stevens is "Alzina Parsons Stevens," in *NAW*. See also FK, "Industrial

Democracy: Women in Trade Unions," *The Outlook*, Dec. 15, 1906, 930–31; and Alzina P. Stevens, "Child Labor," *Proceedings of the Seventh Annual Convention of the International Association of Factory Inspectors of North America, Held at Chicago, Sept. 19–22, 1893* (Cleveland, Ohio: Forest City Printing House, 1894), 46–47. Julia Lathrop later remarked that "when the announcement of these two appointments was made someone remonstrated in a friendly way, saying that two such 'big women' would never be able to work together, to which the governor replied, according to the legend, 'If they are big enough for the job, they will get along together well enough.' The event proved the governor was right" ("Memorial Tribute to Florence Kelley," *The Survey* 67 (March 15, 1932): 677). For Kelley's other appointments, see "Hull House," unidentified newsclipping, [Feb. 1894], Hull House Scrapbook I [1889–1897], JAMC (and *JAP*, reel 81, addendum reel 10). All references to Hull House scrapbooks come from this location in the microfilm. Alexander Bruce (b. 1866) became a professor of law at the University of Wisconsin in 1898 and promoted the enactment and enforcement of child labor laws in that state. See Albert Nelson Marquis, ed., *Who's Who in Chicago* (Chicago: Marquis, 1931), 139. Before working for Kelley's office, John Ela (b. 1837) served as special counsel for Illinois and was a member of the Board of State Commissioners of Public Charities and a state leader in the Democratic Party. See his obituary in *Chicago Daily News*, Dec. 15, 1902, 1; F. B. Wilkie, *The Chicago Bar* (Chicago: Lakeside, 1872), 82; and Rev. David Hough Ela, *Genealogy of the Ela Family* (Manchester, Conn.: E. Ela, 1896), 20.

6. *Hull-House Bulletin*, Dec. 1, 1896, in Hull House Scrapbook III. For Jones's address, see Chicago city directory, 1893. Jones tried to draw Elizabeth Morgan into the group. See Fannie Jones to Elizabeth Morgan, Sept. 21, 1894, TEMC, folder 46.

7. Bisno, *Union Pioneer*, 158. For the names of the inspectors, see "State Factory Inspectors," unidentified newsclipping, [Aug. 1893], NKP. Chicago city directories for 1893 to 1897 show that Bisno lived two blocks south of Hull House in 1893 but moved north to a better neighborhood in 1894. Shortly thereafter, his daughter Beatrice was born. She spent most of her life as personal secretary to Sidney Hillman. Her novel *Tomorrow's Bread* (New York: Liveright, 1938) depicts her father's world. When I interviewed her in Santa Monica, California, in 1981, she said she believed that before her birth her mother had had abortions because

the family could not afford more children but that with her father's employment as an inspector, their economic circumstances changed, and she was born.

8. Issues that labor brought to the Illinois legislature in the 1880s and 1890s included the length of the working day; the prompt and full payment of wages; health, safety, and comfort; accident compensation and employers' liability; child labor; umemployment; the protection of craft workmanship; convict labor; immigration; the legal status of unions; injunctions; arbitration; ballot reform; initiative and referendum; the Illinois Bureau of Labor Statistics; the courts; constitutional revision; education and schools; taxation; and public utilities. See Staley, *History of the Illinois State Federation of Labor*, 150–75. See also Ernest Ludlow Bogart and John Mabry Mathews, *The Centennial History of Illinois*, vol. 5, *The Modern Commonwealth, 1893–1918* (Springfield: Illinois Centennial Commission, 1910), 288–90.

9. M. T. Moloney to FK, State of Illinois, Attorney-General's Office, Springfield, Aug. 7, 1893, in [FK], *First Annual Report* (1894), 7. See also "Sustains Mrs. Kelly," unidentified newsclipping, [Aug. 1893], and "Must Admit Inspectors," unidentified newsclipping, [Aug. 1893], NKP. Moloney's conclusion relied on one portion of the statute that defined *factory* or *workshop* as "any place where goods or products are manufactured or repaired, cleaned or sorted, in whole or in part for sale or for wages." Moloney ignored another section that defined the law's scope more narrowly as a "house, room or place" used "for the purpose of carrying on any process of making, altering, repairing or finishing for sale, or for wages, any coats, vests, trousers, knee-pants, overalls, cloaks, shirts, ladies' waists, purses, feathers, artificial flowers or cigars, or any wearing apparel of any kind whatsoever intended for sale."

10. Bisno, *Union Pioneer*, 148; FK to FE, Hull House, Nov. 21, 1893, IISH; Julia Lathrop, guest editorial, unidentified newsclipping, [ca. Feb. 19, 1932], NKP.

11. JA, *Twenty Years*, 205; FK, *Some Ethical Gains through Legislation* (New York: Macmillan, 1905), 40–41. Forty states passed mothers' pensions laws between 1911 and 1920. See Theda Skocpol, *Protecting Soldiers and Mothers: The Political Origins of Social Policy in the United States* (Cambridge: Harvard University Press, 1992), 9.

12. Those pardoned were Schwab, Fielden, and Neebe. See Wish, "Governor Altgeld Pardons the Anarchists"; Harry Barnard, *Eagle Forgotten: The Life of John Peter Altgeld* (Secaucus, N.J.: Lyle Stuart, 1938), 165–271; Altgeld, *Reasons for Pardoning the Haymarket Anarchists;* and Henry M. Christman, *The Mind and Spirit of John Peter Altgeld: Selected Writings and Addresses* (Urbana: University of Illinois, 1960), 63–104. Addams thought that the pardon "gave the opponents of this most reasonable legislation a quickly utilized opportunity to couple it with that detested word," *anarchy* (JA, *Twenty Years*, 206). Emma Altgeld, a Mount Holyoke graduate, thanked Jessie Lloyd for her invitation to visit Wayside, "I confess that just now . . . your invitation to 'run away and hide' strikes me as being about the best thing the Altgelds could do" (Emma Altgeld to "Mrs. Loyd" [*sic*], Executive Mansion, Springfield, Ill., July 14, 1893, HDLP).

13. For a study of the fair in the context of Chicago popular culture, see James Burkhart Gilbert, *Perfect Cities: Chicago's Utopias of 1893* (Chicago: University of Chicago Press, 1991).

14. FK to CBK, May 27, 1893.

15. "Editor's Study," *Harper's Magazine* 87 (Oct. 1893): 798–802, quoted in Ann E. Feldman, "The Power of Associations: World's Fair Women in 1893" (forthcoming). I am grateful to Ann Feldman for sharing this and other aspects of her work with me. German women who attended the Women's Congresses returned home to found the German umbrella organization, *Bund Deutscher Frauenvereine*, in 1894. See Agnes von Zahn-Harnack, *Die Frauenbewegung: Geschichte, Probleme, Ziele* (Berlin: Deutsche Buch-Gemeinschaft, [1928]), 367 ff. Thomas and Elizabeth Morgan ran a successful hotel for fairgoers, the Morgan House, 6239–41 Madison Avenue. See Thomas Morgan to HDL, July 21, 1893, HDLP. Elizabeth Morgan also took up the practice of law, apprenticing with her husband and serving as "his secretary and notary" ("A Woman Organizer," *News-Record*, July 29, 1894, TEMC, folder 46). For women at the Chicago World's Fair, see Jeanne Madeline Weimann, *The Fair Women: The Story of the Woman's Building, World's Columbian Exposition, Chicago, 1893* (Chicago: Academy Chicago, 1981), though this book contains many inaccuracies. Faith Rogow, *Gone to Another Meeting: The National Council of Jewish Women, 1893–1993* (Tuscaloosa: University of Alabama Press, 1993), describes the founding of the council. Contemporary sources include Mary Kavanaugh Oldham Eagle, ed., *The Congress of Women, Held in the Woman's Building, World's*

Columbian Exposition, Chicago, U.S.A., 1893, with Portraits, Biographies and Addresses (Chicago: Kuhlman, 1894); n.a., *Papers of the Jewish Women's Congress, Held at Chicago, September 4, 5, 6 and 7, 1893* (Philadelphia: Jewish Publication Society of America, 1894); and Marian Shaw, *World's Fair Notes: A Woman Journalist Views Chicago's 1893 Columbian Exposition* (n.p.: Pogo, 1992).

16. See Ida B. Wells-Barnett, *On Lynchings: Southern Horrors, a Red Record, Mob Rule in New Orleans* (New York: New York Age Printing, 1892; reprint, New York: Arno, 1969). See also Mildred I. Thompson, *Ida B. Wells-Barnett: An Exploratory Study of an American Black Woman, 1893–1930* (Brooklyn: Carlson, 1990), 41–49. Harper's and Williams's speeches are in May Wright Sewell, ed., *The World's Congress of Representative Women* (Chicago: Rand, McNally, 1894), 433–37 and 696–711. Fannie Williams also spoke at the World's Parliament of Religions. See Williams, "What Can Religion Further Do to Advance the Condition of the American Negro?" in John Henry Barrows, ed., *World's Parliament of Religions* (Chicago: Parliament Publishing, 1893), 2:1114. For the effect of the fair on the formation of the black women's club movement, see Charles Harris Wesley, *The History of the National Association of Colored Women's Clubs: A Legacy of Service* (Washington, D.C.: National Association of Colored Women's Clubs, 1984), 27–39. When the National Association of Colored Women met in Chicago in 1899, Jane Addams invited the leadership to lunch at Hull House, despite the contemporary taboo against white and black people eating together. A newspaper reported that Addams entertained the women "in a social way" (quoted in Salem, *To Better Our World*, 34). See also Elizabeth Lindsay Davis, *The Story of the Illinois Federation of Colored Women's Clubs* ([Chicago], 1922); Darlene Clark Hine, *Black Women in White: Racial Conflict and Cooperation in the Nursing Profession, 1890–1950* (Bloomington: Indiana University Press, 1989), 28; Wanda Ann Hendricks, "The Politics of Race: Black Women in Illinois, 1890–1920" (Ph.D. diss., Purdue University, 1990); Massa, "Black Women"; Scott, "Most Invisible of All"; and Neverdon-Morton, *Afro-American Women*.

17. Quoted in Mary I. Wood, *History of the General Federation of Women's Clubs* (New York: General Federation of Women's Clubs, 1912), 48, 52. See also ibid., 56; Ruth Bordin, *Frances Willard: A Biography* (Chapel Hill: University of North Carolina Press, 1986), 201; *Papers of the Jewish Women's Congress;* Buechler, *Transformation of the Woman*

Suffrage Movement, 150; and Feldman, "The Power of Associations." Kelley's paper, "The Settlement in Its Relations to Municipal Reform," and her participation in the symposium, "The Settlement in Its Relations to the Labor Movement," are described in Henry B. Learned, "Social Settlements in the United States," *University Extension World* 3 (April 1894): 1101–11.

18. "Labor's Real Voice: Mighty Lakeside Gatherings of the Men Who Want Work," *Chicago Tribune,* Aug. 31, 1893, 1. For the scale of the depression, see Harold Faulkner, *American Economic History* (New York: Harper and Bros., 1924), 503–5. Surprisingly, the 1893 depression has received little attention from political or social historians. An exception is McSeveney, *Politics of Depression.*

19. FK, "Factory Legislation in Illinois" (1894), 8–12. FK's presence was also strong at the convention in subsequent years, reading papers in 1895, 1896, and 1897. See FK, "Child-Labor in Illinois" (1895), 93–97; FK, "The Sweating System" (1897), 58–63; FK, "Evolution of the Illinois Child Labor Law" (1897b), 33–37. By the mid-1890s she and other women factory inspectors had earned the respect of their colleagues. Kelley's voice stood out in a discourse that usually focused on the nuts and bolts of enforcement and avoided larger issues. For example, after Kelley read "Evolution of the Illinois Child Labor Law," the discussion shifted away from her chief point about "the total prohibition of the employment of children to the age of sixteen with compulsory education, manual training and scholarships for needy children" and focused instead on the question of "larger fines and less frequent prosecutions" versus lower fines and more frequent arrests.

20. FK, "Factory Legislation in Illinois," 8–10.

21. FK, "The Sweating-System" (1895), 32.

22. "To Enforce the Law: International Association of Factory Inspectors," unidentified newsclipping, Aug. 24, 1893, Hull House Scrapbook I, 41; "Women Should be Organized Now," unidentified newsclipping, [Sept. 1893], NKP; and FK, "Factory Legislation in Illinois," 10. Perhaps the best example of unskilled workers striking when employers cut wages after hours were reduced is the Lawrence, Massachusetts, strike in 1912. See Foner, *Women and the American Labor Movement,* 426–39.

23. FK, "Factory Legislation in Illinois," 10–12. The chief precedent in hours laws for women— Massachusetts in 1874—also had a distinct effect on both men's and women's hours. See Jeremy Atack and Fred Bateman, "Whom Did Protective

Legislation Protect? Evidence from 1880," Working
Paper no. 33 (Washington, D.C.: National Bureau
of Economic Research, 1991), 18.

24. FK to Joseph Farris, Nov. 27, 1894; FK to
John P. Altgeld (hereafter JPA), Aug. 3, 1895; FK to
JPA, April 17, 1896; and FK to JPA, State of Illinois,
Office of Factory Inspector, Nov. 7, 1893, John Peter
Altgeld Correspondence (hereafter JPAC).

25. FK to RTE, Aug. 20, 1893, RTEP; FK to HDL,
247 Polk St., State of Illinois, Office of Factory
Inspector, Chicago, Oct. 10, 1893, HDLP; FK to RTE,
Aug. 20, 1893. For a literary analysis of these physi-
cal themes, see Mark Seltzer, *Bodies and Machines*
(New York: Routledge, 1992). The newspapers
were the *Herald*, the *Record*, and *Inter Ocean*. The
American Medical Association supported Kelley's
involvement of physicians. See *Journal of the Ameri-
can Medical Association*, Oct. 21, 1893. See also
David Paul Nord, "The Public Community: The
Urbanization of Journalism in Chicago," *Journal of
Urban History* 11 (Aug. 1985), 411–42; John Edward
Erickson, "Newspapers and Social Values: Chicago
Journalism, 1890–1910" (Ph.D. diss., University of
Illinois, Urbana, 1974); and Jon Bekken, "'The Most
Vindictive and Vengeful Power': Labor Confronts
the Chicago Newspaper Trust," *Journalism History*
18 (1992): 11–17.

26. FK to HDL, Oct. 10, 1893; FK to JPA, State
of Illinois, Office of Factory Inspector, Chicago,
Nov. 17, 1893, JPAC; FK to JPA, State of Illinois,
Office of Factory Inspector, Nov. 20, 1893, JPAC.
For the success rate of the indictments, see [FK],
First Annual Report, 20; "Prosecuting the Sweaters,"
Chicago Record, Nov. 9, 1893, NKP; and "Work of
the State Inspectors," *Chicago Record*, Nov. 22, 1893,
NKP. The best overview of factory inspection can
be found in a volume sponsored by the Massachu-
setts State Federation of Women's Clubs and the
Women's Educational and Industrial Union of Bos-
ton: Kingsbury, *Labor Laws and Their Enforcement*.

27. FK, "I Go to Work" (June 1927), 274. FK was
one of two women Bachelor of Laws graduates in
1895. See "Northwestern University Thirty-Seventh
Annual Commencement, June 13, 1895," Northwestern University Archives. All law school graduates
were admitted to the Illinois bar without further examination. See Herman Kogan, *The First Century:
The Chicago Bar Association, 1874–1974* (Chicago:
Rand McNally, 1974), 85. Kelley's admission to the
state bar can be found in the Attorney's Card File,
Clerk's Office, Illinois Supreme Court, Springfield.
For women's entrance into the legal profession at
this time, see Drachman, "Women Lawyers"; and

Isabella Mary Pettus, "The Legal Education of
Women," *Journal of Social Science* 38 (Dec. 1900),
234–44.

28. Appendix B, in [FK], *Fourth Annual Report*
(1897), 248; "Work of the State Inspectors."

29. "Prosecuting the Sweaters."

30. Ibid.

31. FK to CBK, State of Illinois, Office of Factory
Inspector, Feb. 10, 189[4], NKP; HJG, April 20, 1897,
and April 21, 1897, HJGD; "Altgeld's Factory Inspectors," unidentified newsclipping, [*Chicago Tribune*],
n.d. [1893], NKP.

32. "Prosecuting the Sweaters"; "Altgeld's
Factory Inspectors."

33. FK to CBK, State of Illinois, Office of Factory
Inspector, Dec. 31, 1893, and fragment, n.p., n.d.
[1894], NKP.

34. [FK], *First Annual Report*, 44. Kelley's subsequent reports, though more extensive, followed
the same format as the first. These individual descriptions can be matched with the report's "Record
of Prosecutions," which specifies why twenty-two
sweatshop employers and one flour manufacturer
had been fined or charged court costs between
October 21 and December 1, 1893 (20–22).

35. See ibid., 107, 113, 122. The report provided
statistics on men, women, and male and female
children at each of 70 breweries and bottling works,
617 cigar and tobacco workshops, 950 clothing or
shoe manufacturers, 120 workshops making food, 16
making leather goods, 21 meatpackers, 90 laundries,
149 metalworking workshops, 19 paper box makers,
64 printers, 219 woodworking workshops, and 138
miscellaneous producers.

36. [FK], *First Annual Report*, 9, 12, and 8.

37. Ibid., 15.

38. Ibid., 18–19.

39. Ibid., 70; *Third Annual Report*, 127. See
ibid., 23, for FK's list of recommendations. Kelley
also urged that insufficient safeguards be made
illegal in *Second Annual Report*, 26, *Third Annual
Report*, 4–5, and *Fourth Annual Report*, 8. Kelley's
recommendations also called for the prohibition
of dangerous work by children under sixteen; the
prohibition of the employment of children under
sixteen "who cannot read and write simple sentences in the English language"; the prohibition of
night work for women and children; the inclusion
of mercantile establishments in all provisions of the
1893 law; the extension of the eight-hour section
of the law to include male children age fourteen to
sixteen; the addition of two physicians, "of whom
one should be a woman," to the inspectors' staff;

the prohibition of garment manufacturing in any tenement; and the empowerment of inspectors "to require fire escapes, elevator guards, ventilation, sanitation, and the guarding of all dangerous machinery" (ibid., 23). For the assembly's proposals, see "Outlines to the Trade and Labor Assembly, Several Bills to Benefit Workingmen," *Chicago Times Herald*, April 18, 1894, NKP.

40. Mary E. Mumford, "The Place of Women in Municipal Reform," *The Outlook* 49 (March 31, 1894): 588.

41. JA, *Twenty Years*, 159–60; JA to MRS, Aug. 26, 1893. See also *Twenty Years*, 161 and 186. For the bankruptcies, see "Clash with a Mob," *Chicago Tribune*, Aug. 27, 1893, 1. For the role of city hall in aiding the homeless and jobless, see "Hard Luck Stories: Chicago's Unemployed Retail Their Sad Experiences," *Chicago Tribune*, Dec. 10, 1893, 25.

42. FK, *First Annual Report*, 19. See Sidney Fine, "The Eight-Hour Day Movement in the United States, 1888–1891," *Mississippi Valley Historical Review* 40 (Dec. 1953): 441–62; "The Short-Hour Movement," in Bliss, *Encyclopedia of Social Reform*, 1228; Roediger and Foner, *Our Own Time*, 145–61. Prussia limited women's hours to eleven (including one hour for dinner and half an hour for supper). For a contemporary hours strike among skilled workers, see "Cigar Manufacturers on a Strike: The Law Openly Defied," *Chicago Times*, March 30, 1894, NKP. For more on the Illinois law, see Elizabeth Brandeis, "Labor Legislation," in Commons, Lescohier, and Brandeis, *History of Labor*, 3:465; and Clara Mortenson Beyer, *History of Labor Legislation in Three States, Part II. Chronological Development of Labor Legislation for Women in the United States*, Bulletin 66 (Washington, D.C.: U.S. Women's Bureau, Department of Labor, 1932), 203. For the concept of "labor aristocracy," see E. J. Hobsbawm, "The Labour Aristocracy in Nineteenth-Century Britain," in Hobsbawm, *Labouring Men: Studies in the History of Labor* (New York: Basic Books, 1964), 272–315.

43. FK, "Die Fabrik-Gesetzgebung in Illinois" (Factory legislation in Illinois) (1894). *Sozialpolitisches Centralblatt*, the weekly in which Kelley's article was published, was founded by Heinrich Braun in 1892 as a more popular equivalent to *Archiv für Soziale Gesetzgebung und Statistik* (Archive for social legislation and statistics, founded 1888) to help the general reader form "objective and penetrating judgments on actual questions." Both periodicals published a wide range of authors interested in applying Social Democratic ideas to social

problems. Kelley probably read both regularly. See Pierson, *Marxist Intellectuals*, 73–77.

44. Thorstein Veblen described "conspicuous leisure" in *The Theory of the Leisure Class* (New York: Macmillan, 1899). An exemplary study of leisure and changing standards of living is Rosenzweig, *Eight Hours for What We Will*.

45. "Given a Last Warning: Manufacturers Employing Women and Children Adjured to Heed the New Law," unidentified newsclipping, Jan. 6, 1894, NKP. Prolabor papers supported Kelley, writing: "Excessive labor for children is atrocious at all times. Now would be as good a time as any to force a vigorous crusade against it, giving those children who must work reasonable hours and turning over the work thus left undone to those who so sadly need it" ("Child Labor," *Chicago Record*, Dec. 13, 1893, NKP). She also threatened action against merchants who bought goods from New York "made under exactly the same conditions as existed in this city before the passage of the law" (FK to HDL, 247 Polk St., Chicago, Aug. 20, 1893, HDLP). The question of whether women and children were replacing men in the labor force was answered positively by U.S. Bureau of Labor, "Work and Wages of Men, Women and Children, 1895–96," *Annual Report* (Washington, D.C.: GPO, 1896), 11, which found that between the mid-1880s and mid-1890s jobs for males over age eighteen grew by 63 percent while those for females under age eighteen increased by 89 percent.

46. "Mrs. Kelly's Job; Trying to Enforce an Unconstitutional State Law: Thirty Thousand Working Girls Declare the Eight-Hour Day an Injury to Piece Workers," *Chicago Dispatch*, [Feb. 1894], NKP; IMA minutes, Aug. 24, 1893, Illinois Manufacturers' Association Papers (hereafter IMAP), box 1, folder 1.

47. "Attacking the Law: Manufacturers Test the Eight-Hour Labor Statute," *Chicago Tribune*, Jan. 31, 1894, 5; IMA minutes, Feb. 14, 1894, and April 19, 1894, IMAP, box 1, folder 1; "Mrs. Kelly's Job." The IMA helped form the National Association of Manufacturers in 1895, the first annual convention of which was held in Chicago. After 1900 the NAM became Kelley's nemesis. See Albert K. Steigerwalt, *The National Association of Manufacturers, 1895–1914: A Study in Business Leadership* (Ann Arbor: University of Michigan Graduate School of Business Administration, 1964), 37–40. For manufacturers' encouraging sweaters to ignore the law, see "Protected Against Their Will," unidentified newsclipping, [Aug. 1893], NKP. For the IMA's legal expenditures and case selections, see IMAP. See also

Alfred H. Kelley, "A History of the Illinois Manufacturers' Association" (Ph.D. diss., University of
Chicago, 1938), 1–62.

48. "Attacking the Law." See [FK], *Second Annual Report*, 63–67. At that time Mrs. Levy Mayer
ranked prominently in philanthropic activities
among Jewish women in Chicago. See Morris A.
Gutstein, *A Priceless Heritage: The Epic Growth of
Nineteenth Century Chicago Jewry* (New York: Bloch,
1953), 346.

The nine cases the IMA chose to appeal were
William E. Ritchie for employing Mollie Fach, age
twenty-seven, in the manufacture of paper boxes
for more than nine and three-quarter hours a day;
Ritchie for employing Lizzie Furlong, age twenty-
seven, for the same; Ferdinand Bunte for employing
Mary Breen, age twenty, in candy making for nine
hours a day; Joseph E. Tilt for employing Mary C.
Sherlock, age twenty-five, in shoe making for ten
hours a day; Tilt for employing Margaret Taylor,
age twenty, for the same; Lee Drom for employing
Mamie Robinson, age fourteen, in garment making
for eleven and a half hours a day; Drom for employing Hattie Renfranz, age fourteen, for the same;
Louis Eisendrath for employing Mamie Robinson,
age fourteen, in garment making for more than
eight hours a day; and Emil Strouss for employing
Rosa Koeneke, age fourteen, in garment making
for eleven and a half hours a day. See *Ritchie v. the
People*, 155 Ill. 98, 40 N.E. 454, reprinted as John W.
Ela and Andrew Alexander Bruce, *Supreme Court
of Illinois, Southern Grand Division. William E.
Ritchie, Plaintiff in Error vs. the People of the State
of Illinois, Defendant in Error. Involving Constitutionality of the Illinois Factory Law. Brief and Argument
on Behalf of Defendant in Error* (Chicago: Barnard
and Gunthord, [1895]), 50–59. The inspector's brief
noted: "It is fair to assume that the cases brought
here, by the employers, to test the constitutionality
of the law, would not be the ones which we would
present to the court, nor the worst factories, or
even the average ones" (Ela and Bruce, *William E.
Ritchie*, 48).

49. "Labor Law Falls," unidentified newsclipping, [March 15, 1895], NKP. Dating of the event
can be made from JA to Sarah Haldeman, May 4,
1894, Mrs. S. A. Haldeman mss., Indiana University, Bloomington (and *JAP*, reel 2, #1536),
where Addams wrote: "Mrs. Kelley is attending
the Supreme Court, so that it leaves us very short-
handed." See also Edward M. Martin, *The Role of
the Bar in Electing the Bench in Chicago* (Chicago:
University of Chicago Press, 1936), 100–112.

50. Ela and Bruce, *William E. Ritchie*, 9. For the
Massachusetts case, see Sklar, "'The Greater Part
of the Petitioners,'" 109–12; and Kingsbury, *Labor
Laws and Their Enforcement*, 91–125.

51. Ela and Bruce, *William E. Ritchie*, 25. For an
analysis of law as an outcome of struggles among
competing groups, see Robert Gordon, "Critical
Legal Histories," *Stanford Legal Review* 36 (Jan.
1894): 57–125.

52. Ibid., 13.

53. Ibid., 46

54. For the importance of courts, see Arnold
Paul, *Conservative Crisis and the Rule of Law: Attitudes of Bar and Bench, 1887–1895* (Ithaca: Cornell
University Press, 1960); and Keller, *Affairs of State*,
362–70. For differences between the United States
and England, see Hattam, *Labor Visions and State
Power*, 190–203. For more on the U.S.–British
comparison, see Sklar, "Historical Foundations."

55. FK, "Die weibliche Fabrikinspektion"
(Women factory inspectors) (1897), 142; "Mrs.
Kelly's Job."

56. See Philip Corrigan and Derek Sayer, *The
Great Arch: English State Formation as Cultural
Revolution* (New York: Basil Blackwell, 1985), 187.

57. Ela and Bruce, *William E. Ritchie*, 46.

58. For conservatives' invocation of gender to
criticize capitalism, see, for example, Peter Marsh,
"Conservative Conscience," in Marsh, ed., *The Conscience of the Victorian State* (Syracuse: University of
Syracuse Press, 1979), 215–42. For the epistemological revolution at the end of the eighteenth century
that located truth in organic structure rather than
abstract order, see Michel Foucault, *The Order of
Things: An Archeology of the Human Sciences* (New
York: Praeger, 1973). See also Jean Starobinski, "A
Short History of Body Consciousness," *Humanities
in Review* 1 (1982): 22–39; and Anson Rabincach,
*The Human Motor: Energy, Fatigue, and the Origins
of Modernity* (New York: Basic, 1990), 121–23.

59. Wright, *The Industrial Evolution*, 266. In
the United States working women did not express
organized opposition to gender-specific legislation until after 1900. Then opponents came chiefly
from occupations where men predominated and
women's jobs were threatened because they could
not work overtime or because their employers
took advantage of the law as an excuse to exclude
them. In occupations where women predominated,
the main objection arose from reduced wages. In
1909, Florence Kelley spearheaded a movement
for minimum wage legislation for women, which
sought to shore up hours laws with wages laws. For

the most vocal middle-class feminist opposition after 1900, see Ellen C. DuBois, "Working Women, Class Relations, and Suffrage Militance: Harriet Stanton Blatch and the New York Woman Suffrage Movement, 1894–1909," *JAH* 74 (June 1987): 34–58.

In England, where class distinctions were more visible, many middle-class and upper-class suffragists energetically opposed protective labor legislation for women as early as the 1870s and favored an open labor market as the cure for working women's problems. By the late 1890s, however, women affiliated with the British labor movement renounced this position and believed, as one organizer put it, that "without the help of the state, woman cannot secure that place in the commonwealth that she ought to occupy in terms of perfect equality with man" (Annie Marland-Brodie, working-class organizer for the Women's Trade Union League, speaking at the International Congress of Women, 1899, quoted in Feurer, "The Meaning of 'Sisterhood,'" 256). See also Bolt, *The Women's Movements*, 175–76.

Historians of women have generally taken a negative view of protective labor legislation for women. A crucial distinction as to whether the laws were good for women was made in 1925 by Elizabeth Faulkner Baker, *Protective Labor Legislation: With Special Reference to Women in the State of New York* (New York: Columbia University Press, 1925), where she concluded that "in occupations where women predominate, protective laws for women are found to be likely to protect both men and women" (425–26) but in occupations where men dominate, such as printing or street-railway employees, protective laws jeopardized women's jobs. Clara M. Beyer took a positive view in *History of Labor Legislation*, as did Elizabeth Brandeis in "Labor Legislation," in Commons, Lescohier, and Brandeis, *History of Labor*, 3:399–539. For more negative assessments, see Kessler-Harris, *Out to Work*, 180–214; Lehrer, *Origins of Protective Labor Legislation;* Lieberman, "'Their Sisters' Keepers.'" See also Joseph Frederick Tripp, "Progressive Labor Laws in Washington State, 1900–1925" (Ph.D. diss., University of Washington, 1973); Robert Mac-Donald Whaples, "The Shortening of the American Work Week: An Economic and Historical Analysis of Its Context, Causes, and Consequences" (Ph.D. diss., University of Pennsylvania, 1990); Nancy Breen, "Shedding Light on Women's Work and Wages: Consequences of Protective Legislation" (Ph.D. diss., New School for Social Research, 1989); and Dye, *As Equals and as Sisters*, 140–66. Judith A.

Baer, *The Chains of Protection: The Judicial Response to Women's Labor Legislation* (Westport, Conn.: Greenwood, 1978), summarizes secondary sources from the perspective of political science.

The debate continued in the 1980s with Elisabeth M. Landes, "The Effect of State Maximum-Hours Laws on the Employment of Women in 1920," *Journal of Political Economy* 88 (June 1980): 476–94, which argued that legislation limiting hours of work had two effects: it shortened hours for women, but it also limited employment opportunities. Questioning this is Claudia Goldin, "Maximum Hours Legislation and Female Employment in the 1920s: A Reassessment," *Journal of Political Economy* 96 (Feb. 1988): 189–205. Goldin argued that hours legislation reduced the hours for all workers and therefore did not have a sharp differential effect on women's employment opportunities. Supporting her conclusion are Atack and Bateman in "Whom Did Protective Legislation Protect?"

60. For an interpretation of the era as a dialogue between capitalism and socialism, see Martin J. Sklar, *The United States as a Developing Country: Studies in U.S. History in the Progressive Era and the 1920s* (Cambridge: Cambridge University Press, 1992).

61. "Eight-Hour Law Void," *Chicago Evening Post*, Sept. 27, 1893, NKP; "Cigar Manufacturers on a Strike" (Kelley repeated this statement in her *First Annual Report*, 19); "Labor Reform in Illinois," *Chautauqua Assembly Herald*, Aug. 17, 1893, NKP. The best source for changes in laws relating to women and children workers between 1874 and 1893 is [FK], *First Annual Report*, 70–89. See also Sklar, "'The Greater Part of the Petitioners.'"

62. "Why Work Days Should Be Short," *Inter Ocean*, June 19, 1894, NKP. See FK, "Factory Legislation in Illinois." See also Bliss, *Encyclopedia of Social Reform*, s.v. "The Short-Hour Movement," 1228; Sklar, "'The Greater Part of the Petitioners,'" 103–34; Roediger and Foner, *Our Own Time;* Rosenzweig, *Eight Hours for What We Will;* and Ernest Ludlow Bogart and Charles Manfred Thompson, *The Centennial History of Illinois*, vol. 4, *The Industrial State, 1870–1893* (Chicago: McClurg, 1922), 438–80. For the importance of home consumption to organized labor, see S. M. Jelley, "Home the Palladium of Society," in *The Voice of Labor* (Philadelphia: H. J. Smith, 1888), 274–89; and George Gunton, *The Economic and Social Importance of the Eight-Hour Movement* (Washington, D.C.: American Federation of Labor, 1889).

63. "Mrs. Kelly's Job." See Bisno's description of the negotiation process in Illinois Senate and House of Representatives, *Report and Findings of the Joint Committee*, 242–44.

64. "Hit at Sweat Shops," *Chicago Tribune*, April 23, 1894, 7. See "Ellen Martin Henrotin," in *NAW*. Pieceworkers, like those paid hourly wages, thought in terms of the time as well as the task. When asked how many hours they worked, piece-workers replied "ten" at the Illinois sweatshop hearings in 1892, adding that this did not include an additional hour for meals. See Illinois Senate and House of Representatives, *Report and Findings of the Joint Committee*, 32–39.

65. "Hit at Sweat Shops," 7.

66. Cross and Shergold, " 'We Think We Are of the Oppressed,' " 51.

67. Ela and Bruce, *William E. Ritchie*, 51.

68. "Shorter Hours and More Employes," un-identified newsclipping, Jan. 6, 1894, NKP.

69. "Protected Against Their Will"; "Hurts the Woman Worker," unidentified newsclipping, [Nov. 1893], NKP.

70. "Women Against Eight-Hour Law," un-identified newsclipping, Feb. 3, 1894, NKP; John Maguire, quoted in "More Time to Work," *Chicago Tribune*, Feb. 1, 1894, 8. See "Talks to Toilers; Mrs. Charles Henrotin Makes a Radical Speech; Favors a Short Day," unidentified newsclipping, March 28, 1894, TEMC, vol. 2.

11. The Power of a Few Enlightened Persons, 1894–1896

1. [FK], *First Special Report* (1894), 5, 6. See also Earl R. Becker, *A History of Illinois Labor Legislation* (Chicago: University of Chicago Press, 1929), 264–68. Not until twenty years after Kelley began her crusade would the U.S. Supreme Court uphold even the most lenient laws against home manufacture.

2. FK, "I Go to Work" (June 1927), 274. See James H. Cassedy, "The Flamboyant Colonel Waring: An Anti-Contagionist Holds the American Stage in the Age of Pasteur and Koch," *Bulletin of the History of Medicine* 36 (March–April 1962), 163–76; [FK], *First Special Report*, 16. Since the smallpox virus is stable in the dried state and remains viable for long periods of time, it is readily transmitted in cloth. (Before germ theory, most people thought that the chief means by which smallpox was trans-ferred was through the smallpox pustule.) For

similar events in Milwaukee, see John Duffy, *The Sanitarians: A History of American Public Health* (Urbana: University of Illinois Press, 1990), 179–80; and Judith Walzer Leavitt, *The Healthiest City: Mil-waukee and the Politics of Health Reform* (Princeton: Princeton University Press, 1982), 101–7.

3. "Work of the Germs: Sweat Shop District Infected," unidentified newsclipping, April 27, 1894, NKP; "Boycott on Clothing," *Chicago Herald*, May 10, 1894, NKP; "The Smallpox," *The Chicago Mail*, May 10, 1894, NKP. See "Flagrant Cases of Neglect," *Chicago Post*, May 5, 1894, NKP; and "Peril of the City: Danger Lurks in Clothing Made in Sweatshops," *Chicago Tribune*, May 9, 1894, 1. See also "Smallpox Gratis," *The Railway Times*, May 1, 1894, NKP; and "Nests of Contagion," *The Chicago Herald*, April 27, 1894, NKP.

4. [FK], *First Special Report*, 23; "Infected Cloth-ing Destroyed," unidentified newsclipping, May 12, 1894, NKP; "To Avert Quarantine," unidentified newsclipping, May 11, 1894, NKP.

5. Central Council of the Chicago Civic Federa-tion, minutes, May 24, 1895, Chicago Civic Federa-tion Papers, Chicago Historical Society; "Evils of the 'Sweat' Shops," *Chicago Record*, June 18, 1894, NKP; "Will Visit the Pest House: Civic Federation to Make an Investigation," *Chicago Record*, May 23, 1894, NKP; "Miss Florence Kelley," *Chicago Record*, July 25, 1894, NKP. See also "Contagion in Candy: Factory Inspectors Fear Danger," unidentified newsclipping, May 14, 1894, NKP; "Evils of Sweat Shops," *Chicago Record*, May 16, 1894, NKP; "Force to Be Used If Necessary," *Chicago Herald*, May 5, 1894, NKP; "Raid on the Plague," unidentified newsclipping, May 31, 1894, NKP.

6. FK to JPA, State of Illinois, Office of Factory Inspector, June 22, 1894, JPAC.

7. FK to JPA, State of Illinois, Office of Factory Inspector, July 15, 1894, JPAC. Altgeld's reply has not survived but presumably he advised her not to send the report. Later FK told Altgeld she found it strange that counsel for one of her opponents was also "counsel for the city of Chicago" (FK to JPA, State of Illinois, Office of Factory Inspector, Aug. 9, 1894, JPAC). That fall Altgeld advised Kelley: "I find there has been some friction between your office and the city office and that there is good deal of irritation at times. While I do not wish in any man-ner to interfere with your work, I will suggest that it would be conducive to your own peace of mind and be much better all around if all unnecessary friction and irritation can be avoided" (JPA to FK, Nov. 21, 1894, JPAC).

8. "Scores the Health Authorities," *Chicago Tribune,* July 24, 1894, NKP.

9. "Facts Were Hidden," *Inter Ocean,* July 24, 1894, NKP; "The Sweatshops," *Chicago Evening Post,* July 14, 1894, NKP; "The Report of Miss Florence Kelly," *Chicago Herald,* July 25, 1894, NKP; "Miss Florence Kelley," *Chicago Record,* July 25, 1894, NKP; and "Miss Kelly Cold-Shouldered," *The Chicago Journal,* July 24, 1894, NKP. Kelley's report was also covered in "Florence Kelley's Report," *Chicago Record,* July 24, 1894, NKP. See also "Why Not the Troops?" *The Dispatch,* July 24, 1894, NKP.

10. Reynolds was still in charge of the city's department of health in 1904. See Arthur R. Reynolds, *Vital Statistics of the City of Chicago for the Years 1899 to 1903* (Chicago: n.p., 1904). One result of Kelley's campaign was the Chicago School Board's recognition in 1896 of its obligation to protect children's health by preventing the spread of contagious disease in schools. Ten years later this led to the adoption of a school nursing program. See Helen Faye Lyon, "The History of Public Health Nursing in Chicago, 1883–1920" (M.S. thesis, University of Chicago, 1947), 58–64; and JA, "The Visiting Nurse and the Public Schools," *American Journal of Nursing* 8 (Aug. 1908): 918–20.

Michel Foucault has alerted historians to the rise of surveillance and discipline in the modern era, especially relative to the human body. See his *Discipline and Punish: The Birth of the Prison,* trans. Alan Sheridan (New York: Pantheon, 1977). For a feminist critique of Foucault, see Fraser, *Unruly Practices,* 17–68. For a discussion of the multiple positions in which any subject is located, see Joan Scott, "Experience," in Judith Butler and Joan W. Scott, eds., *Feminists Theorize the Political* (New York: Routledge, 1992), 22–40.

11. See Lindsey, *Pullman Strike,* 182; and Wright, "The Chicago Strike, 1894—Boycotts," in *Industrial Evolution,* 313–20. For background on the Pullman community, see Carroll D. Wright, "Pullman," in *The Sixteenth Annual Report of the Massachusetts Bureau of Statistics of Labor* (Boston: Wright and Potter, 1885); and Sarah Lyons Watts, *Order against Chaos: Business Culture and Labor Ideology in America, 1880–1915* (New York: Greenwood, 1993), 37–86. The most complete history of injunctions is Forbath, *Law and the Shaping of the American Labor Movement.* For congressional intention with regard to producers and consumers in framing the Sherman Antitrust Act, see Christopher Grandy, "Original Intent and the Sherman Antitrust Act: A Re-examination of the Consumer-Welfare Hy-

pothesis," *Journal of Economic History* 53 (June 1993): 359–76.

12. FK, "Ein Ruckblick auf den Pullman-Strike" ("Looking back on the Pullman strike") (1894), 55–57; and *United States Strike Commission Report,* Senate Executive Document, No. 7, 53rd Cong., 3rd sess. (Washington, D.C.: GPO, 1895), 426, quoted in Lindsey, *Pullman Strike,* 94.

13. FK, "Ein Ruckblick." For the segregation of black workers in the railway industry, see Jervis Anderson, *A. Philip Randolph: A Biographical Portrait* (New York: Harcourt Brace Jovanovich, 1973).

14. Quoted in Salvatore, *Eugene V. Debs,* 131; FK to HDL, State of Illinois, Office of Factory Inspector, Chicago, July 18, 1894, HDLP. See also Donald L. McMurry, "Labor Policies of the General Managers' Association of Chicago, 1886–1894," *Journal of Economic History* 13 (spring 1953): 145–78; and Commons et al., *History of Labour,* 2:501–9.

15. Lindsey, *Pullman Strike,* 167; JA, *Twenty Years,* 217. See also "First Day of Blood," *Chicago Tribune,* July 8, 1894, 1; and W. T. Stead, *Chicago To-Day: The Labour War in America* (London: "Review of Reviews" Office, 1894; reprint, New York: Arno, 1969).

16. "Women in the Strike," *Chicago Tribune,* July 9, 1894, 3; JA, *Twenty Years,* 228. See also "First Day of Blood," 1; "Rave Like True Reds; Debs' Followers Give Vent to Anarchistic Vaporings," *Chicago Tribune,* July 21, 1894, 1; and Buder, *Pullman,* 183–86. One measure of the lack of middle-class support for the strikers and their sympathizers within the American Railway Union was the disapproval expressed in a major social gospel magazine, see *The Outlook* 49 (June 30, 1894): 185; 50 (July 7, 1894): 9; and 51 (July 14, 1894): 49. Not until 1896 did *The Outlook* speak against the use of injunctions in labor disputes (54 [Sept. 5, 1896]: 720).

17. JA, "A Modern Lear," *The Survey* 29 (Nov. 2, 1912): 135–36. Addams's talk was delivered to the Chicago Woman's Club in 1894, but it was not published until 1912. Addams paraphrased "the injury of one is the concern of all" from Debs's "An injury to one is an injury to all." See Salvatore, *Eugene V. Debs,* 114–46. For more about Addams's arbitration efforts, see *U.S. Strike Commission Report,* xxxix, 459–60, 590, 645–48, quoted in Lindsey, *Pullman Strike,* 230. See also FK, "Ein Ruckblick"; JA, *Twenty Years,* 215; Gerald G. Eggert, *Railroad Labor Disputes: The Beginnings of Federal Strike Policy* (Ann Arbor: University of Michigan Press, 1967), 192–225; and "Labor Is in Doubt; Pullman Company Refuses to Consider Arbitration," *Chicago*

Tribune, July 10, 1894, 1. The inability of government to impose arbitration was described in "Facts of the Strike," *Chicago Tribune,* Aug. 8, 1894, 12. In 1895 the Chicago Civic Federation convened a Congress of Industrial Arbitration and Conciliation, which drafted model legislation for the arbitration of labor disputes and inspired the Illinois General Assembly to enact similar legislation. See also Lowell, *Industrial Arbitration.*

18. FK, "Ein Ruckblick."

19. JA, *Twenty Years,* 217, 214; FK, "Ein Ruckblick," 55; Debs quoted in Salvatore, *Eugene V. Debs,* 135–36. See also "Seeks Gompers Aid," *Chicago Tribune,* July 13, 1894, 1; "Throw a Sop to Debs; Labor Men Vote Him $500 and Then Go Home," *Chicago Tribune,* July 15, 1894, 3; Lindsey, *Pullman Strike,* 227; and Shelton Stromquist, *A Generation of Boomers: The Pattern of Railroad Labor Conflict in Nineteenth-Century America* (Urbana: University of Illinois Press, 1987), 264. For the women scabs, see "Women in the Strike"; and "They Cry for Gore; Amazons Menace the Holland Laundry Girls at Pullman," *Chicago Tribune,* July 21, 1894, 1. For more on women in the Pullman community, see William H. Carwardine, *The Pullman Strike* (Chicago: Charles Kerr, 1894), 75–78. FK's list of convictions in *Second Annual Report* (1895), 62–67, did not include a Pullman conviction.

20. AH, *Exploring the Dangerous Trades,* 62; FK to HDL, July 18, 1894. See also Salvatore, *Eugene V. Debs,* 137–38. Although Kelley's bondsmen met Debs at court, he refused bail as a means of popularizing his cause and remained in jail until his hearing a week later. At the hearing's end he accepted bail worth three thousand dollars. See "Debs Lands in Jail," *Chicago Tribune,* July 18, 1894, 1; Lindsey, *Pullman Strike,* 278–83.

21. FK to HDL, July 18, 1894; and FK to HDL, State of Illinois, Office of Factory Inspector, Chicago, Aug. 1, 1894, HDLP. In 1889 Jessie and Henry Lloyd had constructed a summer home in a portion of Sakonnet, Rhode Island, that was also called Little Compton. See Destler, *Henry Demarest Lloyd,* 212–16, 224, 243.

22. FK to HDL, July 18, 1894.

23. FK, "Ein Ruckblick."

24. Salvatore, *Eugene V. Debs,* 148.

25. FK to HDL, July 18, 1894, and Aug. 1, 1894.

26. Quoted in Chester McArthur Destler, *American Radicalism, 1865–1901: Essays and Documents* (New London: Connecticut College, 1946), 218; FK to HDL [telegram], Chicago, Aug. 13, 1894, HDLP;

FK to "Mrs. Lloyd," State of Illinois, Office of Factory Inspector, Chicago, Oct. 31, 1894; Eugene Debs to HDL, General Offices, American Railway Union, Terre Haute, Aug. 15, 1894, HDLP; and HDL to William Stead, Aug. 21, 1894, HDLP; HDL to FK, Sakonnet, Rhode Island, Aug. 15, 1894, HDLP. Frances Willard agreed that Lloyd should run for Congress, writing him: "It is my humble opinion that you are chosen by the powers invisible as the apostle of our great on-coming movement" (Boston, Oct. 23, 1894, HDLP). Lloyd called the triumph of William Jennings Bryan's silver platform within the Populist movement "the most discouraging experience in my life" (HDL to RTE, [Little Compton], Aug. 3, 1896, HDLP). For a scholarly interpretation of Populism as having lost its vitality by 1895, see Robert C. McMath Jr., *American Populism: A Social History, 1877–1898* (New York: Hill and Wang, 1993). Already distressed by the "equanimity with which the public submit[ted] to the facts" disclosed by his devastating 1894 exposure of Standard Oil in *Wealth against Commonwealth,* Lloyd asked Social Gospel leader Washington Gladden: "And the American People—where is the American People? Is there any such people?" (HDL to Washington Gladden, Winnetka, Dec. 24, 1895, quoted in Lloyd, *Henry Demarest Lloyd,* 1:202). For the People's Party platform in 1896, see Lawrence Goodwyn, *Democratic Promise: The Populist Moment in America* (New York: Oxford University Press, 1976), 470–514; Ruth Bordin, *Frances Willard: A Biography* (Chapel Hill: University of North Carolina Press, 1986), 179–84; Chester McArthur Destler, "The People's Party in Illinois, 1888–1896: A Phase of the Populist Revolt" (Ph.D. diss., University of Chicago, 1932), 109–27; and Schneirov and Suhrbur, *Union Brotherhood,* 58–60.

27. FK to HDL, June 18, 1896, HDLP.

28. Quoted in Lloyd, *Henry Demarest Lloyd,* 1:194. See Henry Demarest Lloyd, "Book Review: *Wealth Against Commonwealth,*" *Altruistic Review* 3 (Dec. 1894): 308–9.

29. FK to "Mrs. Lloyd," Oct. 31, 1894. See Margaret Kelley to FK, Hillside, Wisconsin, Oct. 13, 1894, KFP, box 3.

30. JA to Sarah Anderson, Hull House, June 23, 1894, Jane Addams Papers, Rockford College.

31. Margaret Kelley to FK, Oct. 13, 1894; NK to FK, 434 Chicago Avenue, Oak Park, Feb. 16, 1895, NKP.

32. FK, "The Sweating-System" (1895), 44; JA, "The Settlement as a Factor in the Labor Movement," *HHM&P,* 199.

33. See Charles Booth, *Life and Labour of the People in London* (London: Williams and Norgate, 1891), vol. 2. An edition of five Booth volumes was reprinted by FK's grandson, Augustus M. Kelley, in 1969. Although Booth's study eventually reached seventeen volumes, only volumes one and two appeared before *HHM&P.* See Kevin Bales, "Charles Booth's Survey of Life and Labour of the People in London, 1889–1903," in Bulmer, Bales, and Sklar, *The Social Survey,* 66–110. First used in public health maps in the 1840s, after 1850 such color coding became increasingly feasible through the development of lithographic techniques. Yet not until the 1860s was it widely used—and still primarily for the depiction of urban sanitary conditions. Thus Booth's application of the technique to measure poverty and its extension to nationalities and wages in the Hull House maps represented distinct departures. The major studies containing thematic maps by social reformers between *HHM&P* and the Pittsburgh Survey were Robert Woods, ed., *The City Wilderness: A Settlement Study* (Boston: Patterson Smith, 1898); and Robert A. Woods, ed., *Americans in Process: A Settlement Study by Residents and Associates of the South End House* (Boston: Houghton, Mifflin, 1903). Maps in Woods's 1898 volume were extremely minimal and rudimentary compared to those in *HHM&P,* but improved color-coded maps appeared in the 1903 study. Based on Booth's method of block rather than household analysis, neither these nor the Pittsburgh Survey maps approached the sophisticated detail of the maps in *HHM&P,* although both depicted much larger areas. See, for example, Paul U. Kellogg, "Community and Workshop," in Kellogg, ed., *Wage-Earning Pittsburgh, The Pittsburgh Survey* (New York: Russell Sage Foundation, 1944), 3–30. The most detailed maps in the Pittsburgh Survey appeared in Margaret Byington, *Homestead: The Households of a Mill Town* (New York: Russell Sage Foundation, 1911). See also Cohen, "The Pittsburgh Survey and the Social Survey Movement," in Bulmer, Bales, and Sklar, *The Social Survey,* 245–68; Diner, *A City and Its Universities,* 123–24; and Stephen Kern, *The Culture of Time and Space, 1880–1918* (Cambridge: Harvard University Press, 1983), 133–39.

34. FK TO RTE, State of Illinois, Office of Factory Inspector, July 17, 1894, and Nov. 14, 1894, RTEP.

35. JA TO RTE, Nov. 27, 1894, and Dec. 4, 1894, RTEP. For JA's own reasons for publishing the maps quickly, see JA TO RTE, Chicago, Oct. 31, 1894.

36. FK TO "Mrs. Lloyd," Oct. 31, 1894;. "Factory Inspector Bisno Defeated," *Chicago Herald,* Dec. 14, 1894, NKP; FK to "Miss Williams," 247 W. Polk St., Chicago, Sept. 1, 1894, typed transcription, CLMP.

37. FK to FE, Hull House, Dec. 31, 1894, IISH; FK to Friedrich Sorge, n.p., n.d., quoted in Foner and Chamberlin, *Sorge's Labor Movement,* 122. In the same letter, she also told Sorge that "the big stockyards in Chicago all have introduced the eight-hour day for their 10,000 employees, of which merely 926 are women and children (to whom the law applies)."

Between her New Year's Eve letter and his death from throat cancer in August 1895 at the age of seventy-five, Kelley wrote Engels only one letter (July 1895), which did not refer to the court decision. With that letter she sent him copies of her *Second Annual Report,* the special smallpox report, and "the 7th annual report of the International Convention of Factory Inspectors to which my assistant Mrs. Stevens contributes a valuable paper on Child Labor" (FK TO FE, State of Illinois, Office of Factory Inspector, Chicago, July 28, 1895, IISH).

Butchers, the most skilled stockyard workers, had struck and achieved an eight-hour day in 1886, and women packinghouse workers had their own small union at that time. But by the 1890s employers had reinstituted the ten-hour day, and economic depression helped them crush stockyard unions. See James R. Barrett, *Work and Community in the Jungle: Chicago's Packinghouse Workers, 1894–1922* (Urbana: University of Illinois Press, 1990), 25; Louise Carroll Wade, *Chicago's Pride: The Stockyards, Packingtown, and Environs in the Nineteenth Century* (Urbana: University of Illinois Press, 1987). See also a letter describing declining working conditions and the hiring of more children in the stockyards: "'From the Stockyards': Letter from a Worker Who Was Displaced by a Child," *Chicagoer Arbeiter-Zeitung,* May 12, 1895, in Hartmut Keil and John B. Jentz, eds., *German Workers in Chicago: A Documentary History of Working-Class Culture from 1850 to World War I* (Urbana: University of Illinois Press, 1988), 74–76. For an overview of women in stockyard work, see Edith Abbott and Sophonisba Breckinridge, "Women in Industry: The Chicago Stockyards," *Journal of Political Economy* 19 (Oct. 1911): 632–54.

38. FK to FE, Dec. 31, 1894. Actually, Kelley's records showed that she had nine suits pending on the hours law. See *Second Annual Report,* 67.

39. FK, *Some Ethical Gains through Legislation* (New York: Macmillan, 1905), 44–46, 49, 53.

40. NK, "Early Days at Hull House," 427; "Alton, Ill.," *Daily Republican,,* NKP Jan. 7, 1895; Linn, *Jane*

Addams, 139. See also "To Enforce the Law," *Alton Sentinel*, Jan. 7, 1895, NKP; and "Will Enforce the Child Labor Law," *Chicago Herald*, Jan. 8, 1895, NKP.

41. "Child Labor at Alton," *Chicago Record*, Jan. 26, 1895, NKP; "Alton, Ill."; "Miss Kelley Upheld: Gov. Altgeld Sides with the Factory Inspector," *Chicago Times*, Jan. 13, 1895, NKP; "Will Discharge the Children," *Chicago Herald*, Jan. 15, 1895, NKP; "Will Enforce the Child Labor Law." See also "Mrs. Kelley Will Not Compromise," *Chicago Herald*, Jan. 9, 1895, NKP; and "Mrs. Kelley Makes Complaint," *Chicago Herald*, Jan. 10, 1895, NKP. FK summarized conditions in glassworks in her *Third Annual Report* (1896), 14–18. The struggle against child labor in Illinois's glassworks continued for many years. See JA, "The Operation of the Illinois Child Labor Law," *Annals of the American Academy of Political and Social Science* 27 (March 1906): 327–30. In Pennsylvania the same industry also became a major obstacle to child labor reform. See FK, "Use and Abuse of Factory Inspection," *Proceedings of the National Conference of Charities and Correction* 10 (May 1903): 493–94.

42. FK to Jessie Lloyd, Leland Hotel, Springfield, March 2, 1895, HDLP; NK to FK, Feb. 16, 1895; CBK to FK, Philadelphia, [Feb. 1895], KFP. For Kelley's pessimism about the Supreme Court decision, see "Flaws in the Law: . . . Inspectors Knocked out," *Chicago Tribune*, March 15, 1895, 1.

43. "Opinion of Supreme Court of Illinois, Filed March 18, 1895, *Ritchie vs. the People*," in [FK], *Third Annual Report*, *Ritchie v. the People*, 129–30, 133–34. An 1897 study found that only 114 out of 1,639 state labor laws passed in the previous twenty years had been held unconstitutional, but this included twenty-three out of forty-three areas of labor legislation. See Keller, *Affairs of State*, 407. For another (1896) example of court ideological rigidity resisting regulation in ways that undercut social needs, see Berk, "Adversaries by Design." The Magruder-Haymarket connection was made in Olsen, "From False Paternalism," 1536 n. 62.

44. "Opinion of Supreme Court of Illinois," 133, 134. See "Myra Colby Bradwell," in *NAW*; and DuBois, "Taking the Law." For an analysis of the ability of judges to use women's rights as a means of attacking women's political culture, see Olsen, "From False Paternalism." See also Ernest Ludlow Bogart and John Mabry Mathews, *The Centennial History of Illinois*, vol. 5, *The Modern Commonwealth, 1893–1918* (Springfield: Illinois Centennial Commission, 1910), 320–23. For more on the Illi-

nois Supreme Court, see Keith R. Schlesinger, *The Power that Governs: The Evolution of Judicial Activism in a Midwestern State, 1840–1890* (New York: Garland, 1990), 189–208.

This contest between Kelley and the court set the stage for one hundred years of opposition between equality and difference as strategies for improving the status of American women. Should public policies seeking to benefit women emphasize their similarity to or their difference from men? At its origins, this opposition was clearly class based, pitting advocates for propertied, professional women against those for wage-earning women. This opposition hardened after 1900, but not until well after 1920—some would even say 1970—did the advocates of equality strategies dominate among those seeking to improve the status of working women in the United States. Twentieth-century feminists emphasized the similarity between women and men and, compared to nineteenth-century activists, emphasized individual rather than group forms of personal identity. Seeking to elide rather than validate a collective female identity, women's rights advocates after 1920 increasingly decried nineteenth-century notions of gender difference. By the late 1960s and 1970s, when a second wave equivalent to the nineteenth-century first wave of feminism emerged, gender similarity rather than gender difference was uncontested as the best basis for public policies to benefit women.

In the 1990s, however, feminist legal theorists moved away from unqualified support for equality strategies. Nineteenth-century notions of difference were discredited but so too were twentieth-century notions of equality. Each was viewed as relying on male-specific norms from which females represented deviation. Efforts to transcend the similarity-difference debate vary but might be summarized as trying to view public policy from a female perspective or making the world a better place for women. As this contest heads into the twenty-first century, it appears that notions of difference have managed to incorporate those of similarity and equality in ways that accommodate women's different realities along with hopes for women's greater opportunities, giving voice "not to abstract, ungendered rights but to women's experience" (Katherine De Gama, "A Brave New World? Rights Discourse and the Politics of Reproductive Autonomy," in Anne Bottomley and Joanne Conaghan, eds., *Feminist Theory and Legal Strategy* [London: Blackwell, 1993], 130). In this project,

Florence Kelley can be claimed as a pathbreaker if not as the model feminists want to follow.

Increasingly after 1900 Kelley argued that difference was the best strategy for achieving women's equality. Her dialogue with twentieth-century feminism pushed her in this direction, but from 1882 forward her own vision sought improvements in women's status vis-à-vis men as well as the betterment of working people. See, for example, FK, *Some Ethical Gains,* which is argued on the basis of rights.

For the continued opposition of women unionists and the U.S. Women's Bureau to the Equal Rights Amendment until after 1968, see Cynthia Harrison, *On Account of Sex: The Politics of Women's Issues, 1945–1968* (Berkeley: University of California Press, 1988). The continuing significance of difference in feminist legal and public-policy theory can also be found in: Hester Eisenstein, "Gender as a Category of Analysis," in Eisenstein, *Gender Shock: Practicing Feminism on Two Continents* (Boston: Beacon, 1991); Joan C. Williams, "Deconstructing Gender," and Mary E. Becker, "Prince Charming: Abstract Equality," in Leslie Friedman Goldstein, ed., *Feminist Jurisprudence: The Difference Debate* (Lanham, Md.: Rowman and Littlefield, 1992), 41–146; and Lise Vogel, *Mothers on the Job: Maternity Policy in the U.S. Workplace* (New York: Routledge, 1993). Recent attention to differences among women have highlighted the need for increased attention to differences of social position in achieving social justice. See, for example, Deborah L. Rhode, "The Politics of Paradigms: Gender Difference and Gender Disadvantage," in Gisela Bock and Susan James, eds., *Beyond Equality and Difference: Citizenship, Feminist Politics and Female Subjectivity* (New York: Routledge, 1992), 149–63. For a discussion of the ways in which sameness and difference discourses both disadvantage women by avoiding the issue of human needs, see Carol Lee Bacchi, *Same Difference: Feminism and Sexual Difference* (Winchester, Mass.: Unwin Hyman, 1990).

45. "Levy Mayer Is Highly Gratified, *Chicago Tribune,* March 15, 1895, 1; "Labor Law Falls," unidentified newsclipping, March 15, 1895, NKP; "Supreme Court Punctures the Eight-Hour Act," *Chicago Tribune,* March 15, 1895, 1.

46. "Labor Law Falls"; "Law, Liberty and Humanity," *Chicago Herald,* March 16, 1895, NKP; Stead, *If Christ Came to Chicago,* 402. See also "The Eight-Hour Law," unidentified newsclipping,

[March 16, 1895], NKP; and "That Eight-Hour Law," *Evening Journal,* March 18, 1895, NKP.

47. FK, *Third Annual Report,* 6–7, 19. The *Ritchie* decision was reversed in 1910 in another case involving William Ritchie.

48. "Lengthens the Day," *Chicago Record,* March 16, 1895, NKP.

49. "Will Investigate Child Labor," *The Chronicle,* Nov. 3, 1895, NKP. For the IMA-backed victories, see "Have Their Own Way: A Big Day for Corporations," *Chicago Record,* May 30, 1895, NKP. Although in their public statements IMA leaders declared their support for the regulation of child labor, in fact they opposed any attempt to strengthen child labor laws. The minutes of a meeting on April 17, 1895, opposed Kelley's proposed changes as "inimical to the business interests of the community." See IMAP, box 1, folder 1. For Kelley's child labor proposals, see "Child Labor in Illinois," *The Chronicle,* Aug. 4, 1895, NKP. In 1897 the Illinois child labor law forbade the employment in mercantile institutions of children under sixteen years of age for more than ten hours a day. For this and further changes in 1903 and 1904, see Becker, *History of Illinois Labor Legislation,* 162–63. Kelley's achievements during her last two years in office are summarized in [FK], *Third Annual Report,* and [FK], *Fourth Annual Report* (1897). For the reversal of reform in Chicago after 1897, see Gordon, "Women and the Anti-Child Labor Movement."

50. FK to CBK, 247 West Polk St., Feb. 10, 1896, NKP; FK to CBK, Hull House, Feb. 4, 1896, NKP; FK to CBK, Feb. 10, 1896; FK to "My Dear Mother," State of Illinois, Office of Factory Inspector, June 19, 1896, NKP; Margaret Kelley to Carrie Kelley [Albert Kelley's wife], Hull House, May 30, 1896, KFP, box 3; FK to CBK, Feb. 4, 1896; FK to CBK, Feb. 10, 1896; and FK to CBK, Hull House, Feb. 12, 1897, NKP.

51. Gertrude Tuckwell to JA, Guildford, England, May 21, 1896, PJA (and *JAP,* reel 3, #0151); Sidney Webb to FK, received by JA, PJA (and *JAP,* reel 3, #771). JA to John Weber Addams, London, June 1, 1896, PJA (and *JAP,* reel 3, #0233). See also JA to EGS, London, June 27, 1896, EGSP.

52. FK to HDL, 247 West Polk St., Oct. 1, 1896, HDLP. For more on the election, see Harvey Wish, "John Peter Altgeld and the Election of 1896," *Journal of the Illinois State Historical Society,* 30 (Dec. 1937), 353–84; and Green B. Raum, *History of Illinois Republicanism* (Chicago: Rollins, 1900), 211–19.

12. Feeling the Pinch, 1897–1899

1. FK to CBK, Hull House, Feb. 12, 1897, NKP. See FK to Rufus R. Wade, president, International Association of Factory Inspectors, Aug. 30, 1897, in FK, "Evolution of the Illinois Child Labor Law" (1897b), 33; FK, *Some Ethical Gains through Legislation* (New York: Macmillan, 1905), 57; "Betrayed by Tanner," *Chicago Times-Herald,* Sept. 6, 1897, NKP; and "Governor Tanner's Double-Dealing," *Chicago Times-Herald,* Sept. 7, 1897, NKP.

2. FK to CBK, Hull House, Aug. 14, 1898, NKP; JA to MRS, Aug. 31, 1897, PJA (and *JAP,* reel 3, #0774).

3. JA to MRS, Hull House, Sept. 2, 1897, PJA (and *JAP,* reel 3, #0777); JA to Alice Haldeman, Hull House, Oct. 14, 1897, Mrs. S. A. Haldeman Manuscripts, Indiana University, Bloomington (and *JAP,* reel 3, #0842).

4. JA to MRS, Sept. 2, 1897. For Kelley's apartment hunting, see JA to Alice Haldeman, Oct. 14, 1897.

5. Margaret Kelley to Albert Kelley, Hull House, Dec. 27, 1894, KFP; FK to CBK, Hull House, Dec. 28, 1898, NKP. For the Crerar Library, see "Crerar Will Report," *Chicago Tribune,* July 14, 1894, 14; interview with Crerar librarian quoted in Blumberg, *Florence Kelley,* 163; and Horowitz, *Culture and the City,* 45.

6. FK, "Das Gesetz über Freie Volksbibliotheken" (The free public library law) (1899), 200; FK to CBK, Hull House, Aug. 9, 1898, NKP.

7. FK to CBK, Hull House, June 20, 1898, NKP; FK to CBK, State of Illinois, Office of Factory Inspector, Sept. 15, 1898, NKP.

8. FK to CBK, Sept. 15, 1898.

9. FK to CBK, Hull House, Aug. 27, 1898, NKP; FK to CBK, Hull House, Sept. 21, 1898; FK to CBK, Hull House, Aug. 6, 1898, NKP.

10. FK to CBK, Hull House, Aug. 9, 1898, NKP. Bryn Mawr had the advantage of proximity to Caroline.

11. FK to CBK, Aug. 6, 1898, NKP.

12. FK to CBK, June 20, 1898; JA to MRS, Hull House, Aug. 14, 1899, PJA (and *JAP,* reel 3, #1403).

13. NK, "Early Days at Hull House," 427, 429.

14. JA to MRS, Sept. 2, 1897, PJA (and *JAP,* reel 3, #0777); JA to MRS, Aug. 14, 1899.

15. FK to CBK, Hull House, Oct. 4, 1898, NKP; JA to FK (June 1899), PJA (and *JAP,* reel 3, #1359). FK to CBK, Hull House, Dec. 28, 1898, NKP. For Ko's enrollment at the Lewis Institute, see *First Annual Register of the Lewis Institute. Devoted to Science, Literature, and Technology* (Chicago, 1897)

16. FK to CBK, Hull House, Aug. 24, 1898, NKP; FK to CBK, Hull House, Sept. 21, NKP; FK to Lillian D. Wald (hereafter LDW), Hull House, Jan. 24, 1899, Lillian D. Wald Papers (hereafter LDWP), New York Public Library; FK to CBK, Hull House, June 20, and Sept. 26, 1898, NKP.

17. FK to CBK, Hull House, Sept. 26, and Dec. 28, 1898, NKP.

18. FK to CBK, Hull House, July 24, 1898, NKP, box 2; and FK to CBK, Oct. 4, 1898. For the Webbs' plans to visit, see Sidney Webb to FK, London, Aug. 21, 1897, PJA (and *JAP,* reel 3, #0771).

19. AH, *Exploring the Dangerous Trades,* 60–62.

20. FK to Alexander Bruce, n.d., quoted by Bruce in *Memorial Services for Mrs. Florence Kelley and Miss Julia C. Lathrop,* Hull House, Chicago, May 6, 1932, 19–20, Anita McCormick Blaine Papers, State Historical Society of Wisconsin, Madison.

21. See, for example, Donald Marti, *Women and the Grange: Mutuality and Sisterhood in Rural America, 1866–1920* (Westport, Conn.: Greenwood, 1991).

22. FK, "The Working Child" (1896), 163, 165. The original of the speech can be found in "FK Speeches, typescripts and printed copies," National Consumers' League Records, box D, folder 3, Library of Congress. Another printed version of this talk was more conciliatory, concluding that "the opportunity of the charity worker in this connection is really a large and important one" (FK, "Child Labor" [1897]), 228.

23. AH to "My Dear Little Girl" [Agnes Hamilton], n.p., n.d. [Hull House, June 1898], Hamilton Family Papers [hereafter HFP]); FK to CBK, July 24, 1898.

24. JA to MRS, Hull House, July 18, 1898, PJA (and *JAP,* reel 3, #1131); FK to CBK, Aug. 27, 1898, and July 24, 1898; AH to "My Dear Little Girl," n.d. [June 1898]. For the appointment, see also Lyman Gage to JA, Washington, D.C., July 11, 1898 PJA (and *JAP,* reel 3, #1125). The commission's work was later published as United States Industrial Commission (hereafter USIC), *Report of the Industrial Commission on the Relations and Conditions of Capital and Labor Employed in Manufactures and General Business, Including Testimony, Prepared in Accordance with the Act of Congress Approved June 18, 1898,* 19 vols., (Washington D.C.: GPO, 1900–1902). For more on the USIC, see Clarence Wunderlin, *Visions of a New Industrial Order: American Social and Labor Theory in America's Progressive Era* (New York: Columbia University Press, 1992), 27–45.

25. FK to CBK, Aug. 27, 1898, July 24, Aug. 6, and Sept. 21, 1898. "They are not going to put a woman on it," AH wrote Agnes Hamilton (Hull House, Oct. 11, 1898, HFP).

26. For Jacob Riis, see Jacob A. Riis, "Ruling by the Ten Commandments," in *Theodore Roosevelt, the Citizen* (New York: The Outlook, 1904), 203–29; Riis, *The Making of an American* (New York: Macmillan, 1901), 337–39; Edith Patterson Meyer, *"Not Charity, but Justice": The Story of Jacob A. Riis* (New York: Vanguard, 1974), 192–207; and Howard Lawrence Hurwitz, *Theodore Roosevelt and Labor in New York State, 1880–1900* (New York: Columbia University Press, 1943), 166–231.

27. FK to LDW, Hull House, Jan 24, 1899, LDWP; FK to HDL, Hull House, Jan. 31, 1899, HDLP.

28. FK to MRS, Feb. 4, 1899, PJA (and *JAP,* reel 3, #1287); JA to LDW, Hull House, Feb. 13, 1899, LDWP. TR had written Riis: "Any recommendation she makes against the interests of the employers would be at once met by the cry that 'this is Altgeldism'" (Jan. 23, 1899, Theodore Roosevelt Papers [hereafter TRP], Executive Official, vol. 1). For TR's highly gendered mixture of reformism and nationalism, see his articles "What 'Americanism' Means," *Forum* 17 (April 1894): 196–206; and "The Manly Virtues and Practical Politics," *Forum* 17 (July 1894): 551–57.

Contrary to other accounts of the meeting, Addams visited TR with Maud Nathan; Kelley did not make the trip. See Nathan, *Story of an Epoch-Making Movement,* 55.

29. *New York Sun,* Nov. 1, 1898, quoted in James B. Lane, *Jacob A. Riis and the American City* (Port Washington, N.Y.: Kennikat, 1974), 131–32; quoted in Nathan, *Story of an Epoch-Making Movement,* 55; TR to John Williams, June 2, 1899, TRP, vol. 3; TR to FK, Albany, June 2, 1899, NKP. See also Harold F. Gosnell, *Boss Platt and His New York Machine* (Chicago: University of Chicago Press, 1924), 126.

30. Addams wrote Ely about Kelley's need for work, but he did not produce any live options. See JA to RTE, Hull House, Sept. 6, 1897, RTEP (and *JAP,* reel 3, #0781). Speaking engagements at Madison and Oshkosh did bring Kelley forty dollars. "By saving my vacation, and having it placed to my credit, I can do a good deal of that sort of thing; and it is the most agreeable possible manner of adding to my salary" (FK to CBK, Aug. 9, 1898). She also went to Cincinnati "to lecture and preach" (FK to MRS, Feb. 4, 1899). Only one woman faculty member before 1900, Louise Kellogg of the Department of History, is referred to in Merle Curti and Vernon Carstensen, *The University of Wisconsin: A History, 1848–1925* (Madison: University of Wisconsin, 1949), 1:639; and Helen R. Olin, *The Women of a State University: An Illustration of the Working of Coeducation in the Middle West* (New York: Putnam's, 1909), 293–97. See also the case of Helen Sumner in Kathryn Kish Sklar, "American Female Historians in Social Context: 1775–1930," *FS* 3 (fall 1975): 171–84.

31. "Prof. Ely's Denial," *Chicago Tribune,* Aug. 15, 1894, 7; RTE to HDL, Madison, Wisconsin, June 3, 1895, HDLP. See Ross, *Origins of American Social Science,* 98–140. See also Sklar, "Two Political Cultures in the Progressive Era." Ely told Lloyd that his experience did not shake his faith in "the German doctrine that the state protects freedom against attacks from society. The attack against me, for example, did not come from the state in reality. The demagogue who led it was to be sure for the time being the state superintendent of public instruction but he was that merely owing to an accident of politics." Some male investigators continued to embody those moral visions. For example, Addams wrote to Ely, "Dr. John Graham Brooks from Cambridge has been in Chicago for six weexs. He has been most valuable and inspiring to our plans here. Such a man makes us very discontented with the Chicago University men" (JA to RTE, Feb. 19, 1895, RTEP (and *JAP,* reel 2, 1968).

32. See Harry Liebersohn, *Fate and Utopia in German Sociology, 1870–1923* (Cambridge, Mass.: MIT Press, 1988); Ross, *Origins of American Social Science,* 234–35; and Bannister, *Sociology and Scientism,* 41–44.

33. Deegan, *Jane Addams,* 38, 35.

34. FK's contributions to the *American Journal of Sociology* before 1900 were "Working Boy" (Nov. 1896), "Illinois Child Labor Law" (Jan. 1898), "United States Supreme Court and the Utah Eight Hours' Law" (July 1898), and "Aims and Principles of the Consumers' League" (Nov. 1899). Pieces published after 1900 were "Has Illinois the Best Laws for Protection of Children in Illinois? (10 [Nov. 1904]: 299–314) and "Minimum-Wage Boards" (17 [Nov. 1911]: 303–14). Table 1 of John Sill's unpublished paper "Women's Contributions to the *American Journal of Sociology* during the Editorship of Albion Small" compares the proportion of articles by women and by men published in the first three decades of the *American Journal of Soci-*

ology. He found that of articles on social reform (7.7 percent of the total), 22.5 percent were written by women. For Talbot, Breckinridge, and the School of Social Service Administration see Muncy, *Creating a Female Dominion.* For more on the relationship between academics at the University of Chicago and Hull House, see Andrew Feffer, *The Chicago Pragmatists and American Progressivism* (Ithaca: Cornell University Press, 1993), 91–115.

35. JA to MRS, June 29, 1899, PJA (and *JAP,* reel 3, #1380); FK to LDW, Hull House, July 20, 1899, LDWP. For JA and FK's decision to coteach the course, see JA to MRS, Hull House, Feb. 9, 1899, PJA (and *JAP,* reel 3, #1289). The course, which began on July 5, 1899, was a regular credit course with examinations.

36. FK to LDW, Hull House, Aug. 13, 1899, LDWP; Gertrude Barnum to MRS, Riverside, Ill., Aug. 6, 1899, PJA (and *JAP,* reel 3, #1410).

37. Agnes Hamilton to FK, [Stanford], Jan. 17, 1895, Columbia University. See Albion W. Small and George E. Vincent, *An Introduction to the Study of Society* (New York: American Book Co., 1894). See also Carson, "Agnes Hamilton of Fort Wayne."

38. On FK's appointment by Altgeld in 1893, Friedrich Sorge said that she was "well-known to many party comrades in Germany" and that her appointment "was greeted with great joy" (Foner and Chamberlin, *Sorge's Labor Movement,* 59. See "Heinrich Braun," in *Neue Deutsche Biographie* (Berlin: Duneker and Humblot, 1953), 546; Pierson, *Marxist Intellectuals,* 69–78; Irmela Gorges, "The Social Survey in Germany before 1933," in Bulmer, Bales, and Sklar, *The Social Survey,* 316–39; Anthony Oberschall, *Empirical Social Research in Germany, 1848–1914* (The Hague: Mouton, 1965); and Quataert, *Reluctant Feminists,* 77–80. For *Archiv,* see Pierson, *Marxist Intellectuals,* 73–77; and Arthur Mitzman, *Sociology and Three Sociologists of Imperial Germany* (New Brunswick, N.J.: Transaction, 1973), 121, 146–153. For Braun and Kautsky's differences, see Pierson, *Marxist Intellectuals,* 62; and Steenson, *Karl Kautsky.*

39. Heinrich Braun to FK, Berlin, March 24, 1897, NKP; Heinrich Braun to FK, Berlin, July 24, 1898, NKP.

40. FK to CBK, Sept. 15, 1898, and Aug. 9, 1898.

41. FK, "Die Italiener Chicagos" (Italians in Chicago) (1899), 310–11. Kelley found this paper more demanding than others, writing Caroline, "My long-dragged-out paper on the Italians in Chicago is finished and wrapped for mailing" (FK

to CBK, Aug. 9, 1898). See Carroll D. Wright, *Ninth Special Report of the Commissioner of Labor: The Italians in Chicago, a Social and Economic Study* (Washington: GPO, 1897; reprint, New York: Arno, 1970). For other aspects of the connection between Hull House, Kelley, and the Italian community of the Nineteenth Ward, see Humbert S. Nelli, *The Italians in Chicago, 1880–1930* (New York: Oxford University Press, 1970), 34–35, 100–112.

42. FK, "Die weibliche Fabrikinspektion" (Women factory inspectors) (1897), 129, 136, 138–39, 142.

43. Ibid., 139–41.

44. FK, "Drei Entscheidungen oberster Gerichte" (Three Supreme Court decisions) (1898), 760, 763–65. For other articles by FK in *Archiv* before 1900, see "Die Fabrik-Gesetzgebung der Vereinigten Staaten" (Factory legislation in the United States) (1895), "Die gesetzliche Regelung der Kinderarbeit" (The legal regulation of child labor) (1898), "Das Sweating-system in den Vereinigten Staaten" (The sweating system in the United States) (1898), and "Das Gesetz über freie Volksbibliotheken" (The free public library law) (1899). One more, written before 1900, appeared in 1901: "Das Fabrikinspektorat von New York" (Factory inspectors of New York) (1901).

45. FK, "United States Supreme Court," 33–34.

46. Davis, "Jane Addams vs. the Ward Boss," 251. See also Davis, "Settlement Workers in Politics, 1890–1914"; and Lloyd Wendt and Herman Kogan, *Lords of the Levee: The Story of Bathhouse John and Hinky Dink* (Indianapolis: Bobbs-Merrill, 1943), 91–96.

47. Prior to 1933 and the Federal Emergency Relief Administration, headed by Harry Hopkins, the most important public aid came from "outdoor relief" and institutional care financed under state poor laws. See Katz, *In the Shadow of the Poorhouse,* 36–85; and Lizabeth Cohen, *Making a New Deal: Industrial Workers in Chicago, 1919–1939* (Cambridge: Cambridge University Press, 1991), 62–64. On ward bosses, see Thelen, "Urban Politics"; Jon Teaford, "Finis for Tweed and Steffens: Rewriting the History of Urban Rule," *Reviews in American History* 10 (1982): 133–49; Brown and Halaby, "Machine Politics in America"; Terrance J. McDonald, *The Parameters of Urban Fiscal Policy: Socioeconomic Change and Political Culture in San Francisco, 1860–1906* (Berkeley: University of California Press, 1986); McDonald, "The Burdens of Urban History,"

Studies in American Political Development 3 (1989): 30–55; Teaford, *Unheralded Triumph.*

48. AH to Agnes Hamilton, Hull House, March 30, 1898, HFP. See "To Rule the Schools: Women Who Will Serve on Board of Education," *Chicago Tribune,* May 5, 1894, 16; "Women Feel Joyful: Mrs. Flower Elected U. of Illinois Trustee," *Chicago Tribune,* Nov. 8, 1894, 6; "Republican Women Outline Course of Political Struggle," *Chicago Tribune,* Dec. 13, 1894, 3; "Federated Club's Election," *Chicago Journal,* Oct. 12, 1895, in Hull House Scrapbook III [1889–1897], 24, JAMC (and *JAP,* reel 81, addendum reel 10). For the enduring differences between women's and men's political cultures in Chicago, see Flanagan, "Gender and Urban Political Reform."

49. FK, "Hull House" (July 1898), 566. See Davis, *Spearheads for Reform,* 158; and Davis, "Jane Addams vs. the Ward Boss." Addams herself was appointed garbage inspector in March 1895. "The Ward is really cleaner," she wrote Mary Smith ([Hull House], Aug. 8, 1895, PJA [and *JAP,* reel 2, #1721–24]). For the effects of Chicago's civil service law, see Richard C. Lindberg, *To Serve and Collect: Chicago Politics and Police Corruption from the Lager Beer Riot to the Summerdale Scandal* (New York: Praeger, 1991), 50–52.

50. Joan S. Miller analyzed the success of the Municipal Voters' League, which in 1896 opposed twenty-six of thirty-four candidates running for the Chicago City Council but by 1898 had learned the art of compromise and choosing the lesser of two evils. That year twenty-three of the thirty-five candidates endorsed by the Municipal Voters' League were elected. The league was dominated by men affiliated with the Republican Party. It was not nonpartisan, even though it included some Democrats and Independents. See Miller, "The Politics of Municipal Reform in Chicago during the Progressive Era: The Municipal Voters' League as a Test Case, 1896–1920" (M.A. thesis, Roosevelt University, 1966), 19–20, 27. In the 1892 alderman election, independent candidates stood for election in twenty-five of the city's thirty-four wards; three were elected—in the Sixth, Ninth, and Twenty-first. The one independent candidate who ran in the Nineteenth Ward received 127 votes. In 1897 independent candidates ran in all but one ward; two were elected—in the Twenty-fifth and Thirty-second. Four independent candidates ran in the Nineteenth Ward, receiving a total of 4,468 votes. See *Chicago Daily News,* April 6, 1892, and April 7,

1897. For more on the Municipal Voters' League after 1898, see Hoyt King, "The Reform Movement in Chicago," *Annals of the American Academy of Political and Social Science* 25 (Jan.–June 1905), 33–45.

Chicago's wealthiest businessmen and professionals led the movement for municipal reform within the city's male political culture. For more on the emergence of Progressivism in Chicago's male political culture, see Wiebe, *Businessmen and Reform;* and Donald D. Marks, "Polishing the Gem of the Prairie: The Evolution of Civic Reform Consciousness in Chicago, 1874–1900" (Ph.D. diss., University of Wisconsin, Madison, 1974), 145–87. See also Sidney I. Roberts, "Businessmen in Revolt: Chicago, 1874–1900" (Ph.D. diss., Northwestern University, 1960); and Bruce Grant, *Fight for a City: The Story of the Union League Club of Chicago and Its Times, 1880–1955* (Chicago: Rand McNally, 1955), 141–51. For the Chicago Civic Federation, see Douglas Sutherland, *Fifty Years on the Civic Front* (Chicago: Civic Federation, 1943), 4–7. For the Chicago Commons campaign with illuminating comments on joint efforts with Hull House, see Louise C. Wade, *Graham Taylor: Pioneer for Social Justice, 1851–1938* (Chicago: University of Chicago Press, 1964), 130–35.

51. Nineteenth Ward Improvement Club Papers, University of Illinois, Chicago. The club's first membership list included (in addition to three Hull House residents, Addams, Starr and Kelley), nineteen men and eighteen women. Sara Monoson's otherwise excellent article "The Lady and the Tiger" mistakenly identified the Hull House Men's Club as the sole coordinator of the settlement's electoral challenge. For more criticism of Powers, see "Judge Tuley on Powers," *Chicago Tribune,* April 4, 1896, 3. For the election of 1896, see "Some Pure Men Win," *Chicago Tribune,* April 8, 1896, 2.

52. Ray S. Baker, "Hull House and the Ward Boss," *The Outlook* 58 (March 26, 1898): 771, 769. See also Davis, "Jane Addams vs. the Ward Boss," 250–60; Sidney I. Roberts, "The Municipal Voters' League and Chicago's Boodlers," *Journal of Illinois State Historical Society* 53 (summer 1960): 129; and Roberts, "Businessmen in Revolt." For Pingree, see Melvin G. Holli, *Reform in Detroit: Hazen S. Pingree and Urban Politics* (New York: Oxford University Press, 1969), 54. Pingree specialized in the elimination of corruption in municipal transportation; he was elected governor of Michigan in 1898. For municipal utilities, see Sidney I. Roberts, "Portrait of a

Robber Baron: Charles T. Yerkes," *Business History Review* 35 (autumn 1961): 344–371.

53. FK to CBK, Sept. 21, 1898; and FK to HDL, Hull House, Sept. 26, 1898, HDLP.

54. *Chicago Evening Post*, Feb. 19, 1896, quoted in Davis, "Jane Addams vs. the Ward Boss," 253. Powers claimed to have placed twenty-six hundred ward residents on the city payroll, routinely intervened with judges and jailers, distributed turkeys at Christmas, and arranged decent funerals for the poor. For Addams's analysis of her conflict with Powers, see JA, *Democracy and Social Ethics*, 221–77; and JA, "Ethical Survivals in Municipal Corruption," *International Journal of Ethics* 8 (April 1898): 273–91.

55. FK, "Hull House," 565–66. Neither Kelley nor Addams realized that the Italian community in their ward opposed Powers and that a direct appeal to them might have made all the difference. See Humbert S. Nelli, "John Powers and the Italians: Politics in a Chicago Ward, 1896–1921," *JAH* 57 (June 1970): 67–84. One sign of the growing national strength of reform impulses within male political culture was the creation in July 1899 of the Social Reform Union, which listed four reform governors on its letterhead and invited Kelley to join them as vice president from Illinois. See W. D. P. Bliss to FK, Alhambra, California, July 18, 1899, NKP.

56. FK, "The Working Woman's Need of the Ballot" (1898), 312, 313. Kelley's paper was read at the National-American Woman Suffrage Association's 1898 convention by Mary A. Swift of California. For the 1890 transition of the suffrage movement, see Susan B. Anthony and Ida Husted Harper, eds., *History of Woman Suffrage*, vol. 4, *1883–1900* (Rochester: N.Y.: Susan B. Anthony, 1902; reprint, Salem, N.H.: AYER, 1985), 158–85.

57. AH to Agnes Hamilton, Fort Wayne, Nov. 26, 1898, quoted in Sicherman, *Alice Hamilton*, 127; Charlotte Perkins Gilman, *The Living of Charlotte Perkins Gilman: An Autobiography* (New York: Appleton-Century, 1935), 184; Lane, *To Herland and Beyond*, 183. By 1900 Gilman's book had been reprinted three times, nine times by 1920. During its first five years in print, it was translated into five languages. Charlotte Perkins Stetson did not marry George Houghton Gilman until 1900, so she was known as Mrs. Stetson in 1898. I refer to her as Gilman because that is how she has been known since 1900. See "Charlotte Perkins Stetson Gilman," in *NAW*; and Ceplair, *Charlotte Perkins Gilman;*

and Pittenger, *American Socialists*, 64–88; and Marian K. Towne, "Charlotte Gilman in California," *The Pacific Historian* 28, no. 1 (1984): 4–17.

Gilman declined Addams's invitation to become the head of a new settlement on Chicago's North Side, instead recommending Helen Campbell, who accepted. Gilman and Campbell lived together there for a few months until Gilman suffered a mental collapse. Campbell left the next year. See Mary A. Hill, *Charlotte Perkins Gilman: The Making of a Radical Feminist, 1860–1896* (Philadelphia: Temple University Press, 1980), 272–82; and "Helen Stuart Campbell," in *NAW*.

58. JA to Charlotte Perkins Stetson, Rockford, July 19, 1898, Charlotte Perkins Gilman Collection (hereafter CPGC); FK to Charlotte Perkins Stetson [Gilman], Hull House, July 26, 1898, CPGC.

59. Quoted in Lane, *To Herland and Beyond*, 7. For more on Ward, see Ross, *Origins of American Social Science*, 88–103; Samuel Chugerman, *Lester Ward, The American Aristotle: A Summary and Interpretation of His Sociology* (Durham, N.C.: Duke University Press, 1939; reprint, New York: Octagon, 1965); Clifford H. Scott, *Lester Frank Ward* (Boston: Twayne, 1976); and Henry Steele Commager, introduction to *Lester Ward and the Welfare State* (Indianapolis: Bobbs-Merrill, 1967). For Ward's Washington career, see Michael Lacey, "The Mysteries of Earth-Making Dissolve: A Study of Washington's Intellectual Community and the Origins of American Environmentalism in the Late Nineteenth Century" (Ph.D. diss., George Washington University, 1979). For Gilman's effect on sociological theory, see Thorstein Veblen, "The Barbarian Status of Women," *American Journal of Sociology* 4 (Jan. 1899): 503–14.

60. Gilman, *Women and Economics*, 5, 316, 46; FK to Charlotte Perkins Stetson [Gilman], July 26, 1898.

61. FK to Charlotte Perkins Stetson [Gilman], July 26, 1898.

62. FK to AH, State of Illinois, Office of Factory Inspector, Dec. 8, 1896, HFP. Kelley's 1893 talk, entitled "Formation of a Purchasers' League to Protect Women and Children," was mentioned in Marion Talbot and Lois Rosenberry, *The History of the American Association of University Women, 1881–1931* (Boston: Houghton Mifflin, 1931), 109. In her 1892 essay "Objective Value of a Social Settlement," Jane Addams referred to the aid consumers might exercise in sustaining women's unions in the garment industry if a union could "grow strong enough to offer a label," since "in that case there

would be the hope of co-operation on the part of the consumers" (H. Adams, *Philanthropy and Social Progress*, 50). In "Hull House," FK noted that "the Consumers' League, of which two active members are residents, aims to educate the purchaser as to her influence in the life of the workers, urging the duty of early shopping in conscientiously selected places" (564). For the growth of the consumer culture, see William Leach, *Land of Desire: Merchants, Power and the Rise of a New American Culture* (New York: Pantheon, 1993), 20–25.

See John Graham Brooks, "The Papal Encyclical upon the Labor Question," in *Publications of the American Economic Association* (Baltimore: AEA, 1894), 9:78. For a brief but enlightening summary of one hundred years of papal encyclicals on "the labor question," see the *New York Times*, May 3, 1991, A-10. Brooks's course, announced in *Hull-House Bulletin*, January 1896 (in Hull House Scrapbook III [1889–1897], JAMC [and *JAP*, reel 81, addendum reel 10]), showed that he had much in common with Kelley. Its component parts were "From Theory to Practice," "Social Democracy in Germany," "Social Democracy in the French Communes," "The Rise of Socialism in England," "English Socialism in Practice," "The Outlook of Socialism in the United States." For more on adult education at Hull House, see Colky, "Jane Addams."

63. FK to CBK, Oct. 4, 1898; FK to CBK, Dec. 28, 1898. See Mrs. Charles Russell Lowell, "Consumers' Leagues," *Church Social Union*, Feb. 15, 1898, 22–23; Annie Marion MacLean, "Two Weeks in Department Stores," *American Journal of Sociology* 4 (May 1899): 721–41. Kelley included the "Recommendations for Shoppers" in her 1898 *Archiv* article "Die gesetzliche Regelung der Kinderarbeit" (Child labor laws). One of the other two women Kelley named was Marianna Gay, who, the 1900 census shows, lived with her widowed mother and schoolteacher sister in a seven-family apartment building on Chicago's south side. The third, "Mrs. Smoot," proved impossible to trace.

64. Quoted in Croly, *History of the Woman's Club Movement*, 154. "Ellen Martin Henrotin," in *NAW*, is the best single source. For Henrotin's work at the Chicago World's Fair, see her article "The Woman's Branch of the World's Congress Auxiliary," *Review of Reviews* (May 1893): 419–22; and her essay "The Financial Independence of Women," in Mary Kavanaugh Oldham Eagle, ed., *The Congress of Women Held in the Woman's Building, World's*

Columbian Exposition (Chicago: Kuhlman, 1894), 348–70. In "Financial Independence," she drew on the assistance of Ethelbert Stewart to analyze the proportions of self-supporting working-class and middle-class women. Henrotin's election as president of the General Federation of Women's Clubs (hereafter GFWC) was noted in *Chicago Tribune*, May 12, 1894, 5. For her crucial role in orienting the GFWC toward social reform, see her papers at the Schlesinger Library, Cambridge; Mary I. Wood, *The History of the General Federation of Women's Clubs* (New York: General Federation of Women's Clubs, 1912), 71; Mildred W. Wells, *Unity in Diversity* (Washington, D.C.: General Federation of Women's Clubs, 1953), 54–58; Martin, *Sound of Our Own Voices;* and Blair, *Clubwoman as Feminist*, 102–4. Henrotin also served as president of the National Women's Trade Union League from 1903 to 1907. Her writings include (with Kate Byam Martin) *The Social Status of European and American Women* (Chicago: Charles Kerr, 1887); and *The Attitude of Women's Clubs and Associations*. Kelley may have had a hand in obtaining Carroll Wright's support for this last study, in which Henrotin listed the names, locations, and purposes of 1,283 women's clubs in the United States.

65. For more on the organization of the New York league, see ch. 7 above. For the Boston league's founding meeting, see March and December 1897 minutes, CLMP). The executive committee of the Massachusetts league included "one representative of the Federation of Women's Clubs, and one of the Directors of Working Girls' Clubs" (minutes, June 7, 1897, CLMP). For the Boston Women's Educational and Industrial Union, see Deutsch, "Learning to Talk More Like a Man."

66. JSL, "Consumers' Leagues," *Christian Social Union*, Feb. 15, 1898, quoted in Stewart, *Philanthropic Work of Josephine Shaw Lowell*, 338; Nathan, *Story of an Epoch-Making Movement*, 26–27; minutes, Oct. 21, 1897, CLMP.

67. Minutes, March 1898, CLMP. See also minutes, Feb. 7, and Feb. 24, 1898, CLMP. In 1893 Helen Campbell had called Kelley "one of the ablest workers" in the field of working women's societies and listed five Kelley-derived principles on which such societies should be based, including "institut[ing] a label which shall enable the purchaser to discriminate in favor of goods produced under healthful conditions" (*Women Wage-Earners*, 264). For the union label, see Commons et al., *History of Labour*, 2:266 n. 17. For the debate, see minutes,

May, June 7, Sept. 23, Oct. 7, Oct. 21, 1897, and March 1898, CLMP; and Maud Nathan, "The Consumers' Label," *North American Review* 166 (Feb. 1898): 250–54.

68. Minutes, Feb. 22, 1899, CLMP; Mary Heaton Vorse, "The Watchdog: A Memorial to Margaret Wiesman, Secretary of the Consumers' League of Massachusetts, 1931–1953," typed manuscript, n.p., CLMP, box 31; "The Consumers' League," *New York Times*, May 18, 1898, 4; minutes, May 24, 1898, CLMP.

69. Minutes, Jan. 26, 1899, CLMP. For the search committee, see Stewart, *Philanthropic Work*, 339.

70. n.a., *John Graham Brooks, Helen Lawrence Brooks, 1846–1938: A Memorial* (Boston: privately printed, 1940), 25; Vorse, "The Watchdog," 32–33. For more on Kelley's appointment, see minutes, Jan. 26, 1899, CLMP; Goldmark, *Impatient Crusader*, 56; and National Consumers' League, *Summary Statement of the Work of the First Year of the National Consumers' League*, National Consumers' League Records, Library of Congress. See also "John Graham Brooks," in *The National Cyclopaedia of American Biography* (New York: James T. White, 1940), 449. Brooks had worked closely with elite expressions of women's political culture in New York, including the League for Political Education, which later became Town Hall. At Andover Seminary, Brooks introduced one of the first courses on sociology and inspired Robert A. Woods "to prepare himself to organize" South End House. See *John Graham Brooks*, 7, 24, 28. His German study was published as: John Graham Brooks, *Compulsory Insurance in Germany, Including An Appendix Re-lating to Compulsory Insurance in Other Countries in Europe, Fourth Special Report of the Commissioner of Labor* (Washington: GPO, 1893).

71. FK to Katharine Coman, March 20, 1899, CLMP; Executive Committee of Consumers' League of Massachusetts minutes, March 30, 1899, CLMP. For more on Coman, see *NAW.* Kelley located the power of the ideological symbol (the union label) not in the representation itself but in the social structures sustaining it. For a theoretical treatment of the plastic relationship between ideology and social structures, see Giddens, *Constitution of Society*, 45–49.

72. FK to LDW, Hull House, March 23, 1899, LDWP.

73. FK to LDW, July 20, 1899; JA to MRS, Aug. 14, 1899, PJA (and *JAP*, reel 3, #1404).

74. NK to FK, Hull House, May 31, 1899, "NK letters to FK, 1893–1920," KFP, box 3; AH to FK, [Fort Wayne], June 2, 1899, reprinted in Sicherman, *Alice Hamilton*, 131; JA to FK, Hull House, Sept. 13, 1899, NKP (and *JAP*, reel 3, #1434); JA to FK [June 1899]. Bills from the Hull-House Coffee-House show that Margaret and John resided at Hull House all of August and part of September.

75. JA to FK, [June 1899], NKP (and *JAP*, reel 3, #1359); JA to MRS, Aug. 22 1899, PJA (and JAP, reel 3 #1419); MRS to FK, Sept. 14, 1899, NKP; JA to FK, Nov. 8, 1899, NKP (and *JAP*, reel 3, #1469); JA to FK, Nov. 22, 1899, NKP (and *JAP*, reel 3, #1476); and JA to FK, July 5, 1913, KFP, box 75, folder 56 (and *JAP*, reel 7, #915).

76. FK to CBK, Hull House, Dec. 24, 1899, NKP.

Bibliography

Archival Collections

The author is grateful for permission to quote from manuscripts and records in the following archives.

Amsterdam

International Institute for Social History
    Marx-Engels Collection

Baltimore

Goucher College Special Collections
    Froelicher Collection

Bloomington, Indiana

Indiana University, Lilly Library
    Mrs. S. A. Haldeman Manuscripts

Boston

Boston Public Library, Antislavery Manuscripts
    Papers of Sarah Pugh
Massachusetts Historical Society
    William D. Kelley Letters

Bryn Mawr, Pennsylvania

Mariam Coffin Canaday Library, Bryn Mawr
    College Archives
    M. Carey Thomas Papers

Cambridge

Harvard University, Houghton Library
    William Kelley Correspondence
Radcliffe College, Schlesinger Library
    Consumers' League of Massachusetts Papers
    Charlotte Perkins Gilman Collection
    Hamilton Family Papers
    Ellen M. Henrotin Papers

Chicago

Chicago Historical Society
    Chicago Trade and Labor Assembly Papers
    Chicago Woman's Club Papers
    Citizens' Association of Chicago Papers
    Civic Federation of Chicago Papers
    Illinois Manufacturers' Association Papers
Cook County Court Records
    Divorce Proceedings
Municipal Reference Library
    Journal of the Proceedings of the City Council
    of the City of Chicago
Northwestern University
    Northwestern University Archives
University of Chicago, Regensburg Library, Special
    Collections
    Marion Talbot Papers
University of Illinois at Chicago, University Library,
    Special Collections
    Jane Addams Memorial Collection
    Nineteenth Ward Improvement Club Papers

Durham, North Carolina

Duke University, Special Collections Library
Helen J. Gow Diaries

Fremont, Ohio

Rutherford B. Hayes Presidential Center
Rutherford B. Hayes Papers

Ithaca, New York

Cornell University, Labor-Management Documentation Center, M. P. Catherwood Library
American Association for Labor Legislation Papers
Cornell University Library, Carl A. Kroch Library, Rare and Manuscript Collections
Cornell University Register
Deceased Alumni Records
Emily Howland Papers
Social Science Club Records

Gainesville, Florida

Jane Holland Private Collection

Madison

State Historical Society of Wisconsin
Anita McCormick Blaine Papers
Richard T. Ely Papers
Henry Demarest Lloyd Papers

Minneapolis

University of Minnesota
Social Welfare Archives

New York City

Columbia University, Rare Book and Manuscript Library
Kelley Family Papers
Lillian Wald Papers
The New-York Historical Society
Fairchild Papers
New York Public Library, Astor, Lenox and Tilden Foundations, Rare Books and Manuscripts Division
Nicholas Kelley Papers

Friedrich A. Sorge Papers
Lillian Wald Papers

Northampton, Massachusetts

Smith College, Sophia Smith Collection
Ellen Gates Starr Papers

Philadelphia

Historical Society of Pennsylvania
William D. Kelley Papers
New Century Guild Records
Register of Wills of the City and County of Philadelphia

Rockford, Illinois

Rockford College
Jane Addams Papers

Springfield, Illinois

Illinois State Archives
John Peter Altgeld Correspondence

Swarthmore, Pennsylvania

Swarthmore College Peace Collection
Papers of Jane Addams

Urbana, Illinois

University of Illinois, Illinois Historical Survey
Thomas and Elizabeth Morgan Collection

Washington, D.C.

Library of Congress, Manuscripts Division
Susan B. Anthony Papers
Abraham Lincoln Papers
National Consumers' League Records
Theodore Roosevelt Papers

Zürich

Universität Zürich, Staatsarchiv
Register of Feepayers
Student Register
Stadthaus
Zivilstandsamt, Abteilung Geburten

Complete Writings by Florence Kelley, 1882–1899, and Four Autobiographical Articles, 1926–1927, in Chronological Order.

Within any given year, works identified with month or month and day precede those identified by year only, which follow in alphabetical order.

FK. "On Some Changes in the Legal Status of the Child since Blackstone." *The International Review* 13 (Aug. 1882): 7–98.

———. "Need Our Working Women Despair?" *The International Review* 13 (Nov. 1882): 517–27.

———. "Bismarck's Birthday: A Forced National Gift." *The Times–Philadelphia*, April 25, 1885, 5.

———. "Bismarck's Tariff: The Peasant Proprietor." *The Times–Philadelphia*, May 2, 1885, 3.

———. "Socialism in Germany: Bismarck's Exceptional Laws." *The Times–Philadelphia*, June 21, 1885, 3.

———. "German Workwomen: Taking Part in Politics." *The Times–Philadelphia*, July 5, 1885, 6.

———. "German Schools: Dense Popular Ignorance." *The Times–Philadelphia*, July 19, 1885, 6.

———. "A German Trial: Socialism and Anarchists." *The Times–Philadelphia*, Aug. 2, 1885, 7.

———. "German Education: Overproduction of Intellectual Power and Its Effect upon the Social Order." *The Times–Philadelphia*, Aug. 10, 1885, 3.

———. "Poor Peasants: Grave Problems for Statesmen." *The Times–Philadelphia*, Aug. 16, 1885, 6.

FKW. "Letters from the People." *The New Era* 1 (May 1885): 150–51, 215–16.

———. "Movement among German Workingwomen." *The Woman's Tribune* 2, no. 7 (May 1885): 3.

———. "Letter from Germany." *The Woman's Tribune* 2, no. 9 (July 1885): 1.

———. "Letters from the People: Our Foreign Letter." *The New Era* 1 (July 1885): 215–16.

———. "Correspondence." *The Woman's Tribune* 2, no. 11 (Sept. 1885): 1.

[———]. "Die Sozialdemokratie und die Frage der Frauenarbeit: Ein Beitrag zur Programmfrage" (Social Democracy and the question of women's work: A contribution to the platform question). *Der Sozialdemokrat: Zentral-Organ der deutschen Sozialdemokratie* (Zürich), nos. 33, 34, 35 (Aug. 11, 18, 25, 1886): n.p.

———. "In Defense of Engels." *Workmen's Advocate*, Jan. 29, 1887, 4.

———. "Denouncing LaSallean Views." *Workmen's Advocate*, Feb. 5, 1887, n.p.

[———]. "Jakoby and Democracy: Comparison of Dr. Jakoby's Views with Contemporary Opinion." *Workmen's Advocate*, Feb. 5, 1887, n.p.

———. "The Need of Theoretical Preparation for Philanthropic Work." In a pamphlet with Helen Hiscock Backus, *The Need and the Opportunity for College-Trained Women in Philanthropic Work*, 15–26. New York: New York Association of Collegiate Alumnae, 1887. Also printed as "The Need of Theoretical Preparation for Philanthropic Work. Part I," *The Christian Union* 35, no. 22 (June 2, 1887): 12, and "The Need of Theoretical Preparation for Philanthropic Work. Part II," *The Christian Union* 35, no. 23 (June 9, 1887): 12. Reprinted in Kathryn Kish Sklar, ed., *The Autobiography of Florence Kelley: Notes of Sixty Years*. Chicago: Charles H. Kerr, 1986, 91–104.

———. "A Reply," *The Christian Union* 35, no. 25 (June 23, 1887): 27.

Engels, Frederick. *The Condition of the Working Class in England in 1844*. Translated by FKW. New York: John W. Lovell, 1887.

Jacoby, Johann. *The Object of the Labor Movement: Being A Speech Delivered before His Constituency, January 10, 1870*. Translated with preface by FKW. New York: New York Labor News, 1887. Also printed in *Workmen's Advocate*, Jan. 29, Feb. 5, Feb. 12, and Feb. 19, 1887, n.p.

Marx, Karl. *Free Trade: A Speech Delivered before the Democratic Club, Brussels, Belgium, January 9, 1848, with Extract from La Misère de la Philosophie*. Translated by FKW. Preface by Frederick Engels. Boston: Lee and Shepard, 1888.

FKW. *An Address in Memory of Thomas Paine*. Pittsburgh: Truth Publishing, 1889.

———. *Our Toiling Children*. Chicago: Woman's Temperance Publication Association, 1889. Reprinted in *Pamphlets in Social Science* 4, no. 15, and translated as "Die Lohnsklaverei der amerikanischen Kinder," *Die neue Zeit* 7 (1889): 168–75.

———. "Evils of Child Labor." *Frank Leslie's Illustrated Newspaper* 60 (March 1, 1890): 84.

————. "A Foot Print in New York." *Workmen's Advocate*, March 15, 1890.

FK-W. "White Child Slavery." In "White Child Slavery: A Symposium." *The Arena* 1 (Dec. 1890): 589–603.

FKW. "Child Labor." In *Fifth Annual Report of the Bureau of Labor Statistics of the State of Connecticut for the Year Ending November 30, 1889*, 43–45. Hartford, Conn.: Case, Lockwood and Brainard, 1890.

————. "A Decade of Retrogression." *The Arena* 4 (Aug. 1891): 365–72.

[FK]. "Household Labor." *Union Signal* (Feb. 4, 1892): 1.

————. "Address," in n.a., *The Sunday Problem: Its Present Day Aspects, Physiological, Industrial, Social, Political, and Religious, Papers Presented at the International Congress on Sunday Rest, Chicago, Sept. 28–30, 1893*, 153–55. New York: Baker and Taylor, 1894.

Bureau of Labor Statistics of Illinois. "Working Women in Chicago" and "The Sweating System in Chicago." Parts 1 and 2 in Illinois Bureau of Labor Statistics, *Seventh Biennial Report, 1892*. Springfield, Ill.: H. K. Rokker, State Printer and Binder, 1893.

Illinois Senate and House of Representatives. *Report and Findings of the Joint Committee to Investigate the "Sweat Shop" System, Together with a Transcript of the Testimony Taken by the Committee*. Springfield, Ill.: H. K. Rokker, State Printer and Binder, 1893.

FK. "Factory Legislation in Illinois." In *Proceedings of the Seventh Annual Convention of the International Association of Factory Inspectors of North America, Held at Chicago, Illinois, Sept. 19–22, 1893*, 8–12. Cleveland: Forest City Printing House, 1894.

[————]. *First Annual Report of the Factory Inspectors of Illinois for the Year Ending December 15, 1893*. Springfield, Ill.: State Printers, 1894.

[————]. *First Special Report of the Factory Inspectors of Illinois, on Small-Pox in the Tenement House Sweat-Shops of Chicago, July 1, 1894*. Springfield, Ill.: H. K. Rokker, State Printer and Binder, 1894.

————. "Die Fabrik-Gesetzgebung in Illinois" (Factory legislation in Illinois). *Sozialpolitisches Centralblatt* 3, no. 44 (1894): 521–23.

————. "Ein Ruckblick auf den Pullman-Strike" (Looking back on the Pullman strike). *Sozialpolitisches Centralblatt* 4, no. 5 (1894): 55–57.

Carroll D. Wright, U.S. Commissioner of Labor. *Seventh Special Report: The Slums of Baltimore, Chicago, New York, and Philadelphia*. Washington: GPO, 1894.

FK. "Die Fabrik-Gesetzgebung der Vereinigten Staaten" (Factory legislation in the United States). *Archiv für Soziale Gesetzgebung und Statistik* 8 (1895): 192–209.

————. "The Need of Uniformity in Labor Legislation." In *Proceedings of the Eighth Annual Convention of the International Association of Factory Inspectors of North America, Held at Philadelphia, Pa., September 25–28, 1894*, 21–27. Cleveland: Forest City Printing House, 1895.

[————]. *Second Annual Report of the Factory Inspectors of Illinois for the Year Ending December 15, 1894*. Springfield, Ill.: State Printers, 1895.

[————]. "The Sweating-System." In [Residents of Hull-House], *Hull-House Maps and Papers*, 27–45. Boston: Thomas Y. Crowell, 1895.

———— and Alzina Stevens. "Wage-Earning Children." In [Residents of Hull-House], *Hull-House Maps and Papers*, 49–76. New York: Thomas Y. Crowell, 1895.

————. "Child-Labor in Illinois." In *Proceedings of the Ninth Annual Convention of the International Association of Factory Inspectors of North America held at Providence, R.I., Sept. 3–5, 1895*, 93–97. Cleveland: Forest City Printing House, 1895.

————. "Working Boy." *American Journal of Sociology* 2 (Nov. 1896): 358–68. Also in *Journal of Social Science* (Nov. 1896): 43–51.

[————]. *Third Annual Report of the Factory Inspectors of Illinois for the Year Ending December 15, 1895*. Springfield, Ill.: Ed. F. Hartman, State Printer and Binder, 1896.

————. "The Working Child." *Proceedings of the National Conference of Charities and Corrections at the Twenty-third Annual Session Held in the City of Grand Rapids, Michigan, 1896*, 161–65. Boston: George H. Ellis, 1896.

————. "Child Labor." *Charities Review* 6 (May 1897): 221–29.

————. "Evolution of the Illinois Child Labor Law." In *Eighth Annual Report of the Factory Inspector of the Commonwealth of Pennsylvania for the Year 1897*, 610–15. N.p.: Ray, 1897.

————. "Evolution of the Illinois Child Labor Law." In *Proceedings of the Eleventh Annual Convention of the International Association of Factory Inspectors of North America Held at Detroit, Michigan, Aug. 31 and Sept. 1–2, 1897*, 33–37. Lansing, Mich: Robert Smith Printing, 1897.

[————]. *Fourth Annual Report of the Factory Inspectors of Illinois for the Year Ending December 15, 1896.* Springfield: State Printers, 1897.

————. "The Sweating System." In *Proceedings of the Tenth Annual Convention of the International Association of Factory Inspectors of North America, Held at Toronto, Canada, September 1–3, 1896,* 58–63. Chicago: Harman, Geng, 1897.

————. "Die weibliche Fabrikinspektion in der Vereinigten Staaten" (Women factory inspectors in the United States). *Archiv für Soziale Gesetzgebung und Statistik* 11 (1897): 128–42.

————. "Illinois Child Labor Law." *American Journal of Sociology* 3 (Jan. 1898): 490–501.

————. "Hull House." *New England Magazine* 18 (July 1898): 550–66.

————. "United States Supreme Court and the Utah Eight Hours' Law." *American Journal of Sociology* 4 (July 1898): 21–34.

————. "Address before Convention of Factory Inspectors." In *Report of New York State Factory Inspectors, 1897,* 719. Albany: State Printers, 1898.

————. "Drei Entscheidungen oberster Gerichte über den gesetzlichen Arbeitstag in den Vereinigten Staaten" (Three Supreme Court decisions on the legal limitation of the working day in the United States). *Archiv für Soziale Gesetzgebung und Statistik* 12 (1898): 744–74.

————. "Die gesetzliche Regelung der Kinderarbeit im Staate Illinois" (The legal regulation of child labor in the state of Illinois). *Archiv für Soziale Gesetzgebung und Statistik* 12 (1898): 530–50.

————. "Das Sweating-system in den Vereinigten Staaten" (The sweating system in the United States). *Archiv für Soziale Gesetzgebung und Statistik* 12 (1898): 208–32.

————. "The Working Woman's Need of the Ballot: Speech before the National-American Woman Suffrage Convention, 1898." In Susan B. Anthony and Ida Husted Harper, eds., *History of Woman Suffrage,* vol. 4, *1883–1900,* 311–13. Rochester, N.Y.: Susan B. Anthony, 1902. Reprint, Salem, N.H.: AYER, 1985.

————. "Aims and Principles of the Consumers' League." *American Journal of Sociology* 5 (Nov. 1899): 289–304.

————. "The National Federation of Consumers' Leagues." *The Independent* 51 (Dec. 14, 1899): 3353–55.

————. "Das Gesetz über freie Volksbibliotheken des Staates Illinois" (The free public library law of the state of Illinois). *Archiv für Soziale Gesetzgebung und Statistik* 13 (1899): 193–216.

————. "Die gesetzliche Einschränkung der Heimarbeit in den U.S. von Nordamerika" (The legal restriction of homework in the USA). In Schriften des Vereins für Sozialpolitik, *Hausindustrie und Heimarbeit in Deutschland und Österreich,* 83:183–243. Leipzig: Duncker and Humblot, 1899.

————. "Die Italiener Chicagos" (Chicago's Italians). *Archiv für Soziale Gesetzgebung und Statistik* 13 (1899): 291–313.

————. "Das Fabrikinspektorat von New York und seine Stellung zur Arbeiterschutzgesetzgebung" (Factory inspectors of New York and their place in labor legislation). *Archiv für Soziale Gesetzgebung und Statistik* 16 (1901): 413–49. (Written before 1900.)

————. "My Philadelphia." *Survey Graphic* 57 (Oct. 1, 1926): 7–11, 50–57.

————. "When Co-education Was Young." *Survey Graphic* 57 (Feb. 1, 1927): 557–61.

————. "My Novitiate." *Survey Graphic* 58 (April 1, 1927): 31–35.

————. "I Go to Work." *Survey Graphic* 58 (June 1, 1927): 271–74, 301.

Selected Additional Primary Sources

[Adams, Henry C., ed.]. *Philanthropy and Social Progress: Seven Essays by Miss Jane Addams, Robert A. Woods, Father J. O. S. Huntington, Professor Franklin H. Giddings, and Barnard Bosanquet, Delivered before the School of Applied Ethics at Plymouth, Mass.* New York: Thomas Y. Crowell, 1893.

Addams, Jane. *Democracy and Social Ethics.* New York: Macmillan, 1902. Reprint, edited by Anne Firor Scott, Cambridge: Harvard University Press, 1964.

————. *My Friend, Julia Lathrop.* New York: Macmillan, 1935.

————. "The Objective Value of a Social Settlement" and "The Subjective Necessity for Social Settlements." In [Henry C. Adams, ed.], *Philanthropy and Social Progress.* New York: Thomas Y. Crowell, 1893.

————. *Twenty Years at Hull House.* New York: Macmillan, 1910.

Altgeld, John P. *Reasons for Pardoning the Haymarket Anarchists.* Chicago: n.p., 1893. Reprint, Springfield, Ill.: n.p., 1896; and Chicago: Charles H. Kerr, 1986.

Ames, Azel, Jr. *Sex in Industry: A Plea for the Working Girl.* Boston: James R. Osgood, 1875.

Backus , Helen Hiscock, ed. *The Need and the Opportunity for College-Trained Women in Philanthropic Work.* New York: New York Association of Collegiate Alumnae, 1887.

Bisno, Abraham. *Union Pioneer: An Autobiographical Account of Bisno's Early Life and the Beginnings of Unionism in the Women's Garment Industry.* Madison: University of Wisconsin, 1967.

Bliss, William D. P., ed., *The Encyclopedia of Social Reform.* New York: Funk and Wagnalls, 1897.

———. *The New Encyclopedia of Social Reform.* New York: Funk and Wagnalls, 1910.

Brace, Charles Loring. *The Dangerous Classes of New York and Twenty Years' Work among Them.* New York: Wynkoop and Hallenbeck, 1872.

Brown, Elizabeth Stow. "The Working-Women of New York: Their Health and Occupations." *Journal of Social Science* 24 (April 1888): 72–92.

Butler, Josephine. *The Education and Employment of Women.* London: Macmillan, 1868.

Campbell, Helen. *Prisoners of Poverty: Women Wage-Workers, Their Trades and Their Lives.* Boston: Roberts Bros., 1887.

———. *The Problem of the Poor. A Record of Quiet Work in Unquiet Places.* New York: Fords, Howard and Hulbert, 1882.

———. *Women Wage-Earners: Their Past, Their Present, and Their Future.* Boston: Roberts Bros., 1893. Reprint, New York: Arno, 1972.

Clarke, Edward H. *Sex in Education; or, A Fair Chance for the Girls.* Boston: James R. Osgood, 1873.

Cobbe, Frances Power. "Social Science Congresses, and Women's Part in Them." *Macmillan's Magazine* (Dec. 1861): 81–94.

Comfort, Anna Manning, and George Fisk Comfort, *Woman's Education and Woman's Health: Chiefly in Reply to "Sex in Education."* Syracuse: Thos. W. Durston, 1874.

Croly, Mrs. Jane Cunningham. *The History of the Woman's Club Movement in America.* New York: Henry G. Allen, 1898.

Dall, Caroline Wells [Healey]. *The College, the Market and the Court; Or, Woman's Relation to Education, Labor, and the Law.* Boston: Lee and Shepard, 1867.

Dobkin, Marjorie Housepian, ed. *The Making of a Feminist: Early Journals and Letters of M. Carey Thomas.* Kent, Ohio: Kent State University Press, 1979.

Eaton, Dorman B. *Civil Service in Great Britain: A History of Abuses and Reforms and Their Bearing upon American Politics.* New York: Harper and Bros., 1880.

Elliott, Charles W. "Woman's Work and Woman's Wages." *North American Review* 309 (Aug. 1882): 146–61.

Ely, Richard T. *French and German Socialism in Modern Times.* New York: Harper and Bros., 1880.

———. *Ground Under Our Feet: An Autobiography.* New York: Macmillan, 1938.

———. *The Labor Movement in America.* New York: Thomas Y. Crowell, 1886.

———. *Recent American Socialism.* Baltimore: Johns Hopkins University Press, 1884.

Engels, Friedrich. *The Labor Movement in America. The George Movement. The Knights of Labor. The Socialists.* New York: Louis Weiss, 1887.

———. *Die Lage der arbeitenden Klasse in England, nach eigener Anschauung und authentischen Quellen.* Leipzig: Otto Wigand, 1845.

Fraser, Nancy. *Unruly Practices: Power, Discourse and Gender in Contemporary Social Theory.* Minneapolis: University of Minnesota Press, 1989.

Gilman, Charlotte Perkins. *Women and Economics: A Study of the Economic Relation Between Men and Women as a Factor in Social Evolution.* Boston: Small, Maynard, 1898.

Hamilton, Alice. *Exploring the Dangerous Trades: The Autobiography of Alice Hamilton, M.D.* Boston: Little, Brown, 1943.

Henrotin, Ellen. *The Attitude of Women's Clubs and Associations towards Social Economics.* Bulletin of the U.S. Department of Labor No. 23. Washington, D.C.: GPO, 1899.

Howe, Julia Ward, ed. *Sex and Education: A Reply to Dr. E. H. Clarke's "Sex in Education."* Boston, Mass.: Roberts Bros., 1874.

———. "The Industrial Value of Woman." *North American Review* 135 (Nov. 1882): 433–46.

Illinois Senate and House of Representatives. *Report and Findings of the Joint Committee to Investigate the "Sweat Shop" System, Together with a Transcript of the Testimony Taken by the Committee.* Springfield, Ill.: H. K. Rokker, State Printer and Binder, 1893.

Kelley, Nicholas. "Early Days at Hull House." *Social Service Review* 28 (Dec. 1954): 424–29.

Kelley, William D., *Speeches, Addresses and Letters*

on *Industrial and Financial Questions.* Philadelphia: Henry Carey Baird, 1872.

Livermore, Mary. "Coöperative Womanhood in the State." *North American Review* 153 (Sept. 1891): 283–95.

Lloyd, Caro. *Henry Demarest Lloyd, 1847–1903: A Biography.* 2 vols. New York: G. P. Putnam's Sons, 1912.

Lloyd, Henry Demarest. *A Strike of Millionaires against Miners; or, the Story of Spring Valley.* Chicago: Belford-Clarke, 1890.

———. *Wealth against Commonwealth.* New York: Harper and Bros., 1894.

Lowell, Josephine Shaw, ed. *Industrial Arbitration and Conciliation: Some Chapters from the Industrial History of the Past Thirty Years.* New York: G. P. Putnam's Sons 1893.

Memorial of Sarah Pugh: A Tribute of Respect from Her Cousins. Philadelphia: J. B. Lippincott, 1888.

[Morgan, Elizabeth] Chicago Trade and Labor Assembly. *The New Slavery. Investigation into the Sweating System as Applied to the Manufacture of Wearing Apparel.* Chicago: Detwiler, 1891.

Nathan, Maud. *The Story of an Epoch-Making Movement.* Garden City, N.Y.: Doubleday, Page, 1926.

National Council of Women. *Transactions of the National Council of Women of the United States, Assembled in Washington, D.C., February 22 to 25, 1891.* Philadelphia: J. B. Lippincott, 1891.

[Nelson, Nell]. *The White Slave Girls of Chicago: Nell Nelson's Startling Disclosures of the Cruelties and Iniquities Practiced in the Workshops and Factories of a Great City.* Chicago: Barkley, 1888.

[New Century Guild]. *One Hundredth Anniversary, The New Century Guild, Philadelphia, Pennsylvania, 1882–1982.* Philadelphia: New Century Guild, 1982.

Perkins, Agnes F., ed. *Vocations for the Trained Woman: Opportunities Other than Teaching.* Boston: Women's Educational and Industrial Union, 1910.

Pidgin, Charles F. *History of the Bureau of Statistics of Labor of Massachusetts and of Labor Legislation in that State from 1833 to 1876.* Boston: Wright and Potter, 1876.

Polacheck, Hilda Satt. *I Came a Stranger: The Story of a Hull-House Girl.* Edited by Denna J. Polacheck Epstein. Urbana: University of Illinois Press, 1989.

Powderly, T. V. "The Organization of Labor." *North American Review* 135 (Aug. 1882): 118–26.

[Residents of Hull House]. *Hull-House Maps and Papers: A Presentation of Nationalities and Wages in a Congested District of Chicago, Together with Comments and Essays on Problems Growing Out of the Social Conditions.* Boston: Thomas Y. Crowell, 1895.

Riis, Jacob A. *The Children of the Poor.* New York: C. Scribner, 1892.

———. *How the Other Half Lives: Studies among the Tenements of New York.* New York: Scribner's, 1890.

Sanborn, F. B. "The Three-Fold Aspect of Social Science in America." *Journal of Social Science* 14 (Nov. 1881): 33.

Scudder, Vida. "The Relation of College Women to Social Need." *Association of Collegiate Alumnae Publications,* series 2, no. 30 (Oct. 1890): 1–16.

Stanley, Maude. *Clubs for Working Girls.* London: Macmillan, 1890.

Starrett, Helen Ekin. *After College, What? for Girls.* New York: Thomas Y. Crowell, 1896.

Stead, William T. *If Christ Came to Chicago.* Chicago: Laird and Lee, 1894.

Stewart, William Rhinelander. *The Philanthropic Work of Josephine Shaw Lowell.* New York: Macmillan, 1911.

Swinton, John. *A Momentous Question: The Respective Attitudes of Labor and Capital.* Philadelphia: A. R. Keller, 1895.

Thomas, M. Carey. "Present Tendencies in Women's College and University Education." *Educational Review* 25 (1908): 64–85.

United States Bureau of Education. *The Legal Rights of Children.* Circular of Information No. 3. Washington, D.C.: GPO, 1880.

Van Etten, Ida. *The Condition of Women Workers under the Present Industrial System: An Address, Delivered at the National Convention of the American Federation of Labor, December 8, 1890.* New York: American Federation of Labor, 1891.

Ward, Lester. *Dynamic Sociology; or, Applied Social Science, as Based upon Statistical Sociology and the Less Complex Sciences.* New York: D. Appleton, 1883.

———. "Our Better Halves," *Forum* 6 (1888): 266–75.

Woods, Katharine Pearson. "Life in a College Settlement." *Far and Near* 4 (Jan. 1894): 40–41; (Feb. 1894): 53; (March 1894): 65; (May 1894): 94; (July 1894): 122–23; (Oct. 1894): 166–67.

Wright, Carroll D. *The Industrial Evolution of the United States.* Meadeville, Pa.: Flood and Vincent, 1895.

———. "The Working Girls of Boston." *Fifteenth*

Annual Report of the Massachusetts Bureau of Statistics of Labor, 1884. Boston: Wright and Potter, 1889. Reprint, New York: Arno, 1969.

[————]. "Health Statistics of Female College Graduates, Report of a Special Committee of the Association of Collegiate Alumnae." In *Sixteenth Annual Report of the Massachusetts Bureau of Statistics of Labor 1885.* Boston: Wright and Potter, 1885.

Selected Secondary Sources

Anderson, Margo. "The History of Women and the History of Statistics." *Journal of Women's History* 4 (spring 1992): 14–36.

Antler, Joyce. *The Educated Woman and Professionalization: The Struggle for a New Feminine Identity, 1890–1920.* New York: Garland, 1987.

Attie, Rejean. "'A Swindling Concern': The United States Sanitary Commission and the Northern Female Public, 1861–1865." Ph.D. diss., Columbia University, 1987.

Baker, Jean H. *Affairs of Party: The Political Culture of Northern Democrats in the Mid-Nineteenth Century.* Ithaca: Cornell University Press, 1983.

Baker, Paula. "The Domestication of Politics: Women and American Political Society, 1780–1920." *AHR* 89 (June 1984): 620–47.

Bannister, Robert. *Social Darwinism: Science and Myth in Anglo-American Social Thought.* Philadelphia: Temple University Press, 1979.

————. *Sociology and Scientism: The American Quest for Objectivity, 1880–1940.* Chapel Hill: University of North Carolina Press, 1987.

Behlmer, George K. *Child Abuse and Moral Reform in England, 1870–1908.* Stanford: Stanford University Press, 1982.

Bell, Susan Groag, and Karen M. Offen. *Women, the Family, and Freedom: The Debate in Documents.* 2 vols. Stanford, Calif.: Stanford University Press, 1983.

Benenson, Harold. "Victorian Sexual Ideology and Marx's Theory of the Working Class." *ILWCH* 25 (spring 1984): 1–23.

Bensel, Richard Franklin. *Yankee Leviathan: The Origins of Central State Authority in America, 1859–1877.* Cambridge: Cambridge University Press, 1990.

Benson, Susan Porter. "Business Heads and Sympathizing Hearts: The Women of the Providence Employment Society, 1837–1858." *JSH* 12 (winter 1978): 302–12.

Berk, Gerald. "Adversaries by Design: Railroads and the American State, 1887–1916." *JPH* 5 (1993): 335–54.

Blair, Karen. *The Clubwoman as Feminist: True Womanhood Redefined, 1868–1914.* New York: Holmes and Meier, 1980.

Blumberg, Dorothy Rose. "Dear 'Mr. Engels': Unpublished Letters, 1884–1894, of Florence Kelley (Wischnewetzky) to Friedrich Engels." *LH* 5 (spring 1964): 103–33.

————. *Florence Kelley: The Making of a Social Pioneer.* New York: Augustus M. Kelley, 1966.

Bolt, Christine. *The Women's Movements in the United States and Britain from the 1790s to the 1920s.* Amherst: University of Massachusetts Press, 1993.

Bordin, Ruth. *Woman and Temperance: The Quest for Power and Liberty, 1873–1900.* Philadelphia: Temple University Press, 1981.

Boris, Eileen. *Home to Work: Motherhood and the Politics of Industrial Homework in the United States.* New York: Cambridge University Press, 1994.

Bottomore, Tom. *Sociology and Socialism.* Brighton, Sussex: Wheatsheaf, 1984.

Bottomore, Tom, Laurence Harris, V. G. Kiernan, and Ralph Miliband, eds. *A Dictionary of Marxist Thought.* Cambridge: Harvard University Press, 1983.

Brasch, Walter M. *Forerunners of Revolution: Muckrakers and the American Social Conscience.* Lanham, Md.: University Press of America, 1990.

Bremner, Robert. *From the Depths: The Discovery of Poverty in the United States.* New York: New York University Press, 1967.

Brock, William R. *Investigation and Responsibility: Public Responsibility in the United States, 1865–1900.* Cambridge: Cambridge University Press, 1984.

Brown, Ira. "William D. Kelley and Radical Reconstruction." *PMHB* 85 (July 1961): 316–29.

Brown, James. *The History of Public Assistance in Chicago, 1833–1893.* Chicago: University of Chicago Press, 1941.

Brown, M. Craig, and Charles N. Halaby. "Machine Politics in America, 1870–1945." *Journal of Interdisciplinary History* 17 (winter 1987): 587–612.

Bryan, Mary Lynn McCree, Peter Clark, Jane Colokathis, Beth Durham, Ann D. Gordon, Dorothy Greene Johnson, Gail Miller, Frank A. Ninkovich, David N. Ruchman, Nancy Scote, Lynn Weiner, and Barbara Starr, eds. *Jane*

Addams Papers. Ann Arbor, Mich.: Microfilming Corporation of America, 1985.

Buder, Stanley. *Pullman: An Experiment in Industrial Order and Community Planning, 1880–1930.* New York: Oxford University Press, 1967.

Buechler, Steven M. *The Transformation of the Woman Suffrage Movement: The Case of Illinois, 1850–1920.* New Brunswick: Rutgers University Press, 1986.

Buhle, Mari Jo. *Women and American Socialism, 1870–1920.* Urbana: University of Illinois Press, 1981.

Bulmer, Martin, Kevin Bales, and Kathryn Kish Sklar, eds., *The Social Survey in Historical Perspective, 1880–1940.* Cambridge: Cambridge University Press, 1991.

Campbell, Ballard C. *Representative Democracy: Public Policy and Midwestern Legislatures in the Late Nineteenth Century.* Cambridge: Harvard University Press, 1980.

Carrell, Elizabeth Palmer Hutcheson. "Reflections in a Mirror: The Progressive Woman and the Settlement Experience." Ph.D. diss., University of Texas, 1981.

Carsel, Wilfred. *A History of the Chicago Ladies' Garment Workers' Union.* Chicago: Normandie House, 1940.

Carson, Mina J. "Agnes Hamilton of Fort Wayne: The Education of a Christian Settlement Worker." *Indiana Magazine of History* 80 (March 1984): 1–34.

———. *Settlement Folk: Social Thought and the American Settlement Movement, 1885–1930.* Chicago: University of Chicago Press, 1990.

Cartosio, Bruno. "Strikes and Economics: Working Class Insurgency and the Birth of Labor Historiography in the 1880s." In Dirk Hoerder, ed., *American Labor and Immigration History, 1877–1920s: Recent European Research.* Urbana: University of Illinois Press, 1983.

Cash, Floris Barnett. "Radicals or Realists: African American Women and the Settlement House Spirit in New York City." *Afro-Americans in New York Life and History* 15 (Jan. 1991): 7–17.

Ceplair, Larry, ed. *Charlotte Perkins Gilman: A Nonfiction Reader.* New York: Columbia University Press, 1991.

Cervone, Barbara T. "Rounding Up the Children: Compulsory Education Enforcement in Providence, Rhode Island, 1883–1935." Ed.D. diss., Harvard University, 1983.

Clark, Elizabeth Battelle. "The Politics of God and the Woman's Vote: Religion in the American Suffrage Movement, 1848–1895." Ph.D. diss., Princeton University, 1989.

Clement, Priscilla Ferguson. "Nineteenth-Century Welfare Policy, Programs, and Poor Women: Philadelphia as a Case Study." *FS* 18 (spring 1992): 35–58.

Colky, Michael T. "Jane Addams: Pioneer to Adult Education." Ph.D. diss., Loyola University of Chicago, 1988.

Commons, John R., David J. Saposs, Helen L. Sumner, E. B. Mittelman, H. E. Hoagland, John B. Andrews, Selig Perlman, *History of Labour in the United States.* Vols. 1 and 2. New York: Macmillan, 1918. Reprint, New York: Augustus M. Kelley, 1966.

Commons, John R., Don D. Lescohier, and Elizabeth Brandeis. *History of Labor in the United States, 1896–1932.* Vol. 3. New York: Macmillan, 1935. Reprint, New York: Augustus M. Kelley, 1966.

Conable, Charlotte Williams. *Women at Cornell: The Myth of Equal Education.* Ithaca: Cornell University Press, 1977.

Condran, Gretchen, Henry Williams, and Rose A. Cheney. "The Decline in Mortality in Philadelphia from 1870 to 1930: The Role of Municipal Services." *PMHB* 108 (April 1984): 153–78.

Cooper, Jerry M. "The Army as Strikebreaker — The Railroad Strikes of 1877 and 1894." *LH* 18 (spring 1977): 179–96.

Cross, Gary, and Peter Shergold, "'We Think We Are of the Oppressed': Gender, White Collar Work, and Grievances of Late Nineteenth-Century Women." *LH* 28 (winter 1987): 23–53.

Crunden, Robert M. *Ministers of Reform: The Progressives' Achievement in American Civilization, 1889–1920.* New York: Basic Books, 1982.

Cumbler, John T. "The Politics of Charity: Gender and Class in Late Nineteenth Century Charity Policy." *JSH* 14 (fall 1980): 99–112.

Dann, Martin E. "'Little Citizens': Working Class and Immigrant Children in New York City, 1890–1915." Ph.D. diss., City University of New York, 1978.

Darney, Virginia Grant. "Women and World's Fairs: American International Expositions, 1876–1904." Ph.D. diss., Emory University, 1982.

Davenport, F. Gorvin. "The Sanitation Revolution in Illinois, 1870–1900." *Journal of the Illinois State Historical Society* 66 (autumn 1973): 306–26.

Davis, Allen F. *American Heroine: The Life and*

Legend of Jane Addams. New York: Oxford University Press, 1973.

———. "Jane Addams vs. the Ward Boss." *Journal of Illinois State Historical Society* 53 (fall 1960): 247–65

———. "Settlement Workers in Politics, 1890–1914." *Review of Politics* 26 (Oct. 1964): 505–17.

———. *Spearheads for Reform: The Social Settlements and the Progressive Movement, 1890–1914.* New York: Oxford University Press, 1967.

Davis, Allen F., and Mary Lynn McCree, eds. *Eighty Years at Hull House.* Chicago: Quadrangle Books, 1969.

Deegan, Mary Jo. *Jane Addams and the Men of the Chicago School, 1892–1918.* New Brunswick: Transaction Books, 1988.

Destler, Chester McArthur. *Henry Demarest Lloyd and the Empire of Reform.* Philadelphia: University of Pennsylvania Press, 1963.

Deutsch, Sarah. "Learning to Talk More Like a Man: Boston Women's Class-Bridging Organizations, 1870–1940," *AHR* 97 (April 1992): 379–404.

Dietz, Mary G. "Context Is All: Feminism and Theories of Citizenship." *Daedalus* 116 (fall 1987): 1–24.

Digby-Junger, Richard. "The Gilded Age Journalist as Advocate: Henry Demarest Lloyd and 'Wealth against Commonwealth.'" Ph.D. diss., University of Wisconsin–Madison, 1989.

Diner, Steven J. *A City and Its Universities: Public Policy in Chicago, 1892–1919.* Chapel Hill: University of North Carolina Press, 1980.

Dombrowski, James. *The Early Days of Christian Socialism in America.* New York: Columbia University Press, 1936.

Drachman, Virginia G. "Women Lawyers and the Quest for Professional Identity in Late Nineteenth-Century America." *Michigan Law Review* 88 (Aug. 1990): 2414–43.

DuBois, Ellen Carol. "Taking the Law into Our Own Hands: *Bradwell, Minor,* and Suffrage Militance in the 1870s." In Nancy A. Hewitt and Suzanne Lebsock, eds., *Visible Women: New Essays on American Activism,* 19–40. Urbana: University of Illinois Press, 1993.

Dye, Nancy Schrom. *As Equals and as Sisters: Feminism, the Labor Movement, and the Women's Trade Union League of New York.* Columbia: University of Missouri Press, 1980.

Dye, Nancy Schrom, and Daniel Blake Smith, "Mother Love and Infant Death, 1750–1920." *JAH* 73 (Sept. 1986): 329–53.

Edelstein, T. J. "They Sang 'The Song of the Shirt': The Visual Iconography of the Seamstress." *Victorian Studies* 23 (winter 1980): 183–210.

Eisenberg, Martin Jay. "Compulsory Attendance Legislation in America, 1870–1915." Ph.D. diss., University of Pennsylvania, 1988.

Ensign, Forest Chester. *Compulsory School Attendance and Child Labor: A Study of the Historical Development of Regulations Compelling Attendance and Limiting the Labor of Children in a Selected Group of States.* Iowa City: Athens, 1921.

Farnham, Wallace D. "'The Weakened Spring of Government': A Study in Nineteenth-Century American History." *AHR* 68 (April 1963): 662–80.

Farrell, John C. *Beloved Lady: A History of Jane Addams' Ideas on Reform and Peace.* Baltimore: Johns Hopkins University Press, 1967.

Fastenau, Maureen. "Maternal Government: The Social Settlement Houses and the Politicization of Women's Sphere, 1889–1920." Ph.D. diss., Duke University, 1982.

Fausto-Sterling, Anne. *Myths of Gender: Biological Theories about Women and Men.* New York: Basic Books, 1985.

Feffer, Andrew. "Between Head and Hand: Chicago Pragmatism and Social Reform, 1886 to 1919." Ph.D. diss., University of Pennsylvania, 1987.

Felt, Jeremy. *Hostages of Fortune: Child Labor Reform in New York State.* Syracuse: Syracuse University Press, 1965.

Feurer, Rosemary. "The Meaning of 'Sisterhood': The British Women's Movement and Protective Labor Legislation, 1870–1900." *Victorian Studies* 31 (winter 1988): 233–60.

Fink, Leon. "'Intellectuals' versus 'Workers': Academic Requirements and the Creation of 'Labor History.'" *AHR* 96 (April 1991): 349–431.

———. "The Uses of Political Power: Toward a Theory of the Labor Movement in the Era of the Knights of Labor." In Michael M. Frisch and Daniel Walkowitz, eds., *Working Class America: Essays on Labor, Community, and Society.* Urbana: University of Illinois Press, 1983.

———. *Workingmen's Democracy: The Knights of Labor and American Politics.* Urbana: University of Illinois Press, 1983.

Fish, Virginia Kemp. "The Struggle over Women's Education in the Nineteenth Century: A Social Movement and Countermovement." In Guida West and Rhoda Lois Blumberg, eds., *Women and Social Protest.* New York: Oxford University Press, 1990.

Fitzpatrick, Ellen. *Endless Crusade: Women Social Scientists and Progressive Reform*. New York: Oxford University Press, 1990.

Flanagan, Maureen A. "Gender and Urban Political Reform: The City Club and the Woman's City Club of Chicago in the Progressive Era." *AHR* 95 (Oct. 1990): 1032–50.

Foner, Eric. *Reconstruction: American's Unfinished Revolution, 1863–1877*. New York: Harper and Row, 1988.

Foner, Philip S. *Women and the American Labor Movement: From the First Trade Unions to the Present*. New York: Free, 1979.

Foner, Philip S., and Brewster Chamberlin, eds. *Friedrich A. Sorge's Labor Movement in the United States: A History of the American Working Class from Colonial Times to 1890*. Westport, Conn.: Greenwood, 1977.

Fones-Wolf, Kenneth. "Class, Professionalism and the Early Bureaus of Labor Statistics." *The Insurgent Sociologist* 10 (summer 1980): 38–45.

———. *Trade Union Gospel: Christianity and Labor in Industrial Philadelphia, 1865–1915*. Philadelphia: Temple University Press, 1989.

Forbath, William E. *Law and the Shaping of the American Labor Movement*. Cambridge: Harvard University Press, 1991.

Fox, Richard Wightman. "The Culture of Liberal Protestant Progressivism, 1875–1925." *Journal of Interdisciplinary History* 23 (winter 1993): 639–60.

Frankfort, Roberta. *Collegiate Women: Domesticity and Career in Turn-of-the-Century America*. New York: New York University Press, 1977.

Franzoi, Barbara. *At the Very Least She Pays the Rent: Women and German Industrialization, 1871–1914*. Westport, Conn.: Greenwood, 1985.

Fraser, Nancy. "Women, Welfare, and the Politics of Need Interpretation." In *Unruly Practices: Power, Discourse, and Gender in Contemporary Social Theory*. Minneapolis: University of Minneapolis Press, 1989.

Frederick, Peter J. *Knights of the Golden Rule: The Intellectual as Christian Social Reformer in the 1890s*. Lexington: University of Kentucky Press, 1976.

———. "Vida Dutton Scudder: The Professor as Social Activist." *New England Quarterly* 42 (Sept. 1970): 407–33.

Friedman, Gerald. "The Working Class and the Welfare State: Working-Class Militancy and Its Consequences: Political Responses to Labor Unrest in the United States, 1877–1914." *ILWCH* 40 (fall 1991): 5–17.

Frisch, Michael H., and Daniel J. Walkowitz, eds. *Working Class America: Essays on Labor, Community, and American Society*. Urbana: University of Illinois Press, 1983.

Furner, Mary O. *Advocacy and Objectivity: A Crisis in the Professionalization of American Social Science, 1865–1905*. Lexington: University of Kentucky Press, 1975.

———. "Knowing Capitalism: Public Investigation and the Labor Question in the Long Progressive Era." In Mary O. Furner and Barry Supple, *The State and Economic Knowledge: The American and British Experiences*. Cambridge: Cambridge University Press, 1990.

Furner, Mary O., and Barry Supple. *The State and Economic Knowledge: The American and British Experiences*. Cambridge: Cambridge University Press, 1990.

Gewen, Barry. "The Intellectual Foundations of the Child Labor Reform Movement." Ph.D. diss., Harvard University, 1972.

Giddens, Anthony. *The Constitution of Society*. Berkeley: University of California Press, 1984.

Ginzberg, Lori. *Women and the Work of Benevolence: Morality, Politics and Class in the Nineteenth-Century United States*. New Haven: Yale University Press, 1990.

Girard, Frank, and Ben Perry. *The Socialist Labor Party, 1876–1991: A Short History*. Philadelphia: Livra, 1991.

Glickman, Lawrence. "A Living Wage: Political Economy, Gender, and Consumerism in American Culture, 1880–1925." Ph.D. diss., University of California, Berkeley, 1992.

Goldberg, Judith Lazarus. "Strikes, Organizing, and Change: The Knights of Labor in Philadelphia, 1869–1890." Ph.D. diss., New York University, 1985.

Goldin, Claudia. "The Meaning of College in the Lives of American Women: The Past One-Hundred Years." Working Paper No. 4099. National Bureau of Economic Research. June 1992.

Goldmark, Josephine. *Impatient Crusader: Florence Kelley's Life Story*. Urbana: University of Illinois Press, 1953.

Gordon, Linda. "Black and White Visions of Welfare: Women's Welfare Activism, 1890–1945." *JAH* 78 (Sept. 1991): 559–90.

———. "Social Insurance and Public Assistance: The Influence of Gender in Welfare Thought in the United States, 1890–1935," *AHR* 97 (Feb. 1992), 19–54.

Gordon, Lynn D. *Gender and Higher Education in the Progressive Era.* New Haven: Yale University Press, 1990.

———. "Women and the Anti-Child Labor Movement in Illinois, 1890–1920." *Social Service Review* 51 (June 1977): 229–48.

Gramsci, Antonio. *Selections from the Prison Notebooks.* Translated and edited by Quintin Hoare and Geoffrey Nowell-Smith. London: Lawrence and Wishart, 1971.

Greco, Michael Robert. "William Darrah Kelley: The Ante-Bellum Years." Ph.D. diss., Johns Hopkins University, 1974.

Green, Marguerite. *The National Civic Federation and the American Labor Movement, 1900–1925.* Washington, D.C.: Catholic University of America Press, 1956.

Greenberg, Judith L. "Strikes, Organizing and Change: The Knights of Labor in Philadelphia, 1869–1890." Ph.D. diss., New York University, 1985.

Griffin, Clyde. "Christian Socialism Instructed by Gompers." *LH* 12 (spring 1971): 195–213.

Grossberg, Michael. *Governing the Hearth: Law and the Family in Nineteenth-Century America.* Chapel Hill: University of North Carolina Press, 1985.

Gutman, Herbert G. *Work, Culture, and Society in Industrializing America: Essays in American Working-Class and Social History.* New York: Knopf, 1976.

Habermas, Jürgen. *The Structural Transformation of the Public Sphere.* Translated by T. Berger and F. Lawrence. Cambridge, Mass.: MIT Press, 1989.

Haskell, Thomas L. *The Emergence of Professional Social Science: The American Social Science Association and the Nineteenth-Century Crisis of Authority.* Urbana: University of Illinois Press, 1977.

Hattam, Victoria C. *Labor Visions and State Power: The Origins of Business Unionism in the United States.* Princeton: Princeton University Press, 1993.

Hellerstein, Erna Olafson, Leslie Parker Hume, and Karen M. Offen, eds. *Victorian Women: A Documentary Account of Women's Lives in Nineteenth-Century England, France, and the United States.* Stanford: Stanford University Press, 1981.

Henking, Susan E. "Sociological Christianity and Christian Sociology: The Paradox of Early American Sociology." *Religion and American Culture* 3 (winter 1993): 49–67.

Herreshoff, David. *American Disciples of Marx: From the Age of Jackson to the Progressive Era.* Detroit: Wayne State University Press, 1967.

Hofstadter, Richard. *Social Darwinism in American Thought.* Philadelphia: University of Pennsylvania Press, 1944.

Honeycutt, Karen. "Clara Zetkin: A Left-Wing Socialist and Feminist in Wilhelmian Germany." Ph.D. diss., Columbia University, 1975.

———. "Socialism and Feminism in Imperial Germany." *Signs: A Journal of Culture and Society* 5 (autumn 1979): 30–41.

Hoogenboom, Ari. *Outlawing the Spoils: A History of the Civil Service Reform Movement, 1865–1883.* Urbana: University of Illinois Press, 1961.

Horowitz, Helen Lefkowitz. *Alma Mater: Design and Experience in the Women's Colleges from Their Nineteenth-Century Beginnings to the 1930s.* New York: Knopf, 1984.

———. *Culture and the City: Cultural Philanthropy in Chicago from the 1880s to 1917.* Lexington: University Press of Kentucky, 1976.

———. "Hull-House as Women's Space." *Chicago History* 12 (winter 1983–84): 40–55.

———. "Varieties of Cultural Experience in Jane Addams' Chicago." *HEQ* 14 (spring 1974): 69–86.

Howe, Daniel Walker. *The Political Culture of the American Whigs.* Chicago: University of Chicago Press, 1979.

Hunley, J. D. *The Life and Thought of Friedrich Engels: A Reinterpretation.* New Haven: Yale University Press, 1991.

Hurvitz, Haggai. "American Labor Law and the Doctrine of Entrepreneurial Property Rights: Boycotts, Courts, and the Juridical Reorientation of 1886–1895." *Industrial Relations Law Journal* 8 (1986): 307–61.

James, Edward T., Janet Wilson James, and Paul S. Boyer, eds. *Notable American Women, 1607–1950: A Biographical Dictionary.* 3 vols. Cambridge: Harvard University Press, 1971.

Jeffreys-Jones, Rhodri, and Bruce Collins, eds. *The Growth of Federal Power in American History.* DeKalb, Ill.: Northern Illinois University Press, 1983.

Jensen, Gordon M. "The National Civic Federation: American Business in an Age of Social Change and Social Reform, 1900–1910." Ph.D. diss., Princeton University, 1956.

Johanson, Christine. *Women's Struggle for Higher Education in Russia, 1855–1900.* Kingston, Canada: McGill–Queens University Press, 1987.

Johnson, Oakley C. *Marxism in United States History Before the Russian Revolution, 1876–1917.* New York: Humanities, 1974.

Jones, Gareth Stedman. "Engels and the History of Marxism." In Eric J. Hobsbawm, ed. *The History of Marxism,* vol. 1. Bloomington: Indiana University Press, 1982.

Kalberg, Stephen. "The Commitment to Career Reform: The Settlement Movement Leaders." *Social Service Review* 49 (Dec. 1975): 608–28.

Katz, Esther. "Grace Hoadley Dodge: Women and the Emerging Metropolis, 1856–1914." Ph.D. diss., New York University, 1980.

Katz, Michael. *In the Shadow of the Poorhouse: A Social History of Welfare in America.* New York: Basic Books, 1986.

Katznelson, Ira, and Aristide R. Zolberg, eds. *Working Class Formation: Nineteenth-Century Patterns in Western Europe and the United States.* Princeton: Princeton University Press, 1986.

Keil, Hartmut. "The Impact of Haymarket on German-American Radicalism." *International Labor and Working-Class History* 29 (spring 1986): 14–27.

Keil, Hartmut, and John B. Jentz, eds. *German Workers in Industrial Chicago, 1850–1910: A Comparative Perspective.* DeKalb, Ill.: Northern Illinois University Press, 1983.

Keller, Morton. *Affairs of State: Public Life in Late Nineteenth Century America.* Cambridge: Harvard University Press, 1977.

Kelley, Robert. *The Cultural Pattern in American Politics: The First Century.* New York: Knopf, 1979.

Kenkel, Joseph F. *Progressives and Protection: The Search for a Tariff Policy, 1866–1936.* Lanham, Md.: University Press of America, 1983.

Kessler-Harris, Alice. *Out to Work: A History of Wage-Earning Women in the United States.* New York: Oxford University Press, 1982.

———. *A Woman's Wage: Historical Meanings and Social Consequences.* Lexington: University of Kentucky, 1990.

Kingsbury, Susan M., ed. *Labor Laws and Their Enforcement with Special Reference to Massachusetts.* New York: Longmans, Green, 1911.

Kloppenberg, James T. *Uncertain Victory: Social Democracy and Progressivism in European and American Thought, 1870–1920.* New York: Oxford University Press, 1986.

Koven, Seth, and Sonya Michel. *Mothers of a New World: Maternalist Politics and the Origins of Welfare States.* New York: Routledge, 1993.

Kraus, Harry P. *The Settlement House Movement in New York City, 1886–1914.* New York: Arno, 1980.

Kusmer, Kenneth L. "The Functions of Organized Charity in the Progressive Era: Chicago as a Case Study." *JAH* 60 (Dec. 1973): 657–78.

Kuzmack, Linda Gordon. *Woman's Cause: The Jewish Woman's Movement in England and the United States, 1881–1933.* Columbus: Ohio State University Press, 1990.

Laslett, J. H. M. "Haymarket, Henry George, and the Labor Upsurge in Britain and America during the Late 1880s." *ILWCH* 29 (spring 1986): 68–82.

Lagemann, Ellen Condliffe. *A Generation of Women: Education in the Lives of Progressive Reformers.* Cambridge: Harvard University Press, 1979.

Lane, Ann J. *To Herland and Beyond: The Life and Work of Charlotte Perkins Gilman.* New York: Pantheon, 1990.

Lasch-Quinn, Elisabeth. *Black Neighbors: Race and the Limits of Reform in the American Settlement House Movement, 1890–1945.* Chapel Hill: University of North Carolina Press, 1993.

Laurie, Bruce. *Working People of Philadelphia, 1800–1850.* Philadelphia: Temple University Press, 1980.

Laurie, Bruce, and Mark Schmitz. "Manufacture and Productivity: The Making of an Industrial Base, Philadelphia, 1850–1880." In Theodore Hershberg, ed. *Philadelphia: Work, Space, Family and Group Experience in the Nineteenth Century.* New York: Oxford University Press, 1981.

Leach, William. *True Love and Perfect Union: The Feminist Reform of Sex and Society.* New York: Basic Books, 1980.

Leeman, Richard W. *"Do Everything" Reform: The Oratory of Frances E. Willard.* New York: Greenwood, 1992.

Lehrer, Susan. *Origins of Protective Labor Legislation for Women, 1905–1925.* Albany: State University of New York Press, 1987.

Leiby, James. *Carroll Wright and Labor Reform: The Origin of Labor Statistics.* Cambridge: Harvard University Press, 1960.

Lemons, J. Stanley. *The Woman Citizen: Social Feminism in the 1920s.* Urbana: University of Illinois Press, 1973.

Levine, Daniel. *Jane Addams and the Liberal Tradition.* Madison: State Historical Society of Wisconsin, 1971.

———. *Poverty and Society: The Growth of the American Welfare State in International Com-*

parison. New Brunswick: Rutgers University Press, 1988.

Levine, Susan. *Labor's True Woman: Carpet Weavers, Industrialization, and Labor Reform in the Gilded Age.* Philadelphia: Temple University Press, 1984.

Lieberman, Jacob Andrew. "'Their Sisters' Keepers': The Women's Hours and Wages Movement in the United States, 1890–1925." Ph.D. diss., Columbia University, 1971.

Lindsey, Almont. *The Pullman Strike: The Story of a Unique Experiment and of a Great Labor Upheaval.* Chicago: University of Chicago Press, 1942.

Linn, James Weber. *Jane Addams: A Biography.* New York: Appleton, 1938.

Lorini, Alessandra. "Public Rituals, Race Ideology and the Transformation of Urban Culture: The Making of the New York African-American Community, 1825–1918." Ph.D. diss., Columbia University, 1991.

Lowe, Eugene Yerby. "Richard T. Ely: Herald of a Positive State." Ph.D. diss., Union Theological Seminary, 1987.

Luker, Ralph E. *The Social Gospel in Black and White: American Racial Reform, 1885–1912.* Chapel Hill: University of North Carolina Press, 1991.

Lurie, Jonathan. *The Chicago Board of Trade, 1859–1905: The Dynamics of Self-Regulation.* Urbana: University of Illinois Press, 1979.

McCarthy, Kathleen D. *Noblesse Oblige: Charity and Cultural Philanthropy in Chicago, 1849–1929.* Chicago: University of Chicago Press, 1982.

———, ed. *Lady Bountiful Revisited: Women, Philanthropy, and Power.* New Brunswick: Rutgers University Press, 1990.

McCormick, Richard L. *The Party Period and Public Policy: American Politics from the Age of Jackson to the Progressive Era.* New York: Oxford University Press, 1986.

McSeveney, Samuel T. *The Politics of Depression: Political Behavior in the Northeast, 1893–1896.* New York: Oxford University Press, 1972.

Magee, Mabel Agnes. "The Women's Clothing Industry of Chicago, with Special Reference to Relations between the Manufacturer and the Union, 1880–1926." Ph.D. diss., University of Chicago, 1927.

Maglin, Nan Bauer. "Vida to Florence: 'Comrade and Companion.'" *Frontiers* 4 (fall 1979): 13–20.

Marshall, T. H. *Citizenship and Social Class.* Cambridge: Cambridge University Press, 1950. Reprint, Westport, Conn.: Greenwood, 1973.

Martin, Theodora Penney. *The Sound of Our Own Voices: Women's Study Clubs, 1860–1910.* Boston: Beacon, 1987.

Massa, Anne. "Black Women in the 'White City.'" *Journal of American Studies* 8 (Dec. 1974): 319–37.

May, Martha. "Bread before Roses: American Workingmen, Labor Unions and the Family Wage." In Ruth Milkman, ed., *Women, Work and Protest: A Century of U.S. Women's Labor History.* Boston: Routledge, 1985.

Meckel, Richard A. *Save the Babies: American Public Health Reform and the Prevention of Infant Mortality, 1850–1929.* Baltimore: Johns Hopkins University Press, 1990.

Meyerowitz, Joanne J. *Women Adrift: Independent Wage Earners in Chicago, 1880–1930.* Chicago: University of Chicago Press, 1988.

Miller, Susanne, and Heinrich Potthoff, *A History of German Social Democracy from 1848 to the Present.* New York: St. Martin's, 1986.

Mink, Gwendolyn R. *Old Labor and New Immigrants in American Political Development: Union, Party, and State, 1875–1920.* Ithaca: Cornell University Press, 1986.

Monoson, Sara. "The Lady and the Tiger: Women's Electoral Activism in New York City before Suffrage." *Journal of Women's History* 2 (fall 1990): 100–135.

Montgomery, David. *Beyond Equality: Labor and the Radical Republicans, 1862–1872.* New York: Knopf, 1967.

Morantz, Regina Markell. "Feminism, Professionalism, and Germs: The Thought of Mary Putnam Jacobi and Elizabeth Blackwell." *AQ* 34 (winter 1982): 459–78.

Morris, Jenny. *Women Workers and the Sweated Trades: The Origins of Minimum Wage Legislation.* Brookfield, Vt.: Gower, 1986.

Mouffe, Chantal, ed., *Gramsci and Marxist Theory.* London: Routledge and Kegan Paul, 1979.

Muncy, Robyn. *Creating a Female Dominion in American Reform, 1890–1935.* New York: Oxford University Press, 1991.

Murphy, Teresa. *Ten Hours' Labor: Religion, Reform, and Gender in Early New England.* Ithaca: Cornell University Press, 1992.

Nettleship, Lois. "The Settlement Rationale: A Comparative Study of Samuel Barnett and Jane

Addams, 1870–1914." Ph.D. diss., University of Sussex, n.d. [ca. 1980].

Neverdon-Morton, Cynthia. *Afro-American Women of the South and the Advancement of the Race, 1895–1925*. Knoxville: University of Tennessee Press, 1989.

Newcomer, Mabel. *A Century of Higher Education for American Women*. New York: Harper and Row, 1959.

Nicklas, Floyd William. "William Kelley: The Congressional Years, 1861–1890." Ph.D. diss., Northern Illinois University, 1983.

Nimmons, Julius Franklin. "Social Reform and Moral Uplift in the Black Community, 1890–1910: Social Settlements, Temperance, and Social Purity." Ph.D. diss., Howard University, 1981.

O'Keefe, J. Paul. "The Bond of Perfection: Empirical Method in American Social Reform, 1860's–1880's." Ph.D. diss., University of Wisconsin–Madison, 1979.

Olsen, Frances. "From False Paternalism to False Equality: Judicial Assaults on Feminist Community, Illinois, 1869–1895." *Michigan Law Review* 84 (June 1986): 1518–41.

Parrish, William E. "The Western Sanitary Commission." *Civil War History* 36 (March 1990): 17–35.

Parson, Ruth E. "The Department of Health of the City of Chicago, 1894–1914." M.A. thesis, University of Chicago, 1939.

Pegram, Thomas R. *Partisans and Progressives: Private Interest and Public Policy in Illinois, 1870–1922*. Urbana: University of Illinois Press, 1992.

Perlman, Selig, and Philip Taft. *History of Labor in the United States, 1896–1932*. Vol. 4. New York: Macmillan, 1935. Reprint, New York: Augustus M. Kelley, 1966.

Perrier, Hubert. "The Socialists and the Working Class in New York: 1890–1896." *LH* 22 (fall 1981): 485–511.

Pierce, Bessie Louise. *A History of Chicago*. Vol. 3, *The Rise of a Modern City, 1871–1893*. Chicago: University of Chicago Press, 1957.

Pierson, Stanley. *Marxist Intellectuals and the Working-Class Mentality in Germany, 1887–1912*. Cambridge: Harvard University Press, 1993.

Pittenger, Mark. *American Socialists and Evolutionary Thought, 1870–1920*. Madison: University of Wisconsin Press, 1993.

Pole, J. R. *The Pursuit of Equality in American History*. Berkeley: University of California Press, 1978.

Preston, Samuel H., and Michael R. Haines. *Fatal Years: Child Mortality in Late Nineteenth-Century America*. Princeton: Princeton University Press, 1991.

Quataert, Jean. *Reluctant Feminists in German Social Democracy, 1885–1917*. Princeton: Princeton University Press, 1979.

———. "A Source Analysis in German Women's History: Factory Inspectors' Reports and the Shaping of Working Class Lives, 1878–1914." *Central European History* 16 (June 1983): 99–121.

Rader, Benjamin G. *The Academic Mind and Reform: The Influence of Richard T. Ely in American Life*. Lexington: University of Kentucky Press, 1966.

Rauch, Julia. "Unfriendly Visitors: The Emergence of Scientific Philanthropy in Philadelphia, 1878–1880." Ph.D. diss., Bryn Mawr College, 1974.

Reinders, Robert C. "Toynbee Hall and the American Settlement Movement." *Social Service Review* 56 (March 1982): 39–54.

Reps, John W. *Washington on View: The Nation's Capital since 1790*. Chapel Hill: University of North Carolina Press, 1991.

Roediger, David R., and Philip S. Foner. *Our Own Time: A History of American Labor and the Working Day*. Westport, Conn.: Greenwood, 1989.

Rosenberg, Charles. "The Female Animal: Medical and Biological Views of Women." In *No Other Gods: On Science and American Social Thought*. Baltimore: Johns Hopkins University Press, 1976.

Rosenzweig, Roy. *Eight Hours for What We Will: Workers and Leisure in an Industrial City, 1870–1920*. Cambridge: Cambridge University Press, 1983.

Ross, Dorothy. *The Origins of American Social Science*. Cambridge: Cambridge University Press, 1991.

———. "Socialism and American Liberalism: Academic Thought in the 1880s." *Perspectives in American History* 11 (1977–78): 5–80.

Ross, Steven J. "The Politicization of the Working Class: Production, Ideology, Culture and Politics in Late Nineteenth-Century Cincinnati." *JSH* 11 (May 1986): 171–95.

Rousmaniere, John P. "Cultural Hybrid in the Slums: The College Woman and the Settlement House, 1889–1894." *AQ* 22 (spring 1970): 45–66.

Rury, John L. *Education and Women's Work: Female Schooling and the Division of Labor in Urban America, 1870–1930*. Albany: State University of New York Press, 1991.

Sahli, Nancy. "Smashing: Women's Relationships before the Fall." *Chrysalis* 8 (1979): 17–27.

Salem, Dorothy. *To Better Our World: Black Women in Organized Reform, 1890–1920*. New York: Carlson, 1990.

Salisbury, Robert S. "The Republican Party and Positive Government: 1860–1890." *Mid-America* 68 (Jan. 1986): 15–34.

Salvatore, Nick. *Eugene V. Debs: Citizen and Socialist*. Urbana: University of Illinois Press, 1982.

Scharnau, Ralph. "Elizabeth Morgan, Crusader for Labor Reform." *LH* 14 (summer 1973): 340–51.

Schneider, David M., and Albert Deutsch. "The Public Charities of New York: The Rise of State Supervision after the Civil War." *The Social Service Review* 15 (March 1941): 1–23.

Schneirov, Richard Samuel. "The Knights of Labor in the Chicago Labor Movement and in Municipal Politics, 1877–1887." Ph.D. diss., Northern Illinois University, 1984.

———. "Political Cultures and the Role of the State in Labor's Republic: The View from Chicago, 1848–1877." *LH* 32 (summer 1991): 376–400.

Schneirov, Richard, and Thomas J. Suhrbur. *Union Brotherhood, Union Town: The History of the Carpenters' Union of Chicago, 1863–1987*. Carbondale: Southern Illinois University Press, 1988.

Schofield, Ann. "The Rise of the Pig-Headed Girl: An Analysis of the American Labor Press for Their Attitudes toward Women, 1877–1920." Ph.D. diss., State University of New York, Binghamton, 1980.

Scott, Anne Firor. "Most Invisible of All: Black Women's Voluntary Associations." *The Journal of Southern History* 56 (Feb. 1990): 3–22.

———. *Natural Allies: Women's Associations in American History*. Urbana: University of Illinois Press, 1991.

Scott, Joan W. "Gender: A Useful Category of Historical Analysis." *AHR* 91 (Dec. 1986): 1053–75.

Seifert, Ruth. "The Portrayal of Women in the German-American Labor Movement." In Hartmut Keil, ed. *German Workers' Culture in the United States, 1850 to 1920*. Washington: Smithsonian Institution Press, 1988.

Shaw, Stephanie J. "Black Club Women and the Creation of the National Association of Colored Women." *Journal of Women's History* 3 (fall 1991): 10–25.

Sherrick, Rebecca Louise. "Private Visions, Public Lives: The Hull-House Women in the Progressive Era." Ph.D. diss., Northwestern University, 1980.

Sicherman, Barbara. *Alice Hamilton: A Life in Letters*. Cambridge: Harvard University Press, 1984.

Sklar, Kathryn Kish. "'The Greater Part of the Petitioners Are Female': The Reduction of Women's Working Hours in the Paid Labor Force, 1840–1917." In Gary Cross, ed., *Worktime and Industrialization: An International History*. Philadelphia: Temple University Press, 1988.

———. "The Historical Foundations of Women's Power in the Creation of the American Welfare State, 1830–1930." In Seth Koven and Sonya Michel, eds., *Mothers of a New World: Maternalist Politics and the Origins of Welfare States*. New York: Routledge, 1993.

———. "Hull House in the 1890's: A Community of Women Reformers." *Signs* 10 (summer 1985): 658–77.

———. "Hull-House Maps and Papers: Social Science as Women's Work in the 1890s." In Martin Bulmer, Kevin Bales, and Kathryn Kish Sklar, eds., *The Social Survey in Historical Perspective, 1880–1940*. Cambridge: Cambridge University Press, 1991.

———. "Victorian Women and Domestic Life: Mary Todd Lincoln, Elizabeth Cady Stanton, and Harriet Beecher Stowe." In Cullom Davis, Charles B. Stozier, and Rebecca C. Ward, eds, *The Public and the Private Lincoln: Contemporary Perspectives*, 20–37. Carbondale, Ill.: Southern Illinois University Press, 1979.

———. "Who Funded Hull House?" In Kathleen D. McCarthy, ed., *Lady Bountiful Revisited: Women, Philanthropy, and Power*, 94–115. New Brunswick: Rutgers University Press, 1990.

———, ed. *The Autobiography of Florence Kelley: Notes of Sixty Years*. Chicago: Charles H. Kerr, 1986.

Sklar, Kathryn Kish, Anja Schüler, and Susan Strasser, eds., *A Transatlantic Dialogue: Documents of American and German Women Reformers, 1880–1930*. Washington, D.C.: German Historical Institute, forthcoming.

Skocpol, Theda, and Ann Shola Orloff. "Why Not Equal Protection? Explaining the Politics of Public Social Spending in Britain, 1900–1911, and the United States, 1880s–1920." *American Sociological Review* 49 (Dec. 1984): 726–50.

Skowronek, Stephen. *Building a New American State: The Expansion of National Administrative Capacities, 1877–1920*. New York: Cambridge University Press, 1982.

Smith, Gary Scott. "When Stead Came to Chicago: The 'Social Gospel Novel' and the Chicago Civic Federation." *American Presbyterians* 68 (fall 1990): 193–205.

Solomon, Barbara Miller. *In the Company of Educated Women: A History of Women and Higher Education in America*. New Haven: Yale University Press, 1985.

Sproat, John G. *"The Best Men": Liberal Reformers in the Gilded Age*. New York: Oxford University Press, 1968.

Stansell, Christine. "The Origins of the Sweatshop: Women and Early Industrialization in New York City." In Michael H. Frisch and Daniel J. Walkowitz, eds., *Working-Class America: Essays on Labor, Community, and American Society*. Urbana: University of Illinois Press, 1983.

Staley, Eugene. *History of the Illinois State Federation of Labor*. Chicago: University of Chicago Press, 1930.

Steckel, Richard H. "The Health and Mortality of Women and Children, 1850–1860." *Journal of Economic History* 48 (June 1988): 333–45.

Steenson, Gary P. *After Marx, Before Lenin: Marxism and Socialist Working-Class Parties in Europe, 1884–1914*. Pittsburgh: University of Pittsburgh Press, 1991.

———. *Karl Kautsky, 1854–1938: Marxism in the Classical Years* (Pittsburgh: University of Pittsburgh Press, 1978)

Stokes, Melvyn. "American Progressives and the European Left." *Journal of American Studies* 17 (April 1983): 5–28.

Tax, Meredith. *The Rising of the Women: Feminist Solidarity and Class Conflict, 1880–1917*. New York: Monthly Review Press, 1980.

Teaford, Jon C. *The Unheralded Triumph: City Government in America, 1870–1900*. Baltimore: Johns Hopkins University Press, 1984.

Terborg-Penn, Rosalyn. "Discrimination against Afro-American Women in the Woman's Movement, 1830–1920." In Sharon Harley and Rosalyn Terborg-Penn, eds., *The Afro-American Woman: Struggles and Images*. Port Washington, N.Y.: Kennikat, 1978.

Thelen, David P. *The New Citizenship: Origins of Progressivism in Wisconsin, 1885–1900*. Columbia: University of Missouri Press, 1972.

———. "Urban Politics: Beyond Bosses and Reformers." *Reviews in American History* 7 (Sept. 1979): 406–12.

Thomas, John L. *Alternative America: Henry George, Edward Bellamy, Henry Demarest Lloyd, and the Adversary Tradition*. Cambridge: Harvard University Press, 1983.

Thönnessen, Werner. *The Emancipation of Women: The Rise and Decline of the Women's Movement in German Social Democracy, 1863–1933*. N.p.: Pluto, 1973.

Tomes, Nancy. "The Private Side of Public Health: Sanitary Science, Domestic Hygiene, and the Germ Theory, 1870–1900." *Bulletin of the History of Medicine* 64 (winter 1990): 509–39.

Tomlins, Christopher L. *The State and the Unions: Labor Relations, Law, and the Organized Labor Movement in America, 1880–1960*. Cambridge: Cambridge University Press, 1985.

[Trachtenberg, Alexander, ed.] *Letters to Americans, 1848–1895: A Selection*. New York: International, 1953.

Vicinus, Martha. *Independent Women: Work and Community for Single Women, 1850–1920*. Chicago: University of Chicago Press, 1985.

Wade, Louise. "The Social Gospel Impulse and Chicago Settlement-House Founders." *Chicago Theological Seminary Register* 55 (April 1965): 1–12.

Walsh, Mary Roth. *Doctors Wanted—No Women Need Apply: Sexual Barriers in the Medical Profession, 1835–1975*. New Haven: Yale University Press, 1977.

Watkins, Bari. "The Professors and the Unions: American Academic Social Theory and Labor Reform, 1883–1915." Ph.D. diss., Yale University, 1976.

Weiner, Lynn Y. *From Working Girl to Working Mother: The Female Labor Force in the United States, 1820–1980*. Chapel Hill: University of North Carolina Press, 1985.

———. "'Our Sisters' Keepers': The Minneapolis Woman's Christian Association and Housing for Working Women." *Minnesota History* 46 (spring 1979): 189–200.

Wheelock, Lewis F. "Urban Protestant Reactions to the Chicago Haymarket Affair, 1886–1893." Ph.D. diss., State University of Iowa, 1956.

White, George Cary. "Social Settlements and Immigrant Neighbors, 1886–1914." *Social Service Review* 33 (March 1959): 55–66.

White, Ronald C., Jr., and C. Howard Hopkins. *The Social Gospel: Religion and Reform in Changing America*. Philadelphia: Temple University Press, 1976.

Wiebe, Robert. *The Search for Order, 1877–1920.* New York: Hill and Wang, 1966.

———. *Businessmen and Reform: A Study of the Progressive Movement.* Cambridge: Harvard University Press, 1962.

Williamson, Chilton. *American Suffrage: From Property to Democracy, 1760–1860.* Princeton: Princeton University Press, 1960.

Wish, Harvey. "Governor Altgeld Pardons the Anarchists." *Journal of Illinois State Historical Society* 31 (Dec. 1938): 424–48.

Woody, Thomas. *A History of Women's Education in the United States.* 2 vols. 1929. Reprint, New York: Octagon Books, 1966.

Wormeley, Katherine Prescott. "The Sanitary Commission." In William Quentin Maxwell, *Lincoln's Fifth Wheel: The Political History of the United States Sanitary Commission.* New York: Longmans, Green, 1956.

Zschoche, Sue. "'Preserving Eden': Higher Education, Woman's Sphere, and the First Generation of College Women, 1870–1910." Ph.D. diss., University of Kansas, 1984.

Index

A Note
about the
Author

Kathryn Kish Sklar received her B.A. from Radcliffe College and Harvard University in 1965, and her Ph.D. from the University of Michigan in 1969. She has taught at the University of Michigan and at the University of California, Los Angeles, and at the State University of New York, Binghamton, where she has been Distinguished Professor of History since 1988. She is the recipient of fellowships from the John Simon Guggenheim Foundation, the Center for Advanced Study in the Behavioral and Social Sciences, the National Endowment for the Humanities, the Spencer Foundation, the Woodrow Wilson International Center for Scholars, and the American Association of University Women. She is the author of *Catharine Beecher: A Study in American Domesticity* and other studies in the history of American women; editor of *The Autobiography of Florence Kelley: Notes of Sixty Years;* and co-editor of *U.S. History as Woman's History: New Feminist Essays; The Social Survey Movement in Historical Perspective;* and *Women and Power in American History.*